Developmentally Appropriate Curriculum
Best Practices in Early Childhood Education

FIFTH EDITION

Marjorie J. Kostelnik
University of Nebraska, Lincoln

Anne K. Soderman
Michigan State University

Alice Phipps Whiren
Michigan State University

Boston Columbus Indianapolis New York San Francisco Upper Saddle River
Amsterdam Cape Town Dubai London Madrid Milan Munich Paris Montréal Toronto
Delhi Mexico City São Paulo Sydney Hong Kong Seoul Singapore Taipei Tokyo

Vice President and Editor in Chief: Jeffery W. Johnston
Senior Acquisitions Editor: Julie Peters
Editorial Assistant: Tiffany Bitzel
Development Editor: Bryce Bell
Vice President, Director of Marketing: Quinn Perkson
Marketing Manager: Erica DeLuca
Senior Managing Editor: Pamela D. Bennett
Project Manager: Kerry Rubadue
Senior Operations Supervisor: Matthew Ottenweller
Operations Specialist: Laura Messerly
Senior Art Director: Diane Lorenzo
Text Designer: S4Carlisle Publishing Services

Cover Designer: Ali Mohrman
Photo Coordinator: Sandy Schaefer
Cover Art: Fotosearch
Media Producer: Autumn Benson
Media Project Manager: Rebecca Norsic
Full-Service Project Management:
    S4Carlisle Publishing Services
Composition: S4Carlisle Publishing Services
Printer/Binder: Edwards Brothers
Cover Printer: Lehigh-Phoenix
    Color/Hagerstown
Text Font: Minion Pro

Praxis II* Test is a registered trademark of Educational Testing Service (ETS). This publication is not endorsed or approved by ETS.

Every effort has been made to provide accurate and current Internet information in this book. However, the Internet and information posted on it are constantly changing, so it is inevitable that some of the Internet addresses listed in this textbook will change.

Photo Credits: Krista Greco/Merrill, pp. 1, 211, 214; David Kostelnik, pp. 2, 41, 51, 110, 205, 224, 258, 259 (both), 266, 278, 285, 298, 336, 350, 373, 384, 396, 416, 440, 441, 442, 445, 455, 467, 468, 473, 475 (all), 483; Brian Smith, Photographer, p. 6; Barbara Schwartz/Merrill, pp. 12, 187, 459; Mac H. Brown/Merrill, p. 16; David Mager/Pearson Learning Photo Studio, pp. 22, 27, 37, 84, 248; Annie Pickert/ABMerrill, pp. 34, 448; Photos to Go, pp. 40, 46; Anne Vega/Merrill, p. 57; Karen Mancinelli/Pearson Learning Photo Studio, p. 70; Anthony Magnacca/Merrill, pp. 75, 160, 165, 174, 218, 319, 428; Dorrey A. Cardinale/Parker Boon Productions/Silver Burdett Ginn, p. 78; Laura Bolesta/Merrill, pp. 89, 398; BananaStock, p. 91; Scott Cunningham/Merrill, pp. 98, 142, 272, 293, 334, 430; Nancy Sheehan Photography, pp. 103, 172, 237, 268; T. Lindfors/Lindfors Photography, pp. 118, 311, 464; Shutterstock, p. 122; Todd Yarrington/Merrill, pp. 128, 306; Frank Siteman, p. 141; Keith Weller/USDA Natural Resources Conservation Service, p. 141; Lyssa Towl, pp. 126, 127; Hope Madden/Merrill, p. 206; Katelyn Metzger/Merrill, p. 353; Merrill, p. 363; Valerie Schultz/Merrill, pp. 375, 401; Dan Floss/Merrill, p. 388; Jupiter Unlimited, p. 408; EyeWire Collection/Getty Images–Photodisc, p. 414.

Library of Congress Cataloging-in-Publication Data
Kostelnik, Marjorie J.
  Developmentally appropriate curriculum : best practices in early childhood education / Marjorie J. Kostelnik, Anne K. Soderman, Alice P. Whiren. — 5th ed.
    p. cm.
  Includes bibliographical references and index.
  ISBN 978-0-13-703553-3
  1. Early childhood education—United States. 2. Early childhood education—Curricula—United States. 3. Child development—United States. I. Soderman, Anne Keil. II. Whiren, Alice Phipps. III. Title.
  LB1139.25.K67 2011
  372.21—dc22   2009039846

10 9 8 7 6 5 4 3

ISBN 10:   0-13-703553-5
ISBN 13: 978-0-13-703553-3

Preface

- ❏ What are developmentally appropriate practices, and how effective are they?
- ❏ How can we create the best programs for young children?
- ❏ As early childhood educators, what is our role in shaping children's educational experiences? What is the child's role? What is the role of the family and community?
- ❏ How can we tell if children are actually learning?

Questions such as these are typically asked by early childhood professionals-in-training as well as by seasoned practitioners in the field. Our work with students and increasing numbers of educators probing for answers indicated the need for a comprehensive guide to support the exploration, planning, and implementation of developmentally appropriate programs. Thus, our goal in writing *Developmentally Appropriate Curriculum: Best Practices in Early Childhood Education* was to bring together the best information currently available for developing an integrated approach to curriculum and instruction in the early years. We also hoped to bridge the worlds of child-care and early education, as well as those of preprimary and primary programs. The resulting volume addresses *early childhood professionals-in-training and professionals working in formal group settings with young children from 3 to 8 years old*. We realize that early childhood education spans birth to age 8 years; however, we see infancy and toddlerhood as unique ages within this period, requiring specialized knowledge beyond the scope of this text. For this reason, we did not focus on infants or toddlers in our discussions.

We believe the information in this book will be *valuable to both newcomers to the field and master practitioners*. The ideas in this text have been extensively field tested and found to be effective. All are designed to give you a cohesive view of the *what, why, and how of developmentally appropriate practices*.

Finally, we have had many years of experience working directly with young children and their families and with educators in preprimary and primary settings. We have been in urban, suburban, and rural programs; large–medium and small classes; public, private, not-for-profit, and profit-seeking organizations; half- and full-day programs; preschool classes; and the elementary grades. Currently, all of us are actively engaged in educating young children, the professionals who work with them, or both.

DISTINCTIVE FEATURES OF THIS TEXT

Developmentally Appropriate Curriculum: Best Practices in Early Childhood Education offers instructors and readers several unique features that increase reader understanding and skill development.

- ❏ We treat curriculum as everything that happens to children in early childhood settings. Therefore, the text addresses all aspects of classroom life, including children and adults, the physical and social environments, and teaching and learning from a "whole child" perspective.
- ❏ The concept of developmentally appropriate practices is pervasive throughout the volume. Each chapter addresses principles of age appropriateness, individual appropriateness, and sociocultural appropriateness. All of the DAP material incorporates the latest version of Developmentally Appropriate Practice in Early Childhood (NAEYC, 2009).
- ❏ This book spans the early childhood years from 3 to 8. It provides a comprehensive, cohesive approach that results in greater continuity for children and practitioners.
- ❏ Each chapter progresses clearly from theory and research to practice. There is a strong emphasis on the what, why, and how of teaching.
- ❏ We use developmental domains to address early childhood curriculum. Doing so helps practitioners better understand the link between development and learning and program implementation.
- ❏ Every curriculum chapter includes sample activities.
- ❏ The text addresses individual curricular domains as well as curriculum integration.
- ❏ Detailed directions facilitate the application of developmentally appropriate practices.

❏ National and state standards for learning serve as the basis for curricular goals.

❏ Readers learn a comprehensive approach to conceptualizing, planning, implementing, and evaluating curriculum.

❏ Chapter-end features provide readers the opportunity to extend their understanding of chapter content to their professional lives. *Discussion questions* focus on essential information in each chapter and give readers an opportunity to explore ideas with classmates and colleagues. *Journal recommendations* enhance readers' reflective thinking. *Sample observations* help readers recognize developmentally appropriate practices in operation. *Classroom activities* enable readers to apply chapter content and processes in interactions with children, families, or professionals in the field. If readers complete the *portfolio entries* in each chapter, they will create a comprehensive portfolio, including:

❏ Artifacts (things generated in class and then used in a portfolio)

❏ Reproductions (things reproduced by camera, video, or audio for use in the portfolio)

❏ Productions (things specifically produced for placement in the portfolio) and testimonials (others' attesting to their abilities), all centered on developmentally appropriate practices.

A *standards* section helps readers connect what they are reading with national and state guidelines and expectations for children's learning and behavior. *Certification or licensure exam sample questions* give students an opportunity to apply their knowledge as it might be assessed through the *Praxis II*® Examination in Early Childhood Education or another exam required at the state or local level. This chapter-end activity includes a short case describing a child or teacher, followed by a constructed response question and then by related multiple-choice questions. A rubric for evaluating student answers is provided in the instructor's manual.

WHAT REMAINS THE SAME

Among the popular elements we retained from the previous edition are our focus on developmental domains, a strong research basis for the information provided, and an emphasis on practical applications. This remains very much a "how-to" book. The curriculum chapters include rationales and sample teaching strategies specific to each domain, objectives, issues practitioners face, and illustrative activities. Examples featuring children, families, and professionals from a variety of backgrounds, with a special focus on children with special needs, continue to be a feature of the chapters that compose the book.

NEW TO THIS EDITION

This edition has been extensively updated. The following characterize some of the changes since the last edition:

❏ We have replaced more than one third of the old references with new material dating from 2006 through 2010.

❏ Based on the request of instructors, we have added a glossary to address critical terms introduced in each chapter.

❏ With so much attention focused on national standards, we have expanded and updated the standards material in chapters 2 through 16 to help readers better understand how what they are reading relates to content standards that reach down into early childhood programs.

PEARSON
myeducationlab)

❏ Integrated into the margins are directions to go to MyEducationLab (www.myeducationlab .com), which offers assignable online activities and exercises built around videos and other resources. These resources illustrate and extend chapter concepts and enhance understanding. Students will also find chapter practice assessments in the Study Plan with additional study materials, specifically created for this book.

❏ In chapter 1, we provide a strong rationale for why developmentally appropriate practices (DAP) are more important than ever. The newly published NAEYC document on DAP includes more material on intentional teaching, learning standards, how neuroscience has influenced early childhood education, connecting children to nature, and an increased emphasis on assessment. All of these changes are reflected in our current text.

❏ Although we do not see this as a book on special education, we do believe it is important for all teachers of young children to understand how to support children with special needs in early childhood settings of all kinds. Thus, we have strengthened the inclusion of material on children with special needs in every chapter. For instance, chapter 1 now includes a discussion of an IEP and a description of such a plan for a particular child. Chapters 2, 3, and 4 provide more strategies and examples regarding how children with special needs can best be incorporated in planning and teaching children in small groups and in whole-group activities. In chapter 5, we follow one child who has specific physical needs throughout all aspects of preparing the physical environment and planning the daily routines.

❑ The curriculum domain chapters retain many of the features readers found useful in the last edition. However, new material has been added to each one. All of these chapters now have a feature called "Making Goals Fit," which highlights a curricular goal and how it can be adapted to meet the needs of children ages 3 and 4, 5 and 6, and 7 and 8.

❑ Chapter 9, on the aesthetic domain, places greater emphasis on exploration in the arts, focusing on the aesthetic process more fully as well as how to adapt aesthetic processes and tools for children with special needs.

❑ Readers will find updated sections on children's affective development and emotional intelligence in chapter 10, which covers the affective domain. There is a new section on resilience in young children and another on the particular affective needs of children with disabilities.

❑ Chapter 11, on the cognitive domain, includes a greater emphasis on the interactions among neuroscience, education, and special education. Also, the goals in this chapter have been streamlined and the teaching strategies expanded.

❑ The language domain, covered in chapter 12, provides new material on children who are learning second languages as well as children who have limited English-processing skills.

❑ The physical domain, covered in chapter 13, incorporates the national standards for physical activity and offers a simplified approach to teaching children appropriate health habits.

❑ Chapter 14, which addresses the social domain, has an expanded section on the social studies. It also includes a new feature on the reflective practitioner in relation to children's social development and diversity in the classroom.

❑ Pretend play and construction continue to be combined in chapter 15. Our aim is to highlight the integrative nature of play and its importance at all levels of early childhood education. We have strengthened the rationale on the importance of play and the connection between the curriculum and play.

❑ The chapter on themes and projects, chapter 16, has been updated, with more information about documenting children's learning.

All these revisions address current issues in early childhood curriculum development and implementation. Their inclusion should better prepare readers to face the realities of teaching young children on a day-to-day basis.

FORMAT AND CHAPTER SEQUENCE

Developmentally Appropriate Curriculum: Best Practices in Early Childhood Education has an introduction and four parts. Part 1, Foundations of Early Childhood Education, consists of an introduction to early childhood education today as well as chapters 1 and 2, which address the philosophy of developmentally appropriate practice. Characteristics of the field, the knowledge base associated with developmentally appropriate practice, and critical issues in early childhood education are all outlined in part 1. "Setting the stage for learning" is the focus of part 2, chapters 3 through 8. In these chapters, we describe the overall understandings and skills necessary to create effective programs for young children. We begin with planning, implementing, and organizing small-group, then whole-group, activities. Organizing the physical space and materials used in the classroom, creating a schedule for the day, and determining how to group children to achieve certain aims are discussed next. Child guidance, authentic assessment, and family involvement are treated as fundamental building blocks of effective teaching, with individual chapters devoted to each of these topics. In part 3, chapters 9 through 14, the curriculum is explained within the context of six developmental domains: aesthetic, affective, cognitive, language, physical, and social. Each of the domain chapters has a discussion of theory, research, and educational issues related to children's development and learning in that particular arena, a suggested outline of goals and objectives, teaching strategies that characterize the domain, and examples of classroom activities.

The curriculum domains are presented in alphabetical order to underscore the idea that no one domain is more important than any of the others. Additionally, you may find it useful to know that each domain refers to five kinds of knowledge. These kinds of knowledge are physical, logical-mathematical, representational, social-conventional, and metacognitive. If you are familiar with these terms, reading chapters 9 through 14 in order will make sense. However, if you are unfamiliar with them, read chapter 11 first, in which the terms are explained. The last section of the book is part 4, Integrating Curriculum. This part includes chapters 15 and 16, both focused on creating a cohesive whole. First, we consider the integrative nature of pretend play and construction; second, we consider the integrative aspects of using projects and theme teaching.

STRUCTURAL FEATURES

Each chapter begins with a series of questions that pique readers' interest in the material and provide a framework for reflecting on the chapter's content following an initial reading. In addition, a series of culminating activities enables readers to review and apply the material in their professional lives. Thus, every chapter ends with discussion questions, potential observations to make in early childhood settings, application activities, guidelines for journal entries, suggested items to add to a portfolio, and finally, activities to help readers explore standards for learning that are most relevant to them and the children in their charge. These learning aids will hone readers' understanding and skill and serve as resource materials for the future.

MYEDUCATIONLAB

PEARSON
myeducationlab

The Power of Classroom Practice

Teacher educators who are developing pedagogies for the analysis of teaching and learning contend that analyzing teaching artifacts has three advantages: it enables new teachers time for reflection while still using the real materials of practice; it provides new teachers with experience thinking about and approaching the complexity of the classroom; and in some cases, it can help new teachers and teacher educators develop a shared understanding and common language about teaching . . .
—Darling-Hammond & Bransford, 2005

As Linda Darling-Hammond and her colleagues point out, grounding teacher education in real classrooms—among real teachers and students and among actual examples of students' and teachers' work—is an important, and perhaps even an essential, part of training teachers for the complexities of teaching in today's classrooms. For this reason, we have created a valuable, time-saving website—MyEducationLab—that provides you with the context of real classrooms and artifacts that research on teacher education tells us is so important. The authentic in-class video footage, interactive skill-building exercises and other resources available on MyEducationLab offer you a uniquely valuable teacher education tool.

MyEducationLab is easy to use and integrate into both your assignments and your courses. Wherever you see the MyEducationLab logo in the margins or elsewhere in the text, follow the simple instructions to access the videos, strategies, cases, and artifacts associated with these assignments, activities, and learning units on MyEducationLab. MyEducationLab is organized topically to enhance the coverage of the core concepts discussed in the chapters of your book. For each topic on the course you will find most or all of the following resources:

Connection to National Standards

Now it is easier than ever to see how your coursework is connected to national standards. In each topic of MyEducationLab you will find intended learning outcomes connected to the appropriate national standards for your course. All of the Assignments and Activities and all of the Building Teaching Skills and Dispositions in MyEducationLab are mapped to the appropriate national standards and learning outcomes as well.

Assignments and Activities

Designed to save instructors preparation time, these assignable exercises show concepts in action (through video, cases, or student and teacher artifacts) and then offer thought-provoking questions that probe your understanding of theses concepts or strategies. (Feedback for these assignments is available to the instructor.)

Building Teaching Skills and Dispositions

These learning units help you practice and strengthen skills that are essential to quality teaching. First you are presented with the core skill or concept and then given an opportunity to practice your understanding of this concept multiple times by watching video footage (or interacting with other media) and then critically analyzing the strategy or skill presented.

IRIS Center Resources

The IRIS Center at Vanderbilt University (http://iris.peabody.vanderbilt.edu, funded by the U.S. Department of Education's Office of Special Education Programs [OSEP]) develops training enhancement materials for pre-service and in-service teachers. The Center works with experts from across the country to create challenge-based interactive modules, case study units, and podcasts that provide research-validated information about working with students in inclusive settings. On your MyEducationLab course we have integrated this content where appropriate to enhance the content coverage in your book.

Teacher Talk

This feature links to videos of teachers of the year across the country discussing their personal stories of why they teach. This National Teacher of the Year Program is sponsored by the Council of Chief State School Officers (CCSSO) and focuses public attention on teaching excellence.

General Resources on Your MyEducationLab Course

The *Resources* section on your MyEducationLab course is designed to help you pass your licensure exam, put together an effective portfolio and lesson plan, prepare for and navigate the first year of your teaching career, and understand key educational standards, policies, and laws. This section includes:

- ❑ *Licensure Exams.* Access guidelines for passing the Praxis exam. The Practice Test Exam includes practice questions, case histories, and video case studies.
- ❑ *Portfolio Builder and Lesson Plan Builder.* Create, update, and share portfolios and lesson plans.
- ❑ *Preparing a Portfolio.* Access guidelines for creating a high-quality teaching portfolio that will allow you to practice effective lesson planning.
- ❑ *Licensure and Standards.* Link to state licensure standards and national standards.
- ❑ *Beginning Your Career.* Educate yourself—access tips, advice, and valuable information on:
  - ❑ *Resume Writing and Interviewing.* Expert advice on how to write impressive resumes and prepare for job interviews.
  - ❑ *Your First Year of Teaching.* Practical tips to set up your classroom, manage student behavior, and learn to more easily organize for instruction and assessment.
  - ❑ *Law and Public Policies.* Specific directives and requirements you need to understand under the No Child Left Behind Act and the Individuals with Disabilities Education Improvement Act of 2004.
- ❑ *Special Education Interactive Timeline.* Build your own detailed timelines based on different facets of the history and evolution of special education.

Book-Specific Resources

Study Plan. A MyEducationLab Study Plan is a multiple choice assessment tied to chapter objectives, supported by study material. A well-designed Study Plan offers multiple opportunities to fully master required course content as identified by the objectives in each chapter:

- ❑ *Chapter Objectives* identify the learning outcomes for the chapter and give you targets to shoot for as you read and study.
- ❑ *Multiple Choice Assessments* assess mastery of the content (tied to each chapter objective) by taking the multiple choice quiz as many times as needed. Not only do these quizzes provide

overall scores for each objective, but they also explain why responses to particular items are correct or incorrect.

❑ *Study Material:* Review, Practice and Enrichment gives you a deeper understanding of what you do and do not know related to chapter content. This can be accessed through the Multiple Choice Assessment (after you take a quiz you receive information regarding the chapter content on which you still need practice and review) or through a self-directed method of study. This material includes text excerpts, activities that include hints and feedback, and media assets (video, simulations, cases, etc.).

Visit www.myeducationlab.com for a demonstration of this exciting new online teaching resource.

SUPPLEMENTARY MATERIALS FOR INSTRUCTORS

All of our instructor supplements are posted online at www.pearsonhighered.com. Click on "Educators," then click on "Download Instructor Resources." You may register here and download and print ancillaries.

Online Instructor's Manual

This comprehensive instructor's manual describes how to organize a course by using the textbook; how to find, select, and maintain appropriate field placements for students; how to model skills for students to imitate; and how to provide feedback to students assigned to field placements on campus or in the community. In addition, we have included a series of role-playing activities to be carried out in class. They are designed to show students how to use particular skills prior to implementing them with children and to clarify basic concepts as they emerge during class discussions. In addition, we have provided sample terms and facts instructors can provide students as they write lesson plans in each domain. We have found such content offers a good springboard for students who are just learning the content and processes involved in the six domains. A rubric for self-evaluation of the certification or licensure exam examples offered in the chapter-end activities is also provided here. Finally, the instructor's manual contains a criterion-referenced observation tool, the curriculum skills inventory (CSI). This is a unique feature of *Developmentally Appropriate Curriculum: Best Practices in Early Childhood Education*. The CSI can be used by instructors and practitioners to evaluate the degree to which students demonstrate the skills taught.

Online Test Bank

The Online Test Bank consists of multiple-choice, true–false, short-answer, and essay questions for each chapter.

Pearson MyTest

Pearson MyTest is a powerful assessment generation program that helps instructors easily create and print quizzes and exams. Questions and tests are authored online, allowing ultimate flexibility and the ability to efficiently create and print assessments anytime, anywhere! Instructors can access Pearson MyTest and their test bank files by going to www.pearsonmytest.com to log in, register, or request access. Features of Pearson MyTest include:

Premium assessment content

❑ Draw from a rich library of assessments that complement your Pearson textbook and your course's learning objectives.

❑ Edit questions or tests to fit your specific teaching needs.

Instructor-friendly resources

❑ Easily create and store your own questions, including images, diagrams, and charts using simple drag-and-drop and Word-like controls.

❑ Use additional information provided by Pearson, such as the question's difficulty level or learning objective, to help you quickly build your test.

Time-saving enhancements

❑ Add headers or footers and easily scramble questions and answer choices—all from one simple toolbar.

❑ Quickly create multiple versions of your test or answer key, and when ready, simply save to MS-Word or PDF format and print!

❑ Export your exams for import to Blackboard 6.0, CE (WebCT), or Vista (WebCT)!

Online PowerPoint Slides

For every chapter, a series of PowerPoint slides has been created to highlight key concepts and strategies.

ACKNOWLEDGMENTS

We would like to recognize the major contributions to this text by our colleagues in early childhood education: Barbara M. Rohde, early childhood educator and artist from Durham, North Carolina, wrote chapter 9 for the earlier versions of this text; in addition, she supplied artwork for the classroom floor plans and the pictograph that appear in chapter 5. Laura C. Stein, early childhood consultant, Stein Associates, East Lansing, Michigan, produced chapter 14 for the first four editions of this book. It was an important contribution on which we continue to build. We owe them much for their insights and for helping our ideas come alive on the page. Their influence remains. Michelle Rupiper, director of the Ruth Staples Child Development Laboratory at the University of Nebraska, Lincoln, has joined us in the writing enterprise providing significant contributions to chapters 4, 9, and 16. Carolyn Pope Edwards, professor of Child, Youth and Family Studies and Psychology, University of Nebraska, Lincoln, contributed the section "The Reggio Emilia Approach to Early Childhood Education"; and Ann S. Epstein, director of the early childhood division, HighScope Educational Research Foundation, wrote the portion entitled, "The HighScope Approach to Early Childhood Education." These two segments appear in chapter 1. Sylvia Chard, professor of elementary education, University of Alberta, wrote the material describing the project approach, featured in chapter 16. This work has broadened the scope of the text and has enabled us to present multiple voices describing developmentally appropriate curriculum.

We appreciate the generous assistance of David Kostelnik, photographer, who provided excellent images taken at a number of preschool and elementary sites. We are also indebted to the teachers in the child development laboratories at Michigan State University for their early work on curriculum, for providing continuous and easy access to their classrooms for observation, and for inspiring many of the ideas represented in this book. Teachers in the Ruth Staples Child Development Laboratory School also contributed to our work. We are grateful to Deborah Sharpe, Haslett Public Schools, and Grace Spalding, Department of Family and Child Ecology, for the group times described in chapter 4; and to Donna Howe, head teacher emeritus, for materials related to learning centers (chapter 5) and theme-related material (chapter 16).

We thank the following reviewers for their comments and suggestions: Belinda J. Hardin, University of North Carolina, Greensboro; Carol Hawkins, Youngstown State University; Jane Day Hyche, Gwinnett Technical College; Madhu Lodha, Cabrillo Community College; Tonia Padrick, Brunswick Community College; and Michelle Rupiper, University of Nebraksa, Lincoln.

Julie Peters, our editor at Pearson, was a tremendous support, as were all members of the production team. During the preparation of this manuscript, we discussed our ideas with and received feedback from a number of University of Nebraska and Michigan State University students as well as Head Start, Chapter 1, child-care, preschool, and elementary school teachers and administrators. We heard the concerns of many parents of young children and listened to the children themselves as they responded to diverse program practices in their classrooms. We are especially grateful for all these contributions in shaping our vision of appropriate practices and in motivating us to share this vision with others.

Marjorie Kostelnik
Anne Soderman
Alice Whiren

About the Authors

Marjorie J. Kostelnik is dean of the College of Education and Human Sciences at the University of Nebraska, Lincoln. A former child-care, Head Start, and preschool teacher, as well as elementary school specialist, Dr. Kostelnik has been actively involved in helping educators in early childhood programs explore the implications of developmentally appropriate practices. Her work has taken her to many settings throughout the United States and abroad. Marjorie teaches classes in early childhood inclusive education and is currently on the Coordinating Commission for High Quality Early Childhood Education for the state of Nebraska.

Anne K. Soderman had 14 years of classroom experience working with children in both public and nonpublic educational settings prior to joining Michigan State University in 1979, where she is now professor emeritus. In addition to continuing to consult with schools in international settings, she is currently carrying out an administrative assignment and conducting research on second-language acquisition in Beijing, China. Soderman is also co-author of *Guiding Children's Social Development and Learning,* 6th ed. (2009), *Creating Literacy-Rich Preschools and Kindergartens* (2008), and *Scaffolding Emergent Literacy* (2005).

Alice Phipps Whiren is a professor emeritus of the Department of Family and Child Ecology, Michigan State University. She taught curriculum in early childhood and child development to undergraduate and graduate students and was supervisor of the Child Development Laboratories. Early in her career, she taught young children in an inner-city public school in Michigan. She also served as a Head Start assistant director and has provided a variety of training sessions for preprimary teachers nationally and internationally.

CONTRIBUTOR

Michelle Rupiper is an associate professor of practice and serves as the director of the Ruth Staples Child Development Laboratory at the University of Nebraska, Lincoln (UNL). Having received her doctorate in special education from Teachers College at UNL, Michelle has 25 years of experience working with children and families in a variety of early childhood programs. She is the past president of the Midwest Association for the Education of Young Children and the Nebraska Association for the Education of Young Children. Michelle also consults with early childhood programs across the state of Nebraska.

Brief Contents

Contents

Part 4   Integrating Curriculum   427

Chapter 15   Integrating Curriculum Through Pretend and Construction Play   428

Chapter 16   Integrating Curriculum Through Thematic Planning and Projects   459

INTRODUCTION

If you are a practicing teacher, you probably know the joy of getting a "fan letter" from a child. If you are an aspiring early childhood educator, someday you might get a note like the one Mrs. Howe got from Jiyeon, or you might receive a hug, a smile, or some other sign that you are an important part of a young child's life. Knowing that you make a difference to children and families is one of the best things about being an early childhood professional. Another benefit is knowing that you are helping children at the start of life, a time of amazing potential and tremendous opportunity.

A Good Beginning Is Essential

You know that the beginning is the most important part of any work, especially in the case of a young and tender thing.

—Plato

During the early years, children develop the attitudes toward education and themselves as learners that will stay with them all their lives. As children move through the early childhood period to middle childhood, they reach one of the following conclusions:

School is exciting/challenging/fun, and I am a good learner.

or

School is boring/difficult/painful, and I can't learn.

Children whose conclusions are positive have a strong foundation for subsequent life success. However, the future for children whose school evaluations and self-evaluations are negative is bleak. These children are the most likely to require extensive remedial assistance, encounter mental health problems, endure academic failure, and drop out of school (Cunha & Heckman, 2007; Horowitz, Darling-Hammond, & Bransford, 2005). The particular opinions children form are greatly influenced by their early educational experiences.

As an early childhood professional, you play a major role in shaping these experiences. The more you know about the field you are entering, the better prepared you will be to create effective early childhood programs. This introduction provides an overview of early childhood education today. We define the profession and discuss its significance now and in the future. In addition, we describe the children, families, and professionals who learn together in early childhood settings. Let us begin.

WHAT IS EARLY CHILDHOOD EDUCATION?

Which of the following programs would you classify as early education programs?

> Pre-K classroom
> Second-grade classroom
> Family child-care home

If you answered "All of the above," you were correct. **Early childhood education** involves any group program serving children from birth to age 8 that is designed to promote children's intellectual, social, emotional, language, and physical development and learning (Copple & Bredekamp, 2009). Such education translates into a wide array of programs, including those for infants and toddlers, as well as preschool, kindergarten, and primary programs. These programs may be half day or full day; public or private; enrichment or remedial in focus; targeted at low-, middle-, or high-income families; and administered by a variety of community institutions. Currently more children than ever are involved in early childhood education.

EARLY CHILDHOOD EDUCATION IS GROWING

There has never been a better time to begin a career in early childhood education. The field is growing dramatically (UNESCO, 2007). Today more than half of all the 3- and 4-year-olds in the United States are enrolled in some form of organized early learning program. The number of 5- and 6-year-olds in preschool and kindergarten is even greater, reaching up to 80% of the U.S. population. By age 6, nearly every child in the United States is involved in some form of early childhood education ranging from pre-kindergarten through first grade (U.S. Dept. of Education, 2008). This boom in early education is happening for several reasons:

1. People are becoming increasingly aware that the early years are critical learning years.
2. Increasingly more families want their children to become involved in early learning experiences before mandatory schooling starts.
3. Evidence indicates that high-quality early education has the potential to increase children's lifelong success and provide economic and social benefits to society.

Each of these trends is fueling a demand for more and better early childhood programs and the professionals who work in them.

The Early Years Are Important Learning Years

During early childhood, rapid growth occurs in children's cognitive, linguistic, social, emotional, and physical competence. This lays the foundation for adolescent and adult dispositions, concepts, and skills in every developmental domain. See Table 1 for highlights of the early competencies children are developing from birth to age 8.

Family Interest in Early Education Is Growing

"My neighbor used to look after my daughter, but I really wanted Taylor in a learning environment. I moved her here because I didn't want her watching TV all day. When it comes time for kindergarten, I want her to be prepared."

—Mother of a child in a Pre-K program
Kostelnik & Grady, 2009, p. 2

For the past 40 years there has been steady growth in the number of families seeking out-of-home care for their young children (U.S. Dept. of Education, 2008). This has paralleled an increase in women going to work while their children are very young as well as an increase in single parents needing child-care support (Schulman & Blank, 2009). When arranging care for infants and toddlers, most families seek such care so adult family members can work, go to school, or participate in job training. However, by the time children are 3 years of age, families say that enhanced learning is the number-one reason they want to enroll the children in a formal early childhood program prior to kindergarten or first grade (Barnett & Yarosz, 2007).

TABLE 1 Early Competencies that Form the Foundation for Future Learning	
Developmental Domain	Examples of Significant Competencies Grounded in Early Childhood
Cognitive	❏ Number concepts ❏ Problem-solving strategies ❏ Concepts of time, space, order, patterns, and categories
Linguistic	❏ Language ❏ Communication skills ❏ Associating meaning and print ❏ Emergent literacy
Social	❏ Social awareness ❏ Work habits and attitudes ❏ Prosocial understandings ❏ Development of conscience ❏ Understanding expectations and rules
Emotional	❏ Emotional awareness of self and others ❏ Empathy ❏ Coping strategies
Physical	❏ Body awareness ❏ Attitudes toward food/nutritional habits ❏ Body image ❏ Physical mastery—fine motor/gross motor

Early Intervention Pays Off for Children and Society

Based on four decades of research, we know that high-quality early childhood programs can help children succeed in school and later in life. This is especially true for children who are at high risk for potential school failure due to the burdens of poverty (Karoly et al., 2005; Barnett, 2008). Long-term studies have compared the experiences of low-income children who have gone to preschool with children from similar backgrounds who have not. Preschool alumni are less likely than non-program children to repeat a grade, to be referred to special education programs, or to fail to graduate from high school on time (Cunha & Heckman, 2007). These positive conditions also contribute to a better quality of life years later. At age 40, adults who had participated in a high-quality early childhood program for at least 2 years were less likely to be on welfare or to be chronic lawbreakers than was true for non-preschool going individuals (Schweinhart et al., 2005). As adults, preschool attendees were also more likely to own their own home, to be employed, to have a savings account, and to report higher satisfaction with life. Such positive outcomes benefit the children involved as well as the families and communities in which they live. Families are aware of these benefits; thus, increasingly more families of all kinds are choosing to send their children to "school" early in life.

CHILDREN AND FAMILIES IN EARLY CHILDHOOD EDUCATION

Mary Hughes was making nametags for the children in her class: Juan, Un-Hai, Rachel, Steven, LaTanya, Clarissa, Heidi, Mohammed, Molly, Sally, Keiko, Mark, LeRoy, Indira, Jennifer, and Sasha. As she finished each nametag, she thought about how different each child was. Her students represented many racial, ethnic, and cultural backgrounds. The children varied greatly in terms of their parents' educational level and their families' socioeconomic status. Some children spoke

English, and several spoke languages other than English at home. Some had prior preschool experience, and some had none. Some children lived at home with two parents, some were living in single-parent households, one child lived with his grandparents, and one youngster was a foster child, newly arrived in her foster home. The children also functioned at varying developmental levels. Mary marveled at the group's diversity.

Early Childhood Programs Serve a Diverse Population of Children and Families

Like Mary, you will likely work with a diverse array of children and families throughout your career in early childhood education. You will do so because the United States is becoming more diverse every year. For instance, racial and ethnic diversity has increased substantially in the United States over the past 40 years. According to the U.S. Census Bureau (2008), the population of white children in the United States is declining, while the proportion of children who are non-white is growing (see Figure 1). Also, in many parts of the country, up to 50% of the early childhood population speaks a home language other than English (Espinosa, 2008). Such ethnic and linguistic diversity is predicted to increase in the coming decades.

Family structures are also shifting. Today, children may live in a variety of family arrangements—two-parent families, single-parent families, blended families, extended families, families with opposite-sex parents and families with same-sex parents, adoptive families, and foster families. Overall the percentage of children living in two-parent households has steadily decreased, while the proportion of young children living in single-parent homes has risen (see Figure 2). In 2006, 67% of the children in the United States under the age of 17 lived with two married parents. Of these, the vast majority (90%) lived with their biological or adoptive parents; the other 10% lived with at least one stepparent (U.S. Census Bureau, 2007). Approximately 28% of the children in our country live with only one parent. Of these, 23% live only with their mothers, and 5% live only with their fathers. Another 4% of the families in which young children live are headed by a grandparent. Grandparent-headed households are found in all socioeconomic groups, all ethnicities, and all geographic locations in the country, with more than 4 million children living in intergenerational households (U.S. Census Bureau, 2007).

Income is another differentiating variable among families. Early childhood programs serve families who have limited financial resources as well as families who have large financial reserves. Some programs serve families whose income levels are within the same range; other programs serve families whose socioeconomic circumstances vary widely. All parents ultimately are responsible for food, clothing, shelter, and medical care and for making sure children go to school during the years of mandatory education. Yet, for many families, simply providing the basic essentials of life is a challenge. More than 10.5 million children in the United States live in low-income families. Children living in poverty may have two working parents (54%), one working parent (27%), or no working parents (20%) at home. Poor families are of every race and live in rural, suburban, and urban communities (Douglas-Hall & Chau, 2007).

FIGURE 1   Shifting Population

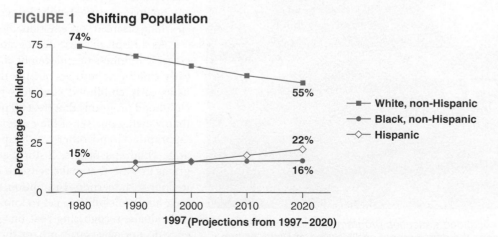

Source: U.S. Census Bureau. Current Population Survey, Annual Social and Economic Supplement. Retrieved January 5, 2008 from http://www.childstats.gov/americaschildren07/famsoc1.asp.

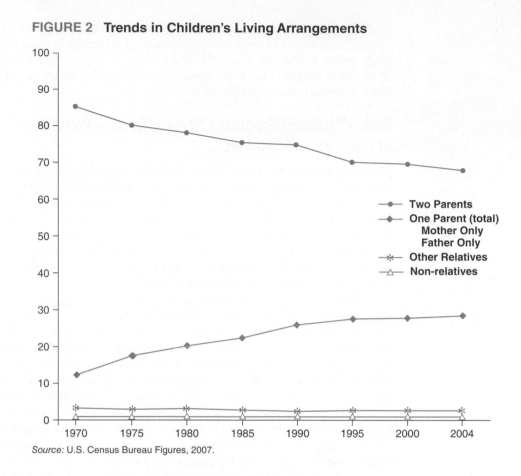

FIGURE 2 **Trends in Children's Living Arrangements**

Source: U.S. Census Bureau Figures, 2007.

Another factor that has influenced diversity in early childhood classrooms is inclusion. Children with disabilities have been provided a free public education in the **least restrictive environment** since 1986. The Individuals with Disabilities Education Act (IDEA) of 1997 provided additional protections to people with disabilities, including freedom from discrimination and equal access to public programs. IDEA was updated in 2004, governing how states and public agencies provide early intervention, special education, and related services to more than 6.5 million infants and toddlers (from birth to age 2) and children and youth (ages 3 to 21) with disabilities. IDEA underscores a U.S. commitment to educate all children, to the maximum extent appropriate, in regular classrooms on a full-time basis. Support services are brought to children as needed; the children are not removed from the early childhood setting to receive the services. Thus, children with disabilities are not clustered into groups of persons with similar disabilities. They are no longer served only in separate classrooms labeled "learning disabled" or "emotionally impaired."

As a result of these demographic and social trends, increasing numbers of children of all kinds are being served in early childhood settings outside their homes. This requires us as early childhood educators to create responsive early childhood programs that treat all people with respect. Rather than viewing one set of life experiences or demographics as "appropriate" and others as "inappropriate," we must integrate children's beliefs, history, and experiences into programs in ways that make sense to children and enable them to flourish as learners. In addition, we must recognize that we have a responsibility to get to know children and families as individuals, recognizing that our personal frames of reference do not necessarily mirror those of all the children and families we serve.

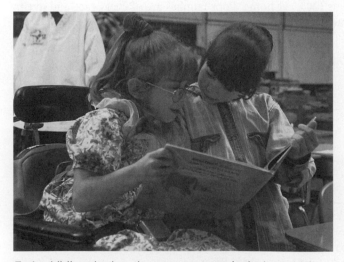

Early childhood education programs are inclusive, which enhances the development and learning of all the children enrolled.

Go to the Assignments and Activities section of Topic 3: Family/Community in the MyEducationLab for your course and complete the activity entitled *Family Influences on Children's School*. Hear what lessons children say their families teach them.

Families Are Children's First Teachers

During early childhood, the immediate context of the family has the greatest influence on the child. The family is responsible for meeting children's physical needs and for socializing the younger generation. Family members provide children with their first social relationships, their models for behaviors and roles, a framework of values and beliefs, and intellectual stimulation (Berns, 2009; Gallagher, 2005). All these functions take place through direct and indirect teaching, in constructive and sometimes destructive ways, more or less successfully. In addition, most environmental influences are channeled to some extent through the family. For instance, through their families, children gain access to economic resources and learn the customs of their cultural group. The first attitudes toward education, work, and society that children encounter are in the family. Parents arrange for out-of-home care and make the initial entrée into a school for their children. They also promote or inhibit opportunities for peer and community contact. If parents are stressed by the hardships of poverty, the uncertainty of losing a job, or the prospects of marital dissolution, their ability to meet the needs of their young children is jeopardized. If parents receive help or support from relatives, friends, or social institutions, the home environment they create for their children may be enhanced.

EARLY CHILDHOOD PROGRAMS VARY IN STRUCTURE AND SCOPE

During your years as an early childhood professional, you will most likely work in a variety of settings and programs. Education programs for young children come in all forms. Programs for young children operate under different funding sources (public or private) and vary in location and size (private home, church or temple, small-group center, or large school). Such programs encompass a wide range of educational philosophies and curricula. Early childhood education programs also vary in their target audience, their scope (full day to half day, full year to partial year, every day to some days), and the training background of key personnel. An overview of the vast array of services currently available is offered in Table 2.

These variations in programs serving young children evolved from distinct needs and traditions. For instance, modern child-care programs were devised in response to societal demands for protected child-care environments during parents' working hours. Historically, child-care programs have emphasized the health and safety of the children enrolled, and, although currently some involve government subsidies, many rely on corporate or private sponsorship and parent fees. Supplementing the learning experiences children have at home has long been the function of the nursery school movement. Usually financed through parent fees, today's preschools have nurturance, enrichment, and school readiness as their primary aims.

More recent early intervention programs such as Head Start, Even Start, and Title I are the result of federally mandated and supported efforts to remediate unfavorable developmental or environmental circumstances. These compensatory education programs focus on a particular segment of the population: children and families who are disadvantaged. Such programs are designed to change children's life opportunities by altering the course of their development for the better. Conversely, primary education reflects a history that emphasizes the commitment of public funds to mass education. The goals of primary education have focused on transmitting society's accumulated knowledge, values, beliefs, and customs to youngsters of all backgrounds and educational needs. Compulsory in some states, not required in others, but available in all, kindergarten straddles the two "worlds" of early childhood. Long considered a transition into formal schooling, kindergarten programs have been the center of much current controversy. Should they be structured more like preschool or more like the elementary grades? Traditionally, more similar to the former than to the latter, today's kindergarten programs vary greatly, depending on the philosophy of the school or district. Awareness that many children have previously attended early education programs and concern about children's subsequent school success have resulted in increasingly adult-centered, academic kindergarten programs (Kostelnik & Grady, 2009; Quintero, 2005). This trend has ignited renewed debate, not yet resolved, about the true function of kindergarten and its role in children's lives. It also has spawned new early childhood programs such as state-funded Pre-k classrooms.

The program variations just described are implemented by a wide array of practitioners trained to work with young children. Let us briefly consider how people become early childhood professionals and what distinguishes a professional from an amateur.

Go to the Assignments and Activities section of Topic 3: Family/Community in the MyEducationLab for your course and complete the activity entitled *How Families Contribute to Head Start*. See how Head Start addresses the needs of young children and their families.

TABLE 2 Early Childhood Education Programs for Children Ages 3–8 Years

Program	Children Served	Ages	Purposes	Funding
Early Head Start	Pregnant women, infants, and toddlers from low-income families	Prenatal to 3 years	Promote healthy pregnancies and enhance child development of very young children	Federal
Even Start	Children from low-income families and children with disabilities	Birth to 7 years	Promote family literacy (child and adult) and overall parent education	Federal
Head Start	Children from low-income families and children with disabilities	3–4 years	Comprehensive early education, health, nutrition and medical services, parent involvement	Federal
Private preschools	Mostly middle class	2–5 years	Enrichment and school readiness experiences	Parent tuition
Parent cooperative preschools	Children of participating parents	2–5 years	Enrichment and school readiness experiences as well as parent education	Parent tuition and in-kind support from families
Faith-based preschools	Children of church, temple, or mosque members	2–5 years	Educational experiences and spiritual training	Church subsidies and parent tuition
State sponsored pre-K programs	Children identified as at risk for economic, developmental, or environmental reasons; in some states, all 4-year-olds whose parents wish to enroll them	4 years	Development of readiness skills for future schooling	State taxes and special allocations
Group child-care homes (varies across states)	All	6 weeks to 12 years	Comprehensive care of children, covering all aspects of development	Varies; sources include employer subsidies; parent tuition; state agencies; the federal government by means of Title XX funds, the USDA Child Care Food Program, and child-care tax credits; and private and charitable organizations.
Family child-care homes (varies across states, ranges from 6–8 or fewer children and one provider)	All	6 weeks to 12 years	Comprehensive care of children, covering all aspects of development	Varies; sources include employer subsidies; parent tuition; state agencies; and the federal government by means of Title XX funds, the USDA Child Care Food Program, and child-care tax credits; and private and charitable organizations.
Center-based child-care	All	6 weeks to 12 years	Comprehensive care, addressing all areas of development, includes full-day and part-time care	Varies; sources include employer subsidies; parent tuition; state agencies; and the federal government by means of Title XX funds, the USDA Child Care Food Program, and child-care tax credits; and private and charitable organizations.

TABLE 2 Early Childhood Education Programs for Children Ages 3–8 Years *(continued)*				
Title I	Children who are educationally disadvantaged (poor, migrants, disabled, neglected, or delinquent)	4–12 years	Supplemental education for children and parents	Federal funds
Kindergarten	All	5–6 years	Introduction to formal schooling	State and local taxes or, in the case of private schools, parent tuition
First, second, and third grade	All	6–8 years	Transmission of society's accumulated knowledge, values, beliefs, and customs to the young	State and local taxes or, in the case of private schools, parent tuition

EARLY CHILDHOOD PROFESSIONALS COME TO THE FIELD IN MANY WAYS

When Scott arrived at Lakeland College, he majored in business administration. After taking some classes, he realized business was not his forte, but he had no clear idea of what he wanted to do. One afternoon he went with some friends to help supervise a Halloween party for kindergartners at the local YMCA. He had a great time with the children. They were fun and so smart. After several more experiences with children at the Y, Scott decided to talk to his adviser about the school's major in early childhood education.

Jackie is the mother of three children. When she began working in a Head Start classroom as a parent volunteer, she became intrigued with preschoolers' development and learning in the classroom. She vowed that someday she would earn her associate's degree in child development. Today, she is close to fulfilling that dream—just one class to go!

Lourdes knew she wanted to have a classroom of her own from the time she was a little girl. She played teacher with her friends and took a child development course in high school. Every chance she had, Lourdes found ways to work with children. She tutored at the local elementary school and participated in the Big Sister program in her town. During her freshman year, Lourdes signed up for courses in early childhood education, determined to make her lifelong dream come true.

What Makes Someone an Early Childhood Professional?

As evidenced by Scott, Jackie, and Lourdes, early childhood educators come to the field in a variety of ways. Some begin their training on the job; others start in a 2- or 4-year institution. Some are hoping to fulfill a long-held goal; others "discover" the field as a result of different life experiences. Whatever their motivation and entry point, individuals eventually decide to move from layperson status to the professional world of early childhood education. This shift is the result of education and training, not simply desire. Thus, certain characteristics differentiate the professional early childhood educator from a layperson (Freeman & Feeney, 2006; Kostelnik, Whiren, Soderman, & Gregory, 2009; Morrison, 2009).

Access to Knowledge. Professionals have access to specialized knowledge and skills that are unavailable to amateurs and that are acquired as a result of prolonged education and specialized training. The Association of Childhood Education International (ACEI), the National Association for the Education of Young Children (NAEYC), the Division for Early Childhood of the Council for Exceptional Children (DEC), and the American Association of Colleges for Teacher Education (AACTE) have made recommendations for the training of professionals in early childhood education. Recommended course content and skills include general studies (humanities, mathematics, technology, social sciences, biological and physical sciences, the arts, physical health and fitness), child development and learning, curriculum development and implementation, family

Go to the Professional Perspectives section of Topic 15: Professionalism/ Ethics in the MyEducation-Lab for your course and watch the video entitled *Advice for Those Entering Early Childhood Education, Parts 1 and 2.* Consider this advice for new teachers entering the field.

and community relationships, assessment and evaluation, professionalism, and field experiences with young children under appropriate supervision.

Although valuable, life experience alone is insufficient to provide the full range of technical know-how and professional skills necessary for maximum effectiveness on the job.

Demonstrated Competence. Professionals also differ from amateurs in having to demonstrate competence in their field before they can enter the profession. The most formalized evidence of mastery requires earning a license or certification, which is usually governed by state or national standards. Slightly less formal monitoring involves having to take tests, pass courses, and demonstrate proficiency either in a practicum setting or on the job. All these experiences occur under the supervision of qualified members of the profession.

Standards of Practice. Professionals perform their duties in keeping with standards of excellence generally accepted for the field. Such standards arise from research and professional reflection. Some standards are enforced through self-monitoring within the profession, whereas others are maintained through governmental regulation. Whatever the case, professional standards provide a gauge by which early childhood practitioners assess their performance and the overall quality of the services they offer children and families.

Lifelong Learning. To keep up with the standards in their field, early childhood professionals constantly upgrade their knowledge and skills both informally and formally. Such efforts include attending workshops, consulting with colleagues, participating in professional organizations, reading professional journals, and pursuing additional schooling. Regardless of the means, professionals treat learning as a lifelong process.

Code of Ethics. Although useful, the personal moral code most people bring to their work is inadequate to govern professional behavior. What is common sense to an individual may or may not be congruent with agreed-on standards within the profession. Thus, professionalism requires adoption of an ethical code of conduct that has been formally approved within the field. Such codes provide guidelines for determining acceptable and unacceptable behavior on the job. Specific ethical codes govern professionals whose work involves children. Although the particulars may vary, all ethics codes focus on ensuring confidentiality; providing safe and beneficial experiences; and treating people with respect regardless of sex, race, culture, religion, and ability. Two early childhood professional organizations that have published code of ethics documents are the **National Association for the Education of Young Children (NAEYC)** and the **Division for Early Childhood (DEC)** of the Council for Exceptional Children. These documents are available at the NAEYC website (www.naeyc.org/about/positions/pdf/PSETH05.pdf) and the DEC website (www.dec-sped.org/index.aspx/About_DEC/PositionConcept_Papers/Ethics).

HOW DOES PROGRAM QUALITY AFFECT EARLY CHILDHOOD EDUCATION?

How will you know if the program in which you are participating benefits young children? According to materials prepared for prospective clients, most early childhood programs claim to be outstanding. Is this true? Let us look at some examples.

A brochure describing the early childhood program at the Westover Child Development Center states:

> *Here at the Westover CDC, we offer a high-quality early childhood program for children from three to five years of age. Our teachers all have degrees in child development or early education. We focus on all aspects of children's learning using a play-based curriculum.*

An advertisement posted on the community bulletin board of a local grocery store reads:

> *High-quality childcare in my home. Loving environment. Lots to do. Fun, safe, reliable. References available.*

A headline of an editorial in a local newspaper states:

> *Blue Ribbon Panel Outlines Criteria for High-Quality Elementary Schools*

Although each example focuses on a different early childhood program, they all mention quality. People who talk about "high quality" are referring to excellence. When something is described as having high quality, we understand that it represents more than the minimum standards and has value exceeding the ordinary. Conversely, "poor quality" suggests an image of substandard conditions and negative outcomes. These variations in quality are particularly important in relation to early childhood education.

Quality Makes a Difference

Quality is a term early childhood professionals often use in describing their programs. Parents, too, are concerned about the quality of their children's education and care. This is true for all families, regardless of background or income level. In recent polls, as many as 97% of the parents surveyed cited quality as a highly important variable in determining which early childhood programs they wanted their child to attend (Raikes et al., 2004; Barnett & Yarosz, 2007). Yet, there is a difference in the quality of education and care that children receive. Some children are in high-quality early childhood programs, but many others have poor quality experiences. High-quality programs benefit children and their families; poor-quality programs are detrimental to them.

Poor-Quality Programs. Every day, thousands of children are subjected to program practices that threaten their immediate health and safety as well as their long-term development and learning (Cost, Quality, and Child Outcomes Study Team, 2000; Raikes et al., 2004). For instance, poor-quality experiences lead to increased behavioral problems and poorer academic progress in children. Such children are also more likely to have poor social skills. These negative effects appear to be long lasting: Evidence of poor quality is apparent as long as 5 years later. To make matters worse, families may not be able to compensate for the negative impact of poor-quality programs, at least for children who spend 20 or more hours a week in such circumstances (Edwards, 2005). Because high-quality care and education may be more expensive, children in low-income families are the most likely to be enrolled in poor-quality programs at both the preprimary and primary levels. In this way, poor-quality programs compound the challenges children living in poverty face.

High-Quality Programs. Children whose education and care are described as high quality enjoy a variety of benefits. Such children demonstrate higher levels of language development, greater social competence, a better ability to regulate their behavior, and better academic performance than do their peers in poor-quality programs (National Research Council, 2001; UNESCO, 2007). Additional evidence indicates that children who have high-quality early childhood program experiences outperform peers who have no such experiences prior to entering school. These results hold true in the short term and across time. Therefore, our aim as early childhood professionals is to create high-quality early childhood programs for children and families. To do this, we must have a better picture of what such programs involve.

What Do High-Quality Programs Look Like?

With so much at stake, we must ask, "What do high-quality programs look like?" Fortunately, there is a growing research base we can draw on for the answer. The essential components of high-quality early childhood programs are given in the following list (Biddle & Berliner, 2002; Stronge, 2002; UNESCO, 2007).

Practitioners are well prepared and well compensated.

❑ Adults have specific training in child development; early childhood education; and subject matter content such as literacy, math, and science.
❑ Adults have specific training in content and subject matter relevant to what they are teaching.
❑ Adults vary their teaching strategies and expectations on the basis of what they believe is age appropriate, individually appropriate, and socially and culturally appropriate for each child.
❑ Adults in higher-quality programs are paid reasonable wages and receive satisfactory benefits.

Staffing is stable.

❑ Teachers remain with the program and the same group of children long enough for children to develop a trusting relationship with an adult outside the home.

Group sizes are small, and a small number of children are assigned to each practitioner.

❑ The group size and adult–child ratios are small enough that children can engage in firsthand interactions with adults, receiving individualized instruction and personal feedback about their learning experiences.

Warm, attentive relationships are established between adults and children.

❑ Adults are warm, respectful, understanding, affectionate, and friendly toward children.
❑ Adults listen to children and comfort, support, and guide them in ways that make sense to children and help them become more successful in their social interactions.

Environments are safe and healthy.

❑ Health and safety provisions are in place to support children's well-being.

Environments are stimulating.

❑ Adequate, appropriate materials are available to support children's explorations and development of more advanced knowledge and skills.
❑ The curriculum is designed to support and enrich children's aesthetic, affective, cognitive, language, physical, and social development and learning.

Family engagement is evident.

❑ The program is designed to support and complement families in their child-rearing role.
❑ Family members are welcome to observe, discuss, and recommend policies and to participate in the program's activities.

There are links to comprehensive community services.

❑ Families are referred and have access to a wide array of services necessary to support their child-rearing responsibilities.

All these quality indicators set the stage for the best possible interactions between children and the early childhood professionals who will help prepare them for the 21st century.

LOOKING TOWARD THE FUTURE

The children with whom you are now working will be adults in a world we have yet to know. Although specific details are difficult to predict, researchers generally agree that to function successfully in the mid-21st century, people will have to demonstrate the following core abilities (Partnership for 21st Century Skills, 2009; Copple & Bredekamp, 2009):

Successful citizens of the 21st century need to know how to work together and be flexible thinkers.

Possess a solid education and be able to apply what they know and can do in relevant situations. Demonstrate knowledge and skills in the areas of literacy, numeracy, science, social studies/civics/global awareness, music and the visual arts, physical education, and health.

Work well with others. Communicate well, respect others, engage with colleagues to resolve differences of opinion, work well across cultures and function well as members of a team.

Act as problem solvers. Analyze situations, make reasoned judgments, and solve new problems.

Utilize skills broadly and engage in flexible thinking. Apply knowledge and skills across multiple areas, generalize knowledge and skills from one situation to another, and regroup and try alternative approaches when standard solutions fail.

Function as information seekers. Gain access to information through various modes, including spoken and written languages, and intelligently use complex new tools and technologies.

Envision themselves as lifelong learners. Continue to learn new approaches, skills, and knowledge as conditions and needs change.

As early childhood educators, we are becoming increasingly aware that in addition to *what* children learn, we must consider *how* children learn so that we can best promote the development of these core abilities (Horowitz et al., 2005; Schickedanz, 2008). In trying to describe how to achieve programs that enhance this kind of learning, educators have created the concept of developmentally appropriate practice. The remainder of this book is devoted to exploring this concept as a means for achieving high quality.

We designed *Developmentally Appropriate Curriculum: Best Practices in Early Childhood Education* to help you develop the knowledge base you will need to function as a professional in the field. While you are reading, we encourage you to reflect on the content in terms of your experiences with children and early childhood programs. We hope you will select some topics to explore further and that you will ask questions and challenge concepts you doubt. Most important, we urge you to use the material provided in this book to develop personal ideas about how to create and implement high-quality programs for children. You are the emerging generation of early childhood educators. We are looking to you to add to our store of knowledge about best practices in early childhood education.

myeducationlab

To check your comprehension on the content covered in the Introduction, go to the Book Specific Resources in the MyEducationLab for your course, select your text, and complete the Study Plan. Here you will be able to take a chapter quiz, receive feedback on your answers, and then access review, practice, and enrichment activities to enhance your understanding of chapter content.

Key Words

PRACTICE FOR YOUR CERTIFICATION OR LICENSURE EXAM

The following items will help you practice applying what you have learned in this chapter. They can help to prepare you for your course exam, the PRAXIS II exam, your state licensure or certification exam, and for working in developmentally appropriate ways with young children.

Early Childhood Programs Today

The Scotts are looking for a child-care program for their 3-year-old son, Tony. They consider three options: a family child-care home, an employer-sponsored child-care center, and a church-based cooperative nursery school. Although the features of each program differ, the Scotts are most interested in finding a high-quality program for their child.

1. **Constructed-response question**
   a. Describe three characteristics of high-quality early childhood programs.
   b. Discuss two ways in which high-quality programs benefit young children. Name two problems experienced by children enrolled in poor-quality programs.

2. **Multiple-choice question**
   Early childhood refers to what ages of children?
   a. birth to age 5
   b. birth to age 8
   c. ages 3 to 5 years
   d. ages 3 to 9 years

PART 1

FOUNDATIONS OF EARLY CHILDHOOD EDUCATION

Chapter 1
**Developmentally Appropriate Practice: An Evolving
Framework for Teaching Young Children**

Chapter 2
**Teaching and Learning in Developmentally
Appropriate Programs**

Developmentally Appropriate Practice

An Evolving Framework for Teaching Young Children

You may wonder:

What do people mean when they say developmentally appropriate practice?
How well do developmentally appropriate practices work?
Should all programs for young children use developmentally appropriate practice?
As a teacher, how will I be using developmentally appropriate practice in my own classroom?

This chapter will help you answer questions about developmentally appropriate practice in early childhood education.

Consider the learning going on in this early childhood classroom.

◆ ◆ *The pretend area has been transformed into a hairdressing shop. The children have created the following signs:*

> *Hr cataz (haircuts) 2$*
> *Shampoo 99c*
> *Karlazz (curlers) 2$ and 99c*
> *Prmz (perms) 2$*

Both boys and girls move into and out of this area and take turns as customers, receptionists, hair-cutters, and cashiers. They enact cutting hair, giving permanents, having manicures, making appointments, writing down appointments, writing out receipts, using the play cash register, and making change.

At the same time, four children are working with a balance scale trying to balance a series of objects against wooden cubes; pairs of children are playing checkers and two are playing Kalah. Players of this African game plan ahead to empty pebbles into each of their pots.

Six children who are building with blocks roll small trucks down an incline and discuss how to build together. One child writes a sign, Dajs HL (Dangerous Hill), and attaches it to the ramp with tape. Three children write in their journals; two mark the water level on a measuring tape attached to a jar under a leaky faucet. A few children sit in the library corner looking at books. Some are finding words they recognize, others are "telling" the story from memory (Fromberg, 2002, p. 17).

All this time, the teacher and an aide are moving among the children, observing, asking questions, modeling problem-solving skills, and helping children to record their findings.

As you can see, this classroom is characterized by action.

◆ ◆ ***Children in action:*** *constructing, creating with multimedia, enjoying books, exploring, experimenting, inventing, finding out, building, and composing throughout the day.*

◆ ◆ ***Teachers in action:*** *holding conversations, guiding activities, questioning children, challenging children's thinking, observing, drawing conclusions, and planning and monitoring children's learning* (Paciorek & Munro, 1999)

Action-oriented practices like these are sometimes described as **developmentally appropriate practices (DAP)**. DAP has had a powerful influence on people's ideas about early childhood education and has moved to center stage in the definition of what constitutes a good program for young children. In this chapter, we explore DAP and what it means for you as an early childhood educator. Let us begin by looking at how and why DAP was created.

WHY IS THERE A NEED FOR DAP?

DAP has evolved to address three significant early childhood issues: lack of universal high-quality early education programs, inappropriate curricula for young children, and growing concerns over lags in achievement among certain groups of children, especially children living in poverty.

17

Program Quality

Quality is a key factor in how much children benefit from early childhood programs. High-quality programs enhance children's development and learning. Poor-quality programs do not. Establishing high-quality programs is not intuitive, nor is it automatic. We know that, regardless of good intentions, many children in the United States (and throughout the world, for that matter) attend mediocre or poor-quality early learning programs (UNICEF, 2008). This has prompted a call to identify and define practices that characterize high quality as an important step in expanding the availability of such programs to young children.

Dealing with Pushdown Curricula

District Drops Recess to Gain More Time for the Basics
Crisis in the Kindergarten: Playtime Disappears
Tutoring for Tots: 3-Year-Olds Prepare for College

These actual headlines illustrate a trend that began in the 1980s and continues today in the United States—**pushdown curriculum** from the primary grades into kindergarten and preschool. Practices that traditionally were not encountered until first grade or later—such as long periods of whole-class instruction, written instruction out of workbooks, and letter grades—have become commonplace in kindergarten and some preschools (Miller & Almon, 2009). First and second graders, too, are often expected to perform tasks previously reserved for the upper grades, such as taking standardized achievement tests and dealing with possible retention.

Societal demands for more academics and a "back to the basics" philosophy have contributed to high-pressure practices like those just described. In 2001, the U.S. Congress passed the No Child Left Behind (NCLB) Act, an initiative aimed at improving learning opportunities for *all* children, K–12. Although the ultimate aims of NCLB are desirable, some applications have been less positive, especially for young children. Throughout the country there is a greater emphasis on academic tasks earlier in life and a belief that earlier is better (Elkind, 2007). Consequently, more young children find themselves sitting at desks, filling out worksheets, and taking tests to get into kindergarten or first grade. Teachers feel pressured to engage in classroom practices they believe are not in the best interests of young children (Wein, 2004). Child advocates are alarmed at what they view as an erosion of childhood and the "miseducation" of the youngest members of society. Physicians report a dramatic increase in the numbers of young children who visit them for stress-related illnesses and conditions. Nationwide, people who understand child development warn that children are being hurried into functioning in ways that do not match their natural modes of learning (Wenner, 2009; National Association for the Education of Young Children, 2009). All of this has signaled a need to describe what practices really are best for young children and what practices detract from helping children succeed in school and in life.

Closing the Achievement Gap

I have children in my class who have never handled a book, never drawn with a crayon, and who are constantly worried about whether or not they will get supper each night. This puts them behind from day one. Years later, I see these same kids and they have never caught up.

—Kindergarten teacher
Kostelnik & Grady, 2009, p. 6

Kindergarten teachers report that one of three children comes to school lacking the basic abilities needed to succeed. Most often, such children come from families living close to or below the poverty line (Douglas-Hall & Chau, 2007). Poverty is the single biggest predictor of low birth weight, malnutrition, poor dental and physical health, stress related to food insecurity and physical safety, homelessness, and child abuse and neglect (Halle, Forry et al., 2009; Shonkoff, 2009). None of these conditions contributes to healthy development or school achievement. Although living in a low-income family does not guarantee school failure, children from such families are more prone to low achievement than are children from more fiscally secure homes, because most families living in poverty have a harder time meeting children's basic physical, social, and cognitive needs. These struggles and lack of opportunities can have a negative impact on children's

FIGURE 1.1   Cognitive Skill Accumulation of Children Born in Families Below and Above the Poverty Line

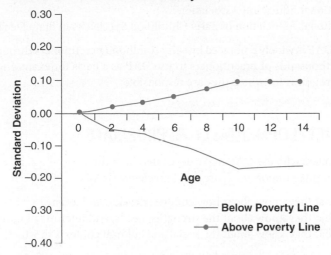

Note: Cognitive skills = numeracy, literacy, problem solving, language

Source: Cunha, F., & Heckman, J. (2007, September). *Investing in disadvantaged young children is good economics and good public policy.* Paper presented at the Telluride Economic Summit on Early Childhood Investment, Telluride, CO.

learning, starting at birth. Figure 1.1 displays the differences in cognitive skill accumulation between children living above and below the poverty line.

By the time most children living in poverty are 5 years of age, they are twice as likely as other children to score at the bottom of their class in literacy, numeracy, and general knowledge. Many enter kindergarten or first grade 19 months to 2 years behind their peers (Lee & Burkham, 2002; Barbarin et al., 2006). Unfortunately, these early lags hinder new skill development, making it hard for children to catch up. This contributes to an achievement gap between children living in poverty and their more financially advantaged peers. That gap continues to widen over the years and is more difficult to alter as children mature. Because the early years are so crucial, there has been a strong push to identify effective early learning strategies to address the needs of *all* children, including children most at risk for school failure.

THE EARLY CHILHDOOD PROFESSION RESPONDS

In response to these circumstances, the NAEYC developed a position paper in 1986 defining the concept of DAP as one means for improving early learning programs. This was quickly followed by an NAEYC book outlining support in the literature for DAP as well as describing examples of appropriate and inappropriate practices for programs serving children ages birth to 8 years (Bredekamp, 1987). These groundbreaking documents resonated with professionals in the field. They prompted action throughout the world and elicited much conversation and debate. As a result, the documents did not remain static, but have been revised twice (in 1997 and in 2009). Each new edition of DAP has incorporated observations and conclusions from professionals in many disciplines as well as the outcomes of relevant research.

PROFESSIONAL SUPPORT FOR DAP

Over the past two decades, the following education associations are among those that have endorsed the principles associated with DAP.

> National Council for the Social Studies
> National Council of Teachers of Mathematics
> International Reading Association
> Association for Childhood Education International
> Council for Exceptional Children

National Association of State Boards of Education
National Association of Elementary School Principals
National Education Association
National Association of Early Childhood Specialists in State Departments of Education

Today, DAP is widely embraced by early childhood practitioners throughout the world. This trend has led thousands of practitioners to use DAP as a basis for examining their practices and those of the programs for which they are responsible.

WHAT IT MEANS TO BE DEVELOPMENTALLY APPROPRIATE

myeducationlab

Go to the Professional Perspectives section of Topic 11: DAP/Teaching Strategies in the MyEducationLab for your course and watch the video entitled *NAEYC Position Statement on Developmentally Appropriate Practice.* Listen to Sue Bredekamp, who helped write the original guidelines, talk about DAP.

Practitioners who use DAP make decisions about the well-being and education of young children based on three important sources of knowledge (NAEYC, 2009).

1. What they know about how children develop and learn
2. What they know about the strengths, needs, and interests of individual children
3. What they know about the social and cultural contexts in which children live

Using this knowledge to guide their thinking, early childhood educators ask themselves, "Is this activity, interaction, or experience age appropriate? Is it individually appropriate? Is it socially and culturally appropriate?"

DAP Is Age Appropriate

Although age is not an absolute measure of a child's capabilities and understandings, it does help establish reasonable expectations of what might be interesting, safe, achievable, and challenging for children (NAEYC, 2009). To address age appropriateness, we first think about what children are like within a general age range. Next, we develop activities, routines, and expectations that accommodate and complement these characteristics. Mrs. Omura, the teacher in the 4-year-old class, is thinking about age appropriateness when she selects wooden puzzles that contain 8 to 25 pieces for the fine-motor area of her classroom. She makes selections on the basis of her observations of the number of pieces 4-year-olds typically find doable but challenging to complete. Mr. Allison, the second-grade teacher, also makes an age-related choice when he chooses jigsaw puzzles consisting of 50 to 100 pieces for the children in his group. He is aware that 7- and 8-year-olds find the more complex puzzles stimulating and fun to try. In both cases, the teachers make decisions about age appropriateness on the basis of their understanding of child development, which they acquired through formal study and classroom observation.

DAP Is Individually Appropriate

All children within a given age group are not alike. Each child is a unique person with an individual pattern and timing of growth, as well as an individual personality and learning style (Berk, 2009). Certain children are more verbal than others, some enjoy solitude, others crave company, some are skillful readers at 5 years of age, others may not achieve reading proficiency until 1 to 2 years later. Children also vary in the kinds and amounts of experiences they have had in relation to the new things they are learning. Each child enters the classroom with differing degrees of familiarity with such things as books, numbers, or puzzles. Sharing, asking for help, or listening to a story are common human interactions with which individual children will be more or less familiar. You can probably think of hundreds of variariations like these, all of which must be considered in designing, implementing, and evaluating activities, interactions, and expectations. It was the concept of individual appropriateness that prompted both Mrs. Omura and Mr. Allison to choose puzzles varied enough in complexity to fit the particular needs of individual children within their classes. These teachers knew that some children would need simpler puzzles to match their current levels of functioning and that other children would benefit from more challenging versions.

Early childhood educators consider individual appropriateness for every child in a group. However, if a class includes one or more children with special needs, the concept is often expanded to include the development of an **individualized education plan (IEP)**. Figure 1.2 provides additional information about an IEP and how it relates to individually appropriate practice.

FIGURE 1.2   Spencer's Individualized Education Plan

Federal law mandates that all children with a documented special need receive special education services early in life. These services must take place in the least restrictive environment possible. For young children, that often includes an early childhood classroom. What services children receive, how services are provided, and the outcomes a child might reasonably be expected to accomplish in a year are described within an individual education plan (IEP). Every IEP includes the same elements: a description of the child's strengths, needs, goals, short-term objectives, special education services, program modifications, and the frequency, duration, and location of the services to be provided. In each case, these elements are *individualized* to address the educational needs of a specific child.

In our example, 4-year-old Spencer is such a child. He has been identified as having autism spectrum disorder (ASD). Spencer likes to play with blocks, draw at the art table, and swing on the tire swing at school. He prefers solitary play and appears not to notice others even if they are playing nearby. If a teacher draws his attention to a peer or an activity, he will join in, but he needs help interacting. Currently, he does not use words, but is learning to use picture cards and simple voice output devices (assistive technology) to communicate. Spencer is enrolled in a special education preschool in the morning, which includes six children who have all been identified as having a special need. In the afternoon, Spencer is in a pre-K classroom, which includes children who are developing typically and children who have special needs.

Spencer's IEP was created in a group meeting that included his mom, dad, and grandmother (who often takes care of him after school). His special education teacher, his pre-K teacher, an occupational therapist, the elementary school principal, and a speech pathologist also attended. The adults first reviewed Spencer's assessment data, noting when his last formal assessment was given and the results. His family offered examples of what he likes to do at home. The teachers brought anecdotal records they had accumulated as well as checklists of behaviors they had observed Spencer display in their classrooms. The pre-K teacher also had work samples of Spencer's art and digital photographs of his block buildings over time.

Together the team created specific social, behavior, and communication goals and objectives for Spencer to address during the year. They agreed that the plan would be reviewed and revised annually. Following are three examples of *individually appropriate goals* identified for Spencer.

IEP Goals

- When shown a motor action by an adult (e.g., shaking a tambourine) and invited to do the same (e.g., "Do what I'm doing!"), Spencer will imitate the adult's actions with an identical object.
- Spencer will request a desired item by giving a picture to an adult or peer.
- Spencer will provide comments at group time with peers using a big mac switch (assistive technology).

Supporting Practices

Both preprimary teachers agreed to incorporate the following *individually appropriate practices* in their classrooms to enhance consistency from one setting to another. Spencer's family will use some of these techniques at home, too.

Create Communication Opportunities

- Program Spencer's big mac switch (assistive technology) to give him general comments/questions to use during play.
  - "Show me what you are doing."
  - "Can I have a turn?"
  - "I want to be next."
- Encourage peers to ask questions and make comments to Spencer.
  - "Laura asks Spencer _____."
  - "Sam tells Spencer _____."

Facilitate Social Opportunities

- If Spencer is playing alone, bring a peer to his play area or ask a peer to invite Spencer to play along.
- When transitioning in the classroom or going outside, have a peer hold Spencer's hand.
- Let Spencer's peers program his big mac by recording their voices.

DAP Is Socially and Culturally Appropriate

We must also look at children and families within the context of their community and culture before we can create meaningful, supportive early childhood programs. Consider the following examples.

Kyoko eats rice for breakfast at home. During a nutrition activity at school, some children insist that rice is only a dinner food. The teacher points out that people eat rice sometimes at breakfast, sometimes at lunch, and sometimes at dinner. Later she reads a story called Everybody Cooks Rice, *which describes people eating rice prepared in various ways and at different meals.*

Several families in the program share a culture in which humility is valued and expressions of group pride are encouraged more than expressions of personal accomplishment. Knowing this, the teacher praises the children as a group for working together to clean up the blocks rather than singling out individuals.

These children are learning by doing.

Powwows are very important in First Nations Cree culture, and most of the children in the Grade 2–3 combined class on a First Nations Reserve in Alberta, Canada, have experienced powwows. However, the teacher realizes that few of them know much about the traditions behind these important community events. This realization prompts her to introduce the topic powwows *for the children to investigate.*

In each preceding situation, early childhood practitioners demonstrated respect for children and their families by taking into account the social and cultural contexts in which they live.

Culture is defined by values, traditions, and beliefs that are shared and passed down from one generation to the next.

> Growing up as members of a family and community, children learn the rules of their culture—explicitly through direct teaching and implicitly through the behavior of those around them. Among the rules they learn are how to show respect, how to interact with people they know well as compared to those they just met, how to organize time and personal space, how to dress, what and when to eat, how to respond to major life transitions and celebrations, how to worship, and countless other behaviors that humans perform with little apparent thought every day. (Bredekamp & Copple, 1997, p. 42)

Because of the amount of variation among people, no single "correct" set of cultural beliefs exists. Instead, adults who work with children must recognize the legitimacy of multiple perspectives, including ones very different from their own (Trawick-Smith, 2009). Lack of cultural awareness by early childhood professionals can lead to erroneous assumptions and potentially negative outcomes for children. Consider the cultural misunderstandings depicted in Figure 1.3.

As noted in Figure 1.3, sitting quietly in class meant different things to people from different cultures. From the principal's cultural perspective, not talking in class signaled a lack of expressive language skills; from the children's perspective, not talking in class represented polite, attentive behavior. Misunderstanding the children's silence could have led to hours of unnecessary intervention, conveyed lack of respect for the children's home values, and undermined the credibility of the practitioners in the eyes of family members. To avoid such negative outcomes, adults who are engaged in DAP work hard to learn about the cultural beliefs of children's families. They understand that the more congruent expectations are between home and the early childhood setting, the more productively children learn. And, as was true for the speech-language pathologist in the earlier story, when they are not sure, they make an effort to find out. Thus, understanding what may be interpreted as meaningful to and respectful of children and their families is a key element in determining DAP.

The Essence of Developmental Appropriateness

Weaving the strands of age appropriateness, individual appropriateness, and sociocultural appropriateness into a cohesive philosophy requires deliberate effort and continuous reflection. First, as educators we must recognize the unique ways in which children are children, not miniature adults.

FIGURE 1.3 Cultural Misunderstandings

A speech–language pathologist in an Inuit school in northern Canada asked a principal—who was not Inuit—to complete a list of children who had speech and language problems in the school. The list contained a third of the students in the program, and next to several names the principal wrote, "Does not talk in class." The speech–language pathologist consulted a local Inuit teacher for help determining how each child functioned in his or her native language. The teacher looked at the principal's notes and said, "Well-raised Inuit children should not talk in class. They should be learning by looking and listening. Not talking doesn't mean they have problems expressing themselves."

Source: Based on "Educating Teachers in Developmentally Appropriate Practice," by F. D. Horowitz, L. Darling-Hammond, and J. Bransford, in *Preparing Teachers for a Changing World*, p. 114, by L. Darling-Hammond and J. Bransford (Eds.), 2005, San Francisco: Jossey-Bass.

Experiences and expectations planned for children should reflect that early childhood is a time of life qualitatively different from that of the later school years and adulthood. This means we must take into account everything we know about how children develop and learn, and match it to the content and strategies planned for them in early childhood programs. Second, we must think of children as individuals, not as a cohort group. This means recognizing that even children who share many similar characteristics are still singular human beings. Finally, we must treat children with respect. This requires us to learn about and value the families, communities, and cultures that shape children's lives. These beliefs form the essence of DAP. As you read the next section of this chapter, consider how these strands are apparent in the practices described.

GENERAL PRACTICES TYPICALLY ASSOCIATED WITH DAP

DAP provides a resource for thinking about, planning, and implementing high-quality programs for young children. It informs our decision making and gives us a basis for continually scrutinizing our professional practices. Within the current NAEYC document, examples of appropriate practices (effective practices supported by research) and contrasting practices (less effective or even harmful strategies) are outlined for infants and toddlers, children ages 3 to 5 years, children ages 5 to 6 years, and children ages 6 through 8 years. (Refer to Table 1.1 for an example.)

As you can tell from Table 1.1, inappropriate practices sometimes reflect errors of omission (never reading aloud to children) as well as errors of commission (interrupting the story with unrelated remarks). Appropriate practices are often defined between these extremes (reading aloud everyday and engaging children in meaningful conversations about the story). The NAEYC document contains hundreds of specific examples of appropriate practices and less appropriate ones. The essence of DAP, however, can be captured in 12 overarching principles (Kostelnik & Grady, 2009; Miller, 2009).

1. Adults develop warm caring relationships with children.
2. Child guidance fosters self-regulation. Adults acknowledge children's positive behaviors, reason with children, and treat their misbehaviors as learning opportunities.
3. Curricula are whole-child focused. Programs address children's aesthetic, emotional, intellectual, language, social, and physical needs.
4. Programs address the learning needs of *all* children, including children who have special needs and those who do not speak English as their home language.
5. Indoor and outdoor environments are safe and stimulating; routines are well suited to the needs of young children.
6. Children have numerous opportunities to learn by doing through hands-on activities that are relevant and meaningful to them.
7. Children are active decision makers in their own learning. They have many opportunities to initiate activities and to make choices about what and how they will learn.
8. Children have many opportunities to play throughout the day.
9. Teachers are intentional in their teaching. They have specific goals in mind for children's learning and use relevant instructional strategies to address those goals.
10. Curricula are integrated across disciplines and developmental domains.
11. Assessment takes place continuously throughout the day and addresses all developmental domains. Adults gather information about what children know and can do through observations, by collecting work samples and by inviting children to document their own learning.
12. Early childhood practitioners establish reciprocal relationships with children's families.

Take a moment to consider the K–1 classroom depicted in Figure 1.4. Which of the 12 principles of DAP just described are illustrated by the children and adults in this program?

Before we move on to other aspects of DAP, consider how developmentally appropriate practice relates to the latest findings in brain science.

TABLE 1.1   Examples of Appropriate Practices and Inappropriate Practices Related to Book Reading with Children Ages 3 to 8

Age Group	Appropriate Practices	Contrasting/Inappropriate Practices
3- to 5-year-olds	Every day teachers read aloud to children, in both small and large groups. To promote children's engagement and comprehension, teachers use strategies such as reading with expression and asking questions (e.g., "What do you think he'll do now?").	Teachers do not regularly read to children. Teachers often interrupt story reading to address unrelated teaching goals, which disrupts the narrative flow and reduces children's comprehension and enjoyment.
5- to 6-year-olds	Teachers provide multiple copies of familiar kindergarten-level texts. Children are encouraged to return to books that have been read aloud to them for independent "browsing." Special time is regularly set aside for independent reading of self-selected familiar texts.	Books in the literacy center seldom change. Multiple copies of books are unavailable for individual reading or reading with a partner. Teachers do not set aside time for independent reading.
6- to 8-year-olds	Teachers read aloud to children each day. For those books that children read on their own, teachers engage children in discussions of interest and importance to them. Taking notes on individual's comments and questions, teachers follow up on these in small groups or individually.	Teachers do most of the talking when books are discussed. Teachers' questions in book discussions with children do not engage them in making inferences, thinking critically, or expressing themselves through use of new knowledge and vocabulary.

Brain Science and DAP

Neuroscientists and pediatric researchers tell us that certain conditions are necessary to promote healthy brain development in young children (National Scientific Council on the Developing Child, 2007 Shonkoff, 2009). These conditions are closely tied to children's day-to-day experiences at home and in the community. For instance, children's brain development is enhanced when adults:

❑ Ensure children's health and safety
❑ Provide appropriate nutrition
❑ Establish close relationships with children
❑ Encourage children to explore and play

FIGURE 1.4   Sam Cooper's K–1 Classroom

Sam Cooper teaches in a class that includes five-through seven-year-olds in a public elementary school. During the few minutes we observe his large, attractive classroom, we see a number of groups containing three to five children busy in several areas of the classroom. Three children are talking to each other as they puzzle over a computer game. Four boys are sitting at a round table, busy with notebooks, crayons, pencils, and markers. One boy explains to us that they are writing in their journals. Sam arrives at that point, and responds to one child's comment about his work with a specific and enthusiastic response that indicates his familiarity with the child's story. He encourages another child to share his idea with a peer, and suggests to a third child that his friend help him figure out his spelling for the word he asked about. Sam surveys the room, and moves over to two girls who are in a heated discussion about balancing objects on a scale. Sam does not interrupt, listening seriously to each child's point of view, nodding thoughtfully, and then asking a question. As the girls try the scales again, Sam looks around at other busy children. He notices a child standing by the bookshelf, moves over to discuss his selection, and speaks with him quietly, finally leaving him after a pat and a smile. A child and adult enter the classroom. Sam moves over to greet them both, and engages in relaxed conversation with the parent, who seems equally relaxed with Sam. Sam gives the children a prearranged signal to gather at the meeting carpet; the parent has been invited in advance to conduct a mini-lesson about American sign language, since children are so interested right now in different methods of communication.

❑ Offer stimulating environments
❑ Establish routines
❑ Minimize stress

Now compare these "brain healthy" conditions to the general practices typically associated with DAP which you just read. What commonalities do you see? What implications does this have for your work with young children? Keep these thoughts in mind as you begin to consider the judgments involved in DAP.

IT REQUIRES JUDGMENT TO DETERMINE DEVELOPMENTAL APPROPRIATENESS

Referring to the practices just outlined, can you determine which of the following situations are developmentally appropriate and which are not?

Twenty 4-year-olds have been in circle time for 40 minutes. DAP or not DAP?

Suzanne wants the easel all to herself. Bianca wants a turn. The first-grade teacher helps the girls develop a timetable for sharing during the next several minutes. DAP or not DAP?

Jamie, a kindergartner, laboriously copies a series of words onto lined paper. DAP or not DAP?

Your first impression may be that a 40-minute circle time is too long for most 4-year-olds and that copy work is not the best way to teach children to write. If so, you probably decided that these scenarios were examples of developmentally inappropriate practices. You may also have assumed that helping two children learn to share clearly illustrates DAP. However, closer scrutiny may prompt you to reassess your original judgments.

For instance, you may revise your opinion about the circle time after learning that the children are enthralled by a storyteller who actively involves them in the storytelling process and that the time has been prolonged in response to the children's request, "Tell us another one." Likewise, helping children to share is usually worthwhile. In this case, however, Suzanne's aunt, uncle, and cousins recently lost most of their belongings in a household fire. They are staying with Suzanne's family, and Suzanne is having to share many things—attention at home, her room, her toys, and some of her clothes. Knowing this, we may determine that making her share the easel today is unnecessarily stressful. Helping Bianca find an alternative activity that will satisfy her desire to paint could be a better course of action for now. A second look at Jamie reveals that he is working hard to copy the words *I love you* for a present he is making for his mom. He is using a model created by another child and is writing on paper he selected himself. Within this context, Jamie's copywork no longer seems questionable.

Scenarios such as these illustrate that determining what does or does not constitute DAP requires more than simply memorizing a set of dos and don'ts or looking at children's activities in isolation. It involves considering every practice within the context in which it is occurring and making a judgment about what is happening to a particular child in a particular place at a particular time. The best judgments are those you make consciously.

Faced with having to determine the extent to which their actions are developmentally appropriate, many early childhood educators ask three questions.

1. Is this practice aligned with what I know about child development and learning?
2. Does this practice take into account children's individual strengths and needs?
3. Does this practice demonstrate respect for children's social and cultural lives?

These queries can address immediate concerns or long-term deliberations. They can stimulate individual thinking or consideration of program practices by an entire staff. In every circumstance, the answer to all three questions should be yes. A no answer to any of them is a strong sign that the practice should be reconsidered, revamped, or discarded. Your response will depend on your interpretation of what is age appropriate, individually appropriate, and socioculturally appropriate for specific children. Your knowledge of child development and learning, your understanding of curriculum, your awareness of family and community relationships, your knowledge of assessment, and your interpretation of your professional role will also influence what you do (NAEYC, 2009). All these factors, combined with an understanding of DAP, should guide early childhood decision making.

DAP HAS HISTORIC ROOTS

The practices associated with developmental appropriateness did not emerge all at once, nor were they the product of any one person's thinking. Certain ideas such as whole-child teaching and hands-on learning evolved over hundreds of years. Table 1.2 provides a brief description of early philosophers and child advocates whose contributions laid a foundation for the general practices that currently characterize DAP classrooms. This list is not complete, but it will give you a sense

TABLE 1.2   People Whose Work Contributed to Current Practices

Person	Contribution
John Amos Comenius (1592–1670) Moravian philosopher	Wrote that multisensory learning was more relevant than verbal learning alone
"All material of learning must be divided according to age levels."	Urged parents to become involved in their children's education
Jean Jacques Rousseau (1712–1778) French philosopher	Recognized individual patterns of development within children
"A child should neither be treated as an irrational animal, nor as a man, but simply as a child."	Promoted the idea that children's natural curiosity was a strong source of learning
	Believed that the school should fit the child, not that the child must fit the school
Robert Owen (1771–1858) Welsh industrialist and social reformer	Created an employer-sponsored infant school that was a forerunner of the North American preschool
"Physical punishment in a rationally conducted infant school will never be required and should be avoided as much as giving children poison in their food."	Favored multiage groupings among children 2, 3, 4, and 5 years
	Focused on hands-on learning and field trips as a way to observe how real things existed in the world
	Emphasized the importance of positive discipline
Friedrich Wilhelm Froebel (1782–1852) German philosopher	Became known as the father of kindergarten
"The prime purpose throughout is not to impart knowledge to the child but to lead the child to observe and think."	Stressed the significance of play and the value of childhood as a time of importance for its own sake, not simply as preparation for adulthood
	Created the first curriculum—including a planned program for children to follow, routines (songs, finger plays, and circle time), and specialized objects for learning (called *gifts*—objects for children to handle)
Maria Montessori (1870–1952) Italian physician	Emphasized active, self-directed learning through play and freedom within limits
"The greatest sign of success for a teacher . . . is to be able to say, 'The children are now working as if I did not exist.'"	Advocated the multiage class
	Created child-scaled furnishings and promoted the use of developmentally appropriate educational materials
Jean Piaget (1896–1980) Swiss psychologist and biologist	Proposed a theory of stages children move through in achieving cognitive maturity
"The principal goal of education is to create [people] who are capable of doing new things, not simply of repeating what other generations have done—[people] who are creative, inventive and discoverers."	Described ways in which children's thinking is qualitatively different from that of adults
	Stressed that children learn through experimentation with objects
Lev Vygotsky (1896–1934) Russian psychologist	Described the influence of language, culture, and social interaction on children's learning
"The only good kind of instruction is that which marches ahead of development and leads it."	Emphasized the importance of appropriate instruction

TABLE 1.2 People Whose Work Contributed to Current Practices *(continued)*

Margaret McMillan (1860–1931) English reformer and teacher "The teacher of little children is not merely giving lessons. She is helping to make a brain and nervous system, and this work is going to determine all that comes after."	First used the term *nursery school* Focused on whole-child learning through play and sensory experience Emphasized working with parents and suggested doing home visits Stressed the importance of specially trained teachers for young children
John Dewey (1859–1952) American educator "Education therefore is a process of living and not a preparation for future living."	Advocated children's learning by doing through hands-on activities, projects, units of study, and a child-centered, integrated curriculum Highlighted the value of play Promoted respect for children's individuality Founded the first "laboratory" school to study child development and teaching through systematic research and practice
Patty Smith Hill (1868–1946) American educator "Observe the children and follow their lead."	Promoted hands-on learning, experimentation, and self-discovery Wrote the song "Happy Birthday" Wrote a kindergarten manual to systematically define best practices for young children Founded the National Committee on Nursery Schools (1926), which eventually became the National Association for the Education of Young Children (NAEYC)

of who helped shape practices in early childhood education today. You will also see that ideas related to DAP have their roots in more than one country.

Now that we considered the basic components of DAP, let us explore the effectiveness of this approach. For any framework to stand the test of time, it must be supported by demonstrable results.

THERE IS EMPIRICAL SUPPORT FOR DEVELOPMENTALLY APPROPRIATE PROGRAMS

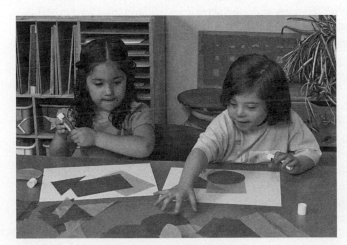

Children in developmentally appropriate classrooms are excited about school and eager to learn.

What began as a feeling for many people is becoming a documented reality. Evidence is mounting that flexible curriculum models, which incorporate DAP principles into their programs, lead to positive educational outcomes for children. In contrast to programs that ignore such principles, DAP-based curricula are more likely to produce long-term gains in children's cognitive development, social and emotional skills, and life-coping capabilities (Montie, Claxton, & Lockhart, 2007; Payton et al., 2008; UNICEF, 2008). Although more remains to be learned, we have a growing body of data supporting the idea that a DAP-oriented philosophy has long-lasting benefits for children. See Figure 1.5 for a brief summary of research findings associated with DAP.

Let's Consider Diversity

At this point you may ask, "How well does DAP contribute to the positive development, learning, and academic success of

FIGURE 1.5   Research Findings Associated with DAP

Several research studies have compared the performance of children in DAP-oriented classrooms with the performance of children in classrooms not characterized by DAP. Here are sample findings related to children's social and cognitive learning:

Social Outcomes

Children whose teachers use DAP tend to exhibit:
   Better social problem-solving skills
   More cooperation
   More favorable attitudes toward school and teachers
   More positive attitudes about themselves as learners

Fewer negative social behaviors
Fewer stress-related behaviors

Cognitive Outcomes

Children whose teachers use DAP tend to exhibit better:
   Creative-thinking skills
   Memory skills
   Mathematical problem-solving skills
   Grasp of mathematical concepts
   Ability to generalize numeracy skills from one situation to another
   Reading comprehension
   Listening skills
   Letter–word identification

Source: Barnett, 2008; Dunn, Beach, & Kontos, 1994; Hart et al., 1998; Jambunathan, Burts, & Pierce, 1999; Mantzicopoulos, Neuharth-Pritchett, & Morelock, 1994; Payton et al., 2008; Sherman & Mueller, 1996; UNICEF, 2008; Wiltz & Klein, 2001.

diverse children? Does DAP work for all? Or, does DAP suit certain children, but not others?" Studies conducted a decade ago seemed to indicate that DAP was widely applicable. Researchers at the time noted that DAP "has the potential to provide strong foundational experiences for males and females from different racial and socioeconomic backgrounds" (Hart, Burts, & Charlesworth, 1997, p. 8). Later studies have borne this out. Over the past 10 years, the beneficial results reported in Figure 1.5 have been found to be true for boys and for girls; for children from higher income families and lower income families; for children of color as well as White children in the United States; and for children in many countries around the world (e.g., Australia, England, France, Greece, Poland, Indonesia, and Thailand) (Bennett, 2008; National Institute of Child Health and Human Development [NICHHD], 2005). Such results indicate that DAP is a promising approach for working with diverse populations of children. However, additional studies specifically structured to answer questions of diversity are necessary before we can say with certainty that DAP meets the needs of *all* the children and families that early childhood educators serve.

DAP PROGRAMS VARY IN STRUCTURE AND CONTENT

LaJoya Gatewood and her husband are looking for an early childhood program in which to enroll their 3-year-old son and 7-year-old daughter. During their search, they visit three facilities, all of which are self-described as using DAP.

The literature for the Burcham Hills Child Development Center states, "We offer a developmentally appropriate array of activities for children designed to foster the development and well-being of the whole child. With the support of caring teachers, children play and experiment, making their own discoveries about the physical and social worlds in which they live. Children learn indoors and outside, in the classroom, at home, and in the neighborhood. Field trips are an integral part of the program as are visits to the classroom by parents and other family members."

During a visit to the Christian Children's Center, they are told, "The philosophy that guides the program at CCC is based on Christian values and developmentally appropriate practice. One of the obvious distinctions of our center is the Christian atmosphere we strive to maintain. Strong efforts are made to incorporate the loving presence of Jesus Christ throughout our program. This includes saying a short prayer before meals, having Bible stories in our book corner and at story times, and teaching children simple Bible verses. We also stress, as Jesus did, the importance of loving and caring for one another. In addition, we appreciate that children develop at varying rates and create programs that allow children to progress at a comfortable pace in learning the skills and concepts necessary for later success in school."

The brochure for the Rosa Parks Community School says, "At the Rosa Parks Community School, children experience a dynamic infusion of African American culture into the early childhood curriculum. Framed within the context of developmentally appropriate practice, children come away with a love of learning and positive self-esteem gained through meaningful activity. Hands-on learning is central to the program. Children learn about Africa and their rich cultural heritage; they learn about African American and African heroes and heroines, music, arts and crafts, and folktales. Teachers come from Africa as well as the United States, and all have first-hand knowledge of African culture."

All these programs have features the Gatewoods like, but each is distinct from the others. The family wonders, "How can programs that differ so greatly all be described as developmentally appropriate?" The answer to their question lies in the fact that DAP is a philosophy, a framework, and an approach to working with children. It is not a single curriculum (Bredekamp & Rosegrant, 1992; Copple & Bredekamp, 2009). Consequently, early childhood programs that incorporate DAP into their overall design vary across program settings and across curriculum models. At the same time, they share a common commitment to the principles that are a hallmark of the DAP philosophy.

DAP Is Adaptable Across Program Settings

The strategies associated with DAP can be carried out in an assortment of early childhood settings—part time or full day; home based, center based, or school based; private or public; nonprofit or for profit. They are applicable to programs serving infants, toddlers, preschoolers, school-age children, children who are linguistically diverse, and children with special needs. DAP can be observed in large programs and in ones that are small, as well as in urban, rural, and suburban locations.

DAP Is Adaptable Across Curriculum Models

Besides varying in their physical characteristics and in clients served, early childhood programs differ in their theoretical foundations. Most of these variations center on differing beliefs about how much either biology or the environment influences child development and learning. These differences in theoretical orientation lead to variations in program models and in the curricula children experience. A brief overview of four theoretical perspectives prevalent among today's early childhood practitioners is offered here.

The Maturationist Perspective. Some practitioners carry out programs designed primarily to support the natural unfolding of children's developmental capacities. From the **maturationist perspective**, they believe that the proper program for each child can best be determined by referring to norms for that age range and providing activities and materials to support children's current levels of functioning. Self-discovery by children rather than adult-initiated experiences dominates the program. Attempts to train children before they are "ready" for certain kinds of learning are believed to be ineffective or even harmful. If children do not seem ready to engage in certain tasks, they are left to "grow into" them without adult intervention. This practice is known as giving children "the gift of time."

A Mental Health Perspective. The work of Sigmund Freud and Erik Erikson underscores the significance of early personality development, giving rise to the view that early childhood programs can help prevent mental illness. Such programs espousing a Freudian/Eriksonian **mental health perspective** use play-based activities to enhance children's sense of well-being. Children are free to choose the activities in which they will participate, all of which emphasize play as a primary vehicle for involvement. Practitioners provide materials such as sand, water, clay, and blocks to help children gain personal satisfaction as they act on their emotions and internal drives. Teachers assume that children will become emotionally functional human beings with support but little direct intervention from adults.

The Behavioral Perspective. Early childhood professionals who focus on children's achieving specific behavioral outcomes (e.g., reciting the alphabet, tying a bow, counting to 10) rather than internal affective processes are described as having a **behavioral perspective**. The programs they create are often associated with teaching children "academics" and basic self-help skills. To achieve their goals, these practitioners rely mostly on direct instruction and external rewards to shape children's behavior in certain directions. Such shaping involves the following steps: (a) targeting a desired behavior, (b) establishing a baseline, (c) selecting relevant reinforcers, (d) sequencing instruction, and (e) systematically applying reinforcers until the goal is achieved.

A Constructionist Perspective. The models described thus far represent polar views of child development and learning. The maturationist and mental health philosophies emphasize the dominant role of biology; the behavioral approach focuses on environmental factors almost exclusively. The constructionist point of view combines the two. Educators espousing a **constructionist perspective** believe that children are holistic beings whose development and learning are influenced both by biology and by children's interactions with the physical world and other people. This point of view maintains that adults and peers are important sources of help and instruction. As they interact with people and objects, children are challenged to explore new ideas and attempt tasks that are slightly beyond their current capabilities. Through such experiences, children gradually master new knowledge and skills. This philosophical orientation suggests that children benefit from opportunities for self-discovery *and* direct instruction and from chances to play freely *as well as* participate in teacher-directed activities. Currently, the constructionist philosophy dominates the early childhood scene, both in terms of research and program implementation.

Although DAP is most closely associated with the constructionist approach to early childhood education, DAP can also be observed in well-executed programs more closely aligned with maturational, mental health, and behavioral orientations. In addition to these theoretical origins, developmentally appropriate programs may be designed around certain life perspectives such as a particular religious or cultural orientation.

To illustrate the variety of programs espousing a DAP perspective, we asked early childhood educators highly involved in the design of two program models to summarize the key elements of their work. The two models they describe are the HighScope approach and the Reggio Emilia approach. As you read these descriptions, consider how each program demonstrates DAP principles in its operations.

▲ ▲

THE HIGHSCOPE EARLY CHILDHOOD CURRICULUM

Ann S. Epstein
HighScope Educational Research Foundation

Origins

The HighScope Curriculum, currently used in settings serving the full range of infants, toddlers, preschoolers, and early elementary–aged children, was originally developed to serve "at-risk" children in Ypsilanti, Michigan. In 1962, the late David P. Weikart and former president of the HighScope Educational Research Foundation, initiated the Perry Preschool Project to see if early education could counteract the persistent school failure of high school students from Ypsilanti's poorest neighborhoods. During this project, teachers worked with 3- and 4-year-old children in a classroom setting for 3 hours a day, conducted daily staff meetings, and made weekly home visits. The basic framework of the HighScope Curriculum emerged with active learning, a plan–do–review process, and small- and large-group activities as its core. A longitudinal study of the students in the Perry Preschool Project through age 40 found the curriculum had positive effects on school achievement and literacy, high school graduation, adult earnings, home ownership, and lifetime arrests. A cost-benefit analysis showed society saves more than $17 for every dollar invested in this high-quality program.

Central Principles

Five basic principles—active learning, supportive adult–child interactions, a materials-rich learning environment, a consistent daily routine, and ongoing child assessment—form the framework of the HighScope Curriculum. Through *active learning*—having direct and immediate experiences and deriving meaning from them through reflection—young children construct knowledge that helps them make sense of their world. The power of active learning comes from personal initiative. Young children act on their innate desire to explore; they ask and search for answers to questions about people, materials, events, and ideas that arouse their curiosity; they solve problems that stand in the way of their goals; and they generate new strategies to try. As they follow their intentions, children develop the knowledge and skills that constitute the curriculum's comprehensive content—detailed and key developmental indicators that guide adult planning and child assessment. Figure 1.6 lists the High-Scope Curriculum content areas.

Active learning depends on *supportive adult–child interactions*. Mindful of the importance of providing a psychologically safe climate for young learners, adults using the HighScope Curriculum strive to be supportive as they converse and interact with children. Throughout the day, guided by an understanding of how young children think and reason, adults scaffold early learning by practicing supportive interaction strategies—sharing control with children, focusing on children's strengths, forming authentic relationships with children, supporting children's ideas, and adopting a problem-solving approach to social conflict. For example, when a child

FIGURE 1.6   HighScope Curriculum Content Areas

Approaches to Learning

Language, Literacy, and Communication

Social and Emotional Development

Physical Development, Health, and Well-Being

Arts and Sciences

    Mathematics
    Science and Technology
    Social Studies
    The Arts: Visual Art, Dramatic Art, and Music

Source: Ann S. Epstein, Senior Director of Curriculum Development, HighScope Educational Research Foundation.

talks, an adult listens attentively; makes related comments and observations; and asks open-ended questions directly related to what the child is doing, thinking, and saying. This interaction style enables the child to confidently express thoughts and feelings, construct an understanding of concepts, and experience partnership in dialogue. Adults rely on encouragement and use a problem-solving approach to deal with everyday classroom situations rather than a child-management system based on praise, punishment, and reward.

Because the *physical setting* has a strong impact on the behavior of children and adults, the HighScope Curriculum places a strong emphasis on planning the layout of the class room or center, selecting appropriate materials, and making them accessible to children. An active learning environment provides children with ongoing opportunities to make choices and decisions. Thus, adults organize the learning space into specific interest areas well stocked with natural, found, commercial, and homemade materials that provide many opportunities each day for children to engage in the key experience in creative, purposeful ways.

In addition to arranging the setting, adults also plan a *consistent daily routine* that supports active learning. The routine enables young children to anticipate what happens next and gives them a great deal of control over what they do during each part of their day. The HighScope daily routine includes the plan–do–review process, which enables children to express their intentions, carry them out, and reflect on what they have done. Small- and large-group times (for younger children) and workshops (for older children) encourage children to explore and experiment with materials and concepts adults have selected based on their daily observations of children's interests, abilities, and the key developmental indicators.

In the HighScope Curriculum, *assessment* includes a range of tasks teachers undertake to ensure that planning for and scaffolding children's learning receive full adult energy and attention. Each day, teachers gather accurate information by observing and interacting with children and taking anecdotal notes based on what they see and hear. Periodically, they use the child observations they have collected to complete a validated and observationally based assessment for each child—the Child Observation Record (COR). Programs also use the validated Program Quality Assessment (PQA) to determine the professional development needs of staff and to monitor and maintain the quality of the program delivered to children and their families.

Where Readers Can Find Out More

The HighScope approach is described in *Essentials of Active Learning in Preschool* (2007) by Ann S. Epstein, and *Educating Young Children* (2008) by Mary Hohmann, David P. Weikart, and Ann S. Epstein, available from HighScope Press, 600 North River, Ypsilanti, MI 48198-2898; www.highscope.org; telephone: 1-800-407-7377; fax: 1-800-442-4329. For up-to-date information about HighScope training, research, publications, and videos, visit the HighScope homepage at www.highscope.org.

▲ ▲

THE REGGIO EMILIA APPROACH TO EARLY CHILDHOOD EDUCATION

Carolyn Pope Edwards
University of Nebraska–Lincoln

Origins

Reggio Emilia is a city in northern Italy where a volunteer group of educators, parents, and children came together after World War II with a shared vision for a new kind of school for young children. After the suffering and destruction of the war, they wanted to offer hope to society and improve life for children and families. Under the leadership of the founding director, Loris Malaguzzi (1920–1994), the system then evolved from a parent cooperative movement into a city-run system of first preschools and then also infant–toddler centers. The system exercises a leadership role in educational innovation in Italy and Europe, and now increasingly the world. Through their experience in the Reggio Emilia preschools, children learn to engage in dialogues and debates with others in a nonviolent and constructive manner and develop problem-solving skills. Children (and families) are also encouraged to express and discuss ideas in open-democratic meetings and to form close, long-term relationships with others in the school. The schools are publicly funded and inclusive, giving first priority to children with disabilities or social service needs.

Goals

The Reggio Emilia approach is not an educational model in the formal sense, with defined methods, teacher certification standards, and accreditation processes. Instead, educators speak of their "experience" and how it can be a source of reflection to others. Loris Malaguzzi was a social constructivist, influenced by progressive educators and psychologists such as Dewey, Piaget, and Vygotsky. He drew a powerful image of the child, who comes into the world social from birth, intelligent, curious, and competent. Malaguzzi's vision, "education based on relationships," focuses on children in relation to people, things, and ideas. The goal is to activate and support children's network of connected ideas and their participation in a world of peers, community members, and the physical environment.

Children, teachers, and parents all have their respective rights to be part of the system, contribute to it, and learn within it. In fact, children are expected to be active and resourceful and to generate changes in the systems in which they are involved. Teachers seek to hold before them this powerful image of the child as they support children in exploring and investigating. Children grow in competence to symbolically represent their ideas and feelings through any of their "hundreds of languages" (expressive, communicative, and cognitive), including words, gestures, drawing, painting, building, sculpture, shadow play, collage, wirework, dramatic play, music, dance, puppets, and computers, that they systemically explore and combine. Adults follow the children's interests and do not provide focused instruction in reading and writing; however, they foster emergent literacy as children record and manipulate their ideas and communicate with others. They try to understand as fully as possible the children's viewpoints and abilities, seeing each child as full of strengths rather than full of needs.

Content/Focus

Teaching and learning are negotiated, emergent processes between adults and children, involving generous time and in-depth revisiting and reviewing. Close, long-term relationships are formed because children and teachers usually stay together in the same group for 3 years, so that a strong link is formed for the child between home and school. Furthermore, long-term, open-ended projects are important vehicles for collaborative work, and these become longer and more elaborate as children grow older and more experienced in this way of learning.

Classroom environments are carefully prepared to offer complexity, beauty, organization, and a sense of well-being and ease. The physical space receives much attention so that it supports exchange and relationships through physical qualities of transparency, reflectiveness, openness, harmony, softness, and light. The space conveys to children, parents, and teachers that their presence is valued and respected. A classroom atmosphere of playfulness and joy should prevail in this kind of environment. Time, too, is treated with special care. Children's own sense of time and their personal rhythm are considered in planning and carrying out activities and projects. Children have time to explore their ideas and hypotheses fully and in-depth. Projects and themes follow the children's ideas and development of concepts. Projects, activities, and experiences such as field trips and celebrations build on one another over time. Children review and revise their original work and ideas, refining them as they have further experiences, consider further questions, notice more details, make more connections, and acquire improved skills. Learning and development advance at their own pace, in widening and deepening cycles of understanding, not step-wise sequences.

Methods

The methods used in the Reggio approach are flexible and allow for input and decision making on the part of all participants. The methods must be adapted to each context and situation, with its own particular history, set of problems, and resources. The most important principle is that teaching should be based on careful observation of children. Teachers begin by actively soliciting children's ideas and thoughts, considering what knowledge, questions, and preferences the children have before formulating plans and projects. Teachers usually work two to a classroom, and collaboration/mentoring is strongly promoted. A *pedagogista* (pedagogical specialist or education coordinator) works with several schools to guarantee high-quality services. In addition, each school usually has a specialist (*atelierista,* specialist trained in the visual arts) to work with teachers and children to encourage expression through different media and symbol systems. Collaboration is encouraged among children through the use of small groups working together in common pursuit of an investigation or a project. These can last for a couple of days, weeks, or months depending on the age and interest level of the children.

Role of the Teacher

Teachers seek to be partners and guides to the children as they learn. They carefully prepare the environment to ensure that it provides strong messages about respect for the children and for their learning. In working with children, teachers play a role of *artful balancing* between engagement and attention. They ask questions to draw out the children's ideas, hypotheses, and theories. Then teachers discuss together what they have recorded and make flexible plans and preparations. They are an endless source of possibilities and provocations to the children. They also act as recorders for the children, helping them trace and revisit their words and actions. Teachers offer new ways of looking at things to children and provide related experiences and materials. They provide instruction in tool and material use when needed, help children to find materials and resources, and scaffold children's learning—sometimes coming in close and interacting actively, sometimes remaining attentively nearby. They also nurture the children's emotional needs and support and develop relationships with each family. They act as advocates for high-quality services to the public and the government.

Role of the Children

Children are active participants in their learning. They make many choices throughout the day, including where to go in their classroom and building and what to work on. In addition to ongoing projects, children engage in many other forms of activity and play, including pretend play, singing, group games, storytelling, reading, cooking, outdoor play, rest, and sociable meals together. They become part of a close-knit group, with their own unique rituals and ways of expressing friendship and affection for one another.

Assessment

Children's progress is tracked in nontraditional ways. Documentation is a cooperative practice that helps teachers listen to and see their children, thus guiding curriculum decisions and fostering professional development through collaborative study and reflection. Teachers keep extensive notes on the children and portfolios of children's individual and group work. Then they construct panels, slide shows, booklets, or videos to record memorable projects and to explore and interpret the learning process. The portfolios are shared with families at the end of the year, and teachers also meet frequently with parents to discuss developmental issues.

Teachers may also prepare diaries, or memory books, to trace the experience of each child in the school, and these become a precious good-bye gift to the family. The memory books help children reflect on themselves as individuals and group members, and help them incorporate their memories into their self-identity and autobiographical narrative of their life. Finally, teachers help older children to create elaborate constructions, artwork, and performances to summarize project learning. Documentation helps teachers to follow and study the ways the group of children develops ideas, theories, and understandings.

There are no checklists of skills, tests, or diagnostic evaluations in a Reggio Emilia program. It is felt that standard assessment tools limit children by focusing on their shortcomings or lack of skills, not their strengths and potential. The research community distinguishes between types of research based on the purposes for which it is conducted. The documentation favored by educators in Reggio Emilia promotes reflective practice and program improvement through formative methods that help educators to better understand their problems, assess the needs of children, and analyze what works and what does not on an ongoing basis. It is intended to assist educators to refine and improve their work in process, not to allow outside audiences to understand outcomes and measure impacts over time.

Where Readers Can Find Out More

The Reggio Emilia approach is described in *The Hundred Languages of Children: The Reggio Emilia Approach: Advanced Reflections* (2nd ed.), edited by C. P. Edwards, L. Gandini, and G. Forman (1998), published by Greenwood Publishing Corporation; and in *Innovations in Early Education: The International Reggio Exchange*, newsletter of the North American Reggio Emilia Alliance (NAREA), at www.reggioalliance.org.

▲ ▲

The HighScope approach and the Reggio Emilia approach are two variations on how DAP might be translated from theory to practice. The curriculum presented in this book will give you additional examples to consider.

THE ONGOING DISCUSSION ABOUT DAP

Although DAP is well accepted in many early childhood quarters, it has not met with universal acceptance. Since its inception, critics have raised thought-provoking questions about DAP. For instance, when DAP was first introduced, it emphasized the principles of age appropriateness and individual appropriateness so much that some people associated DAP only with the maturationist and mental health perspectives described earlier in this chapter (Dickinson, 2002). As a result, many practitioners and critics assumed that in DAP-oriented programs, teachers did very little teaching. Adults were viewed as emotionally supportive but not particularly intellectually

Go to the Assignments and Activities section of Topic 8: Program Models/ Approaches in the MyEducationLab for your course and complete the activity entitled *Reggio Emilia.* Observe a Reggio Emilia classroom in action.

engaged. The same was considered true for the children. Others interpreted the play-based curriculum characteristic of DAP to mean that children simply wandered about early childhood classrooms with little structure or purpose (Fleer, 1995; Lubeck, 1998). This raised concerns that children did not experience enough cognitive challenge in DAP-oriented programs. Teachers and parents also worried that academic subjects such as reading and math were taboo and that children would not learn the basic skills they needed to succeed in elementary school (Hyson, 2003). Additional cautions were voiced by those who believed that DAP might meet the needs of typically developing, European American, middle-class children but not address the needs of children of color, children with disabilities, or children from low-income families (Carta, Schwartz, Atwater, & McConnell, 1993; Wolery, Strain, & Bailey, 1992; Powell, 1994).

As a result of discussions, research, and debate among practitioners and scholars, the concept of DAP has evolved to address many of these concerns. For instance, the latest definitions of DAP continue to stress age appropriateness and individual appropriateness. However, there is a very strong emphasis on sociocultural and linguistic contexts as well. Also, the importance of teachers as intentional planners and doers in relation to children's development and learning is now being described more clearly. Whereas the earliest definitions of DAP focused mostly on child development as the knowledge base for teaching, that base has expanded to more explicitly include knowledge of effective teaching strategies and content knowledge. Furthermore, the newest NAEYC guidelines urge teachers to use strategies that have their roots in all four of the philosophical perspectives prevalent in early childhood today. The notion of children and teachers as active partners in the teaching–learning process continues to be strengthened (Copple & Bredekamp, 2009).

Based on our experiences thus far, we expect that DAP will continue to evolve with time. People will still debate and discuss professional practice. These discussions will play a significant part in advancing the field and in your education as an early childhood professional.

WHAT DOES THE DAP DISCUSSION MEAN FOR EARLY CHILDHOOD PRACTITIONERS?

The ongoing conversation about DAP is not simply a philosophical one being carried out by a few academicians in the field. Every day, people at all levels of the profession are engaged in discussions about DAP—what it is, how to enact it effectively, and how to revise it to better support their work with children and families. This is important for three reasons. First, it tells us that we are part of a "thinking" profession. As early childhood educators, we face many challenges. Some are economic (how to obtain better wages), some are political (how to move children up on the political agenda), and others are physical (how to get through the day without being totally exhausted). However, our work poses intellectual demands as well, requiring clear, creative thinking. Thus, we must continually ask ourselves, "Is our current understanding of DAP comprehensive and inclusive? Does it provide a useful framework? How can DAP be adapted to accommodate the differences among us while maintaining the integrity of its guiding principles?" These critical issues remain open to question and will require our best efforts to answer.

Second, the DAP discussion reminds us that the knowledge base undergirding the field is continually changing. We can never sit back and assume that what we know now is all we will ever need to know. Instead, we must approach our profession as lifelong learners—examining, revising, and expanding our thinking over time.

Finally, the DAP conversation has made clear that a one-size-fits-all approach to teaching and learning is neither functional nor desirable. No single set of strategies is automatically best for every situation. A strategy appropriate for one child may be less appropriate for another child in another circumstance. Instead, we must adapt our methods to fit the strengths and needs of the particular children and families we serve.

Teachers in developmentally appropriate classrooms are often down on the floor with the children.

IMPLICATIONS OF DAP FOR PROFESSIONAL PRACTICE

Now that you are familiar with DAP, take a moment to consider implications this educational philosophy could have for your work with children and families. Also, ask yourself, "How will the issues that surround DAP affect my development as a professional in the field?" Then read the implications we thought of and see how they match your ideas.

As early childhood professionals in training or as practitioners in the field, we should do the following:

❑ Have a thorough knowledge of what DAP is and what it is not
❑ Continually examine our practices, reflecting on our work with children and families and revising our actions in accordance with new knowledge and understandings
❑ Combine our understanding of DAP with knowledge of child development and learning, curriculum goals and content, instructional practices, family and community relationships, assessment, and professionalism to create high-quality programs for children and families
❑ Become adept at articulating the rationale behind our practices and connecting what we do in the classroom to the fundamental principles of DAP
❑ Share information about DAP with parents, colleagues, and community decision-makers
❑ Listen thoughtfully to questions raised and concerns expressed about DAP and strive to clarify points of agreement and disagreement
❑ Recognize that early childhood education is a vital profession in which new ideas are constantly being explored

SUMMARY

myeducationlab

To check your comprehension on the content covered in Chapter 1, go to the Book Specific Resources in the MyEducationLab for your course, select your text, and complete the Study Plan. Here you will be able to take a chapter quiz, receive feedback on your answers, and then access review, practice, and enrichment activities to enhance your understanding of chapter content.

This chapter chronicles an evolving concept in early childhood education: DAP. Developmentally appropriate practices match how children develop and learn with how they are taught. Early learning programs are founded on faith in children's capacity to learn as well as on respect for children as individuals who are shaped by the social and cultural contexts in which they live. Educators working with youngsters aged 3 to 8 years recognize that young children's learning differs significantly from that of older children and adults and approach their work with this understanding in mind. Thus, the application of DAP makes the nature and well-being of children the central focus of professional practice. Research supports the idea that developmentally appropriate programs represent positive educational experiences for young children. Not only do children perform well academically and socially, but their attitudes toward school remain enthusiastic and optimistic. This is not the case for many children enrolled in classes that ignore children's unique educational needs.

DAP has not been without its critics. Concerns voiced over the years have led to revisions in the philosophy and to continued research on the subject. The entire focus of this chapter has been to familiarize you with the basic elements of DAP. As you explore the manifestations of DAP in the chapters that follow, you will repeatedly encounter ideas initially expressed in this chapter. There is no element of early childhood education they do not touch. Teaching and learning strategies, activities and routines, materials, the physical environment, classroom management, methods of family involvement, and assessment procedures are all influenced by the principles of age appropriateness, individual appropriateness, and sociocultural appropriateness.

Key Words

behavioral perspective
constructionist perspective
developmentally appropriate practice (DAP)

individualized education plan (IEP)
maturationist perspective

mental health perspective
pushdown curriculum

Applying What You've Read in This Chapter

1. **Discuss**
   a. On the basis of your reading and your experiences with young children, discuss each of the questions that open this chapter.
   b. Reread the sections on the HighScope approach and the Reggio Emilia approach to early childhood education. Find examples of how these approaches utilize strategies associated with DAP.
   c. Referring to Table 1.2, find the "roots" of the general practices typically associated with DAP described in this chapter.
   d. One reason DAP was introduced in 1986 was to respond to concerns over pushdown curriculum in preschool and the early grades. To what extent do you think this remains the state of affairs in the United States? What should we be doing today?

2. **Observe**
   a. Observe a teacher who has adopted a DAP philosophy. Identify concrete examples of this philosophy in the classroom.
   b. Observe a preschool classroom and a classroom for children older than 5 years of age. Describe ways the adults use the principle of age appropriateness in terms of materials, activities, and routines in each classroom. Identify the similarities and the differences between the two rooms in this regard.

3. **Carry out an activity**
   a. Talk to an early childhood practitioner about how he or she tries to make the children's program age appropriate, individually appropriate, and socioculturally appropriate. Write a summary of your conversation.
   b. Read a journal article about DAP. Is the author in favor of the concept or opposed to it? Describe how convinced you are by the author's position.
   c. Select one of the curricula described in this chapter (maturationist, mental health, behavioral, constructionist). Gather additional information about the approach. Summarize what you discover.
   d. Review written information describing an early childhood program in your community. On the basis of the program's written philosophy and program description, discuss to what extent the program reflects DAP principles.

4. **Create something for your portfolio**
   a. Provide three examples of your work with children: one in which you address the idea of age appropriateness, one in which you demonstrate individual appropriateness, and one that illustrates your efforts related to sociocultural appropriateness.

5. **Add to your journal**
   a. What is the most significant concept about DAP that you learned from your readings and your experience with children?
   b. In what ways have you used DAP in your work with children? What goals do you have for yourself in this regard?

PRACTICE FOR YOUR CERTIFICATION OR LICENSURE EXAM

The following items will help you practice applying what you have learned in this chapter. They can help to prepare you for your course exam, the PRAXIS II exam, your state licensure or certification exam, and for working in developmentally appropriate ways with young children.

Engaging in DAP

Chang is having trouble sitting through the story that the teacher is reading at circle time. The teacher knows the following things about Chang.

> He is 3 years old.
> This is Chang's first day in the program.
> Chang and his family are newly arrived in the United States from South Korea.

1. **Constructed-response question**
   a. Based on your understanding of the principles of DAP, identify which of these pieces of information is important for the teacher to consider in deciding how to best support Chang, and explain how the information you select relates to each principle.
   b. Explain how the concept of judgment will influence your approach to working with Chang.

2. **Multiple-choice question**

   In developmentally appropriate classrooms, what is the role of the teacher?

   a. The teacher and the students are both active and learn from one another.
   b. The teacher structures the room so the children can mostly work on their own without adult intervention.
   c. The teacher works with children mostly in large groups.
   d. The teacher focuses mostly on social and language skills and less on cognition.

Chapter

2

Teaching and Learning in Developmentally Appropriate Programs

How will knowledge of child development affect my teaching?
What teaching strategies are associated with DAP?
How do teachers know what to teach?
What role do national and state standards play in early childhood classrooms?

This chapter on teaching and learning in developmentally appropriate programs will help you answer questions like these.

Working with young children is exciting, exhausting, and rewarding. It is also a tremendous responsibility. This realization hit home with Esme Raji Codell, a first-year teacher in the Chicago Public Schools. On Day 1 of the school year, she looked into the 31 expectant faces of the children in her class and thought, "thirty one chances, thirty one futures" (Codell, 2001, p. 1). That was when she recognized that whatever happened in her classroom that year would influence those children all their lives.

To assume responsibility for teaching young children calls for commitment, patience, and understanding. It also requires knowledge and skills about teaching and learning. This knowledge base has three parts. First, early childhood educators need to know what young children are like. They must understand child development and use this understanding to create early childhood environments where all children can thrive. Second, teachers need to know about the learning process as well as teaching techniques that support learning. Third, they must demonstrate deep knowledge of academic disciplines and related content. Most important, well-prepared teachers combine all three areas of knowledge and skill in their teaching (Neuman, 2007). This holistic approach to teaching and learning, depicted in Figure 2.1, provides the foundation for enacting DAP in early childhood programs. The rest of this chapter is devoted to exploring these essential facets of early education.

EARLY CHILDHOOD EDUCATORS NEED TO KNOW ABOUT CHILD DEVELOPMENT AND LEARNING

A teacher who has a good understanding of child development and learning is more likely to be effective in the classroom; . . . new teachers who have had coursework in learning and development are also more likely to stay in "the field."

—Horowitz et al., 2005, p. 89

Take a moment to consider the following questions.

What are 3-year-olds like? How are they the same as 6-year-olds? How are they different?
When are children most likely to benefit from certain experiences? If a child is scribbling, what might be the next logical step in learning to express ideas in writing?

How might you answer? Although there is more than one "correct" response, the best answers will reflect an awareness of how young children develop and learn. This knowledge is a major factor in the delivery of high-quality programs for children. In fact, teachers who have a solid grounding in child development and learning are more likely to engage in DAP than are individuals who lack this knowledge (Copple & Bredekamp, 2006; Stronge, 2002). Instead of treating their interactions with children as wholly intuitive, they bring factual information to bear on how they think about children and interact with them in the classroom. Thus, early childhood education, like all

FIGURE 2.1 Teaching–Learning Knowledge Base

education, demands well-prepared personnel who appreciate the unique characteristics of the children they serve. Knowledge of child development and learning contributes to this preparation and appreciation. Let us quickly review key principles that will guide your thinking, planning, and teaching.

Children Develop Holistically

Aesthetic, affective, cognitive, language, physical, and social development are all interrelated. Although at times one facet of development may appear to be more dominant than others, in truth, children function in a holistic way. For example, someone observing children engaged in a vigorous game of tag might categorize their activity as purely physical. Yet, the children's ability to play the game is influenced by many developmental processes:

Aesthetic. Appreciating another player's speed, enjoying the rhythm of the game

Affective. Coping with the disappointment of not being "it" right away, accepting compliments and criticism from other players, expressing anger over a disputed call

Cognitive. Determining the sequence in which the game is played, discerning how many children can fit in the space available, remembering who had a chance to be "it" and who did not

Language. Determining what "scripts" to use to get into or out of the game, consulting a game book to clarify a variation called "reverse tag," responding to the teacher's directions

Physical. Running, bobbing, and weaving to tag or to miss being tagged; developing stamina

Social. Negotiating the rules of the game, signaling others about wanting a chance to play, making way for a new player

This holistic picture is true for every task children undertake. Social processes shape cognitive ones, cognitive processes promote or restrict social capabilities, physical processes influence language and cognition, and so on. Consequently, when early childhood teachers think about children, they remember that children are whole human beings whose learning is enhanced when all aspects of child development are addressed in the program. This is referred to as focusing on the "whole child" (National Association of Elementary School Principals [NAESP], 2005; Hendrick & Weissman, 2009).

Child Development Follows an Orderly Sequence

Try putting these developmental milestones in the order in which they tend to appear during childhood.

Fear of ghosts
Fear of animals
Fear of being embarrassed in front of others
Stranger anxiety

What did you decide? Sample progressions like these illustrate the notion of developmental sequence.

Scientists around the world have identified typical sequences of development in every developmental realm (Berk, 2009). Their findings confirm that development is a step-wise process in which understandings, knowledge, and skills build on each other in a predictable order. This is true both for typically developing children and for children with special needs (Filler & Xu, 2006). For instance, before children walk, they first learn to lift their heads, then sit up, then stand with assistance, then crawl, and then stand on their own. Eventually, they toddle, and then run. Similarly, childhood fears tend to emerge in the following order: stranger anxiety, animal fears, fears of ghosts, and later, the fear of potential embarrassment. Maturation provides the broad parameters within which benchmarks like these emerge (e.g., initially children's cognitive structures are such that they recognize only tangible fears such as strangers or animals; later, they become more capable of imagining abstract frights such as embarrassment). Experience also plays a role, modifying and influencing children's progress (e.g., a child with much exposure to dogs may think differently from a child who has no dog experience). Progress from one benchmark to the next happens intermittently, not in a rigid fashion. Individual children may spend more or less time on each one; they may move forward a bit, back a little, then forward again. Some children may even skip steps. In spite of all this individuation, development emerges in roughly the same order in children and initial skills and abilities form the foundation for those yet to come (Copple & Bredekamp, 2009). Knowing these sequences helps teachers understand children's current development and what may likely come next, no matter their age or special needs. These are valuable inputs to the teaching process.

Children Develop at Varying Rates

> *Emahl is 5; so is Lawrence. Emahl was walking at 1 year of age and talking in complete sentences by age 2. However, he still has difficulty sharing people and toys. Lawrence did not walk until he was 14 months old and began talking fluidly only at 3 years of age. He knows several strategies for sharing, however, which he uses well. Emahl and Lawrence are following the same developmental paths but at different rates; both are developing normally.*

This developmental snapshot of Emahl and Lawrence shows that children progress through the same developmental sequences according to their own timetables. Those timetables are a product of maturation and environmental factors and lead to both intra- and interpersonal variations in child development.

Developmental progress is not uniform across domains. Within the same child, different threads of development are at different levels of maturity at any one time. As a result, the same child may struggle to identify the letters in his name, climb nimbly to the highest part of the climber, experience great success cutting with scissors, but also become easily frustrated negotiating a turn at the computer. Such intrapersonal variations are typical in all children.

If you were to chart the development of an entire classroom of children, the time at which each child reached certain milestones would also vary considerably (Trawick-Smith, 2009). Such interpersonal variations may be due to differences in maturity, experience, or special needs. For instance, some first graders come to school in September just starting to make the association between various letters and sounds. Other children can read words and phrases. Still others have no concept of print.

Variations in rates of development are common throughout the elementary years. However, they are most pronounced in young children and contribute to the wide range of behaviors you will see in early childhood classrooms (Copple & Bredekamp, 2006).

Children Learn Best When They Feel Safe and Secure

Children who feel safe and secure learn more easily than children who are worried, angry, or afraid. For young children, psychological security comes from being in the company of warm responsive adults with whom they have close personal relationships (National Scientific Council on the Developing Child [NSCDS], 2004; NAEYC, 2009). Children are most comfortable with adults who obviously like them. Such adults take the time to tune in to what children are saying and doing. They also tolerate childish mistakes. When children see that their families are welcome in the program, hear their home language at school, and see materials and images that reflect their world experience, they feel accepted and valued. Physical security is important, too. If the classroom environment is hazard free and routines are predictable, children can navigate the program with confidence. When teachers set reasonable limits on children's inappropriate behaviors, promote problem solving, and address bullying or aggressive behavior effectively, they create classroom environments that children interpret as supportive and safe (Kostelnik & Grady, 2009). These factors enhance childhood learning, as shown in Figure 2.2.

These second graders share the same birthday but vary in their rates of physical, language, cognitive, and socioemotional development.

Children Are Active Learners

Children in the kindergarten were about to act out the story "Jack and the Beanstalk," when Wally and Eddie disagreed about the relative size of the two rugs.

FIGURE 2.2   Emotions Are Gatekeepers to Learning

Although supporting children's emotional well-being makes common sense, it makes neurological sense, too. Scientists who study brain development tell us emotions influence children's emerging cognitive abilities in either a positive or negative direction (NSCDC, 2007). Positive emotions such as affection, enthusiasm, and pleasure prompt children to be more attentive and emotionally engaged in the learning process (Medina, 2008). Thus, children who feel comfortable and safe are primed to learn. Feelings of fear, loss, or anger, on the other hand, can impede learning if they go on too long. Although everyone experiences these emotions at times with no harm done, if children experience extended periods of fear or distress, their bodies produce elevated levels of the hormone **cortisol** in the brain. Prolonged exposure to cortisol weakens the connections among brain cells, particularly in those parts of the brain responsible for memory and reasoning (NSCDC, 2007). If these toxic conditions become the norm, they can have detrimental effects on brain development and cognitive function. Neuroscience suggests that strong, positive emotional attachments with adult caregivers actually reduce the production of too much cortisol, protecting brain cell connections and promoting learning of all kinds. Physically safe environments also contribute to the positive feelings associated with healthy brain growth.

Source: Adapted from Kostelnik, M. J., & Grady, M. L. (2009). *Getting it right from the start: The principal's guide to early childhood education.* Thousand Oaks, CA: Corwin Press, 107.

Wally: The big rug is the giant's castle. The small rug is Jack's house.

Eddie: Both rugs are the same.

Wally: They can't be the same. Watch me. I'll walk around the rug. Now watch—walk, walk, walk, walk, walk, walk, walk, walk, walk. Okay. Now count the other rug. Walk, walk, walk, walk, walk. See? That one has more walks. (Paley, 1981, p. 13)

In this situation, Wally wasn't satisfied with merely looking at the rugs to determine their size; he was compelled to act on his idea that one was larger than the other and "prove it" bodily. When we say children are active, we literally mean they are people on the move. Recent studies of children's brain development underscore the connection between children's physical activity and their subsequent intellectual functioning (Bjorklund, 2005; Medina, 2008). Young children use their whole bodies as instruments of learning, taking in data through all their senses. As they act on the environment, children connect thought with behavior—exploring, discovering, acquiring, and applying new knowledge and skills.

Children Learn Through Physical Experience, Social Interaction, and Reflection

Physical experiences and social interaction enhance children's learning.

Sung Won is talking to herself as she moves the pieces around trying to complete a three-dimensional puzzle.

Hooey! How can I do it? How come this won't go?

Although she has tried several combinations, one piece seems not to fit anywhere.

Daniel is also working on a puzzle. He is grouping all the pieces by color. Sung Won observes his strategy.

Sung Won notices a bit of pink that flows from one piece to the next. There is pink on the "challenging" piece too.

Wait! Wait! Oh, I know . . .

She slips the piece into place.

Physical Experience with Objects.   Children have a powerful need to make sense of everything they encounter. From birth, their efforts focus on organizing their knowledge more coherently and adapting to environmental demands by directly manipulating, listening to, smelling, tasting, and otherwise acting on objects to see what happens (Medina, 2008). From such investigations children generate a logic or knowledge of the properties of things, how they work, and how they relate to one another. This knowledge comes not simply from the passive act of observing, but also from the more complex mental activity of interpreting and drawing conclusions about what happens. Such conclusions either add to children's existing ideas or cause children to reformulate their thinking.

Social Interaction. Children's experiences with physical objects are further influenced by their interactions with people (Bodrova & Leong, 2007). As children play, talk, and work with peers and adults, they exchange and compare interpretations and ideas. They generate hypotheses, ask questions, and formulate answers (Copple & Bredekamp, 2009). In doing so, they often face contradictions in the way people or objects respond, and these discrepancies force children to extract new understandings from what has occurred. Through such experiences children construct knowledge internally, continually shaping, expanding, and reorganizing their mental structures.

Social experiences also provide children with factual information they cannot construct totally on their own. Through their interactions with others, children learn culturally determined knowledge and skills necessary for successful functioning in society. Examples include the following:

Names of things (door, window, or puerta, ventana)
Historical facts (Martin Luther King's birthday is January 20; you were born in St. Louis)
Customs (when some children are 7 years old, they make their first Holy Communion;
*   some children who lose a tooth hide it under their pillow)*
Rules (wash your hands before eating; walk with scissors)
Skills (how to form the letter A; how to throw a ball correctly)

Reflection. As children interact with objects and people, they reflect on their experiences—what they are doing, how they know what they know, and how their plans compare with their actions (Copple & Bredekamp, 2009). Sometimes this thinking is internal and sometimes children express their ideas aloud as happens when they answer questions like these:

"How did you decide this bridge was longer than that one?"
"What do you want to know about insects? How will you find that out?"
"You thought that container had more. What do you think now?"
"You were going to use blocks and tubes to make your city. Is that what you did?"

Another way children reflect on their experiences occurs when they recall a past event (e.g., collecting leaves in the yard) and then represent that event in some tangible way—with art materials, or with building blocks, or in writing. As children reflect on, represent, and communicate experiences and ideas, they develop greater self-awareness and also deepen and refine their thinking. Although such conscious reflective thinking is most common during the later elementary years, children as young as 3 years begin to engage in the practice (Golbeck, 2006; Amsterlaw, 2006; Copple & Bredekamp, 2009).

Children Are Motivated to Learn Through a Continuous Process of Challenge and Mastery

Discovery brings joy. Exploration creates the need for more discovery, so that more joy can happen. It is a straight up reward system that, if allowed to flourish will continue into the school years. As children get older, they find that learning not only brings them joy, but it also brings them mastery.
—Medina, 2008, p. 273

Young children learn best when they are stimulated and successful in acquiring new knowledge and skills. They love the challenge of learning what they nearly understand but do not quite grasp, and of trying to do what they can almost but not quite achieve immediately. This excitement prompts children to pursue concepts and skills just slightly beyond their current levels of proficiency. It also encourages them to keep striving until they achieve greater competence (Bodrova & Leong, 2007). Children who frequently master new learning tasks remain motivated to learn. They perceive themselves as up to the job, even when it is not easy or instantly attainable. Alternately, youngsters who are overwhelmed by the demands of a task tend to fail. Those who lack stimulation tend to fail as well. In either case, children who fail repeatedly eventually give up (Bredekamp & Copple, 1997). Children who stop trying also stop learning. Adults play a major role in managing the environment and offering learning tasks that stimulate children rather than frustrate them.

Children's Learning Profiles Vary

Although children use all their available senses to learn, they have unique profiles in how they learn best. Consider the following examples.

> *Sarah likes to work on her own.*
> *Consuelo prefers working with a friend.*
> *Wilma has been interested in numbers since toddlerhood.*
> *Carlos has a way with words.*
> *Jerome seems to have a special feel for the outdoors.*
> *Steve enjoys the thrill of competition.*

All of these children are demonstrating different ways of approaching the world, or different **frames of mind**. These frames of mind are also called "intelligences." Based on more than 20 years of research, Howard Gardner has hypothesized that everyone possesses at least eight intelligences. People blend these intelligences into unique learning profiles (Gardner, 1993a). The eight intelligences are linguistic, logical-mathematical, musical, spatial, bodily-kinesthetic, intrapersonal, interpersonal, and naturalistic.

Gardner suggests "each of these areas may develop independently (in the brain), although ultimately they all work together" (Hatch & Gardner, 1988, p. 38). He emphasizes that people possess varying degrees of know-how in all eight categories and that individuals may be "at promise" in some areas while being average or below average in others. The eight intelligences are summarized in Table 2.1.

Differences in learning profiles may also exist because of temperament or cultural factors. For instance, some children think quickly, spontaneously, and impulsively; others are more deliberate. Some children focus on the "big idea"; some think more about the details. Some children constantly look for connections among ideas; others take a single thought and follow it in many directions. Some children organize their thoughts in sequence; others think in a more circular fashion. Some children are socially oriented, working best cooperatively and in groups. Other children value individual achievement and enjoy competition (Trawick-Smith, 2009). All these variations suggest that there is no single way to learn and that there are many ways to be "smart."

Children Learn Through Play

Children do not learn everything through play, but they learn many things through play. Children play at home, at school, and everywhere between. They play with people, things, and ideas. When children are not sleeping, eating, or seeking emotional support from others, they choose to play

TABLE 2.1   Eight Intelligences That Contribute to Children's Learning Styles

Intelligence	Child Learns Best by:
Linguistic *The Word Player*	Reading, writing, and talking
Logical-mathematical *The Questioner*	Exploring patterns and relationships, working with numbers, doing experiments
Spatial *The Visualizer*	Drawing, building, designing, creating things, using the mind's eye
Musical *The Music Lover*	Listening to and making music, using rhythm and melody
Bodily-kinesthetic *The Mover*	Touching, moving, processing knowledge through bodily sensations
Intrapersonal *The Individual*	Working alone; pursuing own interests; being aware of inner moods, intentions, motivations, temperaments, and self-desires
Interpersonal *The Socializer*	Sharing, comparing, relating to others, cooperating
Naturalistic *The Nature Lover*	Observing nature, interacting with plants and animals, perceiving relationships among natural things

and can remain occupied that way for hours. Play is the province of children from the time they are born throughout the elementary school years.

All areas of development are enhanced through children's play activities. Play is the fundamental means by which children gather and process information, learn new skills, and practice old ones (Ginsburg, 2007). Within the context of their play, children come to understand, create, and manipulate symbols as they take on roles and transform objects into something else. Children explore social relationships, too, experimenting with various social roles, discovering points of view in contrast to their own, working out compromises, and negotiating differences. Play enables children to extend their physical skills, language and literacy capabilities, and creative imaginations. The safe haven that play provides for the release of tensions, the expression of emotions, and the exploration of anxiety-producing situations has also been well documented (Wenner, 2009). As a result, there is strong consensus among researchers that play is central to childhood learning.

Practical Implications

Knowing about child development and learning is central to being an effective teacher, and being an effective teacher is central to helping children develop and learn (Horowitz et al., 2005). However, developmental expertise is not sufficient to ensure that early childhood programs are high quality (Mellor, 2007). Practitioners must *connect* what they know with what they do. This connection between theory and practice is illustrated in Table 2.2.

Clearly, your knowledge of child development and learning will be an asset in helping you become a successful teacher. Another crucial element will be your ability to enact effective teaching strategies. Engaging in DAP involves knowing what strategies are possible and when to use them.

TABLE 2.2 Connecting Knowledge of Development and Learning to Teaching Practices

Principles of Child Development and Learning	Developmentally Appropriate Teaching Practices
Children develop holistically	Teachers plan daily activities and routines to address all aspects of children's development—aesthetic, emotional, intellectual, language, physical, and social.
	Teachers create opportunities for children to integrate learning across multiple domains (e.g., mixing language, physical, and social; combining math, science, and reading).
Child development follows an orderly sequence	Practitioners use their knowledge of developmental sequences to gauge whether children are developing as expected and to determine reasonable expectations for children.
	Educators think about developmental sequences in figuring out what next steps will appropriately challenge children as well as what may not be quite reasonable to expect now.
Children develop at varying rates	The daily schedule gives children opportunities to pursue activities at their own pace.
	Activities are repeated throughout the year so children can participate according to their changing needs and abilities.
	Teachers plan activities with multiple learning objectives to address the wide range of development represented in the group.
Children learn best when they feel safe and secure	Teachers develop close, nurturing relationships with children.
	Teachers remain with children over time. Children can easily identify a specific adult from whom to seek help, comfort, attention, and guidance.
	Daily routines are predictable. Changes in routine are explained in advance so children can anticipate what will happen next.
	Activities, transitions, and routines respect children's attention span, need for activity, need for social interaction, and need for attention from caring adults.
	There is two-way communication between teachers and families, and families are welcome at school.

TABLE 2.2   Connecting Knowledge of Development and Learning to Teaching Practices *(continued)*

	Children have access to images, objects, and activities in the early childhood program that reflect their home experiences.
	The early childhood environment complies with the safety requirements of the appropriate licensing or accrediting agency.
	Adults use positive discipline to enhance children's self-esteem, self-control, and problem-solving abilities.
	Teachers address aggression and bullying calmly, firmly, and proactively.
Children are active learners	Children can move about the room freely most of the day. Inactive segments of the day are kept short.
	Children participate in gross motor activities every day.
Children learn through a combination of physical experience, social experience, and reflection	Children handle objects every day. First-hand experiences are evident in every part of the room and in every curricular domain.
	Teachers encourage children to explore and experiment.
	Adults pose questions, offer information, and challenge children's thinking.
	Children have many opportunities to interact with peers.
	Children have chances to document and reflect on their ideas.
Children learn through mastery and challenge	Children engage in activities within or slightly beyond their ability to master. Practitioners simplify, maintain, or extend activities in response to children's demonstrated levels of functioning and comprehension.
	Teachers help children figure out alternative approaches when the task at hand is beyond their current capabilities.
Children's learning profiles vary	Children choose from an array of multisensory activities every day
	The same information and skills are presented in more than one modality (seeing, hearing, touching) and through different types of activities.
	Children have opportunities to play on their own and with others; indoors and outdoors; with natural and manufactured materials.
Children learn through play	Play is integrated throughout the entire day and within all aspects of the program.
	There are a variety of props and other manipulative objects with which children may play.
	Practitioners are joyful and playful as they interact with children.
	Practitioners enhance children's play, sometimes as observers and sometimes as participants.

EARLY CHILDHOOD EDUCATORS NEED TO KNOW ABOUT EFFECTIVE TEACHING STRATEGIES

Teaching is not just talking, and learning is not just listening.

—Horowitz et al., 2005, p. 88

Children develop and learn in many ways, so the strategies that best support them vary too. Following are three examples of different approaches to teaching young children.

A teacher plans for 3-year-olds to match plastic jars to their lids. To support the children's learning, the teacher provides them with a collection of containers and lids that vary in size, color, and shape. Because the children are familiar with the materials, the teacher plans for them to carry out the activity with minimal adult direction. However, she also stops by the area periodically to describe the size, shape, and color of the lids as she talks to the children about their experiences.

The kindergartners at Fairview School have been placing planks to form inclined planes in the block area for several days. They have enjoyed racing their toy cars down the ramps to see how far the cars will go. Capitalizing on their interests, the teacher plans an activity in which children observe, predict, and discover ways to make the cars go farther by varying the ramp angles. The teacher also asks children to analyze and interpret their experimental results. To help the children engage in these scientific processes, the teacher plans what she will do and say to gain the children's attention and to help them recall their past observations of the cars going down the ramps, make predictions about what they think will happen when the ramp angle is changed, and then evaluate their predictions. The procedure combines questioning, informing, listening, paraphrasing, and recording the children's ideas.

Today, Mr. Rosenshine wants to teach the children in his second-grade class new motions to a familiar song. He demonstrates the song first, then has the children imitate his movements several times, then has them catch him making mistakes, and finally has the children do the song independently, without watching him model the actions. He assumes that several repetitions will be necessary before the children will be able to sing the words and do the motions simultaneously on their own.

In each of the preceding activities, the teacher carefully considered the teaching strategies he or she would use to facilitate children's development and learning. The procedures ranged from providing opportunities for exploration to verbally underscoring children's discoveries to developing step-by-step processes. Although these strategies varied in type, complexity, and degree of teacher direction, they were all chosen to match teachers' goals for children's learning.

WHICH TEACHING STRATEGIES ARE BEST?

At one time, educators thought there were certain teaching strategies that were always best no matter the situation (Evans, 1975). Today, we realize that instruction can be more or less appropriate depending on the goals for the activity and individual children's needs. For instance, nondirective strategies that enhance children's exploratory behavior are well suited to children discovering the properties of modeling dough, different ways they can move their bodies, or the operation of levers. However, these approaches are less well suited to children learning the names of the stars, the specific procedures involved in a tornado drill, or the precise rules for a particular game. Which strategies you choose will depend on what you want children to learn. Thus, you must ask yourself, "Which strategies are most suitable for meeting the goals and objectives of this lesson?" When good alignment exists among goals, objectives, and teaching strategies, children benefit. Creating this alignment requires you to become familiar with a wide array of potential teaching strategies.

COMMON TEACHING STRATEGIES

So many teaching strategies are available that outlining them all in this chapter would be impossible. However, we will describe several instructional methods that early childhood professionals commonly use. The first three strategies—sensory engagement, environmental cues, and task analysis— are preparatory methods that shape your planning and teaching before they are carried out. The other strategies are ones you think about in advance but implement only after children are on the scene. All are used alone or in combination to enhance children's development and learning.

Firsthand experiences are best!

Sensory Engagement

All learning begins with perception: seeing, hearing, touching, tasting, and smelling. Thus, children learn best by using all their senses (Medina, 2008; Hendrick & Weissman, 2009). Because most researchers agree about the importance of hands-on learning, you might assume that every activity for young children would naturally include a high level of sensory engagement by children. However, we have seen children sit through a 15-minute talk on the color green (with nothing green in sight), watched children listen to a recording for the sound of an oboe (an instrument they had never seen or heard in person), and listened to children read a story about pomegranates (a fruit with which many had no experience). Thus, we can safely say that sensory engagement is not guaranteed without careful planning.

The most effective means of sensory engagement is firsthand experience. This means you must consider ways to give children direct contact with real objects, people, places, and events (Armstrong, 2006). If you are teaching children about the color green, provide objects of many shades of green for children to see and handle. If you are teaching children to listen for the sound of an oboe, first show them an oboe and let them touch the instrument. Have someone play the instrument while children watch. If you are teaching about pomegranates, show children real pomegranates and give them opportunities to examine them through taste, touch, and smell. If no firsthand experience is possible, seriously reconsider whether the activity is age appropriate. The younger the children, the less you should rely on secondhand experience rather than firsthand involvement. As children mature and express curiosity about people, objects, and events somewhat removed from their immediate experience, continue to plan activities that provide the maximum sensory involvement, keeping the following guidelines in mind.

❏ Firsthand experiences are best.
❏ Firsthand experiences should precede representational or more abstract experiences (e.g., show real fruit prior to pictures of fruit).
❏ Models are more concrete than pictures; pictures are more concrete than words.
❏ Plan activities so that sensory engagement occurs early in the procedure rather than later.

Environmental Cues

Environmental cues signal children about expectations using objects or symbols rather than verbal instructions (Hearron & Hildebrand, 2008). Four chairs around the snack table "tell" children that four children may participate at one time. A sign on the cracker basket with a hand showing three fingers or the numeral 3 indicates that each child may take three crackers. Children can learn to turn on and shut down the computer by referring to a pictograph outlining the appropriate steps. If six children are participating in an art activity in which only two pairs of scissors are available, an unspoken message is that children must share the scissors if everyone is to have the chance to use them. These nonverbal signals support objectives related to independence, cooperation, and self-regulation.

Task Analysis

Task analysis involves identifying a sequence of steps a child might follow to achieve some multistep behavior such as setting the table, getting dressed, or completing a long-division problem (Essa, 2007). Such analyses are necessary to help children gradually accomplish tasks that are too challenging to master all at once. For instance, expecting children to learn how to set an entire table in a single lesson is unrealistic. Instead, teachers analyze the knowledge, skills, and procedures necessary to achieve the goal of setting the table. Then, they create a logical sequence of small steps for children to pursue over time. This analysis is depicted in Figure 2.3. What should be covered early and what comes later becomes clear in the analysis. The principles of developmental direction listed in chapter 3 will provide a useful set of criteria for devising logical sequences around which to create a good task analysis. Other potential sequences are presented in the curriculum portions of this text described in chapters 9 through 14.

FIGURE 2.3 Sample Steps in Setting a Table

1. What is the goal? Set the table.
2. What will the finished arrangement look like?

3. What are the skills or steps involved?
   a. Get out plates.
   b. Put a plate at each person's place.
   c. Fold napkin.
   d. Place napkin to left of each plate.
4. What do children need to know?
   a. Where to find plates
   b. How to fold napkin
   c. Where utensils are positioned
5. What part will I teach first?

Chaining and Successive Approximation

Teachers often use chaining or successive approximation to support children through the steps they have identified as the result of task analysis. Both of these strategies consist of building tasks up a little at a time to support a child in learning a complex set of behaviors (Malott & Trojan, 2008). **Chaining** involves introducing a series or "chain" of behaviors one at a time. As children master the first step, a new step is added and so forth until they successfully demonstrate total completion of a task. In the case of setting the table, on the first day, a child might start by getting out the plates. The next day, the child might get out the plates and put one at each person's place. The third day, napkins could be added to the place setting, and so forth until eventually the child sets the whole table. **Successive approximation** consists of shaping behavior by rewarding children for gradually approximating desired goals (getting more and more accurate). In setting the table, a child might put everything out, but the place settings might be incomplete and the items askew. Initially, the teacher might accept this level of behavior and praise the child for remembering everything and getting it all on the table. Gradually, the child would need to become increasingly precise in what goes where and how neatly the job was done to consider the task complete.

Scaffolding

Scaffolding is the process of providing and then gradually removing external support for children's learning. During the scaffolding process, the original task is not changed, but how the child participates in the task is made easier with assistance. As children take more responsibility for pursuing an objective, assistance is gradually withdrawn (Bodrova & Leong, 2007). For example, Mr. Kaye has planned a counting activity. Children select a bag of "treasures" and count the number of objects inside. As Mr. Kaye works with the children, he notices that Cathleen knows the names of the numbers but counts some objects more than once and others not at all. He recognizes this as a situation in which scaffolding could be used to enhance Cathleen's ability to count accurately. In this case, the teacher might take Cathleen's hand, pointing with her to each object and counting them one at a time, orally. With repetition, Mr. Kaye will stop counting aloud but continue to help Cathleen point to the objects. Eventually, Cathleen will be able to count each object, one at a time, without Mr. Kaye's physical or verbal assistance. The scaffolding process begins with the teacher's providing maximum assistance and taking primary responsibility for pursuing the objective (counting). However, gradually this responsibility shifts to Cathleen until she is able to achieve the objective unassisted. The same principles are at work when children in the kindergarten discover that Sparky, their class pet, has escaped from his cage. The teacher used four steps to scaffold the children's learning:

❑ I do . . . you watch
❑ I do . . . you help
❑ You do . . . I help
❑ You do . . . I watch

Her scaffolding took place over more than one day. See Figure 2.4 for this additional scaffolding example in the language domain.

In other situations, peers may be the source of scaffolding support. Scaffolding techniques could be verbal or physical and could include props or not.

Guided Practice and Repetition

Four-year-old Tony heads for the puzzle area every day. At the beginning of the year, he mostly enjoyed knob puzzles that had a few distinct pieces. Then he moved on to interlocking puzzles that varied in color and shape. Most recently, he has become intrigued with the new floor puzzle of a bus. He has tried this puzzle each day, sometimes on his own, sometimes with other children, and sometimes with the teacher's help. Tony's teacher supports his learning by providing time, space, and materials for him to practice his puzzle-making skills. When she plans for the puzzle area, she considers ways to maintain the children's interest and provide them with appropriate challenges. Each week, she holds over a few favorites from the week before and then adds new puzzles for novelty. She also includes different types of puzzles and puzzles of varying degrees of difficulty. Tony's teacher is using the strategy of **guided practice**.

One basic premise of early childhood education is that children learn through repetition. Real learning does not occur in a single episode. Children need many opportunities to engage concepts, explore ideas, and try out skills to gain mastery. In other words, children need a chance to practice what they are learning and to utilize what they have learned in new situations. Practice takes a variety of forms (Freiberg & Driscoll, 2005; Sarama & Clements, 2006):

❑ Rehearsals (e.g., children hear a story several times, then help the teacher tell it before telling it on their own; children rehearse answering the phone in the housekeeping area; children pretend to put on their outdoor clothing in sequence before trying it with the real items)

FIGURE 2.4   Scaffolding in Action

At their morning meeting, Ms. Ankerson tells her children that their hamster, Sparky, has escaped overnight. She asks, "What can we do to find Sparky?"

High level of teacher support	Scaffolding		Low level of teacher support
I do . . . you watch	**I do . . . you help**	**You do . . . I help**	**You do . . . I watch**
In morning meeting the children and Ms. Ankerson discuss the problem and make plans for how to solve it. As she writes the children's ideas on a chart, she mentions using periods to let people know when to stop reading. She also talks about using capital letters to start a new sentence. She says that names are very special, so Sparky's name will begin with a capital, too.	The next day, the children dictate a "Missing Hamster" story to be read by the principal over the intercom during morning messages. Ms. Ankerson reminds the children that the periods and capital letters will help the principal know when one sentence ends and a new one begins. As she records their thoughts, she calls on various children to use the marker to make the period or the capital letter.	For the day's entry into their journal, the children write about the missing hamster. The children are at varying stages in their development. Ms. Ankerson makes occasional comments on their use of periods and capital letters and offers suggestions as she talks to them about their entries. To help them in spelling words, she draws their attention to the word walls, their own personal word banks, and other resources.	The children create signs at the writing center to post around the school about the missing hamster, one solution to the problem suggested at the morning meeting. Knowing that their messages will be read by others, they seek to write in a way that will be understood. They refer to the sign on Sparky's cage to make sure their spelling is correct and read their messages to Ms. Ankerson for affirmation.

Source: Heroman, C., & Copple, C. (2000). "Teaching in the Kindergarten Year," in D. F. Gullo (Ed), *K Today: Teaching and Learning in the Kindergarten Year.* Washington, DC: NAEYC, 66. Reproduced with permission of the publisher.

❏ Repeating an activity with variations (e.g., the children sort shells one day, sort fruits and vegetables another day, and sort rocks a third day)

❏ Elaborations (e.g., children associate a current skill or event with a previous one; for instance, the children recognize that the process of recording observations of the fish in the aquarium today is similar to the observation records they made last week about insects outdoors)

Practice is most beneficial when the conditions under which it occurs vary slightly from one time to the next. Relevant practice episodes may occur within a day or during several weeks' time. Thus, Tony increases his puzzle-making skills by working on some of the same puzzles, as well as a few new puzzles, as time passes. An-Sook learns to hop by hopping on one foot and then the other; hopping sideways and backward; hopping inside and outside; hopping on even surfaces and uneven surfaces; and hopping alone and with friends. The first graders in Mrs. Harper's room become more proficient at forming their letters by writing in the pretend grocery, making signs to post around the room, writing in their journals, making lists, and writing notes to themselves to help them remember "important stuff." Deliberately setting the stage for these kinds of practice opportunities is essential to DAP.

Invitations

Verbal invitations encourage children to participate in activities by creating openings for them to explore materials or to interact with you or other children. Samples include the following: "Come and see what we're doing here," "Here's a place for you right next to LaKesha," and "Check out the new materials in the reading center. I saw a book I'm sure you'll enjoy." Planning a few invitations in advance is a good idea so that you have a better notion of how to motivate children to try various activities.

Behavior Reflections

Sometimes called information talk or descriptive feedback, **behavior reflections** are verbal descriptions of children's actions (Kostelnik, Whiren, Soderman, & Gregory, 2009). They are nonjudgmental statements made to children regarding some aspect of their actions.

Situation:	Outdoors, a child is sorting leaves into small piles.
Adult:	You found some red and brown leaves. (Or either of the following: You have several different leaves in your piles; You're putting together the leaves that are alike.)
Situation:	Two children are matching lids to jars.
Adult:	You two are working together. (Or: Each of you has found a lid to match a jar; Mareesa, your lid is square. Kyoko, your lid is round. You both found different-shaped lids.)

Behavior reflections help draw children's attention to certain aspects of an experience that they may only faintly perceive and expose them to vocabulary that describes their experience. Such reflections also summarize children's actions in a way that is informative without being intrusive. For instance, children acting on materials might hear their teacher say, "You're stirring the pudding gently, you're making little bubbles" or "When you turned the puzzle piece around, it fit." Summarizations like these do not interrupt children's actions. Youngsters do not have to stop what they are doing to attend to the lesson. However, they do prompt children to focus specifically on their actions, which in turn helps them to recognize and internalize these actions. Behavior reflections may also induce children to explore additional ways of stirring the pudding or turning other pieces in the puzzle to make them fit. Used this way, behavior reflections increase children's self-awareness and understanding.

Paraphrase Reflections

Similar in form to behavior reflections, **paraphrase reflections** are restatements, in your words, of something the child has said. These nonevaluative comments are sometimes referred to as verbal expansions or active listening (Kostelnik et al., 2009). Using words slightly different from those spoken by the child, paraphrase reflections broaden children's vocabulary and grammatical structures. At times, such reflections also prompt children to expand on what they are saying. Verbal expansion helps them to refine and clarify key concepts and messages. When children respond to your reflections, you also gain valuable insights into their thinking. Such insights will influence how you proceed with the activity as well as help shape the direction of future planning. Finally, because paraphrase reflections allow children to take the lead in adult–child conversations, children interpret their use as a signal of adult interest and caring. Such feelings enhance the learning climate in early childhood classrooms.

Situation:	Outdoors, a child is sorting leaves into two piles. He says, "These leaves are pointy. These leaves are round."
Adult:	You found two kinds of leaves. (Or either of the following: You noticed that the edges of the leaves made them look different from each other; You're sorting the leaves according to their shape.)
Child:	These (pointing to three leaves on the side) have holes.
Adult:	You made a special pile just for leaves with holes. You have three piles altogether.

Modeling and Demonstrating

Children learn many things by imitating others (Bandura, 1991; Willis, 2009). Watching a friend play a game, seeing the teacher use a sculpting tool in a certain way, listening to a peer "think aloud" about how to solve a math problem, and observing how one person greets another are all lessons from which children may profit. Even though much of what children imitate is unplanned, teachers can enhance the effectiveness of classroom activities when they deliberately use modeling to help children learn new or appropriate behaviors. For example, when Ms. Pritchard holds a snake gently, she is modeling a positive attitude toward snakes that she hopes the children will emulate. Likewise, when Mrs. Levine visits the pretend restaurant, she models being a customer by sitting down and saying things to the children such as, "Hmm, now what will I have? Do you have a menu? Oh, that sounds good. I'd like a salad and a milkshake. How much will that cost?" Her modeling

The teacher uses effective praise when she says,"You found a way to surprise the reader at the end!"

provides children with examples of how a customer might behave. When Mr. Petricic models looking up information he does not know, he is conveying to children ways of using reference materials to answer questions. Models such as these have the greatest impact when their behavior is obvious to the children. Thus, children are best able to imitate a model with whom they can interact or whose behavior is pointed out to them (Kostelnik et al., 2009). Self-descriptions, such as "I'm not sure how many stomachs a cow has. I'll have to look that up," are useful signals of the modeling that is about to occur. Similarly, peer models are highlighted when teachers say, for example, "Look, John has discovered a new way to use the paint" or "Natalie found another way to add three columns of numbers."

Effective Praise

People often assume that praise automatically promotes children's positive behaviors and encourages children to persist at tasks. Unfortunately, some praise has the potential to lower children's self-confidence and inhibit their achievement (Miller, 2009). Thus, there is a difference between ineffective praise and effective praise. Ineffective praise is general, repetitive, and not genuine. It evaluates children, compares them with one another in unfavorable ways, links their success to luck, and tends to interrupt their work and concentration. Conversely, **effective praise** is specific, acknowledges children's actions, and compares their progress with their past performance. It links their success to effort and ability, is individualized to fit the child and the situation, and is nonintrusive. The differences between ineffective praise and effective praise are illustrated in Table 2.3.

Telling, Explaining, and Informing

During their field trip to the animal barns, Jonathan points to a llama and asks the man who is leading the tour, "What's that?" The man answers, "That's called a llama." Jonathan repeats the new word, "Llama." The children are full of questions: "Where do llamas come from?" "Why do they have such heavy coats?" "Do big llamas have baby llamas?" "How big is the biggest llama in the world?" The tour guide answers each question simply and directly. Simultaneously, he draws the children's attention to the sights, sounds, and smells associated with the llamas. Anyone who wants to may touch the animal's coat, look into the llama's feed trough, and handle some of the feed pellets. When Jonathan sees his mom at the end of the day, the first thing he says is, "Guess what we saw today? A llama! And they get real big and people use their hair to make hats." Obviously, Jonathan is pleased with his newly acquired knowledge.

On their trip to the barn, children discovered that the llama's coat was thick by looking at and touching it. However, they could not discover the name of the animal in the same way—they had

TABLE 2.3   Comparison of Ineffective Praise and Effective Praise

Ineffective Praise	Effective Praise
Good job. Nicely done.	You spent a lot of time on this story. You looked up some important information that made the setting more exciting.
You are a great writer.	You found a way to surprise the reader at the end.
Look at Rodney. Everyone should try to write as neatly as he does.	In this story, you used two words that you never wrote before.
You were lucky to come up with such a good idea.	The time you spent editing paid off. You were able to come up with just the right words to finish your story.
Mary, good job.	Mary, you used a lot of animal sounds in your story.
Carl, good job.	Carl, you added a joke to your story to make it funny.

to be told it was a llama. Information such as the names for things, historical facts, and customary behaviors are learned through social transmission. That is, people tell you either directly, through verbal communication, or indirectly, through books, television, or computer technology. In any case, important information is conveyed to children through telling and explaining.

Effective explanations build on children's firsthand experiences and take place within a context that is meaningful to them. For instance, it is more meaningful to explain how to peel a potato with a real potato in hand as children are preparing vegetable soup, than to try to explain it only in words with no potato to show. Likewise, children benefit when explanations build on what they already know. This is why Ms. Lampley introduces a new game by referring to one already familiar to the children. "Jason and Zach, remember how we make pairs when we play lotto? In this memory game, we will be making pairs, too. Only now the cards will be turned over and we'll have to remember where they are on the table. Let's try it." By explaining new concepts in relation to familiar skills and situations, you can incorporate relevant information into the ongoing conversations you have with children each day.

In early childhood programs, most information is introduced on a just-in-time basis. As children demonstrate a need to know something, the appropriate information is offered. For instance, children in the pretend grocery store get into a squabble over the cash register. Five children want to "work" in the store, but there is only one register. The teacher observes to see whether the children can resolve the difficulty themselves; however, they seem stumped. The only job they know about is the cashier's job. The teacher decides that the time is ripe to offer some useful information. She enters the store, saying, "Hello, I'm the district manager. Have you done an inventory yet? One of the jobs for people who work at the grocery store is to count all the items on the shelves. Another job is to make sure each item has a price tag. Who will make the price tags for our store?" Armed with this new information, the children's play resumes, and the children have a broader idea of the possible roles they might play.

At other times, adults predetermine that they want to teach children certain information. Such decisions may be based on interests previously expressed by children, or they may be dictated by social expectations such as how to wash your hands properly or behave during a fire drill. In any case, teachers plan activities to teach children specific vocabulary, facts, or routines. Teachers convey such information through telling, explaining coupled with modeling, and including some form of hands-on involvement by the children.

In all of these examples, telling, explaining, and informing involves more than merely reciting facts. Information is tied to children's experiences and requires involvement that goes beyond simply listening. Effective teachers look at each activity in terms of the explanations or information that may be necessary to support children's learning. Teachers also make sure they have sufficient background to answer children's questions accurately.

Do-It Signals

Simple directions to children, such as "Look here," "Tell me what you see," "Put together the leaves that are alike," "Find a key that doesn't fit," and "Guess how many are in the jar," are called do-it signals. Beginning with a verb, do-it signals are short statements that prompt children to "do" something. When children follow the do-it direction, their actions demonstrate to the teacher what children do and do not understand. For instance, if, as part of a lesson aimed at examining the parts of fruits, the teacher gives a do-it signal to a boy in her class to show her the rind and he hands her a seed, the child's action tells the teacher the child may not know the difference. The teacher would respond with additional experiences and information as appropriate.

Do-it signals should not be phrased as questions, such as "Can you count to five for me?" or "Who can count to five for me?" Queries like these fail to lead children into action. The appropriate do-it signal would be, "Count to five for me." These kinds of positive statements give children a clear idea of what to do.

Challenges

"Show me how tall you can be." "Make a collage using five different art materials." "Figure out two ways to make this wooden boat sink." Challenges are open-ended variations of do-it signals that motivate children to create their own solutions to teacher-suggested tasks (Epstein, 2007). In this way, challenges provide shared opportunities for children and adults to control activity outcomes. Adults shape the initial direction of the activity, and children determine its application. Challenges can be made in every learning center. Following are some examples for the block area (Neuman & Roskos, 2007, p. 119).

BLOCK CHALLENGES

- Build the tallest tower you can build using ten blocks.
- Build the most stable building that you can build using 12 blocks.
- Make a tall building using only blocks that are triangles (or pyramids).
- Make a pattern using blocks. Ask a friend to make a model just like yours.

A variation on the basic challenge occurs when adults challenge children to think about something in a new or different way. For example, Elliot has divided a set of keys into three groups. One group includes all the round gold keys, a second group has all the angular gold keys, and a third group includes all the silver keys. Having observed Elliot at work, the teacher approaches with a round copper-colored key and says, "I just found this key. Show me where it belongs with the keys that you've sorted." Elliot is now faced with the challenge of reconsidering his groupings to accommodate a new element that does not exactly fit. The children are faced with a similar challenge when they declare that only men can be firefighters. A few days later, the teacher invites a female firefighter to visit the class and talk about her work. Again the children are challenged to reconsider their thinking in light of new evidence that does not match their previous conceptions.

Effective teachers carefully observe and listen to children as they participate in activities. On the basis of the information gleaned directly from the children, teachers plan challenges to stretch children's thinking beyond their current perceptions. As part of the challenge, teachers talk with children, encouraging them to put their thinking into words. Throughout this process, teachers are careful not to expect children to accomplish every challenge during a single activity or to change their thinking immediately simply because they are faced with conflicting information.

Questions

Questions are basic instructional tools common to every early childhood classroom. However, the kinds of questions you ask dictate the quality of children's answers. Effective questions are all of the following:

❑ Purposeful (tied directly to the objectives you are trying to teach)
❑ Thought provoking (go beyond the obvious to stimulate higher levels of thinking)
❑ Clear (understandable)
❑ Brief (to the point)

Questions that meet these standards gain children's attention and help them learn. Those that do not may actually inhibit communication. For example, children stop listening when we ask perfunctory questions just to fill the silence or if we ask rhetorical questions for which no real answer is possible ("How many times have I told you to stop pushing?"). If our questions are long and rambling or if we ask too many questions in a row, children's answers become increasingly short and sometimes stop altogether (Kostelnik, Onaga, et al., 2002). None of these reactions leads to more advanced learning.

Besides quality, another thing to consider about questions is whether they are close ended or open ended (Epstein, 2007). Consider what the following questions have in common.

❑ Have you eaten yet?
❑ What color is your shirt?
❑ Did you remember to bring your boots from home?

Answer: Each of these questions can be answered in one word or with a yes/no response. This makes them all close-ended questions.

TABLE 2.4 Types of Questions and Examples

You Plan to Enhance Children's Ability to:	Sample Questions
Observe	What do you see/hear/smell/taste/feel?
Reconstruct previous experiences	What do you remember about the people at the pizza parlor?
	What happened the last time we put the rock in the sunshine?
Relate cause and effect	What can you do to make it happen?
	What happens when/if you do ____?
	When does it happen?
Predict	What do you think will happen next?
Evaluate	What happened? You thought ____ would happen? How did that compare with what actually happened?
	Which poem is your favorite? Why?
	How will you know the art area is clean enough?
	What will help you decide?
Generalize	Now that you saw what we found when we cut open the lemon, what do you think we will find when we cut open this orange?
Compare	How are they alike/different? Which things go together?
Reason	How did you decide those went together?
Discriminate among objects and events	Which one does not belong? Which one is not an oak tree?
Solve problems	What can we do to find out how many marbles are in the jar?
Quantify	How many? How long? How far?
Imagine something	What would it be like if people had long tails?
Propose alternatives	In what other way could you group these objects?
Utilize factual knowledge	Where do you suppose we could find a worm at this time of year?
Infer	What else can you think of that works like this? Why do you think it happened? How do your observations compare with other children's?
Become aware of their thinking processes	How did you know . . .? What made you decide . . .?
Apply	How can you use what you learned?
Make decisions	What do you think we should do now that we know ____?
Communicate	How can you show/remember/share with others what you did/learned?

Close-ended questions are most appropriate in functional situations in which critical thinking is not necessary (Epstein, 2007). They keep responses short and are meant to get a speedy reply. They are not intended to promote higher levels of thinking or expanded language development. That is the job of open-ended questions. **Open-ended questions** have more than one possible answer. They prompt children to offer opinions or to think in new and different ways (Charlesworth & Lind, 2010). Such questions cannot be answered in a single word; rather, they invite conversation. Because open-ended questions encourage children to think deeply and to use complex language, they are the questions teachers should use most often. In Table 2.4 we offer several categories of open-ended questions for you to incorporate into your instruction.

Besides considering quality and whether questions are closed or open ended, you should think about a few other factors as well (Kilmer & Hofman, 1995; Marzano, 2003).

Limit amount.	Ask only one question at a time. Plan your questions carefully.
Provide time.	Give children enough time to respond to your questions. Wait several seconds for children to answer. Do not appear impatient or undermine their thinking by answering your own questions.
Use do-it signals.	Phrase some of your questions as do-it signals to add variety: "Tell me what happened when we put the snowball in the hot water."
Ask all.	Phrase questions to the entire group of children, not only to individuals: "Let's all think of the ways these two piles of leaves are alike. Jake, you begin."
Listen and reflect.	Listen carefully to children's responses. Acknowledge their remarks by using behavior reflections and paraphrase reflections. Focus on the process of their thinking, not merely the correctness of their response.
Redirect.	If a child's answer seems wrong or off track, follow up by saying, "What made you think . . . ?" or "Tell us more about . . ." Children sometimes make connections that are less obvious to grown-ups.
Address misconceptions.	If the child's answer to a question indicates a true misconception, handle the situation matter-of-factly. Paraphrase the child's idea and then offer more accurate information: "You thought this was an apple because it is red. This is a tomato. Tomatoes are sometimes red, too."

Silence

Six children are in the block area. They have used almost every block for an elaborate building that stretches from one side of the rug to the other. They are laughing and talking to one another, sharing materials, and taking on the roles of construction workers. Mr. Moon observes silently from nearby, noting that Teisha has become part of the group. Today is the first time she has moved into a learning center involving more than one or two children. He writes a quick anecdotal record to remind himself of this milestone. Mr. Moon also notices that the children are sustaining the activity well. He does not interrupt but remains nearby to provide support if needed.

The children and their teacher are investigating a large horseshoe crab shell one of the children brought back from a week at the beach. The teacher has just said, "Tell me what you notice about this big shell." She remains silent for several seconds to give the children a chance to answer.

Coral and Aiysha are engaged in a story-mapping activity in which they are determining the distinguishing characteristics of each character. They are deeply absorbed in their discussion. Their teacher listens attentively for a few moments and then moves to another group of children. The girls continue their analysis.

myeducationlab

Go to the Assignments and Activities section of Topic 10: Planning in the MyEducationLab for your course and complete the activity entitled *Using Guided Learning in a Unit of Study.* Notice the wide range of teaching strategies the teacher uses to support children's learning.

In each of these situations, the teacher used silence to support children's learning. Remaining quiet can be an effective teaching strategy, especially when it is coupled with attentive observation of children and the context in which they are functioning (Kostelnik et al., 2009). Too much adult talk, inappropriate adult talk, or adult talk at the wrong time detracts from a positive learning environment. For instance, researchers have documented that many teachers are too quick to respond to their own questions or too swift to move from one child to the next when a child fails to respond immediately to a question or a do-it signal (Freiberg & Driscoll, 2005). Children need at least 3 to 5 seconds to process what has been said and to formulate a response. Getting into the habit of giving children a few seconds of "wait time" is an effective use of silence. Likewise, children perceive the learning environment as more supportive when teachers refrain from inserting themselves into the center of every interaction and when they avoid interrupting children who are deeply engaged in communicating with one another. In these cases, children interpret the adult's silence as a sign of warmth and respect.

We opened this section on teaching strategies by asking, "Which teaching strategies are best?" As you can see, there are many options from which to choose, and more than one strategy may come to mind in various situations. Considering the strategy alone does not provide enough information to make the most appropriate choice. What makes a strategy "best" is how well it supports the phase of the learning cycle in which each child is engaged.

THE CYCLE OF LEARNING

A naturalist was visiting the Prairie View After School Program to show the children some varieties of turtles that live in their state. He showed box turtles, painted turtles, and red-eared sliders. The children were intrigued.

Penny:	*Those are some funny animals. Can I touch one?*
	The naturalist nods yes, and guides the child's hand to gently touch a small box turtle.
Sam:	*What's that? What's that hole in his head? Can water get in there?*
Naturalist:	*That's his ear. Turtle ears don't have any outside parts. Nothing sticks out, that helps them swim faster. The water doesn't go inside because those ear slits you see are not very wide.*
Collin:	*We have turtles in our pond. That one is just like the ones we have at home. That one is different. I never saw one of those before.*
Celeste:	*Do they bite? Do they eat people?*
Pearl:	*No, they just eat fruit and stuff—you know it falls off the trees and they eat it.*

The children spent the next several minutes watching the turtles, asking questions, and talking about what they saw and knew. Listening carefully, the teacher noticed that each child brought some prior knowledge to the experience. While not all information was accurate, everyone came to the activity with a backlog of concepts that they used in reference to the turtles. Penny had a concept of animals. Sam was aware that turtles might live in water. Collin had prior experience with turtles and could distinguish one kind of turtle from another. Celeste knew animals needed to eat. Pearl knew that turtles didn't eat people. The teacher also observed that the children had different degrees of understanding and accuracy in terms of their learning; some were just becoming aware of turtles, others were eager to acquire more information about turtles, and others had knowledge that they could generalize from one setting (home) to another (the center). All of these observations gave the adult insights into the children's current understandings. Knowing about the cycle of learning guided the teacher's thinking about which teaching strategies she would use to extend children's learning beyond their present realities.

Phases in the Cycle of Learning

The **cycle of learning** describes the process whereby children move from initial awareness of something to gaining new knowledge and skills that they apply in a variety of situations on their own. Movement through the cycle may take days, months, or even years, depending on the circumstances. The cycle of learning consists of five phases, each supporting and leading to the next: awareness, exploration, acquisition, practice, and generalization (Bredekamp & Copple, 1997; Epstein, 2007; Robertson, 2007). These phases are represented in Figure 2.5.

Awareness. The first step in learning anything is to *become aware* that something exists and that it is worth knowing about. In the early childhood years, children become aware of many new things as they interact with people and objects in their daily lives. Adults mediate this awareness through the environments they create and the opportunities they provide for children to experience a variety of events, objects, and people.

FIGURE 2.5 Cycle of Learning

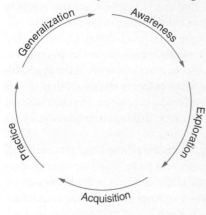

Exploration. Once they are aware of something, children need opportunities to explore the things that capture their attention. The *exploration phase* is a time of self-discovery and occurs as children spontaneously manipulate objects and engage in informal interactions with peers and adults. As children explore, they do the following:

- ❏ Observe, touch, taste, smell, and hear
- ❏ Talk about their experiences
- ❏ Ask questions
- ❏ Collect information
- ❏ Relate current experiences to prior learning
- ❏ Make discoveries
- ❏ Propose explanations
- ❏ Compare their thinking with the thinking of others

Children enjoy practicing new skills with their friends.

❏ Construct new understandings
❏ Create personal meanings and develop understandings that lead them to want to know or do more

Knowledge grows as children mentally organize and reorganize the information they glean from their experiences. Adults facilitate rather than direct the learning process during this child-centered period. Teachers support children's explorations by providing plenty of time and opportunities to experiment and "play around" with objects and materials before asking children to use things in prescribed ways.

Acquisition. Once children have thoroughly explored a phenomenon, they display signs of being ready to move to the *acquisition phase* of learning. Children signal this when they ask, "How do you play this game?" "What comes next?" or "Where do turtles live?" Using a variety of instructional strategies, teachers respond to children's cues. In doing so, they help children refine their understanding, guide children's attention, and help children make new connections. The outcome of acquisition is that children do something—take some form of action (e.g., count, point to something, write a word, draw a map, compare two similar objects). Throughout the acquisition phase, adults "tune in" to the children's learning needs, offering support as children seem to need or desire it.

Practice. After children acquire new knowledge and skills, they enjoy practicing what they have learned. During the *practice phase* of the learning cycle, children use the new behavior or knowledge repeatedly and in a variety of circumstances. We see this in the child who, having learned to play Risk, wants to play repeatedly, enjoying rather than tiring of the repetitions. Children who have just learned to dribble a basketball try it out in the hall, on the playground, in the gym, and on the sidewalk. In most cases, the child's practice is self-motivated and self-initiated. This is how children eventually gain mastery. Teachers facilitate children's practice when they allow children plenty of time to play out the same scenarios repeatedly, when they follow children's lead in repeating activities more than once, and when they vary the practice conditions from one time to the next.

Generalization. Eventually, children have enough grounding to apply their newly developed knowledge or skills to novel (but similar) situations. When this happens, they enter the *generalization phase* of learning. Within this phase, children apply what they have learned in many ways and adjust their thinking to fit new circumstances or demands. This is exemplified by the child who uses the ball-handling skills she acquired and practiced earlier to invent a variation on the traditional basketball game. Teachers promote generalization when they provide children with meaningful opportunities to apply what they have learned in a variety of ways and in new circumstances. In the process of generalizing their newfound knowledge skills, children often make discoveries that prompt them to reenter the cycle of learning at the awareness phase. Take a moment to consider how Raymond proceeds through the cycle of learning while playing lotto, as depicted in Figure 2.6.

LINKING THE CYCLE OF LEARNING TO TEACHING

Accommodating the Needs of Individual Children

Children proceed from awareness to exploration to acquisition to practice to generalization within all realms of learning: aesthetic, affective, cognitive, language, physical, and social. Where they are in the learning cycle depends on their backlog of experiences and understandings as well as the learning opportunities available to them. Therefore, each child's progress within the cycle will differ for various threads within each domain as well as from domain to domain. In other words, children are not in any one phase of learning for everything simultaneously. Instead, youngsters may just be starting to be aware of or explore some concepts or skills while acquiring, practicing, or generalizing others.

Likewise, in making an activity available to a group of children, it is important to remember that each child will differ as to which phase of the learning cycle is occupying his or her attention. For instance, when learning about ladybugs, one child might be involved at the awareness level

FIGURE 2.6   Raymond Learns to Play Lotto

Awareness	Raymond has observed his older sister playing board games with her friends. Raymond notices a lotto game on the shelf in his child-care program and takes it out to look at the pieces.		Over the course of a few weeks, the teacher puts out different lotto games for children to play, such as animal lotto and transportation lotto.
Exploration	Raymond handles the pieces, looks at the different pictures on the lotto cards, and discovers that some cards are identical.	Generalization	Raymond applies what he knows about finding identical pairs to creating functional pairs (e.g., cup to saucer, hammer to nail) in a new lotto game. Raymond discovers that he can make functional pairs in the pretend play area, too. He becomes intrigued with the variety of ways he can make functional pairs with objects throughout the room. In the process of matching shoes to socks, he notices that different shoes have different fasteners and begins to experiment with all these closures. His new awareness and explorations signal his reentry into the cycle of learning with a new idea in mind.
Acquisition	Raymond asks," How do you play this game?" The child-care provider explains the purpose of the game, shows Raymond how to make matches among the cards, and talks about taking turns as part of the play. Raymond plays a game with the adult and then another with the adult and two other children.		
Practice	Raymond plays lotto over and over again for several days.		

because he has not previously encountered ladybugs. Other children may have a general awareness of ladybugs but need time to explore and investigate them. Another child, who has had contact with ladybugs in the past, may be ready to learn some facts about these insects. This child is at the acquisition phase of learning. Yet another child, who knows many facts about ladybugs, may want to practice identifying and temporarily catching the insects outdoors. Other children may know so much about ladybugs that they focus on using what they know to help them better understand other flying insects. These youngsters are at the generalization phase of learning about ladybugs.

To accommodate such differences within and among children, the teacher's planning and teaching must be flexible enough to address all five phases of the learning cycle. Teachers do this by providing children with broad-based, open-ended activities. From these, children extrapolate experiences that correspond to the phase of the cycle of learning most relevant to them. Thus, several children working with puzzles may use them for different purposes—exploration, practice, and so forth. Repeating activities is also a good idea because children need many opportunities to progress through the cycle of learning. Furthermore, teachers must support children in whatever phase of learning they are in for a given activity. They do this by using different instructional strategies as necessary:

❑ Inviting children's interest in something new
❑ Providing varied materials for exploration
❑ Offering feedback, providing information, or asking questions as appropriate in the acquisition phase
❑ Giving children chances to practice what they have learned under different conditions
❑ Encouraging children to generalize what they have learned to new situations

In Table 2.5, you will find sample teaching strategies that typically support each phase of the cycle of learning.

Timing

Children need lots of time to become aware of new ideas and to explore before moving to the acquisition phase of learning. For instance, children who have had few chances to explore flowers in real life will have difficulty learning facts about them immediately. Exploration can take place on previous occasions as well as immediately prior to encountering factual information. The decision to move into acquisition is often signaled by the children (e.g., "Teacher, what's this?" or "How does the water get in the leaves?"). When children start to ask questions about an experience or

TABLE 2.5 Relating the Phases of the Learning Cycle to Teaching Strategies and Children's Responses

Learning Phase	Teaching Strategies	Children's Responses
Awareness	Sensory engagement, environmental cues, invitations, modeling and demonstrating	Notice, perceive, respond
Exploration	Sensory engagement, environmental cues, invitations, behavior and paraphrase reflections, silence	Observe, touch, smell, taste, hear, examine, talk about, ask questions, collect information, make discoveries, compare own thinking with the thinking of others, revise old ideas, construct new meanings
Acquisition	Sensory engagement, environmental cues, task analysis, chaining and successive approximation, scaffolding, invitations, behavior and paraphrase reflections, modeling and demonstrating, effective praise, telling/explaining/informing, do-it signals, challenges, questions, ignore or correct inaccurate responses in conjunction with your task analysis, silence	Carry out an action, adopt new skills, apply new knowledge, extend understandings
Practice	Sensory engagement, environmental cues, chaining and successive approximation, scaffolding, invitations, behavior and paraphrase reflections, guided practice and repetition, effective praise, challenges, questions, silence	Rehearse, repeat, adapt, revise, elaborate, gain mastery
Generalization	Behavior and paraphrase reflections, questions or do-it signals; have child describe his or her thinking, silence	Transfer learning from one situation to another, gain new awareness that prompts reentry into the learning cycle

when they can describe or show some basic understanding of a phenomenon, they are ready to acquire new knowledge and skills. In the acquisition phase, teachers or peers provide instruction, and children do things to demonstrate understanding. After a small amount of instruction has been offered, children practice what they have learned prior to moving on to something else. Eventually, children will generalize or apply what they have learned from one situation to a new one. Often, children's generalization activities occur spontaneously (e.g., children generalize what they have learned about flowers in the garden to blossoms they see growing on trees). At other times, teachers set up experiences that make such generalizations more likely to happen. In any case, teachers recognize that individual children will not progress from awareness to generalization in a single lesson. For this reason, they make sure a variety of activities are available throughout the year and across the curriculum.

Teachers support children's progress through the cycle of learning by carefully observing the knowledge and skills children bring to and demonstrate within each activity. Then, beginning where children are developmentally, teachers provide the supports necessary for children to stretch their performance slightly beyond their current levels of functioning. This is called teaching in the zone of proximal development.

TEACHING IN THE ZONE OF PROXIMAL DEVELOPMENT

The difference between what children can do alone and what they can do while working collaboratively with others or with support from a peer or adult mentor represents the *zone of proximal development* (Bodrova & Leong, 2007; Vygotsky, 1978). Every child can do things with assistance that he or she cannot do solo, and what a child can do while working with others on one occasion, that same child eventually will be able to do with less help or no help in the future (Gronlund, 2006).

FIGURE 2.7 Teaching in the Zone of Proximal Development (ZPD)

Because of the developmental principle of mastery and challenge presented earlier in this chapter, children learn best when teachers provide experiences just beyond what children can do on their own but within what they can do with assistance from someone whose skills are greater. This forward momentum represents higher order learning. For instance, Irma is speaking in two-word phrases (e.g., "Big cookie"). In conversations with Irma, her child-care provider expands the child's sentences, adding more language and grammar than Irma can currently produce ("You have a big cookie" or "You like that big cookie"). If the provider's "lesson" is too complex or beyond Irma's understanding, then Irma will not take it in. However, if Irma can simply "stretch" her thinking to encompass the new language, higher order learning is possible. Under these conditions, she will gradually expand her language skills to a higher level of mastery than she would have been able to manage independently. The relation between Irma's performance and her provider's teaching within the zone of proximal development is depicted in Figure 2.7.

Educators who understand the zone of proximal development recognize that simply giving children access to a variety of experiences is not sufficient to foster optimal learning. Adults monitor such situations to ensure that they are manageable for children. They also provide the assistance necessary to prompt higher order learning. A youngster who is overwhelmed may be unable to understand or apply knowledge gained, regardless of how potentially useful it may be. In contrast, children who experience no challenge beyond their current level of functioning will fail to progress in their understandings and abilities. Thus, learning is most likely to flourish when children feel both successful and stimulated. To support this kind of learning, teachers use the strategy of scaffolding described earlier in this chapter. That is, they utilize one or more teaching strategies to support children and then gradually remove those supports as children demonstrate an increasing ability to perform a task or function on their own.

Until now, we have focused most of our attention on the elements of who, where, why, and how you will be teaching within the context of DAP. Now it is time to consider *what* you will be teaching. That dimension of DAP addresses content—the information and skills children might be expected to learn.

EARLY CHILDHOOD EDUCATORS NEED TO KNOW ABOUT CONTENT

The children were excited about feeding the ducks down by the river. They tossed out bits of crackers and cracked corn and were thrilled as the ducks quickly gobbled up the food. Nikolai asked, "How do ducks eat? Do they have teeth? I can't tell."

The teacher plans a measuring activity. He puts out a variety of measuring tools—rulers, tape measures, yardsticks, and some objects the children can use to make nonstandard measurements, such as colored inch cubes and string.

Marla Murphy reads the Grade 2 Curriculum Standards and finds out that a major science focus for this grade is earth sciences—soil, water, and rocks. She ponders how she will introduce the material and how she will cover the content during the next several weeks.

Every time you answer a question, design an activity, or plan what you will teach children over time, you are addressing curriculum content. Children are curious about many things, and there is much they want to know more about. To enhance children's learning, you need to know a lot about the world yourself so you can offer children accurate information and relevant experiences. Accomplished teachers, therefore, have a rich understanding of multiple subjects (the arts and humanities, mathematics, technology, social sciences, biological and physical sciences, physical health and fitness, human relations, etc.). Such teachers appreciate how knowledge in these disciplines "is created, organized, linked to other disciplines, and applied to real-world settings" (Hyson, 2003, p. 148). They are adept at using tools and methods related to each discipline and can help children pose and solve challenging problems that touch on one or more disciplines at a time. For example, the adult accompanying the children on the field trip to feed the ducks may help the children observe the ducks more closely and make notes or draw pictures about what they observe. She may encourage the children to develop hypotheses about whether ducks have teeth, and help children develop a plan for how to find out more.

All of this knowledge is rooted in the biological sciences and the scientific process. Similarly, the teacher who creates the measuring activity understands the mathematical concepts of standard and nonstandard units of measurement. He anticipates the preconceptions and background knowledge the children may bring to the activity and considers instructional strategies such as using multiple tools to measure, comparing measurements, and graphing the results to further enlarge children's mathematical concepts and skills. As Marla Murphy generates plans for introducing the children to earth science content, she makes decisions about what will be meaningful for her students, what they already know, and how she can provide the firsthand experiences she knows children need. All of this runs counter to the conventional wisdom that adults, by virtue of their maturity and life experience alone, have enough background knowledge to teach young children well. This explains why early childhood professional preparation programs include significant time devoted to general education and study across the disciplines.

ADDRESSING CONTENT IN EARLY CHILDHOOD EDUCATION

There is so much content from which to choose, it is natural to wonder, "How do I decide what to teach?" "What goals should I pursue?" A major source of input will be the children themselves. As children express curiosity about insects, family life, or plants, you will provide experiences to support those interests and expand children's knowledge and skills. Additional teaching around sharing, conflict resolution, and cooperation will occur in the context of daily classroom life. Another source for determining what to teach will be the early learning and **academic standards** that describe what children should know and be able to do from preschool through the early elementary grades.

The desire to create standards for teaching began in K–12 education as educators, families, and community decision makers sought to enhance consistency and continuity of curriculum from one grade to the next. State Departments of Education also wanted to answer the question, "What should children understand and what skills should they be able to demonstrate as a result of their education?" Professional societies (e.g., the National Council of Teachers of Mathematics) developed standards to define critical content in their disciplines and to provide benchmarks for teachers to use to sequence teaching within certain subject areas (Seefeldt, 2005). Today, the standards movement has expanded to include the preprimary years as well. As a result, 49 states have established statewide standards for teaching in the early years. See Table 2.6 for an abbreviated sample of state standards.

BENEFITS OF STANDARDS

Standards provide educators with a credible source for developing early childhood curricula (Seefeldt, 2005). They often come about through the collective thinking of experts in the field, giving practitioners access to an agreed-on agenda for teaching and learning. Discussions about standards can lead to deeper understanding of content and create more shared meaning among those considering them. Because standards delineate what children may reasonably know and do within a given curriculum area over time, they provide resources teachers can refer to in determining if certain goals are more or less appropriate to pursue. Standards, therefore, offer teachers and caregivers useful information directly related to their daily classroom work (Illinois State Board of Education, 2004).

✋ Consult the Standards

TABLE 2.6   Examples of State Standards for Reading (Illinois), Mathematics (Nebraska), and Science (Massachusetts)

Illinois—Preschool Reading (Understanding and Fluency)

Learning Standard A: Apply word analysis and vocabulary skills to comprehend selections

1. Understand that pictures and symbols have meaning and that print carries a message
2. Understand that reading progresses from left to right and top to bottom
3. Identify labels and signs in the environment
4. Identify some letters, including those in own name
5. Make some letter–sound matches

Nebraska—K–1 Mathematics (Numeration/Number Sense)

By the end of first grade, students will:

1. Recognize, write, and orally express the sequential order of the number system.
2. Demonstrate ways of representing numbers and compare relations among numbers.
3. Identify numbers and applications in everyday situations.
4. Demonstrate the value of numbers (0–20) using concrete objects.

Massachusetts—PreK–2 Science (Life Science)

Life Science

1. Recognize that animals (including humans) and plants are living things that grow; reproduce; and need food, air, and water.
2. Differentiate between living and nonliving things. Group both living and nonliving things according to characteristics they share.
3. Recognize that plants and animals have life cycles and that life cycles vary for different living things.
4. Describe ways in which many plants and animals closely resemble their parents in appearance.
5. Recognize that fossils provide us with information about living things that inhabited the earth years ago.
6. Recognize that people and other animals interact with the environment through their sense of sight, hearing, touch, smell, and taste.
7. Recognize changes in appearance that animals and plants go through as seasons change.
8. Identify the ways in which an organism's habitat provides for its basic needs.

Sources: Illinois Early Learning Standards, Illinois State Department of Education, revised August 2004; Nebraska Mathematics Standards Grades K–12, Nebraska Department of Education, adopted December 2000, revised January 2006; Massachusetts Science and Technology/Engineering Curriculum Framework, Massachusetts Department of Education, adopted October 2006.

CHALLENGES IN USING STANDARDS

Children and practitioners benefit when standards are used wisely. However, there are certain challenges in using standards that require attention if the benefits discussed above are to remain real (Gronlund, 2006; Wein, 2004).

Too Many Standards

There are literally thousands of standards for educators to consider. Standards encompass a variety of disciplines and developmental domains. They may also exist at multiple levels, ranging from specific programs (e.g., Head Start) to individual school districts to the state and national groups. Sometimes these standards duplicate one another, sometimes they are complementary, and sometimes they contradict one other. All of this makes the standards maze a challenge for early childhood professionals to navigate.

Scattered Standards

Currently, there is no one place where 100% of the possible standards are conveniently catalogued. Even the standards within a given discipline may be spread out over more than one source. This means practitioners often have to check multiple documents and websites to get a handle on the content within a particular discipline.

Standards That Are Inappropriate for Young Children or an Individual Child

Not every standard is suitable for young children or a particular child. At times, standards are developed by content experts or by committees dominated by individuals focused on older children, without input from early childhood educators. As a result, some standards are not age appropriate. For instance, one school district established the standard that kindergartners should be able to discuss cells as basic units of life, so the children would be "ready" to learn more about animal life as second graders. This standard is too abstract and therefore unrealistic in light of what we know about children's cognitive abilities at this age. Even content that seems age appropriate may not fit the criteria of individual appropriateness and cultural appropriateness that governs DAP depending on children's backgrounds, special needs, and experience.

Standards Implemented in Lockstep Fashion

A major complaint by many practitioners is that they are required to "cover" too many standards too quickly or that they are expected to address standards according to a rigid timetable. These approaches to using standards do not take into account children's individual needs or variations in children's rates of development and learning.

ADDRESSING THE CHALLENGES

Although individual teachers do not control all aspects of the curriculum, early childhood professionals have an obligation to think carefully about standards. Ultimately, each practitioner has to make judgments about which standards to apply and how to do so.

An initial step is to become familiar with standards published by various groups. Readers can access the national standards for a variety of disciplines by going to the Mid-continent Research for Education and Learning (McREL) website (www.mcrel.com) or the websites of individual disciplinary societies. Practitioners in the United States and Canada should also become familiar with the early childhood and grade-level standards adopted by their states and provinces. These are readily available through websites maintained by state and provincial divisions of early childhood education. All of these sites give you access to the original standards developed by content experts and authorities at the state level. Individual school districts and some early childhood programs have their own standards, which their employees need to be familiar with as well.

Sorting through all of these standards can be time consuming. To save you time, we have done some of that work for you by using national and state standards to create goals for the curricular domains presented in chapters 9 through 14. These goals are arranged in sequence from most basic to more challenging and define appropriate curriculum content. Each one addresses expectations for what children should know and be able to do from preschool through Grade 3. You will learn more about how to use the goals when you read chapter 3, "Planning and Implementing Effective Small-Group Activities."

To make sure particular standards are enacted in appropriate ways for young children, teachers ask themselves the following questions (Seefeldt, 2005).

1. From the body of knowledge addressed by this standard, what seems to be most meaningful to children this age? What is most meaningful for these particular children?
2. What facet of this standard might a beginner need to know?
3. What do the children already know about this standard?
4. What about this standard can children learn through firsthand experience?
5. How can this standard be integrated with what children are already experiencing in my classroom? (pp. 22–23)

The challenge of the lockstep curriculum is the most difficult to address. There are no easy answers and early childhood educators sometimes report great stress in having to cope with unrealistic timetables for children's learning. However, research suggests that teachers who keep in mind all three sides of the teaching–learning triangle depicted in Figure 2.1 fare best in coping with this pitfall (Wein, 2004; Gronlund, 2006). They are better able to integrate standards throughout the day and to recognize how child-centered activities naturally support required curriculum content. This connection between standards and children's experiences in a typical early childhood activity is illustrated in Table 2.7, which explains standards addressed by children in a well-equipped art area in a preschool classroom. Note how the same activity can address multiple standards. Adults can take advantage of such activities to observe children's demonstrated skills and to support children in developing knowledge and skills related to the learning expectations and standards for the programs in which they are participating.

❧ Consult the Standards

TABLE 2.7 Addressing Standards in the Art Area

Area	Standard	Experience
	Children:	Children are:
Creative Arts	Develop awareness and appreciation for the visual arts	Painting at the easel, admiring each other's work on their own and with support from an adult
		Looking at picture books that depict the work of various artists
		Responding to questions from peers and adults: "Are there happy colors in this painting? Which ones? Why?"
	Explore and describe art choices	Saying things like "I used red for my screaming mouth" or "I made lots of little circles because it is snowing so hard"
Social-Emotional	Demonstrate self-direction	Using the easel or other art materials by referring to a large pictograph nearby, selecting materials independent of adult direction
	Identify and express feelings	Describing affective elements of their art work, "This is the mommy, she looks happy," "This is the angry dog," using feeling words to describe their aesthetic experiences, "I like blue." "This is fun."
Health, Safety, and Physical Education	Develop self-help skills	Putting on smocks, helping themselves to materials, washing their hands after using play dough
	Develop competence and confidence in activities requiring fine motor skills	Tearing paper for a collage, cutting paper with scissors, using tools such as cookie cutters and rods to shape the play dough, twisting pipe cleaners and wire to make sculptures
Language Arts	Listen to and respond to directions and conversations	Talking with one another about what they are doing and about their experiences
		Responding with corresponding actions when asked to "Pass the scissors" or "Find the picture with the most curvy lines."
	Demonstrate print awareness	Finding the smock with their name on it, following the directions on a pictograph that includes words, reading a picture book about a boy who wants to draw flowers
	Demonstrate emergent writing skills	Writing their names on their artwork, watching while adults label artwork, making labels and directions for projects
Mathematics	Demonstrate an understanding of number and numerical operations	Creating one-to-one correspondence between children and scissors, children and paintbrushes, each place at the table and glue sticks
		Counting the number of items they are using to make a collage, counting how many skinny- and how many thick-tipped brushes are in the box
	Understand patterns, relationships, and classification	Separating collage materials into piles, making patterns with beads and other art materials
	Demonstrate knowledge of sequence and temporal awareness	Saying things like "I put the blue stripe at the top" or "First, I squished the clay flat, then I put the pinecones on."

✋ Consult the Standards

TABLE 2.7   Addressing Standards in the Art Area (continued)

Science	Investigate the properties of objects	Using different kinds of paint, drawing materials, and papers; examining ways to shape the play dough
	Explore the concept of change in both living and nonliving entities	Exploring different ways to thin the paint, observing changes in materials as the paint or glue dries, seeing how colors mix
	Develop inquiry skills	Using language to describe the physical changes they observe, asking questions, predicting how materials will change, testing their ideas
Social Studies	Identify unique characteristics	Making self-portraits, mixing body paint to match the color of their skin, making body tracings, comparing similarities and differences among the portraits
	Are contributing members of the classroom	Helping to clean up, creating visual displays of their artwork, following routines for using the easel

Source: Based on the New Jersey State Department of Education, Preschool Teaching and Learning Expectations, adopted July 2004.

TEACHING WITH STANDARDS IN MIND

Children do not accomplish any standard through a single activity or all in one day. Instead they gradually approximate more and more accurate knowledge and skills as the result of many experiences—some child-initiated, some teacher-led. Consider the Illinois Preschool Reading Standards listed in Table 2.6. Individual children in the class might exhibit the following behaviors related to benchmark 4 of this standard (Gronlund, 2006, p. 35)

Standard A4: Children will identify some letters, including those in their own names

First Steps Toward the Standard:
Children might show awareness of the ABCs by singing the ABC song or by pointing to letters on a page, a puzzle, or a toy when asked (but not necessarily with accuracy).

Making Progress Toward the Standard:
Children might recognize at least the first letter of their names and demonstrate understanding that alphabet letters make up words in the environment by referring to signs and labels in the room and by creating their own signs and labels using a few recognizable letters in the process of writing.

Accomplishing the Standard:
Children might recognize and name some of the letters in their names as well as other letters in environmental print, such as the job chart, books, puzzles, and toys.

Of course, individual children in the class will likely be at different phases in this developmental sequence. Effective teachers observe children carefully to see what they already know and can do, then they put out materials, set up activities, and provide instructional support to help children progress toward accomplishing developmentally appropriate standards and goals. In this case, over the course of the year and depending on children's needs, teachers may do the following:

❏ Sing the alphabet song.
❏ Talk about and point to letters in books, on puzzles or toys, on the child's clothing, or elsewhere in the classroom.
❏ Provide alphabet posters, books, puzzles, hand stamps, and stickers throughout the room so children can be exposed to alphabet letters in different contexts.
❏ Make name cards and name charts to identify helpers for the day or to establish lists for taking turns.
❏ Label children's cubbies or art storage space.
❏ Create alphabet matching games, gross motor activities in which children hop, slide, or gallop from one letter displayed on the floor to another.
❏ Name the letters of children's names as they label pictures in the art area or projects in construction and pretend play.
❏ Provide alphabet games such as bingo and lotto.

Teachers provide these kinds of experiences daily. They also plan specific activities with certain standards in mind. You will learn more about this kind of planning in chapter 3.

SUMMARY

In this chapter, we described the foundations of teaching and learning within a developmentally appropriate framework. Three areas of knowledge and skill were identified: (1) knowledge of child development and learning, (2) knowledge of effective teaching strategies, and (3) knowledge of appropriate content. Activities and routines, materials, the physical environment, classroom management, methods of parental involvement, and assessment procedures are all influenced by these three facets of the teaching–learning triangle.

In terms of child development and learning, certain principles will influence your teaching. These include: children develop holistically, development occurs in orderly sequence, and children develop at varying rates. In addition, children learn best when they feel safe and secure. They are active learners, who learn through a combination of physical experience, social interaction, and reflection as well as through challenge and mastery. Although children's learning styles vary, all children learn much through play.

Because children learn in many ways, the teaching strategies that support their learning vary accordingly. Five common teaching strategies are ensuring children's sensory involvement, performing task analysis, chaining and successive approximation, scaffolding, and guided practice and repetition. These strategies influence activity design and the ways in which tasks are presented to children. Verbal strategies that support children's learning include invitations; behavior and paraphrase reflections; modeling and demonstrating; effective praise; telling, explaining, and informing; do-it signals; challenges; and questions. Silence can also be an effective teaching strategy when it is done to deliberately facilitate children's peer interactions and self-discoveries.

Some teaching strategies are more appropriate in certain situations than are others. Which strategies professionals use depends on the phase of the learning cycle in which children are engaged. The learning cycle begins with awareness and continues through exploration, acquisition, practice, and, finally, generalization. In this last phase, children often become aware of new things, beginning the cycle again.

The third side of the teaching–learning triangle involves appropriate content knowledge. Content is commonly addressed through standards derived at local, state, and national levels. Standards describe the outcomes of what children are expected to know and do as a result of their education experiences. In this book, standards are addressed in the goals associated with each developmental domain.

Now that you know more about teaching and learning in the early childhood classroom, you are ready to set the stage for children's learning. The first step in that process involves planning effective activities for children. That topic is discussed in chapter 3.

PEARSON
myeducationlab

To check your comprehension on the content covered in Chapter 2, go to the Book Specific Resources in the MyEducationLab for your course, select your text, and complete the Study Plan. Here you will be able to take a chapter quiz, receive feedback on your answers, and then access review, practice, and enrichment activities to enhance your understanding of chapter content.

Key Words

academic standards	cycle of learning	paraphrase reflections
behavior reflections	effective praise	scaffolding
chaining	frames of mind	successive approximation
close-ended questions	guided practice	task analysis
cortisol	open-ended questions	

Applying What You've Read in This Chapter

1. **Discuss**
   a. On the basis of your reading and your experiences with young children, discuss each of the questions that open this chapter.

   b. Select two principles of development and learning that you believe are most important for people untrained in early childhood education to know about. Explain your choices and what you would do to emphasize each one.

2. **Observe**
   a. Using Table 2.2 as a reference, observe an early childhood classroom. Identify four practices the teachers are using in the classroom that relate to the principles of child development and learning outlined in the table.
   b. Observe a teacher carrying out an activity with one or more children. Identify three teaching strategies described in this chapter that you see. Provide examples to illustrate your observations.

3. **Carry out an activity**
   a. Review Table 2.2, then add one more DAP strategy to at least four of the principles outlined in the table.
   b. Create a bumper sticker that captures the essence of one of the principles of development and learning described in this chapter.
   c. Refer to Table 2.1. Identify which of the eight intelligences described there most closely match how you learn best. Refer to the teaching strategies outlined in this chapter. Make a list of the strategies that seem to best match your learning profile and provide a short rationale about why.
   d. Refer to Figure 2.5, the "Cycle of Learning." Think of something you have learned to do, such as playing tennis or riding a bike. Describe how you proceeded through the cycle of learning for that particular skill.
   e. Review written information describing an early childhood program in your community. On the basis of the program's written philosophy and program description, discuss to what extent the program is congruent or incongruent with the content described in this chapter.

4. **Create something for your portfolio**
   a. Select a fundamental belief you have about child development and learning. Think both about children in general and specifically about the ages of the children in a program where you are working, volunteering, or doing a practicum. Describe how this belief would affect the following program dimensions: the children's program, staff, materials, physical space, budget, and family involvement. Identify practices that would be incompatible with the belief you chose.

5. **Add to your journal**
   a. Reflect on the extent to which the teaching strategies described in this chapter correspond to what you have observed in the field. What is your reaction to any discrepancies you perceive?
   b. In what ways have you used the cycle of learning in your work with children? What goals do you have for yourself in this regard?

6. **Consult the standards**
   a. Obtain the early childhood standards developed for your state. Identify where you found them. List three standards that seem appropriate for the children with whom you will be working.
   b. Talk to a teacher about how he or she uses state standards while teaching.
   c. Obtain the academic standards for three states. Compare the standards in a single category such as math or reading and describe how the standards are similar or different across the states.

PRACTICE FOR YOUR CERTIFICATION OR LICENSURE EXAM

The following items will help you practice applying what you have learned in this chapter. They can help to prepare you for your course exam, the PRAXIS II exam, your state licensure or certification exam, and for working in developmentally appropriate ways with young children.

Supporting Children's Learning

Rosemary teaches 3- and 4-year-old children in a child-care center. Over time, she observes that although the children begin each day eager to play in the pretend grocery store, they don't seem to know what to do with the materials or each other. They mostly argue over the cash register, grab the food cartons from the shelves and dump them onto the floor. Their play lacks focus, and they seldom talk to one another for real or in a pretend role. It doesn't take long before the area is a mess and the children simply drift away to other activities.

1. **Constructed-response question**

   Rosemary wants to introduce the children to other possibilities and help them play at a higher level.

   a. Describe potential child learning in the pretend grocery store.
   b. Identify three teaching strategies Rosemary could use to support the children's learning in the pretend grocery. Provide examples of verbal scripts to illustrate any verbal strategies you choose.

2. **Multiple-choice question**

   Which of the following teacher behaviors is an example of effective praise?

   a. You are all cooperating so well. That makes me happy.
   b. I like the way you're sharing the cash register.
   c. Good job!
   d. You worked hard to put all the food on the shelves. Now this store is ready for customers.

PART 2

SETTING THE STAGE FOR LEARNING

Chapter

3

Planning and Implementing Effective Small-Group Activities

You may wonder:

Why do teachers write activity plans? Why are written plans necessary?

Is formal planning as important for children in child-care settings and Pre-K programs as it is for children enrolled in elementary school?

As a teacher with my own class, will I have to write the same kind of plans as I am writing now?

What kinds of activities should I be planning for young children?

In this introduction to planning and implementing effective small-group activities, we present information to help you answer questions like these.

◆ ◆ *Estaban Ramirez is student teaching in the kindergarten at Arnold Elementary School. His roommates are amazed at the time and care he puts into writing lesson plans. After all, the children are only 5 and 6 years old. His friends cannot understand how planning for children that age could be so involved.*

People are sometimes surprised at the high level of planning necessary to ensure a smoothly running early childhood classroom. They may erroneously assume that in early childhood settings, little more is needed than simply putting out materials for children to use. However, the difference between providing children with truly educational experiences and merely keeping them busy or entertained is *planning* (Darling-Hammond & Hammerness, 2005; Epstein, 2007). In fact, planning is a key element of *high-quality* early childhood programs, and the ability to plan developmentally appropriate activities distinguishes effective practices from ineffective ones.

WHY PLAN?

Teachers need to know *why* they are teaching *what* they are teaching and *how* they are going to teach. This requires planning (Seefeldt, Castle, & Falconer, 2009). Although the design of teachers' plans varies from program to program, the reasons for planning are universal. Planning helps educators do the following:

- ❑ Organize their thoughts and actions
- ❑ Think creatively about what they want to do
- ❑ Gather needed equipment and materials in advance
- ❑ Connect their teaching to state standards and program goals
- ❑ Address the needs of the "whole child"
- ❑ Tailor activities to accommodate the needs of specific children, including children with special needs and children who are English language learners
- ❑ Address differences among learners
- ❑ Communicate to others what they are doing
- ❑ Identify the standards by which learning and teaching can be accurately and appropriately evaluated

Appropriate planning leads to intentional instruction that benefits young children. Classroom teachers who plan well convey a sense of purpose that children, families, other teachers, and administrators perceive and appreciate. As teachers implement carefully sequenced plans, they gain valuable information about children, materials, teaching methods, and outcomes. As a result, they are better able to keep track of children's progress, noting where advances are being made and where changes in instruction might be necessary. This information contributes to teachers' increased knowledge of the children and provides input teachers use to refine their teaching practices. Thorough planning, therefore, serves as the foundation for effective teaching.

In contrast, inadequate planning often results in chaotic classrooms and/or lackluster programming (Warner & Sower, 2005). Children may wander aimlessly or exhibit inappropriate behavior for lack of anything better to do. If superficial lessons dominate the program, children are not stimulated to learn. They may become bored or discouraged when asked to engage in activities that do not match their abilities. Moreover, the needs of some children may be met, whereas the needs of others may be ignored. In each instance, *poor planning* yields *poor-quality* programs. To prevent these negative results, early childhood practitioners must acquire effective planning skills.

CHARACTERISTICS OF EFFECTIVE PLANNING

Effective planning takes into account individual children and groups of children. It addresses short-term objectives and long-term goals as well as what is currently happening in the classroom and what might be needed in the future. Such planning reflects the teacher's knowledge and understanding of how young children develop and learn and the conditions under which optimal learning takes place. A strong grasp of relevant subject matter is also necessary (Schickedanz, 2008; Stronge, 2002). Additionally, whether applied to a single activity or to the program as a whole, good planning is flexible enough to allow teachers to accommodate children's changing needs over time and to take advantage of teachable moments as they happen. Most importantly, effective planning addresses the unique needs of specific children, at a given time and place.

PLANNING WITH SPECIFIC CHILDREN AND PROGRAMS IN MIND

Good planning is not a "one size fits all" proposition. Readymade plans available online, or borrowed from another teacher, or utilized year after year with little variation are not always educationally sound nor will they automatically work well with every group of children. The best instructional plans meet the unique characteristics (needs, strengths, interests) of the children for whom they are being developed (Epstein, 2007). Effective planners also think about the materials at their disposal; the physical space available to them; what portion of the day might suit the plan best; and the classroom, family, and community cultures that influence the children in their class. Thus, teachers engaged in developmentally appropriate practices recognize the contextual nature of planning. They understand that although a plan may be technically correct, if it is created without considering the specific children involved and the context in which they are learning, it could be developmentally inappropriate. Janet Fowler learned this lesson her first day on the job.

> Janet arrived at the Willow Street Cooperative Preschool in the fall to begin work as the new head teacher. Among the activities she planned for the first week was marble painting at the art table during free-choice time. She wanted to provide an open-ended art activity the children would enjoy. She also thought having them create decorations for the room would be a good way for children to personalize the classroom as well as have fun.
>
> Getting to the classroom early, Janet set up the materials: four metal pie pans, marbles, circles of paper cut to fit the bottom of the pans, baby-food jars half-filled with thick poster paint, plastic spoons for retrieving the marbles from the jars, and smocks. She posted a sign, on which four stick figures were drawn, meaning that four children at a time could participate in the activity. She covered the table with newspaper to protect it and positioned a drying rack nearby on which children could hang their finished paintings. Looking over the area, she felt satisfied that everything was ready and went to the door to greet the children and the parent volunteer as they came into the classroom.
>
> The materials at the art table intrigued the children. However, before Janet could ask everyone to put on a smock, Carl poured some of the paint onto the newspaper, treating it like finger paint. As he tried to push his sleeves out of the way, paint ran down his elbows and onto his shirt. LaTanya tried to roll her marble in a pan with no paper but a lot of paint. As she moved the marble in the pan, paint sloshed over the sides. Soon six or seven children were crowded around the table, trying to get to the materials. Voices rose as children became upset about not getting a turn or stepping in spilled paint. While Janet struggled to help the children, she wondered how she had lost control of the activity so quickly. This problem had not occurred when she had tried the same activity last spring with the 4-year-olds in the Head Start center where she had student taught.

What Janet did not realize was that the children at the Willow Street Cooperative Preschool had never tried marble painting before. Moreover, none of the children had access to similar paints at home. Because poster paints had only rarely been used at the preschool in the past, even returning children had little experience with paint. In addition, the children had never seen signs used to indicate how many children could participate in each area. Although such symbols are generally a good structuring tool, the children did not automatically know what they meant. Finally, Janet forgot that children who are in a classroom from fall to spring know much more about classroom routines and expectations than do youngsters coming together for the first time. Her plan for marble painting, which worked well with the Head Start children in April, was ineffective with these children so early in the year. Although Janet had a technically sound plan, she forgot to consider the contextual nature of planning. To avoid such mistakes, effective planners assume each of the following roles as they plan: information gatherer, goal setter, instructional designer, environmental organizer, evaluator, and writer (Brewer, 2007; Darling-Hammond & Hammerness, 2005).

Teachers as Information Gatherers

Before teachers make any plans, they gather critical information about the children they are teaching. They find out what interests children as well as what knowledge, skills, and understandings children are bringing to the activity. Knowing these things helps teachers make a better match between the lessons they plan and children's educational needs and abilities. In the information gathering role, teachers ask themselves questions like these:

> What previous experiences have children had?
> What are the children interested in knowing or finding out?
> How might children's cultural and linguistic backgrounds influence what is meaningful to them?
> What do children already know, what do they believe, and what can they do?
> What gaps are evident in children's knowledge or skills?

Teachers gather information to answer these questions by observing children, talking with children informally, collecting work samples, and keeping records of children's interactions with materials, peers, and adults. They document children's education experiences visually and verbally. See Figure 3.1 for a simple record one teacher made in the information gathering role. Teachers also talk with families about children's experiences at home and the interests and abilities family members have observed in their children. These information gathering strategies are ongoing and integral to the daily routine.

Teachers as Goal Setters

Identifying appropriate learning goals for children is critical to planning. Which goals teachers choose is influenced by many sources. These include the children themselves, program or school district goals, performance standards in Head Start, state standards, and family/community contexts. Children with identified disabilities have an individualized education plan (IEP), involving academic and functional goals tailored to each child's specific needs. As noted in chapter 1, the IEP influences goal setting as well. Questions like the ones that follow guide teachers as they set goals for children.

> What are families interested in having their children learn?
> What goals does the program or school district have for children?
> What are children's IEP goals?
> What goals have been addressed this week/this year?
> What goals need further attention?
> How does what the children want to know more about relate to other more formal goals?
> What is the primary goal of this activity and how will it support children's development and learning?

Teachers as Instructional Designers

As instructional designers, teachers consider how to address the goals they have chosen within DAP guidelines. Reflecting on what is age appropriate, individually appropriate, and culturally

FIGURE 3.1 A Teacher Documents Children's Learning During Outdoor Play

A Hole in the Sand: Young Children Explore the Natural World
Documented at the Child Saving Institute, Omaha, Nebraska

Panel One
Observing in the sand area, I notice how busy the children are. No one seems to need a teacher's help in any way.

Panel Two
Joshua and Benny are digging in the sand. They dig and dig with hands and shovels, making a hole. "I dug a really big hole," Joshua says. "It's so big I can put my head in it. See!"

Panel Three
Joshua pulls his head out. Benny put his head in. It fits! The boys continue with their play.

Interpretation

Joshua and Benny are exploring the natural world using their own bodies as a frame of reference. They are building on their past experiences with nonstandard measures to find out "how big" the hole really is. It seems that a hole that can fit one's own head is big!

Possible Follow-Up

- *Interview the boys about what is happening in the pictures. What are they curious about—the sand, the size of the hole, or something else altogether?*
- *Keep watching to see if "a hole in the sand" is a one-time experience or the beginning of an increased interest in digging or sand.*
- *We have been measuring things inside, using nonstandard measures such as shoes and teddy bears. Children have recorded that the table is "nine shoes long," the chair is "three shoes high," and the easel is "four teddy bears wide." Now we have a hole that is one head deep. We might measure more things outdoors and move beyond length and height to include depth and volume. We might use various body parts as measuring tools.*

Information from *Documentation Panel Source:* Esterling, L., & Edwards, C. (2008). *A hole in the sand: Young children explore the natural world.* Omaha, NE: Child Saving Institute.

and linguistically appropriate for each child as well as the group are key considerations. Sample questions teachers ask themselves in the design phase include the following:

How does what I know about child development and learning fit this plan?
How will I take into account children's cultural and linguistic backgrounds?
What is the sequence in which learning might logically take place?
What processes/teaching strategies are best suited to addressing this goal?
How will I support children who need extra assistance while still challenging those who are more skilled?
How will I monitor children's learning and document their progress?

Teachers as Organizers

Using information gained through the previous planning phases, teachers organize the physical aspects of instruction. This involves analyzing resources, identifying materials and space needs, as well as addressing potential safety and maintenance issues. The following are typical questions about organization.

What materials are necessary to carry out the plan?

When and where will the plan be implemented?

What will be involved in setting up and cleaning up this activity?

How will I maintain safety?

How many children will participate at one time?

How will I attract/invite children into the activity?

How will I help children transition to the next activity?

What physical adaptations may be necessary to enable every child to participate fully?

Teachers as Evaluators

In the evaluator role, teachers plan how they will assess children's experiences and learning in the activity as well as the effectiveness of their own instruction. To plan well, they must think about what they want to know and how they will find out. Teachers' thinking is guided by these broad questions:

How will I know children are learning?

What progress are individual children making in relation to goals?

What tools will I use to keep track of children's progress?

To what extent does this activity actually support the goals and curriculum standards it is meant to address?

What revisions are necessary to meet children's individual needs?

How did I respond to teachable moments and unexpected learning opportunities?

Based on what happened in this activity, what are logical next steps for the children and for me?

What did I learn about my teaching from carrying out this plan?

Teachers evaluate children's learning experiences and the success of planned activities using multiple strategies such as observing the children and keeping track of their progress using anecdotal records, rating scales, checklists, and children's self-evaluations. Teachers also interview children, ask children to demonstrate simple tasks, and document children's actions and ideas through pictures, words, and sample products (Seefeldt, Castle, & Falconer, 2009). Similarly, teachers reflect on their own instructional experiences, keeping notes and discussing the outcomes of plans with co-workers and family members as appropriate. All of this information feeds back into the planning process and helps to shape future instruction.

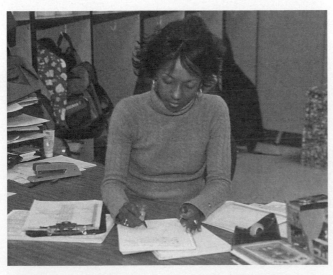

Working through a good learning activity is best done in writing.

Teachers as Writers

Working through the phases of planning just described is best done in writing (Driscoll & Nagel, 2008). Written plans are useful devices that help teachers think about educational activities in detail from start to finish. Putting their ideas down on paper encourages teachers to ensure that all parts of the lesson are addressed, to anticipate potential problems ahead of time, and to perfect instructional strategies before using them in the classroom. This advance preparation enables teachers to approach each lesson with greater confidence and security (Machado & Meyer, 2008). Not only do written plans offer tangible means for checking accuracy and completeness, but repeatedly going through the step-by-step process of writing each part of the lesson creates habits of mind that gradually become internalized. In this way, writing activity plans ultimately helps novice teachers gain practice in thinking more like experienced educators. Written plans also create a permanent record of what activities and objectives have been addressed. Written evaluations will help you remember your successes (or challenges), providing valuable information if you repeat the activity at a later date.

The amount of detail that goes into written plans varies with the writer's experience. In general, inexperienced planners profit from writing their ideas in great detail. As teachers gain practice writing and thinking about planning, the need for extensive written detail gradually decreases. With time, practitioners become more able to think comprehensively while writing only what is necessary for someone else (e.g., a parent volunteer, assistants in the program, or the substitute teacher) to follow their plan successfully. In this way, learning to plan proceeds from representing all of your thinking to conveying only its essence. Planning also shifts from enhancing your own comprehension to helping other people understand what you intend to have happen.

In this text we first present detailed activity plans to help you learn all the necessary steps involved in effective planning. Later, we present an abbreviated form that many experienced teachers use in their day-to-day work with children. Regardless of whether you are a new planner or an experienced one, you must think about certain factors so that you can create developmentally appropriate plans for children. These considerations are basic to all planning.

PLANNING BASICS

Teachers plan activities for solitary children, for small groups of children, and for the entire class to participate in together. All these plans can be thought about in similar ways, with minor variations. In this chapter, we will focus on activity plans in which one or only a few children participate together. Such experiences are frequently offered during small-group times or free-choice periods. It is common for small-group activities to take place within activity centers either indoors or outdoors. Typical centers include language arts, creative arts and construction, science and collections, math and manipulatives, sand or water, gross motor, blocks, and pretend play. You will learn more about specific activity centers in chapter 5. No matter where or when they take place, small-group activities form the building blocks for teachers' daily, weekly, and yearly planning. In chapter 4, we discuss how to plan and implement activities in which the entire class participates at once. How to plan for a week or more at a time is the subject of chapter 16. All the elements that should be incorporated into a typical activity plan are outlined in Figure 3.2. A sample plan follows in Figure 3.3.

FIGURE 3.2 Activity Plan Format

Domain   One of the six curricular domains identified in this text: aesthetic, affective, cognitive, language, physical, and social.

Activity Name   The title of the activity.

Goal   Goals are listed in each of the chapters describing the curriculum. These goals identify desirable behaviors relevant to children's development and learning within the domain.

Objectives   A list of specific instructional objectives leading to the goal and tailored to meet the needs of the children involved.

Content   The content that will be addressed in the activity. This content identifies the terms (vocabulary) and facts relevant to the lesson.

Materials   A list of all necessary props or equipment.

Procedures   A step-by-step description of how to implement the activity. Procedures may include multiple teaching strategies.

Simplifications   Ideas for reducing the complexity or abstractness of the activity. Ways to adapt the activity for children with less experience or special needs.

Extensions   Ideas for making the activity more challenging as children demonstrate the desire and ability to expand their knowledge and skills.

Evaluation   Ways to assess children's learning and the teaching methods used.

FIGURE 3.3   Sample Activity Plan

Domain   Language   **Activity Name**   Turnip Story Sequence

Goal   Children will listen to a story and then discuss the story sequence (chapter 12, The Language Domain, Goal 8).

Objectives

Given an opportunity to hear a story that illustrates a clear sequence of events, the child will:

1. Listen to the story one time through.
2. Name the characters in the story as the teacher points to them.
3. Assist the teacher in retelling the story in the correct sequence.

Content

1. Sequence refers to the order in which events occur.
2. A story describes a series of events that progresses from beginning to end.
3. Changing the sequence of events in a story may change the story's meaning.

Materials   Flannel board; flannel figures corresponding to the characters in the story "The Big, Big Turnip" (see appendix C)

Procedures

Objective 1:   The child will listen to the story one time through.

Invite children to listen to the story "The Big, Big Turnip." Tell the story with enthusiasm and expression, placing the flannel board pieces on the board at appropriate points. Emphasize the characters' names and the sequence in which they appear by repeating them each time a new character is introduced. Leave the characters on the board when the story is over.

Objective 2:   The child will name the characters in the story as the teacher points to them.

Encourage the children to name the characters in order. Point to each one in line, beginning with the farmer. Ask the children to say the character's name when you point to it.

Objective 3:   The child will assist the teacher in retelling the story in the correct sequence.

Hide the characters behind the flannel board. Ask the children to help tell the story by telling you which character to put on the board next.

Repeat this part of the activity more than once. Vary the procedure by giving each child a character that he or she is to put on the board when it is time for that character to appear in the story.

Simplification   Put the flannel board pieces at the bottom of the board, facing the children. Raise them to the top of the board in sequence as you tell the story.

Extension   Tell the story and make mistakes in the sequence. Ask the children to help by correcting mistakes they hear. Ask children to talk about how the meaning of the story changed when the sequence varied. Another option is to encourage children to tell the story on their own.

Evaluation   Using a performance checklist, identify which of the three objectives outlined in this activity plan individual children met. On the basis of your observations of children's participation, describe how this information will influence your future instruction related to story sequence. What objectives do you think the teacher has for the children participating in this activity?

CREATING DEVELOPMENTALLY APPROPRIATE PLANS

All the components of the activity plan described in Figure 3.2 are critical to the planning process. Considered individually, each will make an important contribution to your understanding of how to translate goals for children into developmentally appropriate learning experiences. Taken together, they address the information gatherer, goal setter, instructional designer, organizer, and evaluator roles of the effective planner. Let us recap what must be considered for each element.

Domain

The curriculum described in part 3 of this text is divided into six **domains** representing the various aspects of whole-child learning. Although curriculum integration is our ultimate purpose, we have discovered that planners are most effective when they concentrate on one domain at a time until they are thoroughly familiar with the curriculum and are skilled in writing plans. With this in mind, you will choose a domain within which to write your plan: aesthetic, affective, cognitive, language, physical, or social. Then, you will begin writing.

Activity Name

Each activity should have a name for easy reference now and in the future. It is important to create a title for the activity that is brief but descriptive. Avoid cute names that fail to clarify the main focus of your plan. For instance, if you were writing a counting plan, it would be clearer to title it, "Counting Objects in Our Classroom" than to call it, "Kindergarten Kounting Kapers."

Goal

The **goal** answers the question, "What is the overall purpose of this plan?" It is a broad description of behavior related to children's development and learning within a given domain. Goals are long-term aims that you will address repeatedly during the year. Several goals for each domain are listed in the curriculum chapters in part 3 of this text. For each lesson, you will select *one* goal on which to concentrate within the domain you chose.

Objectives

Objectives are the specific learning behaviors children might logically display in relation to the goal. They describe in precise detail what children are expected to know or do within a particular activity. Well-written objectives are characterized by at least two attributes: (1) the *conditions* under which learning will occur, and (2) a clear statement of the *behavior* children will exhibit as a function of their learning. Here is an example of an objective that contains both parts.

> *"Given an opportunity to participate in a group discussion* about classroom rules, the child will
> (condition)
> *state one idea for a rule."*
> (behavior)

Conditions. The conditions of the objective describe the materials or supports the child will use to engage in the learning process. This is usually the first portion of the objective and often begins with the word *given*.

Here is an example of a condition for a sorting plan:

"Given a set of objects that vary greatly in appearance and other properties, the child will . . ."

See how the conditions change in the following objective that is also focused on sorting:

"Given a set of objects that vary in some properties, but are identical in others, the child will . . ."

Here is an example of a condition for a lesson on exploring earthworms:

"Given a bucket full of soil containing some earthworms, the child will . . ."

See how the conditions change in the following objective that is also about earthworms:

"Given an opportunity to observe and handle an earthworm while hearing an adult describe some of its features, the child will . . ."

As these examples illustrate, conditions may change from one objective to the next, depending on the lesson plan.

Behaviors. The behavior portion of the objective identifies a specific child action that will signify that the objective has been achieved. Objectives are characterized by actions that can be

What objectives do you think the teacher has for the children participating in this activity?

FIGURE 3.4   Action Words for Objectives

Here are some action words you might use in creating objectives. What additional words might you add?

The child will . . .

Circle	Find	Predict
Compare	Hypothesize	Put in order
Count	Identify	Select
Demonstrate	Make	Sequence
Describe	Measure	Sort
Estimate	Name	Tell
Evaluate	Observe	
Explain	Point to	

observed as they occur (Charlesworth & Lind, 2009). Sample behaviors are depicted in bold print below:

The child will:

Sort objects into groups in which the items in each group have at least one attribute in common.
Give a reason for why the objects in each group belong together.
Make a list of the properties that the objects in each group have in common.

The child will:

Search for earthworms by gently pushing aside the soil.
Describe ways the earthworms move.
Name body parts earthworms do not possess.

Additional action words are listed in Figure 3.4. For each lesson plan, we suggest writing at least *three* objectives. All of the objectives should relate to the same goal. They should also be arranged in the logical order in which you think children's learning will occur, progressing from the simplest objective to more challenging ones. More information about how to effectively sequence objectives will be presented later in this chapter. For now, refer to Figure 3.5 for an overview of the difference between a goal and an objective to further enhance your planning skills.

Content

The content identifies information the activity will address. It should be based on a thorough understanding of what the children already know and what would be useful and worthwhile for them to learn. Content addresses terms and facts relevant to the domain and the goal that is the focus of the plan. *Terms* are the vocabulary that describes activity-related objects and events (e.g., a *lamb* is a baby sheep, or *piglet* is the name given to a baby pig). Something known to exist or to have happened is a *fact* (e.g., sheep give birth to lambs, pigs give birth to piglets, all animals give birth to their own kind).

Accurate content is critical to good planning. Successful planners research their terms and facts carefully and write them so that anyone else carrying out the plan will have a clear understanding of its content. We recommend including at least *three* terms, facts, or both to support each lesson plan.

Materials

Each plan needs to include a complete list of the materials required to carry it out. Effective planners consider every item necessary for the setup, implementation, and cleanup phases of each activity. Enough detail should be provided so that someone other than the planner would know what was needed to carry out the activity effectively. Also, if the activity is something the planner has never tried before, it is wise to experiment with the materials prior to using them with the children to gain a true idea of what is needed. For instance, Mr. Buthelezi wanted to create a "tornado in a bottle" as a science experiment. He knew he needed two 2 liter-sized soft-drink bottles, water to partially fill one of the bottles, and tape to hold them together top to top. During a test run, he found that the connection between the two inverted soft-drink bottles leaked after the liquid in the bottles was swirled several times. Duct tape held better than the masking tape he had originally selected. Trying the materials in advance prevented a classroom mess and allowed children to concentrate on the experiment rather than on leaky bottles.

Procedures

The procedures section of the activity plan is a step-by-step description of how the teacher will implement the activity. It outlines the instructional strategies the teacher will use to support children's achievement of each objective. In creating this part of the plan, teachers combine their knowledge of child development and learning with their understanding of effective instruction to determine what teaching strategies are best suited to the lesson and the children involved.

FIGURE 3.5   The Difference Between Goals and Objectives

Goals and objectives work together to guide planning. However, goals are broader in scope than objectives are. They describe what children may be expected to learn over an extended period of time, such as months or even years. Objectives, on the other hand, are specific descriptions of how children may demonstrate learning within an individual lesson. Here are some examples:

Affective Domain

Goal

Children will complete a task they have begun.

Objectives

Given an opportunity to paint at the easel, the child will:

    a. Put on a paint smock.
    b. Select a brush and paints to use.
    c. Paint on the paper.
    d. Hang up his or her painting.

Cognitive Domain

Goal

Children will recognize, describe, and extend patterns such as sequences of sounds and shapes, or simple numerical patterns, and translate patterns from one form of representation to another.

Objectives

Given a set of varied objects and teacher support, the child will:

    a. Explore the objects.
    b. Create an arrangement of objects that repeats certain properties in sequence (e.g., red, blue, red, blue or triangle, square, square, triangle, square, square).
    c. Describe a pattern in words.
    d. Extend a pattern beyond the current pattern.
    e. Duplicate a pattern made of objects using similar objects.
    f. Duplicate a pattern through drawings or symbols.

Language Domain

Goal

Children will create new endings for stories, drawing on logical elements of the original stories.

Objectives

Given a familiar narrative story, the child will:

    a. Read the story from beginning to end.
    b. Retell (in writing or orally) the ending of the story.
    c. Write an alternate ending to the story.
    d. Describe (in writing or orally) how he or she decided what influenced the new ending.

In each of these examples the goals and objectives are closely related to one another and describe children's learning, but with differing degrees of specificity. Educators address the same goal frequently, using the same or different materials and experiences each time. Thus, goals tend to remain somewhat stable over time, whereas objectives change more frequently.

(Refer to the teaching strategies outlined in chapter 2 for examples.) For every objective, teachers determine a set of procedures to support children's learning. The easiest way to do this is to plan the procedures in a stepwise fashion corresponding to the objectives one at a time. This pairing of objectives and procedures is illustrated in the activity plan depicted in Figure 3.3. You may also find it helpful to write both what you will do (short descriptions of teacher behaviors) and what you will say (sample scripts). By carefully planning each step, you are more likely to follow your plan.

Simplifications

Simplifications are ways to modify the activity if the objectives identified in the plan are too advanced or too complex for some children to navigate. There are any number of reasons why this might be the case. A child's lack of experience, differences in age-related abilities, and special needs are all circumstances that might prompt teachers to move into the simplification portion of their plan. Simplifications often represent precursor objectives related to the activity or more rudimentary means of addressing the intermediate goal. For instance, in the earlier example of marble painting, Janet Fowler assumed that children at the Willow Street Cooperative Preschool were familiar with using poster paint. On discovering that her assumption was incorrect, she should have revised (simplified) the activity to make it less complex. One way to do this would have been to take away the pans and the marbles and simply have children experiment with the paint using paper and brushes at the easel (a piece of equipment with which the children were already familiar). After the children became more experienced painters, she could have introduced the marbles and pie tins, knowing that the children would be more successful. In this case, it would have helped if Janet had anticipated that such simplifications might be necessary so that she could have put them into action as soon as she saw that the activity was too difficult for the children to successfully carry out in the original form she had planned.

Simplifications may be used with an entire group of children as illustrated in the Willow Street Cooperative Preschool example or with individual children. For example, a teacher observed that Tanya, a kindergartner whose cerebral palsy made it challenging for her to engage in fine motor tasks, was having a hard time getting the buttons through the holes on her coat completely on her own. The teacher simplified the task by pulling the button partway through the hole and then encouraging Tanya to pull it the rest of the way through. Similarly, a child who was struggling with two-digit addition problems on paper benefited when his teacher simplified the task by giving him Cuisenaire rods to use as an aid in working out the sample problems. In both cases, the overall goal remained the same (buttoning a coat, working on two-digit math problems), but more basic strategies were offered to support children's learning. Such simplifications are often easier to develop when you think about possibilities ahead of time. This also allows you to gather any needed materials in advance. Therefore, we recommend developing at least *one* simplification for each plan you write. Consider your sequence of objectives, and then figure out what might be an even more basic place to begin. Use this idea to develop your simplification strategy.

Extensions

Children who achieve all the objectives identified in a particular plan benefit from trying more advanced steps than the original sequence of objectives covers. Extensions provide ideas for making the lesson more challenging. For instance, if the most advanced objective in a counting plan is for children to count to 100 by 2s and the child can do this easily, it makes sense to encourage the child to count higher or to perhaps try counting by 5s or 10s. Likewise, children who can think of one way to share an item (e.g., taking turns) could be challenged to think of alternative ways to share as well (e.g., trading or using the object together). Youngsters who can write certain words with adult assistance could be helped to develop strategies for remembering how to write these words on their own or for using the words they know how to write to create a simple story. All these strategies enable children to move beyond their current level of functioning to more advanced performance levels in accordance with their needs and abilities. Thinking about extension ideas in advance makes it more likely that those ideas will be well suited to the task and the children. With this in mind, we suggest that you create at least *one* extension for each lesson plan. Try to anticipate the next logical step in the sequence of objectives and use this to shape your extension ideas.

Evaluating and Reflecting on the Lesson

Every activity plan needs to be evaluated. The evaluation serves as both an ending and a beginning to the planning process. Following the implementation of an activity, evaluation information assists teachers in assessing the accuracy of their observations, the lesson content, the effectiveness of teaching methods, and child outcomes. These data help educators to gauge their own learning as well as the children's. In this way, the evaluation brings closure to the activity. However, appropriate evaluation does not simply describe the past; it also provides ideas for the future. What did you discover that will be useful to consider another day? How will you use what you learned? How might you change the direction of your planning? Answers to these questions inform the planning process for the next time.

With these purposes in mind, teachers pose specific evaluation questions and then answer them in writing after the plan has been carried out. Typical evaluation questions are listed in Figure 3.6.

FIGURE 3.6   Typical Evaluation Questions Regarding Children's Learning and Teaching Effectiveness

Children's Participation
1. Who participated in this activity?
2. To what extent was the activity of interest to the children? How do you know?
3. How did you get the children involved in the activity?
4. How accurate were your assumptions?

What Children Learned
1. Which children achieved which objectives?
2. Did children appear to understand the content of the lesson? How do you know?
3. What did children say or do in the activity to demonstrate that they were learning?
4. What indicated that the activity was developmentally appropriate for children in the group?

Teaching Effectiveness
1. How did advance preparation (or lack of it) contribute to the success (or lack of success) of the activity?
2. How did the materials meet the needs of the children who participated?
3. Was the activity carried out as planned? What changes were made and why? Did the changes enhance or detract from the activity?
4. If you were to use this activity again, what would you repeat and what would you change? Why?
5. What activities might be implemented to strengthen children's comprehension?
6. What did you learn from this activity?

The planner may answer some of these questions, other members of the teaching team may address some, and the children may answer others. In this way, evaluation is a dynamic, communal aspect of early childhood education. Most planners *select three or four* evaluation questions to answer for each activity, selecting questions that address both the performance of the teacher and the children. Varying the questions from day to day and from one plan to the next helps teachers glean much information in a short time. This information may be gathered through observations, anecdotal records, performance checklists, rating scales, samples of children's work, participation charts, and children's assessments of their work or progress. More about the specific strategies for gathering evaluative data is described in chapter 7.

ALIGNING ALL THE PARTS OF THE LESSON PLAN

For your activity plan to have the greatest impact, all the parts of the plan must be aligned or be in congruence with each other. That is, each part must relate to and support the other parts. For instance, if the goal focuses on story sequence, as illustrated in Figure 3.3, the objectives should be about story sequence too, not about choosing favorite illustrations or describing the difference between fiction and fact. When a plan is properly aligned, the procedures also will be closely linked to the objectives. If the objective states, "Children will listen to the story one time through," a complementary procedure must be planned that involves reading the story aloud. Likewise, the content portion of the activity should revolve around story sequence (e.g., *sequence* refers to the order in which events in a story occur), not information about how turnips grow in the ground. If growing turnips were what the teacher really wanted children to know about, the goal would be "Children will learn facts about the natural world," and the rest of the plan would support this aim. In addition, in a story sequence activity, the simplifications and extensions should break down the story into smaller steps for children to manage or build on the notion of sequence in a more challenging way. Extensions that have children drawing pictures of turnips or mashing them with a hand masher do not support children's development of the story sequence concept. On the other hand, inviting children to rearrange the sequence of events in the story and discuss how that impacts the ending does expand the children's understanding of story sequence, making it a more appropriate extension for the sequencing lesson. Paying attention to internal alignment adds substance to your plans and gives them a stronger educational foundation.

USING PRINCIPLES OF DEVELOPMENTAL DIRECTION TO ENHANCE YOUR PLANNING

As you can see, the activity plan format described in this chapter requires teachers to identify a logical sequence in which children's learning might occur in relation to a goal. That sequence will range from very basic demonstrations of learning to more advanced levels. At this point you may wonder:

❑ How do educators figure out the order for writing their objectives?
❑ What simplification might fit a certain plan?
❑ What extension makes sense for this activity?

The principles of **developmental direction** will help you answer these questions.

Based on our knowledge of child development and learning, we know that children's understandings and skills proceed from:

❑ Known to unknown
❑ Self to other
❑ Whole to part
❑ Concrete to abstract
❑ Enactive to symbolic
❑ Exploratory to goal directed
❑ Less accurate to more accurate
❑ Simple to complex

These principles describe the typical advancement of the learning process. Initially, learning is informal, concrete, and governed by the child's own rules. Over time, learning becomes more formal, more refined, and more removed in time and space from concrete references. It is also more closely tied to conventional rule systems. This may take place over a period of minutes, days, or years (Heroman & Copple, 2006). Applying principles of developmental direction to your planning will increase the developmental appropriateness of your lessons and, consequently, their effectiveness. Utilizing these principles in your planning will also assist you in supporting each child in your group as you implement your lessons.

Known to Unknown

Children base new learning on what is familiar. They build skills on previously learned behaviors and knowledge. More sophisticated concepts grow out of those that already exist for them. When children can make connections between their prior knowledge and new experiences, the new experiences become meaningful. When children cannot make such links, the experiences are irrelevant. This means teachers must take time to discover what children know and can do prior to introducing new material. The principle of *known to unknown* is why a teacher who wants to introduce the scientific concept of mammals to the children uses examples of mammals common in the children's environment, not animals they have never heard of or have seen only in pictures.

Self to Other

When children are young, all new learning begins with the self: What does this look like to *me?* How does this feel to *me?* How does this fit my experience? Once these issues have been satisfied, children use their personal understandings to better comprehend other people's realities. A teacher who introduces the social studies concept of cultural traditions by beginning with the family traditions children experience at home, before introducing traditions in different parts of the world, is basing the instruction on the principle of *self to other.* The same is true when the teacher introduces a lesson on bullying by first asking children to describe a time when they might have seen or experienced bullying themselves, and then asking them to talk about how other people might feel if they are bullied.

Whole to Part

Children perceive and experience the world in integrated, unified ways, moving from wholes to parts and from general to specific understandings. Only after they have grasped the big idea of an experience do the details become meaningful to them. Hence, children might hear a song several times before differentiating all of the words. Children are better able to discriminate among different kinds of trees if they have a general notion of trees overall. Children's mature understanding of letter–sound associations requires them to have some concept of words first. Introducing too many specifics prematurely or out of context makes the details less relevant.

Because of the *whole to part* principle, early childhood educators offer children a broad array of rich, multisensory experiences in relation to each goal. They repeat activities often, giving children plenty of time to explore and formulate their impressions and conceptualizations. As children express interest and understanding, teachers draw children's attention to relevant details that enlarge youngster's perceptions and challenge them to try alternatives or reconsider old ideas. Conversely, teachers are careful not to teach children skills or facts in isolation. They work from the general to the specific rather than the other way around.

Concrete to Abstract

The most concrete experiences are tangible ones that involve physical contact with real objects. They are those in which children taste, touch, and smell as well as see and hear. The further removed an experience is from this tangible state and the fewer senses children are required to use, the more abstract it becomes. The teacher is using the principle of *concrete to abstract* when considering a variety of approaches to teaching children about leaves. Providing children with real leaves to look at, handle, take apart, smell, and taste is the most concrete way to enhance children's interest in and knowledge about leaves. Giving children pictures to explore or having them cut leaves from magazines is a step removed from the real thing and thus is more abstract. Even further removed is having children watch the teacher point to leaves in a book or on the bulletin board. The most distant and therefore most abstract activity involves having children imagine leaves as the teacher talks about them.

Children throughout the preschool and elementary years benefit from concrete experiences in all developmental domains and across all subject areas. The more unfamiliar the object or phenomenon, the more this is true. The danger in ignoring the *concrete to abstract* principle is that if activity plans rely on abstract approaches too soon, children may parrot what adults tell them, but not truly understand essential concepts. For this reason, teachers in developmentally appropriate classrooms provide children with many firsthand experiences and tangible objects before gradually introducing greater abstraction.

Enactive to Symbolic Representation

Representation refers to how children depict objects, events, and experiences as they think about them and communicate their ideas to others.

The principle of concrete to abstract tells us to start children off by experiencing the "real thing"!

Enactive Representation. When children reconstruct roles (being the parent or an astronaut) and events (feeding the baby or flying to the moon) with their bodies (using gestures, sounds, words, and objects), they are involved in *enactive representation*. This is the most basic form of representing one's experiences and is very common throughout the early childhood years (Driscoll & Nagel, 2008; Lawton, 1987). For instance, following a field trip to feed the ducks, children at the Temple Preschool returned to the classroom imitating duck sounds, waddling, and making "quacking" gestures with their hands. We see enactive representation most often when children are in the pretend-play area, but if we look carefully, we will see it in other parts of the classroom as well. Children may read a story and enact part of it on their own or with others, a child may use "finger counting" to solve a math problem, children may use their bodies to form the length of a whale in a science activity. These are all ways of representing an idea or event using one's body.

Iconic Representation. A more abstract mode of representation involves children's making pictures or constructing three-dimensional images of what they see and think about. These pictures/constructions are *iconic representations*. Youngsters who reproduce or create personal interpretations of objects and events by using art or construction materials such as blocks are demonstrating iconic representation. Thus, following the duck field trip, some youngsters might paint what they saw; others might sculpt duck-like shapes in clay; and still others might use cardboard, wire, and string to re-create the duck pond scene they observed.

Symbolic Representation. The most abstract means of representing an idea or event is *symbolic*. In this mode, children use words and symbols such as signs and numerals to interpret and represent particular phenomena. Youngsters returning from the field trip to see the ducks could represent what occurred on the trip by dictating or writing descriptions of their experiences in words. They might also use numerals to represent the numbers of ducks they saw or fed.

By the time children are toddlers, they engage in all three forms of representation. As children mature, these modes increase in sophistication and are used in increasing numbers of contexts (Bjorklund, 2005). Children may use the three forms singly or in combination (e.g., children in the make-believe grocery act out the roles of customer and cashier, draw pictures on signs for the shelves, write grocery lists, and take inventory; children enact "The Three Billy Goats Gruff," make costumes out of paper bags, create a bridge out of blocks, and write sample scripts of what they are going to say). Throughout the preprimary and early elementary grades, children therefore benefit from access to pretend–play items, art supplies, construction materials, and other representational objects as well as a variety of writing tools and writing surfaces. The enactive to symbolic representation continuum also suggests that children need ample opportunity to explore concepts through enactive and iconic representation prior to relying on symbolic representation alone.

This principle gives us valuable clues about how to simplify and extend activities. For instance, if a child is having difficulty solving a mathematical word problem (symbolic representation), he or she might benefit from simplifying the problem by drawing it on paper (iconic representation) or even representing it by using objects (enactive representation). Conversely, if a child clearly demonstrates understanding of a mathematical principle using concrete objects, he or she might be ready for the challenge of using drawings or letter and number symbols to depict the problem as extensions of the original activity.

Exploratory to Goal Directed

As depicted in the cycle of learning and teaching highlighted in chapter 2, children need many chances to explore objects and behaviors prior to using them in prescribed ways. In some cases, teachers plan days and weeks of exploration prior to introducing certain activities (e.g., children explore manipulating clay and using various tools with clay before being asked to try the "coil" method of making a pot out of clay; children examine and play with the magnets before being asked to use them in a step-by-step problem-solving activity). Even when children are fairly familiar with a material, the first step in most early childhood activities is to give children an opportunity to explore materials and procedures before asking them to engage in more goal-directed activities (e.g., children have a little while to explore the magnifying glasses prior to using them to systematically examine a collection of shells; children explore a variety of objects available at the water table prior to using them in a sink-and-float activity).

Less Accurate to More Accurate

Young children constantly strive to make sense of the world in which they live. They do this by observing, hypothesizing, experimenting, and making deductions about their day-to-day encounters with people and objects. This process is characterized by trial and error and is due to children's relative inexperience and immature thinking; their initial deductions are not always accurate. We can see the *less accurate to more accurate* principle at work when a child who has been told that a certain four-legged furry creature is a "dog," initially draws the conclusion that *all* animals are "dogs." Cognitive theorists remind us that such "mistakes" play an important role in children's mental development. They serve as the catalyst by which children refine their thinking and enlarge it. Each time children encounter events that challenge their deductions (such as interacting with another four-legged furry creature called a cat), they resolve the dilemma by readjusting their thinking to accommodate new information that doesn't fit their old notion (dogs are four-legged furry creatures and cats are too). This mental activity eventually leads to more accurate conclusions. Thus, over time and with experience, the child comes to learn that some furry four-legged animals are dogs, some are cats, some are hamsters, and some are squirrels.

Keeping the *less accurate to more accurate* principle in mind, early childhood educators give children many opportunities to gradually develop more accurate notions of how the world works through direct experience. The procedures portion of each activity plan reflects this understanding, including questions and probes that encourage children to hone their thinking, and opportunities for children to experiment as a way to discover answers that fit their experiences. In addition, activities that involve children developing predictions, evaluating their experiences, solving problems, and determining what they know as well as how they know are featured throughout the day.

Simple to Complex

The principle of *simple to complex* applies to nearly every activity plan teachers write. Simplifying a task makes it smaller or easier to navigate. Based on the other principles cited here, tasks are simplified when they are:

More closely tied to what children already know than to what they don't know
More focused on self than on others
More focused on the whole rather than the parts
More concrete than abstract
More enactive than symbolic
More exploratory than goal directed
More tolerant of inaccuracies

Conversely, an activity becomes more complex when the task is:

More unknown than known
More focused on others than on self
More focused on its component parts than on the whole
More abstract
More symbolic
More goal directed
More focused on what is accurate, and,
When it requires more independence

Complexity increases further as the numbers of variables involved in the task multiply (e.g., it is more challenging to play a lotto game that contains 40 pieces than one that contains 20), and when discriminations among variables become less distinct (e.g., it is easier to match lotto pieces when pairs of matching cards are distinctly different from other pairs than to match pieces in which the pairs are very similar to one another). Also, combining elements is more complex than dealing with them separately (e.g., it is harder to follow multistep directions than to follow directions one step at a time).

APPLYING THE PRINCIPLES OF DEVELOPMENTAL DIRECTION TO YOUR PLANS

Take a moment to consider how the principles of developmental direction in children's learning influenced the Turnip Story Sequence activity plan (shown previously in Figure 3.3). Sample ideas are presented in Table 3.1.

The "Turnip Story" plan could actually make use of all eight principles of developmental direction, depending on how it was carried out and the learning needs of the children. Not every plan will make use of every principle; however, as you design your plans, it is good to consider each principle as you develop the objectives and procedures as well as the simplifications and the extensions. These principles will be especially useful as you consider how to sequence the objectives from most basic to more challenging. As you think about the logical steps the learning may

TABLE 3.1 Applying the Principles of Developmental Direction to Planning	
Principle	**Application to the Turnip Story Sequence Activity Plan Presented in Figure 3.3**
Known to Unknown	This activity was based on a story the children had heard several times before. As children become more adept at identifying characters and at sequencing events in familiar stories, the teacher could introduce less familiar stories for the children to consider.
Self to Other	Some children might be more successful if they had their own flannel board to work with in a one-on-one activity with an adult rather than listening and focusing on other children's contributions in a group.
Whole to Part	First, children heard the story one time through. Next, they focused on parts of the story such as individual characters and events.
Concrete to Abstract	This activity made use of tangible objects (flannel board and flannel figures) for children to manipulate. It would be more abstract for children to retell the story sequence in their own words without the aid of the figures.
Enactive to Symbolic	Once the children were familiar with the story, they might enact it in the pretend-play area. They could make drawings as iconic representations of the story. Eventually, children could reconstruct the story symbolically, using written words.
Exploratory to Goal Directed	The children had many opportunities to explore the use of flannel boards and flannel board figures (in the days preceding this activity) prior to being asked to use these objects in a prescribed way as suggested in the activity plan.
Less Accurate to More Accurate	As children participate in the activity, the teacher will use behavior reflections, paraphrase reflections, and questions to gently guide children toward more complete and more accurate understandings over time.
Simple to Complex	The objectives are in order from most basic to more challenging. Listening to the story is less complex than naming individual characters, and naming the characters is less complex than figuring out the correct sequence of events. All of these steps are simpler than correcting mistakes in the sequence as suggested in the extension or telling the story verbally on their own

take, you will have to make judgments about what behaviors may be involved and the order in which children may logically demonstrate them. While there are few absolutes in carrying out this task, the principles offered here can help you to design instruction more appropriately. As you observe children in the activity, you may have to make adjustments either on the spot or the next time you carry out a similar plan. Over time, you will gradually develop a better understanding of the developmental direction children's learning takes in relation to various goals within each domain.

You now have the basic tools for planning developmentally appropriate activities for young children—a format for writing a lesson plan and information about how to sequence the objectives and procedures that are part of each plan. As you explore the curricular domains presented in this book, you will find there are different types of activities you may choose to support children's learning. The most common of these are described next.

COMMON ACTIVITIES IN EARLY CHILDHOOD PROGRAMS

Early childhood educators plan many different kinds of lessons using the format described in this chapter. Six of the most common types of activities in early childhood education are:

- ❏ Exploratory play
- ❏ Guided discovery
- ❏ Problem solving
- ❏ Discussions
- ❏ Demonstrations
- ❏ Direct instruction

All of these types of activities are appropriate for children ages 3 through 8 years, and all are adaptable to each curricular domain. The most significant way in which they differ from one

FIGURE 3.7 Activity Pyramid

another is the extent to which either children or adults determine processes and outcomes. For some activities, how and what is learned is mostly determined by the children; in other activities, children and teachers share responsibility for how the activity transpires and what ends are achieved; still other activities place primary control for what happens with the adult. Because of what we know about how young children learn best, child-directed experiences and shared activities are much more prevalent in high-quality early childhood programs than are adult-controlled activities. However, all three variations can be used appropriately at one time or another to support children's learning. A summary of these activity types and the relation among them is illustrated in Figure 3.7.

The six activity types addressed in this chapter do not cover all the possibilities, but they do represent the basics around which many other kinds of activities are designed. More specific activities commonly associated with particular domains, such as story mapping or conflict mediation, are addressed in the domain-related chapters to which they apply.

Exploratory Play

Much of what young children learn evolves through playful explorations of the environment. Through self-initiated examinations of people, places, objects, and events, children construct their own knowledge rather than simply taking in information supplied by others. Exploratory play enables children to carry out firsthand investigations, proceeding at their own pace and making most of the decisions about what is done and how and when it is done (Elkind, 2007). Because there are no set answers, children discover things for themselves, taking the activity in whatever direction suits their interests.

Even though children assume primary responsibility for the direction of exploratory play, teachers do more than just make materials available for children to use. Teachers consider which broad experiences they want children to have and the best ways to support children's involvement in these experiences. For instance, Ms. Habibi encourages children's exploration of sand by putting damp sand in the sand table one day, and dry sand on another. She provides various props such as sifters, measuring cups, sieves, containers, shovels, slotted spoons, and non-slotted utensils and gives children plenty of time to engage in the activity. She also invites children to the area, occasionally commenting on what they are doing and saying to acknowledge individuals and support children's involvement.

To enhance children's learning to the fullest, educators offer children a variety of exploratory experiences. They pay careful attention to materials and issues involving safety. For example, at the water table, the teacher may provide a variety of funnels, clear tubing, whisks, and other objects the children might find interesting. Smocks are available and the water table is partially filled with clear water. Because the direction of the activity is primarily up to the children, the adult does not select a single domain or set of objectives for the children to pursue. In exploratory play, teachers rely heavily on the teaching strategies of sensory involvement and environmental cues to stimulate children's interest and enable them to participate freely and safely. They use behavior reflections and paraphrase reflections to acknowledge children's actions and discoveries. They also guide children in using materials safely and interacting peaceably as appropriate. However, because they want exploratory play to remain open-ended, teachers tend to avoid potentially leading strategies such as do-it signals or questions that direct children's thinking in one particular direction.

Guided Discovery

In guided discovery activities, teachers give children the freedom to discover things on their own, yet guide the process so children cannot help but "bump into" target knowledge (Robertson, 2007). Teachers plan these experiences to help children make connections and build concepts

Go to the Video Examples section of Topic 10: Planning in the MyEducationLab for your course and watch the videos entitled *A Scientific Investigation in Preschool: From Tadpole to Frog; Birds: Part 1;* and *Multiple Intelligences in a Project.* Watch how the teacher combines several teaching strategies in each guided discovery activity and how the children's ideas shape the direction the activities take.

through interactions with people and objects. The children's role in guided-discovery activities is to construct knowledge for themselves: making choices and decisions, experimenting and experiencing, raising questions, and finding their own answers (Maxim, 2006). The adult's role is to serve as a resource: emphasizing how to find answers, providing information and tools as necessary, and supporting children as they apply their learning (Copple & Bredekamp, 2009). Both children and adults influence the direction of guided-discovery activities. Adults provide the broad parameters in which learning occurs; children determine the essence of what is learned.

Guided-discovery activities build on exploration, incorporating the additional teaching strategies of modeling, effective praise, telling and explaining, do-it signals, challenges, and questions. Therefore, when the sand table is being used for guided discovery, the activity looks different from when the sand is being used for exploratory play. For instance, Ms. Jamison plans a guided-discovery activity in which she wants children to think about the idea that volume, shape, and color are distinct properties of objects. She sets out several 1-cup measures of different colors and shapes and dampens the sand. As children pack the sand and mold it by using the measuring cups, she comments on the size and shape of the cups and the sand structures the children are building. She also asks questions, such as: "Which measuring cup holds the most? How could you find out? What is the same about these measuring cups? What is different? How do you know? You discovered that the blue cup and the red one hold the same amount of sand. Look at this yellow cup. Will it hold more or less sand than those cups?" Such verbalizations are interspersed with periods of attentive adult silence to allow children opportunities to talk about their ideas and what interests them about the materials and one another. Using this combination of strategies, Ms. Jamison gently guides children's thinking along certain lines but encourages children to come to their own conclusions based on the evidence of their experience. Sometimes the children's conclusions are not scientifically correct. When this happens, Ms. Jamison offers a challenge to stimulate children to think about the objects in new ways. However, because this project is a guided-discovery activity, she ultimately accepts the children's ideas no matter what they are. She does not tell children they are wrong or make them parrot "correct" answers. Instead, she uses what she finds out about children's thought processes to plan guided-practice experiences through which children gradually construct more accurate concepts for themselves. The activity described in Figure 3.3 is a guided-discovery example. Another example of this type of lesson plan can be found in appendix A.

Problem Solving

Problem-solving activities are variations on guided-discovery experiences. Teachers plan such activities to support children's thinking, analyzing, understanding, and reasoning. In these activities, teachers are more concerned with *how* children arrive at answers than in trying to get children to derive a single "right" answer. As children participate in problem-solving lessons, they plan, predict, make decisions, observe the results of their actions, and form conclusions while adults serve as facilitators (Chalufour & Worth, 2003; Epstein, 2008).

Young children are intrigued by all kinds of problems—movement problems (How many different ways can I move from Point A to Point B?), discussion problems (What would happen if . . . ?), strategy problems (What strategies do you need to play a board game?), and skill problems (How many different ways can a set of objects be grouped?). Sometimes these problems arise out of naturally occurring events, upon which adults capitalize (How many children are in our class today? How will you decide what color to paint your truck?). At other times, adults *plan* problem-solving activities to enhance children's learning. The best problems for children to think about engage them in various ways, allow them to gather information concretely, and have more than one possible solution. The more immediate, observable, and obvious the problem, the more easily children can evaluate their actions and come to their own

These children are listening carefully to one another's ideas as they participate in a problem-solving activity.

FIGURE 3.8 **The Basics of Problem Solving**

Steps Involved in Problem-Solving	Problem-Solving Processes
	In this step, children:
Becoming Aware	Notice, observe, wonder, question, identify a problem
Hypothesizing	Think about why things happen, gather information, make predictions, construct reasonable explanations
Experimenting	Take action, test ideas, observe results
Concluding	Reflect on outcomes, explore patterns and relationships, compare, make generalizations about why something happened, develop alternative hypotheses, make plans for further experiments with new hypotheses
Communicating Results	Talk about what happened, record, represent experiences and data

conclusions. All good problems prompt children to analyze, synthesize, and evaluate events, information, and ideas, thereby encouraging children to make new mental connections and construct fresh ideas (Freiberg & Driscoll, 2005; Robertson, 2007). The problem-solving process is similar for every curricular domain. A typical problem-solving sequence is outlined in Figure 3.8.

Mrs. Radechek is giving children opportunities to engage in problem solving when she supplies materials at the water table for children to use in a sink-and-float experiment. Having encouraged children to explore similar materials in the water table on many previous occasions, she prepares to guide them in discovering properties of objects that seem to have a bearing on whether they sink or float. Mrs. Radechek thinks carefully about the materials she will provide as well as what she will say and do to help children proceed through the various phases of problem solving. Her purpose is for children to generate ideas about the following:

❏ *Becoming aware of what they see* (John says, "The bottle cap floats. The plastic boat floats. The rock is on the bottom.")
❏ *Hypothesizing why things happen* (John says, "The blue stuff stays on top. The brown thing sank.")
❏ *Predicting what will happen when another object is placed in the water* (John predicts, "The 'brown' Popsicle stick will sink.")
❏ *Carrying out an experiment and experiencing the outcomes of their predictions* (John says, "It floated.")
❏ *Drawing conclusions and proposing alternative hypotheses* (John says, "Maybe being long is what makes things float.")
❏ *Communicating results and recording their ideas* (John draws a picture of an object that floated; John keeps track of his findings on a chart.)

Although John generated a hypothesis that was incorrect (e.g., color is related to floating and sinking), his investigations eventually led him to reject color as a significant property and switch to something else. By observing, hypothesizing, experimenting, drawing conclusions, and communicating results to others many times and with many variations, John will gradually construct more accurate concepts. In this problem-solving activity, John acted on objects in purposeful ways, applied his notions of how the world works, and reflected on his experiences, with his teacher's help. Mrs. Radechek's role included supporting John's investigation ("Tell me what you see. You noticed the bottle cap is blue and the boat is blue. You've decided being blue is what makes things float") as well as asking questions and offering challenges as appropriate ("What do you think will happen when you put the Popsicle stick in the water?"). The process of problem solving and the thinking it involves was the ultimate purpose of this activity, not having children be able to accurately explain the physics of water displacement (floating). By observing and listening carefully and by applying the principle of less accurate to more accurate thinking, the teacher supported John's concept development and also gleaned valuable information to use for future planning. This sink-and-float activity was one in which adult and child shared control and from which both learned.

The sink-and-float problem-solving activity just described involved children's manipulation of tangible objects and focused on increasing their understanding of the physical world. A similar approach to problem solving can be applied in the social realm as well. Typical steps include the following:

Step 1. Becoming aware of a problem
Step 2. Brainstorming possible solutions

Step 3. Choosing a solution

Step 4. Trying out the plan

Step 5. Evaluating the plan

Children might engage in social problem solving as they generate ideas for rules in the block area, determine how to resolve a conflict between the boys and the girls on the playground, choose a name for the class hamster, or develop an equitable plan for using the computer.

Appendix A provides a sample problem-solving plan.

Discussions

There is much to talk about in early childhood classrooms.

❏ *What is happening in the program?* Who will water the plants? What are ways cooperative reading partners can help each other when someone is absent? Why are some people upset with what is going on in the block area? When will be the best time to celebrate Flopsy Bunny's birthday?

❏ *What is happening to children away from the program?* Jessica has a new baby at her house. Tanya's grandma is visiting. Carlos went to the Panthers game over the weekend. Roger became scared when he heard people yelling and banging outside his window.

❏ *What is happening in the community and world at large?* Children notice many things: There was a big storm last night. A new shopping center is being built. People will be voting next week. Children wonder many things: Can women be firefighters or just men? Why do some trees lose their leaves and other trees do not? What happened to all the dinosaurs? What does it mean to vote?

Discussion implies reciprocal interactions among teachers and children; adults talk to children, children talk to adults, and children talk to one another. Using invitations, reflections, questions, and statements, teachers guide the conversation but encourage children to express themselves and communicate their ideas aloud. Throughout the discussion, teachers talk, but children talk as much as, if not more than, the adults. Sometimes a record is made of the discussion, such as when a group makes a list of classroom rules, generates ideas for names for the guinea pig, or lists suggestions for a new ending to a familiar story. Sometimes no tangible record is made. A sample discussion plan can be found in appendix A.

Demonstrations

Generally, demonstrations involve one person's showing others how something works or how a task is to be carried out. When people demonstrate something, the direction of the activity is completely up to them. Teachers use demonstrations to illustrate instructions, offer children a preview of something they will do later, or open a lesson in a dramatic way. Demonstrations combine do-it signals and modeling and generally consist of three steps: (1) gaining children's attention, (2) showing children something, and (3) prompting children to respond, in words or actions, to what they saw. These steps are summarized in Figure 3.9.

For instance, teachers at the Tree Top Child Development Center open each day with a greeting time, during which they demonstrate one of the materials that will be available to children in the room throughout the free-choice portion of the day. Typical items are games (e.g., lotto, dominoes), experiments (e.g., dissolving substances in water), and novel materials. Today the children will have a chance to scrape vegetables to make "Stone Soup." Their teacher plans to demonstrate the safe way to scrape the potatoes and other items that will go into the soup. She hides some vegetables and a scraper in a

There is much to discuss in the early childhood classroom.

FIGURE 3.9 The Steps Involved in Demonstrations

Step	Sample Adult Cues
Gain Children's Attention	Look up here. See this. Watch me closely. See if you can figure out what I'm doing.
Show Children Something	(Adult carries out an action.)
Prompt Children to Respond	Tell me what you saw. What did you notice? Now you try it. Point to the . . .

paper bag and places it behind her chair. Following one or two opening songs, she pulls out the bag. Giving the children a few introductory hints, she encourages them to guess what they think might be inside (gaining the children's attention). After some guesses are made, she reveals the vegetables and the scraper and proceeds to show the children how to scrape away from their bodies and over a plastic bowl (showing the children something). Finally, she asks the children to make the appropriate scraping motion, as they pretend to scrape a favorite vegetable (children respond). The demonstration ends. The teacher assumes the children will need additional support as they attempt to scrape vegetables for real. However, she is satisfied that she has introduced the safe way to handle the scrapers in a manner children understood and enjoyed.

Demonstrations may constitute an entire activity, as illustrated by the vegetable scraper demonstration. Alternatively, demonstrations are sometimes only a small part of a larger interaction. For instance, a teacher or a peer might demonstrate the proper amount of food to feed the guinea pig, how to reboot the computer, or how to capture air in a jar by putting the jar straight into the water upside down. Even in these brief situations, the same instructional process is followed: gain attention, model, and prompt children to respond in some way. The children's response may be verbal or involve an action of some type, such as shaking out the approximate amount of food, telling the first step in rebooting the computer, or trying to capture air in their jars. When demonstrations of any kind are planned for young children, they must be kept short, and sensory involvement should be ensured early in the procedure. A sample demonstration plan is presented in appendix A.

Direct Instruction

In early childhood classrooms, direct instruction is used to help children learn certain vocabulary, facts, strategies, rules, and routines they might not otherwise discover easily or safely on their own (Freiberg & Driscoll, 2005; Robertson, 2007). Tasks a teacher might choose to address using direct instruction could include proper hand washing procedures, the phonetic rule that words that end in -e have a long vowel sound, or what to do during a fire drill. The advantages of direct instruction are that it is efficient, produces immediate results, teaches children to follow directions, and lends itself to on-the-spot evaluation (Pica, 2000). However, as you can see in Figure 3.7, direct instruction is at the top of the activity pyramid. It is the most structured, teacher-centered form of planning discussed in this chapter. Because young children need a wide array of educational experiences in which they help determine the outcomes, direct instruction should be used sparingly. The best lessons are short and are supplemented by other forms of instruction that give children plenty of opportunities to explore and practice what they are learning directly. Here is an example.

The teacher in the Jackson Elementary School Pre-K class is using direct instruction in this short lesson on animal sounds with a group of four children sitting on a rug with the flannel board. The adult's goal is to teach children to associate a picture with a sound as a pre-reading skill.

Teacher: "Look up here. I have some pictures of farm animals we saw on our field trip."
Children: The children look at the flannel board and individual photographs of a cow, a sheep, a horse, and a chicken.
Teacher: "I'm going to make some animal sounds. Listen. When I make a sound, you point to the animal that makes that sound."
The teacher makes one sound at a time.
Children: The children point to an animal in response to the sound.
Teacher: If a child points to the correct animal, the teacher responds by saying, "That's right, the cow makes the moo sound." If a child points to an incorrect picture, the teacher ignores the response until the child gets it right. Or, the teacher says, "You think the sheep says, 'Moo.' It says, 'Baa.' Let's try again."

TABLE 3.2   Direct-Instruction Steps with Accompanying Oral Cues

Sequence of Steps	Sample Oral Cues
Step 1 Attend Draw children's attention to the task.	Look up here. I have something to tell you. Find a spot where you can see the pictures. Listen to this.
Step 2 Show or tell Show or tell children something.	Here is a _____. This is how to _____. This is what to do first.
Step 3 Differentiate Help children recognize examples and nonexamples.	Which is the _____? Show me something that is not _____.
Step 4 Apply Have children apply what they are learning.	Make a _____. Tell how to _____. Show how to _____. Give me an example of _____. What will happen if _____?

Throughout the lesson the teacher varies his or her voice, facial expressions, and pace of the activity. The teacher also uses gestures, intentional mistakes, surprises, pauses, and enthusiasm to stimulate children's interest and to draw their attention to essential lesson elements. Later in the day the children have a chance to play with the pictures and flannel board on their own. The teacher is pleased to hear the children using the animal sounds (mostly correctly) in association with the pictures.

As just illustrated, direct instruction involves more than simply telling and showing. It includes task analysis, modeling, effective praise, informing and explaining, do-it signals, and challenges. In this type of activity, teachers carry out a series of prescribed steps that lead children toward a particular response (Nelson, Cooper, & Gonzales, 2007). Teachers either ignore inappropriate responses or provide corrective feedback as necessary. This emphasis on working toward a specific response is a significant distinction between direct-instruction and exploratory or guided-discovery activities. In direct instruction, the adult combines a variety of teaching strategies to enable children to be correct most of the time and to lead children through the required steps in such a way that youngsters learn correct responses relatively quickly. Key elements of a typical direct-instruction sequence are outlined in Table 3.2.

An example of a complete direct-instruction activity plan is presented in appendix A.

MAKING AND IMPLEMENTING PLANS

Now that you are familiar with the parts of the lesson plan, the concept of alignment, the principles of developmental direction, and the various activity types commonly used in early childhood programs, you are ready to create and carry out your own plans. As you do so, keep the following guidelines in mind.

❏ Choose a curricular domain within which to plan your activity. Practice writing plans in each of the six domains: aesthetic, affective, cognitive, language, physical, and social.

❏ Do not confine your planning to those domains with which you are most comfortable.

❏ Select a goal that supports the domain you choose. Refer to the list of goals presented in part 3 for each curricular domain. Choose one that fits the learning needs of the children for whom you are planning. The most basic goals are listed first, followed by more advanced goals. Use the initial goals when planning for preschoolers, kindergartners, inexperienced first and second graders, or some children with special needs. Choose goals farther down the list as children gain experience and demonstrate mastery.

❏ Do not write any part of the activity before you choose the goal.

❏ Brainstorm activity ideas that could support the goal you selected. Choose one idea to develop into an activity plan. Make sure the activity is appropriate and of potential interest to children. Consider both developmental factors and contextual factors when making a final choice. As time passes, be sure to plan activities that encompass all six activity types described in this chapter.

❏ Do not select activities just because you have a particular prop or saw a great idea in an activity book. Remember to tailor your plans to meet the specific needs of the children with whom you are working.

❏ Write your plan. At first, write as much detail as possible. After you gain experience, use a shorter format but still think through your plans, referring to all the parts outlined in this chapter. Use the writing process to help you think comprehensively and creatively about the activities you plan.

❏ Do not assume that you will be able to remember everything without writing it down.

❏ Check each portion of your plan for accuracy. Make sure that the individual segments of your plan comply with the definitions presented in Figure 3.2. These definitions should help you develop appropriate activity names, objectives, materials lists, procedures, simplifications, extensions, and evaluation items. Also refer to appendix A for sample plans.

❏ Do not suppose that effective planning happens quickly or easily. It will take time to perfect your planning skills.

❏ Complete your plan. Include all the elements listed in Figures 3.2 and 3.3.

❏ Do not skip or combine parts of the activity plan.

❏ Check that all the elements of your plan are aligned. The activity name, assumptions, content, objectives, procedures, simplifications, extensions, and evaluation should relate to the goal.

❏ Do not assume that alignment happens simply because materials remain constant. To create the necessary curricular congruence throughout the entire activity, keep the goal in mind at all times. Make all parts of the plan relate to it.

❏ Prepare to carry out your plan. Gather materials in advance. Think about who will implement the activity and about when, where, and how to do it. Experiment with unfamiliar activities and rehearse procedures you have not tried before. Anticipate how children might respond, and consider ways of supporting them under these circumstances.

❏ Do not wait until the last minute to collect what you need or to think about how you will prepare, supervise, and clean up after the activity.

❏ Implement your plan. Try to follow the plan as written, adapting as necessary. Make note of the children's participation, the achievement of objectives, and the effectiveness or lack of effectiveness of the teaching methods you chose.

❏ Do not abandon your plan in the excitement of carrying it out. Neither should you rigidly follow a plan merely because of what is written, if children's behavior indicates some changes are necessary. Strike a balance between implementing plans as anticipated and remaining flexible enough to respond to children's cues.

❏ Reflect on the children's learning experiences as well as on your own. Keep written records of what was accomplished. Make notes about what to change next time and how to build on the children's interests and accomplishments. Use this information to create new activity plans and to make records of children's progress.

❏ Do not fail to follow through on what children learn as a result of the activity. For instance, if several children meet all the objectives of the story sequence plan, prepare to move into the extensions another time soon. Avoid thinking that you will remember what you observed. With so much happening every day, forgetting important details is easy. Write anecdotes, keep work samples, and answer the evaluation questions in writing as soon as possible after carrying out the activity to provide a resource for future planning.

SUMMARY

Planning is a key ingredient in creating developmentally appropriate programs for young children. Early childhood professionals use planning for organizational, educational, and accountability purposes. Effective planning requires consideration of many factors simultaneously. These factors include individual children and groups of children as well as past, present, and future needs and expectations. When planning, educators must first think about the children in relation to what is being taught. The initial information gathering step enables teachers to make an appropriate match between instruction and the knowledge, skills, and understandings children bring to the classroom. Following this, early childhood professionals set goals, design the instruction, plan to organize the physical environment, and determine how they will evaluate their plans (both in terms of children's learning and their own). These functions are best expressed in writing. Novice planners write in much detail. More experienced planners keep in mind the same elements of planning that they wrote as beginners but record only the essence of their thinking. The following parts should be included in each activity plan.

1. The curricular domain in which the activity is planned
2. A name for the activity
3. A goal from within the chosen domain
4. At least three objectives focusing on child performance, written in sequence
5. Content covering relevant terms and facts
6. All necessary materials
7. Sample procedures
8. Ideas about how to simplify the activity
9. Ideas about ways to extend the activity
10. Three or four evaluation questions

One way that planners make sure their plans are developmentally appropriate is to ensure all the parts are aligned properly. Another way is to consider the principles of developmental direction: known to unknown, self to other, whole to part, concrete to abstract, enactive to symbolic, exploratory to goal directed, less accurate to more accurate, and simple to complex. Finally, teachers use six common activity types in early childhood: exploratory play, guided discovery, problem solving, discussions, demonstrations, and direct instruction.

myeducationlab

To check your comprehension on the content covered in Chapter 3, go to the Book Specific Resources in the MyEducationLab for your course, select your text, and complete the Study Plan. Here you will be able to take a chapter quiz, receive feedback on your answers, and then access review, practice, and enrichment activities to enhance your understanding of chapter content.

Key Words

developmental direction
domains
goals
objectives

Applying What You've Read in This Chapter

1. **Discuss**
   a. On the basis of your reading and your experiences with young children, discuss each of the questions that open this chapter.
   b. Imagine that you are planning to support children's learning using art materials. The supplies available include modeling dough and various utensils such as forks, spatulas, cookie cutters, and rolling pins. Discuss what you would do to promote children's learning in an exploratory activity. Discuss how your strategies might change if you switched to a problem-solving mode. What kinds of problems might children investigate with the dough?
   c. You observe a classroom in which the children are to learn about the relative size of objects by circling the largest items in rows depicted on a worksheet. How does this activity correspond with your ideas about how children learn best? What other, if any, teaching types might you suggest to support children's learning?

2. **Observe**

   a. Observe the exploratory play of a younger child (younger than 5 years old) and an older child (6, 7, or 8 years old) in an open-ended activity such as sand play, block play, or water play. Describe similarities and differences between the two children in terms of what they say and do in their explorations.

   b. Watch a seasoned practitioner interact with children in an activity for at least 15 minutes. Refer to the activity types outlined in this chapter and identify the type of activity used by the adult. Describe what the adult said and did that fit the definitions offered. Explain your answer.

3. **Carry out an activity**

   a. Refer to the Turnip Story Sequence activity outlined in Figure 3.3. If you were to carry this activity out in an early childhood setting with which you are familiar, what adaptations would you have to make to suit the children in your group? Write out your answers and rework the plan to match.

   b. If you are in a practicum setting, obtain a written activity plan provided by your head teacher.
   Compare the format of that plan with the activity plan format presented in this chapter. Describe the similarities and differences. Are there segments you would like to borrow from either plan that would make the other plan more useful? If so, explain these. If you cannot obtain a written plan from your placement, carry out an activity in your practicum setting. Afterward, develop a written plan for that activity using the format in this chapter.

4. **Create something for your portfolio**

   a. Develop a statement of no more than one page that describes your beliefs about planning and the ways in which you intend to engage in effective planning as you work with children.

   b. Select a written plan that you have implemented with children. Evaluate the effectiveness of your teaching. Finally, write a synopsis of how you might teach the lesson again with the same group of children.

5. **Add to your journal**

   a. What is the most significant concept that you learned about planning and teaching from your readings and your experience with children?

   b. Reflect on the extent to which the content of this chapter corresponds with what you have observed in the field. What is your reaction to any discrepancies you perceive?

   c. What goals do you have for yourself related to planning and teaching activities for young children? How do you intend to pursue these goals?

6. 👋 **Consult the standards**

   a. Refer to the National Mathematics Standards published by the National Council of Teachers of Mathematics. These can be found in the publications entitled *Curriculum and Evaluation Standards for School Mathematics* (1989) and *Principles and Standards for School Mathematics* (2000). Select a subsection of standards to examine (Consider Problem Solving, Number and Operations, or Patterns and Relationships). Consider these standards in light of the Principles of Developmental Direction addressed in this chapter. Describe any evidence of these principles that you see in the standards you selected.

   b. Secure an example of the literacy standards from your state. Find a standard that would be supported by the story sequence activity presented in Figure 3.3.

PRACTICE FOR YOUR CERTIFICATION OR LICENSURE EXAM

The following items will help you practice applying what you have learned in this chapter. They can help to prepare you for your course exam, the PRAXIS II exam, your state licensure or certification exam, and for working in developmentally appropriate ways with young children.

Writing Activity Plans

The kindergarten teachers have a common planning time each week, during which they share new lesson plans with one another. Each teacher writes a draft for the others to go over before using it the next week. Here is an example.

Domain	Aesthetics
Activity Name	Finger Designs in Sand
Goal	Children will respond to basic elements of visual art, such as line, design, and texture.
Content	1. Sand is finely ground bits of stone. 2. Pebbles are small rounded stones that have been worn smooth by erosion. 3. Designs are combinations of lines, shapes, and empty space. 4. Lines may be straight or curved, long or short, thin or thick. 5. Textures range from rough to smooth.
Materials	Large jellyroll pans or cafeteria trays. Coarse sand, fine sand, aquarium gravel

Procedures	1. Prepare in advance by filling each tray almost to the top with one type of sand or stone. 2. Invite children to make designs with their fingers in the different pans. 3. Talk with children about the lines, designs, and textures they are creating. 4. Ask children to make letters of the alphabet in the sand/rocks.
Simplification	Focus on only one element at a time, such as line or texture.
Evaluation	1. What letters did children make?

1. **Constructed-response question**

   a. Identify the primary purpose of this plan. How did you decide?

   b. Based on principles of good planning, suggest three ways to edit the plan to improve it. Explain your revisions.

2. **Multiple-choice question**

   A characteristic of good activity plan objectives are that they:

   a. Are fun for children to do

   b. Describe how children will participate in the activity

   c. Clearly relate to the theme of the day

   d. Describe child behavior/actions

Chapter

4

Planning and Implementing
Effective Group-Time Activities

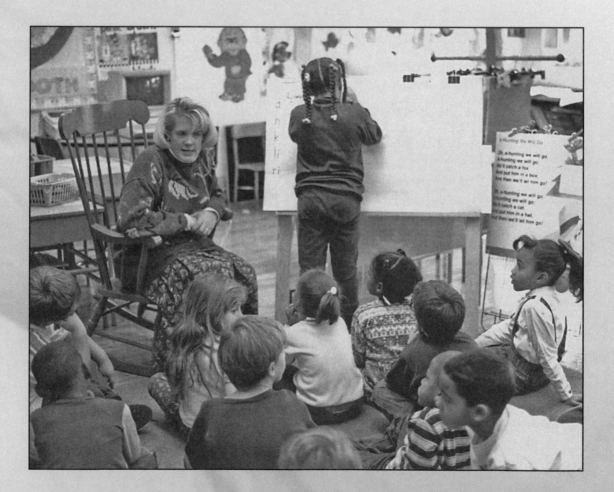

You may wonder:

With so much emphasis on individual learning, how can we create whole-group activities that are developmentally appropriate?

What makes a successful group time for preschoolers?

What kinds of group times are best for school-age children?

What are some pitfalls to avoid when I am carrying out group-time activities in the classroom?

This chapter will help answer your questions about how to plan and implement effective group times with young children.

◆ ◆ *Every day the 3-year-olds come together at about 10:00 in the morning for a 10-minute circle time. Today, the teacher starts by singing, "There was a farmer had a dog, and Bingo was his name-o." The children clap as they join in, singing the familiar song.*

◆ ◆ *A firefighter has come to show the kindergarten children the special equipment firefighters use. Youngsters sit in a circle, trying on hats and boots as the firefighter explains their use. The children are especially intrigued by the oxygen tanks and masks she shows them.*

◆ ◆ *The second graders in Mr. LaFontane's class gather on the rug for a short class meeting on measuring. The teacher invites them to watch as Louie shows how he solved the problem of measuring the size of the class guinea pig.*

The children and adults described above are all participating in **group times**—those portions of the day when all or most of the children gather in one place to share the same learning experience simultaneously. Nearly every preschool through third-grade classroom includes periods such as these. Half-day programs usually incorporate one or two group times each day; full-day programs may have as many as three or four. The curricular focus of a particular group time might be aesthetic, affective, cognitive, linguistic, physical, or social. Consequently, group times incorporate a wide range of activities (Henninger, 2009). On any given day, the whole class may come together to do the following:

❏ Sing, dance, and experience music
❏ Act out stories or hear them read aloud
❏ Play games
❏ Participate in movement activities
❏ Receive instructions
❏ Interact with a resource person
❏ Learn about what is coming next in the day
❏ Discuss a problem in the room
❏ Observe a demonstration
❏ Plan for the session
❏ Report on work or show others what children have accomplished
❏ Reflect on the day

Naturally, adults select only one or two of these activities per group time. Although some aspects of the group-time routine are the same from day to day, others are varied to maintain children's interest and address different aspects of the curriculum.

Carried out appropriately, group times benefit everyone involved. Group times are ideal for conveying important information everyone needs—news about a visitor who is coming, the guinea pig, activities available today, or the upcoming field trip. Group times can facilitate communication because everyone hears the same thing at the same time. Group time also provides a repertoire of common experiences for all children in the class. Most important, they foster cohesive group feelings. Looking around the circle, children see the faces and hear the ideas of all the children in the class, not just a few as in the case of small-group activities. The joyous experience of singing together or dictating a story to which everyone contributes prompts satisfaction and

99

pleasure in one another's company. Children who share their work, talk about their day, or otherwise engage in group discussions construct shared meanings and explore together the give-and-take of group membership. All these experiences foster a sense of community.

In contrast, when whole-group instruction is carried out *inappropriately*, it can be an unpleasant experience dominated by children's lack of attention, distracting behaviors, adult reprimands, and frustration for all (Maag, 2004; McAfee, 1985). The difference between positive and negative whole-group experiences is careful planning and preparation.

PLANNING EFFECTIVE GROUP TIMES

Effective group times have four parts: (1) the opening, focused on gathering and engaging children in the group; (2) the body, focused on the main purpose of the group time; (3) the closing, when the teacher summarizes the activity and guides children into the next portion of the day; and (4) the transitions, the times linking each activity within the group time, and between group time and the other parts of the day. You must consider each segment both separately and in relation to one another to plan effective comprehensive whole-group experiences for children.

The Opening

The primary purpose of the **opening** is to signal the beginning of group time and capture children's interest. It usually consists of two or three short activities (e.g., an action rhyme, followed by a "stretching" poem, followed by a quiet song aimed at bringing the children's energy level down and focusing their attention on the *body* of the group time). Experienced group leaders position themselves at the large-group area to greet children as they arrive. Effective teachers draw children to the group with intriguing, easy to join activities such as fingerplays, movement routines, or humorous poetry. Children are not expected to sit and wait while the adult engages in last-minute cleanup or searches for needed items. As soon as two or three children are ready, the leader begins, rather than waiting until the last child appears. Youngsters who are still engaged in an activity elsewhere soon recognize the opening activities as a signal that group time is about to start. The opening is used to secure children's involvement before moving on to the body of the group time. For example, you might sing a song a few times with variations (e.g., singing the "Eency Weency Spider" using normal pitch, singing it again as a tiny spider with a high-pitched voice, and singing it one last time as a huge spider with a deep-pitched voice). Another strategy is to move fluidly from one song or finger play to another, being careful not to disrupt the flow of the opening by talking between the activities. Thus, the group leader might start by chanting, "Five little hot dogs frying in a pan" (Figure 4.1) and use this finger play as a way to shift into a song involving hand motions, such as "My Finger Is Starting to Wiggle" (Figure 4.2). Likewise, in a second-grade group, the teacher might move from a familiar action rhyme such as "Three Short-Necked Buzzards" (Figure 4.3) to introducing a factual lesson on identifying birds by their beaks and claws. The sequence of activities and the transition from one to another are planned in advance.

FIGURE 4.1 Five Little Hot Dogs

Five little hot dogs frying in a pan (Hold right hand up showing five fingers),
the grease got hot (Hold left hand palm side up, rub with right palm in circular motion),
and one
(Hold up one finger) went bam!
(clap hard)
(Repeat words counting down four, three, two, and one)
No little hot dogs frying in a pan (Hold right hand up showing closed fist),
The grease got hot, and the pan went BAM! (End with BIG CLAP!)

The Body

When most of the children are participating in the opening, the leader moves into the main purpose of the group time. Children's successful participation is supported when they understand what will happen during each step of the group (Hendrick & Weissman, 2010). The **body** of the group time is introduced by telling children about the activity and then inviting their involvement through strategies such as open-ended questions or posing a problem. Props are used to stimulate children's curiosity and interest. For instance, in introducing a guided-discovery activity about animals hatched from eggs, the first-grade teacher shows the children a real egg and says, "Look at what I have. Today you will hear a story all about eggs. While I'm reading the story, listen for the names of animals hatched from eggs.

FIGURE 4.2 My Finger Is Starting to Wiggle
(tune: "The Bear Went Over the Mountain")

My finger is starting to wiggle, my finger is starting
    to wiggle, my finger is starting to wiggle, wiggle
    all around.
My foot is starting to wiggle, my foot is starting to
    wiggle, my foot is starting to wiggle, wiggle all
    around.
(Repeat with different body parts and corresponding
    motions.)

FIGURE 4.3 Three Short-Necked Buzzards
(This rhyme is said while standing.)

Three short-necked buzzards (Hold up three fingers,
    raise shoulders, scrunch neck, resume natural
    posture),
three short-necked buzzards (Repeat motions
    described in preceding line),
three short-necked buzzards (Repeat motions just
    described),
sitting on a dead tree (Hold arms out in an uneven
    position like the branches of a tree, stand on one
    foot).
(Repeat words and motions for two, one, and no
    short-necked buzzards)

Afterward, we'll talk about them." The teacher gives clear, specific directions to the children and uses effective praise to acknowledge appropriate behavior. Teaching strategies such as inviting, reflecting, modeling, telling, explaining, using do-it signals, posing challenges, and asking questions support children's learning during group time. Using an expressive face, voice, and gestures and using props, demonstrations, pictures, humor, and mime are other ways to keep children involved and attentive.

The Closing

The **closing** signals the end of group time and serves as a transition to the next part of the day. Teachers use the closing to summarize key ideas and guide individual children into other learning activities. Instead of simply sending children away from the group, effective teachers direct children toward a different activity. In some cases, teachers explain which activities are available and ask the children to choose one. An alternative is to lightly tap the children one at a time (or use some other signal) to release them from the group. Another option is to say something, such as, "Everyone wearing red may get up and put on their coats to go outside. Now the people wearing blue may get their coats." This approach staggers the children's exit from the area, which enables them to shift more easily from group time to the next scheduled activity (Machado, 2009).

Group-Time Transitions

Group time is a series of short activities connected by **transitions**, which fuse the individual group-time elements into a cohesive whole. For example, a traditional group time might include the following events: introductory song, movement rhyme, short story told with props, stretching rhyme, another song, and exit from group. How well the group flows from beginning to end is dependent upon smooth and interesting transitions. It is at transition points that children become intrigued by what is coming next or their attention begins to wander. Consider the difference between the following transitions from a finger play to the song "Old MacDonald":

Group Leader 1: "Okay, everybody! Let's sing Old MacDonald. Ready? Come on, let's get ready. Okay? One, two, three, Old MacDonald had a farm, Ee-i-ee-i-oh. . . ."

Group Leader 2: (said with great enthusiasm) "There was so much block building going on today! I noticed a lot of you were making pens for the animals. I said to myself, "It looks just like Old MacDonald's farm." Adult begins singing, "Old MacDonald had a farm, Ee-i-ee-i-oh. . . ."

The first example was not interesting and did little to capture the children's attention. The adult's words sounded like directions, not an invitation to become involved. Group Leader 2 capitalized on the children's earlier activity to stimulate their interest and lead them into singing the song. Linking the song to the children and using an expressive voice were two strategies the second adult used to make the transition to music. The leader's words served as a bridge from a finger play she had just finished to a new activity—the song "Old MacDonald."

The element of surprise can be used to capture children's attention during the opening to a group time focused on storytelling (Educational Productions, 1998).

As children come to the group-time area, Gene sits on a chair facing them, holding a small carton of milk and a 4-ounce paper cup in his hands. The children are intrigued.

Taking a dark gray tray lined with waxed paper from under his chair, he balances it on his knees. All the while, he talks softly to the children, describing his actions as he carries them out and explaining that he will be reading a story in just a minute. He goes on to say that his throat is dry, and he wants to take a little drink so that he can read more comfortably.

When children make comments such as "My throat is dry, too," the teacher uses paraphrase reflections to incorporate their remarks into the interaction. "You're thirsty. After group time you may get something to drink at the snack table."

Gene pours a little milk into the paper cup. Taking a sip, he places the cup on the tray and says, "That's better. Now, where is my book? Oh, there it is." He continues to talk, maintaining eye contact with the children the entire time.

Picking up a paperback copy of the book he will read, he says, "One thing you have to be careful of is that you don't end up . . . oh no . . . it spilled. (He gently knocks over the cup on the tray.) Oh well, you know what they say, you can't cry (he pauses dramatically) . . . over spilt milk." Some children say the last words with him in chorus.

The teacher holds the tray where the children can see the milk make little pools of various shapes on the waxed paper. After a moment or two, Gene puts the tray on a nearby shelf. Showing the children the cover of the book, he says, "Today the story happens to be It Looked Like Spilt Milk. *And I just happened to spill my milk. What a coincidence." The children laugh.*

Gene continues, "Well, let's see what this story is all about." Opening the book, he begins to read. The children listen with rapt attention.

This teacher combined words, gestures, and props to capture the children's interest and lead up to the title of the book. This opening was much more fun and did more to help children become engaged than if he had simply said, "Here's today's book. It's called *It Looked Like Spilt Milk.*"

Transitions need not be elaborate. However, they should be planned in advance. You will also want to vary the transitions you use in order to maintain children's attention over time. In effective group times the opening, the body, and the closing flow smoothly, one after the other in a way that makes sense to children and helps them focus on group-time content. Thus, transitions require the same careful planning that goes into selecting the music, stories, demonstrations, and games that make up each portion of group time.

WRITING GROUP-TIME PLANS

Just as with all other forms of planning, whole-group experiences require a written plan. Well-developed plans ensure that each group time has an educational focus and prompt teachers to use a variety of teaching strategies and activity types (Hendrick & Weissman, 2010). Many elements of the activity plan format outlined previously in this book also apply when you are writing plans for group times. However, in this chapter, the format has been adjusted to better support planning decisions unique to whole-group instruction, such as the sequence of each lesson (opening, body, and closing) and the transition from group time to the next event in the day. As with small-group activity plans, when you are first learning to plan group times, you will benefit from writing out all the parts of the plan. Later, you will use a more abbreviated form. A sample plan appropriate for whole-group instruction of all types is presented in Figure 4.4.

GROUP-TIME PREPARATIONS AND STRATEGIES

Location

It is best to locate your group time area away from toy shelves and equipment or temporarily cover attractive items to minimize distractions. The area should be spacious enough for movement activities or whole-group dramatics. Children should be able to easily see the group leader and can sit close enough together to hear one another's voices. Children can be seated in a circle, a clustered group, or a horseshoe-shaped configuration, with the adult facing the group at the open end. Some teachers use a large rug for group time; others mark the group area with tape on the floor in a continuous line or as a series of *X*s. This approach gives each child a specific spot on which to sit. In every case, making sure everyone has enough room to see, hear, and move comfortably without disturbing others is critical. Children who are crammed together pay more attention to protecting personal space or touching their neighbors than focusing on the whole-group activity.

FIGURE 4.4 Sample Group-Time Plan

Date: Monday, March 17   **Activity Name:** Whole-Group Storytelling

Age of Children: 5 to 7 years

Goal: Take on roles and act out interpretations of these roles to tell a familiar story.

Content
1. Stories are sometimes told by one person, sometimes by groups of people.
2. The people or animals portrayed in a story are called the story characters.
3. Storytellers combine words, sounds, facial expressions, gestures, and other body motions to communicate the story.

Materials: None

Opening
1. Sing the songs "Hello Everybody" (incorporate the children's names into the song) and "I Had a Cat and the Cat Pleased Me."
2. Transition to the body by talking about the animals in the song; lead into the animals in the story.

Body
3. Introduce whole-group storytelling: "Earlier this morning you heard me tell the story 'The Three Billy Goats Gruff.' Now, I will tell the story, and we will all act it out together."
4. Set the scene. Briefly review the characters and major events in the story. Explain that each child may be any character he or she wants or may decide to be several in turn (first the "littlest" billy goat, then the middle-size billy goat, and so on). Explain that you will be the storyteller and perhaps take on a role or two as well.
5. Begin the story ("Once upon a time . . ."), and continue the story, moving from event to event until the conclusion.
6. Announce "The End."
7. Transition into the closing by having the children clap for themselves.

Closing
8. Review with the children the ways in which they acted like the billy goats and the troll.
9. Acknowledge the children's participation by using effective praise: "That was fun. You pretended so well. Some children pretended to be the biggest billy goat, some children pretended to be all three billy goats, and some children pretended to be the troll. We will play this story again soon. You can even play it yourselves when we go outside."

Transition to Next Portion of the Day
10. Dismiss the children by shoe color or type to go outdoors.

Evaluation Questions
1. In what ways did children enact their roles?
2. How did the children differ in their interpretation of the three goats?
3. How adequate were the initial directions in helping children to interpret the story successfully? What changes might be necessary in explaining or supporting this activity another time?

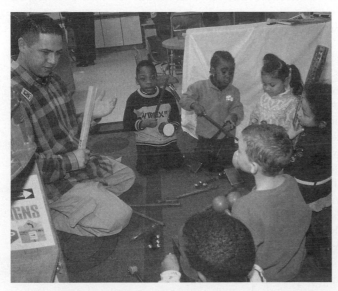

During group time, children gain a sense of community in the classroom.

Focus

Identifying what you want children to learn during whole-group instruction and selecting activities to support your goal is fundamental to planning an effective group time. Failing to choose learning goals leads to confusion, superficial treatment of content, and a haphazard approach to skill development. Unfortunately, trying to address too many goals in one experience yields the same results. Experienced group leaders choose one or two goals around which to plan. As a way to enhance children's understanding and provide some depth of experience, teachers relate one activity to the next. They also vary the curricular focus featured in the body of the group time from day to day. This keeps group times fresh and enables teachers to address different goals across time. Thus, Monday's group time may be dominated by language-related activities, and Tuesday's group time may highlight social learning. On Wednesday, the main focus may shift to the physical domain. See Figure 4.5 for examples of group-time foci that address standards in the visual arts, reading, mathematics, and physical science.

✋ Consult the Standards

FIGURE 4.5   Linking Standards with Group-Time Activities

Source	Standard	Group-Time Activity
Consortium of the National Arts Education Associations	Visual Arts: Children will talk about line, texture, color, and/or space	The teacher shows the children a reproduction of Vincent Van Gogh's painting *Sunflowers*. He invites the children to take turns pointing to examples of the elements; for example, the stems of the flowers could be straight or curved lines. As a follow-up, the teacher passes out a number of smaller painting examples (calendar-size Van Gogh, Klee, Monet, etc.) and asks children to look at the pictures to find the same elements in their examples. Later in the day, as children paint in the art area, the teacher talks to them about the line, texture, color, and space in their own work.
Nebraska Early Childhood Standards—Nebraska Department of Education	Reading: Children will increase their receptive and expressive vocabulary	Children create a group-experience story entitled "The World of Trucks," based on their field trip to a trucking company. The story is begun at group time and children add to it during the week.
National Council of Teachers of Mathematics	Mathematics: Children will create patterns	Children take turns creating clapping patterns
National Science Education Standards (NAS, 1996)	Physical Science: Objects have observable properties	Each child receives a shell to examine closely. Following a discussion of their shells, the children put them all in a basket. Children then retrieve their "own" shells based on the observations they made.

Pace and Variety

Experienced professionals change the pace and variety of each whole-group activity. Quiet segments are followed by more active times, listening is interspersed with doing, child-initiated and shared types of activities counterbalance teacher-directed activities. Activities demanding much concentration or effort by children, such as learning a new song or watching a demonstration, are addressed early in the body of the circle time, when children are still fresh (Hendrick & Weissman, 2010). As the group time winds down, children sing familiar songs and engage in relaxing activities such as stretching or listening to soothing music before starting something new.

Materials

Group times are kept interesting by using a variety of props (Stephens, 1996; Warner & Sower, 2005). Such props may include books, flannel boards, puppets, musical instruments, audiotapes or compact discs, sections of videotape, nature items, real objects, pictures, charts, posters, and storybooks large enough for children to see. Effective group leaders select their materials in advance and are thoroughly familiar with the stories, songs, poems, or instructions they intend to convey. They do not simply pull a book from the shelf at the last minute, nor do they begin a demonstration they have not thought through and practiced ahead of time. These educators carefully select materials, keeping in mind the objectives of the circle time as well as ongoing emphases such as appreciation of diversity. Ms. Richards illustrates this blend of foci when she carries out a demonstration of household utensils by using spatulas, tortilla turners, and chopsticks. This array of real materials is useful in addressing the goal of increasing children's awareness of tools and their function. Such materials also support Ms. Richards's desire for multicultural inclusion. She stores all the necessary items close at hand but out of the children's sight until she needs them. To remind herself of the exact sequence of the activities she planned for group time, Ms. Richards posts a large agenda near the whole-group area, which she glances at periodically to remind herself of what comes next. Other teachers post the words to new songs or poems at eye level near the group area, not only for their reference, but also for the children's.

Preparation

Careful planning and preparation are key to successful group times. Practicing new stories or songs ahead of time increases teachers' confidence and poise. Effective group leaders identify and address potential problems before group time. For example, determining the best place to position the puppet stage so that everyone can see, or arranging the flannel board pieces in the correct order to prevent fumbling with them during the story prevent potential distractions. They rehearse the words they will use for the transition from one group activity to another. Strategies such as these increase the likelihood that group time will proceed smoothly and enjoyably for everyone.

Active Involvement

Firsthand experience is as critical for group time as it is for all other learning activities. Thus, high-interest activities and activities in which children can become actively engaged are desirable for children of all ages. In addition, whole-group instruction is appropriate only when all the children in the group are able to participate in the learning. If the activity is relevant for only certain class members, it is better offered during small-group or learning center–based activity times.

Group-Time Teaching Methods

The teaching strategies described in chapter 2 are applicable to whole-group instruction (ensuring sensory involvement; preparing environmental cues; performing task analysis; using scaffolding; using guided practice; issuing invitations; using behavior and paraphrase reflections; employing effective praise; telling, explaining, and informing; using do-it signals; posing challenges; asking questions; and using silence). Likewise, the activity types described in chapter 3, including exploration, guided discovery, problem solving, discussion, and direct instruction, are applicable to whole-group instruction. Following are additional strategies effective group leaders use regularly (Dodge, Colker, Heroman, & Bickart, 2002; Neuman & Roskos, 2007; Stephens, 1996).

❑ Make whole-group experiences a predictable part of the daily schedule (e.g., group time always follows cleanup or is usually the first activity in the morning or the last activity in the afternoon)
❑ Seat themselves where they can see all the children
❑ Continually scan the group to determine children's interest level and involvement
❑ Ensure all the children can see them (e.g., they do not have children sit in their laps or directly at their sides, where children cannot see the leader's face; some sit on a low chair just a little above the group or on the floor at the front of a horseshoe shape to enable children to focus on what the leader is doing)
❑ Create an atmosphere to support group-time activities (e.g., use audiotaped sounds of a meadow to introduce an insect activity, dim the lights to tell a nighttime story)
❑ Use facial expressions, gestures, and variations in voice to maintain children's attention
❑ Involve children in setting guidelines for appropriate group-time behavior
❑ Clarify the expectations for children's group-time behavior
❑ Pass out materials for children to handle when they need them, not before, and collect them before going on to the next activity
❑ Encourage children to influence the group-time agenda by giving them choices (e.g., children decide which motions to make or choose between two stories to hear or two games to play)
❑ Change, shorten, or eliminate whole-group activities that are not working
❑ Extend or repeat activities that children enjoy
❑ Practice, practice, practice (experience brings effectiveness)

Preparing Other Adults to Support Group-Time Learning

Some teachers have sole responsibility for an entire group of youngsters; others work in a team with staff or volunteers. When multiple people are present during group time, children benefit most when everyone is familiar with the group-time procedures. Although there is no one correct way to do things, adults should have a mutual understanding of their roles and responsibilities during the activity. Typical expectations include the following: (a) Adults sit among the children, not next to each other or off to the side; (b) adults sing along and do the motions; and (c) adults help children focus on the leader or wait their turn to talk. Taking time to define everyone's level of participation, identifying strategies for helping children become engaged, and determining ways to support children who are easily distracted are important in the preparation phase of planning. Likewise, all adults should understand the extent to which children are expected to come to the circle-time activity and what to do if children refuse to participate. The best way to arrive at a mutual understanding is to discuss these issues beforehand and to communicate group-time expectations to both adults and children.

VARIATIONS ON GROUP TIMES

The standard group time carried out in most early childhood programs combines a variety of activities, such as singing songs, listening to stories, and engaging in movement, and typical routines, such as using a job chart or a weather wheel. Specialty groups may also be incorporated into the daily schedule. Specialty-group times are periods of whole-group instruction whose purpose is more specific than that of the general-group times described so far. They are called by names such as greeting time, planning time, music time, and author's circle. Early childhood professionals may regularly use one or more of these specialized group times throughout the week. Some common variations are described as follows.

Greeting Time

Go to the Video Examples section of Topic 10: Planning in the MyEducationLab for your course and watch the video entitled *Setting Up an Investigation: Whole Group Discussion of Apples in Preschool.* Watch a teacher introduce an apple-tasting activity using whole group instruction.

Hello everybody, yes indeed,
hello everybody, yes indeed,
hello everybody, yes indeed,
sing, children, sing!
Hello to Marsha, yes indeed,
hello to LaToya, yes indeed,
hello to Samson, yes indeed,
sing, children, sing.

Greeting time usually occurs at the beginning of the classroom session, welcoming children and helping them make the transition from home to the early childhood program (Graves, Gargiulo, & Sluder, 1996). Children have an opportunity to say hello to one another and share daily news before dispersing into more individualized activities. Greeting time may also be used to introduce activities and materials available during the day. This introduction could simply involve telling children what their choices are, or include demonstrations of materials that children will have a chance to use later in learning centers, individually, or in small groups. Other typical greeting-time activities may include daily routines such as reporting on the weather or asking children to volunteer for classroom jobs such as watering the plants or carrying around the cleanup sign. Greeting time is generally brief and is often followed by free-choice or learning-center time. A second, more traditional, group time usually follows later in the session.

Planning Time

Some children start their day by planning how they will spend a portion of their time in the classroom (High-Scope Educational Foundation, 2005). The purpose of planning time is to encourage children to make decisions and set goals. Plans may be oral or written, using pictures or words. A sample picture plan is presented in Figure 4.6. After children become familiar with the activities that are available during the day, they choose two or three to do and (sometimes) the order in which to do them. At times, only the children make these decisions. In other circumstances, children collaborate with peers or adults in making their choices. Some plans include "have-to" activities (those that the teacher requires) as well as "choice" activities, from which children may freely select. As the day progresses, children periodically refer to their plans to determine how well they are following them. Some programs end with a whole-group closing time during which

FIGURE 4.6   Planning/Reporting

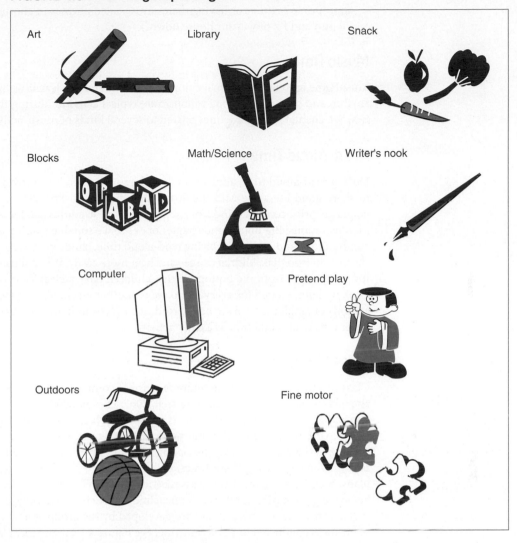

children describe the extent to which they followed plans made earlier in the day. In other programs, this reflection on the day is carried out one-on-one with an adult or in small-group time.

Storytelling Time

"Once upon a time . . ." Few children can resist the enjoyment promised by these words. Everyone likes a good story. Telling a story without a book; telling stories with flannel boards, puppets, or props; and enacting stories through dramatic movement are all activities well suited to whole-group instruction. Effective storytellers use various techniques to capture children's interest and hold it from the beginning of the story to the end (Machado, 2009). They do the following:

- ❏ Choose stories related to the children's interests
- ❏ Tell both familiar and new stories
- ❏ Know their story well (practicing the story beforehand)
- ❏ Use a dramatic voice to get children's attention
- ❏ Maintain eye contact with individual children by continually scanning the group
- ❏ Change the speed, pitch, volume, and rhythm of their voice to correspond to the meaning of the story
- ❏ Articulate each word clearly
- ❏ Use dramatic pauses to build suspense or facilitate transitions between events in the story
- ❏ Change their voice for each character in the story

❏ Provide an opportunity for children to participate in the story by making sounds or appropriate gestures or having them say repeated phrases in chorus (such as "I'll huff and I'll puff and I'll blow your house down")

Music Time

Music time emphasizes mutual enjoyment and interactive learning. Singing, experimenting with rhythm and beat, and moving to music are typical activities during these specialty-group activities. See chapter 9 for guidelines related to several kinds of music activities.

Read-Aloud Time

During read-aloud time, adults read to children. The aim is to provide adult reading models and to share good literature with the group (Neuman & Roskos, 2007). Literacy goals such as oral language, print concepts, and story sense may also be addressed. Picture books with large, colorful illustrations; Big Books; and chapter books make suitable reading materials, depending on the children's age and interests. During read-aloud time, children cluster around the adult, who often sits in a chair so that children can see and hear more easily. When illustrations are shown, the adult turns the pages from the bottom so that children have a clear view of the pictures. Holding the book up high enough for everyone to see is another essential strategy. Books with complex illustrations or small pictures are better read to children individually than in a large group. In many programs, read-aloud time is a daily activity.

Class Meetings

Class meetings contribute to children's sense of community and help engage children in discussion about classroom problems (Gartrell, 2007; Hyson, 2008). Class meetings address topics and issues that directly affect the group as a whole, such as how to manage the use of the new computers, what to do when children tease each other, or what the class iguana's name should be. These meetings are primarily discussion activities in which both adults and children become actively involved. During these times, children explore problems, suggest solutions, and develop plans. As with any group time, class meetings have a clear purpose and established guides for behavior (e.g., one person talks at a time, children listen respectfully, participants have a choice to speak or not). Often these guides are developed by the group as a whole as one of the first orders of business conducted in a class meeting. See Figure 4.7 for an example of the ground rules developed by one group of kindergartners to govern their class meetings during the year. Children as young as 3 years old can successfully participate in short meetings involving the whole group. Such meetings create a sense of community among children, which leads to increased cooperation and ownership of classroom decision making, and over time teachers often find that classroom conflicts are reduced (Hyson, 2008). As children gain maturity and experience, class meetings may be scheduled regularly to ensure smooth classroom functioning and to provide opportunities for children to practice skills associated with democratic living (Seefeldt, Castle, & Falconer, 2010). Reaching consensus, learning to compromise, and making decisions by voting are typical skills that children gain by participating in class meetings.

FIGURE 4.7 Kindergartners' Ground Rules for Class Meetings

Guides for listening and talking at class meetings—developed by Ms. Elliot's kindergartners

Look at people when they are talking
Sit still in group
Listen when someone is talking
One person talking at a time
Make sure everyone who wants to talk has a chance

Brainstorming Groups

K = What do we **know**?
W = What do we **want** to know?
H = **How** do we want to find out?
L = What did we **learn**?
H = **How** did we learn?

The KWHLH formula describes the content of specialty-group times that early childhood professionals use to increase children's understanding and involvement in their learning. Such instruction times are usually tied to a theme or a project that the children are studying. At an initial whole-group gathering, children brainstorm a list of what they know about a particular topic (Mindes, 2006; Obenchain & Morris, 2007). The adult does not comment on the accuracy of what children describe. As a result, the first list often contains both faulty ideas and accurate information. Next, the children create a list of what they want to find out and a third list of how they may obtain answers to their questions. The information on these three lists influences both the teacher's planning and the children's. The children add to the lists or revise them as they investigate the topic. Finally, the group comes together to discuss what they learned and the strategies that led to their increased knowledge. Comparing their original ideas with what they discovered is one way children analyze their learning strategies and the outcomes of their involvement with the topic. An example of a set of KWHLH lists related to spiders that was generated by children in a multiage class (kindergarten through second grade) is presented in Figure 4.8.

Minilessons

On some occasions, you may need to convey specific information to the whole group. Providing instructions about how to carry out a fire drill, demonstrating place value, or teaching children map-reading strategies are examples. Effective minilessons are concise and incorporate all the characteristics of active learning associated with DAP; they are not simply lectures. This kind of whole-group instruction usually precedes small-group or individualized learning experiences that build on what was presented to the entire class. For instance, Felicitas Moreno wants to teach her first-grade class some of the same writing processes professional writers use—gathering ideas before writing; writing more than one draft; revising what they have written; and editing their work for capitalization, punctuation, and spelling with the help of older peers or adults (McGee & Richgels, 2008). With this in mind, she conducts a writer's workshop for a few minutes each morning. Each writer's workshop is a minilesson on a single topic such as how to brainstorm ideas for something to write about or how to put ideas in order from beginning to end. Sometimes Ms. Moreno demonstrates how to do something; sometimes the children work as a group to help one another. These minilessons are followed by a 15-minute writing period during which children work individually or in pairs.

FIGURE 4.8   KWHLH Lists About Spiders

What do we know about spiders?
Spiders are insects.
Spiders make webs.
Spiders crawl on walls.
Spiders are black.
Spiders are sometimes found in basements.

What do we want to know about spiders?
What do spiders do all day?
Why do they make webs?
What are baby spiders called?
How long do spiders live?

How do we want to find out about spiders?
We can look in books.
We can watch spiders outside.
We can look for other places that spiders might live.
We can talk to people who know a lot about spiders.
We can watch a show about spiders.

What did we learn about spiders?
~~Spiders are insects.~~ Spiders are arachnids.
Spiders make webs. Most spiders spin webs. Webs help spiders catch insects to eat. Webs help to keep the spider safe. Some spiders are "wandering" spiders. They do not make webs.
Spiders eat bugs.

Spiders lay eggs.
Spiders crawl on walls.
Spiders are black. They can also be brown, white, and purple.
Most spiders are not poisonous. Do not touch a spider unless you know it is not harmful.
Spiders have eight legs.
Spiders are sometimes found in basements.
Baby spiders are called spiderlings.
Spiders live about 1 year.
Spiders help people by eating insects that are harmful to plants.
People make up stories about pretend spiders like "Anansi."

How did we learn about spiders?
We talked to Mr. Boyle (farmer) and Ms. Kumar (librarian).
We made a spiderweb from string.
We found spiderwebs outside and at school.
We looked in books. We visited the library.
We made our own book about spiders.
We played a spider game.
We made "toothpick" spiders.
We watched two spiders.

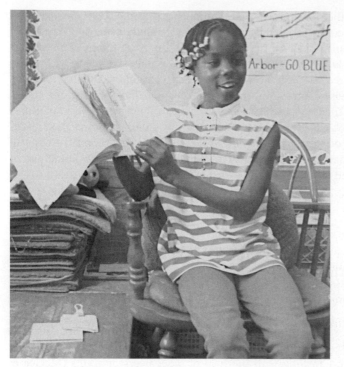

The young writer proudly shares her work from the author's chair.

Author's Chair

Group times featuring the author's chair provide children an opportunity to read something they have written (such as journals or self-designed books) to the group as a whole (McGee & Richgels, 2008). Two or three children who are ready to share their writing are given a chance to read their work. After the reading, listeners ask questions (e.g., "What is going to happen next?" "How did you decide on the name of the story?"). They also provide feedback (e.g., "You thought up a really good title. It told exactly what the story was going to be about." or "The joke you added on the last page was a fun way to end the story." or "Those facts about toads were cool."). Children or adults may offer such comments. Author's chair highlights children's efforts to communicate their thoughts through writing and give group members a chance to celebrate one another's accomplishments.

Reporting Time

Reporting time provides an organized opportunity for children to describe something they have done or to show their work to peers. For instance, the 4-year-olds in Mrs. Reed's class have returned from a field trip to a bakery. Each child has a chance to describe one thing on the trip. All the items are compiled on a master list that is later posted in the room. In John Kamwi's first-grade class, the children meet three times a week in the late afternoon to report on something they have learned that is related to the theme they are studying. Four or five children have a chance to report each day. Their reports may be oral or may include showing the others things they have made or classroom materials (such as books or artifacts) related to what they are talking about. Some children complete a reporting form, such as that presented in Figure 4.6, as a way to record how they spent their time during the day. Reporting time provides closure to the day's activities and fosters a sense of group involvement in each person's efforts.

COMMON QUESTIONS ABOUT GROUP TIME

Should All Children Be Required to Participate in Group Time?

Early childhood professionals are divided in their response to this query. Some teachers believe that the goals of group time are so critical that every child is required to participate to the best of his or her ability. Other practitioners assume that if group time is interesting enough, most children will want to join the group, but believe that children should not be required to do so. Youngsters who do not want to participate may engage in quiet activities away from the group so long as they do not disturb others. Such expectations often vary according to the children's age and developmental abilities. Consequently, younger, less experienced children may have more flexibility about participation than older, more experienced youngsters. Whichever approach is used, the educator's expectations must be based on developmentally appropriate practice and be clear and consistent so that children know what is appropriate and which behaviors demonstrate compliance.

How Can I Facilitate Conversations Among a Large Group of Children?

Many group-time activities involve engaging children in conversation. However, some adults are hesitant to engage in whole-group discussion for fear that they will loose control of the group. Instead, they rigidly enforce a "no talking" rule. Other group leaders attempt discussions only to have them end in chaos or with little accomplished. Both problems can be avoided by helping children learn skills associated with the art of conversation (Freiberg & Driscoll, 2005). These skills can be practiced in small groups of two or three children with an adult at various times of the day, formally or informally, and indoors or outdoors. Prompting discussions with open-ended questions, reminding children about oral turn taking, paraphrasing one child's words to another child, and helping children relate their response to the idea expressed by their peer are all ways to enhance children's conversational abilities.

Introduce whole-group discussions by incorporating children's spontaneous remarks into the normal flow of the group-time activities. Eventually you can move to purposeful group conversations. Use the strategies described in chapter 3 related to guided-participation, problem-solving, and discussion activities. If several children want to speak at once, create a conversation lineup: "First we'll listen to LaVelle, then Duane, then Grace." Periodically remind children of the central question they are answering, and recap what has been said so far. Avoid using closed-ended questions or setting up situations in which there is only one correct answer. Conversations are not oral tests. If a child says something that is obviously incorrect, find something correct in the response, and then add information to make it more accurate and prevent perpetuating the acquisition of erroneous information. For example, during a group discussion about fish, one child pronounced that little fish eat big fish. The teacher replied, "You know that fish sometimes eat each other. I'm not sure who eats whom. Let's spend some time this afternoon finding out if little fish eat big fish or if big fish eat the little ones. During our reporting group, we can tell people what we discovered." Another strategy is to ask for group responses as well as individual replies to questions you pose. Mr. Gogglin does this as part of an estimating activity when he says, "Earlier today, some people thought there might be 100 marbles in this jar. Who here estimates that the number of marbles in this jar is 100?" On a large easel pad nearby, he records the names of children who say they agree or who make some physical sign of agreement. Next, he asks, "Who estimates that there are fewer marbles than that?" Children respond, and he records their names. Returning to a one-person-at-a-time procedure, Mr. Gogglin says, "Stephen, you said you thought there were fewer marbles. Tell us how you decided that."

Finally, keep initial group discussions short. Gradually increase their length and complexity as children become more comfortable and adept.

What Should I Do When Children Interrupt a Story or a Presentation?

The best way to avoid interruptions is to make sure children are comfortable and in a good position to see and hear before you begin. This prevents complaints of "I can't see" or "Teacher, she's squishing me." Another strategy is to tell children before you begin that they will have a chance to talk when you are finished. However, children who make a connection between what you are doing and their own lives may find waiting too difficult. Two options are available when this happens: Incorporate their remarks into the ongoing presentation, or remind them to save their comments for the end. Sometimes the two can be combined. For example, a teacher is reading the book *Green Eggs and Ham,* by Dr. Seuss. Jeremy interrupts excitedly, "I had eggs for breakfast. Mine were scrambled." Immediately, the other children chime in with comments about eggs and breakfast. The teacher treats their remarks as signs of interest and says, "It sounds like you know a lot about eggs and breakfast. Let's hear what Sam did about those green eggs he had, and we'll talk about your eggs when the story is over." She continues reading. This kind of gentle redirection is more helpful and less disruptive than a long discourse on how it is impolite to interrupt. If the children continued, she might momentarily close the book and say something such as "You have lots to say. This story is most fun when you can hear the rhythm of the words. If you keep interrupting, the rhythm will be spoiled. Wait until the story is over; then we will have a good long talk." After the story is over, she waits a moment to savor the mood and then expresses her appreciation to the children for waiting. Turning her attention to Jeremy, she says, "Now, Jeremy, tell me about those eggs you had for breakfast."

What Can Be Done to Support Easily Distractible Children?

If the group as a whole is having difficulty paying attention, it may be a sign that group time has gone on too long or that the content is not relevant or engaging. In these situations, revise your group-time plans on the spot and rethink them for the future. However, if only one or two children consistently have difficulty remaining focused, more targeted techniques are advisable. The following are strategies designed to help children be more successful and get the most out of whole-group experiences.

❑ Tell children what will be happening during group time before you begin. For instance, during cleanup time each day, the teacher tells Carlita the topic or main activity that will be featured at circle time. This prompt helps Carlita make the mental transition from cleanup to group more comfortably.

❑ Have easily distractible children sit near an adult who can cue them as necessary (e.g., "Look up at the book." or "See the shell she is holding." or "Listen for what comes next."). If no other adult is available, the child could sit within arm's length of the leader (not on the leader's lap) to see and hear more clearly, without being the center of attention.

❑ Use scaffolding to help the child function more independently within the group. For instance, the child may begin the year by sitting on an adult's lap. Gradually, supports would be withdrawn by having the child sit next to the adult, then sit one or two people away from the adult, and finally sit anywhere in the circle.

❑ Give the child something for which to watch or listen (e.g., "This is a song about an animal. When I've sung it through, tell me what animal it was about."). This strategy could be implemented privately or with the whole group.

❑ Give the child something to do in the group—turn the pages or pass out the rhythm instruments.

❑ Ask the child to begin by participating in the group and then allow him or her to leave group time midway through and work quietly nearby. Gradually increase the amount of time the child stays with the group.

❑ Break the larger group into smaller groups so that easily distractible children have more opportunities for personal attention, less waiting, and fewer competing stimuli with which to cope.

What Should the Group Leader Do When Children Become Unhappy or Angry During Group Time?

Clarissa is not pleased with the choice of rhythm instruments that are left when it is her turn to select one. Luellen cries when she does not get her favorite colored ribbon for creative movement. Jae Doh becomes angry when he does not get to sit next to a special friend in the circle. In each of these situations, the group leader is faced with having to tend to the needs of an individual child while trying to facilitate the activities for the whole group. Several strategies can be useful in such circumstances.

❑ Ensure that enough materials are available so that even the last child has at least two or three items from which to select. Having a choice is a more palatable option to children than settling for the one that is left. You can also have children trade rhythm instruments or other items midway through the activity. Announce that this will happen before you pass out the materials so that children will know that they will have more than one opportunity to select the object of their choice.

❑ Acknowledge children's emotions with a simple nonevaluative statement. "You really wanted the pink ribbon." "You were hoping to sit next to Carlos at group." When adults underscore children's emotions verbally, they exhibit sensitivity and caring in a way children can understand. This acknowledgment makes children feel heard and accepted. Although such statements do not necessarily resolve the dilemma, they serve as a foundation for eventual problem solving. They also provide some comfort to children for whom no other satisfactory solution is possible at the time.

❑ Problem solve whenever possible. Give children information that may help them deal with their feelings (e.g., "In a few minutes we will be trading ribbons. You will have another chance to get a pink one."). When problems arise among children who have adequate conversational abilities, invite the child or others in the group to help devise a solution either for now or the next time (e.g., "Jae Doh really wants to sit next to Carlos, but so do Ralph and Lauren. What can people do when more than one person wants to sit in the same place?"). This kind of problem solving can take place within the whole group or be carried out quietly between the concerned parties away from the group area. Depending on the flexibility of your agenda, such conversations could occur during group time or afterward.

❑ If other adults are available, solicit their help rather than trying to deal with each problem yourself. Signal the other adult nonverbally or use words: "Mrs. Johnson, please help Jae Doh find a spot to sit." "It looks like Luellen is sad. Please see what comfort you can give her."

❏ When necessary, state clear, matter-of-fact limits. Sometimes children may behave inappropriately. If this happens, acknowledge the child's concern, and then give the child a positive direction about what to do next.

What About Show-and-Tell?

Show-and-tell is a routine whole-group experience in many early childhood classrooms. However, the practice gets mixed reviews from teachers and parents (Hendrick & Weissman, 2010; Spangler, 1997). Show-and-tell may be seen as a means for children to develop both listening and speaking skills, or become the center of attention in an approved way. In contrast, some people express concern that children may become bored by sitting for long periods or may feel coerced into speaking before the group. Still other individuals worry that children develop competitive feelings in the process or feel left out if they think they have nothing worthwhile to share. If teachers choose to implement show-and-tell, they should have a clear curricular goal in mind and then select strategies to match the goal. For example, if the goal relates to listening and speaking, teachers must remember that children initially practice these skills best in small groups. Thus, having one day when groups of three or four children share items from home is a more appropriate strategy than having several children try to show and tell about their items in front of the entire class each day. To minimize the idea that show-and-tell is a time to show off, ask children to bring in items that fit particular criteria, such as something blue, something that begins with the letter *k*, or something you found in your front yard." Also, make sure that children who have no items to share or who forget can find something to talk about by using materials available in the program. Before show-and-tell gets under way, establish simple rules to govern how items will be supervised. Some early childhood educators require that items remain put away until the appointed time. Some teachers ask children to designate in advance whether the item is something the other children in the class can only look at or can touch. Such precautions do much to prevent tears and conflicts. Finally, be prepared to ask children one or two open-ended questions about the items they brought. Telling children in advance what these questions will be helps young children who have difficulty answering on the spot. They do better with some time to think about what they might say.

INCLUDING CHILDREN OF DIFFERENT AGES AND ABILITIES IN WHOLE-GROUP INSTRUCTION

Although the guidelines for whole-group instruction are the same for all children, some accommodations based on age and ability are necessary to enhance children's enjoyment and learning. Younger, less experienced children enjoy group times that share these characteristics:

❏ Are short (10 to 15 minutes long)
❏ Involve a lot of participation
❏ Involve minimal talk
❏ Include short songs and stories
❏ Begin with a familiar activity each time (e.g., a song or finger play the children know well)

Older, more experienced children enjoy group times that are structured as follows:

❏ Are longer (20 to 30 minutes long)
❏ Involve a lot of participation
❏ Include discussion
❏ Include songs with several verses and more complex stories
❏ Involve both familiar and novel activities
❏ Include an element of surprise
❏ Focus on factual information as well as problem solving

Teachers working with children in mixed-age groups must consider all the children in the group rather than simply teaching "to the middle." Such consideration could involve starting with a whole group, implementing a short agenda, then dividing children into smaller groups to better accommodate their varying abilities and interests. Another strategy is to carry out an action-oriented body of the group time with everyone and then invite children who want to stay for a longer story or conversation to do so, but dismiss the others to carry out quiet activities elsewhere in the room.

When including children with special needs, it is important to determine each individual child's ability to participate in the planned activities. Carefully consider the behavior required to successfully participate in the activities planned for group time. Focus on what the child with special needs *can* do when planning activities and incorporate these components in your group time. For example, if a child is not able to hold a rhythm instrument in his or her hand, you could attach bells to the child's wrist using an elastic loop. This would enable the child to independently participate in the activity. It will be important to begin group with an activity each child can successfully complete. Beginning group time with a familiar activity can be comforting for children who require predictability, and signal all children that group time is ready to start. Including the same type of activities in the same order during group time provides children the opportunity to practice skills and master them over time. When introducing new activities in group time, break the activity into steps, demonstrating each one so that all children understand what to do.

Be sure your group-time area is located in space easily accessed by all children and that provides adequate space for movement activities. Children with mobility issues may require more space to participate in movement activities than other children. Seat all children similarly for group time (e.g., all sit in chairs or all sit on the floor) to maximize inclusion of children with special needs. For example, if one child uses a wheelchair, all the children can be seated in chairs for group time. Utilize music, props, movement, dramatic vocal effects and gestures to capture and maintain the child's attention. Some children will benefit from having a "fidget toy" during group time. Small stuffed animals, squishy balls or other items children can manipulate quietly during group assists children in focusing on the group-time activities. Examine your expectations for group time carefully considering the child's ability. It may be appropriate to allow a child with special needs to leave group after a few minutes, gradually lengthening the amount of time as the child gains skills.

Sample group-time plans for younger preschoolers and a mixed-age group of children aged 6 through 8 years are presented in Figure 4.9. Review the sample group times presented in the figure and decide how the two group times are similar and different. Look for evidence of how each group time was tailored to meet the needs of younger or older children.

PITFALLS TO AVOID DURING GROUP-TIME PLANNING

As described previously, whole-group instruction has many potential benefits for children. Unfortunately, these benefits are not always realized. Many of the problems associated with whole-group instruction are averted by careful planning. In the following subsections, we describe a few common mistakes educators make and ways to avoid them.

Failing to Prepare Adequately

There are so many things to do in a day that planning whole-group instruction may seem impossible or unnecessary. Some practitioners assume that changing the songs and the book featured at group time each day is enough variety to maintain children's interest. Others may gather the children and do whatever comes to mind until the whole-group portion of the daily schedule is over. Still others have a general idea of what they want to accomplish but continually interrupt themselves or halt the group because they do not have everything they need immediately at hand. When this happens, children become restless and inattentive. Problems proliferate under these circumstances, and children leave group time having gained little of educational value. The antidote for this problem is to plan ahead for whole-group instruction. Joanne Hendrick (2003), a longtime early childhood teacher and director and professor emerita at the University of Oklahoma, says,

> Providing educationally worthwhile group times takes self-discipline and energy combined with sincere convictions . . . self-discipline to sit down and plan such experiences in advance, energy to carry out plans once they have been made, and conviction that group time is valuable enough to make careful planning a consistent part of the program . . . not just once in a while, but daily. (p. 387)

At first, writing a detailed whole-group plan for each group time will be necessary. As you gain practice and proficiency, your written plans will become briefer, often encompassing only the educational goal and the highlighted feature activity for each whole-group segment of the day.

FIGURE 4.9   Sample Group Times for a 3-Year-Old Group and a Primary School Mixed-Age Group

3-Year-Olds

Date: Monday, August 18   **Activity Name:** Rhythm Stick Fun

Age of Children: 3 years

Goal(s): Explore the use of a musical instrument (rhythm sticks) to make sounds and keep time to the music.

Standard: Source—National Association for Music Education—Children will use rhythm instruments to make sounds alone or with a group.

Content

1. Rhythm sticks are usually played by making a sound on the beat of the music.
2. Beat is the recurring pulse heard or sensed through the music.
3. There is more than one way to play rhythm sticks.
4. Playing rhythm sticks involves knowing when and when not to make sounds.

Materials: Rhythm sticks, enough for two per child and adult

Opening

1. Song, "Everybody, sit down, sit down, sit down, everybody, sit down, sit down here" (tune: "Everybody Do This"). Clap on the beat as you sing.
2. Transition to body—continue song, making motions in time with the beat. "Everybody, clap your hands, clap your hands, clap your hands, everybody, clap your hands, just like me. Everybody, tap your feet . . . everybody, shake your head . . ."

Body

3. Say: "We just sang a song using our hands and feet to make special sounds with the song. We'll sing that song again using musical instruments called rhythm sticks. Watch me as I show you how to use the rhythm sticks."

   Do: Take two of the rhythm sticks and demonstrate to the class how they work. Tap them together quietly, then louder; tap them quickly, then slowly; rub them together in a circular motion to make a gentle swishing sound. Tell the children what you are doing as you make the various sounds.

4. Say: "Before I pass out the sticks, I want to show you a signal that I will use when everyone's sticks must be quiet. When I hold the ends of my rhythm sticks on my shoulders like this, it means be quiet. When I play my sticks, that means it's time for you to play.

   "Now it's time to pass out the sticks. As you get your sticks, place them on your shoulders like this, in the 'be quiet' position."

   Do: Ask the adults to pass out the rhythm sticks, and remind the children to hold the sticks against their shoulders. Model this behavior as the children receive their sticks.

5. Say: "Now that everyone has a rhythm stick, let's practice how to use them. Take your sticks and tap them together like this. Try tapping them fast like this. Now slowly. Tap them loud. Now softly. Rub your sticks together like this to make another kind of soft sound. You're doing a great job! Now let's sing a song while we play our instruments."

   Now sing, "Everybody, tap your sticks, tap your sticks, tap your sticks, everybody, tap your sticks, just like this." Keep singing the song, each time changing the method of tapping the sticks as practiced earlier. Match the way you sing the words with the way you play the sticks. For example, as you are tapping quietly, sing in a very quiet voice.

Closing

6. Say: "We have had a great time playing the rhythm sticks. That was fun. It's time now to pass your rhythm sticks to an adult."

Transition to Next Portion of the Day

7. Say: "Let's get in our jack-in-the-boxes."

   Do: Model huddling low to the floor on hands and knees, face in arms resting on the floor.

   Say: "Jack in the box, you sit so still. Won't you come out? Yes, I will."

   Do: On the last words, pop up on knees, hands outstretched above head. Repeat once more.

   Say: "This time stay in your jack-in-the-box until I tap you. Then you may get up and find a place to play."

   Do: Tap each child one at a time until all have been released from the group.

Evaluation Questions

1. To what extent were children able to use the rhythm sticks as modeled?
2. Did anyone have difficulty finding the beat? If so, what scaffolding strategy might you use to help him or her next time?
3. What future activities will you create based on the children's experience in this activity?

(continued)

FIGURE 4.9 **Sample Group Times for a 3-Year-Old Group and a Primary School Mixed-Age Group** *(continued)*

Primary School Mixed-Age Group

Date: Monday, April 14   **Activity Name:** Global Fun

Age of Children: 6, 7, and 8 years

Goal(s): Gain knowledge related to social studies (maps and globes).

Standard: Source—National Council for the Social Studies—Children will develop knowledge of different earth surfaces and forms.

Content
- ❑ A globe is a sphere on which a map of the earth is drawn.
- ❑ The brown and green shapes on the globe represent land.
- ❑ The blue shapes on the globe represent water.
- ❑ The earth's surface contains more water than land.

Materials: Books in book basket, calendar materials, poem chart with acetate cover, large flat map of the United States, "Waldo" character, state coloring chart, crayons, box with individual cards giving information about each of the 50 states, three plastic globes (about the size of a basketball), very small stickers (enough for each child to have one)

Transition into Opening

- ❑ **Books:** As children enter the room each day, they are greeted by the teacher and then choose books from a book basket on the group-time rug. Children read individually or with other children.

  After 15 minutes the "book leader" collects the books and puts them in the basket while children sing the "book-worm" song.

Opening

- ❑ **Songs/chants:** One or two class favorites

- ❑ **Calendar:** Calendar helper locates yesterday, today, and tomorrow on calendar. Child adds a Popsicle stick to the "ones" box to represent the number of days the children have been in school this year and writes the corresponding numeral.

- ❑ **Poem of the week:** (Poem about traveling) One child points to the words on the poetry chart as the group recites it together. The teacher calls on children to circle and read the words with *th, sh,* or *ch* digraphs.

Transition to Body

- ❑ **Movement activity:** Short stretching exercise that refers to geographic features (climb up the mountain, swim through the sea, etc.)

Body

- ❑ **State review:** Teacher says, "It's Cara's turn to choose a new state. She will move Waldo to a new state on the map of the United States." Cara chooses any state. Teacher asks her why she chose that state, asks the group if they know anything about the state or anyone who lives there, or if anyone has traveled there. Cara locates the state she chose on the coloring map and colors it in any color. Adult pulls the corresponding state card out of the state box and gives children some information about the state. Cara uses the pointer and points to each state previously chosen as children recite the names of the states.

- ❑ **Land or water game:** Adult divides children into three groups. Each group gets a globe.

  Adult explains that this is a globe and that globes are a type of map. Adult uses guided-discovery strategies as children examine globes.

    What do you notice about this object?
    What do you think the colors mean?
    (Adult provides information as necessary.)
    What do you think you see more of—land or water?

  Adult collects globes, puts two aside, and explains: "We're going to play a game to help us locate land and water on the globe. Raise the hand that you write with in the air. Now point to the ceiling with your pointer finger, and I am going to come around and put a sticker on your fingernail. Here are the rules to the game. When you have the globe, decide whom you will roll it to, then call out his or her name. Be sure to roll the globe." Adult demonstrates. "When you catch the globe, look at your sticker finger and decide if it has landed on land or water." Adult writes the words *water* and *land* on the board or on chart paper. "If your finger touches land, I will put a tally mark under that word. If your finger touches water, I will put a tally mark under that word. Which do you predict will have more tally marks, land or water? Why?"

  Group plays game until everyone has had a chance to catch the globe and identify land or water. At the game's end, adult and children count the tally marks and talk about the results.

FIGURE 4.9   Sample Group Times for a 3-Year-Old Group and a Primary School Mixed-Age Group *(continued)*

Closing
❏ Adult lets children know globes will be available if they would like to play the land-and-water game during free-choice time. Suggests the children could see if they get the same basic results each time.

Transition to Next Portion of the Day
❏ Adult briefly describes choices available during free-choice time. Adult asks who would like to start on their journals (and so forth) and then dismisses children in small numbers as they indicate their choices.

Evaluation Questions
❏ To what extent were children able to identify land and water?
❏ How accurate were children's observations?
❏ What unexpected outcomes may have occurred during this group time?
❏ What future activities will you create based on the children's experience in this activity?

Sources: For 3-year-olds: Grace Spalding, Child Development Laboratories, Department of Family and Child Ecology, Michigan State University, East Lansing, Michigan. For primary school mixed-age group: Deborah Sharpe, Wilkshire Early Childhood Center, Haslett Public Schools, Haslett, Michigan.

FIGURE 4.10   Abbreviated Group-Time Agenda

Activity Name: Whole-Group Storytelling

Intermediate Objective(s): Take on roles and act out interpretations of these roles to tell a familiar story.

Opening: Sing the songs "Hello Everybody" and "I Had a Cat and the Cat Pleased Me." Transition to the body: Talk about the animals in the song; lead into the animals in the story.

Body: Introduce whole-group storytelling. Begin "The Three Billy Goats Gruff" story; continue by encouraging children to act out various roles. Announce "The End."

Closing: Review with the children the ways in which they acted like the billy goats and the troll. Acknowledge the children's participation.

Transition to Next Portion of the Day: Dismiss by shoe color or type to go outdoors.

An abbreviated group time agenda for "The Three Billy Goats Gruff" group time featured previously in this chapter is presented in Figure 4.10.

Relying on Whole-Group Instruction to Meet Goals Better Addressed in Smaller Groups

Sometimes practitioners plan activities using a whole-group format when children would benefit more from working on the task with fewer peers. For instance, attending to others and waiting your turn to speak are important receptive-listening skills. Children learn these behaviors just as they learn everything else—gradually. Being expected to wait long enough for 10 or 20 other children to share an idea, have a turn to touch the turtle, or come to the front of the group one at a time is inappropriate for most youngsters aged 3 to 8 years old. Although children need practice improving their turn-taking skills, task analysis would suggest that the wait time must be reduced. One way this can be accomplished is to divide the children into smaller groups for discussions and other turn-taking activities. For example, during scheduled group times, preschoolers could be divided into smaller groups according to the number of adults available. First- and second-grade children could be divided into self-directed groups of four or five children each. Children would complete a task and then reconvene as a whole. For example, the teacher has a variety of seashells for children to examine. Rather than passing the seashells around the entire circle one at a time, she has the children form four smaller groups within the large-group area. Each group is given four or five seashells to examine, which allows the youngsters to handle and look at the seashells with little waiting. After several minutes, all 20 children come together again to share what they observed.

Another strategy is to reserve activities that require much waiting for periods in the day other than group time. This does not mean that children should never have to wait as part of whole-group instruction. However, such periods should be brief.

Selecting Inappropriate Materials

Picture books with illustrations that are too small, too pale, or too busy for children to see clearly; songs that have too many verses; flannel board pieces that do not stick; incomplete items; and equipment that malfunctions are examples of inappropriate group-time materials. Whole-group plans that rely heavily on talk with few other activities are also poor choices. Likewise, items that support the theme but undermine other curricular goals should be avoided or revised to make them more appropriate. This was the case for Marlene, who wanted to teach children about settings in which community workers functioned. Searching through the program's picture file, she found a set of community helper pictures that were large, colorful, and supportive of her main idea. Unfortunately, they depicted only male workers and did not represent the full range of possibilities for boys and girls that Marlene wanted to portray. Rather than being satisfied with the pictures as they were, Marlene sought additional images that included women. This kind of attention to detail helped Marlene ensure that her group-time materials were appropriate both in terms of her short-range objectives (supporting the theme) and her long-range goals (promoting respect for both genders).

Incorporating Too Many Routinized Activities

In some classrooms, daily activities such as using the calendar, completing a weather chart, assigning classroom jobs, having show-and-tell, and taking roll all take place during whole-group instruction. Furthermore, often many of these routines are combined in the same time period. This practice makes group times longer and shortens the time available for other whole-group activities. Consequently, children's enthusiasm for group time may be dulled, children wait long periods, and they are exposed to the core of group-time activities when they are no longer fresh and interested. Several ways to prevent these negative outcomes are available. One is to eliminate some routines. Some early childhood professionals strongly believe activities such as using the calendar and having show-and-tell are developmentally inappropriate because of their abstract nature and their use of procedures that may create competition or unfavorable comparisons among children (Brewer, 2007; Beneke, Ostrosky, & Katz, 2008). However, many practitioners believe that certain classroom rituals add to the predictability of the day and that children benefit from making choices or participating in discussions relative to such matters. No matter which routines you decide are appropriate for the children in your class, consider each in terms of what children are learning and whether whole-group instruction is the best mode for approaching such learning. For instance, attendance could be completed as children arrive, and completing the weather chart could be a learning-center activity instead of a mandatory whole-group endeavor each day. Similarly, show-and-tell could shift from being a whole-group activity to an activity carried out in small groups. In addition, because many programs have more than one group time each day, essential routines can be divided among them. Doing so frees time for children and teachers to engage in other, more varied whole-group activities.

Waiting Too Long to Engage Children in Active Learning

Diane (4 years old): It's [circle time] boring. We just have to be listening, listening, listening, and I don't like that.

—Wiltz & Klein (2001, p. 225)

A long-winded opening that consists of 15 minutes of telling and explaining before the teacher engages in the body of the group time is too long for most children aged 3 to 8 years. Likewise, asking 3- and 4-year-olds to sit through using the calendar, singing four songs, and listening to a story before dancing with scarves is pushing the limits of their abilities. Even youngsters in the first and second grade find sitting so long with no other form of active engagement demanding. Group time is not a synonym for *sit time,* nor should whole-group instruction be passive. Appropriate group times get children actively involved early in the procedure and throughout the gathering. Such engagement can take many forms. For example, children who are singing a song can do the motions, clap or slap their thighs in time to the music, change positions (stand up, sway, crouch, put their hands over their head, and so forth), listen for certain words or phrases in the song, vary the volume and pitch of their voices, vary the speed of the words, and engage in call and response. Children listening to a story can become more active participants by responding with a motion to various instructions within the story, saying a repeated line in chorus, miming some of the characters' actions, or filling in a word or a line as relevant.

The best group times include periods of active involvement.

A guided-discovery activity could include items for children to handle as well as questions to answer throughout the experience, rather than having all the talk at the end of the procedure. During a demonstration, children might watch for certain things to happen or signal the leader in a special way when they note a process is beginning or ending. Youngsters may also talk the leader through a demonstrated procedure, catch the leader making "mistakes," or imitate actions by pantomiming or using objects.

Allowing Group Times to Go on Too Long

Donnie (whining): I don't like doing circle.
Adult: Why?
Donnie: Because it always takes too long.

—Wiltz & Klein (2001, p. 220)

Early childhood professionals have different beliefs regarding the suitability of group time for preschoolers. Some individuals caution against using whole-group instruction with children 3 and 4 years old (Brewer, 2007). Others suggest that such times should last only a few minutes a day and lengthen gradually as children become more experienced (Hendrick & Weissman, 2010). As children in kindergarten and first and second grade develop group-time skills, their overall ability to enjoy and benefit from whole-group activities as long as 20 to 30 minutes increases. However, this is true only when the other criteria defining appropriate group times, such as active involvement and purposeful activity, are maintained. No matter what age the children are, group time is best ended before children lose interest. Thus, group time follows the theatrical adage "Always leave them wanting more." Remember, too, that activities carried out in group time should be repeated or supplemented beyond the whole-group instruction period. For instance, a flannel board story featured during group time could be made available in the library corner for children to use to reenact the story; the materials to conduct an experiment demonstrated at group time could be offered to smaller groups of children later in the day; and the book written, published, and read by a first- or second-grade "author" can be displayed for children to reread on their own.

SUMMARY

Most early childhood classrooms include some whole-group instruction each day. The most common whole-group experiences are group times. Group times can enhance learning across the curriculum and develop a sense of community within the classroom. The extent to which such benefits are derived is directly influenced by the quality of the planning and preparation that go into them. The format for writing group-time plans maintains some of the same planning elements described for other kinds of activity plans. One difference is that the procedures section outlines the opening, the body, and the closing of the activity. Another difference is that a specific strategy is identified for helping children move from group time to the next portion of the day. Group times may be traditional in form or serve specialty functions in early childhood classrooms. Typically, both types of group times are used sometime during the day. Pitfalls to avoid in planning or implementing group-time activities include the following: failing to prepare adequately, using whole-group instruction when an individual or small-group experience would better facilitate children's learning, selecting inappropriate materials, including too many routinized activities during group time, waiting too long to engage children in active learning, and failing to end whole-group instruction soon enough. These mistakes can negate the positive benefits children derive from appropriate group-time learning experiences. However, such problems are avoidable through adequate planning, preparation, practice, and experience.

Key Words

body	group times	transitions
closing	opening	

Applying What You've Read in This Chapter

1. **Discuss**
   a. On the basis of your reading and your experiences with young children, discuss each of the questions that open this chapter.
   b. Discuss three ways in which you could create a group time around the story "The Little Red Hen."
   c. Imagine that a person from the Humane Society has brought a very friendly dog to your classroom to use while he or she is talking about animal care. One of the children is extremely frightened. How will you handle the situation?

2. **Observe**
   a. Watch a group time in an early childhood program. On the basis of your observations, identify the purpose of the group time and create an agenda that corresponds to what you saw. Critique the effectiveness of what you observed.
   b. Observe a group time in an early childhood program. What strategies were used to help children anticipate what was going to happen from the beginning through the end? What instructions did they receive? Critique the effectiveness of what you observed.
   c. Watch a group time in an early childhood program. Identify three ways in which the teacher actively engaged children in the activities. How did individual children respond?

3. **Carry out an activity**
   a. Plan a storytelling group time for a specific group of children. Create a detailed written plan for what you will do. If possible, carry out the group time and evaluate the results in writing. Another option is to ask a friend to observe you and provide feedback.
   b. Plan a group time that involves active movement by the children. Create a detailed written plan for what you will do. If possible, carry out the group time and evaluate the results in writing. Another option is to ask a friend to observe you and provide feedback.

4. **Create something for your portfolio**
   a. Describe a group time that you planned and carried out with children. Identify the learning objectives for children and evaluate the results.
   b. Videotape a group time that you implemented with children. Make the tape no more than 10 to 15 minutes long. On an index card, identify relevant learning objectives for children.

5. **Add to your journal**
   a. What is the most significant concept that you learned about whole-group planning and implementation from your readings and your experience with children?
   b. Reflect on the extent to which the information in this chapter corresponds to what you have observed in the field. What is your reaction to any discrepancies you perceive?
   c. Identify goals for yourself related to whole-group instruction for young children including how you intend to pursue these goals.

6. 🖐 **Consult the standards**
   a. Look up the social studies standards published by the National Council for the Social Studies. These can be obtained in a library or through the NCSS website, www.ncss.org. Identify at least two K–2 social studies standards around which you could develop a group time for young children.
   b. Create a complete group-time agenda from opening to closing for one of the social studies standards you identified above.
   c. Look up the preschool standards for your state. Identify a science or language standard you could address in a group time with young children. Describe the approach you would take.

PRACTICE FOR YOUR CERTIFICATION OR LICENSURE EXAM

The following items will help you practice applying what you have learned in this chapter. They can help to prepare you for your course exam, the PRAXIS II exam, your state licensure or certification exam, and for working in developmentally appropriate ways with young children.

Group Time in the Kindergarten

It is March. The 20 kindergartners in Larry Widener's class are studying the author Beatrix Potter. The children have learned about the author's background, her love of animals, and her talent for drawing. They have enjoyed several Beatrix Potter books in the story corner, including: The Tale of Peter Rabbit, The Tale of Benjamin Bunny, *and* The Tale of Mrs. Tiggy-Winkle. *Today, Larry decides to read* The Tale of Squirrel Nutkin

to the children during group time. It is a lovely book, 4 inches by 5½ inches, with charming pastel drawings. Larry begins the group time by singing a song about rabbits. He follows this with a finger play about squirrels. The children sit in a circle on the rug, participating with enthusiasm. Then Larry introduces the story by reminding the children of the other Beatrix Potter tales they have heard. Larry holds up the book so the children can see the pictures and begins reading. There is much jostling as children strain in to see the pictures. Soon children are inching up closer and closer to the book. Larry stops reading three times to remind children to "sit on their bottoms and to remain in their places." However, before he has read two full pages, the children are crowded around his chair and choruses of "I can't see" are heard throughout the group as some children sit up on their knees to see better. More pushing and shoving occurs as children vie for spots in the front. Larry is frustrated. He loves this story and wants the children to have an enjoyable literary experience; however, he realizes this group time is not working well.

1. **Constructed-response question**

    a. Drawing from your knowledge of appropriate group times, identify the most likely cause of the children's group-time problems. Provide a rationale for your answer.

    b. Identify three strategies Larry could use to enhance the children's learning at a group time that includes *The Tale of Squirrel Nutkin.*

2. **Multiple-choice question**

    Which strategy is *not* likely to be very successful in carrying out a group-time experience with 16 children?

    a. Use changes in voice tone and rhythm to create suspense or drama

    b. Hand out rhythm sticks first thing to capture children's interest

    c. Continually scan the group to determine children's level of interest

    d. Use dramatic hand gestures and animated facial expressions

Chapter

5

Organizing Space, Materials, and Time

You may wonder:

How do I arrange an effective learning environment?
What materials will I need?
How do I develop a schedule for the day?
How can I provide for active learning?

This chapter will help you answer these and other questions about organizing space, materials, and time.

◆ ◆ *A blanket is draped over a sturdy table in the pretend play area, making a tent. Four-year-olds Jenny and Seth enter the area talking loudly and laughing. They peek under the blanket and find the tent empty. Crouching down low they begin to whisper as they enter the cozy space.*
◆ ◆ *Three kindergarten girls, arms locked in unison, march over to the art area to make collages. They see that the art table has four chairs, but two are already occupied. "Come on," announces Sara, "Let's find a place with more room." The girls head over to the block area where a sign with stick figures shows that six children can play. Only one other child is building at the time. The girls happily begin taking blocks off the shelf.*
◆ ◆ *As the primary age children emerge from the building, they eagerly disperse across the playground, some with large balls toward the hard surface area, others with magnifying glasses toward the small meadow at one side of the school.*

As illustrated by the children in these early childhood programs, the physical environment "speaks" to children, influencing what they do, how they behave, and how successfully they achieve their goals (Greenman, 2007). Because children are sensual learners, the physical environment also plays a major role in how children learn and what they come to know. The younger the child, the more this is true. Thus, the physical environment is a powerful force to which early childhood educators must pay particular attention.

PRINCIPLES OF ORGANIZING THE PHYSICAL ENVIRONMENT

Organizing learning spaces indoors and outdoors, providing materials that suit the ages and abilities of all the children in a group, and preparing a daily schedule that promotes optimal learning are important tasks of early childhood professionals. Additionally, each setting should be usable by all of the children, regardless of ability or condition (Americans with Disabilities Act, 2008). This means that reasonable adjustments to the environment must be made so that programs are accessible and available to all.

Alyss is 4 years old and is currently enrolled in a public school preschool program. She is a little person or dwarf, who is quite small for her age, having very short arms and legs. Otherwise she is healthy and competent. Throughout this chapter, her needs will be discussed to assist you in understanding how to meet the individual needs of one child through adjustments to the physical environment.

MEETING THE SPECIAL NEEDS OF YOUNG CHILDREN

Of the two ways in which particular environmental needs of children are accommodated, both are the result of a planning meeting including parents, specialists as needed, building representatives, and teachers. First, an IEP (individual education plan), described in chapter 1, may specify environmental accommodations. Second, a 504 plan (Americans with Disabilities Act) may describe ways to reduce the obstacles for access and participation for a child who does not need additional special intervention. Both types of documents are reviewed annually and updated to reflect the changing needs of the child (Bennett, 2008).

Safety

Safety is the first thing to consider in regard to the physical environment. As an early childhood professional, you will be responsible for overseeing building, room, and playground safety and for teaching children to use materials and equipment safely. Children age 3 to 5 years will need much more careful supervision for all safety practices than children age 6 to 8 years, because the former group is less likely to have learned safe practices well. However, all children during the early childhood period will need help in learning what is safe and what is dangerous. As a result, children should never be left unsupervised. Although this may seem like common sense, it is too often forgotten. In addition to supervising children continuously, there are ways to adjust the physical environment to minimize potential hazards. For instance, adults:

❏ Teach children to use play equipment and materials safely, to put materials where they belong, and to keep pathways clear of tripping hazards.

❏ Scan the area regularly for safety hazards: objects in pathways where children walk or run, clutter near exits, sand or water spilled on hard surfaces, glass or refuse in outdoor play areas, sand or ice on hard-surface walkways. Ensure that materials with loose parts are kept where children expect to find them.

❏ Remove any equipment or materials that appear unsafe. Repair if possible. Report maintenance needs and follow up on them to ensure completion of work.

❏ Use materials, equipment, and playgrounds that are appropriate for the age and abilities of the children.

❏ Make necessary adjustments for children with special needs and empower all children to use materials and resources optimally. Evaluate if the accommodation for one child might pose a hazard for other children.

More specific examples related to each of these guidelines are presented in Table 5.1.

TABLE 5.1 Examples of Safe Practice

INDOOR SAFETY EXAMPLES

1. Cover electrical outlets except when they are in use.

2. Use extension cords, of adequate size, only when necessary. Never string them together for long distances or across pathways.

3. Supervise any electrical appliance in use while children are present.

4. Place tools on high shelves or block off equipment that may be unsafe when an adult is not present. For example, if using a glue gun or an iron for an art project, put the materials in an inaccessible spot as they cool.

5. Place all chemicals (plant fertilizer, cleaning compounds, medicines, etc.) out of the reach of children.

6. Teach children to recognize common symbols indicating a dangerous situation or object, such as the symbols for poison or STOP.

7. Maintain first-aid kits, including plastic gloves and hazardous-waste disposal bags, for treating minor injuries. Use universal precautions when you are exposed to blood, indoors and outdoors (American Public Health Association & American Academy of Pediatrics, 2002).

OUTDOOR SAFETY EXAMPLES

1. Wet metal slides during the summer so that the surface is cool enough for children to slide on, and check that metal is not dangerously cold during the winter.

2. Check the force-absorbent material under climbers, slides, swings, and other equipment to ensure that all hard surfaces on the ground are covered.

3. Check for the possibility of these common hazards: entrapment of the head or other body parts: falls from heights; equipment that can pinch or crush fingers; protrusions; sharp areas; and slippery surfaces or objects in pathways, which lead to abrasions, bruises, and cuts (Allen & Johnson, 1995). Report maintenance needs to the appropriate administrators.

Additional resources on playground safety may be accessed through the following website: www.playgroundsafety.org.

Comfort

Once safety has been addressed, teachers are responsible for ensuring that children can use work and play areas easily and comfortably enough to engage in meaningful activities. Children work best when the temperature is moderate, the air is fresh, and light is adequate. Children tend to be quieter and more socially interactive in less than full-intensity light, but they need the latter for close work. Easy access to water inside and out is also essential for both health and comfort. In addition, young children should have a shaded outdoor play area protected from wind and weather for comfortable activity year round.

Space

Early childhood professionals are responsible for planning the effective use of classroom space. According to national accreditation standards and many state licensing standards, indoor floor space should be at least 35 square feet per child, not counting closets, hallways, and immovable storage units. Outdoor space should be two to three times this number—75 to 105 square feet per child (NAEYC Early Childhood Program Standards and Accreditation Criteria, 2005; Michigan Child Care Licensing Standards, 2005). Greater densities (more children or less space) in the classroom or outdoors are linked to increased aggression, decreased social interaction, and noninvolvement with tasks (Maxwell, 2000). Sometimes facilities that at first glance appear limited can be adapted. For example, in high-ceiling classrooms, a loft holding a listening center on top with a writing center underneath can be used to increase the total space available, making effective use of the vertical space as well as floor space.

The organization of physical space is an effective predictor of program quality because it affects what children can do, determines the ease with which they can carry out their plans, and affects the ways in which they use materials. **Vertical space** defined by walls, the backs of storage units, bulletin boards, and even windows may be used to support children's learning. For example, an interactive word or picture activity could be secured to a window shade mounted on the wall and the shade returned to the rolled-up position when it is not in use.

First, children need **private space** where they can work independently or gain control of their thoughts and feelings. A study carrel, secluded chair, or pile of pillows can meet this need. The coat-storage area, the cubby, and children's school bags are private places where children might store their work and private possessions. Landscaped areas where children can sit near bushes, under trees, or well away from equipment provide private spaces outdoors.

Second, a **small-group space** for two to six children encourages quiet interaction with one another. They are likely to exhibit cooperative and helping behaviors when they are in close personal space (2 feet) and when the task set for the group is noncompetitive. Small-group spaces should vary in size, with secluded spaces for a pair of children as well as for four to six children. Often a small table with the appropriate number of chairs can meet this need. When areas are designed for small groups rather than only for individuals or large groups, behaviors such as wandering, running, fighting over materials, and repeating the same activity many times can be minimized (Kostelnik, Whiren, Soderman, & Gregory, 2009).

Often, the outdoor play equipment determines the configuration of individual and small-group spaces outdoors. Swings may accommodate individuals or two to three children. Usually, climbers accommodate three to five children at a time, depending on the size and the complexity of the climbing structure. Likewise, depending on how it is used, mobile equipment such as tricycles, ladders, and crates may be used by two or more children.

The third kind of space is for a **large group** in which several children listen to stories, sing, engage in games or other movement activities, and share whole-group instruction. Although some common whole-group activities can be carried out while children are seated at desks or tables, having a separate area where children can sit on the floor is preferable. Children can sit closer together, see pictures or demonstrations better, and often feel more like a cohesive group when seated on the floor.

Most outdoor large-group areas are very large, spaced so that children may engage in ball games and other whole-group motor activities. Ideally, a second large outdoor space exists where children can gather comfortably in the shade for demonstrations and discussions.

To structure all three types of space, early childhood professionals must separate them by clear, physical **boundaries**. Storage units, pathways, equipment, low dividers, and even the arrangement of materials on a table can delineate boundaries. As one second-grade teacher indicated, "I painted an old bathtub red, filled it with pillows, and placed it near the window. When a child wishes to be alone, he or she gets a book and sits in the tub. The other children do not bother him or her and neither do I. When ready, the child returns to the ongoing activity." Imaginary boundaries, such as a pretend line between two children sitting side by side at a table, are not effective. Children naturally expect to interact with neighbors. However, they can determine the appropriate number of participants for a specific space by the number of chairs or the amount of floor space within the boundaries. Teachers can also use signs to indicate to children the number of people that an area can accommodate.

Fences, paved surfaces, curbs, sandpits, grass, and other structural features usually establish the boundaries in outdoor areas. Adults may add movable features such as tents, blankets, or orange cones to mark other areas for specific planned events.

Pathways between activity areas allow children to move readily from one activity to another without interfering with the ongoing learning of other children. These pathways must be planned so that the flow of children in the classroom or outdoors is smooth and efficient. Pathways often need to be made wider to accommodate children in wheelchairs or those who use walkers.

Sound

Sound control is an ongoing challenge in programs that encourage independent, cooperative, and learning-center work. A generally noisy environment from which children cannot get relief is not conducive to overall cognitive development, academic achievement, or health (Maxwell, 2000). It is particularly challenging for children with hearing impairments and those with autism. Hard surfaces in the classroom are easy to keep clean but tend to increase noise, and softer surfaces that absorb noise provide a warmer, more resilient surface to touch but are more difficult to maintain. Hard-surface floors are best where there are messy activities or children are likely to track in dirt from outdoors. Carpeted floors are best in areas in which children will be sitting on the floor and playing actively.

With soft, sound-absorbing materials in the classroom, normal noise is diminished. For example, large pillows, instead of chairs, placed on a small carpet can be used in the independent reading area so that children can read aloud without disturbing others nearby. Draperies, carpet, pillows, stuffed animals, and upholstered furniture are all sound absorbent. Another strategy to control sound environmentally is to increase the secluded spaces for one or two children and decrease the number of spaces for six or more children. Use furniture or mobile screens for barriers between activity areas or reduce the floor area of some of the centers.

Equipment and Material Size

Furnishings, tools, and equipment should be appropriate for the size of the children using them. Children experience serious discomfort if their feet do not touch the floor while they are seated

or, conversely, if their knees bump into the table. Outdoor climbers have rungs closer together for 3- to 5-year-olds than for older children. The rate at which preschool children enter into complex play also appears to be related to the size of the space and the child-size structures and equipment in the space (Tegano, 1996). When children have sufficient space to move without interfering with others and experience challenge matched with their size and ability, they engage comfortably with one another and the materials that support play and learning. Alyss is so small that she rarely fits the equipment and facilities provided by the program. Creative accommodations can allow her ease of use and increased self-confidence. These adjustments benefit all of the preschool children.

Mobility

Early childhood professionals are responsible for planning programs that actively involve children and allow them to move from place to place in an orderly manner. Pathways should be wide enough for children to walk on without bumping into

Alyss is able to use the drinking fountain independently with the mobile stairs. The bench facilitates other children who are taller than she is but still too short.

Alyss is able to sit at the table with other children and have her back and feet supported for comfort.

other children or interfering with the work and play of others. Avoid long, empty spaces because they invite running or hurrying. Instead, break up the space by carefully arranging the centers. Some teachers use the center of the room as open space, with learning areas arranged on large tables or clusters of small tables placed so that traffic must move around them.

Attractiveness

An attractive environment is one that appeals to the senses. Texture, color, pattern, design, scent, and sound all contribute to the sense of beauty and place. People shape an environment and are shaped by it (Greenman, 2007). An attractive learning environment is child centered, serene, and exciting. It invites children to engage and provides privacy for reflection. It also reflects the variations of culture and taste, representing the community of children in the room. Ask children in your group what they think would make a space more attractive (Brouette, 2004). Maintain flexibility in changing displays, adding color, incorporating plants, and other strategies that make the room livable.

When adults demonstrate their respect for cleanliness and attractiveness, children are more likely to imitate this desirable behavior. Strive to provide children with a clean and orderly environment free of unpleasant odors. To achieve an orderly environment where children can locate the materials, sit on the floor and look around to gain a keener perspective of the room from the child's viewpoint. Being orderly is not the same as being sterile. Messy activities should occur, animals should be observed, **loose parts** (collections of rocks, leaves, or materials with many pieces), or junk (selected discards such as nuts and bolts, clocks) should be available for exploration and still be in an overall orderly classroom. Avoid clutter in the learning environment both indoors and out.

Encourage children to care for their learning and living environment by putting materials back where they belong and participate in cleaning. This activity is also an opportunity for children to learn classifying, matching, and reading skills if the storage areas are adequately labeled. Keeping working surfaces clean is also a reasonable expectation of children. Before children leave a messy area, encourage them to wipe the surfaces and clean up for the next child's use. Pictographs or written instructions for cleaning and storage also contribute to children's emerging literacy skills because the information is practical, useful, and meaningful to them.

Ultimately, adults must arrange the physical environment to contribute to the ongoing instructional program. Materials, bulletin boards, and pictures should be rotated to reflect various topical themes. Bright touches attract children to the centers where the teacher intends them to become engaged. Both the elements added to attract children and the substance of the learning centers should be changed regularly and reflect the children's changing needs and interests.

Displays may invoke interest, convey information to parents or children, and build a sense of community and pride as children display their work. Good displays make expectations and learning visible, share ideas, help children reflect on their experiences, and learn directly from the environment. Guidelines for an effective display are:

❑ Appropriate vehicle: wall area, display board, cabinet, hanging sign, or computer terminal
❑ Location: at the height and placement most appropriate for audience
❑ Flexibility: ease of displaying materials having two and three dimensions
❑ Safety: types of fasteners and the size and weight of things to be fastened (Greenman, 2007)

Overall, simplicity is key to the entire physical setting. Remove extraneous materials. Each object visible in the room should have a purpose and meaning for the children. When you ask yourself, "Is this contributing to the goal I had in mind?" or "What am I trying to accomplish with this?" you should have a clear, immediate answer. In addition, avoid leaving children's work displayed longer than 1 week; take it down and display other, newer work.

The elements of the physical environment fit together in a comprehensible way and should be designed to make life in that place a rich sensory experience. The effective use of light and children's art displays, plants, art from around the world, and animals adds to the beauty and livability of the

Children have ready access to materials that are stored near where they will use them.

classroom. A classroom that is more homelike and less institutional helps children feel secure and ready to learn. The aesthetic qualities of the classroom provide the children with a code for behavior and for feeling that contributes to their sense of beauty as well (Tarr, 2001; Curtis & Carter, 2003).

Storage

Teachers are responsible for the selection, storage, and display of materials. Objects should be stored near the area where they will be used. Ideally, materials will be in open shelving if children are to have ready access to them, and in closed cupboards or on high shelves if the teacher needs to maintain control of the materials. For example, pencils, paper, scissors, and glue are used daily and should be readily accessible near the tables where they are used. In contrast, finger paint or a microscope might be put away and retrieved as needed. Materials that are small and have many pieces, such as counters, small plastic building blocks, and fabric scraps, should be stored in plastic containers, which hold up well with long-term use. Transparent plastic boxes are a good choice. Mobile storage of the right size and shape is particularly useful for work in centers. Teachers should also consider safety in storage, especially when stacking containers or placing heavy items on high shelves. Alyss may need a small, movable stool to reach materials that other children reach easily. In kindergarten and the primary grades, this will be increasingly important for her.

Easily accessible storage for outdoor learning materials is as essential as for indoor materials. Wheeled toys, tools, containers, sleds, and other materials should be securely stored in a large outdoor shed or a closet opening to the outdoor areas. Children will use the contents more frequently than if they must carry mobile equipment some distance.

Safety, comfort, space, noise control, mobility, attractiveness, and storage are basic elements of the physical environment. Next, we will consider how to combine these elements to create effective learning spaces both indoors and outside.

Arranging the Classroom

Few classrooms are ideal. Consider the organization of the space in the following classrooms: The preschool or kindergarten classroom (Figure 5.1 on page 129) has the advantage of a large adjacent storage area but has numerous corners. When setting up the classroom, the teacher carefully selected the size of the centers located in difficult-to-see spots and the nature of the activities going on in them. The first-grade classroom (Figure 5.2 on page 130) has a more traditional shape and was arranged to accommodate center-based instruction for most of the day. Whole-group instruction occurs in the block area, with the children sitting on the floor. Subject-matter labels are used to denote the activities that are usually located in the various areas of the room, but these designations are not rigid. For example, social studies activities are often located at the center labeled "Spelling," and many science activities are moved to the art table when more space is needed or when more children are at work in the center. A rating scale to assess room arrangement is suggested in Figure 5.3 on page 131 (Dodge, Colker, & Heroman, 2008; Gullo, 1994).

Some states are using a more formal, reliable instrument to assess the quality of the environment in early childhood programs. The Early Childhood Rating Scale-Revised (Hames, Clifford, & Cryer, 1998) helps classroom teachers improve their practices. When teachers understand the criteria, and receive information and support from their administrators, they make substantial improvements in their classroom environments which they maintain over time (Scott-Little, Brown, Hooks, & Marshall, 2008).

Arranging Outdoor Environments

The principles of using the indoor environment to influence development also apply to outdoor environments. The play yard illustrated in Figure 5.4 on page 132 supports several learning centers. Note that many features such as play structures, water sources, hard surfaces, trees, fences, hills, and plantings are fixed.

FIGURE 5.1   Preschool or Kindergarten Classroom

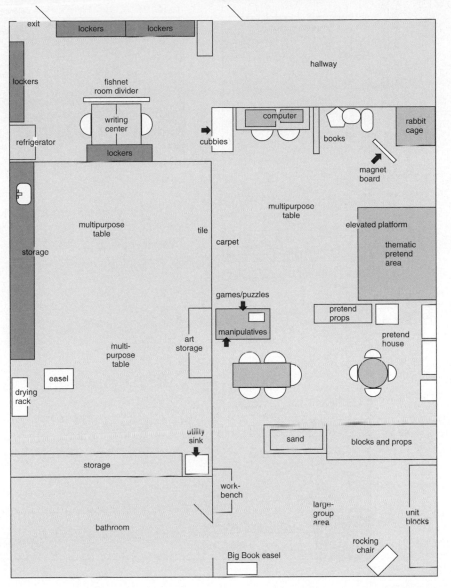

Sand is used under the climbing structure to absorb the force of falls but is also available in the curbed sandbox nearby. The climbing and slide structure is bounded by a hard surface used for wheeled toys. Designed for children younger than 6 years, the structure has short risers, a stair, an arched climbing structure, and a chain climber, leading to various heights of the structure for a variety of challenges. Both a single-person slide and a lower two-person slide provide differences for comfort in high places. A tire-swing structure is adjacent to the climbing apparatus and is large enough for three children. A pretend playhouse at the far end of the yard features a doorway, windows, shelves, and seats. The floor is composed of a force-absorbent material that absorbs heat and light, which makes it free of snow and ice earlier than the turf or sand-covered areas. A picnic table shaded by a large tree is convenient for snacks or table activities. A large shed for storing snow shovels, sand and water toys, wheeled vehicles, water tables, tables, chairs, and other occasionally used equipment is in the corner. Alyss can successfully participate on this playground. If the climbing structure were scaled for 5- to 12-year-olds, much of it would be inaccessible for her.

Play yards that include bushes where children might hide, hills to roll down, grassy lawns to run across, and flowering plants and trees are appealing learning environments. Tiny gardens or clustered plantings, vegetation permitted to grow on fencing, scented herbs and shrubs, and flowers in a playground stimulate young children's senses and curiosity. In one playground a corner

FIGURE 5.2 First-Grade Classroom

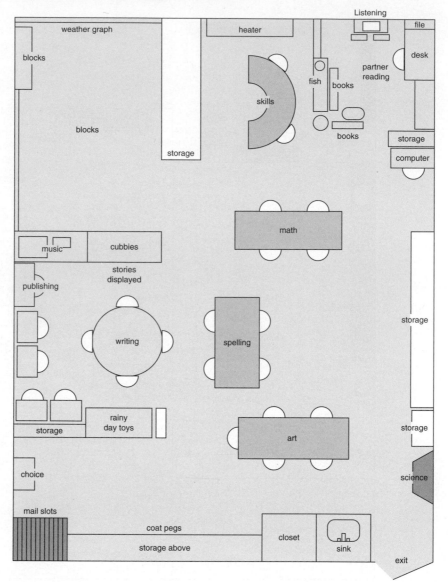

was left alone so that a natural meadow with many different plants and animals thrived there. In another, leaves were left year round to encourage worms which were later studied by the children. A shallow snow saucer left full of water became the home of tadpoles. Children also have a role to play in maintaining the outdoor play–learning environment by watering plants, filling feeders and baths, and picking up paper and other bits of materials that blow into the area (Frost, Talbot, & Monroe, 1990; Starbuck & Olthof, 2008).

Natural playscapes or nature classrooms are on the rise. In these environments, traditional playground equipment is generally absent (or minimally used) and, instead, materials directly from the environment are prominent (see Figure 5.5 on page 133). Hills and gullies are landscaped into the space if they do not occur naturally, providing places to climb, roll, or slide. Flowing water next to soil, sand, and gravel provides children with endless opportunities for exploration as well as the sound of flowing water. These are constructed streams of water that have open access and do not pose the risk of ponds or stagnant water and are often the highlight of such playscapes (Anderson, Corr, Egertson, & Fichter, 2008). Trees providing shade as well as seeds and fruits for birds enhance the landscape as do many plants that are safe and will grow well in the local climate. Plants provide many loose parts such as seed-pods, flowers, fluff, or fruit. Some plants such as pole beans and

FIGURE 5.3   Assess the Physical Arrangement of the Room

To what extent do the following statements describe your classroom?

	Completely	Somewhat	Not Usual
1. Children move from one part of the room to another without interfering with other children.	❑	❑	❑
2. Pathways and boundaries between learning centers are clear.	❑	❑	❑
3. Areas are arranged to encourage active child choice.	❑	❑	❑
4. Storage is labeled and near center so that children can put things away.	❑	❑	❑
5. Shelves are neat and uncluttered.	❑	❑	❑
6. Quiet areas are clustered away from more active, noisy areas.	❑	❑	❑
7. There are places where children may work alone, with a small group, or in a large group.	❑	❑	❑
8. Children and adults can gather comfortably in the large group space.	❑	❑	❑
9. Temporary centers are adjacent to related core centers.	❑	❑	❑
10. Adults see the children all the times.	❑	❑	❑
11. The setting has been checked for safety.	❑	❑	❑
12. Furnishings are child size, clean, and comfortable.	❑	❑	❑
13. Decorations reflect the children's specific backgrounds, experiences, and identities.	❑	❑	❑
14. Differences in ethnicity, ability, culture, and economic conditions are reflected in the books, pictures, and other materials in the classroom.	❑	❑	❑
15. The environment is filled with words, books, and symbols.	❑	❑	❑
16. Children can do things independently in some centers.	❑	❑	❑
17. Children make choices, use materials appropriately and with care, and experience success in most or all centers.	❑	❑	❑
18. There is a convenient place for children to keep personal belongings.	❑	❑	❑
19. Adult areas are separated from child areas.	❑	❑	❑

sunflowers make fine small-group spaces and enclosures; others such as bamboo can be trained into tunnels. Pathways may be of snow, gravel, wooden slabs, or concrete stepping-stones. Many have a stage, which basically is a place that has seating for an audience and a place to perform. The seating may be tree stumps or logs arranged conveniently. A number of these settings have interesting sounds such as wind chimes, hand chimes, or wood drums as well as the natural sounds of birds, wind, and weather. Hideouts may be under a planting of bushes or ornamental grasses, or a lean-to constructed of branches. Most have open areas of grass or meadow filled with local wild plants. Seating is usually benches or slabs of wood at appropriate heights. Often there is a space for deliberate gardening projects (Keeler, 2008). Alyss is able to move with ease in this nature-centered environment; however, the same setting may be more difficult for a child in a wheelchair as the surfaces are not hard and smooth. Nature classrooms have been constructed for elementary schools, preschools, and child-care centers.

Classrooms, playgrounds, and nature classrooms are the larger space components in which learning occurs. Within each of these, professionals must organize materials, plan activities to meet educational goals, supervise the activities, and assess the progress of learners. Learning centers are the vehicle for delivering the curriculum in all of these spaces.

FIGURE 5.4 Playground for Children Under 4 Years of Age

LEARNING CENTERS

Mrs. Lakashul visited a kindergarten group near her home the spring before her child would enter kindergarten. She observed small groups of children busily engaged in a variety of activities. Occasionally one child would leave an area and begin another activity elsewhere. Conversations and the clink of materials could be heard. The teacher stayed with a small group of children for several minutes until she finished showing them how to use the materials and then moved on to another group. Children's writing samples and labeled drawings were displayed on the wall. Children were intensely engaged and obviously enjoying the activities. At the end of the session, Mrs. Lakashul said, "Children love it here, don't they? How do you manage to have so many children so busy at the same time?"

"Oh, children enjoy learning centers. I plan activities for each area, and children accomplish their goals at their own pace," replied Ms. Green.

Learning centers are well-defined interest areas that provide children with a wide range of materials and opportunities to engage in hands-on learning across the curriculum (Stuber, 2007). Each center is carefully constructed to address specific educational goals. Most often children have multiple centers from which to choose at a given time: blocks, creative arts, pretend play, language arts, science, and math are common examples. Because children self-select the activity, the pace, the order and the specific means through which they will approach different learning tasks, learning centers are well suited to their educational needs. Learning centers give children chances to:

❑ Make choices
❑ Move about as needed
❑ Build on previous experience in meaningful ways

FIGURE 5.5   Nature Classroom

Sample Plan: 5,000 square feet

Source: Reprinted with permission from the Arbor Day Foundation and Dimensions Educational Research Foundation (2007). *Learning with Nature Idea Book: Creating Nurturing Outdoor Spaces for Children,* Lincoln, NE: Cuppens, V., Rosenow, N., Wike, J., p. 45.

❏ Progress at their own rates within and among activity areas
❏ Choose activities that fit their particular learning styles and needs at the time
❏ Sustain self-directed activity
❏ Integrate knowledge and skills from one activity to another
❏ Develop concepts and consolidate their learning across the curriculum
❏ Develop skills in working on their own, with peers and with adults

Teachers value learning centers, too, because they make it easier to:

❏ Address children's need for hands-on experiences, mobility and physical activity, social inter-
action, and independence
❏ Accommodate children's varying attention spans and abilities
❏ Build activities around children's individual interests
❏ Move about the room asking probing questions, offering information, and otherwise scaf-
folding children's learning as appropriate
❏ Regularly assess student understanding and skills

Discipline problems, which happen when children are disinterested in an activity or if children's skills are out of sync with whole-group instruction, are minimized when learning centers are included as part of the early childhood day. Children with special needs fit well within a learning-center approach, because coaching and support from the teacher and assistance from one child to another are normal for all children (Genisio & Drecktrah, 2000–2001; Willis, 2009). For all these reasons, national accreditation standards and state licensing requirements in all 50 states require the use of learning centers at the preprimary level, recommending approximately 60 minutes of center-based instruction in half-day programs and two such periods if children attend the program all day. Moreover, many early childhood organizations advocate incorporating learning centers as part of the daily routine for *all* children through age 8 (NAESP, 1998; Stuber, 2007; Copple & Bredekamp, 2009).

CREATING AND USING LEARNING CENTERS

Establishing learning centers is not a guarantee that optimal knowledge and skill building will occur. Children must be taught the skills necessary to effectively use the centers, including the purposes of the centers, ways to exercise self-discipline, and strategies for self-appraisal related to what they are learning. To do this, construct centers with attention to the following six key points.

1. *Organize and implement centers on the basis of your knowledge about the children and their abilities.* For every activity and experience that occurs in a classroom, ask yourself the following questions.
   - ❏ How does this activity center contribute to long-range outcome goals?
   - ❏ What domain-related objectives are met in this activity or experience? What do I hope the children will gain from this?
   - ❏ How does this activity build on most of the children's past knowledge?
   - ❏ Is this the best possible way to present such an idea or concept?
   - ❏ Is this the best possible use of the children's time?
   - ❏ Are the activities, experiences, and materials well matched to the children's developmental levels and interests?
   - ❏ Are the materials and equipment accessible to all the children? Does the activity contribute to meeting the IEP goals of children with special needs?
   - ❏ Does this activity provide an opportunity for children to explore ideas or be creative with the materials?
   - ❏ Does this activity provide learning opportunities for all of the children?
   - ❏ How will I evaluate the effectiveness of this activity or experience?

2. *Keep center activities flexible and adaptable rather than rigid and static.* Although you may have in mind a particular outcome following children's use of materials in a center, you will want to be alert for paths children want to take in their exploration. Children often have good ideas about creative and divergent ways to use available materials. In a well-designed learning center, children can work on domain-related goals established by the teacher while still fulfilling their needs in that or another domain. This flexibility can be accomplished by using basic, open-ended materials stored and available in each area in addition to newly introduced materials.

3. *Provide a diverse array of learning centers daily—and with time—that provide a balance across all developmental domains to achieve a comprehensive curriculum* (Brewer, 2007). In addition, the amount of space needed for a specific center might be altered as children develop. For instance, a language arts center for 3-year-olds might be enlarged and enhanced to provide separate reading, writing, and listening centers for the 5- or 6-year-old.

4. *Take time to introduce children to new activities and materials before children encounter them by themselves.* Some teachers prefer to give children "previews of coming attractions" by letting them know, just before they prepare to leave, what to expect the next day. Other instructors plan an opening or greeting time in their schedules. During this time, they discuss what may be new or unusual, any safety information children need, and any limits on the number of children who can be involved. At this time, they demonstrate the use of particular materials or unfamiliar equipment.

   After children have had opportunities to explore the materials, teachers may want to assign certain tasks to be completed. For example, as part of a thematic unit on clothing, one teacher set up a "shoe shop" center. One of the children's tasks was to weigh one of their shoes with nonstandard weights, record the number on a paper shoe the teacher had provided, and place their work in a shoe box positioned in the area. The teacher demonstrated the activity from start to finish by weighing one of her shoes and having the children count the numbers of weights used. She then recorded the number on one of the paper shoes and placed it in the designated shoe box. The teacher reminded the children that, for this particular activity, they must keep the container of nonstandard weights in the shoe-shop area and limit the use of them that day to the children who were involved in weighing. However, the children were allowed to use the weights to weigh other objects in the shoe-shop area. Besides serving the purpose of knowledge and skill building about use of the materials, such introductions activate children's curiosity and encourage them to visit a particular center.

The focus of a learning center may also be evident to children by the materials that are placed in it. For instance, after children have had experience with rubbings of objects, the teacher may highlight a leaf-rubbing activity by putting all the relevant materials in the middle of the art table. Doing so would draw children's attention to the leaves, crayons, and paper, which would make the activity appear inviting. Yet, children could still have access to other art supplies stored on shelves nearby. Written directions in the form of pictographs, photographs, or words and periodic participation by the teacher are other ways the goals and procedures of an activity could be made clear to children.

5. *Use the area or center space to address different domains over time.* Depending on how teachers structure a learning center and how they set goals, the same materials (e.g., art materials, blocks) could be used to address the cognitive domain one day, the language domain another day, and the social domain yet another. Keep in mind that academic subject areas fit into domains and can be incorporated into any center. For example, reading, writing, viewing, and listening generally occur in all centers though these subjects are also addressed more specifically on a daily basis in specialized centers.

6. *Interact spontaneously with children engaged in center activities.* Enhance, extend, and evaluate learning experiences and developmental outcomes. Hold brief conferences with children about processes and products as children act on the materials in the room. Teachers who choose to be active with the children during this time can also ward off potential difficulties as children work and play together in the chosen context.

EXAMPLES OF CENTERS

The kinds of centers found in any early childhood setting vary dramatically in terms of number, materials and equipment available, and creative ideas generated by both teachers and children. Most of the typical learning centers described in this section may be used either indoors or outdoors if climate and weather permit. The age of the children involved as well as the length of the program day or program year will determine to a large extent the numbers and types of centers to develop.

Key centers are the language arts center; the creative arts and construction center (two- and three-dimensional art or modeling); the science and collections center; the math, manipulative materials, and table games center; a dramatic play area; and a large space for blocks. Frequently, a large, open space has several centers (e.g., blocks; gross-motor activities; music, dance, or games; or group storytelling) set in it during one day, but not at the same time. Some centers may be broken down further into subcenters. For example, a math center may be broken down into a smaller center focusing on classification and set formation and a second center with a focus on shape and symmetry.

Special-interest centers may be set up for shorter periods (1 day to a few weeks), on the basis of the interests of the children and teacher. For example, large-motor-skill equipment such as a climber or a balance beam may be added, particularly when weather limits outdoor use of such equipment. Music, woodworking, and cooking centers, and special collections of one kind or another, are introduced, removed, and then reintroduced periodically. Such centers may require the use of additional adults to monitor and support children's use of materials or space, as might be the case when cooking or tie-dyeing is planned.

All centers share some characteristics regardless of the children's age or the nature of the program. Guidelines for setting up any center are as follows:

❑ Provide displays of materials with labeled plastic containers in open storage on tables or nearby.

❑ Provide a variety of appropriate writing or drawing utensils (pencils, pens, markers, etc.) in every center.

❑ Provide paper of many shapes, sizes, and purposes, such as Post-it note pads, old envelopes, lined paper, small pads, and so on, as appropriate for each center.

❑ Display books, magazines, cookbooks, telephone books, clothing patterns, or other sources of written material prominently in all centers so that children can easily see their purpose. For example, an enlarged floor plan from a housekeeping magazine can stimulate construction in the block area as children read and interpret it.

❑ Provide the tools and materials needed for cleanup, such as sponges in areas where art materials or water is used or brooms and dustpans where play dough or sand is used.

❑ Provide the materials necessary for assessment and recordkeeping for the adult or the children to record children's progress or participation.

❑ Consider the electricity and water sources and the placement of doors, windows, and pathways, as well as potential hazards, throughout the room when placing specific centers in a room.

❑ Introduce new materials and tasks to all the children, and include pictographs, photographs, tape-recorded directions, or other clues so that children can use the center independently. Include directions for the care of materials and for cleanup as appropriate.

❑ Include project-based or theme-related activities in three to four centers each day, and periodically change all centers in a planned way. Every center will need a variation within a 2- to 4-week period, but rarely (if ever) should all centers be changed at once.

❑ Some centers should be self-sustaining, requiring only initial guidance from the teacher. The number of such centers should vary with the children's age and experience.

❑ Include materials necessary to meet the goals of children with IEPs within centers related to those goals. Also include anything needed for a child to adapt to the environment. For instance, Alyss will need a small platform to stand on at easel painting.

❑ Label pictures and materials with English and other languages used by the children, using materials familiar to some children part of the time that are not familiar to others, and select photographs or other artistic works representative of various cultures.

Language Arts Center

The most important rationale for providing language experiences to children through a center-based approach is that doing so supports children's emerging language skills and abilities. This special part of the classroom becomes an arena for children's active learning of language through quality, age-appropriate experiences in listening, reading, writing, drawing, and reenacting stories. In such settings, children can collaborate and compare their products, both with one another and against the rich and diverse literature sources.

Some teachers interact personally with each child daily in this center through the use of brief "mailbox" messages. Children eagerly look forward to checking each day to see what special messages the teacher has left and frequently respond by writing a message to the teacher. At first, the message may be only a word or the child's name and a picture. Children also begin to write notes to one another and answer messages received. Mailbox "messaging" in the language arts center is a highly motivating activity; children enjoy the surprise element of finding and leaving messages and are writing for real purposes (Soderman, Gregory, & McCarty, 2006). Having a real purpose is a powerful factor in children's wanting to develop literacy skills.

Story reenactment may be a part of the language arts center for younger children, but it is frequently an independent center for children in kindergarten and the primary grades. A well-read book and props related to the story that define the characters and the action are essential for the children to enact the story successfully. Sometimes stories are retold with puppets, flannel boards, or other similar strategies.

Listening centers with story tapes and books may be either a periodic addition for younger children or a regular part of the kindergarten and primary classrooms. Overall, the five general guidelines for organizing a language arts center are as follows:

1. Provide materials for all areas of language development: listening, speaking, reading, writing, and viewing.
2. Display the front covers of books rather than the spines.
3. Make a sheet-covered mattress or large pillows available as a comfortable spot for book reading and viewing.
4. Display the alphabet and written messages at the children's eye level when they are seated in the area.
5. Provide books that remain in the area so that children may reread them.

Creative Arts and Construction Center

Young children are naturally drawn to creative arts and construction materials with which they can produce two- and three-dimensional products representing their perceptions, feelings, and ideas. You can often hear children expressing these thoughts aloud as they tactically manipulate a variety of textures, patterns, shapes, and products in the creative arts and construction center. Cows can be any color; the sky is something over their heads, not coming down in a distance to meet a horizon; adults tower over children; and suns are reserved only for happy, warm pictures, not for every picture. In construction activity, children develop increasingly sophisticated skills in manipulating materials, arranging and rearranging them to represent aspects of their world. The teacher's role is (a) to demonstrate the skills that children need to use the materials, (b) to stimulate thinking, and (c) to encourage children's explorations (see chapter 9). Instructors should provide explicit valuing and reinforcement of children's personal expression and private interpretations. Five guidelines for organizing the space and materials follow:

1. Arrange storage units and furnishings near a water source; ensure that traffic does not flow through the center. A corner is desirable.
2. Provide a rack or a table on which wet products may dry.
3. Provide a space in which children's work may be displayed and a system by which work is sent home regularly.
4. Provide materials for maintaining the area, such as sponges, paper towels, and paint smocks to cover clothing.
5. Arrange easels side by side or provide materials at a large table so that children may work alone or together.

Science and Collections Center

Children who are engaged in science discovery observe and manipulate a variety of constructed and natural objects in ways that help them to recognize similarities, differences, and relations among the objects and phenomena. They sniff, look at, listen to, feel, pinch, and, if possible, taste a variety of materials to develop and extend their ability to make careful and accurate observations.

Encouraging children's investigation of natural and constructed phenomena in their world is the primary focus of the science and collections center. Teachers guide children toward an understanding of scientific processes as they have children scan, explore, attend, observe, sort, classify, vary conditions, compare, predict, describe, label, and evaluate outcomes.

To prepare the science and collections center adequately, teachers must become efficient in gathering, taking inventory of, and replacing science resources; protecting children's safety; organizing interesting indoor and outdoor experiences; and arranging the environment. Teachers also need to be alert to the quality of the science experiences they are providing and ensure that such experiences contribute to conceptual growth rather than foster "magical" thinking. Effective science and collections centers always have something active for the child to do, not just objects or media to view.

Although young scientists benefit most from exploring and working with real materials, many good electronic teaching aids are now available and can be stocked near a video or compact disc player for the children's independent use. Exciting full-color, realistic photographs can be selectively displayed in the center. Teachers who want to attract children to a science center will work diligently at setting up attractive, attention-getting displays, using novelty, humor, simplicity, and suspense to draw children (Carin, Bass, & Contant, 2005). The following three guidelines indicate how to set up a science and collections center.

1. Locate the science center according to the nature of the science content. Studies of water volume and pressure require a water source. Work with a prism or shadows require a good light source. Collections may be placed anywhere.
2. Demonstrate the use, care, and storage of the tools.
3. Provide cameras, writing or drawing paper, and pencils for recording observations, and a variety of reference materials with pictures and drawings.

Math and Manipulative Materials Center

Children need a lot of hands-on experience with diverse materials designed to challenge their abilities to perceive similarity and difference in many dimensions. The activities and gaming experiences children encounter in the math and manipulative materials center guide them toward an increasingly complex organization of motor behavior, perceptual development, and mathematical concepts with appropriate language and symbols.

The teacher's role is to deliberately select materials and to structure sequential experiences that enable children to construct concepts and to forgo less mature intuitive thinking. Untimely abstract symbolization interferes with children's understanding. No matter how carefully adults design or simplify the presentation of abstract symbols to young children, they inevitably understand only what they can concretely discern from direct sensory experience. The numeral III or 3 does not have meaning in and of itself until the child has counted three objects several times and then associated the numeral with the quantity of three. The most viable arena in which to give children time for such exploration and application is in a center that highlights activity revolving around patterning, sorting, classifying, varying, comparing, graphing, and connecting quantities and symbols. The objectives and activities outlined in the mathematics section of chapter 11 can be carried out most successfully through organized center activity. In addition, this center may increase fine-motor skills, problem-solving abilities, or memory skills. To organize this center, refer to the following four guidelines.

1. Provide ample materials of varying difficulty levels on the shelves, well spaced for younger children. Cluster similar toys. Materials for all aspects of mathematics and quantitative thinking should be available.
2. Provide a balance of open-ended materials (pegs, Legos, sewing cards), self-correcting materials (wooden cylinders, puzzles, nesting boxes), collectibles (bottle caps, buttons, seashells, baby-food-jar tops), and games (lotto, concentration, and cards).
3. Rotate items from the storage area to the display area regularly. Intentionally select some materials that challenge children's thinking as well as more familiar tasks.
4. To keep interest high, rotate some materials between mornings and afternoons for children in full-day programs.

Blocks Center

Many skills and abilities are fostered in the blocks center because this relatively open-ended material is readily adapted to all developmental domains. For example, fine-motor and gross-motor coordination develop from children's bending, lifting, stacking, balancing, pushing, pulling, and reaching. In addition, increased understanding of directionality; manual dexterity; eye–hand coordination; the ability to configure; problem-solving skills; socialization; and conceptualization of patterns, symmetry, and balance are gained. When appropriate literacy materials are included in the setting, the block center may also provide reading and writing experiences (Schickedanz, 2008). Photographs and sketches of block structures allow the children's constructions to be saved and are an excellent starting point for either taking dictation about the children's work or their writing about their building (Neuman & Roskos, 2007).

Unit blocks and large hollow blocks are critical to an effective block center. They may be supplemented with theme-related materials such as trucks and trains or with other dramatic play props such as hats or hoses. Children frequently make signs to communicate the meaning of their structures. A more comprehensive discussion of using blocks is provided by Wellhousen and Kieff (2001). Seven suggestions for organizing the block center are given next.

1. Arrange storage units around a large space that may be used at other times for whole-group instruction, enclosing three sides of the area to diminish the traffic flow.
2. Locate the area in the noisy part of the room on a firm area rug or a carpet.
3. Label the storage areas with silhouettes of the blocks that should go on each shelf, and provide bins for storing other props that are changed regularly to create interest and stimulate desired play.
4. Establish rules for treating the blocks with care, and encourage safety. Children should take only the blocks they plan to use and construct at least 1 foot from the storage shelves to allow others access. The blocks should remain clean and unmarked.
5. For older children, provide materials for making signs and use floor tape to mark areas for individual play.
6. Provide a variety of other materials for children to use in their constructions, such as sheets, cotton, bottle caps, vehicles, and animal and human figures, appropriately stored on nearby shelving.
7. If the area is also used for large-group instruction, attach fabric (use Velcro fasteners) over the blocks displayed on shelves. Doing so allows the area to be closed and creates a visual boundary, which enables children to focus on the activities in whole-group experiences.

Pretend-Play Center

In the pretend-play center, children interact with one another to reenact their life experiences and play any number of imagined roles. They can pretend to be an authority figure (doctor, teacher, big brother, police officer, mother, or father), someone who has a dangerous or risky profession (soldier, boxer, or race car driver), or even someone who does bad things (robber or monster). They can experiment with cause and effect with only pretend consequences. They integrate and extend their understanding about what happens in particular settings (pizza place, beauty shop, or post office) and build varying perspectives about social, family, and gender roles. In addition to these benefits, children gain self-expression; vocabulary development; a sense of belonging and cooperating; and various modes of social exchanges that require the development of physical, logical, and social knowledge.

The ages and interests of children in the group are important considerations when you are promoting certain activities and experiences in the pretend-play center. For example, younger children may have a need to use the center for housekeeping. They will want relevant props such as dolls, doll furniture, and dress-up clothes. Older children will also enjoy using housekeeping materials occasionally. However, they may be more interested in using the center when it is equipped to simulate other contexts they are learning about in their ever-widening world: stores, space command center, television station, auto repair clinic, restaurant, formal school setting, post office, or hospital. Such equipment is especially necessary for encouraging boys to use the center. Older and younger children may use the same props but enact portrayals in different ways. As children mature, their play may become more realistic. Instead of merely playing at pizza making, they will want to make the real thing and "sell" it to classmates who come in, sit down, order, eat, and pay before leaving.

If space and other resources are available, two pretend-play centers are desirable. The interaction between a theme-related center and a housekeeping center often brings together boys and girls who do not usually choose to work or play together. Opportunities for being creative, interacting socially, and understanding complex relationships (such as that between work and family) are often fostered.

Older primary-aged children often use pretend-play props to stage plays, and they spend much time and energy planning and producing these events. The following six suggestions will assist you in setting up a pretend-play center.

1. Enclose the center with furnishings so that children may easily determine when they are in or out of the center. Avoid lining up the equipment against a wall. A wall may be one boundary, and the equipment may be placed to form a corner or an opposite wall. Placement near the block center often encourages extensions of the play.

2. Add new props and remove others once or twice a week to expand understandings and maintain interest. Younger children may need the same setup for a longer time than will older children.

3. Adjust the pretend-play center to coordinate with thematic units and projects as necessary.

4. Store prop boxes for theme-related pretend play in a closet or on a high shelf. Avoid clutter in the pretend-play center.

5. Encourage primary-age children to bring items to school to use to construct appropriate pretend-play environments for themselves.

6. Include books and material that are relevant to the project or theme that is typically found in the setting, such as a shopping list pad in a housekeeping center or a menu in a restaurant center.

Large-Group Center

Perhaps the large-group center is the space that most develops a spirit of unity within the classroom. In this center, children come together with the teacher as a group for a number of purposes: singing, listening to a story, discussing what will occur or what has happened during the day, writing a group letter to someone, participating in a choral reading or a musical activity, attending to entertainment or information from visitors, or engaging in whole-group games or demonstrations. Thus, lots of enjoyable, safe experiences occur in this center. To develop a space for whole-group instruction, use the following four suggestions.

1. Provide sufficient space to seat children and adults comfortably. Such seating is usually on the floor, so a rug or a carpet is desirable.

2. Close open cupboards or cover other materials to diminish distractions.

3. For young children, create seating spots with floor tape to designate individual places in the group.

4. Arrange a focal point where the teacher and specialized materials are located. Big Books, music players or instruments, and easels for experience stories are typical materials. Bulletin boards with songs and poetry posted on them are also helpful in this center.

Sand and Water Centers

Sand and water have been used for many years in early childhood programs because these materials are so versatile. Children have complete control of the materials, and when accessories are carefully selected, children learn about the flow of fluids, volume, measurement, comparison, observation, and evaluation. Children develop eye–hand coordination during pouring, scrubbing, grasping, and squeezing activities and strengthen small muscles when they are digging, ladling, carrying, and controlling the materials. Usually, children share the area, engaging in conversation and cooperatively using materials. The process is soothing and relaxing as well. This center is often an area where children with special needs prosper because most of them are eager to participate and are successful in doing so. Ideal for children aged 3 to 5 years for exploratory and sensory experiences, the sand and water centers are exceptionally useful for teaching principles of numeric operations when standard measures are used, and concepts such as conservation of volume when containers of various shapes but the same volume are provided. In addition, children's social and language skills may be promoted and other concepts supported when sand and water centers are properly facilitated (Crosser, 1994). Other theme related concepts may also be learned. For example, when the topic is dinosaurs, children learn about paleontologists' role in digging the bones out of the earth by digging up (cleaned and prepared) bones in the sand center. Teachers facilitate learning by preparing the environment, offering information, and gently probing children's thinking about the topic. Conversely, teachers facilitate children's understanding when they listen, comment, and inquire about topics related to activities generated by the children, such as where rivers would flow and where streets would be needed in a sandbox city. Often sand and water centers are provided both indoors and outdoors. The following four guidelines indicate how to set up these centers.

1. Place a covered sand or water table near the source of water and on hard-surface flooring. If a hard surface is not available, place the table on a large, heavy plastic sheet in a carpeted room. Large pans can be used and hung on the walls when not in use if covered tables are not available.

These children are engrossed in caring for worms in the indoor nature center.

2. Provide a covered 5- to 10-gallon plastic pail for storing the sand when water is in the table.
3. If space and resources allow, offer both a sand table and a water table.
4. Rotate accessories used with sand and water regularly in accordance with program goals.

Nature Study Center

Nature study can occur indoors as well as out. Generally, this is a long-term center where children can observe and participate in the care of plants and animals. Some animals that do well indoors are fish, small reptiles, rodents such as hamsters or rats, as well as the occasional visitors to the classroom such as cats and dogs. Children can participate in feeding and watering many of these creatures. Obviously children's health and safety must be a priority in the selection of classroom visitors. Plants indoors contribute to the aesthetics as well as the air quality of the room. Grow lights allow for herbs and flowers to grow easily inside, though windows work very well. In this center, the importance of the full life cycle and the ongoing needs of living things are of great importance.

Plants and small animals such as insects, reptiles, birds, and mice may live in an undisturbed section of the playground so that the natural wild flora and fauna may grow. Not much land is required to provide a place where children might discover worms, insects, and butterflies. The natural environment fascinates children, and much is to be learned from it (National Arbor Day Foundation, 2007). Many cognitive and aesthetic activities may be developed for use in this naturalized setting. In addition, children should develop a sense of respect and responsibility for the natural environment, which also contributes to their quality of life over their lifetime (Woyke, 2004; Keeler, 2008). The Cooperative Extension Service in each region of the United States has written materials related to naturalized gardens and can identify poisonous plants. The eight guidelines for developing this type of center are very general.

1. Place the indoor nature center near natural light and electricity and, if possible, near water.
2. Keep animal food and bedding materials near the center. Cleaning supplies and other chemicals should be stored well away from children.
3. Provide materials to record change over time such as drawing materials or a digital camera.
4. Select an outdoor area away from traffic. Such areas are usually in the back of the schoolyard or lot.
5. If the area is covered with gravel or hard-packed or otherwise inhospitable soil, cultivate the earth and add compost. Worms, dry leaves, and other vegetable materials may also be added to the area.
6. If the area is large enough, transplant shrubs and other plants native to the region that attract butterflies and other insects.
7. Hang and maintain bird feeders.
8. Wait. With time, this area will become an interesting place for children to explore and participate in guided-learning experiences related to the natural environment.

IMPLEMENTING LEARNING CENTERS

Parents, teachers, and administrators may have the following questions about classrooms that devote large segments of time to center activity.

"How can you tell what they're learning?"
"How do you know what children are participating in when they're all over the room?"
"What if a child never visits the language arts center and spends all her time playing with blocks?"
"There are so many materials needed. Where can I get them all?"
"I'm uncomfortable not having any structured time. Do I have to use centers all day long?"

Getting Started

Construction of learning centers depends on (a) the program philosophy; (b) resources such as the number of staff, the materials, and the space available; and (c) any constraints such as a program's established curricular and evaluation requirements. Preplanning involves deciding on the room arrangement, the organization of materials, the number of centers to be used, the amount of time to be allotted to center participation, and the way to introduce the process to children. Early childhood educators beginning to use centers should set up the number and kinds of centers they think they can manage, choosing and maintaining those that need the least direction and contact from the teacher, using familiar materials, and having a clear purpose. Once begun, centers can be changed or elaborated on, or new centers can be developed. Depending on the children's age, they require 2 to 4 weeks to learn the routines and classroom expectations. Once children have been taught appropriate interaction strategies, centers are fun, safe, and stimulating. Later, adults can add to or expand established centers to be more responsive to the children's interests and needs and an expanded curricular framework.

Structuring Self-Sustaining Centers

Although the presence of aides and volunteers in an early childhood classroom can enhance learning-center activity, additional adult support is not always possible, particularly in the primary grades. Many classroom teachers find themselves the only adult overseeing everything that goes on in the classroom. When this is the case, teachers must become skillful at setting up centers that are self-sustaining. The following five guidelines are for enhancing learning-center activity that requires initial guidance only or that allows completely independent action on the part of the children.

1. *Introduce the activity, explaining its purpose and demonstrating proper use of the materials.* Give children the opportunity to ask questions. Tell children where and for how long materials will be available and give necessary reminders about using them cooperatively with others, such as keeping resources only in the learning center so that others can find them.
2. *Introduce new centers and more complex activities only after general center activity has begun.* Work closely with an initial, smaller group of children who can then assist other children who subsequently want to participate. Digital pictures of children going through each step in an activity can be taken, with sequential steps numbered and labeled. Doing so contributes not only to children's autonomy in the classroom but also to their understanding of the sequential nature of activities.
3. *Use a variety of direction-giving strategies,* such as pictographs (Figure 5.6) for very young children and written instructions or oral instructions on the tape recorder for older children.

Some centers should be self-sustaining, requiring only initial guidance from the teacher.

4. *Provide center activities that support the need to practice skills previously taught.* Such practice is particularly useful for youngsters who have missed school or for those who need more repetition to learn new skills.
5. *Structure activities in which children can complete a project independently.* One teacher had planned to make fruit salad with her preschoolers and considered eliminating the activity after she learned that a parent volunteer was ill and would not be able to help. Instead, she altered her original plans slightly. She brought in only soft fruit, put it all in the water table, and provided plastic knives. She put footprints on the floor around the sides of the water table to indicate how many children were allowed to participate at any given time and explained these guidelines to the children in large group before learning-center activities were made available. Thus, she was able to move ahead with the activity with only periodic guidance required on her part.

FIGURE 5.6   Painting-at-the-Easel Pictograph

Source: Drawing by Barbara Rohde. Used with permission.

Deciding How Many Centers to Make Available

The number of centers to operate at any particular time will depend on physical space and the teacher's desire to limit or expand learning options for children. In general, at least 1.5 center activity "slots" should be made available per child; for example, 20 children would require about 30 activity spaces. When there are four chairs at a table and enough materials for four children to work at a time, that activity has four slots. Each puzzle provides one slot unless it is large; then two or three children may work on it at the same time. Blocks usually provide four slots for younger children and six slots for older youngsters if space is available. Teachers frequently use pictographs or numerals to indicate the number of children who can successfully be accommodated at once in a learning center.

Monitoring Children's Use of Centers

In most early childhood programs certain learning centers are available to children every day (e.g., blocks, pretend play, science center), others are offered a little less frequently (e.g., sand/water, wood working). Teachers develop new centers and revise current ones based on their observations of children in center activities and their assessment of how well children are progressing in relation to the educational goals they have established.

Some teachers treat center-based activity times as wholly child-initiated. Children may move from one activity to another at will. Other teachers designate some "have to" centers that children are expected to complete within the day or week (see Table 5.2). Once the required center activities are finished, children may move into other centers of their own choosing.

Adults supervise centers by moving about the room, checking in with children and offering instruction as appropriate. In team teaching situations, one or more adults may be stationed in a particular center or group of centers, carrying out given lessons for some or all of the session. In such

TABLE 5.2 "Have-To" Centers

Painting	Listening	Computer	Reading	Games	Math	Journals	Cooperative Project
Tara	Megan	David	Leroy	Anne	Jerry	Carol	Alyss
Kung Sook	Tom N.	Abdul	Leslie	Sam	Ian	Cal	Sarah
Viola	Mark	Tom W.	Mara	Rashid	Tara	Leroy	Ian
	Barry	Sarah	Cal	Carol	Alyss	Sam	Kung Sook
	Jerry	Alyss	Anne	Tom N.	Abdul	Leslie	David
	Kung Sook		Megan	Viola	Rashid	Mara	
			Mark			Sarah	

circumstances, another adult serves as the "center manager," moving from center to center as needed. In each case, both teachers and children interact with and learn from one another. This learning involves a constant exchange of thoughts and ideas. Teachers observe, listen, instruct, guide, support, and encourage their students. Likewise, children ask questions, suggest alternatives, express interests, and develop plans (Kostelnik & Grady, 2009). In addition, children reflect on their experiences through conversations with adults and peers. They may also keep track of their involvement in learning centers more formally, using a simple checklist or chart such as those depicted in Figure 5.7 and Figure 5.8.

Evaluating Children's Skill Development During Center Time

To check on children's development of basic skills, some teachers select small groups of children with whom to work on specific tasks during learning center time. For example, one teacher noticed that four children were having difficulty leaving spaces between words in their journal writing. During center activity, she asked the four of them to come together to discuss the need for a strategy to help them remember and asked them what could be done. It was interesting that the children offered different solutions. One child suggested putting periods between each word to indicate a space. Another thought that hyphens would be helpful until she remembered simply to leave a space. The important point is that the children were involved in solving the problem rather than relying on the teacher to do so or being told the "correct" way to improve their writing. Before long, the four children began leaving spaces between their words, and the temporary aids they had devised—periods and hyphens—soon disappeared.

Similarly, a teacher of a group of 3- and 4-year-olds noted that a few of the children were having great difficulty using scissors. She invited them to a table on which strips of construction paper and quality scissors were lying and showed them how to cut. By observing each child carefully, she could assist the child with the way he or she held the paper and scissors as needed for the child to acquire the skill.

Clearly activities may be designed so that children demonstrate target skills and where the teacher records individual performance. This is more easily done when children are engaged in a variety of centers and the adult can focus on a few in a "have-to" center (Table 5.2). Additional strategies for assessing children's learning, which could be implemented during learning center time, are discussed in chapter 7.

ADJUSTING THE PHYSICAL ENVIRONMENT

When the physical environment is managed so that children are receiving clear cues as to their expected behavior with materials or in a specific place, the teacher is providing an indirect approach to guidance (Hearron & Hildebrand, 2009). The goals of this strategy are to do the following:

❏ Stimulate learning possibilities
❏ Protect children
❏ Protect equipment
❏ Maintain a peaceful learning environment (Crosser, 1992, p. 27)

FIGURE 5.7   Sample Activity Report

Source: From Donna Howe, Child Development Laboratories, Department of Family and Child Ecology, College of Human Ecology, Michigan State University. Adapted with permission.

Children respond in predictable ways to environmental changes. There are three fundamental ways of changing the environment: The teacher may (1) add something to or (2) remove something from the environment or (3) alter something to make it safer and easier to use correctly.

Adding to the Environment

To improve children's abilities to maintain a clean, orderly, and peaceful classroom, communicate where materials are to be stored or used by:

❑ Putting a colored cube in a plastic bag outside the bin where the inch cubes are stored
❑ Adding drawings for children 3 to 5 years old and labels to shelves for the 6- to 8-year-olds
❑ Adding a sorting tray or a muffin tin to a classification tasks
❑ Providing a hula hoop for a youngster trying to count out 10 sets of seven different objects
❑ Giving children inexpensive meat trays or paper plates to place colored cubes on while they are constructing a pattern without inadvertently interfering with someone else's activity.
❑ Adding placemats to the play-doh activity to define the workspace
❑ Adding signs to indicate the number of children in a center and discuss what that means to limit congestion
❑ Adding the props necessary to pretend play or creative dramatics to help children enact their ideas

FIGURE 5.8 Sample Evaluation Form

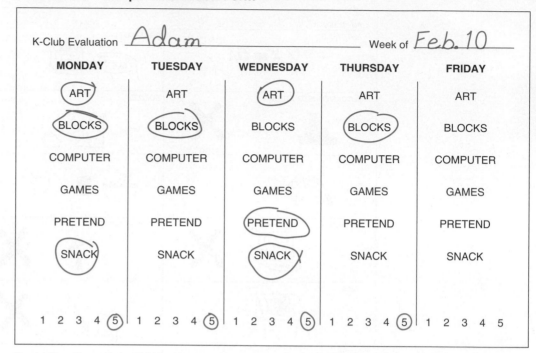

Source: From Donna Howe, Child Development Laboratories, Department of Family and Child Ecology, College of Human Ecology, Michigan State University. Adapted with permission.

❏ Adding stools or other tools that children with special needs require to have access to learning centers. Alyss may need lowered hooks or stools so that she has access to materials.

❏ Adding materials so that all children have something to do outdoors. Because Alyss cannot reach the pedals of a tricycle, a different wheeled vehicle that was propelled by the arms was added as a choice for all children in her program.

Adding reference books and writing materials to various learning centers in the room supports literacy goals. For example, one teacher placed a telephone book in the housekeeping pretend-play area and a children's encyclopedia with the section on hamsters marked and displayed near the hamster cage. Children are basically curious and will use these reference materials, given appropriate support and instruction. One group of first-grade youngsters learned the principle of alphabetical order when a homemade telephone listing of children in the program, paper, and pencils were placed as props in a housekeeping center. They required only occasional assistance in locating desired numbers of friends.

Removing Something from the Environment

Occasionally, simply taking away chairs from an area is sufficient to let children know that fewer than the usual number of children may work in that center at the same time. In a Head Start classroom, the teacher removed 10 pairs of scissors from the basket because she was unable to assist more than six inexperienced children at once. When several youngsters persistently became unruly as they drove their large-wheeled trucks through a kindergarten classroom, the teacher temporarily placed the trucks in storage at the end of the day. In a suburban school, a first-grade teacher removed toys children had brought from home that distracted them from their work. When materials distract children from engaging in profitable experiences, when they pose hazards, or when teachers need to streamline centers to provide behavioral cues, the teachers should remove or reduce materials so that appropriate behavior is most likely to occur. In addition, remove any obstacles to mobility for youngsters who do not see well or who use wheelchairs.

Obviously, materials are added and removed regularly to support the changing learning centers and children's interests. Every center needs to be changed, even in small ways to maintain children's interest and involvement on a regular basis.

Altering the Environment

Indirect child guidance through managing the physical environment sometimes requires ingenuity. A first-grade teacher substituted an electric pencil sharpener for the traditional variety so that children would not grind their pencils to nubs. A kindergarten teacher provided a simple wooden bootjack so that children would no longer use the edge of their lockers to pull off their boots. A teacher of 4-year-olds used a baby cupboard safety device to ensure that the cabinet where plant fertilizers were kept remained closed. Sometimes these adjustments are even simpler: adding detergent to drippy paint to thicken it and make it easier to wash out, placing floor tape on the floor to designate an area in which primary-age children may build with blocks, adding flour to the play-doh that second graders made with incorrect amounts of ingredients.

Adjustments to the environment may be necessary to accommodate the special needs of some children. Teachers can also assist typically developing children to become aware of potential hazards to their peers with special needs and to make the appropriate accommodations.

Teachers must observe their students carefully and adjust the physical environment first if children are failing to engage in productive activities as desired. Play and work can be facilitated in this way without complete reliance on admonitions and oral directions, which can be wearing on children and adults alike.

Center-based learning occurs best in a well-ordered environment in which ample storage is available for each core center; in which children learn to put away materials and use them safely and appropriately; and that is clean, pleasant, and designed for action. All this is feasible by providing the appropriate furnishings, equipment, and materials and by teaching children how to use and care for them.

SELECTING MATERIALS FOR EACH CURRICULAR DOMAIN

Because hands-on learning is a fundamental premise of developmentally appropriate practice, variety in materials is necessary to provide a balanced program. Materials that support literacy, numeric understanding, science, art, music, and other centers last much longer than the workbooks often promoted by publishers. With continuous use, all materials should be added to or replaced as they become lost or broken. In addition, nearly all classrooms have insufficient storage space built in for these materials, so mobile storage; additional shelving high in the room for long-term storage; and plastic containers, bins, or baskets to contain multipiece manipulative items should be obtained early in the acquisition plan.

Programs for 3- to 5-year-olds often begin with appropriate equipment but must include plans for replacement and expansion of choices. Child-care centers have the particularly challenging task of providing interesting materials for the morning and different but appropriate materials for the late afternoon so that children's interest is maintained while their learning progresses. Fortunately, many excellent alternatives are available that address similar competencies. For example, the seriation task of stacking containers can be met with stacking circular cups, hexagon cups, octagon cups, kitty in the keg, square boxes, and Russian nesting dolls. For the preschool child, the perceptually new material is viewed as novel even though the task of ordering remains the same. Children approach and use such playthings with interest and enjoyment.

The NAEYC (www.naeyc.org) and the ACEI (www.acei.org) have publications with detailed lists of materials appropriate for young children. In addition, Clayton and Forton (2001) have an excellent book detailing materials for centers for K–6 classrooms.

GENERAL GUIDELINES FOR THE SELECTION AND USE OF MATERIALS

Teachers must provide materials that are developmentally appropriate and that support hands-on experiences. For example, children learn about plants by growing them. They learn about culture by sharing family traditions within the class. They learn about geography by using a map to find something in the classroom. They learn about reading and writing by participating in functional written communications. In chapters 1, 3, and 4, you reviewed principles of development and how to apply these concepts to adult-planned activities. When a book such as this one is directed to

TABLE 5.3 Examples of Materials Varying from Concrete to Abstract

Concrete	Increasingly Abstract	Abstract
Bulb planted in soil for observation	Photographs of bulb growth	Discussion or graph of plant growth
Parquetry blocks and corresponding colored pattern cards outlining each	Parquetry blocks and black-and-white pattern cards outlining each shape	Parquetry blocks and pattern cards outlining a general shape rather than individual shapes
Unit blocks	Graph paper	Numerals
Field trip	Film or pictures	Letters or words
Cooking activity	Pretend-play kitchen	Picture-book recipe

programs serving a wide range of ages—3 to 8 years—the specific selections are important at each age level. For example, simple balance scales are adequate for 4-year-olds to understand the concepts *heavy* and *light*, but a more accurate scale with weights or a calibrated spring scale is more appropriate for 7- or 8-year-olds who must learn to add and subtract accurately by using it. Both scales provide direct experience with the concepts of *mass, volume,* and *weight.* Regardless of the children's age, teachers have common goals: to facilitate curricular learning, to stimulate interest and curiosity, and to facilitate appropriate social behavior. So that you can implement these goals, some general guides have been developed for your use.

Provide for Firsthand Experiences with Real Things

Children vary greatly in their abilities to handle abstract concepts. Begin instruction by using concrete materials, then use increasingly abstract materials to encourage children to reconstruct their experiences. The presentation in Table 5.3 illustrates concrete materials, bridging materials, and more abstract materials that can be used for this purpose. Children age 3 to 6 years and younger need mostly concrete materials, whereas 6 to 8-year-olds may use a mixture of concrete and a few more abstract materials as a basis for learning. All children, regardless of age, profit from hands-on learning.

Provide Complete, Safe, and Usable Materials

Puzzles with missing pieces, dull scissors, unstable climbing equipment, and broken tools or equipment should be removed, repaired, or replaced. Materials that do not work do not contribute to the learning experience but instead engender frustration and distress. For instance, commercial or homemade learning-center props should be sturdy so that many children can profit from using them. Laminating the pieces to a matching game that are constructed of oak tag or poster board rather than construction paper, which tears easily, is initially more expensive, but the material lasts throughout the activity and may be used often in subsequent years. Additionally, materials must be usable for individual children. For example, the scissors in the first- and second-grade classrooms are too large for Alyss because her hands are tiny in comparison to typically developing children. She will need the smallest size through most of elementary school.

Provide Literacy-Related Materials in All Centers

Children of all ages will use functional literacy materials consistently if they are available: cookbooks and paper to make grocery lists for the housekeeping center, drawing paper and pens to record plant growth, and markers and music-score paper when children are trying out instruments. Books may go anywhere. Children try to use books and other written materials regardless of age. Asking questions and seeking information, children create teachable moments that are ideal for instruction.

Provide Materials Representing National and Local Diversity

Music, art, games, play materials, and photos are available that do the following:

- ❑ Depict men and women in a variety of work roles as well as in the traditional roles
- ❑ Illustrate families of various compositions and ages
- ❑ Show workers in agriculture, business, education, health, and service occupations
- ❑ Portray all races, abilities, and religions of the world respectfully
- ❑ Represent the variety of lifestyles and family incomes honorably
- ❑ Display images and objects that allow all children to feel welcome in the classroom community

When positive images and experiences are included in the day-to-day classroom practices, teachers can help enrich children's understandings of diverse populations (Elgas, Prendeville, Moomaw, & Kretschmer, 2002). Materials should represent people in the classroom, local community, and the country in general.

Demonstrate Proper Use of Materials and Equipment

A simple, direct demonstration of materials and equipment at the time of first use increases the probability of safety and materials conservation. Avoid assuming that children know how to use materials properly. Because the children who come into the learning environment are diverse in their experiences and family resources, such assumptions are not practical. For example, the 5-year-old who may know how to use cellophane tape may not understand the use and function of paste and may have never seen glue. Rarely do young children know how to conserve these products. In addition, the appropriate use of a material such as blocks changes as children learn and mature. Three-year-olds need much space because they generate horizontal structures such as roads or sprawling buildings that are simple enclosures. Seven-year-olds may build successfully in smaller spaces that are about 3 feet square because their constructions are often vertical. Children of all ages need stimulation for their ideas and direction in appropriate behavior while using the center independently or with other children.

Purchase Sturdy, High-Quality Equipment and Materials

A set of hardwood blocks is expensive as an initial purchase, but because they are almost indestructible, they can be used for decades. Housekeeping furnishings made of hardwood and carefully crafted last more than a decade, in contrast with products designed for home use, which last only 3 or 4 years. High-quality materials are also necessary for effective instruction. For example, a toy xylophone, compared with a quality instrument, is lacking in tone and is often off pitch. Administrators and teachers who make long-range plans and purchase high-quality equipment find that durability offsets the initial cost.

Demonstrate Proper Care and Storage of Materials and Supervise Children as They Take on Organizational Tasks

Show children how to wash brushes, wipe tables, roll dough into balls and place it into containers, sort small items into appropriate storage containers, dust if necessary, and wash and wax blocks occasionally. Label shelves or containers with words, symbols, or pictures, depending on the children's age, so that children may put items away. Cleanup and maintenance work is worthy of respect, and children can be taught to take pride in the care and maintenance of their workspace.

Incorporate "Loose Parts" from the Natural Environment and from Discards

Sticks, stones, soil, feathers, seeds and seedpods, industrial discards, and boxes are just some of the very large variety of materials that can be incorporated into center work (Friedman, 2005). If gathered and organized, these materials enrich centers that otherwise are entirely of predictable use materials. Children generally see potentials even when adults do not.

Ensure a Variety of Materials to Support Each Domain

Engage children's interest by changing materials in centers regularly and by offering a variety of materials at any point in time. For example, there are numerous memory games, board games, and counting games. Selecting a variety and rotating them in and out of centers will increase use. Balls come in a variety of sizes; percussion instruments that are commercial and homemade work well and provide greater variation of sounds. Ample books that are informational and narrative fiction appeal to different children over time.

Give Reasons for the Standards You Set for Children's Use of Materials

One first-grade teacher indicated that if she saw someone being careless with materials once, she demonstrated again and reminded the child what should be occurring. She explained that everyone wanted a turn to use the materials, and if they were destroyed, no one else could use them. The children in her group learned that continued misuse of materials led to loss of the privilege of using them. Giving children reasons for the standards helps them understand the principles involved. Individual responsibility and group responsibility are also learned as children develop a work ethic.

Use the Same Materials for Many Purposes

Some materials (blocks, sand, water, clay, and computers with software) are extremely flexible in their use. The same items may be used to meet goals in different domains. In the developmentally appropriate classroom, children are often free to use such materials to meet their personal needs. On other occasions, the teacher guides children's use of materials to address particular curricular goals. For example, collage materials, which have traditionally been associated with aesthetics, can be adapted for use in other domains as well because the material is content free. This concept is illustrated by the sample activities cited in Figure 5.9.

Each activity described in Figure 5.9 is designed for center use. Naturally, when the collage materials are being used for one domain, activities with other materials must be planned for the remaining domains. Notice that the difference in domains is apparent in the strategies and guidance provided by the teacher. This example demonstrates the potential for adults to consider materials flexibly and broadly.

FIGURE 5.9　Collage Materials in Several Domains

Affective Activity: 1-2-3-4-5 Collage
Purpose: To work through a task from beginning to completion
Procedure: Select several items for a collage. Make your collage, show it to a friend, and talk about it. Put your extra materials away, and announce "The end."

Aesthetic Activity: Color Collage
Purpose: To contribute to the aesthetic environment of the school
Procedure: Make a collage in colors you like best. When you are finished, hang up your work for everyone to see and enjoy.

Physical Activity: Snip or Tear Collage
Purpose: To practice fine-motor skills
Procedure: Choose some large paper. Either cut or tear it into little pieces to make your collage.

Language Activity: Texture Collage
Purpose: To increase children's descriptive vocabulary
Procedure: Choose some materials from the box that feel different. Create a collage of many varied textures. Tell someone else as many words as you can think of to describe the textures.

Social Activity: Buddy-Up Collage
Purpose: To practice negotiation skills
Procedure: Each of you will receive a bag containing different collage materials. If you need or want something from someone else's bag, find a way to ask, trade, or share to get what you want.

Cognitive Activity: Number Collage
Purpose: To practice number skills
Procedure: There are four pans of materials from which to choose. Select four items from each pan and glue them onto your paper. You will then have four sets of four.

CREATING A DAILY SCHEDULE

Grandmother Herb came to visit Nathan's nursery school. Happy and eager for her to see his school, he entered the play yard, where he was greeted by a teacher, and moved quickly to the climbing equipment. He climbed, slid, rode tricycles, walked a balance beam, and dug in the sand during this outdoor period. When the teachers began to sing a song, he moved quickly to the stairway where the group gathered before entering the building.

Taking off his own coat, he walked into the room and sat in a large area where others were gathering and looking at picture books. Soon Ms. Eppinger led the children in a finger play, read a short story, and told the children what was in store for the day. Dismissing the youngsters in small groups, the teacher moved through the centers to see that all the children were immersed in their chosen task.

Grandmother Herb watched as Nathan moved independently from one area of the room to another during the center time. She sat next to him while he was working with the play-doh; another child came by with a sign that announced that the children had 5 minutes left. Nathan explained that it was time to put away the materials as he continued to roll out the play-doh and cut it. When his grandmother asked if there was anything she should do, this group of 3-year-olds explained exactly what to do and how as they put the play-doh in a covered container, carried their tools to the sink, wiped off the table, and moved to the large-group area.

Grandmother Herb was astonished that children who had just turned 3 years old could move through the day with such ease, take care of themselves and their materials, and be so independent.

Go to the Assignments and Activities section of Topic 7: Schedules/Routines in the MyEducationLab for your course and complete the activity entitled *Napping Routine for Preschoolers.* Notice the effect of well-established routines on the behavior of children.

How does a child know what to do and when to do it? What makes the movements from one place to the next smooth? Are there principles of planning the day's schedule that can be applied to any group of children? You will understand the answers to these and other questions as you peruse the following sections.

The ultimate goal of preparing a schedule for the day is to provide a social context in which children feel comfortable and secure. Such a schedule allows time for children to begin a task, engage in it, and complete it without hurry or interruption. Routines are predictable so that children feel continuity from one day to the next and from one week to the next. In developing the fundamental plan or daily routines, teachers must consider the pace at which children work, the variety that children need in the mode of instruction and in the groupings of children that work together, and the overall balance of the program.

Routines

Routines are patterns of behavior that, once learned, are incorporated automatically into the daily life of children and adults. Age of children, length of day, and type of program determine the selection of the routine events. In Figure 5.10 on page 152, some sample routines are defined. In the "Sample Schedules" section that follows later, fitting the routines together into a daily schedule for different program types and age groups is illustrated.

Pace

The pace, or speed, of daily activities is determined by the overall schedule of events. Teachers must decide who is to set the pace. When adults set the pace, children change activities when told to do so. Some children may be finished ahead of schedule, and others may be just beginning an activity. Adults generally set the times in the schedule when children must be in a specific place at a specific time, such as mealtimes or times for outdoor play. There are individual differences in the pace of children as well as within one child. For example, Alyss is very quick in learning and completing tasks in a center, but because she has very short legs, she takes longer in getting from one center to another or from indoors to outdoors.

In some classrooms, regular instructional time outdoors is an important part of the daily schedule.

FIGURE 5.10 Typical Routines in Early Childhood Programs

Arrival: Children enter the program from family automobiles, neighborhood streets, or buses. They remove and store outer clothing and move into the classroom.

Morning exercises: Taking attendance, discussing the weather, identifying the date on a calendar, assigning daily tasks such as watering plants or collecting milk or lunch money.

Greeting time: Teachers greet children individually or in a group, introduce the centers available, give assignments, or otherwise convey the plan of the day to the children.

Center time/Free choice/Free play: Children engage in activities designed by the teacher. Often the activities represent all domains of learning.

Limited free choice: A restricted array of choices. This may be used in child-care programs during the long arrival time. Sometimes, particularly with primary grades, a particular domain has many activities from which children choose, such as language arts.

Five-minute warning: This may be a spoken or an unspoken signal given near the end of center time so that children know that projects will soon be put away.

Cleanup: Children put away materials, wipe tables, and attend to room maintenance tasks.

Group time: A planned agenda of whole-group instruction. For younger children, thematic instruction music, a literature experience, or a group motor experience is typical. Any subject matter may be presented to older youngsters.

Transitions: The movement between major time segments when all the children are changing activities. Transitions occur between all major routine segments.

Toileting: This routine is determined mostly by the location of plumbing and the children's age. It always includes getting children to and from the toilet, assisting with clothing if necessary, using the toilet, and hand washing. It may include toilet learning and diapering for younger children or children with special needs.

Meals: Breakfast, snacks, and lunch may be served in either family-style or cafeteria settings. Some children also carry lunches. Hand washing, moving to the lunch area, eating, and cleanup are included.

Naps: Setting up cots; getting comforters such as favored toys, blankets, or sheets; and getting children settled in a quiet darkened area for rest are typical. Some children need to be patted, listen to music, or engage in other forms of comforting to fall asleep.

Journals: Children communicate graphically, initially through drawing, then a combination of words and drawings, and eventually through written communications.

Drop Everything and Read (DEAR): Adults and children engage in individual silent reading.

In other instances, allowing children to set their own pace is appropriate. For example, when some tasks are required and others are optional within a long time segment, children may set their own speed of moving through the planned experiences. One child may complete only the assigned tasks, another child may complete one or two additional activities without feeling any pressure or need to hurry, and a third child may not be able to complete the assigned tasks on a specific day and may need more than 1 day to accomplish the educational goals successfully. Children vary considerably in their learning pace, task completion, need for repetition, and attention and intensity that they bring to each learning experience. Such individual differences in style or pace can best be managed by encouraging self-regulation. However, teachers are responsible for guiding and encouraging children who appear to be disengaged, distracted, or otherwise uninvolved in the program.

Usually, 3- to 5-year-olds thrive in an open setting in which most of their program day has child-paced activities. Many youngsters of this age are just beginning to attain the self-control necessary to pursue a task in depth. Older children respond well to a balanced program of child- and adult-directed activities.

Variety

Learning experiences occur in a variety of group compositions. The size of the group affects the nature of children's and adults' interpersonal interaction as well as the instruction methods. Listening to music or stories and making plans for the day are generally done with the whole class. Specific skills are often learned in small groups determined by the teacher. Usually, groups are formed based on either the observed needs of the children or a balance between more and less skillful children. Once the children have been shown how to do the tasks and all groups are started, the teacher may focus on one or more groups for more intensive instruction. The teacher must monitor the ongoing activity of all the groups when this strategy is being used. During free-choice time, children select both the task and the group. Individual activities may be initiated by either the child or the adult but are carried out by one child working alone. Developmentally appropriate classrooms have daily opportunities for children to work alone, with small groups, and with the whole group.

Variety may also be achieved by changing the purpose, size, composition, and duration of the group. The purpose that a group of children may have for working in a small group may vary, with one group working together to clean an area of the room, a second group working on a common mural, and a third group meeting with the teacher for reading instruction. Children work in pairs, groups of three or four, or casual groupings at centers where the group size varies as children move in and out of the specific center.

The teacher may determine the composition of groups according to the common interests of the children, friendships, or chance. Knowing that some children share a common interest, such as baseball, may provide the perfect vehicle for learning about players, reading scores, or figuring averages. Other small groups may be based on a common skill they have or need to practice. Teachers are also familiar with friendship groups as they form and re-form throughout the year and can take advantage of the established leadership patterns within them. Chance groupings are usually the outgrowth of other factors such as the speed with which children finish a task. Another format is small coaching groups of children in which their abilities are deliberately mixed so that the more capable students may assist their peers in learning. Each type of grouping has specific strengths that allow it to contribute to the total program. The formation and the use of all these groups vary throughout the year as the class needs change.

Variety in the activities and materials used in centers is also important for maintaining interest and enthusiasm in the program. For example, in child-care settings, the selection of clothing in the dress-up area of pretend play can add interest even if the choice of hats and shoes is different during the morning play period than during the afternoon play period.

Balance

A group of kindergarten, first-grade, and second-grade teachers representing a variety of communities identified the following characteristics of a balanced schedule (Kostelnik, 1990):

❑ Short and long time segments
❑ Active and quiet periods
❑ Self-directed and teacher-directed activities

A balance between self-selected activities and small-group, teacher-led activities must be maintained (Copple & Bredekamp, 2009). Children need opportunities to make decisions and develop their unique interests and competencies. Such development is nurtured when they are allowed choices within the curriculum. If all the alternatives are well-planned, wholesome choices consistent with the overall curricular goals, teachers can feel confident that children are learning from the materials and one another as well as from the adults in the program.

The schedule must take into account the balance between physically active tasks and passive tasks. Usually, children function best when vigorous and quiet activities are alternated. For example, outdoor play or gym should follow or precede periods of whole-group instruction. Most young children cannot be physically passive for prolonged periods. Movement that is embedded within a longer period, such as moving to another center or substantial handling of materials, allows for moderate physical involvement.

Children need balance in the amount of time indoors and outdoors. Teachers must provide for outdoor play to promote children's health and fitness. Opportunities to learn desired habits and skills outdoors abound. For example, teachers may take children outside as a component of instruction related to the natural environment. Expectations for appropriate learning and behavior should be consistent inside and outside regardless of who is supervising in either space.

Within time periods, children should have opportunities to explore, acquire skills and information, and practice emerging competencies. Children need chances to focus on materials, interact with their peers, and engage in teacher–child interactions. A rule of thumb is that one third of the time children should engage in large-group activities, one third of the time they should engage in small-group experiences, and one third of the time they should be involved in individual activities (Katz, 1987). Considering how difficult sitting still is for adults, this guideline is probably reasonable for structuring time allotments in any learning environment. When children are given less than 30 minutes to play outdoors, they are unable to attain the higher levels of social and cognitive play (Dempsey & Frost, 1993; Copple & Bredekamp, 2009). The balance of these dimensions varies across age levels and throughout the school year.

Adapting a Schedule That Works for Your Children

Schedules will differ depending on the specific characteristics of the individuals within the group. Some children have less self-control and fewer skills in regulating their behavior than do others. Groups of children are thus likely to be different in their ability to engage in a responsive learning environment. Therefore, even within programs, schedules are not likely to be the same in all classrooms. Also, the time allotments within the daily schedule will change during the year as the children mature. Variations in the daily schedule are also appropriate as seasons and weather alter. Likewise, experienced teachers who know their children well make small adaptations regularly as a result of the children's interest or inability to attend (Bullard, 2010).

Integration

In developmentally appropriate classrooms, teachers attempt to integrate topics in science, health, and social studies and other important segments of information in various ways. Teachers provide reading experiences from information books; set up centers with related activities; and develop full study units on specific topics, such as trees, families, and dental health, that incorporate all the developmental domains. Therefore, separate time segments with these labels generally do not appear in the daily schedule.

Schedule Preparation: A Guide

Following are six guidelines for preparing a schedule.

1. Using a lined piece of paper, write times down the margin in 15-minute intervals (7:30, 7:45, 8:00), then block in and label time segments that are established for your group at the building or center level. These segments may include meals, playground time, and access to library or other specialty teachers.

2. Choose whole-group instruction time segments to facilitate (a) planning groups, (b) giving directions on the use of centers, or (c) sharing experiences with music, literature, and games. A short whole-group activity before center time helps children focus on alternatives and reminds them of their learning goals and responsibilities.

   Keep whole-group sessions short. These activities should not exceed 15 minutes of sedentary time or 20 minutes of active time for 3-year-olds. Whole-group, teacher-directed instruction for 7-year-olds should not exceed 20 to 30 minutes. However, when an activity alternates between hands-on activity and teacher direction, it may be longer and still be successful.

3. Schedule center time so that children have a minimum of 1 hour in which to engage in self-directed learning. Three- and 4-year-olds may need less time at the beginning of the year, and 8-year-olds may be profitably engaged for 2 hours or more. Some teachers schedule independent work by pairs of children at one time of the day and more openly flowing small groups in centers at another time.

4. Indicate when and where in the room or outdoors teacher-directed, small-group instruction will occur. If it is embedded in the center time, carefully consider how to bring children into the small group and supervise the centers. Several sets of small groups working cooperatively on projects may also be planned. Teacher-directed small-group sessions usually last 10 to 15 minutes for the youngest children and 15 to 20 minutes for older children. If more than one activity occurs at the same time, use two columns on your paper. Minimize transitions of the whole group. Confusion, noise, and interpersonal conflicts are common when all children are moving at the same time. The fewer of these transitions, the fewer instances of disruption.

5. Clearly indicate times of cleaning up, putting on and taking off outdoor clothing, performing classroom chores and maintenance tasks, collecting lunch money, taking attendance,

and tending to other responsibilities that the teacher and children share. Although these activities are seldom seen as part of the curriculum, many of them can become important opportunities for children to develop in the affective and social domains.

6. Schedule a closing with the children at the end of each day. Various strategies for doing so are presented in chapter 4. Regardless of how the closing exercise is handled, children find a routine pattern at the end of the day a satisfying finish.

Schedule Implementation

In implementing the schedule, ensure that children know which activity occurs next, where to go, and what to do. Sometimes, schedules need to be planned with individual children in mind (Hemmeter, Ostrosky, Artman, & Kinder, 2008). Alyss, who is very short, cannot keep up with a group of 4-year-olds as they walk down the hallways or on field trips even if she runs. She can start early with an adult, or ride in a wagon if there is substantial distance involved, or the pace of the group should be slower. Expanding the length of times for transitions is helpful, as well as discussing schedules with the children and giving clear communication signals. Signal 5 minutes before center or independent work is to be set aside so that children have an opportunity to bring their work to a close.

Allow for flexibility. If children are to respect their work and the learning of others, they must have an opportunity to complete their tasks. Some small groups will become so interested in their learning activity that they will pursue it much longer if allowed to do so. In general, child-generated learning about topics that truly interest the children lasts much longer than the guides suggested in this chapter. Teacher-controlled learning in which children have less interest may be much shorter in duration.

Prepare children for changes in routines. If the schedule must be altered to respond to the children's needs, the following steps are helpful.

Step 1. Identify the goal to be met by the change in the schedule.

Step 2. Consider more than one alternative change. Can the change be accommodated without altering the whole schedule? Can an addition be made within free-choice or center time and not change the duration or sequence of events?

Step 3. Discuss the changes with the children. Usually telling them briefly the day before and reminding them early on the day of the change are sufficient. Write the change on a poster or the chalkboard for older children, posting the new schedule. An alternative would be to write the current schedule on sentence strips and then rearrange them with the children.

Step 4. If new or more independent behavior will be required of the children, discuss this change with them. Schedule changes are opportunities for addressing affective and social learning goals.

Step 5. Allow time for children to accommodate to the alterations. Three- and 4-year-olds usually require 3 weeks to become comfortable with a new schedule; 6- and 7-year-olds may adapt in half this time.

If possible, plan major schedule changes after holidays or school vacations. Every time children are out of school longer than the weekend, they are experiencing a schedule change. Three- and 4-year-olds may repeat their separation behaviors; 5- and 6-year-olds will take several days to readapt to school. If teachers modify their schedules when children must go through an adjustment period anyway, the number of adjustment times is reduced.

Sample Schedules

The two schedules for 3- to 5-year-old children (Tables 5.4 and 5.5) have long time segments within them. Many activities occur within each of these segments, some of which would be self-selected and others teacher initiated or directed. All choices would be planned according to the curricular goals in this book.

The full-day schedule does not have a precise time for beginning and ending because children arrive and leave gradually. Toileting is normally by demand, with adult reminders. Also, meals are handled both as a part of center time and as a whole-group experience. During the winter months, in many programs the schedules are adjusted so that outdoor play is at the beginning and end of the day to limit the time-consuming process of helping children with snowsuits and boots more than once.

TABLE 5.4   Half-Day Program for 3- to 5-Year-Olds

Minutes	Activity
5–10	Arrival, individual greeting
45–60	Indoor free choice
10	Cleanup, toileting
10–15	Snack
15–20	Group time
30–45	Outdoor play/Indoor gross-motor play
5–10	Review of day/Dismissal

TABLE 5.5   Full-Day Program for 3- and 4-Year-Olds

Minutes	Activity
60	Arrival and limited choice
15	Greeting time; morning exercises
15	Toileting/Hand washing
30–45	Breakfast/Snack
45–60	Free choice: centers
10–15	Cleanup
15–20	Group time
10–20	Transition outdoors, getting wraps
35–45	Outdoor free choice
10	Cleanup outdoors
10–20	Transition indoors/Undressing
10–15	Toileting/Washing hands/Quiet music and looking at picture books
45	Lunch
15	Toileting; getting settled on cots
15	Quiet transition: story record, teacher reading or telling a story, quiet music
45–60	Naps: provisions made for children who wake early or cannot sleep
30	Wake-up time, fold and put away blankets, put on shoes, toileting
45	Indoor free play; open snack as a center
10–15	Cleanup
15–20	Small-group instruction
10–20	Transition outdoors/Getting dressed
60	Outdoor free play: Dismissal occurs gradually as parents arrive to get children.

The kindergarten double session is illustrated in Table 5.6 and is often referred to by elementary schools as full day. It is, however, two half-day sessions with a lunch break between them lasting between 5 and 6 hours in contrast to the 8- to 10-hour schedule in a child-care setting.

The last schedule, shown in Table 5.7, demonstrates the combination of group-reading instruction and center-based instruction. Centers are set up by goal area such as math or social studies or by activities, yet children also have opportunities for teacher-directed instruction in language. The schedules for other primary grades may be constructed similarly.

TABLE 5.6 Kindergarten Schedule: Double Session or "Full Day"

Minutes	Activity
20	Limited choice, lunch count, attendance
15	Morning exercises, planning the day
150	Center time
10	Cleanup
25	Group time
10	Toileting/Transition to lunch
40	Lunch
30	Toileting/Quiet individual activities, films
25	Materials-based math experiences
30	Gym
15	Sharing/Evaluation/Closing
20	Outdoor play/Dismissal

TABLE 5.7 Sample Schedule for First or Second Grade

9:00–9:10	Daily business: attendance, pledge of allegiance or announcements
9:10–9:20	Large group: explain schedule for morning and give directions for how to do independent work
9:20–9:50	Small group: focus on any content or skill that the teacher deems appropriate
9:50–10:15	Large group: motor skills in the gym
10:15–11:45	Children are divided into groups. Give directions for language arts

LANGUAGE ARTS

Start:	10:30	10:50	11:20	
Group:	1	2	3	Creative writing
	2	3	1	Listening/Independent work
	3	1	2	Reading

11:45–12:40	Recess and lunch
12:40–12:45	Attendance; go over schedule for afternoon
12:45–1:05	Large group: calendar (skills: counting, days of week, months, time, etc.), story time
1:05–1:45	Math Their Way: individual or small-group instruction with activities
1:45–2:00	Music (large group): always involves movement
2:00–3:20	Free-choice learning centers or separate time periods, depending on the project, from
2:00–2:20	Science or social studies: varies in form depending on the project
2:20–2:45	Author's Chair: children share their stories in large group
2:45–3:20	Free-choice activity: often based on some type of theme
3:20–3:30	Cleanup and dismissal

SUMMARY

The organizational responsibilities of the teacher using DAP are considerable. Classrooms must be arranged to facilitate quiet movement and to help children maintain a focus on their work. Learning centers must be carefully designed, indoors and outdoors, to meet a variety of goals. Equipment and materials must be chosen to meet the specific curricular goals. Time needs to be organized in the daily schedule, which is generally divided into long blocks, with children moving among carefully selected centers for at least part of every day. The purpose of all organizational work is to prepare the physical, cognitive, aesthetic, and social environment so that opportunities exist for learning and growth-producing interaction among the people in this context. Fortunately, once the basic plans are made and implemented, teachers can concentrate on fine-tuning them to suit particular children and to meet individual needs.

Key Words

boundaries	loose parts	private space
large-group space	natural playscapes	small-group space
learning center	pathways	vertical space

Applying What You've Read in This Chapter

1. **Discuss**
   a. What are the advantages and disadvantages of learning centers as an important part of the early childhood classroom?
   b. Discuss the role of outdoor activity in the healthy development of children.
   c. Refer to the section on scheduling children's days. Discuss the principles that you can derive for organizing the schedule and that can be applied to any group.
   d. How will literacy be properly supported if children participate in center time during the primary grades? Explain how this will be done.
   e. Describe the teacher's role in keeping children safe and healthy by means of the physical environment.
   f. Identify at least two of the eight intelligences discussed in chapter 2 that are the most obviously supported in each of the learning centers described in this chapter.

2. **Observe**
   a. Observe children in a classroom for at least a half day and record the schedule they are currently using. Note the number of whole-group transitions and describe the children's behavior. Also note individual transitions as a child completes one task and goes to another during center time.
   b. Scan a playground in a city park or a schoolyard. Identify features that provide safe activity and features that might pose a hazard. List what should be done to eliminate hazards.
   c. Observe empty classrooms at more than one location. Sketch sample layouts of furnishings and materials and describe how you think the experiences in the various classrooms would differ for the children therein. Discuss your observations with others.

3. **Carry out an activity**
   a. While you are participating as a volunteer or a student in a particular setting, alter the structure of materials or furnishings in some way to influence the children's behavior. Review this chapter to help you decide what you might do.
   b. Carry out the classroom assessment given in Figure 5.3.
   c. Read about the modifications needed in a classroom to meet the needs of little people at www.frontrangelpa.org. Using this information, walk through a primary or preschool classroom and make notes of what should be done to accommodate the needs of a little person.
   d. Use a floor plan provided in this text or that of the classroom where you have had experience. Rearrange the furnishings and explain how this rearrangement would affect the children's behavior. Then try rearranging furnishings to achieve one of the following potential goals.
      ❑ More cooperative behavior
      ❑ More helping and sharing
      ❑ A quieter environment
      ❑ More creativity

4. **Create something for your portfolio**
   a. Develop at least one pictograph to use with young children for a basic routine that you would expect them to implement independently after some initial guidance.
   b. Photograph an area of the room you were able to change to improve the quality and effectiveness of the space.

5. **Add to your journal**
   a. Reflect on the experience you have had in organizing for learning and compare it with what you read in this chapter.
   b. Write a schedule for two different age groups with a rationale for your methods.

6. 🖐 **Consult the standards**
   a. Some states have lists of equipment and materials or a process of determining if there are sufficient materials in a child-care setting. Check your state or an adjacent state to determine what these standards are and how they are assessed.
   b. What procedures does your state (or city) use to provide for the safety of children in primary grades, on playgrounds, or in child-care settings? Such standards are usually found in licensing regulations or are published on websites from the State Department of Education.

PRACTICE FOR YOUR CERTIFICATION OR LICENSURE EXAM

The following items will help you practice applying what you have learned in this chapter. They can help to prepare you for your course exam, the PRAXIS II exam, your state licensure or certification exam, and for working in developmentally appropriate ways with young children.

Organizing Space, Materials, and Time

You have just been employed as a kindergarten teacher. You decide to visit the classroom where you will teach before school starts. When you enter the room, you note the shining floors first and then all of the furnishings and equipment piled high on one side of the room. Cupboards are on one wall and windows on another. A toilet and lavatory open off the wall with cupboards and there is a sink in the countertop. You can see electrical outlets on the wall with no windows or cupboards.

1. **Constructed-response question**

   a. Identify five principles you will use in organizing this space.

   b. List four learning centers that you would most want in the classroom. Describe the materials and equipment you would need for each one and explain how each center will contribute to children's learning.

2. **Multiple-choice question**

   You have introduced a learning center time during the last 45 minutes of the day in a first-grade classroom that is otherwise organized more for adult-initiated activity. The children are noisy and flit from one thing to another. What should you do?

   a. Replace the center time with quiet individual reading

   b. Reduce center time to 20 minutes per day

   c. Introduce the centers to the children each day and include some required centers

   d. Dismiss the children to their centers, one row at a time, reminding them to be quiet and orderly or they will get a check on the board

Chapter

6

Child Guidance in Early Childhood Classrooms

You may wonder:

How can I create a classroom in which children feel safe and respected?
What kinds of rules do I need in my classroom?
What should I do if children have difficulty sharing or taking turns?
Why do children listen better to some adults than to others?

This chapter will help you answer questions like these. All of them are about guiding children's behavior.

When children don't know how to wash their hands, we teach them.
When children don't know how to say the alphabet, we teach them.
When children don't know how to count, we teach them.
When children don't know how to throw a ball, we teach them.
Likewise,
When children don't know how to behave, we teach them.

Adapted from Herner, 1998

The idea of "teaching" children how to behave (rather than expecting them automatically to know how or simply punishing them when they do not) is the hallmark of child guidance in developmentally appropriate classrooms.

WHAT CHILDREN NEED TO KNOW

As young children make the transition from "home child" to "school child," they have much to learn. To be successful both in school and in life, children need a good grasp of many skills (Evans & Rosenbaum, 2008; LePage, Darling-Hammond, & Akar, 2005). Thus, children do best when they:

❏ Express their needs, wants, and feelings constructively
❏ Respond with compassion to others' needs
❏ Calm themselves when angry or upset
❏ Act in a safe and civil manner
❏ Follow rules, routines, and directions
❏ Take proper care of materials
❏ Constructively engage in learning activities
❏ Share, take turns, help, and cooperate
❏ Distinguish acceptable from unacceptable classroom behavior
❏ Regulate and modify their actions based on their understanding of right and wrong

These behaviors "transcend all subject matter commonly taught in school and characterize peak performers in all walks of life" (Costa & Kallick, 2004, p. 52). In fact, these behaviors are so important, they are incorporated in every state's learning standards for young children. See Table 6.1 for examples.

Children do not intuitively know how to behave in all the ways listed in Table 6.1 (Gartrell, 2011; Rightmeyer, 2003). Instead, adults must teach children what is expected and how to conduct themselves appropriately. This requires the same kind of planning and teaching that other aspects of the curriculum demand. Just as teachers provide opportunities for children to learn about science, math, and literacy, they must also provide opportunities for children to learn how to interact with others and manage their behavior independently and in groups. When children make mistakes, early childhood professionals do more than correct children. They teach them appropriate alternative strategies (Bronson, 2006). All of this is done in the hope that children eventually will adopt these more appropriate behaviors and carry them out on their own (Vos & Baumeister, 2004). Thus, in developmentally appropriate classrooms, the ultimate goal of child guidance is for children to become self-regulating.

TABLE 6.1   Early Learning Standards: Expectations for Classroom Behavior Examples

State	Expectation	Benchmarks/Learning Outcomes
New Jersey	Children demonstrate self-direction	Child explores and experiments with a wide variety of developmentally appropriate curriculum–referenced materials and activities
		Child demonstrates self-help skills (e.g., puts blocks away, pours juice, uses soap when washing hands)
		Child moves through classroom routines and activities with minimal teacher direction
Illinois	Children demonstrate respect and responsibility for self and others	Child begins to understand and follow rules
		Child manages transitions and begins to adapt to change in routines
		Child shows empathy and caring for others
		Child uses the classroom environment purposefully and respectfully
Nebraska	Children exhibit self-control	Child attempts to solve problems with other children independently, by negotiation or other socially acceptable means
		Child shows awareness of and responds appropriately to the feelings of others
		Child participates in daily routines without being asked
		Child builds awareness and ability to follow basic health and safety rules
		Child calms self after excitement, expresses strong emotions constructively, and controls aggression

Sources: From *Preschool Teaching & Learning Expectations: Standards of Quality PTM 1503.13*, by New Jersey State Department of Education, 2004, Trenton, NJ: Author; *Illinois Early Learning Standards*, by Illinois State Board of Education, 2004, Springfield, IL: Author; *Nebraska's Early Learning Guidelines 3 to 5 Year Olds*, by Nebraska Department of Education, 2005, Lincoln, NE: Author.

SELF-REGULATION

The after-school kids bound off the buses. They jostle, bump into each other, head for the hall, drop their backpacks, hurry into the lavatories, and race to the snack bar. Some head for the gym to hear the rules for a kickball game—eight-year-old Matt is among them. He listens, attentive and eager, for about five minutes. Then he begins to squirm, look around, and elbow the children next to him. . . . Jeremy, the teacher's aide, steps quietly in behind Matt. "Remember, Matt, be calm. You know how to wait," he whispers. Matt says to himself, "I can wait, I can wait." He gets himself under control and waits for the game to begin.

—Steiner & Whelan, 1995, Dec. 29

In this example, Matt, with the help of a supportive adult, managed to control his natural impulses to fidget. He also resisted the temptation to continue poking his peers. Both are signs that he is developing skills associated with self-regulation. *Self-regulation* is the voluntary, internal control of behavior (Marion, 2010). It involves acting in socially acceptable ways based on reasoning, concern for others, and an understanding of acceptable and unacceptable behavior. People who are self-regulating do not need others to make them do the right thing or to forbid them from engaging in antisocial conduct. Neither are they dependent on external rewards or punishments to guide their actions. Instead, they consider other people's needs and feelings while simultaneously adapting their actions to fit the rules of the society in which they live. Self-regulating children control negative impulses, resist temptation, and delay gratification independent of supervision. They also initiate positive social interactions and undertake constructive social plans without having to be told to do so (Bronson, 2006; Knapczyk, 2004). Refer to Table 6.2 for examples of these behaviors in children's daily lives.

TABLE 6.2 Components of Self-Regulation Exhibited by Young Children

Behavior	Examples
Control negative impulses	Anthony suppresses the urge to strike out in anger when someone accidentally trips him. Hessa refrains from laughing aloud when Anthony falls.
Resist temptation	Jerome walks all the way over to the trash bin to deposit his gum wrapper, even though he is tempted to drop the crumpled paper onto the playground.
Delay gratification	Rachel waits for Marla to finish telling her story before blurting out her own exciting news.
	Steven postpones taking another fruit kabob until everyone else gets one.
Initiate positive social interactions	Shannon comforts Latosha, who is sad about a ruined project.
	Jason shares his glue with a newcomer to the art center.
Make and carry out constructive social plans	Vinny wants a turn with the magnifying glass. He devises a strategy for getting one, such as trading, and then tries bargaining with another child.
	Ashley recognizes that Marcus is having difficulty carrying several balls out to the playground. She helps him by holding the door open.

HOW SELF-REGULATION EVOLVES

Self-regulation evolves gradually in an "outside" to "inside" developmental process (Marion, 2010). That is, children proceed from relying on others to control their behavior for them to eventually achieving greater self-regulation. This gradual shift in control from outside sources to self is a significant developmental task that begins in infancy and continues through adolescence.

The Earliest Days

Infants have no inborn sense of right or wrong. Neither do they have the cognitive and physical skills to control their actions in response to behavior demands, such as, "Let go of the dog's tail," or, "Don't pull on his ears." Through experience and maturation, toddlers and preschoolers gradually learn to respond to controls applied by parents and teachers to behave in certain ways. This form of regulation is called *adherence*.

Adherence (External Regulation)

Children motivated by **adherence** rely on adults to control their actions for them. The most basic form of external control involves physical assistance. Following are some examples.

The parent volunteer holds Melanie on her lap during group time to help her focus on the story. Melanie attends to the story.
The teacher physically separates two children who are fighting on the playground. The children stop pushing each other.
The after-school aide puts her hand over Michael's to keep him from waving the saw around at the workbench. Michael keeps the saw low.

Gradually, children also respond to verbal cues in learning what to do and what not to do. For instance:

The teacher reminds Diego to wash his hands before sitting down for lunch. Diego washes his hands.
Sandra's dad talks her through the steps involved in feeding the iguana. Sandra feeds the iguana correctly.
The teacher's aide provides Joshua with a script of what to say during an argument with Michael. Joshua tells Michael, "I wasn't done yet."

In each of these situations, adults provided the controls that children were not able to exercise on their own.

Another form of adherence occurs when children act in certain ways either to gain rewards or to avoid negative consequences (Wolfgang, 2008). You can see adherence in operation when a child who has been scolded for dumping all the puzzles on the floor stops dropping pieces to avoid additional correction. Likewise, children's desire to receive adult praise, or approval from a peer, may prompt them to use the paints properly or share a toy with another child. In each case, rewards and negative consequences have contributed to children's early differentiations of acceptable and unacceptable actions. Relying on these kinds of external controls is a step beyond having no control at all. It is also a necessary first phase in moving from no self-control to internal regulation. However, adherence has drawbacks that make it an undesirable end unto itself.

Consider the following situation. The children are waiting at the door to go outside. Mr. Martin, their teacher, has promised a smiley-face sticker to children who wait patiently and do not push. Adrianne, who is at the back of the group, wants to be first but quietly stands in place because she wants the sticker. Her behavior is regulated by the promise of the reward, not by concern for her classmates' rights. Under these circumstances, Adrianne will probably follow the teacher's directions at least when he is present. However, because she has no internal basis for following the rule, Adrianne may resort to pushing in front of others if she thinks the teacher is not looking or on another day when no sticker is promised.

Adrianne illustrates the basic problem with adherence. Children who depend on external controls must be monitored constantly. They behave appropriately only in situations in which physical or verbal assistance is readily available and in instances in which the threat of punishment or the promise of a reward is obvious. When such controls are missing, the possibility of misbehavior is great. Having no other means for understanding right and wrong, children lack the self-direction necessary to act appropriately on their own.

Identification (Shared Regulation)

A more advanced degree of self-regulation occurs when children follow a rule to imitate someone they admire. Children's positive actions become their way of emulating the conduct and values of important people in their lives (Goleman, 2006; Grusec, Davidov, & Lundell, 2002). This is called **identification**. Because children identify with nurturing and powerful figures, teachers are often the focus of identification.

Children who rely on identification adopt another person's code of conduct to guide their actions but have little understanding of the reasons behind such behaviors. For instance, influenced by identification, Jacob may wait patiently at the door because a teacher he especially likes advocates this conduct. However, Jacob does not grasp the concept of fairness that waiting represents. In addition, identification requires children to second-guess how another person might behave under certain conditions. If Jacob encounters a situation to which he has never seen the teacher respond, he may not know what to do.

Identification represents shared behavior regulation. Children remain dependent on an outside source to help them control their actions but are beginning to use internal thought processes as well. They do not need constant monitoring. Yet, they still have no way to determine what to do in unfamiliar circumstances. Although identification is more advanced than adherences, it does not represent the highest form of self-control.

Internalization (Self-Regulation)

When children construct a personal sense of right and wrong and act in ways consistent with what they believe to be right, we say they have *internalized* that behavior (Grusec et al., 2002; Bronson, 2006). In other words, children act in certain ways because they think it is the right thing to do, not to gain a reward or the approval of others. They feel concern and a sense of responsibility for the welfare and rights of others as well as for themselves. They also comprehend moral concepts such as justice, truth, and honor. For these reasons, **internalization** represents the ultimate form of self-control.

Sophie demonstrates internalization when she waits her turn to go outside even though she is tempted to push ahead. The reasoning that guides her behavior is that pushing others aside would interfere with their rights. Such interference violates her sense of fairness, which prompts Sophie to remain where she is in the group.

Children who have internalized certain standards of behavior understand the reasons behind acceptable and unacceptable actions. This understanding gives them a reference point for determining

TABLE 6.3   Three Children Waiting to Go Outside

Adrianne	Wants a smiley sticker	Motivated by adherence
Jacob	Wants to be like a favorite teacher	Motivated by identification
Sophie	Wants to be fair	Motivated by internalization

how to behave appropriately in all kinds of situations, even unfamiliar ones. These understandings eliminate the need for constant supervision. For instance, Sophie may transfer her sense of fairness to other activities in which no adult is present, such as taking turns during a game, or making sure everyone gets a turn before the game ends. Moreover, internalized behaviors are long lasting. Children who internalize notions of fair play or honesty will abide by these ideals long after their contacts with certain adults have ended and despite the temptation or opportunity to act otherwise.

See Table 6.3 for a summary of what motivates adherence, identification, and internalization in young children.

DEGREES OF SELF-REGULATION AMONG CHILDREN AND WITHIN THE SAME CHILD

Children achieve self-regulation at rates and in degrees that vary from child to child. Within any group of children, the variations in children's progress toward self-control will be great. For instance, Noelle may take only a few weeks to learn how to behave appropriately at group time. LaRene may take much longer to figure this out. Giovanni may respond easily to gentle verbal reminders to share, whereas Sam may need physical assistance to accomplish this task. In addition, the same child may respond to different motivations in different circumstances (Grusec et al., 2002; Mischel & Ayduk, 2004). That is, Juanita may stay out of the mud to avoid a warning. She may adopt the same attitudes toward cheating as those held by an admired teacher. And, when she accidentally receives too many game tokens, she may return some because keeping them would not feel right. These variations among children are a result of development and experience.

DEVELOPMENTAL INFLUENCES ON SELF-REGULATION

Children's capacity for self-regulation increases with maturity. Although 4- and 5-year-olds can generally regulate themselves in some situations, they do not have the same degree of self-control as 8- and 9-year-olds. Several developmental factors contribute to these age differences, including children's emotional, cognitive, and language development and their memory skills. In each domain, children's increasing understanding and skills emerge according to the following principles of developmental direction.

❑ Simple to complex
❑ Concrete to abstract
❑ Inaccurate to more accurate

Emotional Development

Emotions provide children with strong internal signals about the appropriateness or inappropriateness of their behavior. As children learn to pay attention to these signals, their self-control increases. Two important emotional regulators are empathy and guilt (Hoffman, 2000; Mills, 2005; Thompson, 2006). Empathy prompts children to consider others and to pursue positive actions in response to people's emotions. It tells children, "forge ahead." Guilt conveys the opposite message. It warns children that current, past, or planned actions are inappropriate. It serves as a brake, causing children to reconsider or to stop their actions. By age 3, most children are capable of both empathy and guilt;

Children need adult supervision and support as they develop the emotional and cognitive skills necessary to follow rules on their own.

however, what induces these emotions in preschoolers is different from what triggers them in second and third graders.

Empathy. Empathy is the ability to detect different emotions in others, to feel what another person is feeling and to respond emotionally oneself. It is what induces children to comfort a victim, offer to share, or willingly take turns. The first signs of empathy occur when infants and toddlers mimic the overt signals of distress they witness in others: A 2-year-old cries on hearing another child's sobs. By the age of 3, children recognize that another person's feelings call for more helpful action on their part, such as soothing a peer who has fallen. Preschoolers and kindergartners become increasingly sensitive to others' emotional cues and are better able to respond in useful, though somewhat limited, ways. By the early elementary years, children are more adept at recognizing other's concerns and at employing a greater variety of strategies to offer encouragement, comfort, and support (Miller, 2009).

Guilt. Initially, children experience guilt mostly when they violate a known rule or fail to meet adult expectations (Thompson, 2006). For instance, 4-year-old Carl slaps Selma in a struggle over the cookie cutters. Selma begins to cry. Triumphant over having gained a desired possession, Carl is unmoved by Selma's distress. He experiences no guilt until the teacher reminds him that the rule is "Ask, don't hit" or, "It upsets me when you hurt children." Once he becomes aware of the contradiction between his behavior and the rule, Carl may feel guilty about breaking it and disappointing the teacher. Conversely, if he were 7 or 8 years old, Carl might empathize with Selma's unhappy response and feel remorse at being the source of it (Mills, 2005). This combination of empathy and guilt might even prompt him to do something to make up for his earlier actions. Violating a formal rule would not figure as prominently in his feelings as it had during the preschool years. Instead, Carl would be more focused on the internal distress his actions had caused another person and, as a consequence, himself.

As evidenced by Carl, children gradually respond to empathy and guilt to support their personal notions of right and wrong. This gradual shift from external prompts to internal ones contributes to the inner control that children need to achieve self-regulation. Although it has its beginnings early in life, such complex and "other-oriented" motivation does not fully emerge until adolescence.

Cognitive Development

Children's notions of "good" and "bad" behavior change with age. Whether they judge an action to be right or wrong is influenced by their reasoning powers and the extent to which they comprehend other people's perspectives. The cognitive processes of centration and irreversibility further affect how children conduct themselves.

Reasoning About Right and Wrong. Three- to 6-year-olds make judgments about right and wrong based mainly on whether behaviors are immediately rewarded or punished. Children interpret actions that result in social rewards (e.g., a smile, positive words, getting what they want) as good and those that incur social costs (e.g., a frown, negative words, having their goals blocked) as negative (Bronson, 2006).

Another way young children decide that actions are bad is if they result in physical harm to people or property or if they violate people's rights (Tisak & Block, 1990; Berk, 2009). Hurtful actions such as hitting, breaking things, or calling names are readily identified by children as unacceptable. However, children do not interpret behaviors that disrupt the social order of the group, such as not putting away toys, and those that violate interpersonal trust, such as revealing a secret, as inappropriate until middle childhood.

Because younger children's moral reasoning is still immature, they need support to learn what is expected and why. Adults who state their expectations clearly and offer reasons for expectations help children progress toward self-discipline. The reasons that make the most sense to children ages 3 to 8 years are ones that focus on the following:

❑ Keeping people safe and not hurting people ("Tell him you're angry; don't hit. Hitting hurts.")
❑ Protecting property ("Wear a smock so you don't get paint on your clothes.")
❑ Protecting people's rights ("Everyone needs a turn.")

Perspective-Taking. To interact effectively with others and make accurate judgments about which actions would be right or wrong in certain situations, children must understand what other people think, feel, or know. This involves *perspective-taking* skills. Because these skills are just emerging in the early years, young children sometimes have difficulty putting themselves in another person's shoes. This is a result of being unable, rather than unwilling, to comprehend or predict other people's thoughts and feelings (Berkowitz, 2002). Children frequently assume that others interpret situations just as they do. Not until potential differences are brought to children's attention do they recognize that their perspective is not shared. For this reason, young children benefit from hearing that there is more than one way to look at things (FitzGerald & White, 2003; Goleman, 2006). This information is best supplied as relevant incidents arise ("You want a turn on the tricycle. Harry wants a turn, too." or "You're having fun painting. I'm worried that the paint is getting on your sleeves.").

Sometime between their sixth and eighth birthday, children start realizing that their interpretation of a situation and that of another person might not match (Berk, 2009). Still, they do not always know what the differences are, or they may conclude that variations are a result of the other person's having access to incorrect or incomplete information. As a result, second and third graders often go to great lengths trying to convince others that their view is the logical one. This trait sometimes makes them appear argumentative. On these occasions, adults must remind themselves that such behaviors are an outgrowth of children's immature reasoning, not deliberate obstinacy. In reality, children need to hear the facts of the situation repeated more than once and in varying ways.

Centration. Throughout early childhood, children tend to focus their attention on a select few aspects of an overall situation, neglecting other important features that might help them analyze the situation more accurately or effectively (Berk, 2009; Peterson & Felton-Collins, 1991). This phenomenon, known as *centration*, results in children's having a limited rather than comprehensive perception of social events. This is evident when Rayanne focuses so intently on using the glitter paint for her project that she does not realize that other children are waiting for some or that she is using it all. Centration also prompts children to focus on only one way to achieve their aims. Caleb demonstrates centration when he repeatedly says "Please" to try to get a chance to use the glitter, even though Rayanne ignores him each time. Even when youngsters recognize that their actions are inappropriate or ineffective, they may be unable to generate suitable alternative behaviors without adult guidance. The younger the child, the more this is so. The ability to see an event from more than one angle and to consider several ways to respond accrues only gradually. This ability is enhanced when early childhood professionals point out options to children and help youngsters brainstorm suitable alternatives in problem situations.

Irreversible Thinking. Young children's behavior is further influenced by the sometimes irreversible nature of their thinking. Evidence suggests that children have difficulty mentally reversing physical actions (Waite-Stupiansky, 1997; Slentz & Krogh, 2001). Consequently, children are not adept at contemplating opposite actions, and they have difficulty interrupting ongoing behaviors. It is also difficult for them to respond to directions stated in negative terms. For instance, when Kyley pushes on the door of the toy stove to open it, a parent volunteer calls out, "Don't push." Unfortunately, "Don't push" means little to Kyley. She is unable to mentally transpose the physical act of pushing into its opposite action of pulling and she does not think to stop. She needs assistance to reverse her behavior. This could involve physical help, adult modeling, or a more precise oral direction, such as "Pull the door open." With maturation, children improve in their ability to mentally reverse physical actions, but the influence of irreversible thinking remains evident throughout the preschool and early elementary years. Because irreversibility is such a powerful force in children's thinking, adults must remember to state directions and expectations in positive terms.

Language Development

As children acquire greater and more complex language skills, their capacity for self-control also increases. This is because language contributes to children's understanding of why rules are made and gives them more tools for attaining their goals in socially acceptable ways.

Interpersonal Speech. Many preschoolers come to early childhood programs with a well-developed receptive vocabulary and the ability to express basic needs. Yet, they are not always successful at telling others what they want or responding to oral directions (Jalongo, 2008). Consequently, young children often resort to physical actions to communicate. They may grab, dash away, refuse to answer, push, or strike out rather than use words to express themselves. At such times, children need teacher assistance in determining what to say ("You seem upset. Say to Martha, 'I'm using this now.'" or "You don't want Jonathan to chase you. Say, 'Stop. '"). As the elementary years progress, children become more proficient in both receiving and giving verbal messages. They find words a more satisfactory and precise way to communicate. However, even second and third graders sometimes need guidance in determining the best words to use in emotionally charged circumstances or in situations that are new to them.

Private Speech. In addition to the words they direct toward others, young children use private speech (self-talk) to exercise self-control (Winsler, De Leon, Wallace, Carlton, & Wilson-Quayle, 2003; Winsler, Naglieri, & Manfra, 2006). That is, they reduce frustration, postpone rewards, or remind themselves of what to do by talking aloud to themselves. We hear this when a preschooler says to herself, "Blue shoes, blue shoes" as a reminder of what she is looking for and when a second grader outlines his approach to an assignment in a mumbled tone as a way to help himself plan. The self-talk Matt used to help himself wait through the directions to the kickball game (described in a previous example) further illustrates children's use of private speech to gain control of their actions. When adults hear children talking to themselves, they should allow them to continue rather than asking them to hush. Offering children sample self-talk scripts is another way to help children move toward self-regulation.

Memory Skills

Memory is one more facet of development that influences children's capacity for self-regulation (Bjorklund, 2005; Golbeck, 2006). Initially, young children's memory skills are limited. Their ability to recall the past is episodic and short-term. They often fail to recognize patterns among past events and miss key details in their recollections. Because young children live in the here and now, they are less proficient at drawing on past experience to guide current or future actions. Accordingly, preschoolers tend to "forget" expectations from one day to the next or from one setting to another. To be successful, they need frequent reminders about rules and require overt direction in unfamiliar social situations. As children mature, their memories become more detailed, more connected, and more long lasting. They can organize their thoughts more meaningfully and are better able to draw on past experience to help them think about what to do in current and future situations. By first or second grade, children still benefit from periodic reviews of expectations, but can generally function with less supervision. They are also better able to use cognitive strategies such as repeating, rehearsing, or categorizing information to help them remember when and how to delay gratification, resist temptation, control impulses, and carry out positive social interactions.

HOW EXPERIENCE INFLUENCES SELF-REGULATION

As you can see, development plays a vital role in how well children eventually regulate their behavior. Children's day-to-day experiences with peers and adults also influence the degree to which children achieve greater self-control. The most frequent modes of experience include modeling, instruction, and consequences.

Modeling

One way children learn what is expected of them is by imitating the actions of powerful adults with whom they have strong, affectionate ties (Bandura, 1997; Fox & Lentini, 2006). Early childhood professionals serve as behavior models and through their actions, demonstrate compliance or lack of compliance with certain standards of conduct. The research tells us that social modeling is especially influential in the early years (Berk, 2009). Young children learn potent lessons regarding desirable attitudes and behaviors as well as how to enact them when they see their teachers treat others with kindness, tell the truth, use reasoning as a way to solve problems, or assist someone in need. Alternatively, because youngsters also mimic negative models, they sometimes imitate the aggressive or thoughtless acts committed by those around them.

Instruction

Another way children learn knowledge and skills associated with self-regulation is through instruction. Instruction may be carried out indirectly or through on-the-spot coaching.

Indirect Instruction. Indirect instruction involves all the behind-the-scenes work and planning that ultimately influences young children's behavior. These teaching methods give children opportunities to practice self-regulating skills such as making choices, functioning independently, or following through on personal plans (Hearron & Hildebrand, 2008). For instance, teachers use environmental cues, as described in chapter 2, to signal children what behaviors are expected (e.g., where to put the blocks, how many crackers to take at snack). Similarly, many of the strategies you read about in chapter 5 (e.g., organizing space, setting up equipment in certain ways, and planning the daily routine) help children manage their behavior and get along with peers with minimal adult supervision. For example, when adults make sponges readily available on low shelves it is easier for children to comply with the expectation that everyone participate in cleanup.

On-the-Spot Coaching. What is right, what is wrong, what to do and what not to do are all lessons that can be conveyed effectively to children through on-the-spot-coaching. This form of instruction is provided as relevant situations arise within the context of children's daily interactions. On-the-spot coaching is a powerful teaching strategy because children gain experience at teachable moments in an environment that is supportive, not punitive. Such experience is immediately relevant to children (Kochanska, Aksan, Prisco, & Adams, 2008). Coaching makes use of verbal strategies such as informing and explaining, suggesting, advising, reasoning, encouraging, and clarifying (Weinstein & Mignano, 2007). Typical remarks include, "Catch your cough in your sleeve," "Maybe you could take turns," "Tell him you're angry—don't pinch," "Mr. Ramirez really appreciated when you helped him carry those boxes," and "When you didn't say 'Hi' back, she thought you didn't like her." Physical assistance, modeling and demonstrating, redirecting, distracting, removing children from problem situations, and physical restraint are additional techniques associated with on-the-spot coaching (Wolfgang, 2008).

Consequences

Children also learn how to behave as a result of experiencing consequences. Consequences come in two varieties—positive and negative—and these either reinforce desirable behaviors or penalize negative actions. Such outcomes prompt children to repeat certain behaviors and avoid others (Shiller & O'Flynn, 2008). Children sometimes experience consequences as a natural outgrowth of their actions with no adult intervention. At other times, adults intentionally apply consequences to influence children's behavior.

Positive Consequences. Adults use positive consequences to increase the likelihood that children will repeat desirable acts and behave appropriately in the future (Marzano, 2003; Shiller & O'Flynn, 2008). For example, adults reward children for behaving appropriately by using praise ("You remembered your pictures from home; now you're ready for today's work on animals."). At other times, positive consequences take the form of earned privileges ("You did such a good job watering the plants, tomorrow you can do it all by yourself."). In some circumstances, based on a child's special need for concrete cues, positive consequences may be enacted through tangible means, such as stars on a reward chart.

Negative Consequences. Teachers use negative consequences to reduce the probability that children will repeat undesirable behaviors (Bell, Carr, Denno, Johnson, & Phillips, 2004; Wolfgang, 2008). However, not all negative consequences are effective in promoting self-regulation either. Some negative consequences are so harsh or shameful that they cause children to feel demeaned or fearful. Neither of these reactions leads to a healthy sense of guilt or empathy, both of which are fundamental to self-regulation. In this book, we shall refer to this type of negative consequence as **punishment**. You will learn more about punishment in the next portion of this chapter devoted to adult discipline styles. For now, note that some negative consequences help children learn alternative ways to achieve their goals through the process of being corrected. We will refer to these as **logical consequences** because they teach children logical alternatives to unacceptable behaviors—how to walk instead of run, how to share instead of grab, how to wait instead of interrupting (Charney, 2002; Stephens, 2006). Through logical consequences, children gain valuable information and skills they refer to in future situations.

HOW ADULT DISCIPLINE STYLES INFLUENCE CHILDREN'S SELF-REGULATION

Instructing, modeling, and applying consequences are practices most early childhood professionals use in one way or another. However, these strategies can be combined differently, resulting in distinct adult discipline styles. Four of the most commonly described styles are uninvolved, permissive, authoritarian, and authoritative (Baumrind, 1967, 1973, 1995). Each of these discipline styles is characterized by certain adult attitudes and strategies related to the four social dimensions of control, communication, maturity demands, and nurturance.

1. **Control** is the way and extent to which parents and teachers enforce compliance with their expectations.
2. **Communication** involves how much information adults provide children throughout the guidance process.
3. **Maturity demands** describe the level at which adults set their expectations for children's behavior and compliance.
4. **Nurturance** refers to how much caring and concern is expressed toward children.

Differences among the uninvolved, permissive, authoritarian, and authoritative styles result from varying combinations of these four dimensions (see Figure 6.1).

Uninvolved adults are low in all four dimensions.
Permissive adults are high in nurturance but low in control, make few maturity demands, and engage in minimal communication with children.
Adults employing an *authoritarian* style are high in control and maturity demands and low in communication and nurturance.
Early childhood professionals who are high in all four dimensions demonstrate an *authoritative* style.

Few people personify a "pure" style regardless of which one they adopt. In fact, from time to time, adults may demonstrate behaviors characteristic of all four. However, the majority of grown-ups gravitate toward one style more than the others.

These variations in style have been the subject of research since the late 1960s. Both short-term and long-term child effects have been documented with relatively consistent results over time and across settings (Baumrind, 1967, 1983, 1991; Kochanska, Gross, Lin, & Nichols, 2002; Kochanska et al., 2008; Hart, Newell, & Olsen, 2003). Subsequently, these four styles remain the standard for comparison today (Hetherington, Parke, Gauvin, & Otis Locke, 2009).

FIGURE 6.1 **Differences in Attitudes and Practices Among the Uninvolved, Permissive, Authoritarian, and Authoritative Discipline Styles**

The Uninvolved Discipline Style

"I have little interest in you. Do whatever you want to do."

The **uninvolved discipline style** combines low acceptance and involvement with little control and general indifference to children's well-being (Berk, 2009). Teachers who demonstrate an uninvolved style put little effort into developing relationships with children or guiding their behavior. These adults are egocentric, focusing on their personal needs and agendas before the children's. Their self-absorption may arise for various reasons, including stress, depression, or ill health. Whatever the cause, the outcomes for children are poor. Youngsters lack the security that comes with positive relationships and the comprehension that comes through reasoning. They have no way to determine right from wrong and no opportunity to develop relevant social skills. Youngsters whose lives are dominated by uninvolved adults get a clear message that they are unimportant. None of these circumstances promote self-control. The most common child outcomes of this style are feelings of insecurity and emotional detachment, poor social and emotional skills, as well as disruptive behaviors early in life. Poor emotional self-regulation, truancy, delinquency, and precocious sexuality become evident during adolescence (Aunola & Nurmi, 2005; Kochanska et al., 2002, 2008; Clark & Gross, 2004).

The Permissive Discipline Style

"I care about you. Do whatever you want to do."

Permissive teachers treat children with warmth and affection, sometimes to the point of overindulgence. However, they pay little attention to shaping children's present or future behavior. Some teachers adopt the **permissive discipline style** because they believe that having positive relationships with children is sufficient to get youngsters to behave in socially acceptable ways. Other adults believe that behavior controls stifle children's development. Still others drift into this approach because they do not know how to get children to "listen." Whatever the reason, permissive adults provide little guidance to children about what is acceptable behavior and what is not (Oyserman, Bybee, Mowbray, & Hart-Johnson, 2005). They do not talk with children about how their behavior affects others or help children recognize other people's needs. Because these instructors have low expectations for children's conduct, they give children minimal responsibility and ignore most negative behaviors. If a child engages in gross misconduct, permissive adults use love withdrawal as their primary means of discipline ("I don't like children who hit."). This response temporarily denies children the one social support permissive adults are usually willing to provide—nurturance.

Unfortunately, children subjected to a permissive approach show few signs of self-regulation. This lack of control occurs for several reasons. First, because the impact of their behavior on others is not explained, children fail to develop feelings of guilt and empathy, necessary ingredients for self-control. Second, the fact that youngsters receive few cues about which behaviors are socially acceptable and which are not also means children do not develop the backlog of experience they need to make appropriate decisions in the future. Third, peers and other adults tend to view these children's unrestricted conduct as immature, inconsiderate, and unacceptable. This negative perception contributes to children's feelings of anxiety and low self-esteem. As a result, children who interact mainly with permissive adults tend to be withdrawn, unproductive, and dissatisfied with their lives. By adolescence, the permissive style is correlated with delinquent behavior and poor academic performance (Baumrind, 1995; Hart et al., 2003; Steinberg, Blatt-Eisengart, & Cauffman, 2006). These negative outcomes are similar to those associated with the style that is its direct opposite: the authoritarian style.

The Authoritarian Discipline Style

"Do it because I said so!"

Unlike permissive adults, teachers who use the **authoritarian discipline style** have high standards for children's behavior and exert strong control over children's actions. To achieve these standards and control, they act as strict taskmasters who value children's unquestioning obedience above all else. Theirs is the philosophy of "I say and you obey." Failure to meet their expectations is dealt with swiftly and forcefully, most often through shaming techniques or physical punishment. In either case, their

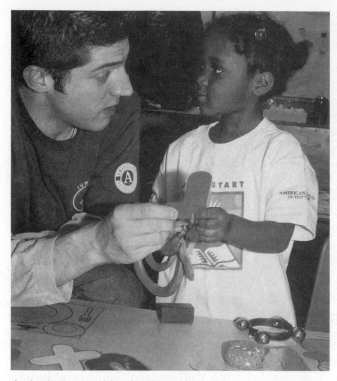

Authoritative teaching begins with positive teacher–child relationships.

goal is to show children who is boss as opposed to helping children consider how their behavior affects others or determining better strategies to use in the future. Not too surprisingly, authoritarian adults have cold, distant relationships with young children. Youngsters view them as harsh disciplinarians who focus more on finding mistakes than on recognizing their efforts to behave appropriately.

The coercive discipline strategies characteristic of the authoritarian style cause children to maintain an external orientation to behavior regulation. In the short term, youngsters act in required ways out of fear or unreasoned obedience, not out of empathy or concern for others. This impedes their ability to develop the reasoning and caring necessary for self-regulation. In the long run, children whose primary experiences are with authoritarian adults tend to become unfriendly, suspicious, resentful, and unhappy. They are often underachievers and exhibit increased incidents of misconduct as well as extreme antisocial behaviors, although to a lesser extent than is generally true for the uninvolved and permissive styles (Baumrind, 1995; Hart et al., 2003; Kochanska et al., 2002, 2008). These outcomes lead to a dismal prognosis for children. A more positive outcome results from the authoritative approach, which we will consider next.

The Authoritative Discipline Style

"I care about you and I have high expectations for your behavior."

Adults who use the **authoritative discipline style** combine the positive dimensions of permissiveness (nurturance) and authoritarianism (maturity demands and control) while avoiding the negative aspects. In addition, teachers rely on some strategies that permissive and authoritarian adults fail to use altogether, such as clear communication and other-oriented reasoning. Early childhood professionals who adopt an authoritative style encourage children to assume appropriate responsibility and get what they need in socially acceptable ways. When children attempt a new skill, adults acknowledge their accomplishments; when children face challenges, teachers help them develop new approaches. These methods contribute to children's feelings of competence and worth. Simultaneously, authoritative teachers establish high standards for children's behavior and are quick to take action to teach them how to strive toward these standards. Explanations, demonstrations, suggestions, and reasoning are the primary guidance strategies they use. When children behave inappropriately, authoritative adults take advantage of these spontaneous opportunities to discuss guilt, empathy, and the perspectives of others (Russel, Mize, & Bissaker, 2004). They also provide on-the-spot coaching to help children recognize acceptable and unacceptable behaviors as well as potential alternatives. This nonpunitive form of child guidance is sometimes called *inductive discipline*, because adults induce children to regulate their behavior on the basis of the impact their actions will have on themselves and others.

The authoritative approach to child guidance is the style most strongly related to the development of self-regulation (Baumrind, 1991; Fox & Lentini, 2006; Hart et al., 2003; Milevsky, Schlechter, Netter, & Keehn, 2007). Children know what is expected of them. They also develop the skills necessary to behave in accordance with that knowledge. Such youngsters tend to be sensitive to others' needs, happy, and cooperative. They are well equipped to resist temptation, delay gratification, and control their negative impulses. They are also better able to maintain positive social interactions and initiate constructive social plans on their own. Unsurprisingly, their behavior is the most internalized of the four patterns of self-regulation described in this text. For all these reasons, children benefit when early childhood professionals adopt an authoritative style.

Adopting an Authoritative Approach to Child Guidance

Authoritative teaching is an effective way to promote self-regulation in children, and is strongly aligned with DAP. Permissive, neglectful, and authoritarian methods are not. Many people formerly believed that teachers' discipline styles were directly related to their personalities or temperaments.

It was further assumed that not much could be done to change a person's natural style (Lewin, Lippitt, & White, 1939). We now know that although adults have personality traits and abilities that seem more in keeping with one style or another, through training and practice, early childhood professionals can learn to be more authoritative (Fox & Lentini, 2006; Kostelnik, Whiren, Soderman, & Gregory, 2009). The following strategies exemplify an authoritative approach. They are listed sequentially so that preventive strategies precede remedial ones.

❏ *Authoritative teachers develop positive relationships with children* (Gallagher & Mayer, 2006; Mawhinney & Sagan, 2007). Relationships are the foundation on which authoritative teaching rests. When children feel close to their teachers, they feel emotionally safe and secure, which enables them to engage the social world with confidence and to learn from their mistakes without undue stress. Close relations with teachers also make it more likely that children will identify with them and adopt the codes of conduct they espouse. Teachers build positive relationships by interacting with each child daily in ways children interpret as supportive, attentive, and enjoyable. To achieve this, teachers do the following:

Greet children by name

Get down to the children's eye level when talking with them

Smile at children often

Laugh with children

Listen carefully to what children have to say

Speak politely to children

Invite children to talk or interact with them

Talk with children about their (the children's) feelings

Assist children in finding constructive ways to express their emotions to others

Comfort children who are unhappy, afraid, or angry

Never coerce, shame, taunt, or physically hurt children for any reason

❏ *Authoritative teachers model desirable behaviors* (Bandura, 1997; Hendrick & Weissman, 2009). This is why they consciously model turn taking, sharing, cooperating, helping, and waiting as well as other actions related to self-regulation. (See Table 6.4 for an example of how teachers model social planning.) As noted in chapter 2, authoritative adults make the most of modeling by drawing children's attention to what they or another model says or does. This helps children recognize critical details they might otherwise miss. For instance, Mr. Collins wants children to copy his gentle handling of the class gerbil, so he verbally describes his actions saying, "Watch how I pick up the gerbil. First, I'll put both hands under her tummy so I don't drop her. See how I'm holding my fingers? This way I don't squeeze her too hard."

❏ *Authoritative teachers emphasize cooperation over competition.* Teachers encourage all children to do their best, but never at one another's expense (Glasgow & Hicks, 2003; Marion, 2010). They avoid pitting one child or group of children against another (e.g., "Let's see who will get the most problems right, the boys or the girls.") and refrain from using competition to motivate children to get things done (e.g., "Let's see who can put away the most blocks." or "Whoever gets the most problems right can pick the game for recess."). Similarly, they do not reinforce one child at the expense of another

---

TABLE 6.4 Modeling Social Planning

TEACHERS MODEL SOCIAL PLANNING WHEN THEY:

❏ Follow through on the promises they make to children

❏ Ask children individually and in groups to discuss potential solutions to problems that arise in the classroom

❏ Work with children to create plans that incorporate children's solutions

❏ Help children evaluate the effectiveness of their plans and make revisions as needed

❏ Encourage children to develop proactive plans involving positive social action (The children plan to learn several "signs" so they can communicate with the custodian who uses sign language; the after-school children make a plan and work together to build a refrigerator carton rocket for the preschoolers in the center or school.)

(e.g., "Cathleen, your paper is so very neat, I wish the rest of the class would try hard like you."). Such competitive strategies may cause children to conclude there can be only one winner and that helping or cooperating with others will sabotage their chances to come out on top. To counteract self-centered thinking, teachers focus on individual progress and group accomplishments instead (e.g., "You got more problems right today than you did yesterday." or "Let's see how quickly we can all put away the blocks."). Remarks like these clear the way for children to come to one another's aid and work together as appropriate. In addition, group rewards encourage children to work as a team to accomplish common goals. Putting up a star for each book read by the class or each act of kindness shown is one way to help children keep track of their progress as a whole and direct their attention to the positive outcomes an entire group can achieve.

❏ *Authoritative teachers help children learn to negotiate to get what they want and resolve their differences peaceably* (Weinstein & Mignano, 2007). Teachers use three approaches to teach negotiation skills. One is to create natural opportunities for children to practice these skills in low-stress situations. For instance, rather than putting the same color of paint on two easels to avoid arguments, Ms. Mullen makes different colors available at each. She then urges the children to find ways to share their resources. Children are encouraged to work things out for themselves with on-the-spot coaching provided by peers or adults.

A second approach is for teachers to use puppets, flannel board stories, storybooks, or skits to illustrate relevant negotiation skills such as sharing, turn taking, and bargaining (Kreidler, 2005; Vance & Weaver, 2002). Children have chances to see both appropriate and inappropriate skill use, evaluate the tactics chosen, and generate ideas for alternative resolutions.

A third strategy is to turn children's everyday disagreements into opportunities for them to learn conflict-resolution techniques. This method is particularly important because even youngsters who can rationally discuss the value of negotiation within the context of a planned activity may forget and resort to aggressive strategies in the heat of actual confrontations. During real disagreements, children benefit from having a mediator assist them through the steps necessary for reconciliation to occur. Mediators are often adults, but they may also be other children in the program (Evans, 2002; Wheeler, 2004). In chapter 14, we provide a step-by-step model of conflict mediation and describe how to teach children effective mediation skills.

❏ *Authoritative teachers involve children in discussing and helping to make classroom rules* (Bronson, 2006; Weinstein & Mignano, 2007). Early childhood professionals hold class meetings and open-ended discussions in which children help to create some of the rules by which everyone in the class will live. Such discussions might begin with the teacher asking, "How can we make our classroom a safe and happy place to learn?" Children's ideas are written on a chart and then posted for all to see. Sample rules created by a group of first graders include:

❏ Be helpful to others
❏ Solve problems with words
❏ Don't laugh when people get hurt or make mistakes
❏ Ask people if you can touch their things before you touch them

Similar discussions are carried on throughout the year so that youngsters may consider the value of their rules over time and revise them as necessary. In this way, children and teachers share responsibility for typical classroom rules and for making sure they are followed.

❏ *Authoritative teachers set limits when children's actions could hurt someone, damage property, or interfere with the rights of others* (Curwin, Mendler, & Mendler, 2008; Levin, 2003). When authoritative teachers see a potential problem brewing, they ask themselves the following three questions.

1. Is the child's behavior unsafe for the child or others?
2. Does the child's behavior threaten to damage property?
3. Does the child's behavior interfere with the rights of others?

Even very young children can help create meaningful rules for the classroom.

If the answer to any of these questions is yes, the teacher knows to intervene. Although individual teachers vary in their interpretation of what makes a situation potentially dangerous or threatening, considering these three questions is a consistent, dependable means for deciding when to set limits on children's behavior.

❏ *Authoritative teachers stop children's unsafe behavior first and then work on resolving the problem that prompted it* (Bell, Carr, Denno, Johnson, & Phillips, 2004; Kreidler, 2005). When children's actions are potentially harmful to themselves or others, authoritative teachers step in immediately to halt dangerous actions. At times, doing so requires physical intervention such as positioning themselves between two angry children or using mild physical restraint. Once the dangerous situation is neutralized and children can focus on what is being said, the adult begins to help children work through the difficulty. Such guidance may be accomplished by holding a conversation, substituting one behavior for another, offering children choices, removing the child from the situation for a brief time, or modifying the environment in some way to allow children to get along more successfully.

❏ *Authoritative teachers focus on problem behaviors that are important enough to deal with each time they occur and ignore those that are not* (Bell et al., 2004; Edwards, 2007). Authoritative teachers only set limits that are important enough to enforce each time the problem behavior arises. They realize that not every minor infraction requires adult intervention. For instance, when Ms. Williams sees a child deliberately ruin another child's artwork, she steps in immediately, reminding children about respecting people's property. Also, she continues to enforce this expectation, day after day, no matter how tired or otherwise occupied she might be. However, although she sometimes finds children's smacking their lips loudly while they eat irritating, many days she does not want to be bothered with restricting this behavior. Because "on again, off again" limits do not provide the consistent enforcement children need to learn them, Ms. Williams tolerates this minor annoyance to address more important issues for the time being. Later, if she determines that children's lip smacking truly interferes with people's rights at the table, she will make "quiet lips" a limit and enforce this rule each day. It is the notion of *importance* that helps authoritative teachers order their priorities and focus on only a few behavior guidelines at a time. This increases the likelihood that children will be able to follow rules and expectations successfully.

❏ *Authoritative teachers remind children of rules matter-of-factly* (Gartrell, 2011; Sigsgaard, 2005). They know that children may forget what constitutes appropriate behavior from one day to the next or from one situation to another. They also realize that although children may grasp that certain behaviors such as running in the classroom are not safe, youngsters may not be able to substitute a more acceptable action without coaching. Teachers' reminders take two forms. First, they talk with children about desirable behaviors at times when infractions are not an issue. This allows children to calmly explore the value and reasons for certain expectations without the added pressure of conflict between their needs or desires and those of others. Second, early childhood professionals remind children of the rules at the moment when the rules are relevant. For example, teachers say, "Remember to walk in the classroom" when children are caught running. In these situations they avoid accusatory statements such as "How many times have I told you not to run inside?" or "You know better than to run in here."

❏ *Authoritative teachers connect reasons to rules* (Bell et al., 2004; Bugental & Goodnow, 1998; Helwig & Turiel, 2002). Reasons underscore the importance of rules and help rules make sense. As children learn the reasons for rules and limits, they gradually internalize those reasons to guide future actions. The most effective reasons correspond to the three questions teachers ask themselves prior to setting a limit: safety, protecting property, and protecting people's rights. Mr. Ramirez is protecting people's rights when he tells Dana, who is shouting across the room to a friend, "Walk over and tell her what you found so other people can concentrate on their work." In this way, he has linked the desired behavior to the rights of others in the class. Simply forbidding Dana to talk "Because I said so" or "Because that's the rule in our room" would be less helpful. Reasons are so essential to children's development of self-regulation that authoritative teachers provide reasons every time they make a rule or intervene to correct a child's mistaken behavior.

See Table 6.5 for more examples of rules linked to reasons.

TABLE 6.5   Rules and Reasons

Rules/Expectations	Reason
"Scrape the carrot away from you. Like this."	Safety: "So the scraper doesn't slip and hurt your hand."
"Say, I don't like it when you hit me."	Safety: "So no one gets hurt or angry."
"Gather by the big tree in the yard after we leave the building when the firebell rings."	Safety: "So we know everyone got out of the building safely."
"Draw on the paper, not in the book."	Property: "So the book is clean for others to read."
"Put the puzzles back on the shelf."	Property: "So the pieces don't get lost."
"Push the computer keys gently."	Property: "So the keys don't break."
"Sit on your bottom."	Rights: "So everyone can see the book."
"Tell her you want a turn."	Rights: "So she can finish using it and then you can have a chance to use it too."
"Give your ideas one person at time"	Rights: "So everyone has a chance to be heard."

❑ *In problem situations, authoritative teachers acknowledge the child's point of view first and then talk about other people's reactions* (Gartrell, 2004; Kostelnik et al., 2009). This strategy follows the developmental principle of self to others. It is exemplified when Mark, eager to use the rolling pin right away, grabs it from Celeste. The teacher physically stops the hurtful action and then says, "Mark, you really wanted that rolling pin." or "You thought it was your turn." The teacher's words are a signal to Mark that she recognizes his needs. Avoiding judgmental language, such as "You are being a naughty boy," she instead focuses on how the situation looks from Mark's point of view. This makes it easier for Mark to listen to the rest of the teacher's message in which she points out how his actions affected Celeste. "Look at Celeste, she is unhappy you grabbed it from her. She wasn't finished using it."

❑ *Authoritative teachers talk about their own emotional reactions to children's behaviors, using "personal messages"* (Kostelnik et al., 2009; Kochanska et al., 2008). These statements serve as a bridge from adherence to identification and are especially powerful with young children. Sometimes called "I statements," personal messages are adult scripts that can be used in both positive and less positive circumstances. They generally consist of three parts: acknowledging the child's perspective, identifying one's own reaction to the child's behavior, and giving a reason for that reaction (linked to safety, rights, or property).

When John shares his blocks with Ali, the teacher says,
1. "You gave Ali some of your blocks." (acknowledgment)
2. "I'm pleased you found some she could use." (adult emotion)
3. "Now each of you has blocks to build the road." (reason)

When Ali knocks John's block tower down, the teacher says,
1. "You had fun knocking down the blocks." (acknowledgment)
2. "I'm concerned John is upset." (adult emotion)
3. "He wanted to keep his tower standing." (reason)

In situations in which behavior change is desirable, authoritative teachers add a fourth part to the "personal message." It consists of a statement that redirects the child's mistaken behavior toward a more constructive alternative.
4. "Next time, ask before you knock down someone else's blocks." or, "Only knock down your own blocks." (redirection)

❑ *Authoritative teachers make positive rules and redirect children's inappropriate behavior by pointing out more acceptable actions to take instead* (Marion, 2010). Teachers recognize that how expectations and redirections are phrased influences how well children comply. Because children often have difficulty reversing ongoing actions or substituting new behaviors for current ones, authoritative adults use positive, specific directives such as, "Put your hands in your pockets" rather than relying on negative statements like, "Don't fidget" or "No pushing." Likewise, they might say, "Sing softly, don't shout," instead of only "Don't shout," so children have a clue about what to do in place of shouting.

❑ *Authoritative teachers use positive consequences to maintain children's desirable behaviors* (Curwin et al., 2008; Wolfgang, 2008). Authoritative teachers recognize the effort required by children to display positive behaviors or compliance, and they take the time to acknowledge these productive outcomes. The most common tool they use is effective praise. As you may remember from chapter 2, effective praise gives children specific feedback about the appropriate behaviors they display and why such actions are desirable. This contributes to children's natural motivation to learn and moves children beyond adherence (Reineke, Sonsteng, & Gartrell, 2008). Ms. Tanimoto is reinforcing Bert's efforts to remember to raise his hand by saying, "Bert, you remembered to raise your hand. That shows you have something to tell us." She does not simply say, "Good job, Bert." The former comment highlights Bert's appropriate behavior in a way that makes sense to him and acknowledges that he has followed a classroom rule. A perfunctory "Good job" comment gives Bert little information he can draw on in the future and will lose its effectiveness over time.

At times, teachers implement positive consequences in the form of earned privileges. For instance, if the rule is "Push the keys on the computer one at a time," children might be told that when they can demonstrate this skill they will be allowed to use the computer on their own. By granting increased independence, the teacher contributes to children's social competence and promotes children's feelings of self-efficacy.

On a few occasions, teachers use tangible rewards, such as stickers or stars on a progress chart, to help certain children develop skills that will eventually contribute to self-regulation. For example, the teacher creates a plan in partnership with a child (and sometimes the child's family) in which the child earns a star for each hour she is able to function in the classroom without shouting out. The visible evidence of her success represented by the sticker may be just what this child needs to recognize her accomplishment and be motivated to control her "shouting" impulses the next hour. As the child gains success, the teacher will gradually replace the stars with privileges or praise. This is done so that children can eventually move from adherence to other forms of motivation such as identification and internalization.

❑ *Authoritative teachers use logical consequences to help children learn more appropriate conduct* (Charles, 2008; Curwin et al., 2008). Logical consequences make an obvious connection between the child's behavior and the resulting intervention. Such consequences help children either try out a desired behavior with adult help or become involved in an effort to restore a problem situation to a more positive state. In each case, children replace an inappropriate action with a more desirable one.

A common form of logical consequence involves **rehearsal** (children approximate or practice a desirable behavior in response to some inappropriate action). For example, if the rule is "Walk; don't run" and Louise runs down the hall, a logical consequence would be to have her retrace her steps and walk. The act of walking approximates the rule and allows Louise to rehearse it physically. This consequence provides a better reminder for the future than simply admonishing her. Similarly, Mr. Collins observes that Mallory is squeezing the guinea pig until it squeals. Knowing that the animal is frightened, he intervenes. Placing his hand lightly on Mallory's, he says, "You're having fun with the guinea pig. I am concerned you might be squeezing too hard. That hurts. Hold him gently, like this." If Mallory cannot loosen her grip, Mr. Collins physically assists her in holding the animal more appropriately. Children who rehearse rules this way increase their chances for knowing how to behave more appropriately the next time.

Sometimes rehearsals are not feasible, so **restitution** is an alternative. When children make genuine amends for their mistaken behavior, they are engaged in restitution. For instance, if Julie draws on the wall, a logical consequence would be for her to wash off the marks. This action returns the wall to a more acceptable state and shows Julie that the unacceptable act of defacing the classroom will not be allowed. This logical consequence is a better solution than simply forbidding Julie to participate in a favorite activity or making her sit away from the group for a while. Although the latter acts demonstrate adult displeasure, they do not teach Julie responsibility toward school property. See Table 6.6 for more examples of logical consequences.

❑ *Authoritative teachers warn children of the logical consequences before enacting them* (Edwards, 2007). Such warnings are given through an either-or statement that repeats the rule and describes

TABLE 6.6   Examples of Logical Consequences

Problem Behavior	Rehearsal/Restitution	Logical Consequence
Maurice keeps poking at Samantha during the story	Rehearsal	Maurice sits with an adult who helps him remain focused on the story
Ji Yeong pushes to get ahead in line	Rehearsal	Ji Yeong is escorted back to her original place in line
Cory hits a child in frustration	Rehearsal	Cory is separated from the victim and sits with an adult to develop a script of what to say instead and then practices using it
	Restitution	Cory gets a wet towel to soothe the child's tears
Karen steps on a child's fingers in the sandbox	Restitution	Karen helps the teacher put ice on the victim's fingers
Troy tears a doll's hair off as he struggles to keep another child from getting the doll	Restitution	Troy helps glue the doll's hair back on
Marie knocks down another child's block building	Restitution	Marie helps the child to rebuild

to the child what will happen if the rule is broken (Kostelnik et al., 2009). For example, if the rule is "Push up your sleeves before you paint," the warning could be "Either push up your sleeves yourself, or I will help you." If the rule is "Wait your turn at the water fountain," the warning might be "Either wait your turn, or go to the end of the line." In both cases, the warning gives children the opportunity and incentive to change their behavior themselves. It also serves as a signal that if they do not comply, the adult will take steps to ensure compliance. Maintaining a calm demeanor is essential so that the warning is a plain statement of fact, not a threat. Its purpose is to provide maximum guidance to children before adult enforcement.

myeducationlab

Go to the Video Examples section of Topic 12: Guiding Children in the MyEducationLab for your course and watch the video entitled *Managing Challenging Behavior: Dealing with Conflict.* A child has difficulty sharing the trains. What authoritative teaching strategies does the teacher use to address this challenging behavior? What rule is the teacher enforcing?

❏ *Authoritative teachers follow through when children fail to comply*   (Charles, 2008). Following through helps children make a connection between the broken rule and a more desirable alternative behavior. Because logical consequences are educational, following through gives children valuable information about how to redirect their behavior. It also shows them that adults mean what they say, which makes the classroom predictable (Curwin et al., 2008; King & Gartrell, 2004).

The follow-through procedure consists of first acknowledging the child's desire within the situation. This acknowledgment is a nonevaluative summary of the event from the child's viewpoint. The next step is to repeat the warning briefly and then declare that the consequence will take place. A sample script follows: "Ralph, you're eager to get a drink. Remember, I said either wait your turn or go to the end of the line. Now go to the end of the line." The teacher waits a moment to see if Ralph can do so himself. If not, the teacher will escort Ralph to the designated spot as a way to maintain enforcement.

Following through in this way must be consistent. Every time the rule is broken, the consequence must be enforced. Rules enforced erratically, varying from situation to situation or from child to child, are rules that children ignore. Authoritative teachers thus insist on only a few rules as a way to maintain consistency.

Rule enforcement must be immediate. Once the teacher gives the warning and a short time for the child to comply, he or she must follow through if compliance does not occur. Long delays between when the child breaks the rule and when the follow-through takes place diminish the educational impact of the consequence.

When warnings are consistently followed by enactment of logical consequences, teachers' actions become predictable to children. Youngsters learn that if they do not comply at the warning stage, a follow-through will take place. This strategy encourages them to respond to the warning without having to experience a consequence directly. Behavior change at this point shows some self-regulation by children, although at the adherence level. Gradually, children learn to use rules and their accompanying reasons as a behavioral guide. In this way, they begin to exercise more control over their conduct while teachers exert less. Thus, children gradually make the transition from external to internal behavior controls.

FIGURE 6.2   Establishing Expectations for Brian—Told by Brian's Teacher

Brian, age 3, came to my Pre-K classroom in August. Not long after that he was officially identified as needing special education for speech and language. He had particular difficulty producing language sounds and had a mild hearing loss.

One of the goals we (his parents, the speech thera-pist, and I) established was to have Brian feel part of the group. This included following basic classroom rules expected of all the children. Sitting at group time was one of these rules. Initially, Brian decided that he absolutely wasn't going to sit with the other children during group time. In the beginning I allowed him some leeway on this because I knew he didn't quite understand the situation. However, once he had some experience with group time, and he still wouldn't comply, I assisted him. I helped him sit down. I made eye contact and I said, "This is group time; you have to stay here a few minutes." We kept group time very short. To help him comply, I would have him sit next to me or next to my aide. Many times I had

him sit on my lap, and she (the aide) would lead the group. As he became better able to sit through the activities, I tried to have him stay there on his own. Each child in my class has a carpet square to designate his or her place to sit or lean. I would help him sit down on his carpet square and say, "This is your space, or, would you like this one? You can have this one. I'll help you sit here."

Sometimes Brian sat and sometimes he didn't. Sometimes we would have to repeat the expectations three or four times. Each time he got up my aide or I would retrieve him. We were very consistent. We knew if we stayed calm and persistent, the day would come when he would sit in group without our help. Some children take a long, long time. We had to follow through with our expectations many times a day. Besides setting limits, we made sure group time was fun too. By midyear, Brian was more successful and found that group time could be an enjoyable part of the day.

Source: Adapted from Kostelnik, M. J., Onaga, E., Rohde, B., & Whiren, A. (2002). *Children with special needs: Lessons for early childhood professionals.* New York: Teachers College Press.

❏ *Authoritative teachers collaborate with family members to promote children's self-regulation* (Barbour, Barbour, & Scully, 2005; Glasgow & Hicks, 2003). Children benefit when all the signifi-cant adults in their lives communicate and work together toward mutual goals. Knowing this, teachers talk with family members about their expectations for children and the guidance strate-gies they use at home. In turn, teachers acquaint families with expectations held for children in the early childhood setting, answering family members' questions honestly and openly. In addition, early childhood staff members talk with family members about mutual ways to help children achieve self-regulation. These conversations are held in a spirit of shared learning and support.

❏ *Authoritative teachers adapt their guidance strategies to accommodate children's special needs* (Brewer, 2007; Allen & Edwards Cowdery, 2008). All young children need to learn how to share, take turns, manage their emotions, respond to the needs of others, and follow certain rules. This includes children with disabilities. The authoritative teaching techniques discussed in this chapter can be used effectively with children whose abilities vary widely. However, adaptations are sometimes required to accommodate children's special needs. Specific accommodations will depend on the child. Naturally, strategies teachers might use to support a child with a hearing impairment may differ from ones used to support a child who has cerebral palsy. Specific ideas about how to guide the development of self-discipline in children who have special needs are derived by consulting with family members, spe-cialists in the field, professional organizations, and the literature (Kostelnik et al., 2009). In many (but not all) cases, it may take some children longer to consistently apply the skills they are learning (Paasche, Gorrill, & Strom, 2004). An example of how one teacher accommodated the special needs of a child in her class while establishing expectations for his behavior at school is illustrated in Figure 6.2.

THE RELATION BETWEEN AUTHORITATIVE TEACHING AND DAP

Although the strategies associated with authoritative teaching are strongly associated with DAP, they alone are not sufficient to equal it. As with all other aspects of early childhood education, early childhood professionals must ask themselves if their expectations and the methods they use to maintain them are age appropriate, individually appropriate, and socially and culturally appro-priate for the children. With these questions in mind, let us consider the following expectation, which is typical in many early childhood classrooms.

At group time, children must raise their hands to speak.

Question: Is this expectation age appropriate?
Answer: This is not an age-appropriate expectation for 3-year-olds, who are just learning to discuss in groups. On the basis of what we know about young children's need for sensory

involvement and movement, group-time activities should not be dominated by oral turn taking and waiting. A better strategy would be to practice such skills in small groups of two or three children. In either case, hand raising is not a particularly useful way to help young children learn to talk together.

Children 7 and 8 years old will be better equipped to respond to this rule. They have both the oral and physical skills necessary to wait and to signal with a raised hand that they desire to speak.

Question: Is this expectation individually appropriate?

Answer: This might be an appropriate expectation for Dan, who has had many opportunities to participate in circle-time conversations and who is feeling relaxed and comfortable in the group. It may be less appropriate for Duwana, who is new to the classroom and is feeling apprehensive about participating in the group conversation.

Question: Is this expectation socially and culturally appropriate?

Answer: This expectation may fit some children's cultural experience. However, it may be less relevant to children whose family and community experiences include a strong emphasis on group response and spontaneous affirmations of things that are being said. Program setting and activity type are other sociocultural factors to consider. Raising your hand to speak may make sense as part of a demonstration, but it may be irrelevant if brainstorming is the group activity underway.

This example illustrates the complexity of guiding children's behavior. There are no "one size fits all" answers. Instead, early childhood professionals continually make judgments about the standards they set and the strategies they use. Adults gear their guidance strategies to match and respect children's current capabilities, simultaneously recognizing that what may work best for one group of children may not be suitable for a second group and that what is effective for one child may not be best for another (Copple & Bredekamp, 2009). In deciding which strategies to use and when, authoritative teachers consider less intrusive alternatives before engaging in those that require more intervention. This approach is illustrated in Figure 6.3, the authoritative teaching continuum (Gordon & Browne, 1996). The initial strategies in the continuum give children maximum control of the situation; the strategies further down the continuum put more control in the adult's hands.

AUTHORITATIVE TEACHING AND THE IMPORTANCE OF TEAMWORK AMONG STAFF

Individual teachers who adopt authoritative methods report increased satisfaction with their teaching and more confidence in working with children. They also report better harmony in the classroom and more frequent incidents of positive behaviors among their students (Weinstein & Mignano, 2007; Kontos & Wilcox-Herzog, 1997). These positive results are multiplied when all personnel in the early childhood setting (full time, part time, paid, and volunteer) collectively and consciously set out to adopt an authoritative approach (Gartrell, 2004). The more successful the adults are in creating an authoritative environment, the more easily children develop the relationships and skills they need to achieve self-regulation.

The essential element in creating an authoritative environment, whether in a single early childhood classroom or in a multiclassroom program, is communication. Communication is fostered when the program includes the following:

❏ A written policy describing how guidance will be addressed in the early childhood setting. This document describes how discipline problems will be prevented, how staff will support children's positive behaviors, and what to do if children engage in inappropriate behavior (Taylor & Baker, 2002). A copy of the policy is provided to every staff member, volunteer, and parent or other relevant family member. Such policies usually include a brief statement of beliefs regarding the importance of self-regulation and the conditions that foster it, a small number of critical rules children and adults have helped to create, and a statement of how the rules will be established and maintained.

❏ Opportunities for staff members and family members to share ideas and work together to promote self-regulation among children. Regular communication occurs between home and the program, including formal and informal interactions.

❏ In-service training that addresses the skills associated with authoritative teaching. Such training involves everyone who works with children in the program, including teachers, bus drivers, cooks, aides, and so forth.

FIGURE 6.3   The Authoritative Teaching Continuum

Least Directive → Most Directive

1. **Watch and listen.** Keep children in view from a short distance. Make yourself available if children want your help, but let them work things out if they can.

2. **Add or take something away** to make a situation easier for children to manage on their own. For instance, too few objects for children to use in the water table could lead to squabbles. Adding a few more might be all that is needed for children to share more successfully. In contrast, too many objects in the water table might make pouring and playing without splashing one another difficult. Removing a few items could make using the materials cooperatively easier for children.

3. **Say what you see.** "It looks like two people want to use the funnel at the same time." "It looks like there's a problem here." "You found a way to share the water wheel. That was a friendly thing to do."

4. **Provide more information.** "You thought he was splashing you on purpose. He was trying to get all that water into that little hole and a lot splashed out. It was an accident." "Sometimes when two people want the same thing at the same time, they decide to share or take turns."

5. **Pose questions and make plans.** "What could you do to solve this problem?" "What could you do instead of hitting her to show you're angry?" "Let's make a plan so this won't happen again."

6. **Give choices.** "John is using the funnel right now. You may use the strainer or the green plastic tubing." "It's cleanup time. You may put away the smocks or drain the water out of the table."

7. **Physically intervene.** Stop hurtful actions such as hitting by catching the child's hands. Hold onto a wiggling child to help him or her hear what you are saying. Separate two children who are pushing.

8. **Help children negotiate problems.** Serve as a translator in the situation. "Did you like it when he scratched you? What could you say to him about that?" "What did you want?" "James, you think it would be okay to take turns. What do you think, Robert?"

9. **Remind children of limits.** "You really wanted the water wheel. It bothers me when you grab to get what you want Ask Jerome for a turn next." "Remember, we have a rule that everyone must share the toys at the center." "I can't let you hit him. Hitting hurts. Say, 'I'm next.'"

10. **Link consequences and actions.** "Either take turns with the water wheel or you'll have to choose something else to do." "If you hit again, you'll have to leave the water table." "You found a way to get everyone's container in the water table. That solved the problem."

11. **Take action in conjunction with the child.** "You're having a hard time remembering to share the things at the water table. Let's look around for another activity for you to do." "You splashed water all over Jenny. Let's get some towels and help her dry off."

12. **Enforce consequences.** "You hit. Now you must leave the water table."

❏ Regularly scheduled times during which team members brainstorm solutions to typical behavioral problems, discuss ways to promote positive child behaviors, and reach a consensus about how certain rules will be interpreted and enforced.

❏ Program policies that are reviewed and revised periodically.

In addition to these strategies, team members might agree to adopt the authoritative strategies outlined in this chapter a few at a time. Colleagues may practice as well as observe and listen to one another and provide supportive feedback regarding successes and ways to improve their skills. The checklist provided in Figure 6.4 is a simple tool that team members could use to guide their observations.

QUESTIONS ADULTS ASK ABOUT PROMOTING SELF-DISCIPLINE IN CHILDREN

Promoting self-regulation among children is challenging. This subject prompts many questions from teachers, administrators, and family members regarding philosophy and implementation. Following are discussions about common issues.

Isn't Just Saying "No" Faster and Better?

When children engage in inappropriate behavior, we may be tempted to simply say "No" or "We don't do that here." Occasionally, these oral shortcuts have the desired effect; children stop misbehaving. Unfortunately, such success is usually short lived, and children repeat the same infractions later. Moreover, children tend to comply only under direct supervision. The moment the adult's back is turned, problem behaviors resume. Authoritative teaching yields a different result; children become more self-disciplined with time. Although following through on logical consequences or

FIGURE 6.4 Authoritative Teaching Skills Rating Scale

Directions: This tool can be used as a self-check measure or as a rating scale completed by an on-site observer. It can be completed in a single 30-minute observation or over multiple observations. Items should be scored according to the following key:

0 = Seldom used or not observed   1 = Sometimes used   2 = Used most of the time

Maximum score = 36

36 to 32 = Expert level: strong performance
31 to 28 = Intermediate level: demonstrates strengths, some areas to improve
27 to 25 = Novice level: needs targeted attention to specific authoritative teaching skills
Below 25 = Much attention needed to achieve authoritative teaching competence

The adult:

_____ Demonstrates interest in children: Greets children individually, says good-bye to each child, invites children to interact, gets down to the children's level when talking with them

_____ Demonstrates respect for children: Listens to children, allows children to finish what they are saying, picks up on children's interests as the subject of conversation, acknowledges children's comments and questions

_____ Offers children choices

_____ Includes children in classroom decisions

_____ States rules that promote safety, protect property, or protect others' rights

_____ States expectations positively: "Ride on the cement" not "Don't ride on the grass"

_____ Suggests alternatives to unacceptable behaviors: "Ask for a turn" or "Walk" instead of "No running inside"

_____ Acknowledges children's positive behaviors

_____ Offers reasons for expectations

_____ States consequences that are immediate

_____ States consequences that are consistent

_____ States consequences that are logical

_____ Uses an appropriate warning prior to enacting a consequence: States the warning as an either-or statement linking the rule to a logical consequence

_____ Follows through on the stated consequence if the child does not comply

_____ Acknowledges the child's viewpoint in problem situations

_____ Intervenes when children are aggressive by stopping the hurtful actions and setting a limit

_____ Uses proximity control: Moves near children to survey the situation and gives children cues to change behavior

_____ Uses gentle restraint: The adult holds one child back from hitting another child

negotiating conflicts may take several minutes, children gain skills from these interactions that they can use again and again. In addition, when you use authoritative strategies such as acknowledging children's positive behavior or offering reasons for rules, you provide mini-lessons both for the children directly involved and for other children nearby. This benefits all.

Shouldn't Children Already Know How to Behave by the Time They Get to Kindergarten and First and Second Grade?

Children do not enter kindergarten, first grade, or second grade having mastered all they need to know about appropriate behavior. Even youngsters who have attended preschool or child care find that elementary school expectations are more structured and elaborate than those they encountered in the past. Many children have never eaten in a lunchroom, walked down a long hallway, or gone to a gym. All these new situations call for new behaviors. As a result, children in the early grades continually experiment with assorted social strategies, discovering what works and what does not and what is permitted and what is not allowed.

Social learning takes time and cannot be hurried. Children are not just memorizing school rules; they are constructing an understanding of what each rule means and applying this concept to their behavior. Consequently, knowing the rules and being able to follow them independently are two important but very different tasks, and the latter is much more challenging than the former. Years, not days or weeks, are necessary for mastery to develop. For these reasons, child guidance deserves special consideration in the early elementary curriculum. Adults cannot simply demand that children act in socially acceptable ways; instead, they must teach children how to do so.

What's the Story on Rewards? I've Heard Some People Say They Are Not Developmentally Appropriate

Today, early childhood professionals have differing opinions about using rewards (positive consequences) with young children. The following chart summarizes contrasting views in the field (Shiller & O'Flynn, 2008; Reineke et al., 2008).

THE CASE FOR REWARDS	THE CASE AGAINST REWARDS
Rewards get children to adherence; this is the first step toward achieving greater self-regulation.	Rewards keep children at adherence; children learn to behave for external reasons such as stickers or praise, rather than for intrinsic satisfaction.
Rewards can help children discern what is desirable behavior.	Rewards can be manipulative.
Rewards can signal children that they have been successful.	Rewards can lose their power over time.
Rewards can provide children with evidence of their increasing competence.	Rewards are not always meaningful to children.

At first these perspectives seem incompatible and mutually exclusive. They imply rewards are either good or bad. However, as is true for most aspects of developmentally appropriate practice, rewards are not "all or nothing" tools. As noted earlier in this chapter, children's motivation to behave in certain ways actually exists on a continuum ranging from motivation that is outside oneself (e.g., adherence) to motivation that comes from deep within (e.g., internalization) (Jalongo, 2007). The strategies teachers use to promote children's positive behavior must consider this continuum as well as counter the weaknesses evident on each side of the either-or dichotomy outlined previously. That is why early childhood educators set up environments and interact with young learners to help children with the following:

1. Gain personal satisfaction from behaving in socially acceptable ways and from developing skills associated with social competence
2. Receive timely and useful feedback regarding their learning and behavior
3. Experience and recognize successes

Positive consequences that are age appropriate, individually appropriate, and culturally appropriate can contribute to these aims, but only when used in combination with the other skills outlined in this chapter.

How Can We Promote Consistency Between the Way Guidance Is Handled in the Early Childhood Setting and How It Is Addressed at Home?

The key to achieving more consistency between home and the program is to establish open channels of communication in which everyone feels valued and respected. The first step is to share basic information. Parents need to know how children will be socialized in the early childhood setting and the rationale for particular goals and strategies. They also need to receive accurate information about their role in the process. Practitioners, in turn, need to know about parents' aspirations for their children and what measures families use to promote these. This kind of information could be exchanged during a home visit, at a program orientation, or through written materials.

Consistency is further enhanced when parents, teachers, and administrators get together to explore values and philosophies. Workshops, parent–teacher conferences, and informal discussions at the classroom or program level are effective ways for school staff and parents to share ideas and problem-solving techniques related to child socialization (Barbour et al., 2008; NAESP, 2005). These times are most productive when the emphasis is on mutual understanding and collaboration.

What Can Be Done When Conflicts Exist Between the Teacher's and Families' Approaches to Discipline?

Many times, the influential people in children's lives have different ideas about how children should behave. Consequently, they may advocate conflicting codes of conduct. For instance, to promote group harmony, program personnel may require children to respond to peer bullying by using nonviolent strategies. Family members, more focused on children's self-defense skills, may encourage them to "fight" when threatened. Both ideas—harmonious living and personal safety—have merit, but they are different and seem to call for incompatible responses from children. This conflict puts children in a dilemma: To obey one set of expectations, they have to violate another.

Contradictory situations such as these might be handled in three different ways. The first is for teachers and family members to discuss their differences honestly and directly, searching for common ground. In the example just described, both parties most likely want children to be safe. They agree on the goal, but their means for achieving it differ. If they recognize their mutual aim, they will have a compatible base from which to explore potential resolutions to the child's predicament.

On other occasions, conflicts arise from differences in style. Teachers sometimes believe they have little in common with parents who hold nonauthoritative attitudes toward discipline. Likewise family members who utilize authoritarian or permissive philosophies may question authoritative techniques. In these cases it helps to emphasize the similarities between philosophies rather than concentrating on discrepancies (Bollin, 1989; Gullo, 2006). Authoritarian and authoritative styles both advocate firm control and high standards; permissive and authoritative styles each promote warm, accepting relationships between children and adults. Discussing authoritative strategies in terms of how they support these overarching principles provides common ground between philosophies.

For instance, adults with authoritarian attitudes may believe that offering children choices is unnecessary because youngsters should simply do as they are told. To help parents feel more comfortable with providing choices for children, the teacher could recommend that the adult first establish boundaries on the child's behavior (such as getting dressed now) and then offer the child a choice (the color of the shirt to wear). This combines an authoritarian value (achieving compliance) with an authoritative value (helping children achieve independence), building a bridge between the two.

A third strategy for reducing children's confusion about contradictory home–program expectations is to help children realize that adults have differing reactions to their behavior. This enables teachers to stress that certain standards may be situation specific: "You're upset. At home you don't have to pick up your things. That may be, but it bothers me when the puzzles are all over the floor. Pieces could be lost. Here at the center everybody is expected to help. Find a puzzle to put away."

On the rare occasions when no mutually satisfactory resolution seems possible, acknowledge that differences exist and make clear to family members how and why authoritative strategies will be used in the program. Children benefit from exposure to authoritative models, even when other adults in their lives are more authoritarian or more permissive. Teachers and administrators who reason with children provide alternative models of interaction and problem solving for children to evaluate and try.

SUMMARY

Young children are not born knowing the rules of society or the settings in which they participate. How to achieve their goals in socially acceptable ways and get along with others are things children have to learn how to do. This learning continues throughout the school years. Parents, teachers, other significant adults in children's lives, and peers all contribute to the lessons children experience during this time. Initially, young children depend on others to direct their behavior for them. However, with time, they learn to respond to rewards and punishments or the moral codes of admired adults as clues about how to behave. These guides are useful and necessary but do not represent the most self-regulated form of social behavior, which occurs only if children treat certain standards of conduct as logical extensions of their beliefs and personal values. We call this *internalization*. Internalization equals self-regulation. Self regulated children grow into ethical, compassionate people who do what they think is right to support their internally constructed perceptions of right and wrong.

The extent to which children exhibit self-regulation is affected by developmental factors such as emotional maturity, cognition, language, and memory. Another influence is children's daily experiences with people. Throughout early childhood, parents and teachers in particular have a tremendous impact on which social behaviors children adopt. These grown-ups use a variety of socialization strategies such as modeling, instruction, and consequences to help children learn acceptable codes of behavior. However, not all adults use or combine these strategies in the same way. Four of the most common variations—uninvolved, permissive, authoritarian, and authoritative—have been the subject of much research. The uninvolved, permissive, and authoritarian styles yield negative results that can undermine self-regulation and positive social adjustment in children. The authoritative style has been most strongly linked to the development of self-regulation. Consequently, much of this chapter is devoted to describing techniques associated with authoritative teaching. Such strategies can be applied in a single classroom or on a program-wide basis.

Key Words

adherence	identification	permissive discipline style
authoritarian discipline style	internalization	punishment
authoritative discipline style	logical consequences	rehearsal
communication	maturity demands	restitution
control	nurturance	uninvolved discipline style

Applying What You've Read in This Chapter

1. **Discuss**
   a. On the basis of your reading and your experiences with young children, discuss each of the questions that open this chapter.
   b. Using ideas and strategies in this chapter, discuss what you might do in the following situations.
      ❏ Jennifer and Marlene each want a rolling pin at the dough table. Only one is available.
      ❏ The pretend-play area is set up for four children. You notice seven children playing there.
      ❏ A parent calls to report that children are rowdy at the bus stop each day. She is worried that some of the younger children will get hurt as older children chase and shove.
      ❏ Sharon slams her book on the table. "I can't read this. I'll never read this. It's too hard," she screams.

2. **Observe**
   a. Observe a group of children in a classroom or outdoors. What are some of the positive behaviors you notice among the children? What are some of the problems they encounter in getting along? How do the children respond to one another in these situations? What implications do your observations have for your approach to child guidance?
   b. Observe a classroom of teachers and children. What are some of the strategies adults use to guide children's behavior? Do these strategies support or detract from the long-range goal of helping children achieve self-regulation?

3. **Carry out an activity**
   a. Interview two early childhood educators who work with children of different ages. Ask them to describe the most common discipline problems they face. How do they solve such problems when they arise?
   b. Attend a community presentation or workshop related to child guidance. What was the presenter's main message? What kinds of questions did people in the audience have? What is your reaction to what you heard?

4. **Create something for your portfolio**
   a. Describe a situation in which you guided a child's behavior. What was the child doing? What did you do? How effective was your approach? What might you do if the same situation arose again?
   b. Ask a supervisor to identify three strengths that you demonstrate in using an authoritative style with children. Also ask him or her to identify one thing you need to work on in the future. Develop a plan to maintain your strengths and improve in the area identified.

5. **Add to your journal**
   a. What is the most significant concept that you learned about promoting self-regulation in children from your readings and your experience with children?
   b. Describe what you would have to do to become more authoritative in your approach to child guidance.

6. ✋ **Consult the standards**
   a. Refer to the Social Studies Standards developed by the National Council for Social Studies (NCSS, 1998), or McREL*Content Knowledge: A Compendium of Standards and Benchmarks for K–12 Education* (Kendall & Marzano, 2004). Identify standards that relate to children's development of self-regulation, K–3. Explain your choices.
   b. Refer to the Early Childhood Learning Standards/ Expectations for your state. Identify standards that relate to children developing self-regulation.

PRACTICE FOR YOUR CERTIFICATION OR LICENSURE EXAM

The following items will help you practice applying what you have learned in this chapter. They can help to prepare you for your course exam, the PRAXIS II exam, your state licensure or certification exam, and for working in developmentally appropriate ways with young children.

Child Guidance

Mr. Sanchez walks into the school library and finds three second graders behind the shelves, cutting pages out of a book about rocks.

1. **Constructed-response question**

   a. Describe one natural and two logical consequences Mr. Sanchez could use in this situation.

   b. Choose the consequence that you think would be best for Mr. Sanchez to apply and provide a rationale for your answer.

2. **Multiple-choice question**

   Which of the following actions does *not* fit the behavior pattern of an authoritarian adult? The adult:

   a. Is flexible
   b. Has high expectations for children's behavior
   c. Is detached
   d. Expects children to obey classroom rules

Chapter

7

Authentic Assessment for Evaluating and Guiding Children's Progress

You may wonder:

How do I keep track of what children are learning in my classroom?
What is meant by *authentic* assessment and how can it be implemented in early childhood classrooms?
What part should standardized tests play in evaluating children's development?
How can information about children's development and learning be organized to give an accurate picture of children's progress?
How can information related to assessment be shared effectively with parents?

This chapter on the assessment and evaluation of young children contains information to help you answer these questions.

◆ ◆ *Gavin Williams knows how important oral language development is for the 3- and 4-year-olds in his classroom. He takes periodic samples of each child's communication, and today, while the children are at free play, he is recording some of the conversation he hears. He notes the oral turn taking going on; the fact that the children are able to sustain a conversational theme; and some of the vocabulary they are using, such as "quart" and "engineer." Marking down Kendra's use of alliteration—"buttery, buttery bundles of corn"—he makes a note to himself to showcase this in large group tomorrow and to invite other children to invent some phrases.*

◆ ◆ *While the children in Ms. McAfee's room are busy at their centers this morning, she is spending a few minutes with each of them, going over their self-appraisal checklists. She helps the children review the early math skills they are working on, showing them how to color in those they have achieved and others she has observed. "Good for you," she tells Juana. "You've learned 2 new skills this month. You have only 3 left on this list, and then you'll have all 10 skills checked. Which one is going to be your special target for the next time we visit about this?"*

◆ ◆ *Mary Descharne is listening as a small group of children practice presenting their portfolios to one another. With her help, they have chosen five of their best pieces of work for the past 3 months, have designed a showcase folder, and will share their work with their family members at a special celebration on Thursday night. The pride they feel is reflected in their faces as they describe why they have chosen a particular piece and the meaning it has for them.*

Each of these teachers is involved in ongoing, strategic, and purposeful assessment and evaluation. Daily, they are active in documenting what the children in their classrooms know and will need to know, the progress being made toward learning and developmental goals, and whether various aspects of the program are supporting each child's growth. For them, assessment is not something that is contrived or something they do *in addition* to their teaching; it has become an integral and useful component of each day.

THE CHANGING FACE OF EARLY CHILDHOOD ASSESSMENT

The need for well-designed assessment and evaluation to help professionals make informed decisions in early childhood education is growing. In addition to learning more about how individual children think, learn, develop, and behave across time, educators need to collect and document information to inform instruction, to identify children who might benefit from special help or additional health services, and to report children's progress to their families. All this constitutes what is known as *assessment,* which takes place primarily through observation, administration of commercial and teacher-constructed tools, and examination of the products that young children create (Morrison, 2006).

Other professionals, funding or regulatory agencies, boards of directors, school boards, legislators, and citizen groups may also require early childhood educators to collect information about the children they are teaching for the following purposes (Egertson, 2008):

❏ To guide children's learning and to inform instruction
❏ To identify children's special needs

❑ To assess the strengths and needs of programs
❑ To hold programs accountable

Connecting assessment to real learning and school improvement in meaningful ways will require our looking at it with new eyes. It must be linked to actual experience in the classroom, and it must become a major component of teacher inservice and ongoing professional development. State and national standards for teacher licensure and program accreditation should require teachers to be competent in integrating learning and assessment (Stiggins, 2007).

In addition, we must become more skillful in designing classroom assessments that will be useful not only to adults for all their purposes, but primarily to the children who are being evaluated. Even very young children need to better understand expectations and to have some understanding of what is needed to reach each of these targets.

RESPONSIBLE EARLY CHILDHOOD ASSESSMENT AND EVALUATION

Often, many professionals tend to use the terms "assessment" and "evaluation" interchangeably when, in fact, they are very different in meaning. **Assessment** is a systematic procedure for obtaining information from observation, interviews, portfolios, projects, tests, and other sources that can be used to make judgments about characteristics of children or programs. **Evaluation** is more complicated. It involves the measurement, comparison, and judgment of the values, quality, or worth of children's work and/or of their schools, teachers, or a specific education program, based upon valid evidence gathered through assessment (Council of Chief State School Officers [CCSSO], 2009). Thus, a truly effective assessment system is more than a collection of separate observations, tests, and formal or informal assessments performed by various professionals at different stages in a child's life. However, in most school systems and communities, such a collection is currently the norm. Often, no connection exists between preprimary screening and assessment and later school entry, other than ensuring that children have had their immunizations. Frequently, valuable information that was gained during well-child screenings or from preschool, child-care, or Head Start attendance is lost or ignored. Such information may include anecdotal records, health histories and records of special needs, records of home visits, checklists relative to oral language development and social skills acquisition, and notations about the emergence of motor skills.

Following entry into kindergarten, there may be little understanding from grade to grade about a child's development other than the general information that is reported in permanent school records or on a child's report cards. Many teachers "start all over" at each grade level in terms of understanding the child's strengths or learning limitations, and sometimes this approach is even purposeful. Ms. Stibble, a second-grade teacher, never looks at previous information about children coming into her room: "I don't want to be biased before they even start!" she exclaims. As a result, she may be wasting costly time in understanding the children's needs.

Well-conceived assessment procedures and tools must be connected to a defined scope and sequence of the curricular skills and concepts children are expected to develop as they move from learning context to learning context. This match, in turn, must be linked with ongoing daily instruction and intervention by the classroom teacher who draws it all together.

Individuals who are implementing evaluation procedures greatly affect the outcome, by design or by default. Assessment and evaluation will be effective only to the extent that attention focuses on the following:

❑ Evaluator's relative subjectivity–objectivity and skills
❑ State of the child at the time of evaluation
❑ Properties of the evaluation setting
❑ Timing of the evaluation
❑ Appropriate selection of data collection tools and strategies
❑ Thoughtful application of outcomes

Assessment and evaluation findings should never become conversational fodder for the teacher's lounge or other public gatherings, and children's limitations should be discussed with others only in terms of how instruction can be modified to minimize them (see Figure 7.1). Confidentiality is the mark of a professional and is supported by the NAEYC code of ethics.

FIGURE 7.1   **Using Children's Strengths and Limitations to Adapt Instruction**

Zai Zai, a child who has recently emigrated to the United States, is enrolled in a local pre-school class for 4-year-olds. Frustrated because of his lack of English and his classmates' unresponsiveness to him, Zai Zai has begun grabbing the arms of children and pinching them. The teacher and school director discuss the problem behavior and also Zai Zai's strengths—his strong desire to play with others and to make friends. Together, they develop a plan to implement immediately:

- Increase adult proximity to and monitoring of Zai Zai
- Provide Zai Zai with scripts for interacting with children
- Implement a consistent verbal response and immediate consequence when Zai Zai's behavior is inappropriate
- Acknowledge Zai Zai's attempts to use the scripts to ask for what he needs or wants from other children
- Meet in 1 week to evaluate the usefulness of the plan

Examining the Evaluator's Subjectivity–Objectivity and Skills

Perhaps nothing is as dangerous in the evaluation process as evaluators who are unaware of their personal biases or lack of evaluation know-how. The latter would include a lack of knowledge about child development and the inability to structure and apply appropriate evaluation strategies. As the classroom teacher, you should be the person who plans and carries out most of the assessment. To do this well, you will want to establish good rapport with individual children and make sure that you are sensitive to any effects that may arise because of differences related to a child's gender, race, ethnic background, and personality. Teachers must also examine as objectively as possible the expectations they bring into the situation and avoid providing spoken and unspoken reinforcement to one child that is not given just as freely to other children.

Obtaining the Child's Best Response

Young children may be difficult to test. They have no concept of the importance attached to the process and most are inexperienced with paper-and-pencil assessment formats. They tire easily, are easily distracted, may have little interest in doing well, may be wary of an evaluator who is unfamiliar, and may simply refuse to cooperate. When English is a second language, children's cultural backgrounds can also affect their performance. Every effort should be made to obtain several samples of the child's best work, performed when the child is at ease, healthy, and motivated. Many problems can be eliminated in early childhood classrooms when evaluation procedures become a normal and less intrusive part of everyday activity.

Choosing an Evaluation Setting

Ideally, early childhood classrooms, where evaluation should take place, are pleasant environments with adequate ventilation, light, and space; pleasing aesthetic qualities; minimal distractions; and modified noise levels. Realistically, these factors are not always optimal. When they are not, both children's learning and their evaluation may be negatively affected. These factors should be considered when educators are planning classroom activities that will serve as a basis for evaluation. Children should not be removed from the classroom to unfamiliar settings for evaluation of activities and events that normally occur in the classroom. However, every effort should be made to ensure that the classroom setting and the ongoing activity in the room at evaluation time do not distract from the children's best efforts.

Determining the Timing of the Evaluation

When doing assessments, you will want to consider two aspects of timing. One is the consistency in the scheduling of skill and behavior sampling. The other is the assessment itself. Some forms of assessment, such as vision and hearing testing and obtaining health records and family profiles, are most helpful when secured as early as possible before interaction with the child begins. Evaluation should be both formative (i.e., ongoing) and summative. Build into your program ongoing methods of collecting daily work samples, as well as opportunities for planned observation and discussion with children. Use more formal measures such as a developmental inventory or running record to measure progress in reading at specified periods during the year. Assessment of skills and behaviors should not be attempted until you have established rapport with children and they have had adequate opportunity to practice the skills and behaviors to be assessed. Assessment should also not be undertaken at certain times of the school year and on school days when children are more likely to be distracted, are less able to concentrate, or are likely to feel rushed (e.g., directly before recess, on the day of a Halloween party, or after returning from vacation).

Selecting Data Collection Strategies and Tools

When we think of testing situations, we usually envision a group of people sitting quietly, taking paper-and-pencil tests. This scenario in early education spells disaster and is developmentally inappropriate. Children may know the answer but may not have developed the skill required to record it correctly or in the right place. In a group setting, they may become confused about what they need to do but be too shy to ask an adult or another child for help.

Before deciding what kinds of strategies or tools are needed, determine the purpose of the assessment.

❏ What do you want to know about this child and how specifically?
❏ Is diagnostic information needed?
❏ How will the data be used?
❏ Who else will need to see and use the data?
❏ If a federal or state granting or funding agency will be involved, will it accept only standardized test results, or are teacher-constructed measures considered valid?
❏ What factors about the child or the testing situation should affect your decision?
❏ How much time can be spared for the evaluation, and when and where should it take place?
❏ Will just one child be evaluated, or a group of children?
❏ Should a direct strategy be used that involves the child, or can an unobtrusive measure work just as well so that the child is unaware of being tested?

Once the basic purpose and related details have been considered, you can select from a number of good evaluation options.

STANDARDIZED TESTING: WHAT PART SHOULD IT PLAY IN EVALUATING CHILDREN'S PROGRESS?

Eight-year-old Lamont is taking a standardized reading test, and it's clear that he's having trouble. With his head bobbing and nose pointing to each word in the passage, he scans back and forth, whispering aloud each of the words. When finished, he moves on to the questions. Slumping down in his chair after a brief time, he throws his pencil down on the test booklet and folds his arms, a defiant look on his face. Only two answers have been bubbled in, but he's had enough.

—Soderman, 2001, p. 55

In every U.S. community today, a great deal rests on positive test outcomes, and the stakes are high to have outcomes skewed toward high-achieving children. Even though standardized tests are constructed so that 50 percent of children will likely test above the mean and 50 percent below, no community finds having too many children (even 50 percent) in the bottom category acceptable. Not surprisingly, concern abounds about the growing mismatch between instruction and children's experiential backgrounds and developmental levels. Educators complain about greater pressure to alter the curriculum and instruction to fit assessment, rather than assessment being used as a tool to measure learning. Perhaps we are growing so accustomed to what has become an acceptable status quo relative to high-pressure assessment that we rarely question whether what we are doing constitutes reasonable and appropriate assessment. As a result, children's well-being in some of our centers, schools, and communities is being disregarded in the drive toward greater accountability.

Standardized testing continues to be a big business in the United States. According to reports, 93 to 105 million standardized tests of achievement, competency, and basic skills are currently administered each year in the United States. In addition to being a financial burden to school districts, standardized testing is time consuming. One estimate indicates that children in second grade now spend a total of 1 month on test preparation and standardized testing per year (McAfee & Leong, 2007, p. 183).

Pressure to achieve greater "educational accountability" has gradually spawned widespread approval of such practices as "teaching to the test" (if not the actual test) and placing heavy emphasis on worksheets, drills, and other inappropriate teaching strategies in early childhood classrooms. All these practices have been designed to raise scores because of the erroneous assumption that high scores on standardized tests equal high rates of learning by the children taking the tests.

Each professional who is involved in selecting or administering a standardized test must take the responsibility of ensuring that the test has proven technical and educational adequacy and is suitable for the population of children being tested. Before one is selected, the following criteria should be considered:

1. Is the test fair for children from all income levels, normed for all racial and ethnic backgrounds represented in the classroom?
2. Is it suitable for children whose primary language is not English?
3. Does the format call for skills children are unlikely to have, such as bubbling in responses?
4. Is it group administered, which makes following directions difficult for young children?
5. Does it call for teaching children in developmentally inappropriate ways so that they are successful on the test but unable to use the information in other ways?
6. Is it a one-shot-only test that would be insensitive to a young child's learning spurts and regressions?

If the test cannot pass these standards, it is likely unsuitable for young children. If so, teachers must vocalize such inappropriateness and suggest alternative ways to collect needed information.

It is important to note that not all standardized screening and assessment of young children should be scrapped. Standardized testing is necessary for both research purposes and diagnostic purposes, and it is reasonable when conducted with the preceding cautions in mind. It can relate how children in one school compare with those across a school district or across the nation, help school districts identify curriculum strengths and weaknesses, and be used to evaluate subsequent efforts to ameliorate these weaknesses (Sattler, 2008).

Diagnostic assessment intended to determine conclusively whether a child has special needs requires multiple types of data and sources. Thus, carefully constructed standardized tests are legitimate tools to consider. They should have **validity**; that is, they should measure what they are intended to measure so that reasonable inferences can be made on the basis of the results. They should have **reliability**, or built-in consistency within the instrument—consistency with time so that a retest within an appropriate time frame would yield the same results and consistency when it is used by more than one person (interrater or interobserver reliability).

Such tools are also helpful in providing a more complete understanding of a child's strengths and weaknesses by allowing teachers to compare the child's performance with an established standard. Standardized testing procedures can help educators document the pre- and postintervention status of groups of children who may be considered at risk because of socioeconomic factors or the geographic context in which they are reared. The tests are not intended to provide in-depth information about the ways children learn or to ameliorate learning disabilities (Sattler, 2008). However, in a relatively limited amount of time, a sample of behavior can be obtained and used to measure developmental status and changes or effects of remediation. The challenge is to find reliable and valid measures, obtain a typical response from the child, and then use the data only in conjunction with other relevant information to evaluate a child's physical, intellectual, social, or psychological abilities and functioning.

WELL-CONSTRUCTED STANDARDIZED TESTS ARE:

Valid. They measure what they are intended to measure.

Reliable. They are consistent and would yield the same results if the child were retested within a reasonable time frame or if the test were administered again by a different person.

The technical aspects of standardized testing are only one consideration. Another is that faulty decisions affecting children's futures are made when too much importance is attached to a particular test or score, even when the test is valid and reliable. Young children do not yet have the ability to question inappropriate assessment procedures. Moreover, many of their parents may not be confident enough to question placement or labeling decisions made by professionals, particularly when "real numbers" and evidence from a standardized test are available to back them up. Therefore, consideration about placing children in special entry programs, resource rooms, and learning groups should be made only after *comprehensive* data have been gathered and evaluated (Individuals with Disabilities Act, 2004).

THE CONCEPT OF AUTHENTIC ASSESSMENT

Because standardized tests have limited use with young children other than for diagnostic or research purposes, this chapter will focus more on authentic or alternative measures that teachers use in natural settings where children work and play. Such measures include the "innumerable and complex ways in which teachers appraise children's learning in the classroom . . . almost any type of assessment other than standardized tests and similar developmental inventories and achievement tests" (McAfee & Leong, 2007). Characteristics of authentic assessment include the following:

✓ *A variety of data is collected across time.* Unlike standardized tests, which provide a "snapshot in time," authentic assessment gauges a child's developmental progress at particular checkpoints against an expected range of maturational behaviors, skills, readiness levels, and concept formation.
✓ *All developmental domains are of interest* and are evaluated, rather than just a child's academic productivity and performance.
✓ *It takes place in the natural learning context* and is conducted by persons familiar to the child.
✓ *It is functional and curriculum embedded* (i.e., it is an integral part of what goes on in the regular classroom and involves children working with everyday objects and materials on everyday performance tasks and in a purposeful pursuit of learning).
✓ *It is based on discovering children's best performance* rather than on documenting what they do not know or cannot do well.
✓ *It is useful for planning classroom instruction* to organize and move children's learning forward.
✓ *It is a shared responsibility* among teachers, children, parents, and other professionals involved in the child's overall development, and effective communication is ongoing among these partners.

Early childhood professionals can accrue important advantages when they systematically and professionally document children's progress with authentic-based assessment as a way to facilitate learning and development. The NAEYC has indicated that to provide an accurate picture of children's capabilities, teachers must observe children across time and use their findings to adjust their curriculum and instruction. In addition, assessment should *not* be used to recommend that children be eliminated from particular programs, retained, or assigned to segregated groups on the basis of ability or developmental maturity. NAEYC's 2006 accreditation standards for assessment of child progress (see Figure 7.2) mandate that assessment results are used to benefit children by informing sound decisions about children, teaching, and program improvement. Figure 7.2 presents the six topic areas for NAEYC's assessment standard 4, followed by an example of some criteria associated with each of the six components. The full text of the document can be found on NAEYC's website.

STRATEGIES FOR AUTHENTIC ASSESSMENT IN THE EARLY CHILDHOOD CLASSROOM

In keeping with the concept and principles of **authentic assessment**, we can employ a number of useful strategies to gather the information we need to determine whether children will need special services and whether they are benefiting from the kinds of learning activities we have planned for them. Data about children is obtained by systematically or informally observing them in the classroom, on the playground or in other school-related venues, and during home visits. We examine products created by the child and take advantage of previously collected records from other sources. Following are a variety of strategies for documenting and organizing this detailed information about young children.

✋ Consult the Standards

FIGURE 7.2   NAEYC Program Standard 4—Assessment of Child Progress

Topic Area 4A: Creating an Assessment Plan

Example of Criteria: Assessments are an integral part of the program and used to support children's learning.

Topic Area 4B: Using Appropriate Assessment Procedures

Example of Criteria: Programs use a variety of assessment methods that are sensitive to and informed by family culture, experiences, children's abilities and disabilities, and home language; are meaningful and accurate; and are used in settings familiar to the children.

Topic Area 4C: Identifying Children's Interests and Needs and Describing Children's Progress

Example of Criteria: All children receive developmental screening that includes the timely screening of all children within three months of program entry; screening instruments that meet professional standards for standardization, reliability, and validity; screening instruments that have normative scores available on a population relevant for the child being screened; screening children's health status and their sensory, language, cognitive, gross-motor, fine-motor, and social–emotional development; a plan for evaluating the effectiveness of the screening program; using the results to make referrals to appropriate professionals, when appropriate, and ensuring that the referrals are followed up.

Topic Area 4D: Adapting Curriculum, Individualizing Teaching, and Informing Program Development

Example of Criteria: Teachers or others who know the children and are able to observe their strengths, interests, and needs on an ongoing basis conduct assessments to inform classroom instruction and to make sound decisions about individual and group curriculum content, teaching approaches, and personal interactions.

Topic Area 4E: Communicating with Families and Involving Families in the Assessment Process

Example of Criteria: Families have ongoing opportunities to share the results of observation from home to contribute to the assessment process.

Source: Standards for Assessment of Child Progress, by National Association for the Education of Young Children, 2005, Washington, DC: Author. Approved April 2005 by NAEYC Governing Board. Reprinted with permission.

Screening and Readiness Procedures

The terms *screening* and *readiness* are not synonymous. **Screening** tools help to sort out children who may need diagnostic assessment and intervention; **readiness** measures assist in determining whether children have acquired characteristics that equip them to come to elementary school with knowledge of *how* to learn. Included are confidence, curiosity, intentionality, self-control, and the ability to relate, communicate, and cooperate. When opting to use screening tools, we need to select only those that have demonstrated **sensitivity**, that is, the accuracy of the test in identifying delayed development. In other words, we do not want to choose one that over-refers children for diagnosis. Well-constructed screening tools also demonstrate **specificity** by identifying children who do not have delays. These help to ensure that children who need further diagnosis are not overlooked (Meisels & Atkins-Burnett, 2005).

Commonly used developmental screening tests include the following (Lipkin, 2006; Wortham, 2008):

Ages and Stages Questionnaire (ASQ)
AGS Early Screening Profiles
Battelle Developmental Inventory (BDI) Screening Test
Bayley Infant Neurodevelopmental Screener (BINS)
Brigance Screener II
Child Development Inventory (CDI)
Child Development Review
Denver II Developmental Screening Test (DDST-II)
Developmental Indicators for the Assessment of Learning (DIAL III)
Early Screening Inventory—Revised (ESI-R)
First Step Screening Test for Evaluating Preschoolers (First Step)
Infant Developmental Inventory
Parents Evaluation of Developmental Status (PEDS)

One area in which some early childhood educators struggle is the effective assessment of incoming kindergarten children to determine whether they are "ready." Currently, many school districts are reassessing earlier scrambles to identify weaknesses in children and are instead turning their energy toward structuring "readiness roundups." These events serve a number of purposes: provide authentic assessment of incoming children (observation and documentation are the primary methods); identify children who may have special needs; allow sharing of necessary information with parents; allow educators to answer parents' questions; help educators determine the number of incoming kindergartners; and provide a friendly, welcoming orientation for both parents and children.

The roundups are held in a regular kindergarten classroom during the spring or summer, and experienced teachers are on hand to observe the children interacting with one another and with materials. Of special interest is how they naturally handle such activities as large-group time and transition times. As a result, children in districts who offer readiness roundups are having a more positive first experience with school. Instead of taking a test, they are able to enjoy engaging activities planned for them. Parents can meet with the school principal and other professionals during this time to become better acquainted with school policy and the ways in which they can work with educators to support their child's successful orientation to school.

In addition to providing a more positive experience for children, the roundup process allows seasoned professionals—preprimary and kindergarten teachers, Chapter 1 supervisors, elementary counselors and principals, speech teachers, school social workers, and psychologists—to observe the children at work and play. For instance, in some districts, the speech teacher is required to interact purposefully with each child for a brief time during this period to obtain a speech/language sample. Visual and auditory screenings are also scheduled to ensure that these primary learning modalities are intact.

Spotting the child who may have difficulties working with other children, adults, or materials is rarely a problem. For these children, additional assessment may be indicated, and a private meeting is scheduled with the child's parents so that educators can learn more about the child's history, present strengths and limitations, and request parent consent for any diagnostic assessment that should be scheduled.

Structured and Nonstructured Observation

One of the most underrated evaluation tools for use with the young child is observational assessment. Here, the objective and experienced eye of someone who is knowledgeable about child development is invaluable. Observational assessment has the following advantages:

❑ It is nonintrusive for the child.
❑ It yields instant, credible information that has on-the-spot utility for improving interactional and instructional strategies with children.
❑ It has important value for formulating hypotheses to evaluate at a later date.
❑ It can be used virtually wherever people are behaving.
❑ It allows the professional to capture, in natural settings, important data that could not be obtained by other methods.

Behavioral observation serves a number of valuable functions in the assessment process by providing a more personalized picture of a child's spontaneous behavior in everyday life settings (classroom, playground, hospital ward, or clinic playroom) than can be obtained from more formal methods (Sattler, 2008). Information about the child's interpersonal behavior and learning style and a systematic record of child behaviors can be used for planning intervention or classroom instruction. In addition, behavioral observation allows for verification of others' reports regarding the child's behavior and for comparisons between behavior in formal settings and that in more naturalistic settings. Such observation also affords us an opportunity to study the behaviors of children who are developmentally disabled and are not easily evaluated by other methods. Powell and Napoliello (2005) note that observational assessment should yield deep knowledge of the student as learner, deep knowledge of the content of instruction, a broad repertoire of effective instructional strategies, and a willingness by educators to engage in collaborative planning, assessment, and reflection.

Young children are particularly good subjects for observations because they have not yet learned to mask their feelings, thoughts, and behaviors very well. The technique also has great utility because it avoids the limitations of paper-and-pencil methods previously described. Being fairly unobtrusive, it requires no cooperation on the child's part. One 4-year-old who was moving through a screening process for kindergarten entry had everyone believing her name was Melissa (her name was Kate, but she preferred the name Melissa). She refused to answer any of the questions until her mother noted what was occurring and intervened, telling her that she had "better take things seriously and quit fooling around!" The teacher who was relating the story said, "She might have been one of our kids tagged for further diagnosis if her mother hadn't clued us in." As it was, Kate turned out to be an exceptionally bright kindergartner.

Observation of children can be seriously flawed when bias or misinterpretation by the evaluator results in poor ratings. For example, if a teacher observes Kate's earlier performance and interprets the behavior as a tendency to lie, then the teacher may allow this interpretation to negatively color future observations of Kate. The **halo effect** occurs, however, if the teacher views Kate's performance as the funny stunt of a highly creative child, then sees Kate more positively in subsequent situations than may be warranted. The **leniency factor** distorts observation differently. The observer would rate not only Kate more highly than would be indicated, but *all* subjects more highly. We see this phenomenon in grade inflation in secondary and postsecondary education in which entire classes of students receive a 4.0 despite distinct differences in performance.

You will want to step back occasionally and observe your program in action. Watch the way your classroom arrangement and organization are affecting children's learning. Note how children interact with other children, materials, and equipment; the comfort level children have in working together and how they express their emotions; and whether the current structure and planning support active, engaged learning (Morrison, 2006). Informal observation methods most useful for doing this include the use of anecdotal records, frequency counts and charts, checklists, rating scales, and participation charts. Multiple observations at different times of the day and week are needed to gain the best picture of a child's abilities, and we need to be careful that all are dated.

Anecdotal Records. Sometimes called narrative records, descriptive narratives, specimen records, continuous narratives, or jottings, **anecdotal records** (see Figures 7.3 and 7.4) contain both typical and unusual behaviors of a child, recorded as they occur. What distinguishes the anecdotal record from the rest, however, is that the anecdotal record is usually a briefer account of a single event and the method used by busy and involved classroom teachers.

Conversely, narratives (which are more often used by clinicians or researchers) usually contain a great deal more information. They are usually a continuous written stream of everything said or done during the observation as well as more in-depth notes about environmental aspects surrounding the behavior; narratives are more often used by clinicians and researchers. We want to emphasize that any single observation cannot and should not lead to solid conclusions about a child's motivations or behavior. Rather, it should serve to develop hypotheses that need to be tested with subsequent observations.

Anecdotal records are most conveniently written on stick-on notes or index cards to be filed. They contain sufficiently detailed descriptions of a particular behavioral event that can then be used with subsequent observations to formulate hypotheses or conclusions about a child's behavior. Included is necessary information about the event, any known stimulus, persons involved,

FIGURE 7.3   Anecdotal Record of Prosocial Behavior

Child's Name: Peter Montoya   **Observer:** M. Cameron
Date: 5/12/09   **Setting:** Haslett Preprimary Classroom
Time: 2:06 P.M.

Peter and Sylvia are seated next to one another at the art table. Both children are drawing on separate papers with markers. Sylvia looks at Peter's drawing and says, "You need a sun." She begins to add a sun to Peter's picture, using an orange marker.
    Peter shouts, "Hey, don't do that. I don't need a sun!"
    Sylvia takes her hand away and says, "Okay. Okay."
    Peter says, "Okay." The children continue to draw side by side.

Interpretation: Peter knows how to express his emotion using words. Sylvia responded to Peter's verbal message in a way that satisfied him.

FIGURE 7.4 Anecdotal Record

Child's Name: Gary Denzell   **Observer:** B. Miller
Date: 10/16/09   **Setting:** Kindergarten Classroom
Time: 10:17 A.M.

Children were asked by Ms. Sharpe to complete a worksheet identifying like and dissimilar objects. Gary continued to play with unit blocks until reminded by Ms. Sharpe to take his place at the table and begin working. He looked up but still did not move. When she moved toward him to get him to comply, he kicked down the block structure he had been making and walked to the table. Ms. Sharpe noted, "That's better." Gary did not respond.

Interpretation: Gary balked when asked to do seatwork. He clearly preferred playing with blocks/trucks. Would there be a better way to "teach" logicomathematical concepts than having him complete a paper–pencil task, which he continues to have difficulty with?

direct quotations if important to understanding the situation, and the child's behavioral responses. Unusual behaviors of any kind are noted. Any subjective inferences or interpretations may be noted but must be kept separate from the observation.

Preschool classrooms and primary classrooms that are structured to include at least an hour of free play per day are excellent environments in which to observe children in this way. To ensure that every child receives a weekly structured observation, some teachers prepare a grid on which all the children's names are listed. Putting the grid on a clipboard, the teacher then spends 15 to 30 minutes circulating in the classroom during center time, directly focusing on four or five children per day and noting behaviors of interest. Teachers may also elect to draw certain children aside during this period to have a brief miniconference about a particular skill or concept and make a note of the interaction. The grid is then cut into individual sections, with the notes on each child dated and stored in the teacher's portfolios for future reference.

Anecdotal observations are particularly useful for noting and improving children's task performance. Watch children as they are involved in a learning activity you've planned for them and look for the following:

✓ How well were they able to handle the materials and task?
✓ What was the nature of errors that were made?
✓ What strategies could be used to optimize learning?
✓ How could the task be simplified or extended to optimize concept learning?
✓ Is the child learning something new?
✓ Is more review or practice needed by some?
✓ What should be taught again, using different materials or a different strategy?
✓ What misunderstandings exist?
✓ How do the children in the group differ in their concepts or ideas?
✓ Can they do something they couldn't do before?
✓ To what extent have they enhanced their competence?

Frequency Counts. Sometimes we have a feeling that a particular behavior is either increasing or decreasing on a day-to-day basis with a child. Occasionally, we may want to collect baseline information before beginning purposeful intervention to alter behavior. **Frequency counts**, or simple tallies of specified behaviors as they occur (see Figure 7.5), can help us document whether our intuition about a situation is correct and can then be charted to display the effects of instituted treatment. For example, a behavior of interest may be a child's aggressive interaction with other children, and a frequency count could document maintenance of, an increase in, or a decrease in the number of incidents of the behavior following intervention. It would also be helpful to document the behaviors at different times during the day (e.g., arrival, center time, large group, lunch) to see if time of day, structure, or particular interactions are problematic. Learning to link assessment data to methods of instruction, climate, intervention, and events and interactions in the classroom is a critical component of good assessment.

Checklists and Inventories. Checklists can range from formal criterion-referenced lists of developmental behaviors and skills to teacher-constructed inventories listing behaviors of interest to

FIGURE 7.5 Tally of Aggressive Interactions

Child's Name: Gary Denzell
Behavior: Aggressive interaction with other children—biting, hitting, spitting, kicking
When: During center activity (9:10–10:15)
Where: Ms. Johnson's room
Observer: B. Miller
Dates: November 17–November 21, 2009

Days	Tally	Total
1	//////	6
2	////	4
3	///	3
4	/	1
5	//	2

FIGURE 7.6 Example of Self-Help Checklist

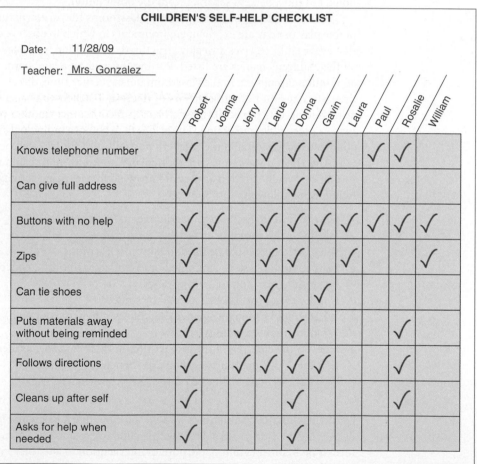

the educator. Checklists allow educators to note both individual achievement and group achievement and usually require a simple check mark (✓) to indicate that the skill or behavior has been noted (see Figure 7.6). Teachers interested in documenting observation of a skill more than once may note the first observation by making a horizontal mark (−), the second with an added vertical mark (+), and additional diagonal lines for subsequent observations of the skill.

Rating Scales and Rubrics. Rating scales are similar to checklists in that lists of behavioral variables are made. They differ in that an *evaluative* component is attached that qualifies behavior or skill acquisition (see Figure 7.7). When a rating scale is used, objectivity can become a problem, and evaluators need to keep this uppermost in mind when rating the child's behaviors. Such scales

FIGURE 7.7 Example of Rating Scale

SOCIAL SKILLS RATINGS SCALE

Date: 4/11/09

Teacher: Mr. Lofy

1 = Skill well developed; color code green
2 = Practiced often but not always; color code blue
3 = Working on; color code yellow
4 = Rarely observed; color code red

	Juan	Jim	Sandra	Jason	Kelly	Amy	Diedra	Eric	Taylor	Regina	Elizabeth	Kerry	Ervin
Developing friendship skills	3	3	1	3	3	1	1	1	3	1	1	3	4
Initiates play/work with others	4	1	1	2	4	2	2	2	4	1	1	3	4
Makes suggestions	4	1	1	3	1	1	2	1	1	1	1	1	4
Takes suggestions	1	3	2	2	3	1	1	2	3	2	2	2	3
Negotiates conflicts (compromises)	3	3	2	3	2	1	2	1	3	2	1	2	4
Is cooperative and helpful	2	2	1	2	3	2	2	1	4	2	2	2	3
Shares materials	2	3	2	2	1	2	1	1	4	2	2	2	3
Gives assistance to others	3	4	2	2	1	2	3	2	4	2	1	2	3
Respects others and their property	2	2	1	2	2	1	2	2	3	2	1	1	3
Conforms to reasonable limits	1	2	1	1	3	2	1	1	2	1	1	1	2
Demonstrates self-control	1	2	1	2	2	2	1	2	2	1	1	2	3
Adapts to new situations	3	3	2	2	3	1	1	2	3	1	2	2	3
Terminates interactions in socially acceptable ways	2	3	1	2	1	1	2	1	3	2	1	3	3
Interacts with new people	3	3	2	3	4	1	1	1	4	1	1	2	4

can be color coded for easier interpretation (e.g., 1 [*skill well developed*] = green, 2 = blue, 3 = yellow, 4 [*skill rarely observed*] = red). Evaluators may choose from a variety of predetermined categories or ranges of behavior, extremes, or opposites. These may be represented by a numbered continuum attached to a specified criterion (e.g., choosing from 0–10, in which 0 = low and 10 = high) or an open continuum (e.g., Extroversion ☐ ☐ ☐ ☐ ☐ ☐ ☐ ☐ ☐ ☐ Introversion).

To increase their objectivity in rating a product, behavior, or skill, individuals can develop rubrics. **Rubrics** are scoring tools that list clearly defined and *observable* criteria to articulate gradations of quality from excellent to poor, high to low, and so on. The criterion to be evaluated is given at the left, and gradations of quality are then listed. The separation between scoring levels

FIGURE 7.8   Rubric for Evaluating My Performance in the Student-Led Conference

Criterion	Quality		
I shared the important features of my work with my parents.	Yes, I shared enough to give them a good sense of my work in all subject areas.	Yes, I shared some but left out other key work samples.	I shared few samples of my work.

should be clear and distinct. For example, a rubric for evaluating the quality of a student-led conference by second graders could be written so that a child could self-evaluate his or her performance (see Figure 7.8). The rubric is shared with and explained in clear, understandable language to children before the project is implemented, which serves a double purpose: It is a performance guide, letting children know what is expected prior to the event; and it is a device they can use afterward to appraise their performance. Rubrics are especially useful in assessment *for* learning because they contain qualitative descriptions of performance criteria that actually guide children's performance during the process of learning (Moskal, 2003; Tierney & Simon, 2004).

Participation Charts.   Time-sample participation charts are useful for recording where children are at a particular time during the school day and with whom they interact most often. Following the preparation of a coded form for documentation purposes, an observer simply notes the location of each child at a designated time. For example, in Figure 7.9 all areas of the classroom have been coded (A–J). Areas assigned to the two supervising adults in the room (Mr. Tanamato is the teacher, and Mrs. Gross is his aide) are identified. The children's names have been recorded down the left side of the form, and designated times when observations are to be made are recorded across the top. In a matter of seconds, the observer can document each child's location at that particular time. After a number of observations have been made, educators can examine these charts to look for patterns in children's interactions with other children and adults, as well as their involvement or noninvolvement in certain activities. For example, using the participation chart in Figure 7.9, a 1-week time sample that documents where 15 children are at five times during the morning's scheduled center activity, a teacher could obtain answers to the following 10 points of interest.

1. You have had the feeling that too many children (more than five at one time) are in the art area. Do you need to structure a rule about this?
2. You suspect that the boys rarely visit the language arts center. Is this true?
3. The children seem to avoid Brian (or vice versa). Is this happening?
4. Mr. Tanamato reports that Sam spends too much time in the bathroom. Does he?
5. You suspect that a few children may be coming to school without breakfast. Who are they?
6. What percentage of the children are visiting the science area each day?
7. The children appear to be avoiding one of the adults. What can you learn about the situation?
8. Some of the children are being dropped off late; you think that you need to document this tardiness so that you can talk to the appropriate parents. Which children are noticeably tardy and not arriving by 8:00?
9. Three boys are best friends. Who?
10. You found whole rolls of toilet paper in a toilet in the bathroom on Tuesday and Friday. Who may need to be watched more closely?

By examining the data collected during the 5 days listed in Figure 7.9, you may draw the following conclusions in response to the preceding questions.

1. No rule seems to be needed about too many children in the art area. Only one incident was recorded.
2. Yes, few boys appear to be working in the language arts center—only Brian every day and Michael on Monday. What can be done to stimulate their interest?
3. Yes, observation indicated that Brian and the other children are not interacting—he is often at lockers or in the bathroom or language arts center, where there are few other children. This situation needs to be observed more carefully so that a cause can be established.
4. We cannot tell whether Sam is spending too much time in the bathroom from this set of observations. Try event sampling for an answer to this question.

FIGURE 7.9 Time-Sample Participation Chart

	Monday 8:15	8:30	9:00	9:15	9:30	Tuesday 8:15	8:30	9:00	9:15	9:30	Wednesday 8:15	8:30	9:00	9:15	9:30	Thursday 8:15	8:30	9:00	9:15	9:30	Friday 8:15	8:30	9:00	9:15	9:30
Brian	A	B	F	J	I	B	A	I	J	J	I	J	B	I	—	H	A	H	I	B	I	J	J	A	I
Amy	C	A	H	D	G	H	A	D	C	C	A	B	H	D	D	D	C	C	A	I	C	C	A	B	D
Kevin	—	|	I	E	E	|	A	|	B	D	|	|	F	E	E	|	B	A	D	D	—	|	B	E	E
Amanda	C	B	D	A	C	C	C	D	E	E	A	F	F	D	D	C	C	C	D	D	D	D	F	F	A
Jenny	A	|	H	D	D	A	H	D	D	F	G	A	C	C	C	A	D	D	D	C	A	G	G	G	E
Joey	—	E	D	D	E	—	|	A	F	C	F	E	E	D	—	H	A	D	F	D	—	|	|	F	D
Bill	D	D	C	C	G	D	B	F	A	C	D	D	B	G	G	A	D	—	F	F	G	G	G	G	D
Sam	D	B	C	C	G	D	B	F	A	C	D	D	B	G	G	A	D	—	F	F	B	G	G	G	D
Sarah	G	G	A	D	D	D	D	C	C	H	D	A	F	|	F	C	C	G	C	G	B	D	C	C	A
Erin	G	G	A	D	H	F	F	D	A	B	A	D	|	H	B	D	D	F	|	D	B	A	D	D	C
Tamera	G	A	D	D	D	D	A	C	C	C	—	A	C	C	C	E	F	F	G	D	A	C	C	D	G
Julio	A	D	C	B	G	A	B	F	A	C	D	B	B	G	G	A	D	—	F	F	A	G	G	H	D
Ahmad	G	G	D	E	E	F	F	A	B	C	|	|	C	H	|	B	F	D	D	A	D	G	E	E	H
Randi	D	|	A	G	G	D	G	D	D	A	|	A	C	H	|	F	C	C	D	A	D	A	B	C	D
Michael	B	J	D	E	E	—	|	I	A	F	|	|	I	D	D	D	D	A	F	F	B	F	D	F	F

A = snack*
B = bathroom
C = dramatic play
D = art center
E = blocks/trucks**

F = manipulatives
G = large motor**
H = science*
I = lockers
J = language arts center

*Mr. Tanamato, MWF; Mrs. Gross, TTh
**Mrs. Gross, MWF; Mr. Tanamato, TTh

5. Jenny and Julio may be coming to school without breakfast. This situation needs to be followed up immediately by talking to the children.

6. Only 20 percent (three) of the children visited the science area last week.

7. Boys are avoiding areas where Mr. Tanamato is stationed, even M, W, and F snack (also science on M, W, F and blocks and large motor on T, Th). Need to follow up.

8. Kevin was tardy on M, T, W, Th, F. Joey was tardy on M, T, F. Michael was tardy on T, W.

9. Bill, Sam, and Julio appear to be best friends and travel from activity to activity together.

10. Kevin and Sam are the only boys who were in the boys' bathroom on both T and F. This situation bears closer watching.

Oral Reading Tests: Running Records

As educators in some school districts move to a literature-based approach to reading in the primary grades as an alternative to basal texts, many of them are looking for a quantitative method for documenting that children are making progress in reading accuracy and in their ability to recognize and correct mistakes without help. One literature-based method for obtaining samples of children's reading accuracy at several times during the year is for the teacher to conduct an individual **oral reading test**, or running record, with individual children. The teacher, using a photocopied or typed version of the age-appropriate story, listens to evaluate the quality of the child's reading, noting mistakes, number of words read, self-corrections, words omitted, words added, and words reversed (see Figure 7.10). Notes are made on comprehension, fluency, and expressiveness in reading, and on the nature of the child's mistakes. These assessments can also be tape-recorded for future reference across time by the teacher and the child or to demonstrate the child's ability to a parent or another professional.

Scoring the oral reading sample (see Figure 7.11) consists of establishing an accuracy rate, a meaningful mistake rate (mistakes that do not destroy syntax or meaning; e.g., *house* for *home*), a self-correction rate, and a comprehension score that ranges from fragmentary understanding (1) to full and complete understanding of the story (4). Such scores, across time, indicate whether the child is improving in accuracy and the ability to self-correct and whether more or less difficult material would be more appropriate. A summary of the process appears in Figure 7.12.

FIGURE 7.10   Analysis of an Oral Reading Sample

Name: Juana Perez
Date: April 4, 2009
Evaluator: Mr. Lofy

Fish Is Fish	Word Total	
AT THE EDGE OF THE <u>WOODS</u> THERE <u>WAS</u> A BIG	10	∕ X
POND, AND <u>THERE</u> A MINNOW AND A TADPOLE	18	X
SWAM AMONG THE WEEDS. THEY WERE <u>INSEPARABLE</u>	25	X
FRIENDS.	26	
ONE MORNING THE TADPOLE <u>DISCOVERED</u> THAT	32	X
DURING THE NIGHT HE HAD <u>GROWN</u> TWO LITTLE LEGS.	41	X
"<u>*LOOK*</u>," HE SAID <u>TRIUMPHANTLY</u>. "LOOK, I AM A FROG!"	50	∕ X
"NONSENSE," SAID THE MINNOW. "*HOW* COULD YOU BE A	59	X
FROG IF ONLY LAST <u>NIGHT</u> YOU WERE A <u>LITTLE</u> TINY FISH,	70	∕ ∕
JUST LIKE ME!"	73	
THEY <u>ARGUED</u> AND ARGUED UNTIL FINALLY THE	80	X
TADPOLE SAID, "FROGS ARE FROGS AND FISH IS FISH	89	
AND THAT'S THAT!"	92	
IN THE WEEKS THAT <u>FOLLOWED</u>, THE TADPOLE GREW	100	∕
TINY FRONT LEGS AND HIS TAIL GOT SMALLER AND	109	
SMALLER.	110	

FIGURE 7.11   Scoring the Oral Reading Sample in Figure 7.10

Name: Juana Perez
Date: April 4, 2009
Evaluator: Mr. Lofy
Literature Category: Level 3

A. Words read: 110
B. Mistakes (X): 8
C. Self-Corrections ($\underline{/}$): 5
D. Meaningful mistakes (/): 0
E. Total corrected/meaningful mistakes (B + C + D)

Accuracy Score: (A − B) ÷ A
(110 − 8 ÷ 110) = .93

Self-Correction Rate: C ÷ E
5 ÷ 13 = .38

Comprehension (1 = fragmentary to 4 = full): 3

Comments: Juana's self-correction abilities are increasing (score on 2/27/09 = .22, score on 4/4/09 = .38). Comprehension was good, and she enjoyed reading to me. According to accuracy rate, literature category is still too difficult. Retest in May.

FIGURE 7.12   Analyzing and Scoring Oral Reading Tapes

Analysis

1. Listen to the tape the child has made.
2. Underline *all* mistakes, writing above printed word what reader actually said.
3. Do not count the same mistake twice.
4. Indicate self-corrections by putting a C above the word and underlining it.
5. Circle any words omitted.
6. Put a caret (^) in the space if an extra word is added, and write the extra word above.
7. If letters or words are reversed, mark with horizontal S (~).
8. Make notes on retelling, comprehension, particular qualities of reading, or problems.
9. In the right margin
   a. indicate a meaningful mistake (does not destroy syntax or meaning) by a slash (/).
   b. indicate a self-corrected mistake by underlining a slash ($\underline{/}$).
   c. indicate a mistake not corrected or that destroys meaning or syntax by a crossed slash (X).

Scoring

1. *Use the following designators:*
   A = Count total number of words read.
   B = Add total number of uncorrected mistakes (X).
   C = Add number of self-corrections ($\underline{/}$).
   D = Add number of meaningful mistakes (/).
   E = Total number of all mistakes (B + C + D).

2. *Obtain accuracy score.* From total number of words read, subtract number of uncorrected and nonmeaningful mistakes. Divide the resulting number by the total number of words read. Thus, use the following formula: [(A − B) ÷ A].

Note: If accuracy rate is less than 95 percent, the child is likely to flounder and lose ability to use strategies ordinarily at his or her disposal. Try an easier text. If 100 percent accuracy, suggest a more difficult text to child.

3. Obtain self-correction rate. Divide number of self-corrections (C) by total number of all mistakes (E). Thus, use the following formula: [C ÷ E].

Note: The self-correction rate assesses a child's determination to make sense of what is being read. The higher the percentage, the more the child is gaining meaning from reading.

4. Determine comprehension or retelling score, using the following criteria:
   1 = fragmentary understanding
   2 = partial understanding
   3 = fairly complete understanding
   4 = full and complete understanding; ability to make inferences from what is read

Note: Oral reading tapes may be passed on from a teacher in one grade to a teacher in another so that the teachers can assess a child's reading progress with time. It is important to use only one tape for each child, date each entry, and use the same scoring criteria across a school district so that interpretation of children's scores will be valid. It should be noted when a child is moving to a more difficult level of reading material, for it is expected that a child's accuracy and self-correction scores will temporarily decrease until the child increases skills at the new level.

Teacher–Child Miniconferences

Holding brief, one-on-one conferencing sessions between teacher and child about particular aspects of the child's work is an evaluation method that can be used to further follow up on any of the methods described to this point. The teacher may ask questions to probe the child's thinking about the products, clarify concepts that are still fuzzy in the child's mind, and learn more about what the child is interested in working on in the future. Information gathering is most effective when teachers offer open-ended requests such as "Tell me how you figured this out" or "This part is especially interesting. Tell me how you thought of that." Discussions that take place in small- and large-group meetings between children and the teacher also yield information about children's conceptualization that can be useful for more in-depth planning and assessment.

The Ecomap

Finding out about the child's world outside the classroom can enhance assessment, particularly when this is done early in the year, perhaps in preparation for the initial fall conference between teachers and children's parents. The **ecomap** (see Figure 7.13) is a paper-and-pencil exercise

FIGURE 7.13 Ecomap: The Child's Developmental Contexts

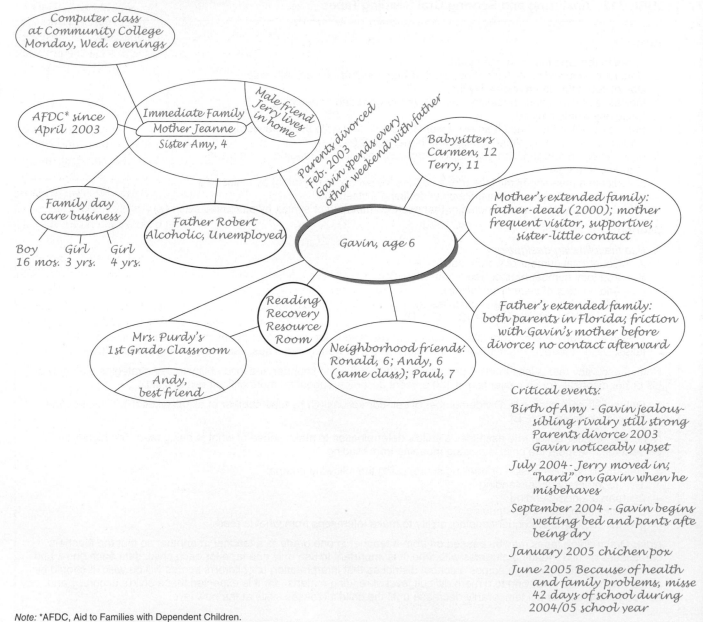

Note: *AFDC, Aid to Families with Dependent Children.

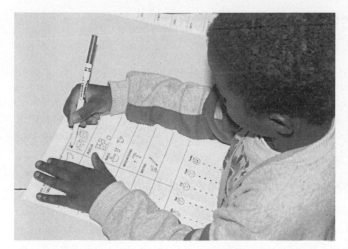

Maurice is indicating how he spent his time at school and will evaluate whether his day was terrific, good, okay, sad, or terrible.

designed to provide a simple, visual overview of the child's experience in the family and community. The teacher invites the parent(s) to sketch out the child's ecomap and to begin by drawing a circle in the middle of the paper and placing the child's name in the center. Other circles representing the most salient systems in the child's life (e.g., immediate family members living both in and outside the household, as well as extended family—grandparents; influential aunts, uncles, etc.) are then placed around the center circle and connected by lines.

Other connections related to health care, recreation, extracurricular activities, parents' workplaces, the child's best friends outside school, child care, and so forth can be added to provide more information. As the connections are drawn, the teacher may elicit additional information about any connections that seem to be highly problematic or supportive for either the child or the parent. In this way, the teacher becomes acquainted with the way children spend their time and energy outside the classroom. Also revealed is the qualitative nature of the various contexts, which provides a better understanding of a child's special needs or of life events that may be affecting the child's classroom performance. Parents who have participated in the exercise have reported that it allowed them to establish better rapport with the teacher and feelings of collaboration. Others have said the process made them more aware that even a very young child's world can be fairly complex.

Self-Appraisal by the Child

Children are rarely challenged to evaluate their own progress, yet doing so is important. Besides conferencing with the teacher periodically about their work, they can learn to document involvement in the classroom by using checklists that have been developed in many of the domains. For example, skills in a certain area (e.g., physical development, social–emotional development, or emergent writing) may be listed (see Figure 7.14), with spaces that can be dated by the teacher or student and then colored in by the child as a skill is achieved. As the year progresses, children are reminded about maintaining the skill every time they make entries and are reinforced as they see the number of skills adding up on the checklist.

Teachers will want to produce self-evaluation checklists that list a range and number of skills so that every child will be able to check or color in at least a few skill blocks at the beginning. Skills to be acquired should be reasonably within a child's reach, given more time and practice. For children who are progressing more slowly, a checklist that breaks down the skills more finely and recognizes smaller gains in development should be devised. For younger children, pictographs and a rebus are helpful.

FIGURE 7.14   A Form for Child's Self-Appraisal

Date: 6/12/09	9/27	12/5	2/14	4/12	5/10
I can zip.					
I play and work with others.					
I share with others.					
I help clean up.					
I put materials away after using them.					
I try new things.					
I am helpful to others.					

ORGANIZATION AND USE OF AUTHENTIC ASSESSMENT AND EVALUATION DATA: PORTFOLIOS AND STUDENT-LED CONFERENCES

In a local school district, an early childhood education committee has been given the task of structuring a districtwide portfolio and student-led conferencing process. Maggie Williams, a first-grade teacher, is serving as the facilitator and summarizing a list of concerns that committee members have raised: Will parents accept the new process? Should standardized and unit testing be continued? Should all teachers be required to implement the process? How involved should the children be? What products should be saved and included?

Portfolios: Matching Assessment with How Children Learn

The reasons for developing portfolios in child care and education are many and include the following (Martin, 2007, p. 231):

❏ Document a child's development
❏ Record key features of a child's learning
❏ Store relevant formal documents
❏ Demonstrate a child's abilities
❏ Reveal the interactions between children
❏ Collate children's artwork and work samples
❏ Identify children's special needs
❏ Document for purposes of accountability
❏ Show the program's success and effectiveness in meeting children's needs
❏ Record stages of curriculum delivery
❏ Help student teachers understand children's development
❏ Assess developmental progress
❏ Evaluate children's learning outcomes
❏ Provide opportunity for teacher reflection
❏ Encourage children's reflection and self-evaluation
❏ Communicate with parents
❏ Design curriculum and guidance strategies

Perhaps the most important item listed is encouraging children's reflection and self-evaluation on their work. Children are delighted when they see for themselves how they have grown, and there is no better way to allow them to do so than to keep their dated work samples and other artifacts to compare today's work with yesterday's. When children show their dossier, portfolio, or process folios of work to others, teachers can share in their obvious mixture of pure delight and heavy seriousness as children select their personal best to let others know how they are progressing.

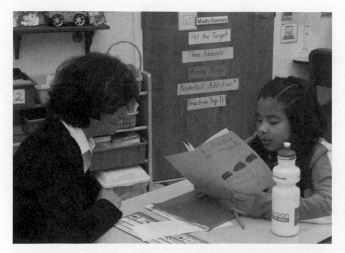

Portfolios are useful for noting development across time in various domains.

Samples may include a child's drawings, paintings, video or audio tapes, maps, graphs, descriptions and photographs of projects and friends, charts, webs, and written work—in short, anything that meaningfully depicts their progress. The process promotes developmentally appropriate instruction in that it requires professionals to plan performance-based evaluation activities from which products can be collected intermittently during the school year and to allow children adequate time and guidance to work on relevant artifacts for their portfolios.

The most compelling feature of portfolios is that they focus more on what children *can* do, whereas traditional assessment focuses primarily on what they cannot do or cannot do well. Beginning as general collections of their work, portfolios are then reduced to selections that the children think are representative of their progress.

Most school districts that implement the portfolio assessment system have several types of portfolios for each child coexisting in a classroom at any one time (see Figure 7.15).

FIGURE 7.15   Types of Portfolios

Type of Portfolio	Description
Individual Portfolio	These are kept in the classroom, and children store dated work samples selected by the teacher and children from their daily work. Decision should be made about what is to be collected and how often. These will be the general collections from which children will choose several work samples to include in their "showcase" portfolios at a later time.
Showcase or Student-Led Portfolio	Children choose favorite pieces of work or work that represents what they believe is their best effort. This can be done with or without the help of the teacher; however, the process is more effective when children are asked to explain to the teacher why they selected each of the pieces. Teachers may also want to add a selection that they feel represents the child's best efforts.
Teacher Portfolio	This is a separate folder from either of the two above. It consists of manilla folders for each of the children, which may contain copies of work from the child's individual portfolio, checklists and inventories of skill development, anecdotal notes made by the teacher, correspondence from parents or other professionals, or other information the teacher believes is illustrative of the child's academic or personal growth. These are not shared at the student-led conferences but may be useful if parents want to confer later with the teacher or if the teacher needs to confer with other professionals who are involved in educational planning for the child.
Program or Institutional Portfolio	This portfolio is maintained from year to year and grade to grade. It is a specified collection of the child's work for the period of time the child is in a particular school. Contents are a few particular items agreed on by staff that are collected at each grade level for all children at consistent times during each year (see Figure 7.16 for examples). All folders are cleaned of extraneous contents at year end and sent back to the office for dispersion to the child's next teacher the following year.
Digital/Electronic Portfolio	Increasingly, with children's developing technology skills, schools are helping children develop electronic collections of their work. These may contain PowerPoints, simple web pages developed by older children, scanned samples of children's written work and drawings, or videos of a student's performance or a group performance. Ethical issues include the extent to which technology should shape the process, excluding identifiable personal material, and who shares responsibility for controlling contents (Martin, 2007, p. 231).

FIGURE 7.16   Examples of Portfolio Contents at Grade Level

Grade Level	Example of Portfolio Contents
Preschool/Kindergarten	Self-portrait at beginning and end of the year Social Skills Checklist, checked three times per year Self-Appraisal Checklist, completed by the child each month Ecomap, collected in initial conference with parent Humpty Dumpty drawing/writing sample, beginning and end of year Clifford attribute chart, October and April Picture of child interacting with others in an activity
Grade 1	Concept of Print Inventory, October and April Self-portraits, beginning and end of year Three samples of child's best writing, October, February, May Math story problem written in the spring Inventories of literacy and math progress, checked October, February, May Picture of the child with favorite friend(s)

Some elementary schools hold a celebration evening for children who will be going on the next year to a middle school and present the children and their families with these longitudinal, comprehensive collections of their work. Such collections are highly valued because they paint a picture of significant growth by children as they move through the elementary years. One child who was looking back at some of the earliest entries grinned broadly and remarked, "I was such a baby then!" When schools are implementing new instructional practices, the portfolios help determine whether children's skills are improving with time.

When introducing the portfolio process to the children in your classroom, you may consider bringing in professionals who keep some sort of portfolio (e.g., photographers, models, architects, artists, journalists, or educators) to lead a discussion about why people have portfolios. Because a sense of ownership will be important, children should brainstorm about the kinds of representative samples to save during the year. When children are working on pieces for the portfolio, you will want to remind them about qualitative aspects of the work and the importance of their best effort.

Storage for easy access is important. Some teachers have obtained large, individual pizza boxes in which children store their work. Other educators have had children make portfolios out of large pieces of sturdy tagboard. With large classes of children, two or three places can be established in the room for folder storage so that children do not have to wait in long lines to place daily work in their portfolios.

You may want to negotiate with the children the selection of pieces for their showcase portfolios or have this remain wholly the child's choice. At the time of selection, the child communicates with you the reasons that he or she considers a particular piece to be a good choice. The dated pieces should always be arranged chronologically so that they indicate growth. For very young children, maybe only three to five pieces should be included. Primary-age children can be helped to select samples of work from each curriculum area and to categorize the material for the viewer. If able, children may also construct a preface, a table of contents, or labels to tell the reader how the materials were developed or organized.

Decorated or personalized showcase portfolios can be simple or elaborate, depending on the children's skill and motivation. Teachers can encourage children to customize them as creatively as possible and to take pride in the uniqueness of their personality or work style. As soon as children can write, they can include a statement of purpose for or an introduction to the portfolio. One child wrote, "Dear reader: My portfolio contains art work, journals, center work, writing pieces, and spelling sheets. This is work I adore, so please try not to rip it" (Soderman, Gregory, & McCarty, 2005).

Student-Led Conferences: Bringing Parents and Others into the Process

Whenever our hard work is acknowledged by others, it is enormously satisfying. That's what makes student-led conferencing such a powerful mechanism for evalution of children's growth. Such conferencing encourages children to reflect on what they have produced and to think about their goals. It is a celebration in which parents and interested others can view a child's accomplishments firsthand, make supportive comments and suggestions, exchange information, and be actively involved in the child's work world. Instead of being cut out of the process (as in traditional parent–teacher conferencing), the child is not only brought into the process, but, appropriately, takes center stage. Instead of the teacher's relating simple scores or grades to parents and telling about work that was not produced, the onus is put on the child to present evidence of growth and achievement during a specific time period. It is the children's celebration. Student-led conferencing comprises three stages: (1) a preparatory period, (2) implementation of the conference, and (3) a debriefing period.

Getting Ready for the Big Event. At specific times during the school year, anywhere from once to quarterly, teachers and children plan for a portfolio conference. The teacher sets a convenient time for parents to attend (one that does not conflict with other community events or with parents' work schedules), helps children to select and organize materials, sends out written invitations, plans for pictures to be taken, organizes child care and transportation if necessary, and informs the parents about the process. Schedules can be drawn up to ensure that the teacher has adequate time to meet each family. An optimal structure is to have four or five families in the room at one time for 20 to 30 minutes, depending on the class size. Preprimary and kindergarten teachers who have two classes per day will want to schedule two separate evenings to accommodate parents comfortably.

The teacher will want to stress the importance of parents' remembering to be only positive because the work they will be viewing is their child's personal best at that particular time. If parents are inexperienced with the process, professionals can provide examples of questions parents may ask children during the conference (e.g., "Which piece is your favorite? Why?" "What are your goals for the next work period?" "What do you think is the most important thing you've learned this year?" "What do you enjoy most about school this year? What do you find most difficult?").

In addition to selecting pieces for their showcase portfolio, children may practice communicating about their work by showing their portfolios to a classmate (a portfolio buddy) and to someone else in another class before the conference. They may role-play introducing their family members to the teacher, write invitations, and plan with the teacher how to restructure the classroom environment for the evening. For example, children can make posters celebrating the event, table decorations, and decorated paper tablecloths. They can make a parent guest book for written feedback, make refreshments, make a welcome sign for the door, and help select soft, instrumental music to be played in the background. They may also help clean and organize the classroom for the event. Children also discuss with their teacher the activities that might be of special interest to their parents: sharing their favorite books (and showing off their improving reading skills), including their parents in their classroom center experiences, reviewing their journals, participating in group projects, and viewing videos showing them at work in the classroom.

Documentation Boards. Student-led conferences are perfect venues for displaying documentation boards, which are becoming increasingly popular. At the Child Development Laboratories at Michigan State University, these three-sided boards, with panels approximately 2 × 5 feet, line the hallways outside the early childhood classrooms during student-conferencing days. They contain documentation of the exciting learning that has transpired during particular projects. Although each board is unique, it contains a description of the curricular goals and objectives that received special attention during the project. Also included are pictures of the children involved in working on included activities, narratives by the children about certain concepts and skills they were learning, and brief written perspectives by the teacher. Three-dimensional artifacts produced by the children during the project are also labeled and arranged on the table near the boards, providing additional evidence of completed work for parents and others to view. Family members spend a great deal of time examining the boards prior to and following their conference time. The boards are also available for viewing by university faculty coming into the school for research and by members of the public who might be visiting the laboratories, creating interest in the school's approach to early education. The boards are then archived and may be brought out to share with other classes of children or adults who are involved in similar projects.

Celebrating. Because of their extensive involvement in the preparatory phase, children are very excited about the celebration—perhaps even a little nervous. As in the case of the artist, photographer, architect, writer, and scientist, the work in which they have so much personal investment is about to be viewed and evaluated by others. Even very young children can be encouraged to introduce their parents to the teacher and then to read a favorite book with their parents, engage a parent in a favorite classroom activity or game, share their journal, and look through the portfolio. As children mature, student-led conferencing can become more sophisticated. However, the evening should maintain an air of celebration and be as enjoyable as possible for all.

In many school districts where attendance at parent–teacher conferences has been extremely low, administrators report that nearly 100 percent of parents attend student-led conferencing because they find it so enjoyable. Moreover, because their children are the presenters, non-English-speaking parents do not experience the extreme language barriers that keep them away from parent–teacher conferences. Because the focus is on what the children *did* accomplish and they feel grown up in taking on the role of presenter, most children share the feelings of one second grader who exclaimed to her teacher the next morning, "That was fun! When are we going to do it again?"

Debriefing. How Was It? A written follow-up to thank parents for attending and to find out what they enjoyed or did not enjoy about the conference is important so that future portfolio celebrations can be improved. A brief survey sheet can be included in the thank-you note, including such questions as "What did you like about the conference? Is there anything you would like to see changed? How has your child responded to the student-led conference? Would you like to see this type of conference format continue in the future? Why or why not?" A place for comments and suggestions can also be included (Soderman et al., 2005).

The teacher will want to schedule time with individual or small groups of children to discuss their reactions to the conference and even have children who can write fill out evaluation forms. Eric, a first grader, drew a picture of himself playing a board game with his parents, all three with huge smiles on their faces, which said a lot about his experience. He titled his page

"CONNFORNS [CONFERENCE]" and wrote, "I like when I plad games. I like when I sode (showed) my Mom & Dad my fobler (folder). I like when I sode them the room." Children may discuss their favorite aspect of the conferences and what they will do differently the next time, and they may suggest changes to make for the next conference during the preparatory or implementation phases.

Portfolios and student-led conferencing help children connect schoolwork with real purposes for learning skills, help them recognize their strengths and weaknesses, and help them see learning as sequential and connected with effort—life skills that are just as important as the academic skills being evaluated. Teachers take on a different role; instead of telling parents about the learner, they allow the learner to play the lead role. This requires teachers to become facilitators, consultants, and knowledgeable guides in children's learning. Parents are brought intimately into an interactive evaluative process that is more meaningful, more pleasurable, and more productive in terms of understanding and appreciating their child's growing abilities. The portfolio process is more effective when it includes student-led conferencing and when schools and school systems have institutionalized the practice across the entire period of children's school careers.

ASSESSING AND EVALUATING CHILDREN'S PROGRAMS

It would be a mistake not to take a careful look at the environment in which children are learning, including the social-emotional climate, the setup of the classroom, the approach to instruction and assessment, and parent involvement—in short, the entire program. When done carefully, program evaluation can be a good indicator of success and is usually conducted for one or more of the following purposes (Bagnato, 2007, 258):

Describe and quantify program features
Highlight successful program practices
Improve weak program practices
Demonstrate individual child and family progress
Demonstrate success across groups of children and families
Align program missions and standards with expected outcomes
Document program quality, impact, and outcomes to funding agents/stakeholders
for self-advocacy

There are a number of standardized measures and assessment tools for doing so, and a listing of those most often used by researchers and state and local early childhood educators can be found by accessing the U.S. Department of Education's 2007 Regional Educational Laboratory at the University of North Carolina, Greensboro (Brown, Scott-Little, Amvade & Wynn, 2007). This comprehensive report lists key instruments, criteria for selecting an instrument, and recommendations for assessment or diagnostic use. Most important is choosing one that corresponds closely to the program goals, and choosing valid and reliable instruments that are culturally and linguistically appropriate for children and families participating in the program.

SUMMARY

Developmentally appropriate early childhood evaluation is necessary for documenting young children's growth and for providing sound information for program planning in the primary grades. Formulating an effective evaluation strategy to measure children's progress requires the following:

1. Early childhood educators with a solid understanding of the many facets of child development
2. Appropriate and authentic evaluation strategies for measuring children's engagement in activities and developmental progress with time
3. Effective use of evaluation data to improve the quality of each child's educational experiences and growth
4. A useful structure for organizing and sharing obtained formative and summative information with relevant others (i.e., the children, parents, other educational staff working currently or in the future with the child and administration)

myeducationlab

To check your comprehension on the content covered in Chapter 7, go to the Book Specific Resources in the MyEducationLab for your course, select your text, and complete the Study Plan. Here you will be able to take a chapter quiz, receive feedback on your answers, and then access review, practice, and enrichment activities to enhance your understanding of chapter content.

Although standardized tests can help us understand and plan for the child with special needs, information gained from them should be used only along with other equally valid sources. Single scores on standardized tests should never be used in isolation to direct or redirect the lives of young children; nor should they be used to structure children into homogeneous settings when the children could be better served in regular programs and with their peers. In general, authentic assessment methods are preferred in early childhood education.

Findings from evaluating children's work should be used. Although this may seem obvious, testing and evaluation often do not go beyond collecting scores to assign grades or make comparisons across classes or schools. The process should always culminate in a plan by the teacher to structure learning experiences for the child. Results may also help the professional to note the strengths and weaknesses of classroom instruction and guidance. Findings should be considered in the context of the teacher's knowledge of the child and influence the timing and nature of the next evaluation.

All assessment findings should be carefully cataloged for future use, and information should be kept confidential except when it is used to support the young child's educational experience. In the hands of professionals who are knowledgeable about child development, curriculum planning, and early childhood assessment, effective evaluation can become one of the tools needed to plan advantageous beginnings for children and the kinds of classroom experiences that will lead to sustained curiosity and a desire for lifelong learning.

Key Words

anecdotal records	halo effect	screening
assessment	leniency factor	sensitivity
authentic assessment	oral reading test	specificity
ecomap	readiness	validity
evaluation	reliability	
frequency counts	rubrics	

Applying What You've Read in This Chapter

1. **Discuss**
   a. Return to the questions that opened this chapter. On the basis of your reading and your experiences, discuss your response to each question in detail.
   b. If you were interviewing for an early childhood teaching position and a member of the interviewing team asked you what you know about authentic assessment and how you would implement it, how would you answer?

2. **Observe**
   a. Arrange to view the portfolios of a class of first graders and a class of third graders in a local elementary school in which student-led conferencing is used.
   b. Ask for permission to observe implementation of the process. Determine the following:
      1. What products were kept in the portfolios? How does this differ between the first graders and the third graders?
      2. During the conferencing, what role do the children play? What role does the teacher play? In what ways is the process an effective way to share information? In what ways could it be improved?

3. **Carry out an activity**
   a. Carry out a reading accuracy test with a second grader, using the process described in this chapter. Use Leo Leonni's

Fish Is Fish as the text. What is the child's accuracy score? What is the child's self-correction rate? How would you score the child's comprehension? Summarize what you learned about the child's literacy skills.
   b. Using the information you gained about ecomaps in this chapter, ask the parents of one or more children in a nearby early childhood education setting if you may interview them. What can you discover about the child that might be helpful in working with that child in an educational context?

4. **Create something for your portfolio**
   a. Develop a position statement about the need for more authentic assessment of children in the early childhood classroom. Give reasons why it supports developmentally appropriate educational practices.
   b. Create a subsection on your ability to assess and evaluate the progress of young children. Include a listing and brief description of a number of authentic methods. Carry out as many of these methods as you can with a child of the appropriate age. Summarize the results of each assessment procedure and attach a copy of the child's work.

5. **Add to your journal**
   a. What are your earliest memories of taking tests? How well do you do today when you are taking tests? What are your strengths and limitations?
   b. How confident do you feel about implementing authentic assessment and evaluation strategies? In what area do you need more information or practice?
6. ✋ **Consult the standards**
   a. Look on the Web for a copy of your own state standards for assessment of young children. Compare them with those that have been crafted by NAEYC (see Figure 7.1 in this chapter). How do they compare? How comprehensive is each document? Are there any omissions in one set of documents or the other that you believe are critical to effective assessment?

PRACTICE FOR YOUR CERTIFICATION OR LICENSURE EXAM

The following items will help you practice applying what you have learned in this chapter. They can help to prepare you for your course exam, the PRAXIS II exam, your state licensure or certification exam, and for working in developmentally appropriate ways with young children.

The principal of Wexford Community Schools has asked his staff to consider the implementation of a portfolios and student-led conferencing system in the school. Several teachers have expressed their concern about going in this direction. "It's going to mean more work for us, and we're already overwhelmed," says one. Other comments center on whether children in the school can handle the responsibilities involved in keeping portfolios and whether parents will accept this as an alternative to regularly scheduled conferences and report cards.

1. **Constructed-response question**

   a. If you were a member of this elementary school staff, would you have additional concerns about implementation of portfolios and student-led conferencing beyond those already expressed above?
   b. How would you begin to actually put such a process into effect in your classroom and how would you want to work with children, parents, and other teachers in your building to make it a more efficient process?

2. **Multiple-choice question**

   Authentic assessment calls for collecting a variety of data across time and over all developmental domains, use of data for planning classroom instruction, embedding assessment in children's regular classroom activity, and involving children and parents in the process. Consider each of the following types of assessment. In what ways is each able to be consistent with authentic assessment?

   a. Standardized assessment tests.
   b. Portfolios and student-led conferencing.
   c. End-of-the unit textbook and workbook assessments.

Chapter

8

Strengthening Developmentally Appropriate Programs Through Family Engagement

You may wonder:

What does *family engagement* really mean?
Why are people so interested in involving parents or other family members in early childhood programs?
How should I respond to family members who seem unable or unwilling to become involved in the program?
What are effective strategies for working with families as partners in children's education?

This chapter on building family partnerships in early childhood education will help you answer questions like these.

◆ ◆ *A tear trickled down Tish Kelley's cheek. The mother of a 3-year-old, she thought that on the first day of preschool, her daughter would cling to her at least a little. However, Joelle Kelley entered the classroom happily, eager to play with the toys and the other children. "'Bye, mom; you can go now," she said. Tish sighed, "Only 3 years old and already she doesn't need me."*
◆ ◆ *During a home visit with the kindergarten teacher, Patrick's father explains that Patrick has been diagnosed with attention deficit disorder. He stresses that Patrick is a loving child who needs plenty of affection, simple directions, and clear boundaries.*
◆ ◆ *At a school-sponsored curriculum night, Kathy Hale, a parent of a first grader, mentions that she is a weaver. She says, "My daughter loves to watch the loom in action. Would you like me to come in sometime and show the children how to weave?"*

Imagine that you are the teacher in each of these scenarios. Take a moment to consider the family members you have just met. They are all different. Yet, they are also alike in the following ways.

❏ Each of them is a significant person in a young child's life.
❏ Each has an emotional investment in that child.
❏ All have ideas and opinions about raising and educating young children.
❏ Each family member has the potential to become more actively involved in the early childhood program in which his or her child participates.

What you do and say in situations like those just described will influence the degree to which families will feel welcome in your classroom and the extent to which they will become active in their children's education. For this reason, you must think carefully about your relationships with children's families and about how you might encourage them to become involved in early childhood programs. **Family members** are all those in the child's life to whom the young child is attached, generally including parents, stepparents, grandparents, and partners of parents who have an ongoing regular relationship to the child.

THE CHANGING NATURE OF FAMILY ENGAGEMENT IN EARLY CHILDHOOD EDUCATION

The notion of engaging parents or other significant family members in children's early education is not new. For years, connecting home and school has been a fundamental aim of parent cooperative nursery schools, Head Start, and other early intervention programs. Accumulated research indicates that family involvement in children's programs is critical to the educational success of children (Kniepkamp, 2005; Daniel, 2009). Therefore, national accreditation standards identify it as a necessary component of high-quality early childhood programs (NAEYC, 2007) for children birth to five years. Likewise, state licensing standards as well as state curriculum standards emphasize engaging family members in their children's early education. In addition, the National

Association of State Boards of Education (NASBE, 1988; reissued 2004) recommends that all education programs serving children aged 3 through 8 years do the following:

❏ Promote an environment in which family members are valued as primary influences in their children's lives and as essential partners in early education.
❏ Recognize that the self-esteem of parents/significant family members is integral to children's development and should be enhanced by the family's positive interaction with the program.
❏ Include family members in decision making about their own child and the overall early childhood program.
❏ Assure opportunities and access for family members to observe and volunteer in the classroom.
❏ Promote an exchange of information and ideas between family members and teachers.
❏ Provide a gradual and supportive transition process from home to school for children entering school for the first time. (p. 19)

Such guidelines capture the spirit of family engagement espoused in this chapter.

When we talk about family engagement, early childhood professionals think not only about children's biological parents, but also *any* person who has primary responsibility for making decisions about the well-being of each child. This includes stepparents, adult partners of biological parents, grandparents, and foster parents. Moreover, family engagement is viewed as a continuous process that incorporates parents and other extended family members in the *total* educational program, including planning, implementation, and assessment (Bredekamp & Copple, 2009). As a result, family members and early childhood professionals form an alliance in which they develop a common understanding of what children are like—how children develop, how they behave, the challenges they face, and how they can be helped to meet these challenges. Adults also come to a shared conception of what good education is—what it looks like, how it operates, what it strives to achieve, what it requires, and what it precludes. When such alliances occur, family members and teachers learn together, mutually supporting each other in their efforts to make life more meaningful for the children and themselves (Goldberg, 1997).

The coalition between family members and teachers can take place in several ways and with varying degrees of participation by both groups. Joyce Epstein, a leading researcher on the subject, identified five categories of family partnering that range from lesser to greater ties between home and the program (see Table 8.1).

The desirability of all five types of family engagement is currently so well accepted that the federal government now mandates inclusion of parents and other significant family members as

TABLE 8.1 Five Types of Family Engagement with Examples

	Definition
Type 1: Childrearing	Professional staff member facilitates the development of skills leading to improved learning at home. Adults in the family acquire knowledge and skills that enable them to supervise, teach, and guide children.
Type 2: Communicating	Professional staff member communicates effectively with family members. Family members receive and respond to the messages from the program.
Type 3: Volunteering	Professional staff member solicits assistance from family members and organizes the work they are to do. Family members participate in the classrooms with the children and attend workshops or other programs for their own benefit.
Type 4: Learning at Home	Professional staff member provides family members with strategies to assist the child's learning at home. Family members assist the children, monitor homework, and coordinate family learning opportunities with program-based experiences.
Type 5: Representing Other Families	Professional staff recruits and prepares family members for decision-making roles at all levels: program, district, and state. Family members become active in community or advocacy activities that monitor or advise programs.

Source: Adapted from "Five Types of Parent Involvement: Linking Practices and Outcomes." In J. L. Epstein, *School, Family, and Community Partnerships: Your Handbook for Action* (2009). Thousand Oaks, CA: Corwin Press.

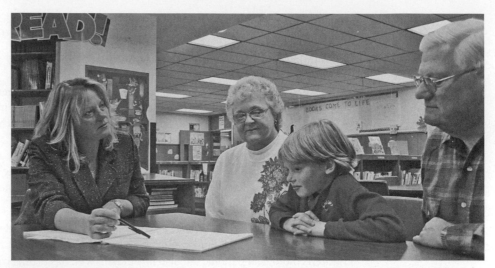

Adult family members should feel welcome in the program so that they will be involved in the child's learning.

participants, advisers, and knowledgeable consumers of services in all phases of Project Head Start, in the education of children with disabilities (Individuals with Disabilities Education Act, 2004), and in federally administered child care (U.S. Department of Education 2009). Increasingly, state governments have followed suit. As a result, in early childhood programs across the United States, family members are involved in children's education at all levels—from tutors at home to classroom participants, from volunteers to paid employees, from advisers to program decision makers. Those involved include first-time parents, teenage parents, older parents, single parents, dual-career parents, stepparents, parents of children with disabilities, grandparents, foster parents, aunts, uncles, and older brothers and sisters (Chang, Salazar, & DeLeong, 1994; Gullo, 2006). Moreover, although originally targeted at programs for very young children, family participation efforts have reached beyond such programs into elementary, middle, and high schools (Weinstein & Mignano, 2006). All this has transpired because we as educators have discovered that children, parents, and programs benefit immensely when family members take an active part in young children's education.

BARRIERS TO FAMILY ENGAGEMENT

With all the benefits that result from family engagement, you might expect that both teachers and families would be eager to partner. Yet, frequently families and professionals have misperceptions about each other that hinder the development of effective home–school relations (see Table 8.2) (Gonzalez-Mena & Widmeyer Eyer, 2008). They may also interpret different ways of doing things as wrong or as subtle criticisms of their approaches or as deliberate attempts to undermine their goals. None of these perceptions foster feelings of trust and cooperation.

Further barriers to productive home–school relationships develop when families have the following experiences (Weinstein & Mignano, 2006; Berger, 2008).

❑ They believe that their lack of formal teaching skills prevents them from making meaningful contributions.
❑ Family members are unsure of what to do to get involved.
❑ They get the message that their involvement is of little worth because they are asked to do only menial tasks (cutting string for an activity, putting out napkins, bringing the cupcakes to parties).
❑ They assume that the only thing programs want help with is fundraising.
❑ They interpret program invitations to get involved as insincere because no one gets back to them when they offer their time.
❑ Family members feel like they are intruders when they visit the program.
❑ They believe no one in the program appreciates the time they put into children's learning at home.

TABLE 8.2 Mutual Misperceptions of Teachers and Families	
Teachers Wonder Why Family Members	**Families Wonder Why Teachers**
Tend to linger after saying good-bye to their child. (Don't families know this makes the separation process more difficult?)	Are in such a rush to get them out of the room. (Don't teachers know this makes the separation process more difficult?)
Push for academics too soon. (Don't families know how children learn?)	Do not make the program more like "real" school. (Don't teachers know I want my child to learn?)
Get upset when their child gets dirty. (Can't families see this is a sign of learning?)	Do not keep their children cleaner. (Can't teachers see this is a sign of learning?)
Do not do a better job teaching children to behave. (They can't control him at home but want us to control him in the program.)	Do not do a better job teaching children to behave. (They can't control him in the program but want us to control him at home.)
Always criticize them. (Can't families see we're doing our best?)	Always criticize them. (Can't teachers see we're doing our best?)

These obstacles to family engagement are intensified among low-income families, who often feel stigmatized by society, and who may have had unfavorable school experiences of their own. Unfortunately, their negative perceptions are reinforced if teachers and administrators appear to be insensitive to the family's incredible financial and work constraints or get in contact with them only when their children are having problems (Magnuson & Duncan, 2002). These negative encounters contribute to families' feelings of shame, anger, distrust, and hopelessness, all of which detract from their motivation to become involved in their children's education.

Some additional barriers to family engagement have practical considerations. For instance, schedule conflicts arise when the activities are at times when parents are unavailable to participate. Families that are temporarily homeless are hard to reach and may be very concerned about maintaining custody of their children. Poor working families, dual-career families, and single-parent families frequently experience *role overload* (Weinraub, Horvath, & Gringlas, 2002). This basically means that there is too much to do and no time to do all of it. Regardless of family members' level of interest in partnering with professionals for the well-being of their children, they inevitably experience time and energy constraints (Bracey, 2001). Likewise, immigrant families and others whose primary language is not English often encounter communication challenges, as do English-speaking families when teachers use jargon (Eldridge, 2001). In addition, families raised in other cultures may be unaccustomed to any type of parent involvement and do not always know how to respond because the practice is atypical for their cultural group. Additionally, recent immigrants may be concerned about their own or their children's legal status and may be hesitant to get involved.

In addition to all of this, family engagement requires a lot of the teacher's time, and teachers are already busy. Moreover, it is discouraging when families are unresponsive to program efforts to become involved. As a result both families and programs sometimes miss opportunities to enhance children's learning through greater family engagement.

Both a readjustment of the attitudes of educators and family members and more concerted efforts to emphasize the partnership aspects of family engagement are needed if these obstacles are to be overcome. Evidence currently indicates that the early years are the optimal period in which to address such problems (Briggs, Jalongo, & Brown, 2006). As you read through this chapter, you will learn how to overcome common barriers and to support families.

CHARACTERISTICS OF EFFECTIVE FAMILY ENGAGEMENT

As educators have become increasingly aware of the benefits of family engagement and the obstacles that sometimes hinder its development, their attention has shifted from answering the query "Why?" to exploring the question "How?" Consequently, recent research has focused on discovering variables that characterize effective family engagement efforts. From these studies, four key elements have been identified: collaboration, variety, intensity, and individuation. A brief overview of each follows.

Collaboration

Collaborative relations between early childhood personnel and families are most apt to develop when families and teachers recognize each other's importance in the child's life. Because neither school nor family has the resources to do the entire job of educating the young, it is not in the best interests of either to attempt to duplicate each other's efforts. Rather, children's education is enhanced when home and school see themselves as distinct entities, performing complementary, interconnected functions (Berns, 2009). Family members have special information regarding their children (Driscoll & Nagel, 2008).

❏ Interests
❏ Play activities
❏ Eating habits
❏ Family experiences
❏ Previous educational or child-care experiences
❏ Kinds of playthings
❏ Influence of extended family members

❏ Fears
❏ Response to stress
❏ Difficulties
❏ Health
❏ Family reading patterns
❏ TV viewing habits
❏ Home discipline

Teachers can provide family members with equally useful and important information (Driscoll & Nagel, 2008):

❏ Interactions with peers
❏ Strengths and limitations
❏ Favorite activities
❏ Response to success and failure

❏ Memory
❏ Persistence at tasks
❏ Leadership/follower roles
❏ Contributions to the group

Collaboration is enhanced when mutual respect and open communication exists between professionals and families and when they both work together to enhance children's learning (Brewer, 2007; Epstein, 2009). Thus, family engagement represents a balance of power between families and teachers—a partnership. In this partnership, each member is valued and recognized as a "child expert." Families know their own child better than anyone else does. Teachers know many different children and have specialized knowledge of child development, program content, and educational strategies. When family members and teachers combine their areas of expertise, collaboration becomes a reality.

Variety

Lisa Digby is the room mother for her son's second-grade classroom. She belongs to the PTO and the library committee. Whenever a job needs doing at school, Mrs. Digby can be counted on to help.

Carole Wilson has been to school once, the day she enrolled her daughter for kindergarten. She works an 8-hour shift at a shirt factory and has a part-time job at Red's, a local convenience store. She has little time to spend at school volunteering.

If you were to talk to these mothers, you would find that both are keenly interested in their child's early education, and both want to be included in some way. However, what works for one will not necessarily suit the other.

Family members differ in the extent to which they are willing or able to take part in educational programs and in how they want to be included. Consequently, effective family engagement encompasses a variety of means by which family members can participate and does not require all family members to be involved in the same ways, at the same time, or to the same degree (Epstein, 2009).

FIGURE 8.1   Variable Characteristics of Parental Engagement

Kind of Contact
Predetermined agenda – – – Informal structure
Scheduled – – – Spontaneous
Face-to-face – – – Indirect

Format
Written – – – Spoken
Goal directed – – – Open ended
Presentation or discussion – – – Hands-on experience

Purpose
Provide input – – – Elicit input – – – Collaborate
Establish, maintain, or change – – – Relationships, goals, or strategies

Who Initiates
Child – – – Family member – – – Program personnel

Location
Home – – – Program – – – Community

Frequency
One time event – – – Repeated events – – – Continuous

Resources Required
Little time and energy – – – Lots of time and energy
General skills – – – Specialized skills

Role of Family Member
Receiver of information – – – Program supporter – – – Audience – – – Home tutor – – –
Classroom participant – – – Co-learner – – – Decision maker – – – Advocate

Variety can be considered in terms of the kinds of contacts that occur between home and program, the format they take, the purpose for which exchanges are made, who initiates them, where they occur, how frequently they occur, the type of parental response necessary for success to be achieved, and the resources required for participation. These variations are outlined in Figure 8.1.

More variety across the whole array of contacts is better. When a broad mixture of family engagement opportunities is created, educators demonstrate their interest in and acceptance of many kinds of families. Also, families receive visible proof that they may contribute according to their preferences, talents, resources, and degree of comfort (Berger, 2008). For example, varying the location from the school to a public library may encourage family members who are uncomfortable in schools to attend an event related to story reading in addition to helping them get library cards for themselves and other family members.

Intensity

The more we get together, together, together,
The more we get together, the happier we'll be.

This familiar children's song makes an important point that can be applied to family engagement. Parental participation outcomes are more likely to be positive if contacts are more frequent (NAESP, 2005). Regular, focused contact is necessary to promote the development of trusting relationships between parents and practitioners. Also, when opportunities for engagement are numerous, families can more easily find entrées to programs that better suit their needs and interests. Frequent, varied contact across time conveys the message that the educators value parents and that parental inclusion is not simply tolerated but welcomed and expected.

Individuation

Educational programs are most likely to elicit a positive response from families when opportunities for participation are tailored to meet families' particular needs and perceptions (Epstein, 2009). No one formula for family engagement, and no single program, can be generalized successfully to every population. Instead, the best outcomes emerge when a match exists between

Show genuine interest by listening carefully and responding respectfully.

what early childhood programs set out to do and what families want, when congruence exists between the strategies implemented and those to which family members feel receptive. When program designers consider family constraints such as child care and transportation needs, employment obligations, and economic, psychological, or physical stress, the chances for collaboration improve; as collaboration becomes greater, so do opportunities for individuation.

As you might assume, families are more likely to become partners in their children's education when practitioners take into account collaboration, variety, intensity, and individuation. Because these dimensions of family engagement are so important, they provide the backdrop for the rest of this chapter. Next, you will read about specific strategies for creating partnerships with families around children's early education.

EFFECTIVE FAMILY ENGAGEMENT TECHNIQUES

All the strategies suggested in this section may be used in individual classrooms or generalized to whole programs. We have listed about 50 ideas to give you a wide array of options to consider. However, note that no single educator would institute every strategy. A more likely approach would be to adapt one or two ideas from each of several categories to create a comprehensive family engagement plan. Such plans would be individualized to meet the needs of the children, families, and staff members within your program. Regardless of how simple or elaborate a family engagement plan might be, the goal is always the same: to reach out to families and help them feel included and an integral part of their child's education (NAESP, 2005). The first step is always the same, too: to establish positive relationships with families.

Establishing Relationships with Families

It's important to me that families know as much as they can about me so that they can feel comfortable leaving their child with me. It's not easy leaving your child with a stranger.

—Texia Thorne, teacher

I think they're terrific. The teachers seem to care not only for my children, but they care about me. When I come in looking tired, they ask me, "How are you doing? What can I do to help you? How are you feeling?"

—Debbie King, Kristine's mom

No matter what your position is in an early childhood program—practitioner-in-training, teacher, or administrator—you can begin to establish positive relationships with the families of the children in your group. The following simple guidelines will help you to forge closer ties with the most significant people in children's lives.

Show that you truly care about each child. An old Danish proverb states, "Who takes the child by the hand takes the mother by the heart." Keep this message constantly in mind and recognize that, first and foremost, families want early childhood professionals to pay attention to their children and treat them as special (Reisman, 1996). To show that you care, treat each child as an important, valued human being by your words and deeds each day. Recognize, also, that a loving education includes ensuring that children go outdoors with all the clothing their family sent that day, that children's noses get wiped, that children's tear-stained faces get washed, and that notes from home are read and answered. Oversights of these "details" speak volumes to families and may give the unintended impression that you are too busy or uninterested.

Make personal contact with families. No substitute exists for face-to-face communication between people. If you are fortunate enough to work in an early childhood program in which families come into the building to drop off or retrieve their children, take advantage of these times to greet family members, inquire about their day, and have a friendly word. This means being available rather than rushing around making last-minute preparations or focusing solely on getting the children into their coats to go home. If you do not see families regularly, take advantage of the times when you do see them. Mingle with family members at program events rather than chatting with your colleagues. Greet family members and see that they have activities to do or people with whom to talk. Family members who are not English speakers still recognize "Hello, Mrs. Garcia," and respond to smiles and nods of recognition.

Treat parents and other family members as individuals. Communicate with them on a one-to-one basis, not only in groups. Use an adult interpreter with families whose primary language is not English. Periodically provide time for family members to talk with you privately. Interact with them as interesting adults, not simply as Felicia's mom or Pedro's dad.

Show genuine interest in family members by listening carefully and responding. A real barrier occurs when family members form the impression that early childhood personnel are too busy or too distant to give much thought to what family members are thinking or feeling. Dispel this notion by doing the following:

❏ *Provide openings for family members to share their concerns or inquire about their child's program experience.* "What changes have you seen in Jack recently?" "What are Anne's favorite play activities at home?" "Do you have anything you're wondering about regarding Suman's development?"

❏ *Ask questions relevant to family comments.* Invite family members to elaborate on what they are saying. Reply, "Tell me more about that" or "Then what happened?" Such comments help family members to feel heard and valued.

❏ *Respond to family members' questions honestly and directly.* If you do not know the answer to something, say so. Promise to find out. Then do it.

Be courteous to family members. Treat family members with consideration and respect. Pay attention to nonverbal behaviors (e.g., facial expressions, posture, and gestures) and words. Implement the following strategies daily.

❏ *Greet family members when you see them.* Address them by their proper names, using *Mr., Ms., Mrs.,* or *Dr.* Pronounce family names correctly. Use the correct surname for each adult. Adult surnames may differ from the child's surname.

❏ *Avoid using professional jargon unnecessarily.* Using **jargon**, or technical terminology, that people do not understand implies an unequal relationship and sometimes makes families feel unwelcome or uncomfortable talking with you. Use familiar words to explain what you mean (e.g., talk about "children working together" instead of "cooperative learning"; "pretend play" instead of "imitation and symbolic play"; "acknowledging the child's point of view" instead of "reflective listening").

❏ *Avoid addressing notices and newsletters to be sent home with the words "Dear Parents."* Doing so implies that all children in the program are living in two-parent families. A more inclusive salutation would be "Dear Family Members."

❏ *Arrange to have program materials translated in the home languages of the families in your classroom.* Provide a translator (perhaps a family member from another family) to facilitate conversations between you and new families whose home language you do not speak. Learn a few words in each family's home language. If family members feel embarrassed about their English skills, one strategy that is sometimes helpful is to share how frustrated you "feel at not being able to communicate in the parents' language. This helps to break down any tinge of superior/inferior perceptions from the relationship, and keeps both of you on the same level as human beings" (Lee, 1997, p. 58).

Honor family confidentiality. Mrs. LaRosa's husband left her this morning. Shannon O'Malley is thinking about going back to school. Vincent Kaminski has been diagnosed with a serious illness. Family members trust you to keep private information to yourself. Remember that personal information should never be shared with anyone not directly involved in the problem, including co-workers, members of other families, and outside friends. Not only is violating this trust unethical, but doing so could ruin your relationship with the family and that family member's relationship with educators in the program forever.

Focus on family strengths (stability of family routines, monitoring of electronic viewing, establishing homework expectations, demonstrating literacy usage, establishing and monitoring reasonable expectations for the children). Early childhood professionals enhance the possibilities for relationship building when they look for family strengths rather than focusing solely on what appear to be family faults (Driscoll & Nagel, 2008). You can achieve this in several ways:

❑ *Concentrate on what family members can do, not only on what they have difficulty accomplishing.* Identify one strength for each family in your class. Find ways to build on these strengths during the year.

❑ *Catch yourself using judgmental labels.* When this happens, try to think of the families in alternative ways. For instance, initially you might think, "Sarah comes from a 'broken' home." Shift to a more positive perspective: "Sarah comes from a family in which her grandmother is tremendously supportive." You need not totally ignore family problems or concerns, but you should avoid labeling families and thinking of them in a deficit mode.

❑ *Listen respectfully when children share information about their family with you.* Be careful to avoid making judgmental comments such as "How awful" or "I wouldn't boast about that." Instead, reflect children's feelings about what they have shared (e.g., "You sound excited" or "That worried you").

❑ *Make sure classroom materials reflect the cultural groups and family compositions of the families in your group.* Taking this approach provides a visible sign that you value each child's family.

❑ *Consider situations from the family's viewpoint.* For instance, a parent who is having difficulty separating from his or her child at nursery school is not simply being uncooperative. Rather, the parent may be feeling guilty about leaving the child or worried that the child is not getting the attention he or she would receive at home. Likewise, a parent who fails to respond to a telephone call from the educator may be overwhelmed by work demands, not simply uninterested in his or her child. If it becomes necessary to refer a child for special education assessment, family members may be distressed, deny the possibility, or be angry at the program. Often such information shatters the families' hopes for their child and vision of the future. Trying to see things from each family member's perspective will help you to appreciate family circumstances and find alternative, more effective means of communicating.

❑ *Provide positive feedback to families about their children's progress and their child-rearing successes.* Offer family members information illustrating children's increasing abilities. For instance, knowing that Ruby's mother was concerned about Ruby's skills in relating to other children, the teacher sent home a note saying the following: "Today, Ruby offered her turn at the computer to a child who was eager to get involved before time ran out. She did this all on her own. I thought you'd enjoy hearing about her growing awareness of the needs of others." Comments or brief notes about issues that you and the family are working on together go a long way toward helping families feel like partners in the educational process.

Share control with families. If family members are to become truly involved, we must be willing to include them as partners in the educational process (Hohmann & Weikart, 2002). You can communicate this desire to families in several ways:

❑ *Take your cues from family members.* If they indicate a desire to communicate in certain ways, follow through. If the message seems to be, "I'm not ready," avoid pushing too hard. Wait awhile and then try again. Interact with families in ways that seem to feel most comfortable to them. Some family members will appreciate a telephone call, others would prefer that you communicate in writing, and still others would like an in-person conference. Try to accommodate these preferences as best you can.

❑ *Learn from family members.* Watch how a mother interacts with her child: What words does she use, and what nonverbal behaviors do you see that seem to be effective? Imitate these in your behavior with the child. Ask family members about their children. How do they help the child make transitions at home? What are the child's special interests? For children with serious difficulty in communication, ask how the families communicate with them. This kind of information could be a tremendous help in facilitating your communication with each child and indicates to families that you value their knowledge and skills.

❑ *Collaborate with family members on decisions regarding their child's educational experience.* Be honest and clear about the child's achievement and behavior. Deciding together on certain goals for children and strategies for achieving these goals is an important component of shared control, as is including family members in finding solutions to problems. Avoid announcing what you plan to do to address certain issues in the classroom. Instead, if you see a problem developing in which help from home would be useful (e.g., Samantha is having difficulty separating from her mother; Doug is not paying attention to directions in class; Marcel is getting into fights with children on the playground), initiate a dialogue with the appropriate family members and invite them to work with you to find a solution (Gonzalez-Mena & Widmeyer Eyer, 2008). Clarify the issues where you are not able to share in making decisions. For example, many programs no longer celebrate religious holidays as a strategy to make all families feel included. Teachers are not in the position to compromise on state or program standards either, but they may adjust how these are met. When you engage in these practices, shared control clearly translates into shared decision making.

Make frequent attempts to include families in children's early education. Begin by planning several simple contacts throughout the year rather than depending on one elaborate event. Offer some one-time engagement opportunities (such as an orientation or a hands-on workshop) as well as a few that encourage sustained participation (such as issuing a weekly newsletter, inviting family members to volunteer in the classroom each month, or asking for periodic help with materials at home).

Offer many ways for families to become involved in their children's education. Remember to diversify the kinds of contacts you make, the format they take, their purpose, and their location. Invite specific family members to participate in specific activities such as sharing their hobby or work. Also, vary the role that family members assume as well as the time, energy, and physical resources required. Make sure to create opportunities related to all five types of family engagement (see Table 8.1).

Tailor the engagement strategies you select to meet the needs of the families with whom you are working now. Ask yourself questions like these:

> Which families are likely to be able to attend a daytime meeting about child discipline? Who would find a night session better?
> Which families will find a chili supper and a short meeting on supporting literacy at home most appropriate? Who might prefer a Saturday workshop?
> Who might find a support group of adults their own age who are experiencing similar challenges helpful?
> Who might like a social event that includes all members of the family?

Avoid relying on the same approaches every year without considering how family needs differ from family to family and from year to year. For instance, last year, a Saturday-morning pancake breakfast was just the event to stimulate family interest and enjoyment of the program. However, this year, the children have been creating a classroom museum. A visit by family members to take a tour of the project might be a better match between the children's interests and their desire to include their families in their investigations.

Gathering Information from Families

Vivian Paley, a former kindergarten teacher and noted author, told the story of a father who came to school to share with the children memories of his childhood. Inviting family members to tell family stories was one way she found to gather family information that was comfortable for adults and valuable for children:

> "I was born in a small village near Calcutta in India," Vijay's father tells the class. "We had a sliver of a stream that ran along between our village and the forest. From the moment our summer holidays began, all the children played in the stream. We built dams out of stones to make the water tumble faster and we sailed pieces of wood, pretending they were ships on the ocean. One day

my cousin Kishore screamed that he saw a bear in the woods and we all ran home. Then he said it was a joke and we were all angry with him. However, we didn't want to waste time being angry because soon it would be time to return to school. And, so, every day, if our mothers wanted to find us, they knew we would be playing in the stream."

    We stare at Mr. Shah as we had never seen him before. Then we look at Vijay, our shy Vijay, and he is grinning. "There!" his smile seems to be saying. "Now you see how much there is to know about me." (Paley, 1995, p. 46)

Information may be gathered from families informally (e.g., chatting with families at drop-off time and pick-up time or making conversation at program events) as well as in more formal ways. A few basic strategies are outlined next.

Use enrollment or intake information as a way to learn more about the families of the children in your classroom. When families first enroll, they are often asked to supply information about their child in writing on an enrollment form or orally through an initial intake interview. Typical questions that families are asked are presented in Figure 8.2.

Throughout the program year, invite family members to share anecdotes and information about their child. This information might be used as the basis for classroom activities and to increase your knowledge of the child and his or her family. Word such requests as invitations to share information, not as commands to meet your expectations.

Ask for input from family members about their learning goals for their children. Give them a short list of program-related goals for children. Ask them to indicate which of these goals they

FIGURE 8.2   Family Information of Interest to Educators

Family Structure

❑ How many children are in your family?
❑ Who lives in your household?
❑ Who else takes care of your child during the day or on weekends?
❑ How are decisions made in your family?

Child Rearing

❑ What words does your child use for urination? Bowel movement? Private body parts?
❑ Describe your child's eating schedule.
❑ What food does your child like or dislike? Are there any foods to which your child is allergic?
❑ Describe your child's sleeping schedule.
❑ How do you put your child to sleep?
❑ How does your child react when he or she is angry or unhappy? Excited or confused?
❑ How does your child relax or comfort himself or herself?
❑ What are your child's favorite activities?
   How do you handle the following situations?
   Toilet training
   Sharing
   Messy play (paints, sand, water)
   Sex roles
   Racial concerns
❑ Whom does your child play with at home?
❑ What rules do you have for your child at home?
❑ What do you do to teach your child to behave?
❑ What are your child's responsibilities at home?
❑ Are there other things you think we should know about your child?

Family Culture

❑ What is your ethnic or cultural background?
❑ What languages are spoken in your home?
❑ What traditions, objects, or foods symbolize your family?

Sources: Based on *Parents as Partners in Education* (6th ed.), by E. H. Berger, 2008, Upper Saddle River, NJ: Merrill/Prentice Hall; *Anti-Bias Education for Young Children and Ourselves*, by L. Derman-Sparks and J. O. Edwards, 2010 Washington, DC: National Association for the Education of Young Children; *Roots and Wings: Affirming Culture in Early Childhood Settings*, by S. York, 2005, St. Paul, MN: Toys 'n Things Press.

FIGURE 8.3   Family Interest Survey

Your Name _____

Child's Name _____

We are delighted that you and your child are enrolled at Central School this year. We look forward to working with you. As you know, we encourage family members to be involved in our program as much as possible. To give us an idea of ways you would like to become a partner in the educational process, please check your areas of interest below. Thank you. We look forward to partnering with you.

Potential Family Interests

_____   Working with my child at home

_____   Sending in materials from home

_____   Translating materials for families in the program

_____   Reviewing materials for the program

_____   Building or making materials for the program

_____   Helping with the family toy-lending library

_____   Helping to find potential field trip sites or community visitors

_____   Helping with community trips

_____   Working with the teaching team to develop ideas for the classroom

_____   Planning special events in the community

_____   Planning special events at the center

_____   Attending events for parents

_____   Serving as a family "mentor"

_____   Attending a family-to-family support group

_____   Serving on the parent advisory council

deem most important for their child. Collect the information and use it in designing classroom activities. Refer to family members' lists periodically, and use them as the basis for some of your communications with families throughout the year.

Find out about family interests and discover ways in which family members might like to become involved in the early childhood program. Recently, a mother asked if she could visit her child's kindergarten class for the morning. The teacher, very pleased, said yes and assigned the parent to the art table. Several weeks later, by happenstance, the teacher learned that the mother was an accomplished cabinetmaker. Although the mother had enjoyed the art area, the teacher regretted missing an opportunity to have this mother help the children with some real woodworking skills. This oversight was not a major problem; however, it points out the importance of knowing each family member's talents and interests and making plans with these interests in mind. See Figure 8.3.

Seek out cultural information. Read about the cultural heritage of the families you serve and then check with them to see if what you learned through reading accurately reflects their practices and beliefs (Derman-Sparks & Edwards, 2010). Attend a cultural festival involving families in your group. A very honest, open approach would be to ask parents if what you read was true and if their family held a particular belief or practice. Ask more and assume less. If you are genuinely attempting to understand the culture and to bridge the inevitable gaps, family members are usually pleased to help and support your efforts.

Ask for evaluative feedback from families throughout the year. Let families know that their opinions count. Suggestion boxes near the program entrance, short questionnaires sent home that can be returned anonymously in a postage-paid envelope, written or oral evaluations administered at the end of workshops or other school events, and e-mail or telephone surveys conducted by staff or parents are some methods that prompt family input. Another effective strategy is to hold family–teacher forums once or twice a year at school. These regularly scheduled,

Provide family members with the information that they need to become partners in the educational process.

informal gatherings give family members and teachers a chance to evaluate the program together. Loosely structured around a broad topic, such as children's personal safety issues or promoting children's problem-solving skills, they provide for mutual exploration of educational ideas and strategies. Moreover, family members may ask questions and make suggestions for changes or additions to early childhood programs in an atmosphere in which such communication is clearly welcome.

Read the individual education plans for children with special needs as well as conferring with family members as soon as possible. Attend the planning meetings with parents of children who will enter your group. Regardless, you should know the goals for the child and use the assessment information that is available so that the child's progress will be supported optimally in your setting. Family members are experts in the needs of their own children and may provide useful information on strategies to support their specific child.

As a follow-up to these evaluation efforts, let family members know that you intend to act on some of their suggestions. Later, inform them (through a program newsletter or at a group meeting) of changes that have resulted from family input.

Keeping Families Informed

Is my child happy? Is my child learning?
How are you addressing reading in the classroom?
I don't understand my child's new report card.
Where are the letter grades we used to get in school?

These are typical questions that family members have about their child's early experiences. Anticipating such questions and communicating relevant information to families is an important part of being an early childhood professional. How you respond to unanticipated requests for information will also be important.

Develop written materials for your classroom in which you make clear your desire to include families in their children's early education. Provide specific guidelines for the form that family engagement could take and how home–school contacts might evolve. For example, let families know they are welcome to visit the classroom or that jobs will be available that they can do at home if they choose. Send these materials home to families and review them during a home visit or a program orientation at the school or center.

Acquaint family members with your educational philosophy, the content of the curriculum, program goals, and the expectations you have for children in your classroom. Integrate this content into a beginning-of-the-year family orientation as well as into any written materials (e.g., handbook, program brochure, written bulletins, web pages, or of program activities) sent home describing the curriculum. Offer examples of classroom activities that family members might see or hear about. Use hands-on activities to help family members better understand the materials in the classroom and their relation to children's learning. Use video materials on your website that explain components of your program.

Include nondiscrimination and inclusion policies that explicitly state that all families are welcome in the program (Gelnaw, 2005). Provide some examples of families that have attended in the past, such as those described earlier in the chapter. Display children's books that represent the full array of families in the program, including those headed by grandparents, single fathers, same-sexed parents, and those of cultural or racial minorities. Include examples of children and parents who have disabling conditions.

Familiarize families with a typical day for children in the program. Family members feel more comfortable with the program if they can envision how their child spends his or her time there. At the least, families should receive a copy of your daily schedule that outlines the timing of classroom events and explains the general purpose of each segment. Some teachers also utilize a slide or video presentation that illustrates how children in their class move through the day. Motivated to attend by seeing pictures of their child, parents leave having learned more about the early childhood program and its philosophy. A similar outcome occurs when educators put on a "miniday," in the evening or on the weekend, during which parents proceed through an abbreviated but total schedule in their child's company. Children are proud to lead their mom, dad, or grandparent through the routine, and family members gain insights into their child's classroom participation. Some programs provide this type of information via their website.

Periodically write one- or two-line notes regarding children's positive program experiences. Send these "happy notes" home with the child to demonstrate your interest in both the child and the parent (Berger, 2008). A child's first journey to the top of the climber, an enthusiastic creative-writing experience, or the child's pride in knowing many new facts about insects is a good occasion for a short, handwritten note from you. If you write one note every other day, the families in a class of 30 children could receive three or four such contacts in a year. Be sure to include all children from all families, especially those whose positive experiences are less frequent.

Create a weekly or monthly newsletter to inform families about the program and the children's experiences away from home. This simple form of communication can familiarize families with what is happening in the classroom, provide family members with ideas for subjects to talk about with their youngsters at home, and stimulate family members to engage in home-based learning with their children.

Preprimary-level teachers usually write the newsletters themselves. Newsletters designed for the early elementary grades may include contributions from the children (Berger, 2008). In either case, make newsletters short and visually interesting by using subheadings and graphics. Avoid overcrowding and use a 12-point font for easier reading. Divide the content into sections in which items are highlighted by outlining, indenting, using boldface, capitalizing, or changing typeface. Keep the focus on the children. More effective newsletters have suggestions that engage family members in child learning.

The newsletter content may include one or more of the following items.

❑ A review of the children's experiences at the center or school since the last newsletter
❑ A description of activities children will take part in throughout the next several days or weeks
❑ Specific, practical examples of how family members could address or reinforce children's learning at home
❑ Relevant classroom, family, or community news
❑ Invitations to family members to participate in the classroom, donate materials, or suggest upcoming classroom events

Stay in touch with family members who seem unresponsive. Avoid stereotyping family members as uncaring or impossible to work with. Remain pleasant when you see them. Periodically send notes home to let families know about their children's positive participation in program-based activities. Continue to offer simple, easy-to-do suggestions for home-based participation. Keep the input from the program as positive as possible, and make few demands. You might not see immediate results.

Use electronic communication whenever appropriate. Scanners, digital cameras, camcorders, e-mails, discussion list servs, pod casts, and websites can all help communicate information to parents. Opportunities to communicate faster and reach family members at work or at home are available. A few programs offer continuous online viewing of what occurs in a classroom for family members with protected pass codes. For some, this is an unacceptable invasion of the child's privacy. On the other hand, family members seem to like the opportunity to check on their young children while in a program.

A good website covers program goals and policies, information related to enrollment, opportunities for families to become involved, nondiscrimination positions, short "in classroom" video clips (with adult permissions), and referral resources that families can connect to directly as needed, such as local support groups for grandparents who are raising grandchildren (Orb & Davey, 2005). Setting aside time to keep a classroom website current and to read the responses of family members is important (Mitchell, Foulger & Wetzel, 2009) (see Figure 8.4).

Establishing Two-Way Communication Between Families and the Program

Both teachers and families have valuable contributions to offer each other: insights, information, ideas, and support. The back-and-forth flow of communication helps both of them develop a more complete picture of the child and their role in that child's early education. Thus, the concept of two-way communication between persons at home and those in the formal group setting is a critical element of DAP.

FIGURE 8.4   Tips for Using Electronic Communications

❏ Seek permission from the parents before sending e-mails.
❏ When sending e-mail to multiple receivers, avoid identifying family members to other persons by using the nickname function in the software program or by avoiding the public display of all addresses via the e-mail program.
❏ Determine if the family member would like the electronic communication to arrive at work or at home.
❏ Use black type on a white background, with at least a 12-point font so that recipients can easily read the message.
❏ Take the time to individualize the monthly newsletter for each family, with a digital photo of the family's child engaged in a current learning experience.
❏ Provide at home education activities on a classroom website.
❏ Create a family response link or form on the web pages to elicit comments, questions, and feedback.
❏ Prepare carefully constructed newsletters off-line, using a good word-processing program. The same standards of quality writing apply to electronic delivery as to delivery by post or child backpack.
❏ Place classroom documentation on a section of the website. Photographs of *all* children and relevant explanations should be included. Focus on children's learning.
❏ Provide noncustodial parents and grandparents access codes for protected websites unless there is a court restriction.
❏ If you are willing to engage in communication by e-mail or texting, specify a time and day when you would be available. You still must establish some boundaries between home and work.
❏ Don't contact someone immediately just because you can. If the communication is expected, it won't be as likely to end up being sent to the junk box by the e-mail screening program.

TABLE 8.3 Home–Program Communication	
Ways to Convey General Program Information	**Ways to Convey Specific Information About Individual Children**
A program handbook	Enrollment forms
A videotape of program activities	Telephone calls
Orientation meetings	Home visits
Home visits	Greeting and pickup routines
Newsletters	"Happy notes"
Bulletin boards	Photos of children engaged in activities
Program visits and program observation by family members	Family–teacher notebooks kept for individual children
Educational programs for families	Regular and special conferences
Web pages	Photos and commentary in documentation
Social events for families	
Articles sent home to families	
Family–teacher forums	

Vary the communication strategies you use rather than relying on a single method. Table 8.3 provides a summary of communication strategies by type. The general information is about the program and the specific is about their child in particular.

Take advantage of arrival and departure routines as a time to establish two-way communication with families. As one child-care provider stated,

> It's great to have family conferences, but those happen only once in a while. Most of my communicating with parents goes on in the five minutes I see them at 8:00 a.m. or the 5 minutes at 5:30 p.m. That's when I develop rapport with them, get in tidbits about child development, and try to problem-solve because parents are always in a hurry. Yet those five minutes add up. Before you know it we've been having weeks of minicontacts, day after day, and we have come to know a lot about one another and about the child as well (Sciarra & Dorsey, 2007, p. 355).

Establish telephone hours during which you and family members may call. Set aside 1 or 2 hours each week for this purpose, varying and dividing the time between 2 or more days, and notify them of your availability as well as the telephone number where you can be reached (at home or at the program). Also ask family members to indicate which time might be the most convenient for a call from you. It is important to set some boundaries as well. Parents should not be able to phone or text you any time of day and expect an immediate response.

Early in the year, establish a positive basis for communication by calling each family to briefly introduce yourself and share a short, happy anecdote about the child. This practice does much to dispel some family members' dread that a call from a teacher always means trouble. It also enables parents to get in contact with you more easily as needs arise. Make it a goal to touch base in this way with each child's family two or three times a year.

Create a notebook for an individual child through which family members and staff communicate as it is sent back and forth between the child's home and the program. Write brief anecdotes to the parent regarding the child's school experience. Encourage family members to write about home events (e.g., visitors, changes in routine, illness, disruptions, accomplishments, and interests) that might influence the child's performance in the program. A line or two conveyed once or twice a week between the home and school settings can do much to expand family

FIGURE 8.5 Example of Family–Teacher Communication Through Notebook Entries

---

1-6-10

Sarah had a wonderful Christmas vacation. We spent the last week in Miami—temps 80–84 degrees, sunny, swimming every day. She is not eager to be back, I'm afraid. We tried to tell her that kids who live in Florida have to go to school and don't get to swim all day and go out every night to dinner with Grandma & Grandpa. She's not convinced.

Mrs. G. (Mom)

1-6-10

Hi. Welcome back. Sarah is "stacking" in her wheelchair—is there a change in seating? Just curious. She ate a good lunch.

Leslie (special ed. teacher)

1-6-10

I hate to be out of it—please define stacking. Sarah spent today at a tea party with Michelle and Kelly and Lara. They discussed vacations, served "milkshakes" and muffins. Ryan asked Sarah several times to come and see his block structure. She finally agreed.

Dana (child-care teacher)

1-9-10

Dana, "stacking" is a postural problem where the head is tilted back and her shoulders are flopped forward. Sarah will sit up if we say "Can you pick your shoulders up better?" or anything similar, and she's very proud that she's able to do so.

Leslie

1-16-10

Sarah is bringing dinosaur stickers for sharing—the other kids can have one to take home.

Mrs. G.

1-16-10

Stickers were a hit! Sarah would also like to share with her Adams School friends. Sarah enjoyed reaching for and grasping scarves in the gym. She chose pink ones (we didn't have purple). She elected to "supervise" the art area, where Michelle and Kyle asked her for choices for the Boxosaurus decorations.

Dana

---

members' and the teacher's knowledge about the child and each other. This strategy is particularly effective when children participate in multiple educational settings outside the home, such as after-school child care or a special education program. Sample entries are provided in Figure 8.5 for Sarah, a 5-year-old with cerebral palsy who attends a special education class in the morning and an after-school child-care program in the afternoon.

Carry out home visits as a way to get to know children and family members in surroundings familiar to them. Although time consuming, such contacts are a powerful means of demonstrating interest in the child and his or her family as well as your willingness to move out of the formal educational setting into a setting in which parents are in charge (Weinstein & Mignano, 2006; Delisio, 2008). Visiting children at home also enables you to meet other family members or persons living there and to observe the child in this context.

Home visits benefit family members by giving them a chance to talk to the teacher privately and exclusively. Parents or other important adults in the child's life may feel more comfortable voicing certain concerns in the confines of their home than they would at school. When these visits are conducted early in the child's participation in the program, children have the advantage of meeting their teacher in the setting in which they are most confident. When they arrive at the center or school, the teacher is already familiar to them.

Despite all these potentially favorable outcomes, some family members are uneasy with home visits. They may be ashamed of where they live, fear that their child will misbehave, or suspect that the teacher is merely prying into their private affairs. To avoid aggravating such negative perceptions, give families the option of holding the visit at another place (e.g., coffee shop, playground, church,

FIGURE 8.6   Home-Visit Hints

Before getting in contact with families, determine the purpose of your visit. Some teachers choose to focus primarily on meeting and working with the child; others prefer to make the adult family member their major focus. Still others decide to split their attention somewhat evenly between the two.

Create a format for your time in the home that supports your purpose in going there. A sample agenda for the third option cited above might be as follows:

1. Arrive.
2. Greet family member and child.
3. Chat with family member a few moments. Give him or her program forms to fill out and a short description of how children spend the day at the center or school. Usually these are written materials, but some programs offer information on audiocassette for parents who cannot read.
4. Explain that next you would like to get acquainted with the child and that you will have a chance to talk to the family member in about 15 minutes.
5. Play and talk with the child while family member is writing, reading, or listening. Use modeling dough you brought with you as a play material.
6. Give the child markers and paper you brought with you and ask him or her to draw a picture that you can take back to school to hang up in the room.
7. While the child draws, talk with family member(s) about concerns, interests, and questions.
8. Close by taking a photograph of the child and family member(s) to put in the child's cubby or in a school album.

Supplies needed:

Map with directions to child's residence
Markers
Paper
Modeling dough
Digital camera
Audiocassette tape player

In a letter, inform families of your intention to carry out home visits. Explain the purpose of the visit, how long it will last (not more than an hour), and potential home visit dates from which they might choose.

Follow up on the letter with a telephone call a few days later to arrange a mutually convenient time for your visit and to obtain directions.

Carry out each home visit at the appointed time.

Follow the visit with a short note of thanks to the family for allowing you to come, and include a positive comment regarding the time you spent together.

or community center) or postpone your visit until you have established a relationship in other ways and the family is more receptive to your coming (Berger, 2008).

Teachers, too, may have qualms about visiting children's homes. They may feel unsafe in certain neighborhoods or believe that the hours invested will prove too many. In addition, program personnel may have concerns about teacher time and additional compensation. Having teachers work in pairs, keeping in touch with program personnel via cell phone before and after each visit, scheduling visits during staff development days, and securing small grants to support travel costs are ways some programs and school districts have addressed these issues (Delisio, 2008). As a result, home-visit programs continue to be part of many early childhood programs. Suggestions for conducting successful home visits are offered in Figure 8.6.

Structure family conferences to emphasize collaboration between family members and teachers. Consider the following points as you plan each conference (Berger, 2008; Gonzalez-Mena & Widmeyer Eyer, 2008):

Planning

❏ Create a pleasant written or e-mail invitation in which family members have options for scheduling times. Arrange for a translator if needed. Send it at least 2 weeks in advance of the anticipated event.

FIGURE 8.7 Potential Family Conference Questions

Sample Teacher Questions

1. How does your child seem to feel about school?
2. Which activities or parts of the day does your child talk about at home?
3. Which children does your child talk about at home?
4. How does your child spend his or her free time?
5. Is there anything that your child dreads?
6. What are your child's interests and favorite activities outside school?

Sample Family Questions

1. How has my child adjusted to school routines?
2. How well does my child get along with other children? Who seems to be his or her best friends?
3. How does my child react to discipline? What methods do you use to promote self-discipline and cooperation?
4. Are there any skills you are working on at school that I/we might support at home?
5. Are there any areas in which my child needs special help?
6. Does my child display any special interests or talents at school that we might support at home?
7. Does my child seem to be self-confident, happy, and secure? If not, what do you think the home or program can do to increase his or her feelings of self-worth?

myeducationlab

Go to the Assignments and Activities section of Topic 5: Assessment/ Observation and complete the activity entitled *Communicating about Children's Learning.* Reflect on the strategies that the teacher uses in planning and implementing a parent conference.

❑ Provide family members with sample questions that they might ask you as well as examples of questions that you might ask them (see Figure 8.7). When providing these, assure parents that they are just samples and do not preclude any other inquiries parents may have.

❑ Confirm each appointment with a brief, personal telephone call, a genial e-mail, or a short note to let them know you are looking forward to meeting with them.

❑ Allow enough time for each conference to ensure a genuine exchange of ideas and information.

❑ Secure a private, comfortable place in which to conduct the conference. Some grandparents may have difficulty in child-size seating, so use adult-size furniture.

❑ Prepare by reviewing the goals from previous meetings, individual educational plans, or prioritized goals of the family. Gather and organize your assessment information, work samples, or other materials that will enable you to provide the parents with accurate information.

❑ Write out a draft of a list of potential IEP goals for the coming year for the annual review of these goals.

Implementing

❑ Greet family members and thank them for coming. Take time to engage in welcoming social rituals such as offering a cup of tea or chatting for a few moments before beginning the more factual content of the conference.

❑ Begin on a positive note by conveying a pleasant anecdote about the child.

❑ Briefly outline the major areas you hope to cover. Ask family members if they have items they would like to add. Mention that the purpose of this conference is to exchange ideas. Urge family members to ask questions or interject their comments as you go.

❑ Throughout the conference, refer to the goals the family members signified as most important on the personalized goal sheet they filled out at the beginning of the year. Provide evidence of the child's progress in these areas. Add other goals that parallel your focus.

❑ Avoid broad generalizations such as "She is doing just fine." Tell parents the details that lead you to the conclusion.

❑ Be specific about what the child has accomplished and how he or she has succeeded. Include family contributions to the child's success such as, "Your idea of practicing the fire drill with Harry when other children were not here was very successful. He was able to cope with it that first time and was successful when the whole school did a fire drill."

❑ Keep the conference as conversational as possible, eliciting comments from family members as you go.

❑ Answer family members' questions directly, honestly, and tactfully. Avoid using jargon and judgmental terms to describe the child. Deal in specifics rather than generalities, and base your discussion on objective observations and concrete examples of work.

Concluding
- ❏ End on a positive note.
- ❏ Collaborate on future goals and strategies.
- ❏ Clarify and summarize the discussion.
- ❏ Make notes of agreements and of things you have said that you would do.
- ❏ Make plans to continue talking in the future.
- ❏ Follow up on any agreed-on strategies such as sending spelling words home.

Partner with families to support linguistically diverse children. Ask family members whose primary language is not English to teach you some words and phrases that could be useful for interacting with the child as he or she enters the program. Invite family members to the program to tell stories, sing songs in their home language, and share other oral traditions typical of their family. Encourage families to bring music, objects, or foods into the classroom to share and talk about. Ask them to provide storybooks, newspapers, and magazines printed in their home language for use in the classroom. When working with older children, provide ways in which family members can use their primary language to help their children with program-related assignments or activities at home. Create a home library that includes a variety of print materials written in families' home languages for children to borrow. Make the importance of the child's home language clear to the child and therefore to you. Stress that although children will be learning English in the formal group setting, such learning does not require children to abandon or reject the language of the home (Kostelnik et al., 2009).

Make contact with noncustodial parents. Provide opportunities for noncustodial parents to participate in home visits, open houses, and other school activities when possible, unless they are prohibited by a court order. Mail newsletters and web address to those who live elsewhere.

Work with family members to support the development and learning of children with special needs. All family members have the potential to learn and grow with their children. More than most families, families of children with disabilities are forced to confront similarities and differences and to reexamine their assumptions and values. One crucial aspect of your job is to support such families, as they become contributing members of the educational team. To do this, use the techniques you have learned so far as well as the strategies described next:

- ❏ *Gather and share information regarding all aspects of the child's development and learning.* Children with disabilities are whole beings. They cannot be summed up by a single label such as "hearing impaired" or "language delayed." When you talk to families, avoid focusing on only the child's disability. Talk about the whole child.
- ❏ *Treat families of children with disabilities with respect, not pity.* Families are families first and the family of a child with a disability second. They will have many of the same strengths, needs, concerns, hopes, and dreams expressed by other families in your class. Keep these in mind as you communicate with them.
- ❏ *Listen empathically as families express feelings about their child.* Family members have many reactions to their child's disability. Some deny the reality of the situation. Others feel angry, helpless, or depressed. Others are proud of their child and his or her accomplishments. In every case, the best approach is to listen without giving a lot of advice or telling families how to feel. Paraphrase reflections (described in chapter 2) are an excellent tool that shows your interest and effort to understand.
- ❏ *Expect families to vary in their expectations for their child.* Some families may believe the child has enough problems already. Such families often have low expectations for children's performance in the early childhood program. Other families view a disability as something to be overcome. They may expect their child to excel beyond normal development and learning for any child that age. Many families fall somewhere between those extremes (Kostelnik et al., 2002). Respond with sensitivity to these variations. There is no one "right" attitude. Accept families as they are and help them, as you would any other family, to determine reasonable expectations for their children.
- ❏ *Learn about the child's disability.* You do not need to be an expert on every form of disability, but you do need to know how to obtain relevant information. Ask family members to tell you about their children and how they work with them at home. Read articles and books about

various disabling conditions. Locate human resources in your community to support children and families in educational settings if a child has a disability.

❏ *Work cooperatively with other professionals involved in the child's life.* Often children with disabilities take part in a wide array of services involving professionals from varying agencies and backgrounds. You will be one member of this team. You may participate in a formal planning process with other team members and the family. However, many times, coordination may become difficult or communication may break down. Make an effort to communicate with the other helping professionals in children's lives. If possible, coordinate conferences with the specialist assigned and talk to families together. The traveling notebook described in Figure 8.5 is one means of maintaining communication.

Integrating Families into the Program

> Hanging at the top of the stairs at the Cesar Chavez School is a large quilt containing more than 100 fabric squares—each one different. Some are colored with fabric crayons, others are stitched or sewn, and still others have been embroidered or quilted. This quilt came about through a cooperative effort of families, staff, and children. Each family and staff member received a plain cloth square on which he or she could sew, cut and paste, or draw a picture or some other symbol that captured his or her feelings about the Cesar Chavez School. Families could work on the squares at home or at workshops in which family members, along with the children, were given materials and guidance about how to create a square of their choosing. Emphasis was placed on participation by many people rather than on achievement of a perfect final product. As a result, even children and adults who believed they lacked arts and crafts talent were enticed into participating in the project. The quilt required several months to complete. Today it hangs as a warm and loving tribute to the community spirit of the Cesar Chavez School. It is also visible proof that families, children, and staff are partners in the educational process.

The quilt at the Cesar Chavez School is a good example of how educators in one early childhood setting integrated families into the ongoing life of the program. Following are additional strategies that you can use.

Institute an open-door policy in which family members are welcome to come to the classroom or program unannounced. Invite family members to watch or participate in the classroom, and provide simple guidelines so that family guests will know what to expect from you and the children while they are on-site. For instance, make them aware of locations from which they can observe unobtrusively. Clearly indicate the times when you are available to chat and the times when your attention must be focused on the children. Snack time, the story time before recess or nap, and outdoor times are periods of the day when parent visitors might easily be accommodated.

Invite family members to visit the classroom for particular occasions. These times might be incorporated into a whole-group social affair such as a family–child breakfast or a Sunday afternoon open house. Fathers attend family activities more frequently than any other type of program activity (Turbiville, Umbarger, & Guthrie, 2000). Invite family members to share in a certain classroom activity such as making applesauce or planting seeds. Consider asking individual parents to become involved in a specific project (e.g., making bread or listening to children read). In every case, let families know they are welcome and that their presence will enrich the program. Issue your invitations far enough in advance for family members to arrange to be there. Follow up each visit by asking family members to fill out a reaction sheet on which they can briefly record their impressions, suggestions, and questions. This evaluation lets families know that their opinions are valued.

Encourage family members to participate in the classroom as volunteer teachers for part or all of a day. Issue an invitation in which you describe the volunteer role. Clearly indicate that family members, by virtue of their life experiences, have the skills necessary to do the job. Follow up by speaking to individual family members about how they might become involved. Fathers are more likely to respond to a specific, personal invitation than to a more global invitation (Turbiville et al., 2000). Support volunteers by using the suggestions outlined in Figure 8.8.

FIGURE 8.8   Guidelines for Working with Family Members as Teachers in the Classroom

❏ *Establish clear guidelines for family volunteers regarding their responsibilities in the classroom.* Offer specific suggestions as to what volunteers are to do and a rationale for delegated responsibilities. An activity card with this information could be prepared and then handed to a different parent day after day. Read the card aloud, or prepare an illustrated chart if the parent is an uncertain reader. An example of such a card is offered below.

Welcome! Today please:

1. Greet children and help them find name tags. Goal: Children will demonstrate that they have a feeling of belonging in a new place and recognize they can get meaning from print (how their name looks).
2. Supervise matching game. Goal: for children to notice similarities and differences.
3. Join the children at lunch. Encourage them to pour and serve themselves. Goal: Children will demonstrate a growing ability to care for themselves and meet their own needs.

❏ *Take time to demonstrate some of the activities family members are to supervise that day.*
❏ *Help family members feel welcome in the classroom.* Introduce them to the children and provide youngsters with name tags so that parents can interact with them more comfortably.
❏ *Inform family members that when they volunteer in the classroom, all children in the group will view them as a teacher.* Remind the child that Mom, Dad, or Grandma will be helping many children and will have special responsibilities throughout the day. This helps clarify the adult's role for Mom, Dad, or Grandma and the child.
❏ *Talk with family members about how to handle some potentially disruptive situations in the classroom.* Also discuss what to do if their child is involved. When this latter issue is ignored until it happens, some family members may fail to act or may overreact out of embarrassment. Neither response is conducive to the family members' feeling comfortable at school.
❏ *Give family volunteers in the classroom meaningful tasks to carry out:* helping children in the pretend-play area, engaging children in conversation, assisting children at the snack table. Avoid requesting them to do only busywork like washing the easel and brushes or cutting straws for a future fine-motor activity. If family members are to become partners in the educational process, they must be given real responsibilities from which they can derive genuine satisfaction.
❏ *Notice family members' successes in the classroom and comment on family members' helpfulness and effectiveness.* Describe their work in terms of better class functioning and individual child learning. This will underscore their value to the educational process.

Involve family members in making classroom collections or materials either for their use or for children to use at school. Ask parents or grandparents to donate a song, story, or recipe that is a family favorite. Collect these items from family members individually (in writing or in person) or plan a program event in which such items are shared. A potluck dinner or a family songfest in which children also participate may pave the way for beginning such a collection. In each case, these collections are tangible evidence of parents' contributions to the program. They can be assembled with minimum hardship to either families or staff. Moreover, such collections signal to family members that their cultural traditions are valued by educators and are worth sharing with others.

Create home-based alternatives to on-site volunteering. For instance, ask family members to volunteer to prepare materials at home, make arrangements for field trips and with resource people, coordinate parent discussion groups, find resource materials at the library, compare prices of certain types of materials or equipment at local stores, or react to activity plans that will eventually be used in the classroom.

Provide home-based learning activities for family members and children to do together. This strategy is appropriate for all families but especially for those whose time is limited because of employment and family constraints. However, to achieve positive outcomes, families require clear expectations and guidelines about what to do. Provide written, audio or podcast directions. For each activity, invite family members to also tell you how easy it was to do and how much they and their children enjoyed it. Offer feedback to families about how their assistance at home is affecting their child's learning. A story book in a nylon bag with follow-up ideas written on a card has been successful in fostering literacy development in young children (Burningham & Dever, 2005). Similarly, activities related to a child's IEP goals could be sent home.

Send children's work home (Morrison, 2009). Attach a note about the work. Occasionally ask parents to return a note about what they think of the child's work.

Show genuine pleasure in every family member's attempts, no matter how large or small, to support the children's education. Continually let families know how much you appreciate the time and effort they put into their child's education, not just because their help allows you to do a better job but also because the children benefit so greatly. In addition, in classroom newsletters or community newspapers, acknowledge family contributions. Families may also be officially recognized at program events or with tangible tokens of appreciation such as certificates, plaques, or thank-you notes from the children.

Involving Men in Early Childhood Programs

Mr. Wasserman had just returned home with his 4-year-old daughter and told his wife, "I don't want to pick Gwennie up at the child-care center anymore."

Mrs. Wasserman inquired, "Why not?"

"I went in and got her, put on her coat, looked for her bag, and none of the teachers even said hello or looked at me. They said hi to all the mothers and told them about their kid's day. If we ever want to know what is happening, you will have to go yourself."

Michael begged his father to go to the parent conference with his mother. When his parents both agreed to go, he was extremely pleased. On their way home, Michael's dad said, "I don't know why Michael wanted me to go. I was the only father there."

The desire to include men in the early education program has arisen fairly recently. Although women have joined the workforce, a corresponding increase in the participation of fathers whose wives are employed has increased very slowly (Berger, 2008). However, the essential roles of both men and women in the development and education of children are now more fully understood. Male involvement in children's education is associated with higher achievement and with social competence (Fagen, 2000; Berger, 2008).

In general, the barriers to participation by men are similar to those for women. However, men face even more barriers and more formidable barriers. For instance, are men actually welcome in programs? The experience reported by Mr. Wasserman is unfortunately all too common. There appears to be ambivalence between the desire that teachers express and their behavior. Fathers are also ambivalent, as Michael's dad expressed. When neither the teachers nor the fathers (men) are confident that they know what to do and why they are doing it, the fact that fewer men than women are involved, except at home, is not surprising.

Furthermore, men and women have different interaction styles with children and with each other. Children flourish with a combination of styles of interaction of both men and women. Most men are individualistic and competitive, whereas most women focus more on relationship building. The issue of male power is a considerable part of teachers' hesitancy to involve men in their programs (Turbiville et al., 2000).

Because women compose the largest portion of early childhood educators, these professionals in the field must overcome such barriers. Fortunately, when early childhood professionals are committed to including men in their programs and have the support and training necessary to plan and implement appropriate strategies, male participation increases (McBride, Rane, & Bae, 2001).

The principles of collaboration, variety, intensity, and individuation are valid for both men and women. However, men are much more likely to respond to a direct request for assistance than for a general request for parental participation. A short video on the website that features a father interacting in the program can be encouraging to other men. Requests for participation must be compatible with work schedules or tasks that can be completed in the father's home. Strategies for gathering information, inviting interaction, and recognizing contributions should be directed to the important men in children's lives as well as the women. Even a separate interest survey for men is appropriate (Levine, 2004).

Establishing relationships, gathering information, and keeping families informed are also important if the fathers' engagement is to be optimal. Thus, educators may have to institute dual parental contact for children whose parents do not share a household. Men report a desire for school involvement, believe that they have some responsibility to be involved, and find the loss of contact with and on behalf of children to be one of the most difficult aspects of parental separation (Baker & McMurray, 1998). Therefore, information should be gathered for noncustodial parents as well as for the parents who are the primary caregivers. Sending notices of meetings, scheduling conferences, and asking for participation by mail to noncustodial parents all support the connection between the child and the parent.

Activities planned specifically for men or with men's interests in mind have been successful in some programs. For example, educators in one program held a special workshop on motor skills on a Saturday morning. Both men and women attended, although more men attended than had ever attended any other event. Similarly, at Edgewood Primary School, educators held a special celebration for children and the important men in their lives. Children invited grandfathers, fathers, stepfathers, and other males who were special to them. This event was held in the evening and was planned to engage adults and children in lively, beneficial activities.

Involving men in early childhood programs continues to be a challenge, even in programs in which some success has been achieved. However, when the early childhood educators are committed and follow through to the implementation stage, progress is made toward achieving this goal.

Providing Family Education

At a recent get-together for the families in her room, Consuelo Montoya invited the participants to give her ideas about topics they would like to explore in the coming months. Families brainstormed five ideas. Next, Consuelo put up a sign at the entrance to her room, asking family members to put a mark by the idea they most wanted to have a chance to talk about. Families who could not come to the room in person were invited to telephone in their preferences. Following are the results:

> *Consuelo Montoya's Classroom—Family Topics Wish List*
> *Sibling Rivalry = ////////////*
> *Healthy Snacks Kids Will Eat = /////*
> *Celebrating Family Traditions = ////////*
> *How to Help Children Make Friends = /////////////////*
> *Taming the TV Monster = ////////*

On the basis of these outcomes, Consuelo plans to organize a workshop entitled "How to Help Children Make Friends." She and another teacher will gather ideas and information for families and then share it during a family education evening at the center. A workshop on sibling rivalry could come next. For that workshop, Consuelo is thinking of inviting family members to talk about what they do at home when the bickering starts.

This example was one teacher's approach to developing family education opportunities for families of children enrolled in her classroom. Many other ways are available for educators to carry out this important facet of family engagement. Following are some guidelines for how to begin.

Conduct a simple needs assessment of family member concerns and interests related to child rearing and other family issues. This process could be carried out for only your classroom, among several classes, or on a programwide basis.

You can proceed in several ways. One way is to invite family members to a brainstorming session in which mutual concerns are generated. A second approach is to conduct a brief written or telephone survey in which family members identify the issues that are most important to them. A third technique is to provide family members with a broad range of potential issues that could be addressed and then ask them to indicate which are most important to them. The summary of the results can then be used to provide direction for future parental education efforts.

Deal with the most pressing needs for the group early. However, a word of caution is advisable: Avoid simply going with the notion of majority rule. Instead, look at the concerns in terms of various demographic subgroupings such as low-income families or single-parent households. For example, a workshop on sibling rivalry or children and television would be of interest to a broad range of families in your class, whereas blended families might find the following two topics pertinent: (1) living with other people's children and (2) dealing with stepparent stereotypes. Addressing both general and specific concerns in your plan will give it the widest possible appeal and will be more sensitive to all families served by the program.

Invite family members to educational workshops that involve both them and the child. Consider using a format in which children receive child care half the time while their family members discuss program-related information with other family members and staff. The second half of the session could be devoted to parents and children's working together, practicing skills, or creating make-it-and-take-it items for use at home.

Encourage family members to support student learning at home.
❑ Send books and materials for home use.
❑ Give clear, written directions for homework. Put homework assignments on the school website so that parents can check in daily.
❑ Suggest strategies that parents can use to help children with homework such as scheduling a time and place to do it, providing adequate lighting, checking to see if it is done as well as instructional strategies.
❑ Send home learning kits such as activity packets that parents and children can do together or have activity packets that can be checked out by the family from the school media center.

Help family members anticipate typical developmental changes throughout the early childhood period. Knowing what to expect empowers family members to respond appropriately when such changes occur and makes them more confident teachers of their children. A note home to families, a brief discussion in the classroom newsletter, a small-group discussion, and an organized workshop on a related topic are a few ways to get this kind of information home. Chatting informally with family members individually and frequently is another valuable way to convey developmental information to parents. These personal contacts are especially useful because teachers can provide appropriate information and answer questions with a specific child in mind.

Provide general information about child development and learning, in take-home form, to family members. Books, pamphlets, cassettes, and videotapes can be made available through a parent lending library. In a box easily accessible to parents, file articles culled from magazines, newsletters, and early childhood journals such as *Young Children, Day Care and Early Education,* and *Childhood Education*. Provide more than one copy of each article so that you can recommend relevant readings and parents can take them home with no obligation to return them. Periodically send home a note highlighting new material available for parents to borrow or keep. Identify a few good websites on child growth and development and enable linkages from the program website. Organize family discussions around one or more of these reading topics or give family members a checklist on which they can indicate whether they would like a particular article sent home with their child.

Tailor the method of delivery to your families. The timing of the meeting, the content, and the method of delivery should all be consistent with meeting the needs of the adult members of the family. For example, it might be more effective if health-related information were delivered by a health professional. This might be a presentation followed by questions. However, many topics such as sibling fighting might be best as a discussion and may be led by a teacher or administrator who understands development and guidance. For meeting the social needs of family members who work, a morning breakfast with a very short "thought for the day" might be most effective.

HELPING FAMILIES AND CHILDREN MAKE A SUCCESSFUL TRANSITION

Many children experience a major shift in programs when they move from preschool to kindergarten (Deyell-Gingold, 2006) or first grade (Gullo, 2006). There is often a change of building, staff, school climate, and numbers and ages of other children and may be changes in numbers of adults and children in the classroom. Continuity of education is the ideal, but may not be the practice. What makes for a smoother transition?

- ❑ Children who are socially adjusted (skilled play behavior, ability to enter play groups, and communication skills) have better transitions than children who are rejected (rough play, arguing, trying to have own way and less cooperative).
- ❑ Children whose parents expect their children to do well in preschool and kindergarten do better than those with low expectations.
- ❑ Children experiencing developmentally appropriate classrooms and practices in both programs also have smoother transitions.
- ❑ Children in programs from preschool through first grade that view the transition as an ongoing process by fostering family–school connections, child–school connections, peer connections, and classroom–classroom connections enjoy smoother transition experiences (Gullo, 2006).

Teachers can prepare families to be more successful by doing some of the following (Morrison, 2009; Deyell-Gingold, 2006):

- ❑ Empower parents to speak as advocates for their children, learn how to work with school staff, and learn about volunteer opportunities in the new program. Parents who know their strengths and needs are more confident in the new situation.
- ❑ Alert family members about the different expectations in the new program such as different standards, dress, program expectations, and parent–teacher interactions. The transition between kindergarten and first grade can also be stressful for children and supported by families.
- ❑ Let parents know what the child will need, such as packed lunches, pencils, or crayons, well ahead of time.
- ❑ Suggest that parents take their child into the new building when the program is not in session and show the child where his or her room will be, where coats are hung, where lunch is eaten, and where the bathrooms are located.
- ❑ Invite local kindergarten or first-grade teachers into a parent program so that they can share information and meet parents in the spring before children go to school.
- ❑ Exchange visits with a local kindergarten or hold a kindergarten day where preschool children visit a kindergarten and engage in their activities for a morning. This is more probable if most of the children will be entering one kindergarten rather than dispersing across several. Likewise, kindergarten children profit from interactions with the first first-grade teachers and children.
- ❑ Share information about programs and individual children with professionals in the receiving programs. When children are in one type of program such as a community child care program and move to another program, written parental permission to transfer records or information is required. Explain this to parents and provide the appropriate forms well in advance. Information is passed on between grade levels within a school without written parental permission (McGann & Clark, 2007).
- ❑ Read books about kindergarten and riding the bus.
- ❑ Discuss bus safety rules with parents and children so they know what to expect.
- ❑ Encourage parents to arrange for an older child to accompany the kindergarten child on the first school bus

Facilitate the transition between prekindergarten to kindergarten for children and families.

trip and to see that he or she gets on and off the bus safety and at the correct stop. Alternatively, the parent may help the child on the bus, drive to the school and assist the child off the bus and into the school on the first day.

❏ Discuss with the parents their concerns as their child goes into kindergarten or first grade.

The transition between preschool programs and kindergarten can be a stressful time and is smoother when the children, family members, and teachers coordinate their efforts in making the transition easier. Bilingual families and families whose children have special needs may need additional support as well as more advanced planning for the transition.

Facilitating Family-to-Family Support

A group of parents was seated at a picnic table for the Sugar Hill Child Development Center end-of-year potluck dinner. Eventually the conversation turned to what they liked best about the program. In addition to the satisfaction many of the parents derived from watching their children develop and learn in a happy, safe, and stimulating program, they most appreciated having a chance to talk with members of other families who were coping with some of the same child-rearing challenges.

"I just want to talk with a grown-up sometimes. Not about the office or my work, but about how they get their kid to take vitamins or what if she doesn't want to kiss Grandma."

"It's easy to feel like you're the only one whose child is or isn't doing something. (Remember Tim and the shoes?) But here there are other parents I can talk to. . . . Makes you feel less alone."

These families voiced one of the most significant benefits of family involvement: the opportunity to get to know and interact with the members of other families responsible for raising a child. Such positive outcomes are more likely to occur when educators in early childhood programs take deliberate steps to help families make these contacts.

Arrange opportunities for family members to talk with one another informally. Plan some casual get-togethers whose primary aim is to provide family members with an opportunity to build their social networks and communicate with their peers. Make sure to include an unstructured break to facilitate family-to-family conversation during more formally scheduled events. Strong evidence indicates that these informal exchanges are just as valuable to family members as the regularly scheduled program is (Powell, 1989). In fact, for single parents, strengthening informal social networks may be the most effective means of eliciting their involvement in their children's education. The same is true for families whose home language is not English. Linking parents who speak the same language and encouraging informal support networks helps create a sense of belonging that families appreciate (Lee, 1997).

Work with other teachers, parents, and administrators to organize a family-to-family mentoring program. Pairing new families with family members already familiar with program philosophy and practices helps ease the entrée of newcomers and gives established families a responsible, important means of involvement. This strategy may be particularly important for immigrant families and those whose home language is not English. Give the mentors guidelines about how to fulfill their role. Some of their duties might include the following:

❏ Calling new family members to welcome them and answer their initial questions
❏ Arranging to meet new families prior to beginning the program and provide a tour of the facility
❏ Inviting new families to accompany them to open houses or orientation sessions held early in the year
❏ Translating relevant program materials or serving as translators during family conferences or other program-related gatherings
❏ Checking in periodically to answer questions and provide information as needed

Talk to your program administrator about creating peer support groups for teen parents, single parents, working parents, and families of children with disabilities, and noncustodial parents and grandparents who are raising their grandchildren. Suggest that your program promote support groups by providing not only the location for group meetings, but also child care during the time such groups meet. If such groups are already part of your program, make sure individual parents in your class know about them. If only a grandparent heads one family unit, you will likely find other settings that can provide this support electronically or in person in the community.

SUMMARY

myeducationlab

To check your comprehension on the content covered in Chapter 8, go to the Book Specific Resources in the MyEducationLab for your course, select your text, and complete the Study Plan. Here you will be able to take a chapter quiz, receive feedback on your answers, and then access review, practice, and enrichment activities to enhance your understanding of chapter content.

Practitioners and family members who work together create a strong foundation for developmentally appropriate programs for young children. The principles of collaboration, variety, intensity, and individuation provide a framework for thinking about successful approaches to including families. On the basis of these principles, various strategies for increasing family engagement are suggested. The guidelines we selected highlight the broad repertoire of skills you will need to work more effectively with families. However, you will not use all of these strategies in any single year. Although many questions remain as to how to reach and involve all families, the inclusion of the child's family will continue to remain a high priority among educators of young children. Our job as early childhood professionals is to continue investigating alternative methods of engaging family members and to welcome them as full-fledged partners in the educational process.

This chapter is the last in part 2. You now have a wide array of tools to use to design a developmentally appropriate curriculum for young children, including small- and whole-group planning and implementation skills, organizational and time-management skills, guidance strategies, and techniques for including family members in children's early education. Part 3, which follows, focuses on the curriculum.

Key Words

collaboration

family members

jargon

Applying What You've Read in This Chapter

1. **Discuss**
   a. On the basis of your reading and your experiences with families, discuss each of the questions that open this chapter.
   b. Assume that you are a teacher of 4-year-olds. Leon's grandmother will be volunteering in your classroom today. What will you do to ensure that the experience is positive for Leon, his grandmother, and yourself?
   c. Describe how you would apply the principles of age appropriateness, individual appropriateness, and sociocultural appropriateness to the concept of family engagement.
   d. Describe how you would use the various strategies for planning and communicating about an urgent matter like a threat in the community or a fire in the building.
   e. How can you make your communication strategies sensitive to the many diverse families who have children in your program, such as single fathers, same-gender parents, grandparents raising grandchildren, and adoptive or foster parents?
   f. How would you adjust your parent engagement strategies if the families of children were recent immigrants?

2. **Observe**
   a. Observe a program in which family members volunteer in the classroom. What does the head teacher do to make the experience a success for families, children, and staff?
   b. Arrange to accompany an early childhood professional on a home visit. What is the purpose of the visit from the practitioner's perspective? Describe what the practitioner does to address this purpose. Explain how the family responded and whether the original purpose was achieved. Were any additional outcomes accomplished? What were they?
   c. Observe a family engagement event at an early childhood program. Describe the purpose of the event, how families learned about it, and the support strategies designed to facilitate their engagement. Use Figure 8.1 to guide your description. Describe what occurred during the event and family reactions to it.

3. **Carry out an activity**
   a. Think about an early childhood setting in which you are or have been involved. Create a comprehensive family involvement plan for this program by choosing one or two strategies from at least three categories listed in this chapter. Provide reasons for your choices.
   b. Interview an early childhood educator about his or her work with families. Ask the practitioner to describe some of the methods he or she uses to help families feel welcome and involved in their child's education.
   c. Identify a cultural background belonging to one or several families in your program that varies from yours. Find a community event or resource through which you might learn more about this cultural group. Participate and describe what you discovered about the culture and about yourself.

d. Think back on your own childhood education experiences and make note of how your family may have been involved or could have been involved.

4. **Create something for your portfolio**
   a. Take pictures and record families' reactions to a family engagement activity you planned.
   b. Create a family newsletter for a specific group of children. Provide a written rationale for why you developed your newsletter as you did.

5. **Add to your journal**
   a. What is the most significant concept that you learned about family engagement from your readings and your experience with children and families?
   b. Make a list of the most pressing concerns you have about family engagement. Describe what you will do to address your concerns.

c. Describe a positive interaction you had with a family. What made it work? Describe a less successful interaction. What went awry, and how might you avoid a poor outcome in the future?

6. ✋ **Consult the standards**
   a. Look up the early childhood standards adopted by your state or a state that borders your own. Identify and make note of the sections of those standards that promote family engagement.
   b. Look up the NAEYC Early Childhood Program Standards and Accreditation Criteria that were approved by the NAEYC Governing Board in April 2005. Refer to www.naeyc.org/accreditation/050415.asp to obtain these. Find the standards that refer to family engagement and describe what those standards mean for early childhood professionals.

PRACTICE FOR YOUR CERTIFICATION OR LICENSURE EXAM

The following items will help you practice applying what you have learned in this chapter. They can help to prepare you for your course exam, the PRAXIS II exam, your state licensure or certification exam, and for working in developmentally appropriate ways with young children.

Family Engagement

1. **Constructed-response question**

   You are encouraging the families of the children in your first-grade class to partner with you in helping their children develop an interest in the natural world.

   a. Define what it means to partner with families and explain why this is important.
   b. Describe in detail two effective forms of communication that you could use to elicit family support.

2. **Multiple-choice question**

   Ms. Brown did not respond to a request for a home visit at the beginning of the program. You have not heard from her at all, nor has she attended a meeting or responded to you or the program for 3 months. What is the best course of action?

   a. Keep a log of parental participation and turn it in to the administrator.
   b. Spend more of your time and attention on those who did respond or came to meetings and less on people like Ms. Brown.
   c. Continue inviting participation and begin offering activities on the weekend or in the evening.
   d. Send a note home addressed to Ms. Brown, explaining how her lack of engagement is negatively impacting her child.

PART 3

THE CURRICULUM

◆ ◆ *As a prospective parent is being shown around the center, she asks the director, "What kind of curriculum do you follow?"*

◆ ◆ *The first-, second-, and third-grade teachers have been called together to reexamine the social studies curriculum for the lower elementary grades. There is much discussion about how this curriculum should look in comparison to the upper elementary curriculum.*

◆ ◆ *The program staff have spent an exciting day learning about children's self-esteem. The question they want answered is, "How can we best address self-esteem within our curriculum?"*

◆ ◆ *As part of the accreditation process for the school, the early childhood coordinator is asked to submit a copy of the curriculum for review.*

Curriculum is something educators frequently talk about, yet it can mean different things to different people. When some individuals discuss curriculum, they are simply referring to the goals and objectives of the program. Others have in mind a written plan for student learning or a syllabus that lists topics of study and how these topics will be taught (Brewer, 2006). Still others equate curriculum with certain materials or types of activities. The form the curriculum takes can also vary from detailed written descriptions, to sets of beliefs and experiences that can be understood only by observing the program in action. Because so many interpretations of the term *curriculum* exist, we will clarify how this term relates to the curriculum detailed in the next six chapters.

DEFINING THE CURRICULUM

Curriculum is all the organized educational experiences provided for children by the early childhood program. These experiences can take place inside the classroom or beyond, involving educators, family members, and other people in the community. In its written form, curriculum includes stated goals and objectives, strategies and activities aimed at supporting all aspects of children's development and learning, and methods of assessing children's progress and program effectiveness.

Formulated within a framework of developmental appropriateness, the curriculum described in the following chapters represents one interpretation of how to educate children aged 3 through 8 years. Hereafter, it is referred to as the *Children's Comprehensive Curriculum*. The Children's Comprehensive Curriculum has a twofold purpose: (1) to help children develop the knowledge, skills, attitudes, and dispositions essential to becoming happy, contributing members of society, and (2) to give educators the tools necessary to facilitate such learning. Originally developed by faculty in the Department of Family and Child Ecology at Michigan State University, the Children's Comprehensive Curriculum has been implemented and evaluated in the Child Development Laboratories on campus since 1988. Variations of it have been adopted by preschool, child care, Head Start, Chapter 1, and preprimary special education programs throughout the Midwest. Educators in numerous school districts have also used this curriculum as the basis for redesigning their goals, objectives, and methods for teaching children in kindergarten through fifth grade. The version offered in this book is a combination of these adaptations.

Why Use the Children's Comprehensive Curriculum?

The Children's Comprehensive Curriculum is divided into six domains: aesthetic, affective, cognitive, language, physical, and social. Considered individually, these domains represent major facets of child development. Although we realize that no one aspect of development can be isolated from the rest, we have found that purposeful planning for each domain results in a more comprehensive approach to instruction. Taken altogether, the entire array represents a "whole-child" approach to teaching. It unites an understanding of what is (i.e., how children develop and learn) with value statements of what ought to be (i.e., goals and objectives for children's development and learning now and in the future), with methods for achieving these aims (i.e., teaching strategies and activities). A brief overview of each domain within the Children's Comprehensive Curriculum is presented in Table 1.

Why Emphasize Developmental Domains over Subjects?

Practitioners more accustomed to the traditional subject-matter designations of art, math, science, reading, social studies, and physical education may question the child-oriented categories of developmental domains. They may wonder whether the material included within the following chapters will meet their needs and to what extent domains relate to their work with children.

TABLE 1	**Curricular Domains Within the Children's Comprehensive Curriculum**
Domain	**Developmental Focus**
Aesthetic	Appreciation of the arts and enjoyment of sensory experiences
Affective	Trust, autonomy, initiative, industry, self-awareness, self-esteem
Cognitive	Perception, physical knowledge, logical-mathematical knowledge, social-conventional knowledge, scientific understanding, critical-thinking skills
Language	Receptive language, listening skills, expressive language, reading, and writing
Physical	Fine- and gross-motor skills, body awareness, physical health
Social	Social skills, socialization, social studies

Although standard curriculum divisions are comfortable because they are familiar, subject matter alone is not a sufficient source of curriculum. Too often it leads to fragmented, isolated skill development or the exclusion of other kinds of knowledge and skills essential to children's ultimate success in society. Consequently, a subject-matter orientation is not comprehensive enough to suit our purposes. We prefer to emphasize a broader range of perceptions, dispositions, knowledge, and skills. For instance, art and music are covered under aesthetics, but so too are dance and other sensory experiences. The affective domain includes learning processes related to self-awareness and self-esteem, but also the development of independence and a sense of industry. Science and math are components of the cognitive domain but also included are problem solving, critical thinking, and perception. Reading is found within the language domain, as are listening, speaking, and writing. The physical domain encompasses gross- and fine-motor skills, health, and body image. Incorporated within the social domain are social studies content, and processes and skills fundamental to children's increased social competence.

As children participate in the six developmental domains, they experience a comprehensive educational curriculum that goes beyond the subject-oriented programs characteristic of many primary schools. The domain-focused curriculum also transcends the traditional materials-based programs associated with numerous preprimary settings.

Why Emphasize Developmental Domains over Materials?

Several philosophers throughout the history of early childhood education have advocated including certain materials to enhance particular learning goals for children. Froebel's gifts; Montessori's pink tower; and Hartley, Frank, and Goldenson's emphasis on blocks, water, and clay are typical examples. In each case the teacher's role was closely tied to facilitating children's use of these items. In the past, many teachers began to take a passive role, treating the curriculum as inherent in the materials. Today a more interactive approach as described in chapters 1 and 2 is proposed.

Nevertheless, many practitioners still assume that if they have the proper equipment, the instructional aspect of the program will take care of itself. When teachers make this assumption, goals for children's learning are often unspecified or ambiguous, and teachers may neglect to sufficiently challenge children. Instead, their main focus becomes one of monitoring children for appropriate materials use. Although having carefully selected materials and equipment is a necessary ingredient of quality children's programs, it is not a sufficient foundation for the curriculum (Bredekamp & Copple, 2009). Materials supplement the curriculum; they do not equal it. Moreover, the same materials can be used to support learning across domains. This broader view distinguishes a domain-focused curriculum from a materials-based approach.

DESCRIBING THE STRUCTURE OF CHAPTERS 9 THROUGH 14

Each of the next six chapters focuses on a single curricular domain. Each chapter includes these segments:

I. **Introduction**—This part of the chapter describes the importance of the domain to children and its relevance to early childhood education.

II. **Issues**—A brief discussion of current educational issues related to the domain and how they might be addressed in early childhood programs follows.

III. **Purpose and Goals**—For each domain, a purpose and a list of goals are presented. The purpose is a global statement about the idealized long-range educational outcome of the domain. Purposes are lifelong in intent, spanning an individual's entire educational experience. They are equally applicable to children in preprimary programs, elementary school, and middle or high school and beyond. Knowing the purpose for each domain helps educators keep sight of "the big picture," giving them a focus that goes beyond any one particular skill or bit of knowledge. Purposes are guideposts educators can use to gauge how well their instructional practices support long-term aims as well as more immediate outcomes.

Each purpose is further subdivided into several goals. The goals identify distinctive categories of behavior relative to children's development and learning within the domain. Based on national standards relevant to each domain, they help educators recognize domain-related skill patterns and concepts and outline the content and processes around which practitioners should plan classroom instruction. In this guide, the goals are listed in sequence from most fundamental to most complex. Consequently, the goals can be used as a guide for sequencing learning experiences for each domain. Their purpose is to give teachers needed direction in planning while simultaneously allowing them the autonomy to decide how best to address each goal in light of children's interests and capabilities. Thus, teachers can use the goals as a source of activity ideas. Such activities could include classroom routines, children's use of classroom materials to explore objects and concepts, and teacher-initiated lessons. A diagram depicting the relationship among the purpose, the goals, and activities for a sample domain is offered in Table 2.

TABLE 2 The Relation Among the Purpose, Selected Goals, and Sample Activities for the Physical Domain

Purpose	Goals	Sample Activities
For children to achieve physical competence and develop knowledge, attitudes, skills, and behaviors related to a healthy lifestyle	1. Develop awareness of the location of their body parts.	a. Sing and act out the "Head, Shoulders, Knees, and Toes" song. b. Make body tracings, labeling external body parts. c. Play the Hokey Pokey game, emphasizing left and right. d. Make body tracings, labeling internal body parts.
	2. Engage in activities that require balance.	a. Walk the balance beam. b. Play the Statue game. c. Use stilts. d. Ride a two-wheel bicycle.
	3. Practice fine-motor skills.	a. Move small objects with kitchen tongs. b. String beads. c. Make letters in sand on trays. d. Cut out snowflakes.
	4. Learn health and safety procedures.	a. Brush their teeth each day. b. Sing "This is the way we wash our face" to the tune of "Here We Go "Round the Mulberry Bush." c. Play the Red Light, Green Light game. d. Read a story about "good touch and bad touch."

Once teachers have selected activities that address their chosen goals, they can identify more specific instructional objectives (e.g., behavioral objectives) suited to the learning needs of children in their class. We believe that these objectives are best created by individuals who know the children well. For this reason, we have not attempted to identify these objectives in this guide.

IV. **Teaching Strategies**—This segment offers practical strategies teachers can use to address the domain in their classrooms. The suggested techniques were developed by practitioners in the field and represent concrete ways to operationalize the goals and objectives.

V. **Activity Suggestions**—Each of the curriculum-focused chapters ends with a selection of sample activities that support the domain. All activities include the following components.

   a. Activity name
   b. Goal to which the activity relates
   c. Recommended materials
   d. General procedure for carrying out the activity with 5- to 6-year-olds
   e. Suggestions for simplifying the activity for 3- to 4-year-olds
   f. Suggestions for extending the activity for 7- to 8-year-olds

These activity suggestions are illustrative, not exhaustive, examples of the types of activities and lessons teachers can plan for use inside and outside the classroom. However, we have tried to present a broad array of activities that cover the range of goals within the domain.

RECONCILING THE USE OF DOMAINS WITH OTHER CURRICULAR APPROACHES

Some practitioners work in programs in which the curricular focus is established on a programwide or even a statewide basis. Teachers faced with having to reconcile a more traditional subject-based or materials-based curriculum with domains have two options. First, they can advocate for a domain-focused orientation within their organization. Second, they can look for ways to integrate their current curricular approach with that suggested in this book. Most often this involves including subjects or materials under the broader construct of domains. For instance, some school districts have adopted the six curricular domains along with the purpose and goals for each. Next, committees have examined current subject-related instructional objectives to determine their appropriateness and the extent to which they support a particular domain. On the basis of the committees' recommendations, suitable revisions in objectives, classroom practices, and assessment tools are enacted. Individual practitioners can pursue a similar path, clustering subjects under domains and then evaluating their instructional practices in terms of the purpose of each.

Likewise, practitioners accustomed to thinking of curriculum as materials have begun by taking equipment standard to their program and generating ideas for using the material to support goals within various domains. For instance, blocks can be used to address objectives in any of the six curricular domains. This process can be repeated with other objects such as art materials, puzzles, small manipulative items, sand, and water. An example of this method of integration was provided in chapter 5.

In conclusion, as educators in more and more programs consider adopting policies and procedures to support DAP, the notion of curricular domains will become increasingly common. One purpose of this text is to help educators better understand this approach to curriculum planning and implementation. The best way to begin is to examine what each domain entails, starting with the aesthetic domain.

Chapter

9

The Aesthetic Domain

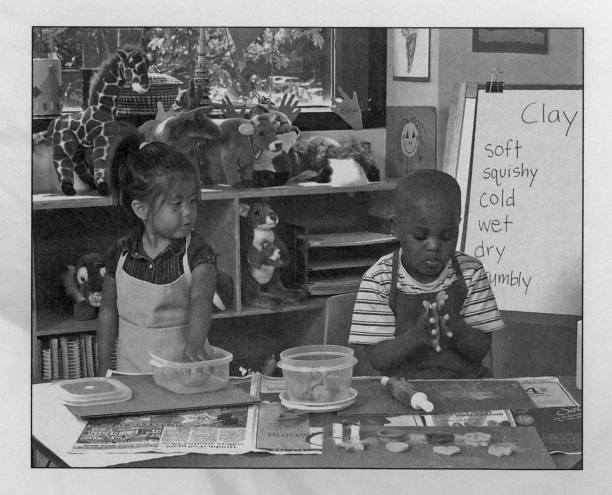

You may wonder:

What is meant by *aesthetics*?
What are *the arts*?
Why is aesthetic education important for children's learning?
What can I do to enhance children's aesthetic development?

In this chapter we present information to help answer your questions about facilitating children's aesthetic interests and participation.

◆ ◆ *The children have created a "tent" in the preschool room by using a blanket draped over a folding table. Maggie and Joy decide to take the xylophone, the bells, and a drum into the tent. "We're making a tent band, Mr. Jordan!" they say as they crawl under the edge of the blanket. He smiles as he hears their creative musical play and listens to their laughter. He decides to ask the children to tell about their band at sharing time.*

◆ ◆ *Mrs. Gerhard carefully uncovers a large print of the painting* An Afternoon at La Grande Jatte, *by Georges Seurat. "Tell me what you see in this painting," she says. The 5-year-olds seated on the floor kneel to look more closely. Luke announces, "This is good work. I like it." Gillian says, "It's a happy earth." Antonio agrees, "I like this. Lots of color and a cat." The teacher nods. DaJuan points to the corner, "I see boats." Shawnna notices, "There's a lady trying to catch a fish." Kyle leans in and says, "I see a monkey and a dog." Their teacher smiles and says, "You're looking very carefully; I wonder what you think the artist was trying to tell us in this painting." Tiara shouts, "It's about a wedding! There's the wedding girl!"*

◆ ◆ *Four-year-old Caleb looks from rock to rock on the tray, searching for his favorite. He notices that the rocks are different colors, some are smooth, and some sparkle when water is poured over them. Picking one up, he announces, "Here it is. This is my best." Mr. Rey says, "You chose rock number 14, Caleb. Tell me what you like about this rock and I'll write it on our chart."*

◆ ◆ *Luis and Rachel stand in front of their teacher's aide, Mrs. Oppenheimer, as she strums chords softly on the guitar. The children listen and watch intently. Luis's head and shoulders begin to sway from side to side. He moves slowly to the music, responding to the gentle rhythms.*

◆ ◆ *Amber's preschool group is dramatizing the story "The Three Billy Goats Gruff." She decides to be one of the goats going across the bridge. She practices using her best billy goat voice to say, "It is I, Big Billy Goat Gruff."*

◆ ◆ *The first graders in Ms. Fernandez's class have been working in small groups for 15 minutes. Izayah's group is working together making trees for the class mural. The children are busy discussing what trees look like and cutting, arranging, and gluing paper shapes they have produced. Izayah decides his tree needs more leaves; he searches through the scrap box for the colors he wants. "Mine will be very leafy," he says with pride.*

Each child just described is involved in aesthetic activities appropriate for early childhood. In this chapter, we explore the idea that involvement in the arts is important for every child and should be a fundamental part of the curriculum.

AESTHETICS DEFINED

The word **aesthetics** refers to the ability to perceive through the senses. The Consortium of National Arts Education Associations (CNAEA, 1994) defines aesthetics as "a branch of philosophy that focuses on the nature of beauty, the nature and value of art, and the inquiry process and human responses associated with these topics" (p. 82). Mayesky (2009) describes aesthetics as an appreciation of beauty and a feeling of wonder. Aesthetics can also be defined as the love and pursuit of beauty as found in art, movement, music, and life (Schirrmacher & Fox, 2009). In simple terms, aesthetics is a person's ability to perceive, be sensitive to, and appreciate beauty in nature and creations in the arts.

THE ARTS DEFINED

The term **arts** is used for both the creative work and the process of producing the creative work. The arts fall into four broad categories: visual arts, performing arts, usable arts, and literary arts. **Visual arts** include drawing, painting, sculpture, printmaking, mosaics, collage, and numerous others. **Performing arts** include singing, dancing, playing instruments, dramatics, storytelling, puppetry, and many others. **Usable arts** (or crafts) include weaving, ceramics, pottery, knitting, jewelry making, and many others. **Literary arts** include writing stories, poems, plays, jokes, skits, essays, novels, and several others.

SCOPE OF THIS CHAPTER

As you might guess, aesthetic learning encompasses a broad range of experiences related to different art forms and appreciation of natural beauty. The CNAEA (1994) indicated that dance, music, theater, and visual arts are the basic areas of importance in arts education. Therefore, to make this chapter manageable, we refer to those four basic areas in the arts: dance, music, drama, and visual arts. Although we provide many examples, other activities involving the natural world, performing arts, storytelling, poetry, and movement can be found in other chapters throughout the book. For example, activities related to nature are found in chapter 11; storytelling activities are in chapter 15; movement activities are found in chapter 13. For our purposes, literary arts are included in chapter 12. Teachers can also transform many activities into aesthetic experiences for children by selecting an aesthetic objective (e.g., "Contribute to the aesthetic environment").

AESTHETIC EDUCATION FOR YOUNG CHILDREN

Aesthetic education in early childhood is a deliberate effort by teachers to provide experiences in nature and the arts, nurture awareness of the arts, foster appreciation of the arts, and develop skills in evaluating art forms. Children learn about the arts by responding to them and by creating their own art.

Therefore, aesthetic experiences may be either responsive or productive (Figure 9.1). Table 9.1 provides an overview of both types of experiences and suggests activities included in each.

Responsive aesthetic experiences refer to the way the child reacts to art or nature. They involve the child recognizing the beauty of nature, appreciating art and nature, and forming judgments, what they like and do not like. For example, recall the activities described at the beginning of this chapter. Joy and Maggie were playing with and responding to musical sounds. The children exploring the painting were learning to appreciate visual art. Caleb, who was inspecting rocks, was learning to appreciate natural beauty and forming his preferences. Luis and Rachel were learning to appreciate the performing art of guitar playing. Each of these children was involved in responsive aesthetic learning. Responsive experiences include discovery, exposure, and evaluation activities.

Discovery activities, such as Caleb's examining rocks, provide opportunities to respond to natural beauty. Young children explore the details of natural objects such as frost on a window, a beautiful spiderweb, the petals of a rose, leaves, insects, trees, shells, or clouds through their senses. They discover by looking, listening, smelling, touching, and sometimes tasting. Activities like these can result in greater appreciation of nature and recognition of beautiful things.

Exposure activities, such as Luis and Rachel's exposure to the guitar, broaden their familiarity with the arts. These activities provide opportunities for children, as observers and consumers of art, to listen to a variety of music, experience dance or dramatic performances, or view the visual arts in many forms.

FIGURE 9.1   Aesthetic Development Model

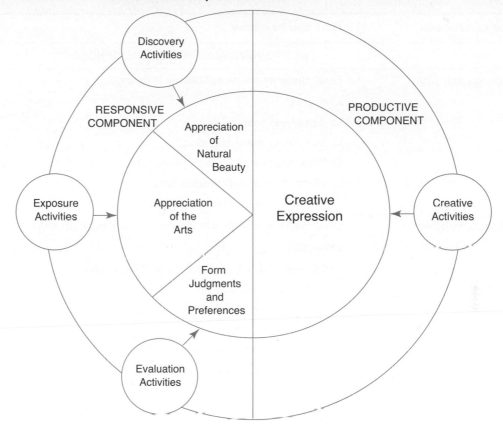

Evaluation activities, such as the 5-year-olds examining the painting, encourage children to discuss and make judgments about a variety of visual art, music, dance, and drama forms. Students may decide how to judge the art (such as "It uses color in a pleasing way." or "It delivers a message.") and express their preferences on the basis of those criteria. Through such activities children learn that different art appeals to different people, and that each person's view is valid.

Productive aesthetic experiences involve the child in *creative art activities,* which engage the child actively with a variety of materials, props, instruments, and tools useful for making visual art, music, drama, or dance. These activities stimulate creativity and provide opportunities for self-expression. Painting a picture, gluing felt pieces into a pleasing design, or experimenting with movement to music are examples of creative art activities. At the beginning of this chapter, Joy and Maggie were creating a band through their play, Amber was participating in a simple drama, and Izayah was working on a paper mural; all these children were engaged in creative expression and productive aesthetic experiences.

Many times, children create their own aesthetic activities through play, and skilled teachers notice such actions and guide their learning. Sometimes teachers introduce a number of activities to achieve several goals. The following example shows how one teacher used a series of three aesthetic activities to teach children to become familiar with, evaluate, and create their own art. For example:

> *Mrs. Gonzalez's first graders are learning about air. This week, their focus is on things that move in the air. The teacher asks if anyone has seen art that moves in the air. Children suggest kites and hot-air balloons. She hangs several mobiles (a seashell mobile, a wooden bird mobile from Mexico, and a baby's nursery mobile made of stuffed cloth shapes) in the classroom. The children examine the mobiles and discuss their individual experiences with mobiles. They notice the shapes, colors, and effects of air movement (an exposure activity).*
>
> *The next day, Mrs. Gonzalez shows the class a picture of a famous mobile,* Lobster Trap and Fish Tail, *by Alexander Calder. She asks the children to imagine how it was made and to tell what they like about it (an evaluation activity). Later, Mrs. Gonzalez encourages the class to look at books showing other mobiles.*

TABLE 9.1 Responsive and Productive Aesthetic Experiences

Type of Activities	Goal and Examples
	RESPONSIVE AESTHETIC EXPERIENCES
Discovery activities	*Goal:* Show awareness of beauty in nature
	Examples:
	❑ Observing beautiful fish
	❑ Examining interesting rocks
	❑ Watching cloud formations in the sky
	❑ Discovering beauty in spiderwebs
	❑ Smelling flowers, grass, or spices
Exposure activities	*Goal:* Become familiar with different types of each art form
	Examples:
	❑ Looking at details in paintings or photographs
	❑ Touching a sculpture
	❑ Watching a dance
	❑ Listening to a choir
	❑ Watching a dramatic performance
Evaluation activities	*Goal:* Participate in aesthetic criticism
	Examples:
	❑ Comparing several baskets
	❑ Selecting the best collage for a portfolio
	❑ Choosing a favorite song
	❑ Telling characteristics liked about a dance
	PRODUCTIVE AESTHETIC EXPERIENCES
Creative activities	*Goal:* Use a variety of materials, tools, techniques, and processes in the arts
	Examples:
	❑ Playing an instrument
	❑ Dancing
	❑ Finger painting
	❑ Singing a song
	❑ Playing a role in a drama

On the third afternoon, Mrs. Gonzalez displays a collection of materials (a variety of paper, hole punches, markers, thin wooden dowels, and string), and the class discusses ways they could use them to make their own mobiles. By now, students have many ideas for their mobiles; some ask for assistance in attaching and suspending the shapes, but most of them work independently (a creative activity). As the students finish, they hang their unique mobiles throughout the classroom and examine one another's work.

Importance of Aesthetic Learning

Some people lack appreciation for the arts, considering them to be "soft" domains. However, aesthetic learning in general, including all of the arts, is highly integral to children's cognitive and academic achievement (C. Seefeldt, 2005). For example, an emphasis on beauty and the wonder of nature helps children respond emotionally and make connections to the natural environment.

These early affective connections to the natural world can form a foundation for social consciousness, care, and knowledge (Kemple & Johnson, 2002).

There are many reasons to engage children in the arts. The arts foster development of skills such as patience, persistence, eye–hand coordination, and good work habits, and they provide children with opportunities to experience success (Alvino, 2000). Integrating the arts with other areas such as language, math, and science can add hands-on excitement to learning and create richer experiences for children (Clements & Wachowiak, 2010). Participating in creative activities allows children to develop and refine skills related to perceptual abilities, making choices, and solving problems. Such activities also provide an effective outlet for children to express their feelings when they may not have the language skills to do so.

Connections between music and math are well known (Geist & Geist, 2008). Music uses patterns such as repeated melodies, rhythms, and refrains. For many children, music helps make math concepts meaningful because they learn to notice a pattern and predict what comes next in the pattern (Edelson & Johnson, 2003/04). Students have also demonstrated mathematical understanding through writing poetry (Whitin & Piwko, 2008), exhibiting a connection between the literary arts and the cognitive domain.

The creative arts can contribute to a prosocial climate in the group. For example, children who sing together, create puppets together, play musical instruments and dance together are more likely to behave cooperatively in other circumstances. Activities such as these build group cohesion and social solidarity.

In addition, learning in other domains is greatly enhanced through the arts. The arts and their relationship to learning in other domains is complex and interactive (Deasy, 2002). Gardner's theory of multiple intelligences indicates that many children learn best in ways other than the linguistic, mathematical, or logical approach. Youngsters frequently make connections to learning more readily through kinesthetic, tactile, auditory, interpersonal, and spatial experiences. Gardner's work helps us expand our view of nonverbal forms of knowledge to include musical, bodily-kinesthetic, spatial, and visual forms. In other words, aesthetic activities provide ways to explore these forms of knowing. The arts are integral to a high-quality education and must be included in the curriculum in order for students to succeed both in school and later in life (Arts Education Partnership, 2004).

RELATIONSHIP BETWEEN AESTHETIC LEARNING AND KNOWING

For children to develop into successful, contributing members of society, they must be able to think and create. Connections between aesthetics and thinking are well established. We have only to look at the creative communication of thought and ideas in the work by young children attending the schools of Reggio Emilia, Italy, to see this connection (see Chapter 1). In Reggio Emilia, the arts are not a separate part of the curriculum, but are a way for children to experience problem solving (C. Seefeldt, 2005). Children in these schools engage in the arts by gathering information, reformulating it, and expressing their knowledge through original representations. The creative process involves noticing relationships, redefining the elements, and reorganizing the parts into something new.

Teachers should plan a range of experiences for children to explore materials used in aesthetic activities. For very young or inexperienced children, teachers should encourage sensory exploration without much teacher direction or interference. As children gain experience with the materials, teachers can build on earlier general explorations by further exploring a specific medium. Encourage children to determine how the medium can be used, what tools are needed to work with the medium, or how to create certain effects using the medium and tools. During this phase, teachers can provide instruction on how to use certain tools or techniques in order to build children's confidence and interest in the materials.

Physical Knowledge Through Aesthetic Activities

Discovery of the physical properties of materials contributes to "physical knowledge." For example, by using musical instruments, students learn about how they feel and the variety of sounds they make. Through playing with movement, children become aware of body positions, gestures, the feel of movement, control of their limbs, and the physical characteristics of dance. By playing with materials such as play-doh (this is actually a brand versus dough which would refer to home made as well), children learn what the medium feels like and they observe changes (Swartz, 2005). For example, by using their fingers or tools, children learn that play-doh is soft, spongy, cool, and can change in shape. With greater experimentation, they learn what happens to play-doh when it is combined with water or heat, and how it dries hard if it is not kept in a container.

Logical-Mathematical Knowledge Through Aesthetic Activities

In productive and responsive aesthetic experiences, children consider logical-mathematical relations. For example, while drawing a picture, the child may think about sizes, shapes, placement next to, under, or over areas. In dance, he may consider where his body is in space (up high, down low) or how his body is in relation to others around him (such as next to, between, behind, first, last). While involved in music, the child learns to consider loudness, speed, and pitch in relation to music made by others. Through drama, the child learns how her character fits into and relates to other characters in the story. These understandings are the fundamentals of logical-mathematical knowledge. Therefore, when a kindergartner adds blue scribbles above a self-portrait, he uses logical-mathematical knowledge to express his relationship to the sky. Playing instruments or singing songs involves the use of rhythm, beat, long and short tones, and loud and quiet sounds—all mathematically based. Similarly, when a child engages in dance, the child practices slower and faster, higher and lower movements, and matches his or her motions to the teacher's movements. All of these examples involve logical-mathematical knowledge.

When teachers use the vocabulary of the arts (Figure 9.2), they give children richer language to use for describing, comparing, evaluating, and expressing preferences in the arts. Using terms such as *color* and *line*, or *tone* and *rhythm*, helps children understand the elements of art or music. With older children, teachers can more specifically focus activities on the elements.

Representational Knowledge Through Aesthetic Activities

Representing thoughts and feelings is an important way to learn, and engaging in the creative arts is to communicate, think, and feel (Drew & Rankin, 2004). We extend children's ideas when we encourage them to represent their thoughts using art materials, **creative movement,** or music. Children take different perspectives when using different mediums. Original visual art, music, drama, or dance requires the person to think of an experience, an idea, or a feeling and express it by manipulating the elements of the medium. In other words, learning within the arts involves representing something with something else. The use of different media encourages children to notice different details of the item or experience they are representing. The activity is highly symbolic and involves the learner in focused representational thought. Being able to imagine something that is not present and then finding ways to express it concretely to others is a major cognitive accomplishment (Koster, 2009).

Social-Conventional Knowledge Through Aesthetic Activities

Through social-conventional knowledge we teach understanding and respect for cultural traditions, history, and heritage. Experiences with music, visual arts, dance, and dramatics serve as symbols of cultural identity for children. Presenting activities that demonstrate respect for various cultures, customs, and traditions assists children in developing a sense of community. Children learn that art represents the ideas and feelings of other people as they view, discuss, and explore art from different cultures (Koster, 2009).

Social-conventional knowledge is part of aesthetics when the learner acquires concepts and understandings related to the arts in society (see Table 9.2). For example, the names and characteristics of cultural dances such as ballet, polka, hula, waltz, tango, or square dance are passed from generation to generation as social-conventional knowledge. Moreover, when teachers expose children to art forms by using words such as *portrait, landscape, still life, print, watercolor, sand*

FIGURE 9.2   Commonly Used Terms in the Arts

Teachers use descriptive words that point out various aspects of the arts. Through repeated use, children learn to recognize and use these terms. Here are some common terms.

Visual Arts Terms	How They Can Be Used
Line	A mark that continues a dot made by a tool on a surface. "Look at the way that fork makes zigzag *lines* in the clay." "Josh, you decided to paint curvy *lines* with the green paint."
Color	A characteristic or visual sensation of light. Hue is the color name. "What *colors* do you see in this painting?" "How do you think these bright *colors* would look on black paper?"
Shape	Form; the outside edge of an object or an enclosed space. "Can you find the circle *shapes* in this design?" "Angie is making her own abstract *shapes* with tissue paper."
Texture	The surface quality or how an object feels or looks. "Which wallpaper has a rough *texture*?" "You made the *texture* of the grass in your picture look really soft."
Composition	Design; the arrangement and organization of the parts. "You filled your paper with a busy *design*." "Marcie, you worked hard on the *composition* of your collage."
Pattern	Recurring sequence of elements such as shapes or color. "You're making *patterns* with that sponge." "Can you find a *pattern* in this picture?"

Music Terms	How They Can Be Used
Beat	The steady pulse of music. "Notice how the *beat* changes from fast to slow." "Let's clap to the *beat* of this march."
Pitch	The key or keynote of a tune. "Listen and try to sing the same *pitch*." "You noticed we sang high and then low *pitches*."
Melody	The tune or how tones move up and down in music. "You made up your own *melody*." "When I hummed the tune, you recognized the *melody*."
Rhythm	Groupings of long and short musical sounds. "Clap this *rhythm*." "Your *rhythm* sticks tapped the *rhythm*."
Dynamics	Volume; the way music changes in intensity or loudness of sound. "We can hear the music *dynamics*." "When the *volume* goes down, make your arms go down."
Tempo	Relative speed of the musical piece. "This waltz has a fast *tempo*." "Let's slow the *tempo* to a walk."
Mood	The interaction of music and emotion. "How does the *mood* of this music make you feel?" "This music sounds like a happy *mood*."

Source: Adapted from *How to Work with Standards in the Early Childhood Classroom* (p. 74), by C. Seefeldt, 2005, New York: Teachers College Press.

painting, mosaic, appliqué, and *collage,* they utilize social-conventional knowledge. The art of drama has many conventions, such as monologue, dialogue, skit, and rehearsal, and many dramatic techniques to learn. When children learn appropriate audience behavior for musical performances or learn what is expected when they visit an art museum or gallery, they are learning social-conventional knowledge.

TABLE 9.2   Factual Content in the Arts

SAMPLE CONTENT FOR ART

1. Art is a representation of feelings, mood, or a message created by a person for enjoyment and to enhance people's lives.
2. An artist is a person who creates art.
3. Anyone can be an artist: men, women, boys, and girls can be artists.
4. Art is the way something is made (the process) and what is made (the product).
5. Art is created all over the world in all cultures.
6. Artists use tools and materials that are special for their kind of art.
7. Art that people see and/or touch is called visual art; painting, sculpture, and drawing are some examples.
8. Art that people listen to or watch is called performance art: music, drama, and dance are some examples.
9. Art that people use in their lives is called usable art or crafts; pottery, basketry, and quilting are some examples.
10. People have preferences in art; what someone likes is not always liked by others.

SAMPLE CONTENT FOR MUSIC

1. Music is a combination of agreeable sounds.
2. The pitch of music can be high, middle, or low.
3. The tempo of music can be fast, moderate, or slow.
4. People make musical tones with their voices or instruments.
5. Some instruments are played by striking, some by blowing, and some by strumming.
6. People all over the world make music.
7. Some music has words called lyrics.
8. Music can convey a mood or message.

SAMPLE CONTENT FOR DANCE

1. Choreography is the art of creating and arranging dances.
2. A complete turn of the body executed on one leg is called a pirouette.
3. Freestyle dancing is moving to music with no fixed structure.
4. Dance is an important part of many cultures.

SAMPLE CONTENT FOR DRAMA

1. Drama is a story that is acted out.
2. The scenery and staging of a dramatic production is called a set.
3. Blocking is the movement of actions on a stage.
4. Props are the items used by the actors in a dramatic production.

Metacognition in Aesthetic Learning

A simple way to define *metacognition* is "thinking about thinking." Teachers help children think about their own thought processes by asking carefully chosen questions at appropriate times. In aesthetic learning, metacognitive processing is valuable for organizing thinking, making decisions about a sequence of steps, or helping students to develop greater insight into their self-expressive work. When a teacher responds to a child's unique idea by asking, "How did you figure that out?" the teacher encourages the child to consider the process that he or she used to arrive at a particular solution. Other questions that stimulate similar thinking are, "How did you know?" "What clues are you using to help find your answer?" and "What made you choose that instead of this?"

CHILDREN'S ACQUISITION OF A FUNDAMENTAL KNOWLEDGE BASE FOR AESTHETIC DEVELOPMENT

Young children are naturally curious; because of this curiosity, they enjoy exploring nature, are motivated to create art and music, delight in the movement of dance, and spend hours in meaningful dramatic play. At first, the process of manipulating materials is more important to them than the product created. A child's early art, music, dance, or drama is made without regard to the effect of their work on others. Later, children feel a greater need to communicate ideas and meaning becomes more important. Children also begin to evaluate their work according to emerging aesthetic standards based on developing tastes and combined with messages received from others. Aesthetic milestones in the development of aesthetic preferences, musical interests, vocal music, instrumental music, creative movement, visual representations, and drama are described in this section.

Development of Aesthetic Preferences

Children's early aesthetic responses begin with sensory exploration of objects and sounds. Preferences for a particular texture or smell, such as the soft edge on a blanket or a particular beloved toy, may be noticed. By age 5 years, children's preferences for certain kinds of music begin to surface. Many children as young as 3 or 4 years begin to make choices from their environment, gathering and exploring collections of particular objects such as stones, seashells, or buttons. At a later stage, these collections become more sophisticated and must be acquired by deliberate searches. For some children the treasured objects may be bottle caps, coins, or baseball cards. Other children are fascinated by special dolls, toy horses, and so forth. In addition, children are likely to enjoy spontaneous conversations about these special objects and demonstrate beginning levels of adult aesthetic evaluative behaviors—describing, analyzing, interpreting, and judging—but they often need help organizing their comments and applying criteria.

Development of Musical Interests

In infancy, the appeal of music is usually the quality of sound. Babies often show interest when adults sing to them, in the sound of bells, and in soft music. As children grow and are exposed to various musical experiences, their interests broaden to include the element of melody. They learn to prefer what they are familiar with, particularly enjoying songs with repetition, in which the same melody is heard repeatedly. Examples include "Twinkle, Twinkle, Little Star" and "Old MacDonald Had a Farm." Later, children develop a keener interest in pitch—recognizing when sounds go up or down and discriminating when sounds have changed. Very young children have difficulty attending to more than one musical dimension (such as volume, rhythm, beat, or tempo) simultaneously, and when asked to make decisions about what they hear, they do not respond with any degree of accuracy. By age 5 or 6 years, many children demonstrate understanding of sound contrasts such as high–low, loud–soft, and up–down. Likewise, 6-year-olds can identify pairs of chords as same or different. Although educators understand that within any group of children of a given age, a wide range of musical abilities will be found, educators also know that musical interest and appreciation can be enhanced through a variety of regular musical experiences.

Development of Vocal Music (Singing) Behaviors

Babies explore musical sounds through vocal play and experimentation. Toddlers are able to discriminate among sounds and may sing or hum while engaged in play (Henniger, 2009). By 3 years of age, many youngsters, if encouraged to express themselves musically, begin to impose structure on their improvisations by repeating selected patterns. The pitch range of young children's spontaneous singing can be extensive. However, when children are learning songs by imitation, a more limited range seems to be most comfortable. Many 3-year-olds can sing whole songs and develop a large repertoire, and many have a favorite song. As they gain vocal control, children expand their range of usable pitches and can produce melodies more accurately. Later, they are able to fit together diverse rhythm patterns and appear to sense the function of form. By age 5 years, many children can use a steady, accurate beat, melody, and rhythm repetitions in their singing. The process of learning to sing in tune depends on opportunities, encouragement, and positive feedback so that they know they are matching pitches. Children in the early primary grades can learn songs that are reasonably complex. Songs with greater demands on memory and sequencing skills are not beyond most 6- to 8-year-olds.

Development of Instrumental Music Interests

Early in life, infants begin to intentionally make sounds by kicking or hitting objects. Toddlers gain pleasure from making sounds with musical instruments or other objects, and by the time children are 3 years of age they can play simple rhythm instruments with a basic understanding of beat (Henniger, 2009). By age 3 years, children are creating patterns by repetitions, and by age 5 years, they can make a steady beat. Four- to 6-year-olds are ready for more group experiences involving exploration of rhythm and melody instruments. Soon after, they become interested in the "right way" to play simple instruments. By age 6 years, some children begin to imitate conventional music patterns, and unfortunately, they may lose some creative spontaneity. Youngsters at this stage benefit not only from plenty of opportunities to freely explore instruments, but also from encouragement to improvise melodies and create their own music.

Development of Creative Movement and Dance Interests

From the earliest days of life, babies respond to music through body movement. Even newborns become more active when lively music is played and calmer when slower, quieter music is played. Infants sway and bounce, and by age 18 months, they clap, tap, and spin in larger spaces. Two-year-olds tend to respond actively to rhythmic music, but each at his or her tempo. Three-year-olds gain greater coordination in movement; they enjoy moving creatively with others and participating in singing games that involve movement. Preschoolers are motivated to move to music, but their movements are not always synchronized and they tend to limit their movements to repetition of a few patterns (Epstein, 2007). From age 4 to 6 years, children increase their ability to clap and march in response to a steady beat, and enjoy participating in action songs such as "Shake My Sillies Out" and "Here We Go, Looby-Loo." They are becoming more skilled at synchronizing movement with the rhythmic beat of music. By age 6 to 8 years, children have mastered basic movements and can match these movements to music. They can also invent their own movements to music and are better able to follow more complex movement sequences (Mayesky, 2009).

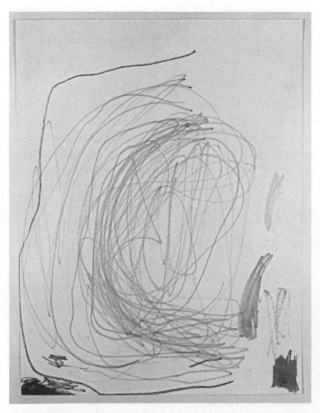

The scribble stage

Development of Visual Art Expression

Children's visual art changes and develops new characteristics as they mature and have more experiences. Children go through a similar pattern of artistic growth everywhere in the world, but individual children go through the sequences at different rates and have unique outcomes (Koster, 2009). Toddlers take pleasure in the physical movement of a crayon, pencil, or marker and gradually notice the resulting marks they make on paper. Children's drawings eventually change from random scribbling to controlled scribbles by the time the children reach age 4 years. Between ages 4 and 7 years, children develop a set of visual symbols of their own invention to represent familiar concepts that they apply to various media. They learn that their creations communicate messages to other people and begin to value the product. By age 8 years, a youngster can create drawings that are more complex and involve multiple views and details. These children are interested in many forms of artistic expression, and with encouragement, continue to refine their visual perceptions as they mature. In Lowenfeld and Brittain's (1965) classic work on creativity and learning, these researchers described developmental stages of visual art representation from toddlerhood to adolescence (see Table 9.3). Descriptions of artistic stages are useful as guides for expectations at various ages and stages of development. However, variations in development and children's previous experiences with the arts make a difference in progress among children.

The preschematic stage

The schematic stage

TABLE 9.3   Stages of Visual Art Representation

Age Range (yr)	Stage[a]	Description
	Scribbling	**Beginnings of Self-Expression**
2–4	Early scribbling	Disordered scribbles. Purely kinesthetic. Child is establishing motor coordination.
	Middle scribbling	Controlled scribbles. Child notices a connection between motions and resulting marks. Variety of motions increases. Color becomes useful to distinguish marks from background.
	Late scribbling	Child begins naming scribbles. Child's thinking changes from kinesthetic responding to having mental pictures. Child connects marks with world around him or her. Choice of color begins to have some meaning to child.
	Preschematic	**First Representational Attempts**
4–7	Early preschematic	Child controls motions to produce simple symbols that relate to his or her visual world (e.g., circle, vertical and horizontal lines). Symbols change often. Objects are randomly placed. Color choice relates to emotional reactions. Child produces a "person" symbol.
	Late preschematic	Child gains better motor control, which allows for experimentation with a variety of symbols. Exaggeration of certain symbols indicates importance. Color choices continue to relate to emotional reactions.
	Schematic	**Achievement of Form Concepts**
7–9	Schematic	Child arrives at highly individualized visual symbols (or schemata) that satisfy him or her and are used repeatedly. Schemata represent child's active knowledge of objects; schemata change only when meaningful experiences influence child's thinking. Spatial relationships are not random.

[a]For descriptions of later stages—Dawning Realism: The Gang Age (9–11 yr.), The Pseudo-Naturalistic Stage (11–13 yr.), and Adolescence Art (13–17 yr.)—see Lowenfeld and Brittain (1965).

TABLE 9.4   Examples of Aesthetic Activities for Growing Children

Aesthetic Component	Activities by Age Group		
	1- TO 3-YEAR-OLDS	3- TO 5-YEAR-OLDS	6- TO 8-YEAR-OLDS
Aesthetic preferences	Exploring natural objects, music, child-appropriate art objects (wood toys, dolls, bells)	Exploring and collecting objects, describing what they like about valued objects and own work	Exploring; collecting; describing; analyzing; interpreting; and evaluating objects, own work, and others' work
Musical interests	Lullabies, musical toys, songs with repetitions, simple melodies (e.g., "Ring Around the Rosie")	Repetitive and cumulative songs, more complex melodies; guided music listening	Wide variety of song types; beginning to relate music to moods; interest in musical notation
Vocal music interests	Songs with simple tunes that repeat (e.g., "Twinkle, Twinkle, Little Star"), songs that use child's name ("Hello, Everybody")	Improvising, singing while swinging, songs with repetitions, substituting words (e.g., "Mary Wore a Red Dress")	Singing more complex songs (e.g., "Swingin' on a Star"), silly songs (e.g., "A Peanut Sat on a Railroad Track"), rounds (e.g., "Make New Friends"); musical notation
Instrumental music interests	Manipulating objects with sounds (e.g., bell, xylophone, tambourine, triangle)	Simple instruments, music with defined beat and rhythm, cooperative instruments; improvising	Imitation of established melodies and rhythms; some improvisation; using instruments with own songs
Creative movement and dance behaviors	Spontaneous movement to music using arms and legs	Singing and dancing games (e.g., "The Farmer in the Dell"), action songs (e.g., "Bingo"; "Head, Shoulders, Knees, and Toes"); using props	Improvising; simple folk dances; organized dance instruction

Sources: Adapted from *The Arts in Children's Lives: Aesthetic Education in Early Childhood,* by M. R. Jalongo and L. N. Stamp, 1997, Needham Heights, MA: Allyn & Bacon.

Development of Enactment or Dramatic Behaviors

Infants enjoy beginning enactment in such games as "This Little Piggy" and "Peek-a-Boo." By age 1 year, most children can enact simple gestures meaning "eat" or "sleep." By age 2 years, children are attempting to enact simple finger plays such as "The Eensy Weensy Spider" and are using real-life objects to take on familiar caregiving roles such as feeding or rocking a baby. Children from age 3 years to age 5 years become capable of deferred imitation; that is, they imitate movements of objects they have experienced in the past, even when the model is not present (Inhelder & Piaget, 1964). The amounts of pretend play and imaginative role-playing greatly increase during this period. Children 6 to 8 years old demonstrate continued interest in fantasy, but they demonstrate an emerging emphasis on nonfiction accounts of experiences in their play. As children learn to read and write, they may write and perform their own creative dramas, if they are encouraged. They also seek more elaborate props and begin to participate in more formal types of drama. Development affects the kinds of aesthetic activities (Table 9.4) in which children are likely to engage.

AESTHETIC LEARNING AND THE TEACHER'S ROLE

Teachers influence the extent to which their students value the arts and can provide a background of experiences that free children to become creative producers and tasteful consumers of the arts as adults. Teachers who are most effective: (a) provide consistently high-quality creative art experiences for their students, (b) share their enthusiasm by talking about beauty in nature and the arts with children, (c) provide opportunities and support for creative dramatics, (d) integrate art and music into the curriculum, (e) encourage individual expression, and (f) strive to become more creative themselves.

CURRENT EDUCATIONAL ISSUES

Teachers and administrators are faced with many issues that affect their thinking, planning, and implementation of educational programs for young children. Some of the current concerns dealing with aesthetic development are discussed in this section.

Teaching the Arts Without Special Training

I have to teach art and music in my kindergarten classroom, but I don't have the training. Isn't it best to leave those things to the specialists?

Teachers need not be artists or musicians to teach children to appreciate the arts and be aware of beauty in their natural surroundings. Any personally productive experiences that teachers have had, whether writing a paper in college, decorating a home, or planning a flower garden layout, can help them identify with the act of creating.

Teachers who believe that the arts and a love of natural beauty are important, who openly demonstrate these attitudes, and who encourage children to involve themselves in creative endeavors do much to influence children's positive attitudes and aesthetic development, regardless of the teachers' specialized background or training. In addition, teachers are wise to use specialists if they are available. Observing strategies specialists use to motivate children and respond to their work, and gaining information about materials and techniques, can be useful for teachers. However, teachers should avoid relying on specialists to provide the bulk of aesthetic experiences they offer. Classroom teachers have a unique understanding of the needs and interests of the children they teach, and can utilize this knowledge to plan weekly aesthetic activities for their particular group of youngsters. Children benefit from frequent opportunities for singing, making their own art, dancing, and enacting drama, in both planned and spontaneous activities.

Teaching the Arts by Using Adult-Designed Products

I have a number of art projects I do. The parents love it when the kids bring home their paper turkeys all decorated the way I do. What's the harm?

Sometimes teachers fall into the trap of presenting an activity with a particular product in mind, one either designed by the teacher or found in a book. They erroneously believe they are providing creative art. For example, well-meaning Ms. Karley introduces an activity: "Today we're all going to make turkeys just like this one (holding up a completed brown-paper tracing of a hand, with four fingers colored as feathers, and a head indicated with an eye colored on the thumb). First, you trace your hand on the paper I'll pass out, then take your red crayon and . . . ." Some children enjoy following the directions but may think that the art project is not theirs. Many children find they cannot meet the adult standard that is set. When children are expected to follow step-by-step directions, severely limited to the teacher's ideas, choice of materials, and techniques, they are forced to produce something that most likely holds no meaning for them. This situation can cause frustration and feelings of inadequacy as the children recognize that their finished product does not look just like the teacher's.

Ms. Karley's good intentions for a fun activity result in children with negative attitudes about art and convince children that they are incapable. Focusing on the product limits any creative thinking children may have brought to the activity because imaginative approaches are not reinforced. Even though a teacher may say that they do not expect children to follow their pattern exactly, this is not the message that is communicated to the children.

Let's consider how this activity could be presented in a way that encourages more creative thinking and results: Mr. Tiehl holds up a large photograph of a real turkey. He asks, "What do you notice about the turkey? Look carefully at the neck; did you notice that reddish-orange piece of skin? What else do you notice? Has anyone ever seen a turkey? What did it look like?" He listens, responding to children's thinking. "Okay, you had really good ideas. Today during work time, you may choose to go to the art table and make your own turkey. Remember, everyone's will be different because we all have our own ideas. There are some materials on the shelf nearby to use [pointing to baskets and trays holding a variety of paper, crayons, scissors, glue sticks, markers, yarn, real feathers, pipe cleaners, and scrap paper]. If you want to use something that is not on the

myeducationlab

Go to the Video Examples section of Topic 9: Content Areas/Lessons and Activities in the MyEducationLab for your course and watch the video entitled *Creative Arts*. Watch for the various roles of the teacher in supporting children's aesthetic learning. How might these roles differ depending on the age or experience of the children in the group?

shelf, just ask me. I will come back and see how you are doing in a while. Your turkey could be big or little, fat or thin, whatever you decide. Now who will be the first four at the center?" Children who are interested and motivated readily move to the art table. Those who want to make something different that day are also encouraged to take a turn. Finished works are hung or put aside to dry. The children produce a flock of unique creations that are personally satisfying. Children watch one another work, notice new things, and learn from one another. Mr. Tiehl has used the photograph as the only model for the children to follow and has facilitated children's learning instead of limiting it to an adult-designed stereotype.

Responding to Children's Creative Products

I don't know what to say to kids when they show me their art. I don't want to say the wrong thing.

Traditionally, adults respond in a variety of ways to children's creations. Researchers have analyzed the impact of six kinds of adult responses: complimentary, judgmental, valuing, questioning, probing, and correcting (Schirrmacher & Fox, 2009). Each response affects the way the child thinks about art, some in positive ways but many in negative ways. Table 9.5 provides a summary of the impact of traditional adult responses to young children's creative work.

Frequently, adults think children want an oral response to their work, when an unspoken signal such as a smile or a nod would be sufficient. However, when an oral response is requested—such as when the child asks, "Teacher, how do you like my picture?"—adults should avoid looking for representation (adult realism) and use a more effective approach. By focusing on one of the elements of the arts (e.g., line, color, texture), we encourage aesthetic awareness and open a dialogue if the child is comfortable discussing his or her work. Think about what you see in the child's work. Comment on line, symmetry, composition, or perspective in the work. How did the child create the work? Comment on the materials, medium, or tools used by the child (e.g., "You used a wide brush to make strong, thick lines in your painting."). Judiciously using probing responses also encourage children to talk about their work from their perspective. Listen to what the child says, and respond in terms of what is said, remaining interested but nonjudgmental. This is an excellent time to utilize the teaching strategy of paraphrase reflections. When children use obviously recognizable symbols, teachers should still remain as objective as possible. Indicate understanding of the meaning, but avoid showing preference for realism over abstract art. Be nonjudgmental and focus and the process and effort of the work rather than the end product. Table 9.6 provides examples of effective adult responses to children's art.

TABLE 9.5   Impact of Traditional Adult Responses to Children's Art

Response	Example	Impact on Child
Complimentary	"Very nice."	Cuts off discussion.
Judgmental	"Great work, Joey."	Empty comment with overuse. Child thinks anything he or she does is terrific, no matter how little effort is put forth.
Valuing	"I like that very much."	Puts emphasis on the product, not on the process. Too often rewards what is recognizable by adults; ignores personal expression that is not.
Questioning	"What is it?"	Insists it be something; disregards abstract expression. Disappoints the artist, who thinks its identity is obvious.
Probing	"Tell me all about your picture."	Encourages child to discuss; avoids passing judgment on child's work. Assumes that the child will enjoy and learn from verbalizing ideas.
Correcting	"Very good, but the grass should be green."	Assumes that the child must copy reality. Discourages creative expression.

TABLE 9.6   Effective Responses to Children's Aesthetic Products

Response	Examples	Impact on Child
Acknowledge effort.	"You worked a long time on it."	My hard work is noticed.
Recognize use of aesthetic elements.	"You used lots of different shapes." "The bright yellow areas look even brighter next to the dark gray ones."	Yes, I did. I didn't notice that. That looks good to me.
Indicate understanding of symbols.	"I noticed your tree has lots of fruit." "The people in your picture are standing in the rain."	Good; you know what I mean.
Acknowledge child's feelings.	"You're pretty proud of your collage." "You're disappointed with your painting."	I don't have to feel the same way about all my art.
Ask for information.	"Show me a part you like." "Tell me something about your picture."	I can tell things about my art that only I know.
Broaden child's self-concept.	"You really like animals."	Yes, I guess I do.
Recognize progress.	"This is the third drawing you've made about our field trip."	I've accomplished a lot.

PURPOSE AND GOALS

Planning activities in the arts is easier when teachers consider specific goals. The National Standards for Arts Education, published by CNAEA (1994), along with the Music Education Standards from the Music Educators National Conference (MENC, 1994), provide a set of useful goals for teachers to use.

Purpose

The purpose is: For children to become aware of beauty in nature and art, to appreciate and participate in creative arts to achieve personally meaningful ends.

Goals

As children progress toward the goal, they will:

1. Show awareness of beauty in nature
2. Experience various art forms (music, dance, drama, and visual art)
3. Become familiar with different types of each art form (e.g., types of dance such as ballet, tap, folk, and square)
4. Use a variety of materials, tools, techniques, and processes in the arts (visual art, music, dance, and drama)
5. Recognize and respond to basic elements of art (e.g., line, color, shape, texture, composition, pattern)
6. Recognize and respond to basic elements of music (e.g., beat, pitch, melody, rhythm, dynamics, tempo, mood)
7. Talk about aesthetic experiences
8. Participate with others to create music, dance, drama, and visual art
9. Recognize that music, dance, drama, and visual art are means of communication
10. Recognize themselves as artists
11. Participate in aesthetic criticism (describe, analyze, interpret, and judge)
12. Contribute to the aesthetic environment
13. Begin to recognize the arts as a lifelong pursuit
14. Begin to appreciate the arts in relation to history and culture
15. Connect the arts and other curricular areas

MAKING GOALS FIT

Table 9.7 illustrates how the same goal can be implemented with children of different ages or abilities. By utilizing different techniques or strategies teachers can provide appropriate experiences for all children related a specific goal.

TABLE 9.7 Adapting Materials for Use with Different Ages

Goal #4	Example of Activity for 3- to 4-Year-Olds	Example of Activity for 5- to 6-Year-Olds	Example of Activity for 7- to 8-Year-Olds
Use a variety of materials, tools, techniques, and processes in the arts	Encourage children to use hands and fingers to pinch and pull clay. Introduce simple tools such as clay hammers.	Introduce technique such as making a pinch pot.	Introduce technique of coiling to make coil pot.

TEACHING STRATEGIES

The following teaching strategies will help you plan meaningful aesthetic experiences for children.

1. **Model your own aesthetic enthusiasm.** Respond to the aesthetic qualities of the world around you. Point out the beauty you see in the sky, trees, rocks, and other natural objects. Talk about discoveries you made in the arts that you enjoy. For example, tell children about a time that you performed in or went to see a play; describe how music that you heard recently made you feel; tell about playing an instrument or singing with friends; or describe how excited you were at the local art fair.

2. **Prepare an aesthetics-friendly classroom environment.** Use the physical classroom to provide aesthetic experiences by displaying children's artwork at their eye level. Occasionally play music for pure enjoyment during other activities. Model singing for pleasure at various times of the day, such as transition or departure times, and encourage children to do the same. Remove clutter and use low shelf tops as places for displaying plants; sculpture; a beautiful basket; or items of natural beauty such as driftwood, a flower arrangement, or colorful rocks. Rotate interesting reproductions of famous artists' work in the classroom as a decoration, and use it in art appreciation discussions.

3. **Organize a creative arts center.** Maintain basic supplies in labeled containers, allowing easy access by the children. Presenting materials in an organized and pleasing fashion makes it easy for children to both find what they are looking for and to put materials away when they are finished. Store the more specialized supplies for occasional use. Basic materials (see the following list) should be plentiful and easily accessible for regular use by the children. Some early childhood educators constantly introduce new and different media to youngsters. These teachers are reluctant to offer the same materials two days in a row, perhaps for fear children will become bored. However, children who are continually faced with new media are never able to gain control over, or develop skill in the use of, any one medium. Children need many opportunities to practice with basic media in order to use the material for true self-expression. With this is mind, teachers should provide young children with frequent opportunities to use basic art materials so that they can develop this sense of mastery. Teachers should introduce basic materials, such as those listed next, and make them available regularly. For example, painting at the easel should be offered almost daily. Finger painting should be offered several times a month. Materials for drawing (crayons, pencils, or markers) on paper, as well as construction paper and scissors, should be provided daily. It will also be important to ensure that materials are age appropriate and of suitable quality. For example, scissors that will not cut or markers that are dried out are quite frustrating for children.

Basic Art Materials for Young Children (see also Figure 9.3)
- ❏ Tempera paints (at least the primary colors [red, yellow, blue], white, and black)
- ❏ Watercolor paints (paint boxes with refillable colors, or larger paint cakes)
- ❏ Finger paints (at least the primary colors) with finger-paint paper
- ❏ Drawing materials (crayons, pencils, markers)

❏ Paper (manila paper, newsprint, construction paper—white and a variety of colors)
❏ Art chalk (like pastels, softer than blackboard and sidewalk chalk)
❏ Glue (white, nontoxic), paste, glue sticks
❏ Modeling clay
❏ Modeling dough (homemade is easy; see Figure 9.4)

Basic Tools for Art

❏ Paintbrushes—various sizes and shapes
❏ Paint containers (cups with covers)
❏ Rollers, sponges, other objects used to apply paint
❏ Tape (transparent, masking)
❏ Scissors (select appropriate for age of children)
❏ Staplers
❏ Paper fasteners
❏ Hole punches
❏ Recycled plastic containers of various sizes
❏ Wood tongue depressors or craft sticks
❏ Rulers
❏ Supply of newspapers

FIGURE 9.3   Inappropriate Art Materials for Young Children

Some art materials are not appropriate for young children to use because they are unsafe or contain ingredients that can pose a threat to children if the materials are used without strict adult supervision:

❏ Oil-based paints
❏ Inks that are not water soluble
❏ Leaded paints of any kind
❏ Turpentine, paint thinners
❏ Asbestos products
❏ Chemically treated wood
❏ Toxic products or products that create toxic fumes, such as some adhesives
❏ Permanent markers

FIGURE 9.4   Recipes for Modeling Dough

Soft Dough
2 c. flour
1/2 c. salt
2 T. alum
3–5 drops food coloring
2 T. cooking oil
2 c. water

Boil water. Add salt and food coloring. Mix in oil, alum, and flour. Knead. Store in airtight container.

Baker's Clay Dough
1 1/2 c. salt
4 c. flour
1 1/2 c. water
1 tsp. alum

Mix dry ingredients; add water gradually. When a ball forms, knead dough well; add water if too crumbly. Shape. Bake at 325°F until hard.

Hardening Dough
1 c. water
3 c. salt
1 c. cornstarch

Mix water and salt; place pan over medium heat. Gradually mix in cornstarch; heat until mixture thickens into a mass. Cool on aluminum foil before kneading.

The following materials can add variety and inspire creativity in art activities. Make these materials available when they are needed or requested.

Variety or Occasional Materials and Tools for Art

- ❑ Wood glue
- ❑ Glue–paste mixture (white school glue and white paste combined 1 to 1)
- ❑ Variety papers (paper towels, tissue paper, waxed paper, crepe paper, tinfoil, cellophane, coffee filters, etc.)
- ❑ Pipe cleaners
- ❑ Powdered paint
- ❑ Straws (plastic or paper)
- ❑ Thread, yarn, ribbon, string
- ❑ Wire
- ❑ Cardboard scraps
- ❑ Liquid starch (apply to manila paper for wet-chalk drawings)
- ❑ Wood scraps
- ❑ Glitter
- ❑ Recycled clean socks, T-shirts, gloves
- ❑ Cardboard boxes (such as salt, oatmeal, gift, shoe, milk, toothpaste)
- ❑ New or sanitized plastic foam meat trays
- ❑ Colored sand (mix powdered paint into play sand)
- ❑ Natural objects (leaves, stones, seeds, seashells, acorns, gourds, etc.)
- ❑ Paper cups, paper plates, paper napkins
- ❑ Paper tubes (paper towel, toilet paper)
- ❑ Magazines, wallpaper pieces
- ❑ Squeeze bottles
- ❑ Egg cartons
- ❑ Spray can tops, jar lids, milk jug lids, other plastic lids
- ❑ Old, sanitized toothbrushes
- ❑ Other small bits (buttons, sequins, beads, feathers, lace)

4. **Provide a variety of music-supporting materials.** Young children need a rich musical environment in which to grow (MENC, 1994). When children have many opportunities to explore and create with basic rhythm instruments, experiment with a variety of pitched instruments, and listen to many kinds of music, their enjoyment of and participation in musical experiences are greatly enhanced. The following music materials are recommended for early childhood programs.

Basic Rhythm Instruments

- ❑ Rhythm sticks (wooden dowels, lengths of broom handles, wooden spoons, heavy straws, or heavy paper towel rolls)
- ❑ Maracas
- ❑ Triangles
- ❑ Jingle bells
- ❑ Sand blocks
- ❑ Tambourines
- ❑ Cymbals
- ❑ Drums

Basic Pitched Instruments

- ❑ Xylophones
- ❑ Tone bells
- ❑ Simple wooden or plastic recorders
- ❑ Kazoos

Other Music Materials

- ❑ Compact disc (CD) player with a collection of musical CDs
- ❑ Simple cassette-tape recorder that can be used by children; tapes
- ❑ Chord instruments (such as guitar, autoharp, piano, keyboard)—these add interest and variety to children's singing but are not necessary for musical success in the classroom

Children learn from exploring a variety of musical sounds.

5. **Provide a variety of creative movement props.** Movement is an important musical response because it is unspoken and allows the teacher to better understand the aspects of the music that the child is sensing (Bredekamp & Rosegrant, 1995). Simple props can motivate creative movement exploration.

Props for Creative Movement and Dance
- ❏ Plastic hoops
- ❏ Scarves of various colors
- ❏ Streamers or flags (e.g., crepe paper or strips of tissue paper attached to short, safe handles such as wide craft sticks or straws)
- ❏ Rhythm sticks
- ❏ Tambourines
- ❏ Paper towel rolls
- ❏ Pom-poms
- ❏ Batons

6. **Provide props for creative dramatics,** such as:
- ❏ Props that suggest roles: fire helmets, short hoses, maps, boots, badges; cash register, play money, empty food containers, menus, plastic dishes, apron, play money, trays; steering wheel, earphones, board with knobs and dials
- ❏ Props related to familiar stories: "The Three Little Pigs"—sticks tied together, cardboard bricks, ears, pot; "The Three Bears"—three different-sized bowls, spoon, three chairs, three pillows; "Caps for Sale"—felt rounds in various colors, monkey tails, chairs
- ❏ Lengths of fabric in a variety of textures and colors that can be draped by children to create costumes.
- ❏ Props that stimulate imaginative stories: wand, top hat, cloak, crown, skirts, vests, purses, wallets, telephones, microphone, animal noses, masks, stuffed animals, hand puppets, and finger puppets

7. **Value all aspects of the creative expression process.** No matter what stage of development the child is in, teachers should recognize and value that level. Individual developmental differences are expected in any group of children. The way adults respond to the child's aesthetic products (e.g., the drawing, the dance, the song, or the dramatic production) will have lasting effects on the individual. Adult responses to children's attempts at creative expression either help establish an environment of acceptance and encouragement or clearly indicate to children that their own ideas are not valued. In general, teachers should use praise judiciously. Be flexible and prepared for unique actions and products, such as when Anthony uses the props intended for "The Three Billy Goats Gruff" to create his own story about the planet Mars. Observe; engage the child in dialogue about his or her creation, showing interest and asking questions such as "Tell me about your people from Mars." or "How did you get the idea to create a space station on Mars?" Show children you value their creative experimentation and encourage their own ideas in aesthetic activities, especially if these ideas are different from others' or yours. Use words such as "Your picture doesn't have to look like Matthew's. It's much more interesting when each person uses their own ideas!"

8. **Teach children to respect and care for materials.** Teachers should demonstrate how to clean and store materials properly. For example, rhythm instruments should be carefully placed into storage containers at the end of the activity. Paintbrushes should be washed carefully and laid flat or handle down to dry. Watercolor paint boxes or paint cakes should be rinsed with clear water and left open to dry. Teach children to replace caps on markers to preserve their moisture for longer use. Paper scraps large enough to be used another day should be kept in a scrap collection box and recycled. Presenting materials in a carefully organized manner demonstrates the value of art supplies and encourages children to care for the materials.

9. **Involve children in daily musical experiences.** All children sing; they begin as soon as they gain sufficient control over their voice to talk. Even teachers with little musical training, or those who believe they have a less than adequate singing ability, can share the joy of music with children. At various times throughout the day, such as at transition times, during cleanup, at the opening of group meetings, or at the end of the day, teachers should sing songs with the class, play a recorded piece of music as background, or encourage children to clap along as they tap out rhythms with a tambourine.

FIGURE 9.5   Techniques to Teach Young Children

Depending on the ages and experience of the children, the following are some techniques that should be demonstrated.

Visual Arts Techniques

Pasting
Gluing
Cutting
Tearing
Folding
Finger painting
Washing the brush between colors
Hanging or laying wet paintings to dry
Pressing light and hard with crayons
Twist-attaching pipe cleaners
Stapling
Hole punching
Tying
Printing by pressing down and pulling up
Kneading
Weaving

Music Techniques

Handling instruments carefully
Starting and stopping
Passing out and collecting instruments
Listening for the beat or rhythm
Quiet and loud
Fast and slow
High and low
Directing and following
Being the audience

Dance/Drama Techniques

Finding your own space
Moving without bumping into others
Moving high and low
Moving fast and slow
Sliding your feet
Walking, marching, skipping
Moving forward and backward
Movements such as swaying, jumping, bouncing
Using your body to express feelings
Starting and stopping

10. **Motivate children's creativity in a variety of ways.**

   ❏ Demonstrate techniques that are new to children. Show ways to manipulate the tools and substances to achieve particular effects. Do not demonstrate how to make a picture or a recognizable product. Allow children to create their own ideas by using the techniques you demonstrate. For example, show the children how to use a glue stick or how to twist two pipe cleaners together (see Figure 9.5).

   ❏ Use motivational talk. Following demonstrations, engage children in discussions that encourage them to suggest ideas using the technique or material demonstrated. For example, say, "Using this way to flatten and roll the clay, think about what you might make; who has an idea?" or "Now that you know how to use the tape player, what song will you record onto your tape?" Write their ideas on a list.

   ❏ Role-play ideas. One of the best ways young children learn about something is to experience the concept with their whole body. Children's artwork increases in creativity and detail following role-playing experiences. Using children's ideas, suggest they move like tall trees blowing in the wind, be a wave crashing to the shore, or crouch like tiny mice in the grass. Afterward, children can apply these ideas to making pictures, performing a drama, or creating a dance.

   ❏ Collect and mount photographs of real objects and events to help children make connections to prior knowledge, notice more detail, and break down simplistic ideas they may have formulated through other experiences. For example, shown a picture of a thunderstorm, children can use the rhythm instruments to create their own storm with great gusto.

   ❏ Encourage imagining. Young children are not bound to reality, and teachers can encourage creativity by supporting imaginative thought and expression. For very young children this might be simple pretend play. Teachers can suggest older children change their perspective, such as imagining what they could see when looking down from a tall tree or while flying over the rooftops, or what it would be like walking on a distant planet.

Demonstrating new techniques motivates interest and creative thinking.

11. **Use the outdoor environment to stimulate aesthetic awareness and creativity.** Perhaps as a result of technology,

overscheduling, or parental fears, today's children have less of a relationship with nature than prior generations did (Louv, 2005). As a result, they need caregivers who understand the value of outdoors for play, enjoyment, and appreciation of the natural world. On the playground, during a field trip to the park, or while on neighborhood walks, encourage children to point out beautiful things they see.

12. Connect creative experiences to concepts children are exploring. Mrs. Martin's kindergartners are learning about opposites (such as high–low, fast–slow, big–small, warm–cool). After brainstorming examples, she challenges them to use creative movement or art materials to show two opposite words they select.

13. Explore the materials before asking children to use them. Spend a few minutes with novel materials before introducing them to the children. Become familiar with what they can do and discover problems children may encounter. For example, if the paint is too runny, add thick paint or detergent. If the autoharp is out of tune, take time to tune it to make the sounds more appealing.

14. Demonstrate techniques or processes (series of techniques) that are new to the children. Children need to be shown how to use materials and tools in order to create the effect they desire. Teachers should demonstrate new techniques to children and then provide plenty of time to experiment and explore with the materials. Children will also require opportunities to revisit techniques in order to gain mastery. Demonstrations could include cutting, gluing, sanding, rolling, or strumming the strings of an instrument.

15. Discover and use picture-book illustrations as works of art. Every year, new and wonderful children's books are published that contain stunning examples of visual artistic expression. Teachers should share at least one beautiful book with their students each day. Help children (a) discover the joy of art available to hold in your hand, and (b) explore and recognize techniques used by the illustrator. Before (or after) reading the story each day, take time to introduce at least one picture as a piece of art, discussing the visual qualities they see. What child has ever read Maurice Sendak's *Where the Wild Things Are* (Sendak, 1963), Lois Ehlert's *Eating the Alphabet: Fruits and Vegetables from A to Z* (Ehlert, 1989), or Cynthia Rylant's *The Relatives Came* (Rylant, 1985) without pausing to look at the incredible pictures? Teachers should treat books as priceless gifts and each illustration as a gem to be treasured. This demonstration of appreciation can influence children to develop a lifelong interest in collecting good art and owning beautiful books.

> **Other Activities Using Book Illustrations**
> ❏ Use the art-related ideas in picture books to help children explore their own ideas. Use books such as *Mouse Paint*, by Ellen Stoll Walsh (1989), or *Don't Touch*, by Suzy Kline (1985).
> ❏ Explore the various ways in which a particular subject is depicted by different artists; for example, grandmothers, as portrayed in picture books such as *Charlie and Grandma,* by Sally Ward (1986); *Gifts*, by Jo Ellen Bogart (1994); *My Grammy,* by Marsha Kibbey (1988); and *Bigmama's*, by Donald Crews (1991).
> ❏ Notice and imitate an illustrator's use of materials or technique, such as painted papers in any book by Eric Carle; collage in any book by Lois Ehlert; use of colored clay as in *Gifts*, by Jo Ellen Bogart (1994); or use of a watercolor technique as in pictures by Leo Lionni.

16. Use different kinds of questions to help children describe, analyze, interpret, and judge works in the arts. Questions can extend children's ability to respond to the arts. Using various kinds of questions regarding the arts, elicit a variety of kinds of thinking from children.

> ❏ *Cognitive memory questions* motivate thinking about facts (e.g., "What did you see in that painting?" "What animals did you hear in that song?" "What are some words to describe this dance?").
> ❏ *Convergent questions*, or *closed questions*, have expected answers (e.g., "What color was used most in this painting?" "What kinds of lines are used in this part?").
> ❏ *Divergent questions,* or *open-ended questions,* have many possible answers (e.g., "Why do you think the artist used black in his picture?" "How does this music make you feel? Why?").
> ❏ *Evaluative questions* ask for children's values (e.g., "What part of that dance did you like the best?" "Which finger painting is your favorite? Why?").

17. Involve all the children in the arts. The arts provide opportunities for success for all students, regardless of their abilities. Aesthetic experiences should allow for a wide range of exploration and creative expression. Including young children with disabilities in creative activities

TABLE 9.8   Sample Adaptations for Children with Special Needs

Challenge	Adaptation	Examples
Weak grasp	Build up writing instrument, provide short/stubby implements	Pencil grips, thin foam secured by tape, foam curler, break chalk or pencil into shorter pieces
Need for structure	Eliminate use of glue/tape	Sticky collage base (contact paper), glue sticks, stickers
	Limit material choices	One or two collage materials at a time
	Small containers for materials	Butter, yogurt containers
Scissor difficulty	Scissors sizing	Wrap tape around loops to make them bulkier
	Scissors alternatives	Encourage tearing, adaptive scissors
	Thicker paper, weighted or textured paper	Sandpaper, wallpaper
	Position paper to encourage correct hand position	Tape top of paper to wall
Limited use of hands, arms and fingers	Proper child positioning	Provide foot support and chair that holds child upright, three-ring binder for forearm support, provide correct table height
	Stabilize learning materials	Tape paper down, place paper in shirt-size box
	Alternative drawing methods	Salt trays, funnel painter
Limited vision	Provide visual contrast	Add dark colors to glue, use dark colors on light paper
	Increase tactile feedback	Add sawdust or sand to paint
Tactile sensitivity	Squeeze paint	Thicken paint and put in squeeze bottle, spread finger paint with tool or provide plastic gloves

requires effective teaching strategies to ensure success. These strategies include modifying materials to meet individual needs, and providing adequate space and time for children to engage in an activity (Mitchell, 2005). Children with motor, orthopedic or visual impairments may require additional space or environmental modifications to participate in creative movement activities. Teachers should plan ample time for children with special needs to explore materials and complete activities. Activities with various visual art media and music should be adapted to allow as much participation as possible according to the child's individual needs. Table 9.8 provides examples of how some art activities could be adapted to better include children with a range of abilities.

18. **Provide aesthetic activities as a stress reduction technique.** Aesthetic activities can provide an outlet for children to express and process their fears. For example, children can conquer their fear of the wolf in the *Three Little Pigs* by taking on that role in a child-directed drama, or paint a picture to express their feelings about an incident they experienced. Tactile activities such as finger painting, clay, and play-doh can be calming for young children. Following traumatic events such as a natural disaster or September 11, 2001, teachers can provide children opportunities to explore their feelings, such as the first-grade teacher who facilitated her class in writing and illustrating the book, *September 12th We Knew Everything Would Be Alright* (Scholastic, 2002).

PITFALLS TO AVOID

Don't Focus on Making a Model When Demonstrating

Avoid making a recognizable product when you are demonstrating the technique. For example, show the children appropriate ways to apply glue to Styrofoam, focusing on where it is most needed and the amount to use. Keep focused on the technique you are teaching versus a recognizable product. Whatever the teacher makes will establish an extremely strong model, and children may feel they must copy it. Children will believe that this is the result the teacher wants and abandon their own ideas. Even very creative individuals have difficulty thinking beyond what their teacher shows them as "the correct way." Instead, focus on the technique, then ask the children to tell how they will use the materials.

> ### A Teacher Demonstrates Technique
>
> Mr. Sanders gathers the 4-year-olds together to demonstrate the technique of crayon resist. He wants them to realize that the harder the crayon is pressed, the better their drawing will show through the paint. Using white paper and a variety of crayon colors, he shows them how to press really hard with the crayons. Then he makes some very light lines to show what *not* to do with the crayons. During the demonstration, he is careful not to make recognizable pictures as he wants them to use their own creative ideas. As he paints over the lines with watery dark paint, he guides the children to notice which lines showed up the best. After the demonstration, he asks children to tell what kinds of pictures they might make by using this technique. The children are motivated to think of their own ideas.

Don't Hurry Children

Give children plenty of time to explore, experiment, and become familiar with materials in an unhurried, uninterrupted, and unstructured way, without insisting that they "make something." This is especially important if the materials are new to the children, they will need to determine what they can do with the materials and how they might use them. Children also need time to repeat aesthetic experiences over and over, including time to watch others who are engaged.

Don't Waste Children's Time

Don't fill children's art time with coloring sheets and other adult-designed activities aimed at making specific objects. When teachers present activities such as these, they communicate to children that child-created art is not sufficient, resulting in decreased motivation for creating original works (Seefeldt & Wasik, 2006). These activities rob children of valuable time for developing skills and using marks to create meaning (Kolbe & Smyth, 2000).

Avoid Overdirecting

Accept children's ideas for creative movement, art expression, music, and drama. Avoid the temptation to give your ideas too readily. Remember that creative activities should provide opportunities for self expression. Expect students to individually respond in different ways to suggestions from you or to the music or materials.

Don't Reinforce Only a Realistic Approach

Children recognize when teachers truly value individual differences. Teachers who reward (in spoken or unspoken ways) only pictures that are realistic and recognizable, ignoring more abstract expressions, severely limit young children's creative expression of thoughts, feelings, and events. Young children often experiment with materials without intending to relate their finished product to reality. They may be fascinated by the way the colors change when they touch each other, or how the sand sticks to the glue and not to the paper. Adults who insist that they "see something" in children's pictures impose the value of realism that can force children into this singular mode of expression and the frustration of such limits. When we focus on the artistic elements of the work (such as color, lines, arrangement of shapes), or the effort expended by the artist, children see that they are free to use whatever means of expression they want, without worrying that their work will be devalued.

Use Praise Sparingly

Many adults fall into the trap of lavishing children with unconditional, false praise, thinking that they are reinforcing continued creative expressions. However, overuse of praise can actually decrease a child's motivation (Koster, 2009). Recall our discussion of effective praise in chapter 3. Linking effort and success is a much more effective strategy than empty praise.

APPROACHES TO TEACHING THE ARTS

Different approaches can be taken to teaching anything. Some approaches are more teacher controlled, some are more child controlled, and others share the control between teacher and child. Just as these approaches can be applied to teaching in general, they also apply to teaching in the arts. The three approaches can be thought of as a continuum from closed to open. The more aspects of the activity the teacher controls, the more closed it is for the child. The fewer aspects of the activity the teacher chooses, and the more choices a child is given, the more open the experience. Figure 9.6 shows this continuum of teaching approaches and how it relates to the arts. Notice the variety of dimensions of the art activity that can be more or less controlled by the teacher: *Materials* include all physical objects and tools needed for the activity. *Techniques* are how the materials are used. *Subject* is the topic or theme of the activity—for example, birds. The *product* is what the finished work will look or sound like—for example, a map, a picture, or an ornament.

Consider examples of the three teaching approaches. For our purposes, the examples will relate to visual art; however, teaching any of the arts (music, creative movement, drama, dance) applies.

Mr. Stein plans a finger-painting activity that is completely *teacher controlled*. He chooses the paper, cuts it to 8 × 11 inches, and selects blue paint (the materials). He describes the technique of applying blue paint with a spoon and using fingers to spread it on the paper. He tells the children they will all be making pictures of the sky (the subject) and that their paintings (the product) will be hung on the wall when they are dry. As the children paint, he reminds them of the way they are supposed to work, discouraging "messing around" with the paint, redirecting children to "make their sky pictures." All the children produce similar blue paintings. After their paintings dry, most children have difficulty differentiating which painting belongs to whom. Some children toss their paintings into the trash. Children react negatively to the experience.

Ms. Porter's approach to art is completely *child controlled*. Children are free to work with any materials they want, using whatever techniques they devise. They may select any subject and produce any product they want. Ms. Porter does not enter the art area, assuming that doing so would interfere with children's creativity. Today, during free-choice time, a few children enter the art area, look around, and then leave. One child spends her whole free-choice time in the area, using markers, scissors, yarn, and glue to make a picture for her mom. Ms. Porter notices that few children use the art area, even though they have many choices, and she wonders why.

Mrs. Alvarez's approach to art is *shared control*. She plans some aspects of the activity but leaves many aspects open for children to choose. She arranges newspaper on one end of the art table and lays smocks on three chairs. She prepares plastic containers of red, blue, yellow, and white finger paint, placing them on the newspaper with a plastic spoon in each. She wets a clean sponge and puts it on a dish near the paint. She also lays a pencil and one piece of finger-paint paper in front of each chair. As children arrive, she gathers them together and demonstrates how to use the materials if they choose to finger-paint today. As

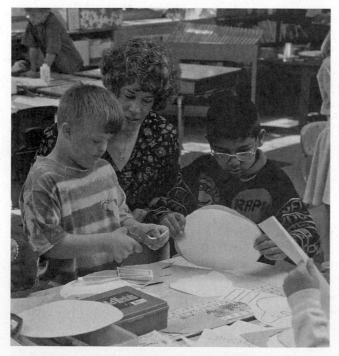

All children benefit from aesthetic experiences.

FIGURE 9.6 **Continuum of Teaching Approaches**

Teacher Controlled _____	**Shared Control** _____	**Child Controlled**
Teacher chooses all materials		Child chooses materials
Teacher chooses techniques		Child chooses techniques
Teacher chooses subject		Child chooses subject
Teacher's product		Child's product

she moves the red paint on her paper, she purposely does not make a recognizable picture but instead focuses on a variety of ways to move her fingers in the paint, hoping that doing so will inspire additional thinking. As several children show interest in the activity, she suggests that they begin a waiting list because there is room for only three children to finger paint at a time. During the morning, she checks in to see how the painting is progressing. She notes that most of the children have signed up to paint. She points out that Michelle found her own way to use her fingers in the paint. She remarks that each painting is unique. Jae Young chooses to use the other end of the table to make his creation out of crepe paper, construction paper, and glue that he finds in labeled containers on the art shelf. Mrs. Alvarez smiles and gives them a thumbs-up. When their creations are dry, the children easily find their own and are eager to tell about them. Later, many of the children write or dictate a story about their experience. Mrs. Alvarez facilitates learning through the physical setup, demonstration, discussion, and choices. Her teaching approach provides a balance of teacher control and child control as well as independence and sensitive intervention without her monopolizing the activity. She has motivated children to think and solve problems; has taught them about technique, sharing, and cooperation; and has given them new insights into themselves as artists.

ACTIVITY SUGGESTIONS

As described in chapter 3, six generic activity types form the basis for planning and teaching. Following are examples of some of these activity types as they apply to the aesthetic domain.

Aren't They Beautiful? (For Children of All Ages)

Goal 1 Show awareness of beauty in nature.

Materials Natural objects such as real flowers, real shells, a real plant, stones, a real rabbit, etc.

Procedure Bring in something natural that you consider beautiful. Gather children together and talk about the object, how pretty the object is, how the object makes you feel and adds to your life. Be enthusiastic about the experience. Ask children to express what they like about it.

To Simplify Talk to children one by one as they show interest in the object.

To Extend Give children several days to experience the object in an appropriate manner. Then gather them together to discuss it. Follow up by encouraging them to draw about it.

Artists in Our Town (For Children of All Ages)

Goal 2 Experience various art forms (music, dance, drama, and visual art).

Materials Varies depending on what kind of artist visits

Procedure Invite a visual artist, a musician, a dancer, or an actor (one of the parents or a community person) to visit the class. Ask this person to bring samples of his or her work and the tools necessary to perform the work. Ask your guest to demonstrate the art form and discuss how he or she became interested in this type of art. Encourage children to ask questions.

To Simplify Keep the presentation short (10 minutes). Arrange the artist and his or her tools in an area of the classroom where children can talk with him or her during free-choice time.

To Extend Send a note home to parents asking them to help their child find someone they know (in their family or neighborhood) who is an artist, a musician, a dancer, or an actor. Explain that your objective is to help children understand more about art in the culture. Ask them to help their child talk to this person and find out information about him or her (e.g., What kind of artist are you? How did you get interested in that? How old were you when you started?). Provide time for children to report to the class about the artist they found, or invite the artists to come as visitors.

Field Trip to Art Museum (For Children of All Ages)

Goal 3 Become familiar with different types of each art form (visual art).

Materials Postcard prints with suggestion cards

Procedure Arrange to take the class to an art gallery. Visit ahead of time, taking note of which pieces would interest the group. Purchase postcard prints of some of the artwork. Distribute these to small-group leaders, along with suggestions for things to point out. Encourage the groups to move slowly through the exhibits, looking for the artwork depicted on the postcards. Move among the small groups, asking questions to motivate children to notice variety in the use of materials, subject matter, and kinds of art (paintings, drawings, sculpture, carved designs, etc.) represented.

To Simplify Go for a short time. Arrange for very small groups or pairs of children assigned to each adult. Prepare adults to look at things in general, stopping to analyze the pieces that interest the children.

To Extend Plan a longer visit. Prepare children for some particular pieces of artwork that they will see. Analyze these pieces carefully as the children discover them. Plan follow-up activities of drawing or painting something they remember.

Listen to This! (For Older or More Experienced Children)

Goal 3 Become familiar with different types of each art form (music).

Materials Tape recorder, collection of short passages of various kinds of music

Procedure Arrange a tape recorder or CD player and a collection of musical pieces in a quiet corner of the room. Encourage children to take turns listening to the music selections alone or with a friend. To focus attention on appreciation of the range of types of music, select music that varies greatly, such as folk, rock, classical piano, catchy tunes from commercials, television theme songs, marching band music, part of a symphony, chamber music, and jazz. If you are making your own tape, organize the selections with blank spaces between them so that children can easily distinguish beginnings and endings.

To Simplify Limit the number of music types to two or three.

To Extend Ask children to bring in samples of types of music that they enjoy at home. Encourage parents to contribute to a collection of samples, especially requesting music from various cultures.

Let's Stick Together (For Older or More Experienced Children)

Goal 4 Use a variety of materials, tools, techniques, and processes in the arts (visual art).

Materials Clay, cutting tools, water

Procedure Potter's clay offers opportunities for three-dimensional sculpture and ceramic design. However, occasionally in the drying process, attached pieces fall off. Discuss this fact with the children, and demonstrate a process in which clay pieces are attached so that this will not happen. Prepare two pieces of clay to attach. Using a tool that makes shallow cuts (such as a table knife, fork, or wooden ceramic tool), crosshatch lines into the surfaces to be joined. Then apply plain water with a finger to wet both scored surfaces and produce a slippery "glue." Press the pieces together and blend the clay to completely cover the line of attachment. Give children clay, tools, and water, and encourage them to practice attaching pieces.

To Simplify Offer children large (fist-sized) pieces to attach; set these aside to dry.

To Extend Invite children to think of things that have parts (e.g., animals have legs, a head, and a tail) to attach. Brainstorm ideas. Encourage them to work on their own creations, using the technique demonstrated.

Object Prints (For Younger or Less Experienced Children)

Goal 4 Use a variety of materials, tools, techniques, and processes in the arts (visual art).

Materials Paint, pans, sponges, paper towels, collection of interesting objects, paper

Procedure Introduce object printing by demonstrating the down–up motion used to make prints on paper with various objects. Prepare several shallow pans of paint in a variety of colors. Pour the paint onto flat sponges or layers of paper towels, and offer a selection of interesting objects (wooden spools or other wooden shapes, small pieces of sponge, dowels, potato mashers, corrugated cardboard pieces, cotton swabs, forks, plastic cups, a small pine tree bough, pine cones, etc.) to print with. Provide large-size paper to print on, giving children a selection of colors. Encourage children to experiment with the various objects and to fill their paper with interesting printed shapes.

To Simplify Limit the number of objects or the number of paint colors. Hammer a nail into wooden shapes to make them easier to manipulate.

To Extend When the prints are dry, ask children to try to recall which object they used to make an individual shape on the print. Another time, have children make their own collections of objects to print.

Oh-Up! Oh-Down! (For Children of All Ages)

Goal 4 Use a variety of materials, tools, techniques, and processes in the arts (drama).

Materials None

Procedure After reading or hearing a story that the children particularly enjoyed, suggest that the group stand up and form a circle or stand facing each other. Tell children that they are going to use their bodies to become people, animals, or objects in the story. Teach them signals to use to begin and end their dramatic interpretations: "Oh-up" means to stand up and begin; "Oh-down" means to stop and crouch down. Have everyone go down into a crouch; then say, "When we come up, we're all going to be (e.g., the papa bear tasting his porridge). Oh-up! . . . (do it with them) . . . Oh-down!" Orally reinforce creative ideas that children use. Repeat the procedure, using other ideas. Encourage children to participate, but do not force them. If some children insist on watching, select a place nearby where they may easily join in if they change their mind.

To Simplify Select ideas that are obvious and easy to visualize (e.g., "Be the baby bear crying over his broken chair" or "Be Goldilocks going to sleep in the bed"). Do this for a short time and end before the children become tired.

To Extend After the obvious ideas, select some ideas that are more subtle (e.g., "Be the chair that breaks when Goldilocks sits down" or "Be the door that opens when she knocks"). Let children take turns being the leader, suggesting ideas. Alternatively, use this as a warm-up exercise before having the children act out the whole story as a class.

Name That Tune (For Younger or Less Experienced Children)

Goal 6 Recognize and respond to basic elements of music (melody).

Materials None

Procedure Teach and practice singing a number of simple children's songs with the children, such as "The Eency Weency Spider," "She'll Be Comin' 'Round the Mountain," "Mary Had a Little Lamb," "Yankee Doodle," "Old MacDonald Had a Farm." After the tunes have become familiar to the children, explain that you are going to play a game with the class. Hum without using the words (or use a kazoo) to create the melodies, asking children to listen and name each song.

To Simplify Use short, simple songs that children know well.

To Extend Teach the class some new songs and try this exercise. Try it again the following day, without singing them with words first.

Feel the Beat (For Younger or Less Experienced Children)

Goal 6 Recognize and respond to basic elements of music (beat and tempo).

Materials Recorded music with a strong beat, rhythm sticks or tubes, tambourine

Procedure Play a number of recorded instrumental selections with an obvious beat (a steady pulse) and a variety of tempos (relative speed of the beat). An audiotape demonstrating different kinds of music can be made with pauses between short musical segments. Play the tape and respond to the beat with your hands (clap hands, slap thighs). Have the children begin in a sitting position, and say, "Listen to the music. Feel the beat. Clap on the beat with me." Do not expect young children to match the beat exactly. Next, suggest that children move their hands a different way to the beat (punch the air, point a finger, wave, etc.). Suggest that the children move more of their body to the beat (nod their head, shrug their shoulders, sway their hips, step in place, walk to the beat).

To Simplify For children who do not feel the beat, help them by placing their hands over yours as you clap. Then switch, having your hands cover theirs. Try using an oral cue on the beat to help children become more aware. Say, "Beat-beat-beat-beat-beat" or "Clap-clap-clap-clap." Younger children are better able to keep time with a moderate tempo than with a slower tempo.

To Extend Offer children simple rhythm instruments on which to tap the beat of the music, such as rhythm sticks or empty paper towel tubes. Demonstrate tapping on the floor, softly on a shoe, or on the thigh. Explain the terms *beat* and *tempo*; play a game in which children take turns demonstrating a fast tempo, a slow tempo, and a medium tempo by hitting a tambourine as everyone else moves in time to the beat.

Pitch Play (For Older or More Experienced Children)

Goal 6 Recognize and respond to basic elements of music (pitch).

Materials Pitched instruments (such as a xylophone)

Procedure Show children how sounds can be high or low by playing one of each on the xylophone. Then sing the same sounds, "Da-da" (high–low), matching the pitches. Teach children how to have musical "conversations" using matching pitches, with one person leading and the others responding like an echo. Tell the children to listen to what you sing, then echo back what they heard, using the same sounds (matching pitches). Begin with one word that has two syllables, like *hello*. Sing the first syllable high; sing the second low. The leader sings, "Hel-lo" (high and low). Response: "Hel-lo" (high-low). Practice this using various words, like "el-bow," "fing-er," "tooth-paste," "meat-ball," or phrases like "play-ball," "slide-down," "go-slow," and so on. Change the pitches for variety; use low–high sometimes. Then, use phrases with three words or sounds, such as "go-out-side" (high–high–low) or "eat-ice-cream" (low–low–high), until it becomes easy. Next, have the child lead, and you reply with different words but matched pitches. The leader sings, "Hel-lo." Response: "Hi-there" or "Hi-Carl." Finally, switch roles again and have the student make up his or her response to your lead, still matching your pitches.

To Simplify Start simple, using one-pitch conversations.

To Extend Use two sets of pitched instruments, such as bells or xylophones, using the same procedure: One leads, the other echoes using the instruments instead of singing voices or in addition to singing voices. Be sure to start with two pitches that are very different (high–low) and gradually use those that are more difficult to distinguish (high–middle or middle–low).

Art Talk (For Children of All Ages)

Goal 7 Talk about aesthetic experiences.

Materials None

Procedure Plan an aesthetic experience for the class, such as experimenting with watercolor paints on wet paper or listening to the music of *Fantasia* on tape. Afterward, gather children together to discuss what they remember, know, think, and value about the experience. Ask questions such as "What did you see or hear? What do you remember about that?" (cognitive memory questions), "What colors of paint were we using today?" (convergent question), "What words can we use to describe different parts of this music?" (divergent question), and "How did you like this activity?" (evaluative question).

To Simplify Ask only one or two questions. Keep the discussion short but listen to everyone's reply.

To Extend Follow up the discussion by having children draw, write, or dictate their feelings and thoughts about the experience.

What Does It Mean? (For Older or More Experienced Children)

Goal 9 Recognize that music, dance, drama, and visual art are means of communication.

Materials A sign, reproductions of paintings, crayons or markers, paper

Procedure Point to a written sign or message in your classroom. Read it aloud and ask what the message tells us. Discuss the fact that some art, music, and dance communicate ideas to an audience without using words. Show children a print of a painting that has an appropriate and understandable message, such as Degas's *The Rehearsal* (Phaidon, 1994, p. 123), depicting ballet dancers; Picasso's *Weeping Woman* (Phaidon, 1994, p. 356); or Homer's *Breezing Up* (Phaidon, 1994, p. 227), showing boys sailing. Do not tell children the title. Ask them to look carefully, notice details about the picture, and tell what they think the artist was communicating. Let students know that there are no "right" answers, that anyone's ideas can be valid, and that sometimes the same work has many messages. Accept all ideas. Later, tell children about how each piece of art has a title, which helps us to understand the message of the picture. Tell the children the title of the picture and listen to children's comments. Follow this by providing familiar drawing materials (crayons or markers and paper) and suggest that children make a picture with a message. Display the pictures and give students time to look at and speculate about what message each might be communicating. Ask each artist to tell what the message is and to give the work a title. Display titles with their pictures.

To Simplify Relate the concept of artistic messages to other unspoken messages such as gestures, facial expressions, and body language. Use the obvious messages, and use examples that communicate more obviously.

To Extend Show an example of a painting in which the message is less obvious, more abstract, and nonrepresentational, such as Mondrian's *Composition* (Phaidon, 1994, p. 321), a design of geometric shapes, or Miro's *Women, Bird by Moonlight* (Phaidon, 1994, p. 317), a colorful work with lively shapes open to many interpretations. Encourage children to offer opinions about what the artist is communicating.

My Own Song (For Children of All Ages)

Goal 10 Recognize themselves as artists.

Materials None

Procedure Model and encourage children to select familiar tunes and sing their own words to them. For example, to the tune of "Frère Jacques," or "Are You Sleeping?" sing, "Going home now, going home now, going home, going home, going going home, going going home, going home, going home."

To Simplify Suggest that children sing their name using the melody of a familiar, simple song, such as "Mary, Mary, Mary, Mary, Mary, Mary, Mary, Mary, . . ."

To Extend Encourage children to use more extensive personal descriptions with the melody. "Frère Jacques" can sound like "My name's Sandy, my name's Sandy, how are you, how are you, I live in a yellow house with a dog named Patches, I like school, I like school."

SUMMARY

Teaching through the arts is a satisfying process. When children engage in arts that are truly meaningful to them, so-called art from the heart, teachers share the excitement of these creative experiences. Seeing children express wonder at the beauty of butterfly wings gives us hope for future adults who appreciate nature. Encouraging children to respectfully handle a wooden sculpture or to listen to the "March of the Toy Soldiers" with their eyes closed inspires imagination and creative thinking. Supporting children as they examine samples of wallpaper to decide what they like and do not like focuses children on the notion that art is all around them and that they can have preferences that are worthwhile. Recognizing that a child has grown in his or her ability to create music, art, dance, or drama helps teachers realize the power of the arts to enrich lives.

Key Words

aesthetics	literary arts	usable arts
arts	performing arts	visual arts

Applying What You've Read in This Chapter

1. **Discuss**
   a. After considering the value of creative art, think about how you feel about using coloring books and coloring pages with young children. Discuss your thinking with a partner, giving a rational argument for your stance.
   b. Obtain an example of a child's artwork. Consider several ways in which you, as his or her teacher, could respond appropriately to the child's work. Tell how each response may affect the child.
   c. Talk about the ways in which teachers can use music in the classroom. List as many ways as you can think of.

2. **Observe**
   a. Locate a program or a school that has an arts (art, music, dance, creative movement, or drama) specialist working with the children. Arrange to observe as the specialist works with a group. Take notes on the strategies, techniques, and content of the lesson. Discuss your observations. How does what you observed relate to the goals and objectives for the arts in this chapter?

3. **Carry out an activity**
   a. Plan a music activity using musical instruments to teach two of the following musical concepts: beat, rhythm, tempo, and pitch. Carry out the activity with a group of children. Consider how the children responded. Evaluate your results.
   b. Select a familiar story for children to enact. Make, or encourage children to make, a collection of props that will stimulate them to act out the story. Plan how you will introduce the story and props to the children and how you will motivate them to participate in the activity. Help children think of the gestures, movement, and dialogue that would help tell the story.

4. **Create something for your portfolio**
   a. Review the three teaching approaches described in this chapter. Think about which approach you will primarily use with the arts and why. Create a statement describing your choice and tell how it fits with your philosophy of education.

5. **Add to your journal**
   a. Consider your background in the arts. What formal and informal experiences did you have as a child? Were they positive or negative? Think about your current participation in the arts. What experiences influenced this participation? Consider how this affects your disposition toward teaching the arts.

6. **Consult the standards**
   a. Locate a set of standards that relates to the arts or aesthetic learning. Read through the standards and select one or two that apply to the age group that you teach. Decide how you could use these to plan an art activity for young children. The standards referred to in this chapter (CNAEA, 1994; MENC, 1994) are available online at the ArtsEdge website: http://artsedge.kennedy-center.org/teach/standards/

Others to use:

Mid-Continent Research in Education and Learning (MCREL). (2005). *PreK–12 Standards: Keys to Learning.* Aurora, CO: Author. www.mcrel.org

Kendall, J. S., & Marzano, R. J. (2004). *Content Knowledge: A Compendium of Standards and Benchmarks for K–12 Education.* Aurora, CO: MCREL. www.mcrel.org

CTB/McGraw-Hill. (2003). *Pre-K Standards.* New York: Author. www.ctb.com

PRACTICE FOR YOUR CERTIFICATION OR LICENSURE EXAM

The following items will help you practice applying what you have learned in this chapter. They can help to prepare you for your course exam, the PRAXIS II exam, your state licensure or certification exam, and for working in developmentally appropriate ways with young children.

Aesthetic Development and the Curriculum

1. Constructed-response question

   A teacher in the second grade is doing a unit on farm animals. She plans an art activity in which children are to trace a shape of a sheep, cut it out, and then glue cotton balls on it.

   a. Based on your knowledge of children's aesthetic development, describe three ways this lesson could be improved.

   b. Describe why you would make the changes you suggest.

2. Multiple-choice question

   What is the least effective strategy for implementing a music activity with young children?

   a. Look like you are enjoying singing and being with the children.
   b. Start the song and expect the children to follow along.
   c. Know the song well.
   d. Use visuals and props.

Chapter
10

The Affective Domain

You may wonder:

How do emotions develop in young children?

How do children develop self-awareness and a secure sense of self?

What is emotional intelligence? Can I foster it in my classroom?

How can I help children who are not coping well with stress to develop greater resilience?

Is affective development different in children who have special needs?

In this chapter we present information to help answer your questions about the affective domain. Learning about one's **emotions**, understanding another person's feelings, acquiring a concept of self, and developing self-efficacy are hallmarks of the affective domain. Consider these children:

◆ ◆ *The preschoolers at Franklin School have been following a picture chart that tells them step-by-step how to proceed from washing their hands to getting snack to cleaning up. By mid-November, most of the children are able to follow the routine from start to finish with only a few reminders. The teacher initiates an activity in which children reflect on their growing ability to "do snack" on their own. She also mentions the children's increasing independence in a newsletter home to families.*

◆ ◆ *The children in Mr. Kent's classroom are debriefing about the student-led conferences that were held the day before:*

"I liked when I showed my parents the room," shares Ian.

"Yeah, and my dad said he could see I was a lot better in math than the last conference. I was such a baby then!" notes Nicole.

"I think we should do this again next week!" says Jorge excitedly.

Mr. Kent grins broadly and tells the class, "You all practiced introducing your parents to me, and every one of you remembered to do it—every single one of you! You helped make this conference a big success."

◆ ◆ *In Ms. Roehlpartan's first-grade classroom, the children have just viewed a DVD on space rockets, and she has invited them to draw pictures of a rocket and create a story. She reminds them to put their names and the date on their pictures so that today's work can be saved in their writing portfolios. As she draws near to watch Michael, he glances up at her and then quickly covers the poorly scrawled name he has written in the upper left corner. He keeps his name covered, covertly watching until she moves on and only then withdrawing his hand. Mrs. Roehlpartan realizes that 6-year-old Michael is ashamed of his efforts to print and uncomfortable in having her see it. She thinks, "I've got to address this situation, but I will need to do it sensitively."*

In educational settings in which professionals take an active role in supporting children's affective development, we can see numerous examples of their efforts: a teacher comforting a preschooler who is distressed that her mother has left, a principal talking with worried children about their teacher who has been hospitalized, a teacher offering genuine praise to a child who has worked carefully through a challenging math story problem, and a teacher helping a child develop an oral script that might assist the child in entering a play group of peers.

Such educators recognize that facilitating emotional health and resilience in young children begins with establishing a warm and supportive school and classroom environment. In addition, they know they must actively build components into the everyday curriculum that promote children's growth in managing intense feelings and emotions, understanding others' feelings, becoming self-aware, making personal decisions, and handling stress. Emotional development is obviously complex and hugely important in whether or not children learn to communicate well with others, develop personal insight and assertiveness, learn self-acceptance, and take personal responsibility (Lantieri, 2008). Teachers play a major part in this process.

EMERGENCE OF THE EMOTIONAL SELF

Learning appropriate ways to express every aspect of their personality is one of the most complex jobs young children have. Children work daily on refining their self-help and social skills, mastering unfamiliar tasks, exploring their emotions, and coping with tensions. The stage for their being able to develop these skills is set in early infancy and continues throughout the early childhood years and beyond.

Erik Erikson aptly labeled the earliest developmental stage from birth to approximately 12–18 months as "Trust vs. Mistrust" (see Table 10.1) and then described additional stages that emerge in a cumulative fashion in the early years from birth to age 12 and thereafter. He theorized that human development ranges on a continuum characterized by opposite emotional poles in each of the stages. During all stages, human beings have a central task on which to work and need guidance and support from key others in their lives. When children are mostly successful in moving through these various stages, their overall affective development tends to fall toward the positive emotional pole; conversely, when they are unable to successfully resolve conflict and tensions that arise between the emotional extremes, development is likely to fall toward the negative emotional pole. This affects future resolution of emotional tensions. It should be noted that successful task completion during a particular stage does not guarantee that children will sail through subsequent stages or challenging events later on in life; however, they are less vulnerable and more resilient when they have developed the competencies demanded at each of the stages.

"Phillip, you look pretty glum, today," noted his teacher.
"My mom said we're moving to Kansas," Phillip shared. "It's really far away, and I don't want to go. If I do, I'll miss everyone here at school, but I have to," he lamented. "The only good thing is that my Grandma and Grandpa Selby live there."
"It sounds as if this is something that's causing both unhappy and happy feelings at the same time," said his teacher, "but that your feelings right now are mostly sad."

Not until middle elementary school do children begin to understand that such events as their parents' divorce or moving to another town can cause both positive emotions and negative emotions and that people can hold contrasting feelings simultaneously about other persons, objects, or situations. However, even with this understanding, children may experience considerable confusion and a sense of anxiety about not having a clear-cut response (Kostelnik et al., 2009).

TABLE 10.1   Erikson's Stage Theory of Emotional Development

Age	Stage	Developmental Task	Key Relationships
Infancy–18 months	Trust vs. Mistrust	Establish a trusting relationship with a primary caregiver, to develop trust in self, others, and the world as a place where needs are met	Primary caregiver, usually the mother
18 months–3 years	Autonomy vs. Shame and Doubt	Strive for independence	Parents/family caregivers
3–6 years	Initiative vs. Guilt	Plan and carry out activities; learn society's boundaries	Family caregivers
6–12 years	Industry vs. Inferiority	Be productive and successful	Teachers/peers
12–20 years	Identity vs. Role Confusion	Establish social and occupational identities	Peers
20–40 years	Intimacy vs. Isolation	Form strong friendships and achieve a sense of love and companionship	Friends/lovers/spouse/partner
40–65 years	Generativity vs. Stagnation	Be productive in terms of family and work	Spouse/partner/children/culture
65+ years	Ego Integrity vs. Despair	Look back at life as meaningful and productive	Family/friends/society

Source: Information from Kostelnik, M. J., Whiren, A. P., Soderman, A. K., & Gregory, K. (2009). *Guiding children's social development: Theory to practice* (6th ed.). Albany, NY: Delmar.

Children younger than 10 years generally do not associate the *source* of their emotions with what happens in their minds. Rather, there is a more simplistic and direct linking of their emotional state to their physical state of being. If they miss a parent or are hungry, tired, or injured, they perceive emotions such as sadness, irritability, anger, or fearfulness as directly resulting from the situation rather than from what they *think* about the situation or how to interpret it. They are also unaware that a person can feel certain emotions internally but mask them externally. Thus, children at this stage of emotional development may not be alert for subtle cues in others' responses to them when their social behavior is inappropriate or "thoughtless."

Children pay a great deal of attention to how key adults in their lives respond to their negative emotions. If our response to a simple tumble is relaxed, they quickly get back into the play. However, if their emotions run more deeply and we ignore them, respond with a lack of empathy, or deny their feelings ("It's nothing!), children may begin to doubt themselves, fail to share their deeper emotions again with others, and even become disconnected from their emotions. When they lose the capacity to share how they are feeling with others, they lose a critical coping strategy. Also, because our gut-level negative emotions (fear, anxiety, dread, dismay, panic, suspicion, and wariness) serve to inform us of danger and the need to be vigilant, children who learn to keep their emotions inside also lose an important coping tool (Ginsburg, 2006).

Developing **empathy**, or the ability to understand another person's feelings by feeling the same emotion, is a critical component of emotional development. This calls for being able to imagine what a person must be feeling like and demonstrating caring, compassion, and altruism when we see that others are hurt, troubled, or need help. Even toddlers demonstrate concern when they see another child upset, a parent not feeling well, or someone who has been hurt. Teachers are effective in helping young children develop this important sense of others when they model empathy and caring behavior, describe actions they are taking to comfort someone else, acknowledge and label children's feelings ("Sophie is sad because her cat ran away yesterday. I think she needs a hug."), and encourage children to help one another in the classroom (Epstein, 2009).

SELF-AWARENESS AND SENSE OF COMPETENCE

The children in Betty Wescott's kindergarten class are busy making "business cards," an activity she created so that children would learn to write their last names as well as their first names. She tells them to begin thinking about cleaning up to go out for recess in 5 minutes. "Awwww," says Guiliano. "We're working. We have to finish. Then we can go out."

"Right!" agrees Eamonn. "When we're done, then we can go."

Each day of a child's life is filled with interactions with others, which may be more or less successful. Each incident provides children with a mini-lesson, building **self-awareness** about who they are and how others see them. Five-year-old Brian's reluctance to join in with other children is seen by his teacher as a need to build social strategies; to his father, it is a source of irritation and "sissiness." The second graders in Mrs. Milan's class mostly sit in silence when she is not speaking and wait to respond to her directions. Conversely, those in the second-grade classroom down the hall are encouraged by their teacher to be independent, to be self-reliant, and to rely on their own thinking as much as possible (Gestwicki, 2010). Cumulatively, these isolated but potent forces result in children's building an internal picture of themselves as capable and valued or as inept and relatively unimportant.

Like everything else in an organism, an individual's concept of self develops and changes during the life span; however, evidence indicates that a person's **global self-concept**—all the beliefs a person has about him- or herself—is structured fairly early in life and appears to be well developed by the time a child is 8 or 9 years old. Components of the self—one's perceptions about how competent one is intellectually, physically, emotionally, and so forth—are known as **self-esteem**. These evolve from children's many interactions with others, the demands that are placed on them, and the emotions that result from these experiences.

For children experiencing day-to-day encouragement to actively explore in a safe, supportive, high-quality environment, increased confidence and competence are likely to be the outcome. For example, before leaving for the day, Kendal shares work she's completed at school that day with her teacher who takes time to point out positive aspects: "You're really enjoying writing. Your stories are your own creation, and look here—you've learned to put in adjectives. That's a big step." In this way, children come to understand themselves. They know who they are, what they can do, what they *want* to do, how to react to things, which things to avoid, and which things to gravitate toward.

Children who develop healthy self-esteem have an accurate mental image of self. Rather than being self-absorbed, narcissistic, and craving attention from others, they have a realistic sense of self-efficacy and competence. This comes from genuine feedback, respect, and support from the adults in their lives as well as opportunities to reflect on their behavior and accomplishments (Epstein, 2009).

Feelings of self-worth are reflected in a child's overt behavior in the classroom, in the peer group, and on the playground. Clues and patterns that indicate whether a child is experiencing low self-esteem are substantiated in children's negative self-statements ("I'm rotten at this!" "I can never get anything right!"); elaborate defenses to protect a fragile ego ("I didn't even want to be chosen because I hate kickball!"); problematic behavior (unrealistic fear, unjustified anger, continued lying, conceit, overconcern with past or future); avoidance of play, projects, or working with others; or lack of interest in appearance, cleanliness, and care of possessions.

Children's perceptions of themselves are the result of a mirroring process as they interact with important others in their world. High self-esteem comes from:

❑ Realizing that others like your ideas and will follow your lead
❑ Being warmly accepted as a person in your own world
❑ Peoples' willingness to listen and take you seriously
❑ Feeling that other people enjoy being with you
❑ Being acknowledged and appreciated for exactly who you are
❑ Doing things that you find interesting and important
❑ Knowing that you can trust people to be concerned about your feelings and needs
❑ Experiencing time and time again, year in and year out, that the important people in your life take time just for you—to listen, to explain things, to relax with you, to share confidences, to find moments every day in which friendship can flourish (Roberts, 2006).

By the time they are ready for kindergarten, many 5-year-olds have developed a sense of how others value their efforts to explore ideas, carry out plans, gain information, and master new skills. Children who have developed a strong sense of initiative enjoy gaining increased competence. They seek ways to use their energy in appropriate and constructive ways and take pride in cooperating with others in skill-building activities. Conversely, children who have experienced less nurturing care in the early stages of development are less likely to initiate activity on their own or be successful in ventures to do so. They may have problems related to task completion, and these children often demonstrate less ability in problem solving or decision making. They may hang back in play or act so aggressively that they fail to establish meaningful friendships. For example, a 4-year-old boy who had grown bored watching his mother try on eyeglass frames in an optometrist's office began teasing a little girl standing by her mother, who was also trying on frames. Even though his behavior became highly inappropriate and annoying to others, his mother ignored what he was doing. At one point, the small girl said to the child, "You're bad!" Surprisingly, the tone of her voice brought an abrupt stop to his teasing. He looked confused for a minute and then went to his mother to report the affront.

"She said I'm bad," he complained.

"Well, you *are* bad," said his mother, not even looking at him. The long-term effect of this kind of response on a child's self-image is unfortunately predictable, especially when it is combined with little or no effort to provide him with more appropriate behavioral skills.

As primary-age children develop a more sophisticated intellectual capacity, they become better equipped to evaluate their social skills and status in light of others' behavior and expectations. In developing a consolidated sense of themselves, children watch others' compliance and transgressions and the consequential approval or disapproval of such behavior. They listen to evaluations of their actions and others' actions and begin to formulate a rudimentary understanding of others' desires, beliefs, and emotions.

When the children in Ms. Brennan's room get ready for snack, they each have a job to do. Some wash tables, some distribute cups, plates, and napkins, and some place food on serving plates after washing their hands. Everyone waits to eat until all have gathered, and each pours from the small pitchers she's made available. All children clear their own places and can do so without reminders now. "What an independent and responsible team you are!" declares Ms. Brennan today.

From the preschool years until preadolescence, children are absorbed with developing responsibility and living up to the reasonable expectations of people with whom they have contact. They learn that doing so requires effort on their part and that making poor choices about following through on such tasks as homework and household chores results in others' disappointment or disdain.

To the extent that children feel free to assert themselves in everyday interactions with peers, teachers, parents, and others and are reinforced for efforts at skill building and successful accomplishments, they develop a positive attitude about learning. When their efforts are discouraged, ignored, or short-circuited by others, a sense of inferiority results, which causes them to veer away from challenges and responsibilities or to behave in a hostile and socially inappropriate manner. These behaviors, although frustrating to professionals working with these children, are simply natural defensive mechanisms in youngsters who have experienced significant contact with others who are largely insensitive to and unsupportive of their developmental needs. Although most educators empathically recognize the root cause of such behavior, the conduct of poorly nurtured children is often disruptive and time consuming. It has a negative impact on their progress and interferes with other children's progress. As a result, professionals sometimes find themselves feeling some ambivalence toward these children who are so difficult to manage on a day-to-day basis.

Concepts of Emotional Intelligence

Helping young children develop good social and emotional skills early in life predicts their long-term emotional health and well-being. They are less vulnerable later on to school failure, depression, violence, drug and alcohol abuse, and other serious mental health problems.

Daniel Goleman (1997), author of *Emotional Intelligence*, suggests that without forming the concrete skills required to identify and manage our emotions, we are less well equipped to communicate effectively with others. When children have trouble making solid connections between their feelings and thinking, they are less able to resolve conflicts in a nonviolent way, be empathic toward others, or remain optimistic in the face of setbacks. Their ability to operationalize intrapersonal intelligence—that is, becoming emotionally "smart"—results in greater happiness, confidence, and capability. They are nicer to be around, more likely to make friends, and more likely to *be* a friend to others. Five basic sets of skills constitute **emotional intelligence** (see Table 10.2). When taught and mastered, they are beneficial in every avenue of a child's life (Lantieri, 2008; Elias, 2006).

> *Hiro demonstrates extremely high emotional intelligence. At age 5, he attends a dual-immersion preschool which has almost equal numbers of children whose primary language is Spanish or English. Fluent in both, he frequently and spontaneously offers help to new children entering the classroom who cannot speak one of the languages and helps them enter play with other children. "Hiro is my secret weapon," laughs his teacher.*

TABLE 10.2 Basic Skills for Emotional Intelligence

Skill Set	Emotional Intelligence Component
Self-Awareness	The ability to identify your thoughts, feelings, and strengths; understanding and recognizing how thoughts, feelings, and strengths influence your choices and actions
Social Awareness	The capacity to recognize and understand others' thoughts and feelings; developing empathy; ability to take the perspective of others
Self-Management	The ability to manage your emotions so that they facilitate rather than interfere with the task at hand; setting long- and short-term goals; dealing with obstacles that may come your way
Responsible Decision Making	The skill to generate, implement, and evaluate positive and informed solutions to problems; tendency to consider the long-term consequences of your actions for yourself and others
Relationship Skills	The ability to resist negative peer pressure and to resolve conflicts in such a way that you maintain healthy and rewarding connections with individuals and groups

Sources: Elias, M. J. (2006). "The connection between academic and social-emotional learning." In M. J. Elias and H. Arnold., *The Educator's Guide to Emotional Intelligence and Academic Achievement.* Thousand Oaks, CA: Corwin Press.

As in every other developmental domain, children are active in constructing a knowledge base they will use in every internal and external operation related to their emerging emotional structures. Included are the following:

- ❏ *Physical Knowledge* With adult guidance, children become increasingly aware of their tendencies to react and behave under certain conditions and gain awareness about their dispositions, capabilities, and abilities (Who am I? What do I feel and under what circumstances? When do I feel valued, secure, and most comfortable? When are the times that I feel most uncomfortable and who am I with during those times?).
- ❏ *Logical-mathematical knowledge* Along with increasing cognition, children develop the logical organization to deal with incoming affective information (How am I like others? How am I different from others?) and to recognize and contrast the distinct and recurrent patterns in their behavior and that of others.
- ❏ *Representational knowledge* This increases as children learn new ways to express their inner emotional thoughts and feelings through the increased use of speech as language develops, through the refined use of body language, and through written expression as literacy skills emerge.
- ❏ *Social conventional knowledge* Here, children are intensely interested in learning more about how others view them; what the rules and boundaries are for socially acceptable ways of behaving; and more about gender, ethnicity, and interpersonal applications. Children copy behaviors they see that others use successfully to get what they need or want and discard other behaviors, which they perceive are not valued by others.
- ❏ *Metacognitive knowledge* Children increase their metacognitive abilities by putting their sensory channel modalities to work to investigate emotional cause and effect. As they do so, they grow in their conscious conceptualization of their emotional strength and limitations (self-awareness, self-esteem, self-concept), develop better instincts about themselves and others, and acquire strategies to affect their emotions and those of others. For example, Patrick is a child who develops friends easily and has a well-developed sense of fairness. Recently, when a classmate was having a tough time learning to work a yo-yo, several of the other children laughed. Patrick said sternly to his peers, "No laughing! He's trying, and it's hard." Patrick is able to put himself in the place of his struggling classmate and also has the courage to challenge and effectively stem the potentially hurtful behavior of others.

Stress and Resilience: How Children React to Overwhelming Emotional Demand

All the aspects of affective development discussed so far, in combination with the quality of care the child experiences, result in a child's ability to cope with perceived demands in the environment. Some children have little ability to bounce back from negative experiences, whereas others seem to have tremendous resilience.

Coping with "Normal Life Stressors"

Children experience emotional demands from any number of sources (see Table 10.3). When stressful situations persist for long periods and when the child is unable to experience relief, symptoms may appear, such as increased irritability, depression, anxiety, sleep disturbances, somatic problems, or a dramatic increase or decrease in appetite. Highly stressed children *look* stressed. Significant and long-standing tension may manifest in the quality of speech, as dark circles under the eyes, in the child's posture, and occasionally in compulsive behaviors. When a child is unable to cope, behavioral disorders and increased psychological vulnerability may result. We see this in mental and conduct disorders, school failure, and psychosomatic illness.

Children in Toxic and Violent Environments

You may find that one or more children in your classroom are experiencing fairly traumatic childhoods in home situations that you cannot change; also, some may be experiencing horrendous situations that they choose to keep secret but that clearly manifest themselves in the child's ability to

TABLE 10.3 Examples of Childhood Stressors

Type of Stressor	Examples of Potential Sources of Stress
Individual Stressors	Disabling conditions
	Inadequate or unbalanced diet
	Difficult personality
	Unreasonable push to grow up and be independent of adult support
	Lack of exercise to release tension or be fit
	Too many extracurricular activities
	Heavy exposure to television; unmonitored use of video games, television
Intrafamilial Stressors	Birth of a sibling
	Death of a loved one or pet
	Parents change of job or heavy involvement in work
	Moving to a new home or place
	Marital transition of parents
	Poverty
	Abuse, neglect
Extrafamilial Stressors	Unsatisfactory child care
	Poor match between child's developmental levels and school's expectations
	Lack of appreciation of cultural differences by others
	Negative peer relationship at school or in neighborhood
	Birthday parties or sleepovers at someone else's home
	Unsafe factors in the community
	Fast-paced society in which children live

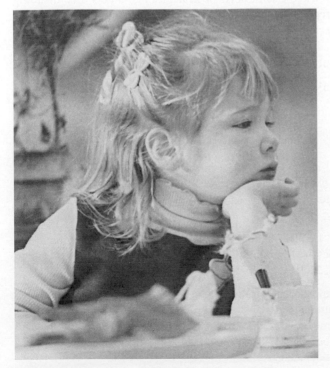

Stress can overwhelm children as well as adults.

trust or relate well to others. In Figure 10.1, consider the testimony of an adult who was a first or second grader in *someone's* classroom while living in a situation where genuine terror was commonly experienced.

Accumulating evidence from studies of adults who suffered such childhoods conclude that these early negative experiences appear to be woven into the individual's very soul, sometimes for life, and that the journey to health is a long and difficult one. Perhaps a child will be making a part of that journey in your classroom. Many individuals who remember particularly painful family experiences when they were children identify teachers as those who were helpful in their being able to survive and transcend horrific situations.

James Garbarino (2008) writes about children worldwide who have had encounters with natural disasters such as a hurricane like Katrina, wars, terrorist incidences, and community brutality (e.g., drive-by and school shootings). He details the lives of untreated children who are abused or who watch the abuse of others, the effects of poverty, gender abuse, children growing up in homeless centers and detention camps, and those who exist in spiritual voids. While we consider these extreme situations, they must be acknowledged, no matter how uncomfortable they make us. Garbarino suggests that doing the "right thing" for children in these situations is often neither

FIGURE 10.1   Continuing Memories of a Painful Childhood

I'm not sure where to start. I remember once sitting at the dinner table, getting ready to eat and my sister was to say grace, so she started and my dad slapped her across the face. He told her she was wrong and to do it over. She started again and he slapped her again. This went on over and over, faster and faster for what seemed like a half hour. I remember sitting there (I was about 6 or 7), across from her; I was paralyzed. I just kept praying, "Get it right." The problem was, she was doing it right, just the way we learned it in Sunday school. I wanted to help her, but I was so scared and so small. She had long blonde hair. . . . It kept flying back and forth when he hit her across the face, then it would stick to her tears; her face was so red.

   Apparently my brother told him to stop, but Dad said to sit down or else. My sister has quickly pointed out that "he stood up for me." I think she wanted me to do something. What could I do?

simple nor easy, "not intellectually, not emotionally." Children everywhere should be ensured of the fundamental rights to grow up feeling safe, to be protected from social toxicity, abuse, war, and political violence, and to be freed from the morally destabilizing effects of poverty.

   Without additional help, children who are unable to cope effectively will barely be able to benefit from what is going on in the classroom academically and socially. Nor do children necessarily benefit from a teacher offering quick fixes, dictating "appropriate" responses, or pushing them to talk when they are not ready to do so. Helping the child to replace ineffective strategies calls for a patient and carefully planned approach from the teacher who utilizes many of the guidelines suggested subsequently in this chapter. When additional focused attention and support are not helpful, other professionals need to be drawn in to help the child modify his or her emotional upset and responses.

Developing Resilience

Evidence indicates that children who are most effective in coping with *normal* stressors (e.g., getting up and dressing in time for the school bus, being disappointed once in a while, or being left out of a play opportunity) learn how to cope with the larger issues. Also, children who can find or generate more alternatives for coping usually do much better and build confidence in managing stressful situations.

   In coping with stressors, children use the same sorts of strategies that adults use, including such defense mechanisms as denial, regression, withdrawal, and impulsive acting out. However, as is true for adults, these behaviors in children are clear-cut signs that they need additional or different skills in perceiving or dealing adequately with a situation. Other red flags that signal that children are out of coping strategies include (Ginsburg, 2006):

❏ Problems in completing school work
❏ Not wanting to attend school
❏ Sleep problems
❏ Age-inappropriate behavior
❏ Outbursts and tantrums
❏ Changes in eating habits
❏ Isolation/withdrawal
❏ Inability to make or maintain friends
❏ Physical symptoms

   How can we determine whether a child is emotionally healthy? Even when children seem troubled, the chances are good that they are functioning in a healthy manner if they are able to do the following (Hendrick & Weissman, 2009):

❏ Work on emotional tasks that are appropriate for their age
❏ Depart from their family without undue stress
❏ Form an attachment with at least one other adult in the setting
❏ Learn to conform to routines without undue fuss
❏ Become deeply involved in play
❏ Settle down and concentrate

❑ Interact with others in an appropriate and nonaggressive way
❑ Access a full range of feelings and deal with them in an age-appropriate way

We can expect that there will be occasional bumps in the road in terms of any child's emotional health and development. Even so, children vary significantly in their abilities to cope with challenging environments and events. Some recover quickly from adversity, seemingly with no leftover adverse affects. Others do not demonstrate this kind of buoyancy and need to develop additional resilience.

Resilience is not the same as invulnerability. It is the "capacity to rise above difficult circumstances, the trait that allows us all to exist in this less-than-perfect world while moving forward with reasonable optimism and confidence. Blanketing children with protection while reinforcing their strengths requires our belief in the following concepts" (Ginsburg, 2006).

❑ To be strong, children need unconditional love, absolute security, and a deep connection to at least one adult.
❑ Children live up or down to adults' expectations of them.
❑ Listening to children attentively is more important than any words adults can say. This applies to routine situations as well as times of crisis.
❑ Nothing adults say is as important as what children see them doing on a daily basis.
❑ Children can only take positive steps when they have the confidence to do so. They gain that confidence when they have solid reasons to believe they are competent.
❑ If children are to develop the strength to overcome challenges, they need to know that they can control what happens to them.
❑ Children with a wide range of positive coping strategies will be prepared to overcome almost anything and far less likely to try many of the risk behaviors that adults fear.

Evidence suggests that teachers can build better resilience in young children by using the following six strategies in their early childhood classrooms.

1. *Build in more opportunities for play.* Play provides children with opportunities to problem solve, socialize, exercise leadership and following skills, and build communication skills. It allows them to engage in give-and-take with their peers and reduce tension. It also provides them with a chance to experiment with controlling people and objects. These abilities are key in determining whether a child builds the capacity to recover from conditions that might be predictive of failure.

2. *Modify children's difficult behavior without sending a message that the child is not okay.* This calls for helping children develop ways in which they can regulate their behavior and emotions as well as acknowledging their efforts and successes. If you find a child's behavior has become a growing source of irritation for yourself or others in the classroom, try to recast the behavior in a more positive light (Josh has a *lot* of energy!) in order to redirect your perspective and that of the child's peers in a more supportive direction.

3. *Teach them to become effective problem solvers, which translates into the power of independence.* Find a way to have conversations with each child about what he or she wants to accomplish and build steps needed to get there.

4. *Teach them ways to better express their thoughts, ideas, and feelings.* Discuss ways in which each child is unique and strong. Help them document those characteristics and then refer to such characteristics at times when they need additional support.

5. *Build rapport and connectedness in the classroom.* As much as possible, create within each child a spirit of being a special and valued member of the team. Along with this, help each child to increase his or her capacity for appreciating, caring for, and empathizing with others.

6. *Know what goes on in children's lives outside the classroom, what supports they have, and which ones they are missing.* Be willing to advocate for the kinds of interventions needed to reduce risk factors and increase protective factors.

Children want to be competent and recognized by others as competent. Educators can take advantage of this natural motivation of children by guiding them toward more fully integrated intrapersonal and interpersonal strengths. This calls for an adequate focus in your program on the development of self-awareness; cooperative relationships; mutual respect; and a climate of fairness, caring, and participation. In addition, educators in truly effective schools work closely with families and the community *before* children enter the formal system. These linkages with families must be maintained and strengthened as children move through the developmental tasks of early childhood and into adolescence and young adulthood.

AFFECTIVE DEVELOPMENT IN CHILDREN WITH SPECIAL NEEDS

*Ezra is a child with **Down syndrome**, a condition resulting from an extra copy of chromosome 21. When he first joined the kindergarten class at Willow Elementary School, he was rarely without his adult aide at his side. Now, in April, he has learned the routines well enough that he has become fairly independent. His friendship with his classmate Kyra has also been a supportive factor.*

Go to the Assignments and Activities section of Topic 2: Child Development and Learning in the MyEducationLab for your course and complete the activity entitled *Emotional Development among English Language Learners.* What do teachers need to consider in promoting the self-efficacy of English Language Learners in their classrooms?

The inclusion of children with special needs in early childhood programs was initially met with mixed reactions by professionals unfamiliar with children who have disabilities. However, with respect to supporting their emotional development, children with disabilities are similar in many respects to children without disabilities. They need and want affiliations with others, nurturing relationships, and stimulating and enjoyable classroom experiences. A frequent error that educators make is to focus on the child's physical or cognitive progress and to forget that the child has affective needs as well.

Remember that earlier in this chapter, we outlined the critical components that promote feelings of self-worth in children. They have to know they are accepted and valued by others, that they are viewed as competent, and that they have control over important aspects of their life. Without additional support, children with special needs are exceptionally vulnerable in each of these areas.

Any number of childhood disorders may hamper affective development. Included are conditions categorized as *pervasive developmental disorders (PDDs),* which are not only marked impairments in social reciprocity and communication, but also behavioral abnormalities. These disorders may coexist with other disabilities such as mental retardation, inattention, hyperactivity, or epilepsy. Because there is such diversity in the numbers of conditions across and within disability categories, teachers in inclusion classrooms will be more successful when they work closely with special educators to identify the accommodations and modifications needed to support children with disabilities (Chamberlain, 2008). Following are a few of the more common special conditions experienced in the regular classroom.

Autism

Carrey, a preschooler who has been diagnosed with autism, often struggled in novel situations. If the school day was altered for the purpose of an assembly or if a substitute teacher showed up in his classroom, he often shrieked, paced, or crouched under his desk. His teachers tried everything from teaching relaxation techniques to reading Social Stories, to providing peer support and encouragement, but nothing seemed effective. Then Carrey's teacher, Ms. Soderberg, came up with a strategy that related to his area of fascination: James Bond films. When Carrey was struggling, Ms. Soderberg (or the substitute) would tell him, "Change is good. James Bond changes from Sean Connery to Roger Moore to Timothy Dalton to Pierce Brosnan to Daniel Craig, and each one is as good, if not better, than the next!" Carrey agreed with the statement but still had a hard time dealing with change in the moment. His teachers taught him the strategy of chanting all the actors in the order they played Bond, to bring his anxiety under control. The chant went something like this: "Change is okay. Something new can be just as good if not better. Connery, Moore, Dalton, Brosnan, Craig." Other students in his class knew the chant, too, and whispered it to Carrey or with him in difficult moments.

—Kluth & Schwarz, 2008

Autism is the most widely known PDD. Children with autism may exhibit such behaviors as repetitive motor mannerisms (e.g., hand or finger flapping), persistent preoccupation with parts of objects, a delay in language development or repetitive use of language, lack of make-believe or socially initiated play, lack of eye contact, and failure to develop peer relationships (American Psychiatric Association [DSM-IV-TR], 2000).

One critical goal is to teach skills that extend the child's ability to interact well with others and adapt in social situations. Children with autism may not demonstrate appropriate facial expressions to match the situation at hand or their expressions and emotional reactions to events may be more extreme than their peers. They may also be oblivious to the feelings or intentions of others. It's important to teach other children in the class how to initiate social interaction with children with autism and to try again if the child ignores them at first.

Most important in this arena, children with autistic disorders need to understand that behavior carries meaning. They will likely need help in modifying socially inappropriate gestures; building communication skills; establishing daily routines; and extinguishing negative, destructive, or aggressive behaviors that cause others to reject them. Finally, they need teachers who are willing to gain access to information and the increasing numbers of helpful materials being developed for teachers dealing with behavioral difficulties in young children.

Professionals working with children who exhibit autistic behaviors have better outcomes when they ease the child into new situations, strategize to capture the child's attention without forcing it, teach and model social and play skills purposefully, redirect swiftly by giving clear verbal signals, and distract the child away from negative behaviors, fixations, and withdrawal from others by encouraging involvement in more acceptable activity (Kostelnik et al., 2009).

Attention Deficit Hyperactivity Disorder

Mrs. Emmons, 7-year-old Phillip's second grade teacher, is aware of his history of being disruptive, not following directions, blurting out silly comments, and moving from activity to activity without any focus. She realizes that she cannot completely erase Phillip's low frustration tolerance and inability to recognize the consequences of his behavior. However, she is committed to stemming further failure as much as possible. She notes, "Both Phillip and I have learned a lot about ADHD this year. It's not always easy, but it's not big enough to lick either one of us, either."

Attention deficit hyperactivity disorder (ADHD) other neurobiological syndromes that appear in early childhood may have pervasive and long-lasting negative effects on affective and social development. Researchers believe that in 80 percent of the cases of ADHD, the disorder results from heredity rather than negative parenting or poverty (although these factors may further complicate the condition). These impairments often lead to academic underachievement and problems with adaptive skills in daily living, with communication, and with the social skills necessary for self-sufficiency. Children with ADHD are more vulnerable to peer rejection and are at increased risk for physical abuse because of their difficult behaviors. So that their chances for success are increased, they need to be in classrooms in which teachers are knowledgeable about behavior management strategies and coaching—and can deliver such help sensitively and in age-appropriate ways to help children build self-confidence and self-management skills. Close communication and coordination with the child's family is also critical (Batshaw, Pellegrino, & Roizen, 2007).

Sensory Processing Disorders

Aurora is 5 years old. She refuses to eat snacks and the lunches that are offered at school, and it is obvious that the smell of certain foods is actually offensive to her. She often slouches across the table when involved in tasks and must be reminded to sit up in large group where she prefers sprawling on the floor. She often refuses to participate in outdoor activities that many of her classmates enjoy, preferring to spend her time day after day on the swings. Her parents find her behavior frustrating and feel guilty and embarrassed that they have had little success in "handling her better." Her teacher finds her disruptive, challenging, and "immature." Both her parents and her teacher feel they are failing to make any difference in Aurora's behavior and that it's time to consult a professional who can help them better understand this self-absorbed, nonadaptive, and disorganized little girl.

Sometimes referred to as "out-of-sync" or "sensory sensitive," children with **sensory processing disorders** may exhibit overresponsiveness or underresponsiveness to touch or movement, sound, sights, taste, or smell. They may be highly sensitive to certain tactile experiences—labels in their clothing, having their hair combed, brushing their teeth, lighting, colors, and certain tactile activities. They may have difficulty in gauging the strength of their movements or recognizing personal space. This may be a child who is constantly in motion or one who moves through the day mostly in a dreamlike state, showing little interest in the world or people around her. Children with sensory processing disorders are inclined toward awkward posture, seem careless, and are frequently accident prone. Though the problem is connected to a central nervous system tendency to misinterpret or fail to pick up on sensory messages, the condition often goes undiagnosed or is frequently misdiagnosed. Two resources can be extremely helpful to classroom professionals in terms of recognizing symptoms, understanding what can go amiss, evaluation, and treatment: C. S. Kranowitz's *The Out-of-Sync Child* (New York: The Berkley Publishing Group, 2006); and K. A. Smith and K. R. Gouze's *The Sensory Sensitive Child* (New York: HarperCollins Publishers, 2004). Included in their suggestions are the following helpful tips:

❑ See the child's problems and behaviors through a sensory lens to better understand what the child is experiencing.
❑ Establish good rapport with the child so that there is good will between the two of you, which aids in working out difficulties.
❑ Provide large amounts of genuine praise to counterbalance praise/criticism ratios. Be specific about the child's accomplishment so the child will know what behaviors to continue.
❑ Pick your battles and turn down the "emotional heat." Sensory sensitivity interferes with children's ability to regulate their emotions and their behavior. Younger children need extra support as they develop strategies for internal control.
❑ Monitor your thoughts about the child's behavior. Negative thoughts about why the child cannot be more cooperative only serve to arouse your anger, impatience, and sense of hopelessness. Try to think of the child with a sensory processing disorder as doing his or her best and disappointment about relapses as a signal to identify a still-missing piece of the puzzle.
❑ Structure "chill-outs" rather than "time-outs" for both the child and yourself. Find a way to give a highly frustrated child additional space or a way to calm down, using a neutral, nonjudgmental voice. Remove yourself from a conversation that is going nowhere, and provide these chill-outs *before* things get too emotionally hot, if possible.
❑ Plan ahead and stick to a routine as much as possible. Because they often feel so internally disorganized, children with sensory processing problems may need external organization more than other children in your classroom.
❑ Empathize with the child's parents who are confronted daily with the incompatibility of the child's sensitivities and other family members' needs, habits, and personalities (Smith & Gouze, 2004).

English Language Learners

Sue Yeun, a kindergartner at Wilkshire Elementary, has come from Seoul, South Korea, and has been in the United States for only 3 months. An English language learner, she spends much of her time at the writing center on her own, where she practices drawing pictures of her cat and writing its name in Korean. She is sometimes frustrated trying to express herself to children who do not share her language. In large group, Ms. Parr plans to read Helen Recorvits's My Name is Yoon, *a tale about a young Korean girl who prefers to write her name in Korean but is told by her father that she must learn to write in English. Ms. Parr has also gone a step further and has invited in a Korean student from the nearby university who will translate the text into Korean simultaneously so that Sue Yuen can understand this engaging story that is so close to her own situation.*

Few classrooms exist today that do not include children who are new to our country. Children who are **English language learners (ELLs)** have special needs in terms of their English language deficits and cultural differences. Providing optimal emotional support and learning opportunities for bilingual learners requires that professionals do the following:

❑ Reflect on their attitudes and perspectives toward linguistic and cultural diversity
❑ Learn more about the languages and cultures represented in their classrooms
❑ Monitor their behavior for direct or indirect behaviors that might indicate low expectations for linguistically diverse students

❑ Examine ways in which linguistically diverse students are assessed

❑ Examine their own culture and their students' culture with respect to family structure, life cycle, interpersonal role/relationships, discipline, time and space, religion, food, health/hygiene, and history/tradition/holidays (Otto, 2009)

Begin with the families of English language learners to gain information. What suggestions do they have for working with their children? Can they help you learn basic greetings and expressions to aid in communication with their child and them?

In supporting the English language learner in your classroom, make certain that you acknowledge that continued development of the child's primary language at home is important. Have patience while the child develops enough receptive language to begin using English; meanwhile, provide scripts and words the child can use to interact with others. Provide them with physical cues to know when their behavior is inappropriate or when you will be calling on them. Be thoughtful about pairing them up with other students in the classroom in cooperative learning opportunities. If possible, use interpreters from the community who can help the child with initial acclimatization. Review the materials you are using to see if they acknowledge the diversity that is reflected in the children who are participating in your classroom (Santos, 2004).

CURRENT EDUCATIONAL ISSUES

Although everyone agrees that good emotional health is necessary for effective functioning and a positive quality of life, not everyone agrees that classroom teachers should be actively involved in guiding the development of children in this arena. Several issues form the basis of this opposition.

Including Affective Education in the Curriculum

Some parents in our school oppose having affective education included in the curriculum, saying that academic achievement should be the primary and only concern in an educational context and that affective development should be left as the legitimate province of the family.

This sort of attitude goes against not only a philosophical concern for the overall development of young children, but also the principles of DAP. Children are moving out of the family's care and into the extrafamilial arena earlier and earlier, with professionals in child-care centers and educational settings assuming increasing responsibility for nurturing children as well as educating and keeping them safe. Increasing numbers of children are coming into the school setting with poorly formed attachments. They are in need of both emotional resources and a warm, trusting relationship to correct the direction of their affective development. Richard Weissbourd, author of *The Vulnerable Child* (1997), identified school conditions necessary for children to find a capacity for work, love, and play. They need protection from destruction and prejudice, a continuous relationship with a consistently attentive and caring adult, opportunities in school and in the community for real achievement, and strong friendships with adults and other children.

Potential Lack of Professional Competence

I'm often being asked by parents for advice about guiding their child's emotional development at home. I usually feel competent in knowing what to suggest, but don't know if I should just recommend that they seek the advice of a child psychologist or counselor.

In the past and in particular institutions of higher learning, much of teacher training focused on academic content and methods, with only cursory attention to the affective and social domains. More attention was given to structuring consequences for negative behavior than to developing children's self-esteem or establishing a positive classroom climate in which to nurture emotional development. As a result, many beginning teachers felt ill-equipped to deal with children's affective and social problems and relied heavily on artificial methods for keeping children "under control." Rarely did they feel equipped to offer advice to parents.

Currently, program standards in early childhood education maintain that preservice teachers be trained to understand developmental sequences and to work with all children in a sensitive and supportive way. Teachers also learn strategies for intervention when children lack emotional stability and social skills and are made aware of the need to design an atmosphere of trust and experiences for children that will actively enhance positive development. Similarly, effective public school systems are providing in-service aid to teachers so that they can help children develop more positive self-esteem, find appropriate outlets for strong feelings, deal with natural and acquired fears, and learn conflict management. In short, affective development is not left purely to chance. In good early childhood programs, it is considered as important as academic aspects, and well-trained and sensitive teachers are viewed as critical. However, if you're ever unsure about how to respond to parents, be honest and recommend that they contact another professional.

Appropriate and Inappropriate Touch in Early Childhood Settings

I think that children in my classroom need occasional hugs and a lot of encouragement, but given some of the things I've seen in the newspaper today, I'm almost afraid to touch a child.

One issue frequently raised by educators about providing nurturance to children and satisfying their affective needs is the concern that hugging children, patting them on the back, or letting a young child sit on the teacher's lap could result in allegations of inappropriate contact. A number of wrongful accusations have caused administrators of many early childhood programs to take a defensive posture, which has led to taboos against any hugging, patting, or touching and has thereby shortchanged the children. As a way to avoid cutting out this essential aspect of a school program and to protect educators from precarious positions, some researchers have suggested that the need for a warm, caring relationship between the teacher and the children be fully communicated to parents and the community; that children be instructed about "good touch, bad touch." We agree that hugs, touches, and appropriate, short personal conversations are necessary, but they should be provided only when others are present.

Acquiring Self-Esteem: Can It Be Taught or Must It Be Developed?

Our school is thinking of instituting a purchased curriculum to develop self-esteem in children. I don't want to spend the half hour per day this would require, and believe that the overall emotional climate that I establish in my classroom will be more effective than this artificial approach.

Another major issue regarding the affective domain is the misconception that self-esteem is something that is provided for children—that simply giving children everything they want, frequently telling them how special they are, and engaging them in 15-minute sessions of self-esteem building endows them with healthy dollops of self-esteem that they can then draw on when it is needed during future challenges. This approach does not work. In fact, such an approach may negate children's understanding the relation among hard work, true accomplishment, and feelings of self-worth. Nongenuine praise and ignoring a lack of effort can diminish motivation in children. Young children are in the process of developing an internalized sense of others' values, and they will eventually compare or evaluate their worth against this standard. To create a context in which good self-esteem is nurtured, adults must take the time each day to observe children's real accomplishments and make sure to comment on them. They need to provide the guidance children need to develop internal control and make healthy choices. All this must take place in an atmosphere in which adults demonstrate warmth, respect, acceptance, authority, and empathy (Kostelnik et al., 2009). In addition to taking advantage of spontaneous opportunities to support children's emotional development, teachers will want to actively plan experiences to aid children's understanding and capabilities in this domain.

PURPOSE AND GOALS FOR AFFECTIVE DEVELOPMENT

Goals for affective development have been drawn from research and best practice for guiding children's emotional intelligence, resilience, and intrapersonal well-being.

Purpose

The purpose of affective development is for children to see themselves as valued and capable.

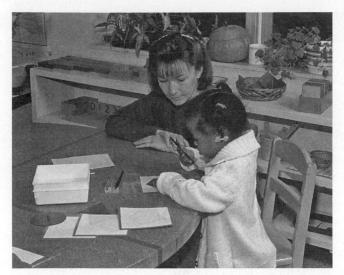

Give children adequate time and encouragement to finish tasks themselves.

Goals

As children progress, they will:

1. Demonstrate trust in others.
2. Identify emotions.
3. Acquire and use language to express their emotions.
4. Understand how circumstances and events influence personal emotions.
5. Make connections between their emotions, facial expressions, body language, and behavior.
6. Accept constructive criticism.
7. Understand they can affect how others feel, that people feel friendly toward those who act friendly toward them.
8. Learn satisfying and effective strategies for coping with personal emotions and tensions.
9. Regulate their emotions in a constructive manner when in emotionally charged situations.
10. Develop situational knowledge, identifying contextual cues to moderate and adjust their behavior.
11. Make reasonable attempts to master situations that are difficult for them.
12. Control their behavior without external reminders.
13. Recover aptly from setbacks and disappointments.
14. Increase their understanding of fair and unfair, right and wrong, kind and unkind behavior.
15. Demonstrate empathy for others.
16. Make choices and then experience the consequences of personal decisions.
17. Evaluate their accomplishments and set new standards and goals.
18. Demonstrate increasing awareness of the concepts of possession and ownership.
19. Assert their rights appropriately.
20. Demonstrate a growing ability to care for themselves, their personal belongings, and to meet their own needs.
21. Demonstrate care and respect for classroom materials.
22. Contribute to classroom maintenance.
23. Demonstrate increasing independence in using age-appropriate materials and tools.
24. Begin and pursue a task independently.
25. Complete a task they have begun.
26. Experience the pleasure of work.
27. Demonstrate knowledge of factors that contribute to quality work (i.e., time, care, effort, responsibility).
28. Identify characteristics and qualities that make them unique.
29. Explore similarities and differences among people as a way to gain personal insight.
30. Increase their knowledge, understanding, and appreciation of their cultural heritage.
31. Develop comfortable relationships beyond the family.
32. Demonstrate feelings of belonging and security in the school environment and community.
33. Value and use respectful language regarding gender, family, culture, abilities, and race.
34. Imagine and speak of future potential for themselves.

Before leaving this section, choose several goals in the affective domain. Refer to Table 10.1 at the beginning of the chapter, where we outlined Erikson's stage theory of emotional development. Which stage is supported by each goal? Are there goals for each of the first four stages?

AFFECTIVE TEACHING STRATEGIES

1. **Promote children's emotional awareness and sense of worth.** Talk with children about their emotions, even when it's not always comfortable to do so. Structure activities and experiences specifically to build awareness of situations and events that influence emotions (Brewer, 2007). Keep in mind that children aren't always certain why they're feeling as intensely as they are about an event. Help children learn to acknowledge and label their feelings as they participate in

MAKING GOALS FIT

As in other domains, we can use the same goal with different age groups of children or with children in varying stages of affective development. Table 10.4 is an example of how the goal, to begin and pursue a task independently (24), can be adapted to three different age groups.

TABLE 10.4 Beginning and Pursuing a Task Independently

Goal #24	Example of Activity for 3- to 4-Year-Olds	Example of Activity for 5- to 6-Year-Olds	Example of Activity for 7- to 8-Year-Olds
Begin and pursue a task independently	Upon entry into school each morning, hang coat in cubbie without a reminder; clear snack materials and push in chair before going outside; listen for clean-up song and help restore materials without being asked to do so.	During large-group time, listen carefully to instructions for small-group work; following large-group time, move to appropriate small group, gather needed materials, and maintain focus on task; ask for assistance from peer before asking teacher.	Understand directions for homework; gather needed materials before leaving school; follow through to complete assignment independently at home; return to school the next day, having completed the work in a quality manner; share accomplishments as appropriate with teacher and classmates.

classroom activities. "You look upset." "You're enjoying writing that story." "You want a chance for another turn." "You're disappointed you didn't get a turn yet," and so forth. Use a wide array of "feelings" words that represent variations on happy, mad, sad, and afraid. Be careful not to jump to conclusions about why children are feeling a certain way.

2. **Help children find satisfying ways to express their emotions to others and to assert themselves appropriately.** Assist children in identifying what other people look like and sound like when they are angry, not interested, or frustrated. Provide sample scripts to help children express their emotions and needs. For example, when a child needs to learn to express feelings to another child, he or she might be advised, "Tell Gemil, 'I don't like it when you grab things from me. I wasn't finished with the puppet. Please give it back to me.'" (See Figure 10.2 for additional scripts children can be taught to use.)

3. **Choose literature in which the characters respond to emotions in a variety of ways, and discuss how they felt and acted.** Primary-age children may be helped to express their feelings through writing. Select examples of literature that illustrate how children have written about their frustrations or stresses and learned to cope more effectively with them through writing. Have children dramatize situations in which anger or frustration is handled appropriately. Use puppets to model using language rather than hitting to express anger. With older children, model different responses to frustrations such as not winning a race or a game.

FIGURE 10.2 Scripts to Increase Children's Legitimate Assertive Behavior to Protect Property or Self

I'm not finished using this yet. You can have it later.
This is mine. It's not for sharing. Sorry.
Stop calling me names. I don't like it.
No, I won't give you this. I still need it.
No pushing!
Cutting in line is not allowed.
You forgot my turn.
We can't both use it at the same time. You can have it in a minute. Then I'll use it again when you're through.

4. Provide empathy for children's fears and concerns. These fears and concerns may be imagined (fear of monsters), realistic (fear that someone will make fun of them), or learned (apprehension about visiting the doctor). Familiarize yourself with information about children's fears, and provide a safe and supportive context in which children can gradually work through them. Help by acknowledging the child's discomfort and offering physical or spoken consolation.

5. Examine your own emotional reactions and how you model stress and problem solving to children when you are under pressure. Evaluate whether your sense of humor is alive and making the classroom a pleasurable place in which to spend time.

6. Help children develop greater self-understanding. Use the behavior and paraphrase reflections you learned in chapter 2 to make nonjudgmental observations about children's actions and words as a way to support children's growing self-awareness. For example: "You wrote a story about a magic rocket." "You are building a tall tower." "You used lots of colors in your painting." "You found a new way to solve that math problem."

7. Create activities in which children explore their physical and social qualities. Examples might include body tracings, self-portraits, autobiographical stories and sketches, projects around personal family traditions, or conversations in which children identify personal preferences and qualities (e.g., I like _____, or My favorite _____ is _____, or I feel unhappy when _____ occurs). Invite children to assess their personal qualities in relation to fictional or nonfictional literary characters (e.g., Curious George, Miss Rumphias, Benjamin Franklin, an astronaut); invite children to describe themselves in relation to a particular characteristic (talkative, quiet, energetic, assertive, curious, tolerant, patient), noting: "A lot like me, a little like me, not like me." Repeat this often, focusing on a variety of characteristics over time.

8. Document children's progress. Take photos of the children as they participate in classroom activities. Invite children to reflect on what they see in the photos and to create captions or narratives, describing what they are doing. Collect some products the children make, captioning these as well in the children's own words. Display documentation boards so children can refer to them and talk about projects they have carried out over time. Invite children to explain their work to others (e.g., peers, family members, older or younger students). Refer to Chapters 7 and 16 for further information about documentation.

9. Promote children's ability to meet age-appropriate expectations for self-discipline. Notice when children exhibit self-control (resisting temptation, controlling their impulses, delaying gratification, or carrying out proactive plans). Use positive consequences to bring these constructive behaviors to children's attention.

10. Be patient, firm, and objective when you are helping children modify their behavior. View children's inappropriate behavior as a gap in their knowledge or skills. Rather than expecting immediate change, identify steps in progress, giving children reinforcement when you see them trying to correct a particular behavior. Use subtle cues to remind children that their behavior is close to exceeding limits. When possible, allow children opportunities to assess the situation, determine what should be done, experience consequences, and modify their behavior in a positive direction. Model respectful interaction and a firm tone of voice when modifying children's behavior. Be careful to maintain objectivity in situations where children are in conflict with others, reflecting what you see and not how you feel about what you are observing.

11. Set effective limits with clearly defined expectations. Involve children in structuring classroom rules, and apply natural and logical consequences consistently when rules are not observed. See Chapter 6 for more information in this regard.

12. Never ignore difficult behaviors or problems such as lying, stealing, or cruelty to self or others. Watch for any bullying that goes on or for children who make fun of other children or isolate them from play. When children demonstrate a pattern of difficult behaviors and are unresponsive to your attempts to modify them using authoritative teaching methods, seek help by working with other professionals who have more specific expertise.

13. Establish an emotionally supportive, low-stress environment. Help children make smooth and comfortable transitions into the program. Establish a predictable schedule and provide a daily overview of the day's activities, including any changes in routine, notice of visitors, and so forth. Establish a stimulus-reduced area in which children who are seeking quiet can work. Balance quiet and active experiences so that children are not emotionally or physically overloaded. Evaluate the room for visual and auditory stimulation, as well as noise levels, lighting, and temperature.

14. **Enhance children's growing sense of autonomy and initiative by giving them frequent opportunities to make choices and decisions.**
    - ❏ Offer many different choices to children each day. Anticipate situations in which choices could be offered, and plan what those choices will be.
    - ❏ Take advantage of naturally occurring situations in which to offer choices. Ask children which side of the circle they would like to sit on or whether they would like to pass out the tambourines or the rhythm sticks.
    - ❏ Offer choices using positive statements. Give children acceptable alternatives rather than telling them what they cannot choose. It would be better to say, "You can use the blocks to make something like a road, a house, or a rocket" than to say, "You can make anything except a gun."
    - ❏ Offer choices for which you are willing to accept either alternative the child selects. Pick alternatives with which you are equally comfortable. For example, "You can either use my story starter today or develop an idea you have yourself." "You choose: watering plants or feeding the fish."
    - ❏ Allow children ample time to make their decisions. When making choices, children sometimes vacillate between options. Allow them time to do this rather than rushing them. Give youngsters a time frame within which to think, saying, "I'll check back with you in a few minutes to see what you've decided," or "While you're finishing your painting, you can decide which area to clean up," or "I'll ask Suzy what she wants to do, and then I'll get back to you." Allow children to change their minds if the follow-through on the decision has not yet begun.
    - ❏ Assist children in accepting responsibility for the choices they make. Once children have made a decision, and it is in process, help them stay with and follow through on their choice.
    - ❏ Be careful about providing too many choices or overloading children with decision-making "opportunities" that are meaningless or are better made by adults.

15. **Use scaffolding techniques to challenge children to perform tasks slightly beyond what they can easily do on their own.** Gauge the amount of support and challenge necessary for optimal growth, slowly decreasing support as children move toward increasing their **autonomy.** Support children in their efforts to try new or uncomfortable tasks. Talk about their efforts, and praise their courage and determination to try, not just the results. Develop a ready bank of reinforcing and encouraging phrases, such as the following, to support children in this process.
    - ❏ You worked so hard to figure that out. I'm proud of you!
    - ❏ I'm happy to see you cooperating like that.
    - ❏ It's such a pleasure working with you because you try so hard.
    - ❏ That's really an improvement!
    - ❏ Hey, I can see that you've been practicing and that it's paying off.
    - ❏ You are really burning those old neurons today!
    - ❏ Now that's what I call a terrific job. You've remembered to leave spaces between every single word.
    - ❏ You've completed your homework every day this week. Good for you!
    - ❏ That was a very friendly and caring thing to do.
    - ❏ Wow! You figured it out.
    - ❏ You have to feel really proud of yourself. It took meeting the problem head on, and you did it!

16. **Help children evaluate their accomplishments.** Encourage children to reflect on how well they defined the problem, whether they thought about all the alternatives, whether they persisted long enough, what turned out well, and what they might do differently the next time. Also, provide opportunities and formats for self-appraisal. Conference with them and provide task-specific feedback and questions to help them identify what they have learned and the next steps to enhance their learning. Focus on what has been accomplished compared to what was intended. "Did this picture/experiment/piece of writing turn out the way you planned?" You may also point out that the child could do something, given the effort: "You chose a harder puzzle this time, and you completed it." Sometimes, children need to have feedback on how to assess if they have accomplished a task. Ask them in advance questions such as, "How can you be sure that your answer on each subtraction problem is correct?" "What do you think makes a good experiment?" When children

focus on the negative, accept their statements and then ask, "How do you wish it were different? What could you do to change it?" Help students set goals for what they can change and be more accepting of what they cannot. Ultimately, children will learn to provide feedback to themselves, but this takes much practice and experience. Praise children's accomplishments and, to build self-esteem, use genuine praise and more reinforcement than negative criticism. Give children adequate time and encouragement to finish tasks for themselves. Guide children toward continual self-examination of their growth and work rather than relying on only the teacher's or their parents' evaluation. Involve them in producing self-appraisal reports prior to parent or family conferences.

17. **Make it easy for children to use materials and equipment independently.**
    ❏ Set aside a portion of each day in which children may engage in free-choice, self-initiated activities.
    ❏ Establish a specific location for materials so that children know where to find them and where to put them away. Maintain the storage area in an orderly fashion so that children will know what it is supposed to look like. Mark storage areas with words, symbols, or pictures as needed to identify materials that should be located there.
    ❏ Demonstrate the proper care of materials and equipment. If necessary, tell the children exactly what to do while demonstrating step by step, and then take the materials or equipment out again so that the children can imitate the behavior.
    ❏ Supervise the process of putting materials and equipment away properly, giving reminders as necessary; praise children who are achieving the standard and those who are helping others do so. Allow children to choose between two or three tasks as they carry out their work.

18. **When working with children with disabilities, avoid the tendency to overprotect them so that they can develop autonomy as much as possible.** Assist children only when assistance is needed. When possible, encourage children who are not disabled to seek help from children with disabilities. Doing so helps both the child with the disability and the child who is not disabled to build the perception that an existing disability should not be the central focus when an individual is evaluating another person's abilities.

    For children who have difficulty controlling impulsivity because of neurological disorders that manifest themselves behaviorally (e.g., ADHD, autistic-like disorders, conduct disorders), use such approaches as nonpunitive separation to remove the child from an overstimulating situation. Provide reinforcement for staying on task and provide frequent goal-setting sessions and helpful, concrete suggestions for more appropriate behavior.

19. **Watch for signs of stress in children who are learning English and provide sensitive support.**
    ❏ Wait a bit longer for an answer.
    ❏ Pronounce their name correctly in their language and learn a few words to say to them in their own language, such as "Good morning" and "See you tomorrow."
    ❏ Provide scripts for them.
    ❏ Use a lot of body language and facial expression to get your message across.
    ❏ Make statements or requests that are brief and easy to understand.
    ❏ Restate, enlarge on, and recast their language.

20. **Design activities in which the primary purpose is to teach children to use various tools and equipment in the classroom.** Give children real tools to use—art, carpentry, literary, math, and science tools; musical instruments; and technology equipment. If you are not sure how to use certain tools properly, find out or invite someone into your classroom to demonstrate. Show children how to use tools and equipment appropriately, effectively, and safely.

21. **Set up activities in which children follow step-by-step procedures to completion.** Use pictographs, verbal instructions, or written directions to guide children's actions. Have children use simple checklists to chart their progress. Invite children to report on the results. Begin with simple two- or three-step plans and gradually increase the number of steps and complexity of the tasks. Allow ample time for children to complete such work on their own.

22. **Give children opportunities to carry out classroom jobs.** Encourage them to clean up after themselves when possible and to assist others who need help. Create a job chart for children to use each day. Select certain jobs that children can carry out to help in the classroom—watering the plants, restocking materials, feeding fish, monitoring an area to make sure that materials are

Provide opportunities for children to describe their emotions.

returned to their appropriate places, collecting lunch money, and so forth. Explain or demonstrate each job and create a way for children to choose and alternate among jobs.

23. Help children develop plans of their own to follow. Involve children in planning, implementing, and evaluating some class activities and decisions. Walk children through simple planning steps such as deciding on a goal, developing steps to achieve that goal, following the plan, reporting on how well the plan worked, and possibly revising the plan for the future. Use open-ended questions to support children's thinking, such as, "How will you accomplish this?" "What materials will you need?" "Are there other ways to accomplish the same thing?" "What steps will you need to take to be able to do this?"

24. Help children develop standards. For instance, invite children to select their "best work" to be included in their portfolios or for display. Ask what criteria they will use to determine "best." Similarly, invite children to develop a list of criteria they will use to determine if their cleanup efforts are sufficient. In other words, what constitutes a "clean room"? (Materials are put away, the caps are on the markers, drawers are closed, etc.) Record these on a checklist to which children can refer.

25. Support children as they learn more about themselves in terms of gender, abilities, and culture. Provide children with opportunities to interact with adult members and other children of their gender and culture as well as other cultures. Plan visits to various work sites, and invite people to explain a variety of occupations, including those that are nontraditional. Monitor program materials and routines to avoid reinforcing negative stereotypes. Create activities that challenge stereotypes and prejudice. An important first step for all of us is to evaluate realistically the status of our own biases and how these prejudices might influence our interactions with others in both formal and nonformal settings. We also need to survey the kinds of activities and materials used in the classroom to make sure that boys and girls, children of varying abilities, and children of differing cultures have access to materials and activities that are relevant to their experiences.

ACTIVITY SUGGESTIONS

We Get Angry . . . (For Children of All Ages)

Goal 4 Understand how circumstances and events influence personal emotions.

Materials Children's books about anger (e.g., *When I'm Angry*, by Barbara Gardiner and Jane Aaron; *Alexander and the Terrible, Horrible, No Good, Very Bad Day*, by Judith Viorst; *Attila the Angry*, by Marjorie Weinman Sharmat; *Let's Be Enemies*, by Janice May Udry; *The Sorely Trying Day*, by Russell Hoban; *The Hating Book*, by Charlotte Zolotow)

Procedure After you have read some books about anger and have discussed with them the feeling of anger, have the children share examples of moments and events when they have felt angry. Discuss ways in which the characters deal with the situations to help them get rid of the angry feelings. Talk about positive and negative strategies people use when they are trying to get rid of angry feelings.

To Simplify After reading the stories, talk about what made the main character angry or upset.

To Extend Write the title "We Get Angry When . . ." at the top of a large sheet of paper on the easel. List examples or write a class experience story as the children share their ideas. Older children could write and illustrate individual "I Get Angry When . . ." booklets.

Happy Faces (For Younger or Less Experienced Children)

Goal 5 Make connections between their emotions, facial expressions, body language, and behavior.

Materials Paper plates with tongue depressor handles attached to them, yarn for hair, markers, crayons, glue, construction paper, facial features cut out of magazines (be sure to use magazines with pictures of many different races of children and adults)

Procedure In the art center, spread out materials. Help the children use the materials to make puppets with happy faces, providing suggestions but not giving them a model to copy. Encourage them to talk about how they feel inside when they are wearing a happy face or how they feel when someone else looks at them with a happy face.

To Simplify With extremely young children, provide prepared puppets and encourage them to discuss feelings that go along with happy faces.

To Extend Have older children write and stage a puppet show about an especially joyous situation. Extend children's ability to identify body language expressions of happiness. Have them hold the stick puppets in front of their faces as they march up and down, repeating this chant in happy voices (to the tune, "Here We Go 'Round the Mulberry Bush"):

This is my happy face, happy face, happy face.
This is my happy face being worn at school today.
This is my happy march, happy march, happy march.
This is my happy march taking place at school today.

Toy Land Relaxation (For Younger or Less Experienced Children)

Goal 8 Learn satisfying and effective strategies for coping with personal emotions and tensions.

Materials Hinged toy figure, flexible cloth figures, taped musical selections for marching and relaxing, tape player

Procedure To help children become familiar with and contrast feelings of bodily relaxation and tension, talk with them about how our bodies are hinged together. Help them discover where these "hinges" are located (neck, wrist, fingers, ankles, toes, and waist) and how stiff and tight their bodies feel when the hinges are all "locked up" because they are angry, unhappy, or overly tired. Contrast this with what happens when these same hinges are loose when they are relaxed or happy by having the children relax each locked body hinge, starting with the neck, then the waist, wrists, and so on, reminding them to sit down carefully as their body becomes increasingly limp.

To Simplify Demonstrate the process of locking up and loosening up with toys such as stiff, inflexible robots and limp cloth dolls or animals.

To Extend To increase children's sense of contrast, use marching music and practice being stiff robots; then switch to some peaceful, relaxing music, and encourage children to slow everything down and become completely limp and relaxed. Discuss with children other states they have experienced and how their bodies felt at the time, what their facial expressions may have been, what they may have said, or how they may have behaved (e.g., being angry vs. being happy and relaxed). For a follow-up activity, have children choose pictures from magazines that depict faces of people who seem "tight," angry, and hurried and those in which people seem "loose," happy, and relaxed.

I Can! (For Older or More Experienced Children)

Goal 17 Evaluate their accomplishments and set new standards and goals.

Materials Large empty juice cans, colored paper strips, markers, blank booklets, paste or glue

Procedure Provide or have children each bring in a large empty juice can that has been washed and checked for any sharp edges. Have them place a label around the can that says "I CAN!" and then decorate the can so that each is individual. As they learn and demonstrate a new skill, have them fill out a special colored paper strip, dictating or writing the skill and dating it. Have them put the strips in the can.

(continued)

To Simplify Watch for children who fail to recognize their accomplishments. Remind these children that small gains also need to be recorded, and help them identify some of these gains or set goals that can be accomplished.

To Extend At the end of each month, have the children transfer their "I CAN!" slips into an ongoing booklet, denoting the beginning of each month (e.g., "In November, I learned to do these things") and pasting in the strips following the heading. The pages could also be illustrated in some way. The booklets become a vehicle for children's self-assessment. They can also become one piece of a portfolio, shared with a portfolio buddy or the entire group, and shared with parents at conferences or open houses.

We're Learning to Do So Many Things (For Younger or Less Experienced Children)

Goal 17 Evaluate their accomplishments and set new standards and goals.

Materials Large precut hand on easel, markers, blank booklets

Procedure Tell the children, "Just think of how many things you do every day from the time you get up in the morning until you go to bed." Place a large precut hand on the easel. Tell the children, "Sometimes when someone is able to do a lot of different things, we say they are 'pretty handy.'" Ask them what they think the expression means, and discuss the many ways we use our hands to accomplish what we need to. Label the precut hand "We Are Pretty Handy." Encourage the children to think of skills they have developed, print them on the hand, and then have the group decide where to place it in the classroom.

To Simplify For children who have difficulty thinking of things they do, have the group suggest something they can probably do.

To Extend Have the children construct an individual booklet that contains about 10 pages, titled "Learning to Be Handy." Have them work on completing the pages by drawing their hands on each page and then listing a separate skill they have learned on each of the fingers (e.g., "I brush my teeth," "I can count to 25," "I fix my own cereal," "I make my bed," "I feed my dog").

I Can Get There All by Myself (For Older or More Experienced Children)

Goal 26 Experience the pleasure of work.

Materials Paper, markers, scissors, glue

Procedure Demonstrate to children how to draw a simple map from your home to the school. As you draw it, talk about several landmarks on the way. Draw them in and label them. Draw a clock by the house, noting the time (on the hour or half hour) that you usually leave for school. After drawing the school, add a clock by it indicating (again, on the hour or half hour) what time you usually arrive. Tell the children, "This is a map of the way I come to school every day. The clocks indicate the time I leave for school and the time I arrive. Each of you gets to school each day by walking or riding in a car or bus. That means you have to get ready to leave by a certain time and then get to this classroom by the time school is ready to start." Invite each child to construct a simple map showing their home, the school, and a route between.

To Simplify Tell the children that you would like to construct a classroom map showing the school and the way to each of their homes and that you need their help in drawing their houses. Have them make just a picture of their homes on individual pieces of paper and cut around them. Construct a simple mural showing just larger cross streets, and help the children paste their homes east, west, south, or north of the cross streets.

To Extend Have the children also indicate the approximate time (half hour or hour) that they leave their homes and arrive at school. Have them draw a more elaborate route between home and school on an individual basis. Have them take part in constructing the classroom mural that integrates all their homes in relation to the school.

All About Me Book (For Children of All Ages)

Goal 28 Identify characteristics and qualities that make them unique.

Materials Paper, scissors, magazines, writing tools

Procedure Have the children describe themselves on paper, then bind the pages together in a book. Pages suggestions include the following:

"This is me"—a self-portrait
"This is my family"—a family portrait
"Here is my hand"—a hand tracing
"Some things that I can do"—a dictated or written list of skills
"My favorite foods"
"My favorite animals"—magazine picture cutouts

To Simplify Have the child dictate words to teachers or classroom aides. Create fewer pages.

To Extend Have the children decide what should go on each page. Have the children write in narrative form for each page to extend the information provided about themselves (e.g., "Here is my hand. Ten things I can do with my hands include sorting silverware from the dishwasher, . . ." Have them further illustrate each page.

Match Mate (For Younger or Less Experienced Children)

Goal 29 Explore similarities and differences among people as a way to gain personal insight.

Materials None

Procedure Play this as a circle game. Pick one child to be in the center. Teach the children the following song, to the tune, "Ring Around the Rosie":

Match Mate, Match Mate,
Looking for a Match Mate,
Match Mate,
Match Mate,
You are it!

As the children sing and hold hands, the "center" child moves around the circle, stopping in front of someone on the words, "You are it!" The other children then guess in what way the two children match. The child who was chosen as the "mate" will then become "it" for the next round.

To Simplify Teacher chooses child to be "it" and just chants the words with the other children while the "it" child chooses a mate. The teacher describes the ways in which the two children are alike.

To Extend The "center" child selects a mate on the basis of two or three matching characteristics, and the children describe these to the group.

SUMMARY

Young children have much to learn about themselves and the effect they have on others. What they learn in the early years from parents, teachers, and peers becomes vitally important in their later ability to form and maintain relationships; work and play well with others; and feel valued, confident, and competent in any number of situations. While there are many teachable moments in the classroom to scaffold children's emotional competence over time, teachers must also actively plan classroom experiences in the affective domain. Even children in the worst situations can develop increasing competence that counters other negative messages they are receiving.

The development of emotional strength and stability, a lifelong task, is interdependent with children's cognitive, physical, and social development. Because children spend major amounts of time in extrafamilial settings and because they are moving into these contexts earlier and earlier, good early childhood learning environments are those in which aesthetic, affective, physical, and social development are valued as highly as academic aspects of learning. Caring professionals who are able to structure positive learning climates, who actively promote children's emotional development and sense of self-worth, and who foster children's competence are key players in facilitating positive affective outcomes for young children. Also critical is the sensitivity of caring adults to differences in personality, gender, ethnicity, and race in the children and families with whom they work.

Key Words

attention deficit hyperactivity disorder	emotions	self-awareness
autism	empathy	self-esteem
autonomy	English language learner (ELL)	sensory processing disorders
Down syndrome	global self-concept	
emotional intelligence	resilience	

Applying What You've Read in This Chapter

1. **Discuss**
   a. Review each of the opening questions in this chapter.
   b. In what way does the acquisition of self-esteem depend more on internal factors than on external factors?

2. **Observe**
   a. Arrange to visit an early childhood classroom and observe the following:
      1. The overall affective climate in the classroom. What contributes most noticeably to it? What detracts from it?
      2. Evidence that the teacher supports children on an individual basis as well as a cohort group. Cite specific examples of how he or she does this.

3. **Carry out an activity**
   a. Read Daniel Goleman's book, *Emotional Intelligence* (1997). Find out what he believes is the cost of emotional illiteracy.
   b. Interview one or more principals of an elementary school. Ask to see how affective development is planned for in the curriculum. Ask, "How is this translated into everyday instruction? Could you give me some specific examples?"
   c. Survey 10 parents about affective education and whether they believe that it should be part of the school curriculum or left for families to provide for their children. What are their reasons for their preference?
   d. Survey one child at each level, preschool through third grade, to find out how involved each is in terms of extracurricular activities. How much television does each

child watch? How much leisure time does each have, and how does he or she spend it?

4. **Create something for your portfolio**
   a. Develop a lesson plan for the affective domain.
   b. Write a brief position paper outlining your beliefs about the importance of planning for affective development in the early childhood classroom.

5. **Add to your journal**
   a. How well is your emotional intelligence or intrapersonal intelligence developed? Because this is a lifelong process, are there areas that need attention? How can you address needed skill building?
   b. When you feel overly stressed or overwhelmed, what strategies do you use to reduce stress for the short term? for the long term? How do you react physically to undue stress? psychologically? behaviorally?
   c. In what temperament category would you place yourself: easy, slow to warm up, difficult, or none of the three? What characteristics make you believe that this conclusion is appropriate?

6. **Consult the standards**
   State standards often outline academic standards but do not include those for social and affective development. Check out the standards for your own state and two other states in the United States. What do the standards include in terms of affective development? How comprehensive are they? How do they compare with the goals for children outlined in this chapter?

PRACTICE FOR YOUR CERTIFICATION OR LICENSURE EXAM

The following items will help you practice applying what you have learned in this chapter. They can help to prepare you for your course exam, the PRAXIS II exam, your state licensure or certification exam, and for working in developmentally appropriate ways with young children.

To give children more choices in her classroom, Ms. Canady has set up a white board on which she has listed the morning's centers, letting children sign up for their first center as soon as they come into the room. Some children who ride the bus arrive after the walkers and are complaining that their first choice is always filled by the time they get to school. Wanting the children to have an opportunity for engagement and involvement, she allows the children at center time to remain in a center all morning if they wish. Again, some children are complaining that they don't get a chance to have a turn in the center they really want.

1. **Constructed-response question**

    Providing choice to children is a genuine priority for Ms. Canady. Yet, it seems the more choices she provides for the children, the more complaints they have about not having a choice.

    a. What can Ms. Canady do to improve her ability to provide children with opportunities for choices during center time and eliminate some of the issues the children have identified?

    b. Identify several other opportunities Ms. Canady can provide to offer genuine choices for the children in her classroom.

2. **Multiple-choice question**

    Martin is a child who seems limited in his ability to make good learning choices during the morning center time. He rarely stays long in any of the centers, gets out additional materials that he does not put away, and does not complete any of the work he begins in any of the centers. What would you do to improve the situation for Martin?

    Choose one of the following options and then explain why you believe it would be the *least effective* option.

    a. Eliminate choices during center time for Martin, providing him with a schedule each morning for center work where he must complete something at each center before moving on to the next.

    b. For a week, have Martin accompany Sarah, who makes good center learning choices. Then give him an opportunity to see if he has learned how to make better choices.

    c. Tell Martin that if he cannot make better choices at center time, you will have some seat work ready for him to do instead.

    d. Observe Martin's center participation closely, jotting down some information. Where does he spend the most time? The least amount of time? Whom does he prefer to work with or by? Does he lack the skill to participate in the activities? Is he able to concentrate for the time necessary to complete a task? Does he know how to use the materials or tools? From these notes, develop a plan to guide Martin's center participation.

Chapter

11

The Cognitive Domain

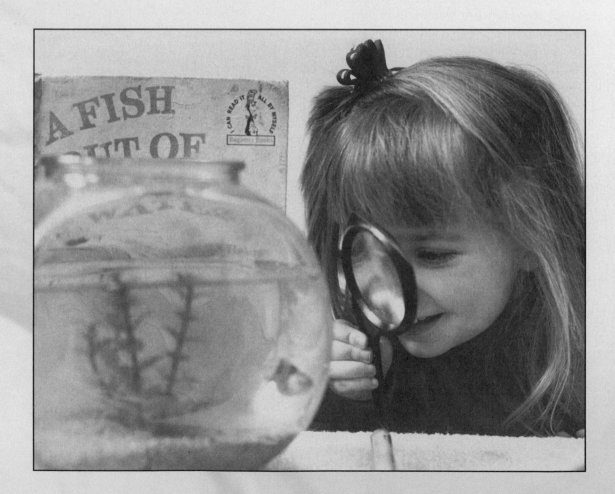

You may wonder:

How do current neuroscience discoveries about the brain contribute to our understanding of children's cognitive development?

What was the process of cognitive maturation that brought you to this point in your development? How "smart" are you, and in what ways are you "smart"?

What components make up a fundamental knowledge base for children's cognitive development? What do children need to know to be proficient thinkers?

What should our goals be for science and mathematics education in the early years? Is hands-on activity alone sufficient to accomplish these goals?

In this chapter on the cognitive domain, we present information to help you answer the preceding questions:

◆ ◆ *In a discussion with a group of kindergartners after reading* It Looked Like Spilt Milk *(by Charles G. Shaw; 1947, HarperCollins), Ms. Linscott asks the children, "How do you think clouds stay up in the sky?"*

"They're stuck up there 'cause they're made out of white stuff . . . out of lots of white glue and stuff!" offers Kiley.

"And sometimes they fall down at night and the next day it's all sun and no clouds in the sky . . . just all sun!" adds Latonya helpfully.

Young children's thinking is dramatically different from that of older children and adults, and this fact is illustrated repeatedly by young children's "cute" but inaccurate statements. They literally see the world from an entirely different perspective. Their fascinating journey toward more mature thinking comprises a combination of inherent capacities, accumulated experiences, and the quality of their relationships with others who accompany them on this journey.

Clearly, everything is cognitive! While a good part of this chapter will be focused on science and mathematics, the maturation of the complex processes of the human mind that lead to "knowing" in all domains of development will also be described (Berk, 2007). Because of the roundabout fashion in which the intellect evolves, promising new directions in early childhood education that support the integration of various learning domains and experiential learning have enormous potential. They are made even more effective when each child's cognitive levels are matched carefully with classroom learning experiences and when professionals are sensitive to the negative effects of overchallenging or underchallenging the children in their care.

COGNITIVE MATURATION

Contributions of Neuroscience to Understanding Children's Cognitive Development

A father comforts a crying newborn. A mother plays peekaboo with her 10-month-old. A child-care provider reads to a toddler. And in a matter of seconds, thousands of cells in these children's growing brains respond. Some brain cells are "turned on," triggered by this particular experience. Many existing connections among brain cells are strengthened. At the same time, new connections are formed, adding a bit more definition and complexity to the intricate circuitry that will remain largely in place for the rest of these children's lives (Shore, 2003).

The early years are a time of rapid brain growth and development in children's lives. Neurobiologists have documented that the human brain contains some 50 billion neurons at birth and that at least 10 billion of these neural cells continue a process of connecting with one another in a series of plateau and acceleration periods. Because of a gene called **CREB,** which stimulates the number of connections made by each axon, each one of these cells has the capacity to connect with a thousand others, laying out the complex neural pathways by which children develop

FIGURE 11.1   Neuronal Growth

Neurons at Birth   Neurons at 6 Months   Neurons at 2 Years

language, mathematical understanding, social interaction, emotional growth, and aesthetic intelligence.

Connections at birth and even at 6 months are relatively sparse and immature (see Figure 11.1). By age 2, however, connections have multiplied significantly through a process called **synaptogenesis**, and by age 3, a child will have twice as many brain connections as an adult (Shonkoff, Boyce & McEwen, 2009). Somewhere between 2 and 3 years of age, a necessary process called **pruning** begins and continues. Less-used synapses are "weeded out," while other connections continue to build and strengthen. This results in a more "efficient" brain as children grow toward adolescence.

The fatty myelin sheath that covers the nerves is almost fully formed in most children by age 6. This allows for faster, smoother electrochemical impulse transmission and the beginning of more sophisticated thinking patterns. Visual pathways are myelinized within the first 6 months of life, and auditory myelination is completed by 4 to 5 years of age. The gender differences in myelination account for greater achievement in females between 6 and 29 years of age in language skills and reading (Nelson, Thomas, & deHaan, 2006; Santrock, 2007).

Both biology and experience play an important role in brain development. For example, a child's repeated experiences of interacting with the same caregiver eventually lead the child to recognize and form attachments to that person. With added variation in experience, new neural circuitry is created and greater differentiation occurs in the child's ability to discriminate between objects, people, and events.

Intersections between Neuroscience and Education. Since the 1970s, when anatomic study of the brain began in earnest, we have learned more about the human brain than in all of recorded history prior to then (Kornhaber, Fierros, & Veenema, 2005). Much of the knowledge that had been learned about brain development before the 1970s remained generally in the realm of medicine and was viewed as unimportant for educators, but this is no longer true. Information about brain development and behavior, the potentially negative effects of risky environments on young children, and links between brain research findings and children's cognitive development are now salient and hot topics in the fields of early childhood and special education.

In forging new frontiers into how the mind works, neurobiology provides valuable insights into planning for young children. We know that a brain does not simply grow larger as our toes and fingers do; instead, it forms particular connections that are unique to each individual, depending on the quality and repetition of stimulating multisensory experiences encountered in the early years (Begley, 1997). These repeated experiences strengthen specific synapses with time. In turn, such experiences ultimately produce the mature brain and corresponding abilities and capabilities in the child.

Because of technological advances in **neuroscience** today, we can literally "see" brain activity we once knew very little about. One of the most promising finds in this last decade has been the suspected presence of a mirror neuron system in human beings (Sylwester, 2006; Ramachandran, 2006). Neuroscientists believe that mirror neurons help to explain how infants learn to speak, how children develop empathy for others, and why we enjoy participating in sports and artistic activities or watching others do so. They believe that we are able to learn new skills because this system supports the cognitive functions that rely on imitation rather than simply on verbal explanations (e.g., seeing someone else jump, clapping our hands, acquiring a new language, learning to tie our shoes, or watching someone make wontons). This part of the brain may be most responsive to emotionally arousing stimuli, causing us to pay attention or become bored and look for other stimuli. It is more highly activated when we experience emotions or when we see another person experience emotions such as happiness, anger, and pain. It may mediate our understanding of situations where we have auditory clues but an absence of visual cues. For example, in early evening, Josh hears a car driving into the garage and then the door opening. Though he can't see his father yet, he yells, "Mom, Daddy's home!"

Special educators who are trying to determine the root causes of autism are especially excited about these studies. To date, anatomical differences in the cortical areas of the brain suspected of housing mirror neurons have been found in adults with autism spectrum disorders as contrasted

---

"BRAINY" TERMINOLOGY

Neuron a cell, usually consisting of a cell body, axon, and dendrite that transmits nerve impulses

Axon an extension of a neuron that transmits impulses outward from the cell body

Dendrite a branched extension of a nerve cell neuron that receives electrical signals and conducts those signals to other neurons

Synapse junction between two nerve cells that transmit signals

CREB a gene that stimulates synapses to transmit signals

Synaptogenesis growth of connections between neurons and brain circuitry; also known as "arborization"

Pruning elimination of infrequently used and weak neural pathways

Myelin a fatty substance that surrounds and insulates nerve fibers, enabling smooth transmission of nerve impulses

Mirror neurons type of brain cell that fires equally when we perform a certain action or when we watch others perform the same action; neurons that allow us to "feel" what others may be feeling in a certain situation

Cognition the mental process of acquiring knowledge by the use of reasoning, intuition, or perception

Simplified Model of a Neuron

---

with nonautistic adults; the mirror neuron–related areas are significantly thinner in those who have been diagnosed as autistic and are correlated with symptom severity on the autism spectrum. Studies using **neuroimaging technologies,** such as functional magnetic resonance imaging (fMRI), positron emission tomography (PET), electroencephalography, and magnetoencephalography, have indicated that children with autism demonstrate less activity in these areas of the brain when imitating others. These neuroimaging technologies have also become important in determining whether exposure to certain interventions (say, in the case of reading disorders) are effective or not. To date, a number of well-constructed studies support the hypothesis that this neural system exists, though findings continue to be controversial (Sylwester, 2006).

Challenges to Optimal Development. Just as we know that high-quality early environments set in motion positive trajectories for cognitive development, we've become more certain of other factors that have a strongly *negative* influence. Some of these may occur genetically as life begins, setting off any number of disorders that can influence later cognition. In addition, poor prenatal nutrition, maternal drug and alcohol use, and several maternal chronic illnesses can result in problematic fetal brain development and loss of cognitive potential. Children diagnosed with mental retardation generally have substantially subaverage intellectual functioning that negatively affects their ability to function in daily life (see Figure 11.2). Cases of severe mental retardation can usually be attributed to a biological origin. In most cases of mild mental retardation, the causes remain unclear. However, both genetic components and socioeconomic factors, such as poverty and undernutrition, often contribute to the prevalence (Batshaw, Pellegrino, & Roizen, 2007).

Traumatic and chaotic environments also negatively affect neural connections and cognitive growth in young children being reared in risky situations. Elevated stress hormones such as cortisol result in diminished brain growth in regions of the brain related to memory, learning, and emotional attachment; simultaneously, arousal is increased in other regions related to hyperactivity, anxiety, impulsive behavior, attention regulation, and self-control (Scott, 2008). Even if a child's environment does not contain overt abuse or serious neglect, it may be one in which the

FIGURE 11.2   Example of Teaching a Child with a Cognitive Domain Challenge

Colin

Colin, a 7-year-old in first grade, was diagnosed with mild mental retardation at age 4 years. Early in his development, his parents had suspected a problem because of speech, language, and motor delays. While he has required special education services for the past 3 years, he has been able to do fairly well in regular classes. Recently, his teacher has noted that Colin is having increasing difficulty with any task requiring memorization, particularly in math. She has also observed that he seems to have more difficulty when math tasks are broken into parts than when he is presented with all parts of the task at once. This seems odd to her, but Colin appears to be better at simultaneously processing what needs to be done. His teacher requests that Colin be reevaluated in order to better understand the learning challenges that he is having currently. She also notes to his parents, "Despite his learning problems in math, he's doing especially well in reading. Colin and I are working on strategies for the difficulties he's having in math. All in all, he's having a pretty good year, and I think a closer look will allow us to continue making progress."

child is simply deprived of the kind of stimulating experiences that produce the most fertile minds (Newberger, 2008).

Research results now remove any doubt about the effect of inadequate environments and early experiences; such results yield serious implications for parents, policy makers, and early childhood educators. Children need and benefit from high-quality learning experiences spent with nurturing adults. Meanwhile, parents are more pressed for time than ever, and quality child care for working parents remains a problem in terms of both availability and cost. Likewise, although we have made inroads into providing a better match between children's cognitive levels and primary classroom experiences, many children are still sitting in classrooms in which a serious gap exists between professional knowledge about cognitive development and instructional practice.

Brain to Mind: Neural Development and Cognitive Processing

Neural development equips children for **cognitive processing**. Although procedures such as fMRI allow us to better understand the way the physical brain operates during completion of an intellectual task, the way in which human beings actually think, reason, and develop language and other cognitive processes remains locked in theory. A number of influential theorists have offered differing accounts of how thinking, reasoning, language, and other cognitive processes develop. The contributions and criticisms of these theories have been outlined by Santrock (2007) as follows:

Contributions of Cognitive Theories
- ❏ The cognitive theories emphasize the individual's active construction of understanding.
- ❏ The cognitive theories underscore the value of examining developmental changes in children's thinking.
- ❏ The information-processing approach offers detailed descriptions of cognitive processes. (p. 25)

Criticisms of Cognitive Theories
- ❏ There is skepticism about whether children develop cognitive skills during particular stages and in the way Piaget envisioned. Howard Gardner, noted Harvard psychologist, has noted that Piaget is important not because he got it all right, but because he was the first person to portray children's intellectual development in detail and because people continued to address the questions that Piaget himself first addressed.
- ❏ The cognitive theories do not give adequate attention to individual variations in cognitive development.
- ❏ The information-processing approach does not provide an adequate description of developmental changes in cognition.
- ❏ Psychoanalytic theorists argue that the cognitive theories underrate the importance of unconscious thought.

Some of the most well-known cognitive theorists are introduced in Table 11.1. In reviewing their ideas, think about your own development: how you learned to function on a day-to-day

TABLE 11.1   Cognitive Theorists

Theorist	Ideas About Cognitive Development
Swiss psychologist **Jean Piaget** 1896–1980 Cognitive Constructivist	"Intelligence is an adaptation. Life is a continuous creation of increasingly complex forms and a progressive balancing of these forms with the environment" (from *Origins of Intelligence in Children*, 1952). Different ages and stages bring about differing capacity to think more abstractly, idealistically, and logically. Intelligence is based on logical and mathematical knowledge that is invented by each child, that is, constructed by each child from within. The four age-related stages are: sensorimotor (birth to 2), preoperational (2–7), concrete operational (7–11), and formal operational (11 through adolescence). Children actively construct ideas about the world as they go through these stages. Development, according to Piaget, leads the ability to learn.
Russian psychologist **Lev Vygotsky** 1896–1934 Social–Cultural Constructivist	Knowledge, according to Vygotsky, is not generated from within; rather, learning stimulates and leads development. Culture and social interaction collaboratively guide cognitive development. Memory, attitudes, and reasoning involve the use of inventions of society, such as language, mathematical systems, and memory strategies. Human beings act within zones of proximal development (ZPD), moving through a series of learned tasks that can be performed maximally only with the help of more accomplished persons. The theory is non-stage specific.
Stanford University professor **Albert Bandura** 1925– Theory of Reciprocal Determinism	Bandura is considered "the father of the cognitive movement." He believes that one's environment causes one's behavior, but that the world and a person's behavior cause each other. Observational and social learning and modeling form the basis for his theory. Individuals perform a series of discrete mental operations on incoming information and then mentally store the conclusions drawn from the process. These are used to operate on subsequent social experiences and, in turn, influence future behavior. His belief is that there are reciprocal interactions among behavior, the person/cognition, and the environment, with behavior influencing cognition and vice versa. Environment and biological conditions influence one another.
Carnegie Mellon Teresa Heinz Professor of Cognitive Psychology **Robert Siegler** 1949– Information Processing Approach to Cognition	Siegler sees the physical brain as analogous to computer hardware and cognition as analogous to software. Cognition involves three components: encoding, automaticity, and strategy construction. Children must encode information, paying attention to relevant information and ignoring the nonrelevant. For the information to become useful, the process must become automatic. There is controversy over whether speed in processing information is due to gained experience or biological maturation, such as myelination. Individuals manipulate information, monitor it, and strategize about it. They gradually increase their capacity to process it, which allows for increasingly complex knowledge and skills. Siegler rejects behavioral theory.

Source: Adapted from *A Topical Approach to Life Span Development* (3rd ed.), by J. W. Santrock, 2007, Boston: McGraw-Hill.

Adults can facilitate children's higher-order thinking though scaffolding.

basis; how you now learn new information and ways of behaving; how you think through challenges you encounter; ways you *prefer* to learn; and intellectual tasks and topics that hold or do not hold your interest. Which of the theories do you believe best allows you to understand your abilities to make decisions, to adapt and cope with changing events in your life, and to generally act in the way you do? What do you believe accounts for the *variations* in the way that people you know process information? How powerful do you think unconscious thought is in the way you process information? What implications do the beliefs of each of the following theorists about how children learn have for your teaching?

Howard Gardner, of course, has made us more thoughtful about the possibility that human beings may be intelligent in different ways with his concept of multiple intelligences (verbal/linguistic, logical/mathematical, bodily/kinesthetic, visual/spatial, musical/rhythmic, interpersonal, intrapersonal, and environmentalist/naturalist). Intelligence, he notes, is more complex than mere capacity for storing, retrieving, and processing information, and while some persons demonstrate intelligence in all eight areas, some areas are usually stronger than others in most people (Gallenstein, 2003). Robert Sternberg's (2006) triarchic theory of intelligence (that we are either primarily analytical, creative, or practical in terms of our intelligence) also offers insightful ideas about cognitive formation and application.

One common principle here seems to be that knowledge cannot come in neatly packaged sets of understandings which can be passively given to children. When such packaging is attempted, we risk short-circuiting in-depth or true understanding of phenomena in children because we cut them off from the intriguing and engaging work of concept formation. In short, we cut off their active thinking.

CHILDREN'S ACQUISITION OF A FUNDAMENTAL KNOWLEDGE BASE FOR COGNITIVE DEVELOPMENT

myeducationlab

Go to the Assignments and Activities section of Topic 8: Program Models/Approaches in the MyEducationLab for your course and complete the activity entitled *Understanding Developmentally Appropriate Practice through Cognitive Development.* Watch how adults promote the cognitive development of infants and toddlers.

To this point, we have focused on how children come to know things. Now we turn to what they *need* to know. A necessary knowledge base comprises primarily five subgroups, as displayed in Figure 11.3 (DeVries & Kohlberg, 1990).

1. **Physical knowledge**—observable attributes of objects and physical phenomena: size, color, shape, weight, texture, tendencies under varying conditions (e.g., objects roll downhill; snow is cold; sugar is sweet; spiders have eight legs).

2. **Logical-mathematical knowledge**—relations between objects, and phenomena deriving from observation; developing a logical organization to deal more effectively with incoming knowledge, including matching, classifying (subclasses and supraclasses), patterning, seriating, numbering (counting, one-to-one correspondence, equivalence of groups of numbers, invariance of number), using space in relations to the body (vertical and horizontal coordinates; right and left, in-front and behind coordinates; depth and distance coordinates; topological—closed or open shapes, inclusion–exclusion, proximity, order—and Euclidean geometric—lines, angles, equalities, parallelism, distance perspectives), and using time (order of events and length of events).

3. **Representational knowledge**—imaginative expression of symbolic thought that represents the child's mental world; manipulation of images, art, symbols, and language to stand for objects, events, and concepts; competence in restructuring an experience in another way through symbolic representation (dramatic and creative play, rhythmic movement, imitation, construction of two- and three- dimensional models) and sign representation, which evolves through spoken language and then written language as follows:

   ❏ Using names for objects in the environment
   ❏ Using words to identify the properties and functions of objects
   ❏ Using words to denote location in space and time
   ❏ Using words that describe relations (comparing, describing differences and similarities, enumerating, measuring, and ordering)
   ❏ Using words to relate physical knowledge
   ❏ Using words to relate social knowledge
   ❏ Using words to tell events and stories
   ❏ Using words to relate personal feelings and thoughts

4. **Social-conventional knowledge**—cultural and societal conventions, rules, and viewpoints transmitted to children by family, society, school, and peers to guide behavior related to other individuals, institutions, and the use of goods and services (e.g., 911 is a number to call if someone is in danger; some families have more than one mother and father; many Jewish families celebrate Hanukkah; most people finish high school; farmers produce most of our food).

5. **Metacognition**—proficient strategies for monitoring your thinking processes. Becoming an effective problem solver requires that children develop this unique cognitive quality. It is activated and enhanced when we help them develop the requisite skills needed for critical and fair thinking, mental flexibility, organization of their ideas, and application of the many essential components of

FIGURE 11.3   Cognitive Wheel

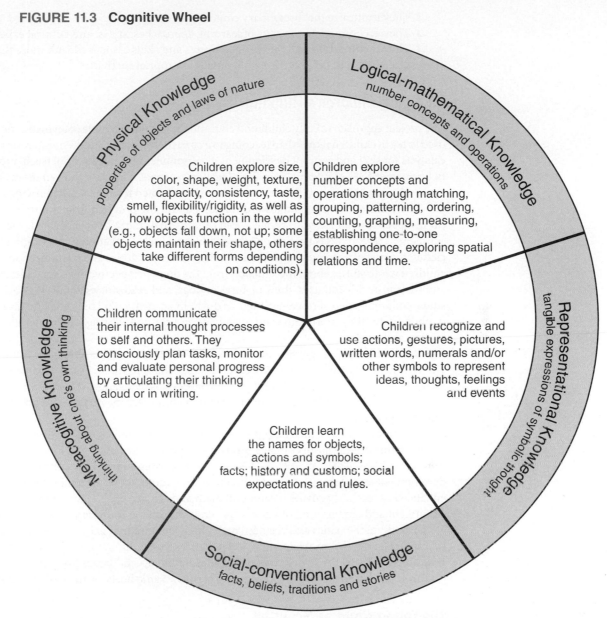

Source: Adapted from Kostelnik, M. J., & Grady, M. L. (2009). *Getting it right from the start: The principal's guide to early childhood education.* Thousand Oaks, CA: Corwin Press, 22.

learning (McAfee & Leong, 2006). The use of Socratic or open-ended questioning can move children away from fragmented, fuzzy, and inconsistent thinking by challenging them as appropriate:

❑ "How do you know that?"
❑ "Where did you find that out?"
❑ "Why do you think someone would do that?"
❑ "When would that not be true?"
❑ "Is there another way to think about that?"
❑ "How would you explain that to someone else who wanted to learn it?"

Children are the best source of topics that interest them, and skillful teachers mobilize children's enthusiasm for learning when they design interdisciplinary "anchors." These anchors are complex problems that children think are worth solving and that capture their desire to learn a set of relevant skills and concepts. Such anchors can be invented or natural, as long as they fulfill the following requirements (Barab & Landa, 1997).

❑ They capture children's imagination.
❑ They are perceived as important by learners.

❏ They legitimize the disciplinary content they integrate.

❏ They accommodate a variety of learning approaches, styles, and cultural experiences.

❏ They require children to draw on concepts and skills associated with more than one discipline; and generate developmentally appropriate activities.

Engaging Children's Thinking

The project approach to early childhood education is just one example of an instructional approach used to teach children rather than teaching to a curriculum. It uses children's interests as worthwhile catalysts for skill and concept development. For example, a primary-school teacher asked children to bring in articles of interest from their local newspapers. The class showed more than a passing interest in an article about the community's concern related to an increase in roving packs of dogs.

The children were guided toward thinking about the problem from a number of hypothetical perspectives and asked to create a web of ideas that might be investigated. Included in their subsequent research was finding out about rabies and rabies treatment, the origin of humane societies, the cost of keeping dogs and other animals, and the duties and training of dogcatchers. The children wrote stories about the situation from the dogs' perspective, investigated varieties of dogs and their histories and uses, drew pictures of dogs, and read stories about dogs. All during their study, children's interest remained high, as did their academic skill building and understanding of methods of finding information and organizing and communicating it to one another and to their teacher and parents.

Researchers have suggested that each child's brain is a "rich, layered, messy, unplanned jungle ecosystem" (Sylwester, 2006). We're certain that children thrive best in a learning context that includes many sensory, cultural, and problem layers closely related to the real-world environment in which they live. It is the environment that best stimulates the neural networks that are genetically linked to it.

As children develop their cognitive abilities, they will acquire general reasoning skills that will enable them to solve more complex problems, expand their perceptual abilities, and think critically about ideas. These abilities are necessary for children to function well and progress in every developmental domain. In the early childhood classroom, however, abilities will be purposefully enhanced as teachers provide meaningful math and science experiences directed at new concept attainment and organization of knowledge. Problem solving is the common factor that brings together both mathematics and science curriculum, and children gain dramatically when teachers (a) capture and design problem-solving experiences that children find engaging and in which they *want* to participate; (b) structure opportunities for small- and large-group problem solving; and (c) use games and daily-living problems, rather than worksheets, as the basis for lessons.

The Young Child as Scientist

Children are full of questions and expend a great deal of their energy on discovering how things work, what people do, and how they can become more competent players in the general scheme of life. They have a driving need to learn how electric outlets work, how toilets flush, how things open and close, where bubbles go, how seashore waves "melt" sand castles, and how whales can stay underwater so long without breathing.

Preschool children act on their intense curiosity by observing, trying out simple operations, and questioning adults, repeatedly. For these children, events simply happen or happen by magic. They turn on the television and Barney appears. They ride with their family in the car at night, and the moon follows them—amazing!

Later, as neural pathways mature and primary-age children gain experience and information, their understanding of cause and effect is more often correct, although still limited. So that children can build a consistent picture of the physical world, effective educators consider children's prior knowledge base and relate new learning experiences to this base. They also modify their planning of new and subsequent experiences for individual children and small groups, based on what children know—and want to know. Doing so also calls for evaluating any misconceptions children have about a particular phenomenon, and young children have a lot of them.

To develop the concepts and skills needed to comprehend their world from an accurate and scientific perspective, preschoolers and elementary children need teachers who have a basic

PEARSON
myeducationlab

Go to the Video Examples section of Topic 9: Content Areas/Lessons and Activities in the MyEducationLab for your course and watch the video entitled *Science*. How do we provide developmentally appropriate science activities for young children?

understanding about scientific concepts that children need to explore. They benefit when their teachers have a view of science as a dynamic process that must involve science inquiry. Children also need access to thoughtfully selected materials and many opportunities to work with and observe scientific phenomena. Finally, they expand concepts quickly when teachers structure time for them to revisit, represent, discuss, and demonstrate the experiences they have with specially selected materials (Moriarty, 2002).

"Doing" Science in the Preschool Years. Science is the process of finding out and a system for organizing and reporting discoveries (Lind, 2004). When children in either a preschool or elementary classroom are in the process of observing, thinking, and reflecting on actions and events, they are doing science. When they are organizing factual information into more meaningful concepts, problem solving, and acting on their curiosity, they are doing science. In trying to understand how the work of scientists is related to their lives and investigations, they are doing science. They would *not* be doing science if they were merely listening to the teacher talk about science or reading about it in a textbook.

As you provide meaningful opportunities for the children in your classroom to be actively involved in the scientific process by forming hypotheses, collecting data, and formulating and testing their conclusions, you offer them the basic skills they will need for lifelong "sciencing." These include multisensory observing, questioning, comparing, organizing, measuring, communicating, experimenting, relating (drawing abstractions from concrete data), inferring, and applying. In the early childhood classroom, we can increase the effectiveness of these opportunities by making sure that we respect children's current abilities and potential capabilities.

Debriefing after each science activity to evaluate the kinds of concepts young children are forming is a necessary strategy for building integrity into our instructional planning. This helps children realize that science is more than a collection of activities and already-known facts. They need to know that the solution to problems or new discoveries can sometimes spring from intuitive feelings about a particular phenomenon, as well as from already documented laws, theories, and principles. Thus, children should be encouraged to think creatively and divergently (in many directions) as well as convergently (centered on already-known facts) in their problem finding and problem solving. These cognitive skills are those that the American Association for the Advancement of Science believes are critical for living in a complex world.

Age-appropriate science concepts are those we would typically expect children to understand at particular ages, according to our knowledge of child development norms and our experience with young children. Preschoolers probably function best when we spontaneously provide science experiences related to their outdoor play (spiders, insects, plants, soil, sand, and water) and natural interest in animals and animal homes. Sue Edland, a teacher in Lansing's Pleasant View Elementary School, takes advantage of that by frequently asking children to observe the living things she brings into her kindergarten classroom and then to write about their observations in their journals (see Figure 11.4). During the morning meeting, she introduces what she has brought in that day, a caterpillar, and invites the children to especially notice its physical characteristics (e.g., color, presence of hair, number of legs and where they're attached) and behaviors (how and what it eats, how it moves from one place to another, whether it has a favorite place in the terrarium or moves about in much of the space, how active it is at different times during the day). She shows the children two different information books she has brought in and reads a brief portion of a page from each, pointing out the real-life pictures of varieties of caterpillars and their habitats. "I'll put these books over by the terrarium for your use this morning, along with this hand lens and penlight [connecting tools] that will give you a better look," she says, "and I'll also put Eric Carle's *The Very Hungry Caterpillar* there as well." One child later wrote in his journal, "The catrpilrs [caterpillars] ar eting the lvs. The catrpilrs ar mving. The catrpilrs ar sleping," enhancing both his science concepts and his writing capacity.

Science in the Early Primary Years. As children move into the primary grades and progress in conceptual depth and complexity, teachers can engage them in doing a great deal more of the recording, written communication, and presentation of their findings; building collections of natural materials; constructing dioramas; and using information books for guided study, focused reading, and vocabulary building. Science should continue to be primarily a hands-on activity, which can include gardening, hatching eggs, studying pond life, and so forth. Science curricula are

FIGURE 11.4 A Concept List in the Life Sciences

Building the Young Child's Concepts About Living Things

Characteristics of living things

Living things have a number of basic characteristics that are easily observable, such as color, size, and structure. Noticing these characteristics can lead children to wonder more deeply, for example, about how a cricket's color might help it survive, or why an oak tree might have so many acorns.

Living and nonliving

All things on earth are either living or nonliving. Living things share certain characteristics (for instance, they grow and reproduce) that will become more evident to children as they acquire experience. Children have common misunderstandings, such as that to be alive, something must move. Thus, plants do not appear to be living to children, while cars might be considered alive.

Needs of living things

Living things must have certain needs met if they are to survive, grow, develop, and reproduce. Animals need food, water, air, and a space in which to live. Plants need light, water, air, and space in which to grow.

Life cycle

All living things have a life cycle that includes a beginning (birth for animals, germination for plants), growth, development, and death. All living things also reproduce, creating a cycle that maintains the species.

Diversity and variation

There is tremendous diversity of plant and animal species on earth. In a vacant lot, you might see spiders, ants, pill bugs, grasses, weeds, bushes, and so on. Within each kind of living thing, you will see variation. For instance, not all worms, snails, or oak trees are exactly the same.

Habitat

The habitat is the part of the total environment that a particular living thing uses to meet all of its basic needs. For example, a worm's habitat can be a small patch of earth, while a rabbit will need enough space to find plants to eat and places in which to hide from predators. Each of these habitats provides for all of the worm's or rabbit's needs.

available that provide age-appropriate activity suggestions for elementary children, notably those that came out of such projects as the Elementary Science Study (ESS), the Science Curriculum Improvement Study (SCIS), the Science-A-Process Approach (SAPA), and the American Association for the Advancement of Science's *Benchmarks for Science Literacy*.

Using Inquiry as an Instructional Approach. Developing young scientists who think and behave like scientists in the real world requires teaching both process (**inquiry**) and content. The process involves providing children with multiple, high-quality experiences, consistently moving through the following sequence:

1. *Observation.* Inquiry involves teaching children to be effective and systematic observers of objects and materials in their world, the position and motion of objects, as well as characteristics of organisms, their life cycles, and how organisms and environments interact. Teachers advance inquiry skills by modeling observation, offering children tools and strategies, providing scaffolding to generate active thinking, and structuring opportunities for practice.

2. *Formulation of questions, based on observation.* Socratic questioning (Why do you think . . . ? How do you think . . . ? What would happen if . . . ?) spurs on children's focused attention, particularly when paired with additional hands-on experiences. Correcting children verbally does not have the same power as providing new information through experiences (Chalufour & Worth, 2003).

3. *Developing a workable hypothesis.* Inquiry also involves directed teaching about how to frame and articulate connected questions. Again, this takes time and requires good modeling on the part of the teacher, as well as classroom experiences that foster cause and effect, trial and error. Making sure that children feel psychologically safe to experiment, to make choices and correct mistakes, and to have their opinions respected is part of good modeling.

4. *Devising a strategy for testing it.* Actual investigation to try out their ideas is another necessary component in the inquiry process. This requires an adequately stocked classroom and goal-directed fieldwork that is often extended beyond the classroom.

5. *Analyze and draw conclusions from collected data.* Once investigations have taken place, children should have time and guidance in analyzing their findings. What did they find out

and what does it mean to them? What misconceptions are still operating? What conclusions can be drawn?

6. *Articulating findings to others.* This is where children need guidance in how to talk about what they found that they feel is important. They will need to organize the information in some useful way and communicate their outcomes to others.

True inquiry, of course, requires a teacher to go beyond setting up a simple science display or contrived experiment without directed attention or follow up. These inquiry skills can be put into motion again and again to have children advance their understanding of the "big areas" of science, with use of the following:

❏ Earth sciences (weather; space; ecology; major features of the earth)
❏ Physical sciences (change in matter; forces affecting motion, balance, direction, speed, light, heat, and sound; magnetism; electricity; physical properties and characteristics of phenomena)
❏ Life sciences (characteristics of living plants and animals; life cycles and processes; basic needs, habitats, and relations)

Integrating Science Across the Curriculum. Teaching children about basic concepts in science is a natural catalyst for curriculum integration. For example, when the children in Mr. Mishler's room became interested in the dandelions cropping up in a field near the school, their investigations led them to drawing and writing about their magnifications and dissections of the plants and plant roots, measuring and graphing lengths of stems they found, estimating and counting the numbers of emerging plants, and painting the fascinating yellows and greens of the new plants and the plants that had already gone to seed. The children classified the leaves of dandelions and other plants, discussed and formulated a definition of what constitutes a weed and what constitutes a flower, read and constructed poems about flowers and fauna, and performed for another class the silly song that Mr. Mishler wrote about dandelions. They began using the correct term for the yellow substance that came off on their fingers and chins when they were handling the dandelions and discovered the purpose of the substance in the life cycle of plants. They experimented with creating a yellow dye and methods for removing it from swatches of material. Mr. Mishler includes different genres of children's literature for the children's science, including picture books and selected pages from information books. He is always careful to make sure that the nonfiction books are accurate or to point out any inaccuracies to the children. The children's excitement about their investigations is enhanced by the number of engaging pictures and interestingly displayed books that appear in special places in the classroom.

Clearly, all curricular activity could spring from science; at the least, good sciencing requires integration of activities and experiences from all other learning domains. The depth and breadth of children's learning will depend on hands-on opportunities to collect a wide variety of information and guidance in integrating this knowledge through reflective discussion about what they discover.

Using a more in-depth, theme-repetitive approach toward science education that can lead to higher order problem-solving skills rather than rote memorization should be a priority in good science teaching. Another priority should be to help children make connections between science and real-world issues. Once children have developed the basic skills of observing, inferring, and experimenting, they should be encouraged to engage in scientific inquiry, a process that requires them to think about and interpret what they are gaining through the many sensory-experience activities in the early childhood classroom.

Remember that teaching with a hands-on approach to science does not automatically teach problem solving and inquiry. Also necessary is the teacher's ability to ask good, open-ended questions and to provide well-planned activities involving guided discovery, problem solving, and social inquiry. For example, when Ms. Villareal asks children to use the paper bear tracks she has developed to measure the distance between the "bear den" and the dramatic play center, she is simply using a hands-on approach. However, when she tells them, "Find some way to measure the distance from the bear den to the dramatic play center and then report to the group on how you did this and what you found out," she is engaging the children in inquiry. The first approach simply has children carrying out a process she designed. The second encourages children to develop scientific skills that will become enormously useful to them—discovering a way to gather data when they need to problem solve, mentally organizing the information, and effectively articulating it to someone else.

The Young Child as Mathematician

For young children, mathematics is everywhere. It is a natural and integral part of their world. They see numerals everywhere—on their house, on the clock, on the cereal box, on their play telephone, on the car, and in books. Many of their favorite finger plays, songs, and rhymes, which are used to encourage language, also develop math vocabulary and concepts: "Ten Little Monkeys Jumping on the Bed," "One, Two, Buckle My Shoe," "Eency Weency Spider," "The Grand Old Duke of York" (Smith, 2008). Favorite books, such as Jon Scieszka and Lane Smith's *Math Curse*, Eric Carle's *Rooster's Off to See the World*, and Pat Hutchins's *The Doorbell Rang*, help shape children's early perspectives about the relations among different components of mathematics and their connection to every aspect of children's lives. At home, in preschools, and in elementary schools, young children sit at the computer, interacting with such characters as Zack the cabdriver and Chester the lazy raccoon, who take them through a variety of math activities in Infinity City or into fractions and decimals in a program called *Math Keys* (Minnesota Educational Computing Corporation [MECC]; Macintosh/Windows).

Every teacher can sympathize with the frustration felt by a child who cannot solve apparently straightforward and simple arithmetic problems. It is not only effort that gives some children facility with numbers, but an awareness of relationships that enables them to interpret new problems in terms of results that they remember. Children who have this awareness and the ability to work flexibly to solve number problems are said to have a "feel" for numbers or "number sense." What characterizes children with "number sense" is their ability to make generalizations about the patterns and processes that they have met, and to link new information to their existing knowledge (Anghileri, 2006).

Today, mathematics instruction is less about teaching basic computation and more about helping students become flexible thinkers who are comfortable with all areas of mathematics and are able to apply mathematical ideas and skills to a range of problem-solving situations (Burns, 2007). Your role is to bridge each child's informal knowledge of mathematics with more formal concepts of mathematical knowledge and thinking. How you arrange the environment, the opportunities you present for real problem solving, the methods you model, and the way in which you allow children to use materials and work together will all be crucial factors in how well children learn to become critical thinkers and problem solvers. Will they be sitting still and only listening to you or will they be learning through engaging physical, mental, and social activities? Will mathematical problem solving become an integral part of center and daily activity in the operation of your classroom or relegated just to the math time slot on your daily schedule? Will debriefing, comparing findings, and talking about processes for arriving at answers become as important a part of your mathematics program as getting the right answer and the activities themselves?

By watching, listening, and copying, children will initially learn isolated facts, but they need to be encouraged right from the beginning to see how numbers are used differently and also the connections that underlie their use. If you were to do this, you would teach a child that the written symbols 0, 1, 2, 3, 4, 5, 6, 7, 8, 9 are called *numerals*. They stand for a *number* value or amount. The number 5 can be associated with five objects, 6 with six objects, and so on. We can help children recognize that 5 always comes before 6 and always after 4, and that 4 can be a pattern of $1 + 1 + 1 + 1$ or a pattern of $2 + 2$ or "double 2" or 6 minus 2 (Anghileri, 2006). What is important is that children not become rigid in their thinking and unable to see the meaning making that can be so much fun in working with numbers, shapes and space, patterns, classification, seriation, problem solving, and other aspects of mathematics.

Diversity in race, ethnicity, social class, gender, out-of-school experiences, and modality-related learning styles is critical to consider when we are designing developmentally appropriate classrooms (Charlesworth, Lind, & Lind, 2009). Even prior to kindergarten, some children understand that a counting sequence indicates increasingly larger quantities; others can also identify objects to 10, recognize some numerals, and identify coins and geometric shapes. Some kindergartners may even solve simple addition and subtraction problems in their heads. Other children in the same classroom may never have seen a computer, and their math vocabulary may be limited to the words *big* and *little*.

Even though wide differences can be found in any one classroom of children, preschoolers and early primary-age children share one characteristic: Their conceptualization is limited by thinking parameters common to the preoperational period (i.e., centration, egocentrism, and irreversibility). Thus, most children have a considerable amount of work to do before they will truly understand what "fiveness" is all about, as well as other logical-mathematical concepts. For example, although a child may be able to demonstrate "counting," he or she may have no true understanding of the hierarchical nature of counting.

Building Basic Concepts in Mathematics in the Early Years. As with other mathematical concepts, children's understanding of counting moves through a sequence governed by the following set of principles (Hohmann and Weikart, 1998).

1. *One-to-one principle.* Using one and only one number name (such as "one, two, three") for each number counted.
2. *Stable-order principle.* Using the number names in a stable order, such as "one, two, three" even though the order may be unconventional, such as "six, eleven, fifteen."
3. *Cardinal principle.* Using the last number name spoken to describe the number of objects in the set, "One, two, three . . . Three snakes!"
4. *Abstraction principle.* Counting part of a mixed set of items, for example, counting the red blocks in a building made of multicolored blocks.
5. *Order-irrelevance principle.* Recognizing that the order in which objects are counted is irrelevant. Six balls are always six balls no matter which one you count first. (p. 482)

Moreover, the child's logic may not yet be developed enough to know that a rearrangement of the same objects leaves the number or amount unchanged. For example, 4-year-old Chelsey was presented with two rows of five pennies each and asked to count each row. She did so, counting the pennies one at a time, and said there were five pennies in each row. When asked, "Are there the same number in each row, or does one row have more?" she methodically counted again and responded, "They're the same." As she watched, the pennies in the second row were spread farther apart from one another. When asked, "Now is there the same number in each row, or does one row have more?" she quickly pointed to the second row and said with confidence, "This one has more!" Chelsey was obviously centering on the length of the two rows and was unable to think about the difference in spacing at the same time. With this kind of understanding, Chelsey did not yet have an anchor for making decisions about the use of number.

Young children are eager to build on their basic concepts of logical-mathematical knowledge. Many of these concepts, such as comparing, classifying, and measuring, are needed as the child grows conceptually in other developmental domains, including the affective, social, and aesthetic arenas. Similarly, concepts the child is developing in other areas, such as science (observing, communicating, inferring, predicting, hypothesizing, defining, and controlling variables) and language (higher, slower, warm, hardest, longest, and juicier), will be important for logical-mathematical extensions (Charlesworth, Lind, & Lind, 2009).

At first, a child gains mathematical knowledge through naturalistic experiences completely controlled by the child; these experiences are complemented by informal, exploratory activity in which adults offer comments or ask questions. Young children need a prolonged period of informal exploration before they can form basic concepts about shape, one-to-one correspondence, size, weight, texture, and amount. For the preschooler, this exploration occurs through such natural activities as building with blocks; pouring water; working with sand, puzzles, and play-doh; cooking; and matching, sorting, and seriating objects. In interacting with adults and one another during such activities, they also extend their foundational math vocabulary, picking up words used for comparison, position, direction, sequence, shape, time, and number (Smith, 2008).

A basic math vocabulary should be developed during this period for preschoolers and kindergarten children that includes the following:

❑ Words that describe positions in space (*over, under; above, below; inside, outside*)
❑ Words that describe amounts (*more, less; most, least; quarter, half, whole*)

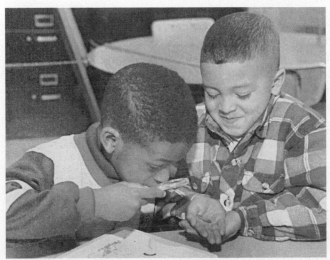
Pairing children in cooperative learning situations enhances concept building.

❑ Words that describe size (*large, small; smaller than, larger than*)
❑ Words that name shapes and parts of shapes (*rectangle, square, circle, triangle, line, angle, arc*)
❑ Comparative vocabulary (*-er, -est*)
❑ Speed vocabulary (*fast, slow; quick*)

Eventually, activity that is wholly hands-on is replaced by more structured acquisition of mathematical concepts. However, most school systems are incorporating early childhood mathematics programs that continue to include manipulatives and open-ended questioning as important learning components.

Since "math avoidance" among girls begins very early, you will want to purposefully structure classroom activities in such a way as to make sure you are "catching" the girls' interest in mathematical activity, as well as the boys'. What are ways to engage them at working with blocks, technology, and mathematical problem solving so that activities aren't contrived or forced? What kinds of problems, games, and activities appeal to the girls in your classroom in developing math concepts? If certain children don't choose to participate in these, how can you restructure them to build continuing competencies in children?

CURRENT EDUCATIONAL ISSUES

Making sense of all the information we currently have about cognitive development and experiential considerations is a complex but critical task for early childhood educators to tackle if children are to become effective, lifelong learners. Despite the extensive work to reform early learning contexts and ensure qualitatively better outcomes for children, a number of controversial issues persist.

Using a Constructivist Approach versus Direct Instruction

I struggle with how much to allow my kindergartners to discover on their own and when to use direct instruction to teach a math or science concept. What's the answer?

This leads us to one of the most important questions being asked in early childhood education today. Should teachers be directly teaching young children or is their role only to support children as they construct knowledge? We make a mistake when we construct programs that favor one approach over another. Evidence indicates that young children can develop highly efficient skills to solve math or science problems without understanding what lies behind the process they have used. Although they can demonstrate expertise in getting the "right answer," they are often hard pressed to explain the procedure to someone else or to transfer the discrete skills to other situations or problems. Because the brain requires a great deal of repetition so that it can detect patterns, concept formation is better ensured when children experience both variety and repetition in not only logical-mathematical activities, but also the follow-up discussion that has been recommended for making sense of their findings. Thus, professionals must develop classroom experiences that help children make meaningful connections through enriched, thematic, and real-life experiences rather than cutting off such connections by "bits and pieces" instruction (Association for Supervision and Curriculum Development, 2008).

A recent observation in an Oakland County, Michigan, kindergarten class at math time provides some insight into this dilemma. In this case, the teacher missed a great opportunity to extend children's understanding through scaffolding and reflective discussion:

Many of the children were actively involved with manipulatives while the teacher worked on sorting with a small group of youngsters. She passed a container filled with interesting objects around the group and asked each child to select two that were similar in some way. She then asked each child to tell the others how his or her objects were the same. Although every child was successful in choosing two objects that were similar in some way, not one child could tell her the similar feature. Clearly, though, some children had an understanding of the salient characteristic because they attempted to show it nonorally. For example, one child, who had selected a quarter and a plate, used his finger to trace a circle in the air. However, he did not have a name for this characteristic. The teacher then complimented the children on their selections and excused them from the group.

Effective teaching requires the early childhood educator to play many roles in the classroom, as described previously in chapter 3. In addition to being a facilitator and learning guide, the teacher must also be active in transferring existing knowledge that children cannot discover on their own. In this case, children needed vocabulary (social-conventional knowledge) to help them articulate what they were trying so hard to describe. The teacher could have involved the other children in helping to label the circle that was being drawn in the air. She could also have said, "Excellent, Jamel. You're representing a circle in the air. Is its shape square or round? Are your two objects square or round?" Although many thoughtful, well-meaning early childhood teachers are struggling with this issue, direct instruction is an appropriate and necessary component in early childhood classrooms as we help children work on problems they find interesting to study.

Using Calculators and Computers in the Early Childhood Classroom

How appropriate is it to have young children spending time in the classroom with computers, and don't calculators actually shortcut the development of mathematical thinking?

Becoming knowledgeable about the growing number of technological tools available must be a requirement for today's learner. The questions related to their use include how early children should be introduced to them, how much time should be allocated to their use at the expense of other learning, and whether they should be allowed in "testing" situations or only in follow-up practice once conceptualization has been fixed.

Despite the widespread use of calculators, teachers and parents continue to resist their use in school. Many people believe that children who are allowed to use them will fail to develop a conceptual understanding of mathematics operations. The results of more than 80 studies on this issue firmly dispute this idea. These results indicate that using calculators in instruction and testing sharpens children's performance, problem-solving ability, and affective attitudes about mathematics (Kennedy, Tipps, & Johnson, 2009).

Although young children need to learn to estimate and calculate problems mentally (mental math), they must eventually learn to do paper-and-pencil math and to use a calculator. Each of them should have access to a calculator, and the calculators they are given should have easy-to-read numbers found directly on the keys, easy-to-depress keys that move distinctly when depressed, four functions with an automatic constant for addition, and solar power (Smith, 2008). Even very young children can use such calculators in the dramatic-play center and the math and science centers. Just as they are taught other skills with tools, they should be allowed to explore and practice with calculators, which are sure to become an increasingly important and helpful tool in their understanding number operation.

Similarly, computers can enhance learning and should be considered a necessary piece of equipment in the early childhood classroom, providing games and simulations that aid problem solving, and allowing students to use some fairly engaging tutorial programs for skill building and practice. Teachers need to be astute with respect to selecting software that is operationally easy to use. Not only should it be entertaining, but it also should teach a skill, process, or concept. Professionals also need to observe the children carefully to ensure that they can understand the task involved and are not just pushing buttons.

There are a number of publications that offer technical, instructional, and practical aspects of computer programming with young children, including *Arithmetic Teacher, Child Care Information Exchange, School Science and Mathematics, Journal of Computers in Mathematics and Science Teaching,* and *Instructor* magazine's monthly feature on technology (Kennedy et al., 2009).

Using Worksheets and Workbooks as a Primary Teaching Mode for Mathematics

Some parents in our school are pushing to have us use workbooks. What rationale can I provide for my principal about why I prefer not to use workbooks or dittos?

Sometimes parents and others see worksheets in the early years as an indication that the program is truly more educational or academic in nature than other programs and that teachers are introducing children to "real work" (Worthington & Carruthers, 2004). They question the value of using them, particularly as a mode to find out what children know for a number of reasons.

❏ The children have no ownership of the content of the worksheet.
❏ They are also confined by layout; the child has to fit into the worksheet organization and way of doing mathematics.

❑ Most worksheets have closed questions and only one answer.
❑ Worksheets do not tell what a child knows about mathematics and the way he or she is thinking.
❑ Worksheets do not reveal what the child can do but often what the child cannot do.
❑ Young children can often get bewildered in finding the sense in a worksheet.
❑ The match of worksheet to child is difficult and children can work below their actual ability.
❑ Worksheets that claim to be "teaching" mathematics have sometimes very little mathematics in them to assess (e.g., the typical worksheet with the numeral 2 in dots for the children to go over, accompanied by two large balloons to color in). The child might respond to the teacher's question, "How many balloons?" This takes 3 seconds and the child traces around the numeral and colors in the balloons. The coloring takes 20 minutes or more. The exercise is really coloring in and not mathematics!

We feel the same way about the use of workbooks in the preprimary and early grades. A teacher may want to use an example given in a workbook, re-create it on a white board, and present the problem to groups of children for discussion. A child who has little concept of what is being asked for initially may learn a great deal by listening to children and the teacher talk about a problem presented and watch as the solution is obtained; however, to go back and work independently on workbook pages that call for knowledge the child does not yet have is a waste of that child's time and effort. The only thing we can be sure we're teaching in a case like that is that mathematics is stressful and to be avoided. Interestingly, children like workbooks for all kinds of reasons. That doesn't mean they're good for them or effective in providing skill building or assessment of learning.

Constructing Optimal Environments

Effective early childhood classrooms are those in which children have many opportunities to express their thoughts, wishes, and ideas to one another as well as to adults. The best early childhood classroom exists in an active, well-prepared, workshop-like environment. A truly effective early childhood classroom must be carefully constructed by a professional who understands that young children are eager to learn and will respond responsibly when they are given the freedom, resources, and guidance necessary. Efforts should be made to match what happens in the classroom as nearly as possible to what happens in the child's mind and to provide both familiar and slightly discrepant logical-mathematical problems that relate to children's experience and engage their interest. Moreover, to be able to act effectively on a full range of later problems, children must maintain an appreciation of their ability to think divergently, creatively, and imaginatively in addition to developing convergent modes of thinking. This kind of approach to information seeking and problem solving cannot result from learning a narrow set of learning strategies for information processing (Gardner et al., 2006).

NATIONAL EXPECTATIONS AND STANDARDS

At present, almost all states already have or are in the process of developing standards to guide the quality of instruction and assessment in early childhood education. In addition, in most of the academic domains such as literacy, math, science, and social studies, national professional organizations have also created sets of standards that outline what students should be learning, quality of teacher preparation, and quality of system delivery.

For science, the National Research Council (NRC) and National Academy of Science (NAS) formulated the 1996 National Science Education Standards: Observe, Interact, Change, Learn. In addition, standards work in science has been done for preschool curriculum by CTB/McGraw-Hill (2002) and McREL (Kendall & Marzano, 2004). The standards for science encompass both inquiry, or the processes of science, and content, as reflected in the science competencies outlined next in this chapter.

In mathematics, much of the momentum for moving toward a more comprehensive, useful, and meaningful instructional approach has been provided by the leadership of the National Council of Teachers of Mathematics (NCTM), which formulated the 1989 Curriculum and Evaluation Standards for School Mathematics for grades K–4, 5–8, and 9–12. Together with the NAEYC, the NCTM has published a position statement that includes preschool-age children for the first time

(NCTM, 2000). The overall goals of the Standards (see the Goals for Mathematics subsection next in this chapter) are for children to learn to value mathematics, become confident in their ability to perform mathematics, become mathematical problem solvers, learn to communicate mathematically, and learn to reason mathematically. This document clearly states that rote memorization is obsolete. Students are to process information more actively, develop the kind of skills and understandings that will allow broad application in a number of fields, and learn to use tools such as calculators and computers for problem solving. Instruction should grow out of genuine problems of interest to children, and teachers are to engage children in small-group and paired activities. Educators are also mandated to follow up on classroom activity, discussing with children the methodologies the children have developed for their problem solving and what they have learned (Kennedy, Tipps, & Johnson, 2009).

Ongoing authentic assessment is the primary strategy suggested for documenting children's conceptual understanding and includes anecdotal records taken during observation and interviews and from work samples (drawings, graphs, sketches, and written work), inventories, and the child's self-appraisals collected in a portfolio. Assessment and evaluation should include strategies to determine a child's conceptual understanding of operations as well as his or her ability to work through problems by applying the "rules."

To promote optimal development of these concepts, effective teachers equip their classrooms with a wide variety of well-chosen, interesting manipulative materials that invite exploring, sorting, combining, and experimenting. Minimally, these include interlocking counting cubes, linking materials in a variety of colors and shapes, measuring instruments, play money, geoboards, tangrams, geometric models, attribute blocks, collections (keys, buttons, seashells, plastic animals, and bottle tops), beads, timers and clocks, base 10 materials, and probability devices (dice, spinners, etc.).

Effective teachers also structure many opportunities for children to hear the correct names for conventional tags again and again, especially those that cause children problems (e.g., in 11, there is no "teen" sound; in 20, there is no "2" sound), which promotes understanding, proficiency, and the language needed to describe operations. Such teachers involve children in activities especially contrived to promote a framework for mathematical thinking and problem solving. Teachers monitor and nurture this understanding by posing good questions to help children notice discrepancies and come closer and closer to the correct answer. They encourage children to think about the relevant pieces of information needed to solve problems and challenge them to think of other ways to find an answer or defend their proposed solutions. Many of the experiences the children have are gamelike, including board games, dice, cards, bingo games, lotto, and measurement of real aspects of the near environment. Other experiences come naturally out of the everyday operation of the classroom, which helps children perceive mathematics as relevant and useful rather than as something to memorize and repeat (Brewer, 2004).

As with science, every aspect of the curriculum can and should be used to promote logical-mathematical conceptualization. The integration of linguistic and mathematical thinking—having children write about mathematics—is an especially good technique for encouraging children to examine their ideas and reflect on what they have learned (Burns, 2007). Children should be challenged to think mathematically, rather than just arithmetically, and inquiry and discussion about why a fact is so should replace the practice of just "getting the right answer." In this way, children develop internal rules and principles to help them understand number and number relations in our base 10 system of numbers. This internalized comprehension can then be used in other situations, such as those requiring understanding of multiple digits or place value. Children who are given the correct answer repeatedly do not necessarily discover why a fact is so. Thus, they are left with little ability to make use of the information without a helping adult to continue to do the headwork. Teachers who encourage memorization of math facts without teaching some simple but helpful rules or "tricks" to remember produce children who learn arithmetic at the expense of learning mathematics (Baroody & Dowker, 2003).

PURPOSE AND GOALS FOR THE COGNITIVE DOMAIN

Goals in the cognitive domain are drawn from and consistent with those published by the National Academy of Science (NAS) and National Council for the Teaching of Mathematics. (NCTM).

Purpose

The aim of the cognitive domain is for children to acquire, apply, adapt, integrate, and evaluate knowledge as they construct new or expanded concepts.

Goals for Science and Other Cognitive Functions

As children progress, they will:

1. Examine the observable properties of man-made and natural objects, using their multisensory abilities.
2. Learn and apply the scientific process.
3. Explore firsthand a variety of cause-and-effect relations.
4. Demonstrate an awareness of the interdependence of all things in the world.
5. Develop and refine their skills to communicate findings.
6. Become aware of their thought processes, building more accurate, complete, and complex concepts with time.
7. Recognize that knowledge and data come in many forms and can be organized and displayed in diverse ways.
8. Acquire knowledge related to a variety of technology and become competent in using it.
9. Acquire scientific knowledge related to the life sciences.
10. Acquire scientific knowledge related to the physical sciences.
11. Acquire scientific knowledge related to the earth sciences.
12. Explore a variety of scientific equipment, such as simple machines, magnets, and measuring instruments.
13. Use scientific equipment appropriately and safely.
14. Develop and use an accurate vocabulary related to scientific events, objects, and processes.
15. Participate in recording scientific data.

Goals for Mathematics

As children progress, they will:

16. Understand numbers, ways of representing numbers, relations among numbers, and number systems.
17. Understand meanings of mathematical operations and how operations relate to one another.
18. Compute fluently and make reasonable estimates.
19. Recognize, describe, and extend patterns.
20. Sort, classify, and order objects by size, number, and other properties.
21. Represent and analyze mathematical structures, using algebraic symbols.
22. Add and subtract whole numbers, using objects, pictures, and symbols.
23. Describe change in various contexts.
24. Analyze characteristics and properties of two- and three-dimensional geometric shapes.
25. Specify locations and describe spatial relations.
26. Recognize symmetrical shapes in a variety of positions.
27. Use visualization, spatial reasoning, and geometric modeling.
28. Understand measurable attributes of objects and the units, systems, and processes of measurement.
29. Apply appropriate techniques, tools, and formulas to determine measurements.
30. Formulate and ask questions using data.
31. Select and use appropriate statistical methods to analyze data.
32. Develop and evaluate inferences and predictions that are based on data.
33. Understand and apply basic concepts of probability.
34. Understand and represent commonly used fractions.

MAKING GOALS FIT

In order to be effective in teaching young children about physical science, we need to carefully design activities that are age-appropriate (see Table 11.2).

TABLE 11.2 Teaching Age-Appropriate Physical Science Concepts

Goal #10	Example of Activity for 3- to 4-Year-Olds	Example of Activity for 5- to 6-Year-Olds	Example of Activity for 7- to 8-Year-Olds
Children will acquire scientific knowledge related to the physical sciences.	Understand the effect of push and pull through exploration of a variety of magnets and materials.	Construct and observe objects that spin; describe some of the variables that influence the spinning of objects.	Measure the forces between two magnets as the distance between them changes; illustrate and describe this in your science journal.

TEACHING STRATEGIES

The most important fact to keep in mind when you are teaching preprimary- and primary-age children is that the minds of these children are evolving—and if they are to build a solid and reliable cognitive base, we cannot do all the thinking for them. Teachers who fail to appreciate the young child's need to construct knowledge may diminish his or her potential development. Conversely, teachers who go overboard in minimizing their role in the child's developing intellect, morality, and personality also err. A teacher does not promote understanding by permitting students' constructions to stand even though they clash with experts' constructions. Rather than waiting for correct scientific entities and ideas to be constructed and validated, teachers need to find a way to provide developmentally appropriate experiences to challenge children's misconceptions (Gardner, 2006).

In the early years, children need to be taught by professionals who are knowledgeable about constructing environments conducive to learning. Instead of imposing their predetermined goals, these teachers provide materials, activities, and suggestions that encourage initiative and independent pursuit. Such teachers allow children adequate time to explore, investigate, reflect, and ask questions. They differentiate effectively between teaching strategies that promote logical-mathematical and physical knowledge and those needed to extend social-conventional knowledge in young children (Kamii & DeVries, 1977). This approach calls for, in the former case, refraining from providing the correct answer, challenging children to think about what it might be, and having them follow through by investigating and evaluating their ideas. In the latter case, when extending social-conventional knowledge, good teachers respond to a child's inquiries with correct information; if they are not sure what the answer is, they are honest about not knowing and then work with the child to obtain the information needed. Following are eight additional ideas for structuring a fertile climate for learning.

1. **Encourage intellectual autonomy when expanding children's general cognitive skills.** Use projects and themes that are drawn from the children's interests and that offer a broad and integrative framework for interaction to effectively set the scene. The concept of using hands-on experiences and activity for developing the young child's conceptual thinking will be especially important. Introduce every concept with real objects first, and plan several related experiences to reinforce a given concept rather than presenting isolated activities at random. Emphasize the process rather than solely the products of children's thinking.

Questioning used to stimulate their thinking or to discover why children have categorized, sequenced, or solved a problem in a certain way should be open ended. Allow children to reach their own conclusions regarding cause-and-effect relations, and the answers they offer should be accepted. When children make errors, plan further experiences or suggest other approaches that might help the children discover the correct answer or have more success with individual tasks. However, when children are having difficulty with a concept or with demonstrating proficiency, help them break a task into more manageable parts and introduce them to the next step in the sequence when doing so would be helpful. Teach particular skills and facts in contexts relevant to children.

2. **Develop children's ability to move out of a comfort zone with respect to inaccurate concepts.** Cardellichio and Field (1997) underscored the teacher's role in closing the gaps between children's "spontaneous constructs" and scientific constructs by providing the child with enough data to force them to challenge misconceptions and create strong, accurate conceptualizations. Such gap closing can be accomplished through well-constructed activities used along with information books, resource persons, field trips, and provocative questioning. These researchers also suggested the following seven strategies for encouraging cognitive development and divergent thinking.

    a. *Hypothetical thinking:* This is a powerful technique to create new information. Einstein developed his theory of relativity by asking, "What would it look like to ride on a beam of light?" For example, a teacher might ask, "What would happen if you . . . ?" "What if . . . ?" The key is not in asking the organized question but in the follow-up questions such as "What if this had happened?" "What if this had not occurred?" "What if this were not true?" "What if I could find out how to do something I can't do right now?"

    b. *Reversal:* Here, you turn the current perspective upside down. For example, say, "What if you had your mother's role and she had yours?" "What if we slept during the day and stayed awake at night?" "What if we always ate our dessert before we ate the rest of our dinner?" "What if children ran the schools and teachers were students? What would it be like?" "What if we had only summer clothes to wear in the winter and winter clothes to wear in the summer?"

    c. *Application of different symbol systems:* Instead of using words to tell something, ask children to create a song, act it out, or develop another set of symbols to use in place of a current set.

    d. *Analogy:* Look for correspondences to create new insight about both elements in an analogy. Say, "What is like this?" "How is this like . . . ?"

    e. *Analysis of point of view:* Determine why someone holds a particular opinion or belief. Say, "What harm might occur if we . . . ?" "What do you think one of your parents might think about that?" "Who would love it if . . . ?" "What if the wolf turned out to be . . . ?"

    f. *Completion:* Give the beginning of a story and ask children to form the ending; give the ending of a story and ask children to form the beginning or the middle.

    g. *Use of graphic organizers (charts, tables, information webs, Venn diagrams, and flowcharts):* These organizers promote children's comprehension and vocabulary development, eliminate oversimplification, and extend children's understanding of the complexity of relations, events, and so forth. They help to make relations among concepts concrete and explicit.

3. **Place more emphasis on children's understanding of concepts than on rote learning.** Keep in mind that children's development of logical-mathematical concepts follows a predictable pattern. Always begin teaching new concepts by using concrete experiences. Provide a variety of manipulatives (real objects) to be used for sorting, classifying, comparing, estimating, predicting, patterning, graphing, measuring, counting, adding and subtracting, understanding parts and wholes, and gaining concepts of number, conservation of number, quantity, shapes, mass, and volume. When involving children in making mathematical equations, provide sets of real objects in addition to materials such as number stamps and number cards before paper-and-pencil tasks are introduced. Circulate among children, observing how they are approaching tasks, and structuring brief miniconferences to check their understanding of the targeted concept.

After children have had numerous concrete experiences, introduce representational concepts (e.g., pictures or drawn figures). Introduce abstract experiences last (e.g., abstract symbols such as $2 + ? = 5$). Allow children ample opportunities to explore a given material before asking them to use it in a prescribed way. Present the same mathematical concepts and skills on many occasions and in many ways (e.g., drawing numerals in the air, in sand, in salt, in finger paint, on the chalkboard, and on paper). Involve them in playing a variety of games using cards and dice.

4. **Integrate science and mathematical concepts and skills throughout all areas of the early childhood curriculum.** Link logical-mathematical activities with social studies and language arts as well as with pretend-play, affective, aesthetic, physical, and construction activities as often as possible.

5. **Extend children's science and mathematical vocabulary.** Use a wide variety of accurate terms when talking with children about their day-to-day experiences (e.g., number; mass; size; shape; position of objects in space, relations among objects; and changes in the functioning, position, or characteristics of objects).

6. **Use everyday experiences in the classroom to help children connect science and mathematics to daily living and see it as useful and necessary.** Capitalize on problems that occur naturally in the classroom, school, or community that can capture children's curiosity.

   Incorporate mathematical tools into classroom routines (e.g., calendars, clocks, rulers, coins, scales, measuring cups, graphs). Practice addition and subtraction in natural settings without symbols, encouraging children to use headwork to solve problems. Draw children's attention to aspects of daily work and play in the classroom that utilize mathematical concepts (e.g., durations of time—5 minutes until cleanup, 15 minutes for recess, and 2 weeks off for spring vacation).

   Introduce scientific concepts by building on the everyday experiences in the lives of the children in your class. Make available a wide array of natural materials through which children can explore the physical world. Examples include collections of natural objects (seashells, rocks, and bird nests), live animals (fish, guinea pigs, and insects), plants, and scientific tools (scales, magnifiers, and magnets). Take advantage of spontaneous events to highlight scientific ideas. Emphasize children's discovery of principles of cause and effect by allowing them to draw conclusions based on their experiences with real objects. Select scientific themes that include both first-time experiences for children and experiences with which children are familiar.

7. **Develop positive learning attitudes and practices in the classroom.** Model an interested, curious, enthusiastic attitude toward science, and encourage children's curiosity by providing them with numerous hands-on scientific experiences and relevant demonstrations. Carry out scientific demonstrations with groups small enough that children can become actively involved and can feel free to ask questions about what they are observing. Help children to observe more carefully by first directing their attention to a particular aspect of an object or a phenomenon and then asking them to describe what they see (e.g., "Look up at the sky. Tell me what you see."). Encourage children to make predictions by asking them, "What will happen next?" and hypothesize and draw conclusions by asking them, "Why do you think that happened?" Convey only accurate scientific terms, facts, and principles to children, checking out any information about which you or the children are unsure. Help children recognize many sources of scientific information, such as books, their experiences, and resource people.

8. **Use collections as a way to extend and assess children's ability to categorize, classify, and display information.** Give children individual or group opportunities to create collections of natural objects (e.g., rocks, shells, leaves, stones) or man-made objects found in the environment (e.g., buttons, nuts and bolts, keys and locks, textures of cloth, sets of magnets). Offer them guidance on collecting objects and what may be appropriate or inappropriate to collect. Provide opportunities for children to display and tell about their collections.

myeducationlab

To check your comprehension on the content covered in Chapter 11, go to the Book Specific Resources in the MyEducationLab for your course, select your text, and complete the Study Plan. Here you will be able to take a chapter quiz, receive feedback on your answers, and then access review, practice, and enrichment activities to enhance your understanding of chapter content.

ACTIVITY SUGGESTIONS

Science Activities

Soil Samples (For Younger or Less Experienced Children)

Goal 1 Examine the observable properties of man-made and natural objects, using their multisensory abilities.

Materials Containers for gathering soil samples, trowels for digging, plastic wrap, magnifying glasses, pots and molds, water glasses, water pitcher, quickly sprouting seeds, paper, markers

Procedure Help children gather a number of kinds of soil samples—such as sand, gravel, clay, and loam—placing each sample in a different container and covering with plastic wrap to retain moisture. Before the soil samples have time to dry out, place them on separate sheets of paper for examination. (*Note:* Working with small groups of children is recommended so that subtle changes can easily be observed.)

(continued)

To simplify Invite the children to use magnifying glasses to observe differences in the samples. Have the children rub the samples between their thumb and forefinger to note differences in texture. Ask them to smell the samples to detect any differences in smell. Provide a number of pots and molds and suggest that they try to mold the samples. Discuss with them which samples seem to hold together better than others and why this might be so.

To extend Examine the various samples to determine how much air they contain by filling separate water glasses with each of the soil samples and leaving some room at the top to add water. Slowly pour in water from the water pitcher and watch as it soaks in and displaces any air, helping the children to note the size and frequency of bubbles. Assign a team of children to each soil sample and have them carefully examine the pile for organic components such as stones, insects, and leaves. Have each team note the kinds of components they find, decide how to record their findings, and then report their findings to other teams. Place samples of each kind of soil in pots. Water to see if any weeds will sprout. Record findings. Place quickly sprouting seeds (one variety) in various samples and have children note which kinds of soil promote the best growth. In another experiment, have children test different growing conditions by altering light, water, and heat (Nickelsburg, 1976).

Sniff Test (For Younger or Less Experienced Children)

Goal 1a Examine the observable properties of man-made and natural objects, using their multisensory abilities.

Materials One set of small vials, each with a particular and unique smell (e.g., flower, perfume, lemon, orange, garlic, coffee, extracts); a second set of vials with the same scents; blindfold; magazines

Procedure Have the children form a circle. Choose one child to be blindfolded in the center. Distribute one set of vials among children in outer circle. The blindfolded child is given one vial from the second set and must move around the circle, using his or her sense of smell to find the matching vial and identify what he or she is smelling.

To simplify Have children individually match each container to magazine pictures of the source of the scent.

To extend Enlarge the variety of scents. Choose scents within categories (e.g., all flower scents, all fruit scents, or all coffee scents). Design a similar activity to test sense of taste.

---

*What's the Solution? (For Younger or Less Experienced Children)**

Goal 3 Explore firsthand a variety of cause-and-effect relations.

Materials Sand, salt, water, two clear jars, coffee filters, teaspoon measure, spoon for stirring, other materials (e.g., sugar, baking soda, coffee, cornstarch, dirt, gravel, beans, tempera paint), paper, pencils

Procedure Explain to the children that sometimes things mix together without changing. Sometimes the things being mixed turn into something new, which is then called a *solution*. Have children fill one of the jars with very warm water, add 1 teaspoon of sand, and stir for 30 seconds. What happens to the sand? Then have them hold the filter over the mouth of the empty jar. Empty the first jar into the filter. What is left in the filter? What is left in the jar? Ask whether they have created a solution, reminding them of the definition of the term. Next, have them empty and clean both jars and repeat their experiment, this time using a teaspoon of salt instead of sand. What is left in the filter? What is in the jar? Where is the salt? What happens to the salt? Have they created a solution or not?

To simplify Carry out the experiment using only the salt.

To extend Have them experiment with other materials such as sugar, baking soda, coffee, cornstarch (use $\frac{1}{2}$ cup cornstarch and $\frac{1}{2}$ cup water to produce an interesting goo), dirt, gravel, beans, and tempera paint. Have children who are able record their findings in their science journals. Have children construct a chart on which they differentiate materials that dissolve from those that do not.

---

*Source: Adapted from Scholastic's *The Magic*.

Mystery Box (For Younger or Less Experienced Children)

Goal 5 Develop and refine their skills to communicate findings.

Materials Box; set of related objects

Procedure "Hide" several objects in a box. Provide oral clues to the children about the identities of the objects. Invite the children to ask you questions about the objects to discover what is in the box.

To simplify Place only one object in the box. Select an object with which all the children are familiar.

To extend Place several objects in the box that are different but have one characteristic in common (e.g., all are articles of clothing). Have one of the children take on the role of "clue giver."

Plants or Animals (For Older or More Experienced Children)

Goal 9 Acquire scientific knowledge related to the life sciences.

Materials A variety of laminated pictures of foods (e.g., milk, fruit, vegetables, hot dogs, bread, cheese, hamburger, beans); two boxes, one labeled "Plants" and another labeled "Animals"; paper; pencils or pens

Procedure Discuss with the children that all living things need food and that some food comes from plants and some from animals. Have the children sort the food according to their sources. Once the foods are sorted, have the children make a list of the foods in each category.

To simplify Sort the foods without listing them.

To extend Have the children find out how green plants get their food. How is this different from the way animals get their food? Ask children if they can think of foods they eat that are a combination of plant and animal (e.g., spaghetti with meatballs).

Me and My Shadow (For Older or More Experienced Children)[†]

Goal 10 Acquire scientific knowledge related to the physical sciences.

Materials *Me and My Shadow,* by Arthur Dorros (Scholastic); one of the following for each child: piece of cardboard or stiff paper from which to make a cutout of a shape or figure, pencil, thread spool, adhesive tape, large piece of white paper, crayons or markers; assorted materials (e.g., construction paper, waxed paper); pens or pencils

Procedure After reading *Me and My Shadow,* have children make a cutout figure (person, bear, horse, etc.), use the tape to attach the cutout figure to the eraser end of the pencil, and then stick the pointed end of the pencil in their thread spool. Ask them to predict what will happen when the figure is placed in the sun. On a sunny morning, have them go outside and place the figure in the center of a large piece of paper. Have them use different-colored markers or crayons to trace the shadow on their paper at approximately 10:00 A.M., noon, and 2:00 P.M. Discuss with them how the shadows changed during the day.

To simplify Supply cutout figures.

To extend Have the children determine how to block the shadow made by the figure by using assorted materials (construction paper, waxed paper, plastic wrap, tissue paper, etc.). Have them describe what happens with each type of material. Have children measure the length of the shadows made at 10:00 A.M., noon, and 2:00 P.M. and describe what happens. Older children can write about the outcomes in their science journals. Provide information books about shadows and have children look up information about how shadows are formed. Have children construct drawings of the shadows formed at particular times of the day.

[†]Source: Adapted from Brainard and Wrubel (1993).

In and Out of Balance (For Younger or Less Experienced Children)

Goal 15 Participate in recording scientific data.

Materials Balance scale, wooden blocks, spoon, Ping-Pong ball, pencils or pens, other objects

Procedure Ask the children to carry out a series of experiments to see which weighs more: (a) a wooden block or a Ping-Pong ball, (b) a Ping-Pong ball or a spoon, (c) a spoon or a wooden block. Have them draw the results of each experiment in their science journals, numbering and dating each experiment.

To simplify Have them discriminate between only two objects.

To extend* Have them choose other objects that are more difficult to discriminate visually, recording their predictions prior to the experiment, then their findings.

*Source: Adapted from Hein and Price (1994).

Mathematics Activities

Place-Value Pocket Game (For Older or More Experienced Children)

Goal 16 Understand numbers, ways of representing numbers, relations among numbers, and number systems.

Materials A series of laminated cards on which individual numerals 1–9 are written; pocket charts with six slots labeled (from right to left): "ones," "tens," "hundreds," "thousands," "ten thousands," and "hundred thousands"

Procedure In small or large groups, choose individual children to play the game. Hand a child two or three numeral cards (fewer cards for a child with a less developed understanding) to form a two- or three-digit number. For example, hand the child the numerals 2, 3, and 6. Say, "Form a number that has 6 hundreds, 3 tens, and 2 ones [632]. Now tell us the number you have made." Have children suggest any corrections if needed and tell why they are needed. Have the child select another card and play the game again. Vary the number of cards given to a child by matching it to individual performance level. Children will build skills by watching higher degrees of performance demonstrated by other children.

To simplify Demonstrate the game before asking children to play. Use only one or two places. Place numeral cards, noting the place for each, then ask the children to tell the number you have made. Once they understand place value, place two or three numeral cards, and then ask whether the cards represent a number you say to them.

To extend When the children are ready, challenge them to play up to the hundred thousands place.

Count and Match (For Younger or Less Experienced Children)

Goal 16 Understand numbers, ways of representing numbers, relations among numbers, and number systems.

Materials Magazines, scissors, magnifying glasses, cards with numerals and representative symbols, blank cards, glue or paste

Procedure Have the children gather pictures that clearly display a certain number of objects (e.g., number of teeth in a smiling face, number of birds flying in a flock, or number of boats sailing on a river). Have children pair up, and tell them to look at the picture, count the objects, and then match the picture to a card with the numeral identifying the number of objects. Magnifying glasses can be supplied to help children distinguish the numbers of objects more clearly.

To simplify Use cards displaying only the numerals 1 to 5 and including matching round circles or other graphics to represent the number indicated.

To extend Provide materials for matching numbers of objects beyond five. Have children search through magazines for pictures that can be matched with particular numeral cards. These can be pasted on cards, mixed up, and then sorted by children into appropriate piles coordinated with the appropriate numeral cards.

✏ *Grouping and Sorting (For Younger or Less Experienced Children)*

Goal 20 Sort, classify, and order objects by size, number, and other properties.

Materials Sets of objects that can be grouped on the basis of size, shape, color, pattern, or position

Procedure Give children daily opportunities to classify a variety of objects. Remember that there are no right or wrong ways for children to classify. Instead, emphasize the process by which children reach their conclusions. Use the following script to guide your instruction:

> "Show me a way to put these into groups that are alike."
> "Good. You found a way to sort the objects."
> "Tell me why these things [point to one grouping] go together." (Repeat for each grouping and accept the children's answer for each.)
> "Show another way to sort the objects into piles."

To simplify Use fewer objects with more obvious grouping possibilities.

To extend Provide greater numbers of objects and those with more than one common characteristic so that children will discover more sophisticated combinations (e.g., grouping all yellow objects that have something to do with transportation).

✏ *Pictorial Story Problems (For Younger or Less Experienced Children)*

Goal 22 Add and subtract whole numbers, using objects, pictures, and symbols.

Materials Pictorial scenes and sets of related objects, blank number strips, markers

Procedure Give children individual pictorial scenes, such as an apple tree or a field, a barn and corral, or a seashore. Invite children to place selected objects on a particular scene and to tell an arithmetic story problem about what they have just depicted (e.g., "There were five apples on the tree, and three fell on the ground. How many apples were there in all?").

To simplify Use only a few objects. Demonstrate a simple addition problem.

To extend Use more objects. Invite children to think of as many combinations as possible. Have children develop written number strips for each combination after it is concretely constructed (e.g., $2 + 5 = 7$; $3 + 4 = 7$; $1 + 6 = 7$; $10 - 3 = 7$). Children may also work with partners, with one child thinking of and constructing the problem and the other child checking the work and developing a written number strip.

✏ *Bull's-Eye! (For Older or More Experienced Children)**

Goal 29 Apply appropriate techniques, tools, and formulas to determine measurements.

Materials A set of laminated cards with a numeral between 1 and 100 on each card, a set of cards with a numeral between 100 and 1,000 on each card, a set with a numeral between 1,000 and 10,000 on each card, calculators, paper, pencils or markers

Procedure Using a set of cards selected according to children's abilities, group three or four children together to play the game. Each child draws two to four cards (as agreed on by the group) and mentally estimates the sum of the numbers, which is written down. Each student then uses a calculator to find the sum and checks with the others. If correct (Bull's Eye!), the child receives a point. The child with the most points at the end of the time or after five rounds is the winner.

To simplify Limit numerals to 1–50.

To extend Have children use calculators to determine the difference between each sum and each estimate. The difference between the two numbers becomes a score. After five rounds, the group sums the scores for each player, and the player with the lowest sum is the winner.

---

*Source: Adapted from Kennedy, Tipps, & Johnson (2009).

Fraction Fun (For Older or More Experienced Children)

Goal 34 Understand and represent commonly used fractions.

Materials Unifix cubes or bear counters in two colors, graph paper, markers in same two colors as cubes or counters

Procedure Have children line up six same-color cubes or bears. Ask them to make additional rows, substituting one more cube of the opposite color in each additional row until they get down to a seventh row made up entirely of the opposite color. Ask children what they notice (e.g., the colors look like stairs). Ask, "How many cubes are in the first row? What fractional part of our whole is the different-colored cube in the second row (1/6)? In the third row?" and so on.

To simplify Begin with only four blocks in the first row, asking questions appropriate for the children's current understanding.

To extend For older children, ask, "What fractional part of our whole is the different-colored cube in the first row (0/6)?" Use 10 blocks as a starter row. Have children make up fraction word problems to go along with their display (e.g., "If there were 10 apples, and Mother used 8 of them to make a pie, what fraction of the apples is left?"). Have children represent their two-color fractions on graph paper. Have children show and write their fractions. Ask, "What fraction is more of the bar, 2/10 or 8/10?" Note, "8/10 is bigger than 2/10. We show this as 8/10 > 2/10."

SUMMARY

Cognitive development in the young child is a complex process. Outcomes depend on the quality of children's experiences both inside and outside the formal classroom as they move through a series of psychosocial and neurobiological changes.

Children's ability to acquire knowledge and then use it effectively to plan, monitor, and evaluate their capabilities is better ensured when they have developed and can maintain a measure of confidence in themselves and in others. This type of confidence results when they are nurtured by adults who understand the critical interrelation between cognition and all other areas of development.

Learning environments that stimulate optimal cognitive growth are those in which curricular construction is guided by sensitivity to variations in development, in which children are encouraged to be both independent and collaborative learners, and in which high task involvement is motivated through the presentation of diverse and engaging activities that young thinkers and doers perceive to be personally useful.

Key Words

abstraction principle	logical-mathematical knowledge	order-irrelevance principle
axon	metacognition	physical knowledge
cardinal principle	mirror neurons	pruning
cognition	myelin	representational knowledge
cognitive processing	neuroimaging technologies	social conventional knowledge
CREB	neuron	stable-order principle
dendrite	neuroscience	synapse
inquiry	one-to-one principle	synaptogenesis

Applying What You've Read in This Chapter

1. **Discuss**
   a. How does theory about how people learn influence our approach to introducing math and science concepts in the early childhood classroom?
   b. Which of the cognitive theorists' ideas most closely coincide with your own in terms of how people learn?
   c. How does inquiry go beyond process learning? What are some strategies that encourage inquiry?

2. **Observe**
   a. Make an appointment to observe the classroom of an experienced early childhood teacher. What is the instructional approach for the cognitive domain? What

logical-mathematical materials are present in the classroom? How does the teacher use the outdoor environment? Are children encouraged to discuss their findings and how they arrived at their answers or simply involved in activities?

3. **Carry out an activity**
   a. Identify upcoming specialized trainings or courses in manipulative math or hands-on science. Plan to attend one this year and try at least five of the ideas with a group of young children.
   b. Keep a journal for 1 week. What kinds of problem solving were you called on to do that involved the use of the math or science concepts described in this chapter?
   c. With a small group of school-age children, ask, "Can you prove at least three things that happen or don't happen when water freezes?" How do they react? What do they say they will do to find the answer? Discuss how this approach might yield different results than those obtained by simply asking the children to fill a container with water, freeze it, and then explain what happens.

4. **Create something to put in your portfolio**
   a. Develop a math-based lesson plan based on the format provided in this text.

b. Develop a cognitive- or science-based lesson plan based on the format provided in this text.

5. **Add to your journal**
   a. Think about your early experiences with math and science. Did you take higher level courses in secondary school and college? Were you encouraged to do so? Do you think your strengths or limitations in this area have had an effect on your professional development?
   b. How aware are you of the way you approach problem solving on an everyday basis? How adept are you at analyzing problems? How rational or logical are you in problem solving? How adaptable are you in your thinking? How fair minded are you in judging others? Think of a specific example of your behavior when you answer each of these questions.

6. 🖐 **Consult the standards**
   a. Go to the Internet and search for "Science Standards." What two organizations emerge as the leaders in advancing science standards? In what way do science standards serve as goals for development in multiple domains? Choose an example of three of these and discuss how they are critical in terms of general cognition, rather than just science.

PRACTICE FOR YOUR CERTIFICATION OR LICENSURE EXAM

The following items will help you practice applying what you have learned in this chapter. They can help to prepare you for your course exam, the PRAXIS II exam, your state licensure or certification exam, and for working in developmentally appropriate ways with young children.

Children younger than 5 years old are often influenced by what is known as "perceptual salience," that is, their perceptions dominate their understanding, and seeing is believing. They don't automatically know what older children come to know—that number, mass, distance, volume, and area remain constant despite change in appearance and that you can undo operations.

At a summer camp craft class, 9-year-old Juana and her 3-year-old brother Carl had created a sculpture from toothpicks and marshmallows. Each child had been given 20 marshmallows and 10 toothpicks to create what he or she wanted. Carl, after completing a "spaceship" with his materials, began pestering Juana for more toothpicks and marshmallows to make a different spaceship because he did not like the one he had created. "Just use the ones you have!" she replied testily. Carl looked down in a confused way at the unwanted creation, thought again about the other one he had in mind, and cried, "But they're all gone. I don't have no more!"

1. **Constructed-response question**

   From Juana's viewpoint, it was possible to construct a new product from materials available. From Carl's, it was not.

   a. Describe a strategy you would use to move Carl toward greater understanding about

undoing an operation. What exactly would you say other than, "You didn't like the spaceship you made anyway. Let's take it apart and make a new one."

   b. Explain why 9-year-old Juana might be impatient with Carl's perspective.

2. **Multiple-choice question**

   The cognitive theorists presented in Table 11.1 in this chapter share both similarities and differences in the way they believe children develop concepts about their world. Which of the following is most consistent with that of Russian psychologist Lev Vygotsky?

   a. Carl will eventually come to develop the concept of undoing operations, simply by growing older rather than by additional experiences like this one right now.
   b. Carl would benefit most from his camp counselor helping him to focus on what is relevant in this case, that is, that the original materials can be used in another way.
   c. Carl's camp counselor could structure a series of activities for the children, cementing their understanding at successively sophisticated levels.
   d. Carl would benefit enormously by having a number of additional experiences just like this one and from having someone ask Socratic questions to help him come nearer and nearer to a correct conclusion.

The Language Domain

You may wonder:

How does oral language develop in young children?

What is the connection between oral language, phonological and phonemic awareness, and emerging reading and writing?

How can I enhance young children's emerging literacy skills in developmentally appropriate ways?

What is meant by a balanced literacy program?

How can I integrate language experiences across the entire curriculum?

I n this chapter, information is presented to help you answer these questions.

◆ ◆ *Three-year-old John listens intently at his Head Start center as the dental hygienist explains why brushing our teeth is necessary to prevent tartar from forming. He watches as she shows pictures of brownish tartar that has collected on some teeth. Later, he is playing with the family cat and exclaims, "Mom, look! Snowball has tartar sauce on his teeth!"*

◆ ◆ *Five-year-old Nancy draws a picture of herself as a ballet dancer. When her teacher asks her to write a story about her picture, she does so by drawing a series of round shapes next to the picture, but no letters or words. She explains, "I can write, but it takes too long, so I make these."*

◆ ◆ *Seven-year-old Ethan is still struggling with his reading. He has trouble isolating sounds within words and reads so slowly that all academic subjects have become difficult for him.*

All these children are in varying stages of language and literacy development. The quality of this development hinges on their neurological maturity, early and subsequent experiences in language exposure, interactions with others that focus on the use of print, and engaging opportunities to apply newly developing and higher level understandings in a variety of situations.

The intersection between language and literacy acquisition is a complex, continuous, and interactive process that drives children from rudimentary understandings to increasing sophistication (Rumelhart, 1994). Critical components of the language domain and necessary skills that must be built include the following:

❏ Listening and viewing—paying attention to communication that is heard or visually represented

❏ Speaking—developing an adequate vocabulary and primary language structure to communicate needs and ideas to others

❏ Reading—making meaning from texts through the use of prior knowledge, semantics, syntax, visual, aural, and tactile clues

❏ Writing—gaining understanding of an alphabet system to communicate with others across time and space

All of these components must be made meaningful and useful to children if they are to become fully literate. Most influential will be the important adults in a young child's life. From them, the child learns how language structure is modeled, begins to discover the purposes for communicating with others, and is motivated to do so (Soderman, Gregory, & McCarty, 2005).

ORAL LANGUAGE DEVELOPMENT

Alexander, at age 2 years, is already attuned to three languages. His maternal grandmother has come to the United States from Hungary to live with the family and care for him while his parents work. Because she speaks little English, the language she and Alexander have begun to share is Hungarian. His favorite playmate is a slightly older toddler who lives next door, Hao Hao, whose primary language is Chinese. When crossing the street on the way to the playground with his grandmother, his friend Hao Hao, and Hao Hao's mother, Alexander

The foundation for language is built early through informal interaction with others.

remembers and repeats his grandmother's warning: "Vigyázz . . . kocsi! (Careful . . . car!)." At the playground, when he shares a sand toy with Hao Hao, his mother reminds Hao Hao to tell Alexander, "Xiè-xie (Thank you)." Alexander looks thoughtful for a moment and then repeats the words over and over to himself softly as he fills his pail with sand, "Xiè-xie, xiè-xie." That evening, when asked by his grandmother, "Megfürdik? (take a bath?)," he shakes his head and responds, "Nem (No)," and then looks at his English-speaking father and says, "No!" just to be sure everyone understands that he is not yet ready to begin his bedtime ritual.

Even with a variety of multicultural influences, Alexander's English language development at age 24 months is on target. His *receptive vocabulary* (i.e., the number of words he understands) contains about 300 words. His *expressive vocabulary* (i.e., words he uses to express himself) is clearly not as large but seems to be exploding as he demonstrates a few new words each day. He is learning that he can use language for various purposes: to satisfy his needs and wants (instrumental), to control others (regulatory), to create interactions with others (interactional), to express his personal thoughts and opinions (personal), to create imaginary worlds (imaginative), to seek information (heuristic), and to communicate information to others (informative). By the time Alexander is 6 or 7 years old, he will have a remarkable, adultlike grasp of the grammar, syntax, vocabulary, noun phrases, meaning, and pronunciation that make up his primary languages. He will accomplish all this without ever being wholly aware of language forms and structures. His creative ability to imitate and pick up on the patterns, rhythms, and meanings of language is believed to be primarily the result of innate tendencies.

Solid research documents human language as a built-in, genetic predisposition that is hardwired into the brain. As far as we know, only human beings can acquire language, although many other species develop strategies for communication (Lightfoot, Cole, & Cole, 2008). Some human developmental processes are *experience expected* and others are *experience dependent*. Speech and language appear to be both, but are largely experience expected. They would develop even when there is deprivation or overstimulation in the child's environment; they seem impervious to both. The eventual quantity (vocabulary development) and quality (syntax and ability to elaborate) of the child's language development depend on exposure and stimulation. Thus, we talk, sing, and read to young children to save brain synapses from elimination, not to cause new synapses to form (Bruer, 2003).

Red Flags in Early Speech and Language Development

By age 2, some children, mostly boys, are noticeably lagging in speech or language development. During the preschool years, children develop the ability to articulate sounds, with /p/ and /b/ being the earliest and others such as /r/ and /l/ taking as long as 6 years of age to fully develop. Listeners who are not familiar with a child's speech patterns may be expected to undersand only 25 percent of what a 1-year-old says, 50 percent of what a 2-year-old says, and 100 percent of what a 4-year-old says. Even then, however, not all sounds are produced accurately, and there may still be disruptions of fluency and rhythm (Batshaw, Pellegrino, & Roizen, 2007). Seventy-five percent of all expressive language delays resolve by the time children enter school. The remaining 25 percent often signal more serious and long-lasting problems (Figure 12.1) such as those resulting from congenital or acquired hearing impairments or problems in the cognitive, sensorimotor, psychological, emotional, or environmental systems (e.g., poverty, nonverbal family, bilingual home, or repeated and untreated ear infections) (Kalb & Namuth, 1997). Parents and caregivers of young children who are not keeping up with their peers in language development frequently take a wait-and-see approach rather than seek intervention.

Mispronunciations are common in the preschool years, primarily because of a lack of auditory discrimination. A quarter of all children have difficulty untangling consonant sounds in their primary language even as late as 7 years of age, and this difficulty is often reflected in their

FIGURE 12.1   Teaching Language Skills to a Child with Special Needs

Theresa

Theresa, a 4-year-old, has been blind since birth. Because of a severe case of respiratory distress syndrome, she had required high levels of oxygen for many weeks as a premature infant. By the time she was 4 months old, she had been diagnosed with retrolental fibroplasia. Subsequent lags in development resulted in delayed speech, although her performance on the Peabody Picture Vocabulary Test–III (PPVT–III) for receptive language appeared normal. By age 4 years, her behavior had become difficult. She reacted strongly against change and, when frustrated, she would hold her breath, scream, rock, and bang her head.

When Theresa was enrolled in a school program with children who could see, her teacher, Ms. Wing, was unsure about whether she, not Theresa, could cope. The blindness was less of a problem than the temper tantrums. Ms. Wing found that the best resource she had for trying to turn the situation around was Theresa's parents, who had begun to attend some classes to help them with training Theresa at home.

Strategies that the parents and the teacher agreed to implement involved removing Theresa to a quiet place when she began screaming and telling her that she would have to stay there until she could rejoin the group without frightening the other children. When she began rocking or banging behaviors, Ms. Wing and Theresa's parents quickly involved her in other tasks. Gradually, with all the adults in her life reacting consistently and helpfully, Theresa's behavior both at school and at home began to improve, and she became more independent.

Knowing that Theresa would have to rely on Braille for reading and heavily on her auditory strengths for vocabulary, Ms. Wing introduced a larger number of tactile activities in her classroom. She has worked not only with Theresa, but also with the other children on becoming especially astute listeners. "This is a skill that all the children in my classroom need in order to become good communicators and more highly successful readers and writers later on," notes Ms. Wing.

---

spelling and articulation blunders. Thus, we sometimes see children pronouncing *then* as "ven" (see Figure 12.2) and *birthday* as "birfvay." *And* is often pronounced as "ad," *spaghetti* is more frequently than not said "busketti," and words such as *trouble* and *tree* are heard and spelled as "chrubel" and "chree." Problems in dysfluency that frequently occur in 3- and 4-year-olds, such as primary stuttering, are often labeled *hesitant speech*. This type of speech results from children's having to focus cognitively on *how* they are communicating something rather than on *what* they want to say. Listening patiently for them to speak usually gives them the time they need to communicate.

Many speech-language pathologists agree that speech or language therapy is unwarranted prior to kindergarten, especially if the child is showing good comprehension and using gestures to communicate. However, children who are clearly frustrated at being unable to communicate their feelings and needs may be in danger of developing behavioral problems or withdrawing from others (Kalb & Namuth, 1997). Also, children progress through a *speech readiness period*, beginning at approximately age 9 months and extending until age 2 years, in which they appear to be most receptive to learning language. Although apparent problems may seem to resolve later, some experts believe that too much developing cognition may be lost in the interim because language and developing cognition are so closely intertwined. Moreover, children who are not speaking effectively by school entry often lack the ability to interact successfully with others in the learning context. Behaviors of a preschool child that may signal more serious long-term outcomes include the following:

❑ Does not turn when spoken to, recognize words for common items, or use sounds other than crying to get attention
❑ Does not respond to changes in tone of voice or look around for sources of sound, such as a ringing doorbell
❑ Cannot point to pictures in a book that are named or understand simple questions
❑ Cannot understand differences in meaning (e.g., *up* and *down*), follow two requests, string together two or more words, or name common objects

FIGURE 12.2   Auditory Discrimination That Is Not Yet Fully Developed

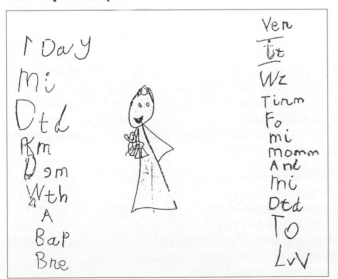

"One day my daddy came home with a baby bunny. Then (Ven) it was time for my mommy and my daddy to leave."

❏ Does not answer simple "who," "what," and "where" questions
❏ Cannot be understood by people outside the family
❏ Cannot use four-word sentences or pronounce most individual sounds in words correctly

The bottom line in determining the seriousness of abnormal speech and language development in children prior to age 5 years seems to lie in ensuring that from early infancy on, a child's receptive language is intact and that the child is demonstrating comprehension reasonably appropriate for his or her age level, good intelligibility, and a willingness to be engaged with others in his or her daily activities. If delays persist until kindergarten, most pediatricians recommend speech therapy (Cowley, 1997).

CHILDREN'S ACQUISITION OF LITERACY

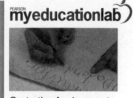

myeducationlab

Go to the Assignments and Activities section of Topic 9: Content Areas/ Lessons and Activities in the MyEducationLab for your course and complete the activity entitled *Promoting Literacy*. What do various theorists believe about language and literacy?

Before continuing to read this chapter, take a moment to reflect. Can you remember learning to read and write? What specific memories and mental pictures are you *immediately* aware of related to the process?

When we are asked to reflect on our earliest literacy experiences, many of us think about sitting in a formal reading group at approximately 5 to 6 years of age. A basal text (early reader) is being used, and individual children in the group are being called on to read brief portions of the text. The teacher is there to correct mistakes and help the reader along.

How closely does this description match what flashed through *your* mind when you were considering the preceding questions? Usually forgotten or discounted are the many other experiences that we had in infancy and early childhood—listening to stories; seeing pictorial representations; and becoming familiar with letters, words, and other print experiences before we had any formal reading instruction. Most important was the extent to which our parents and others communicated with us, elaborated on our efforts to communicate with them, encouraged our practicing language, and modeled correct grammar usage, moving us along a continuum of oral language development (Soderman & Farrell, 2008).

In infancy, children become increasingly sensitive to the sounds, rhythm, and intonation of language around them. With their built-in cognitive mechanisms, they move from initially making just throaty sounds to babbling at 4 months of age and then imitating a broader range of sounds by age 8 months. Around this time, they are already beginning to narrow their "ear" to the distinctive set of individual sounds constituting our primary language. By 1 year of age, children proudly show off with several words and babbled sentences that mean something to them but not necessarily to anyone else. Then, because of a heady growth of neural connections prior to age 18 months, an explosion of receptive language occurs, during which they may learn as many as 12 words a day. At about 20 months old, they realize that everything in their world has a name, and "What's that?" becomes a favorite question (Otto, 2009).

Children who are developing second languages acquire them in much the same way, first beginning to recognize recurring sound patterns, language chunks, and often-heard words or phrases. Through social interaction, they venture in certain situations to attempt words and phrases, often mixing them together with words from their primary language. Once a child acquires 50 to 100 words for objects and actions in the second language and begins to use them functionally and exhange them, the new language takes off quickly (Soderman & Oshio, 2008).

Those of us who reached the upper limits of early language development were fortunate to have had many of the following rich literacy experiences:

❏ Leafing through cardboard picture books as an infant
❏ Nestling into a lap and being read favorite stories
❏ Watching television programs such as *Sesame Street*
❏ Observing others while they were reading and writing
❏ Playing "school" with other children, perhaps being challenged by an older sibling to name as many "B–buh" words as we could think of
❏ Drawing pictures and scribbling with chalk on the sidewalk
❏ Excitedly pointing out a favorite place to eat because we knew its name started with a huge *M or B*

❑ Looking at newspapers, magazines, and other print around our homes
❑ Making our names and other words in finger paint or sand
❑ Deciphering secret codes from friends
❑ Reading comic books
❑ Rhyming silly words
❑ Being fascinated with the sound and corresponding written version of certain words (even "naughty" words)
❑ Picking out specific letters on license plates while riding in the car
❑ Identifying our first few sight words correctly without anyone else's help

The Importance of Phonological Awareness

As young children mature, their interactions with others support the growth of oral language and early **phonological awareness.** This is the understanding that oral language can be divided into smaller components and manipulated (van Kleeck, Gillam, & Hoffman, 2006) (see Table 12.1), It is an auditory and oral process that grows in complexity during early childhood, beginning with an ability to "hear" and then generate rhymes. Subsequently, children gain an understanding of segmentation in sentences (ex. [Little Miss Muffet] [sat on a tuffet]; [Jack and Jill] [went up the hill] and the ability to recognize individually segmented syllables (Car-o-lyn, grow-ing). With time, they acquire the concept of onset and rime (f . . . an, p . . . an, m . . . an) which leads to the

TABLE 12.1   Literacy Terminology, Definitions, and Related Activities

Term	Definition	Example of Activities to Promote Development
Alphabetic Awareness	Knowledge of letters of the alphabet and understanding that they correspond to spoken sounds in the language, and that left-to-right spellings of printed words represent phonemes from first to last	Collecting objects with same beginning sounds; writing experiences; ABC books
Alliteration	A string of words that begin with the same sound	Listening to and generating tongue twisters that begin with the same letters and sounds (e.g., "Suzy sells seashells . . ."); making up silly poems, using a particular letter; reading alliteration books
Graphemes	The letter symbols in an alphabet	Learning letter shapes, letter names, letter sounds; letter writing; distinguishing upper- and lowercase letters; learning to distinguish letters
Onset and Rime	Onsets are the beginning sounds of words. Rimes (consisting of 37 phonograms) begin with a vowel and share the same spelling endings (e.g., -at, -ack, -ing)	Recognizing and generating word families (e.g., *mat, sat, fat, rat, hat* or *sing, wing, thing, ring*)
Phonemes	Discrete sounds in a language	Games to identify words that start or end with same or different sounds; clapping the numbers of syllables in a word; stretching out words; exaggerating individual sounds in words
Phonemic Awareness	Awareness that the speech stream consists of a sequence of sounds or phonemes	Separating names and words into syllables or beats; blending sounds into words; segmenting words into sounds
Phonics	A tool to help make concrete connections between individual graphemes and their associated sounds and to understand vowel and consonant patterns	Decoding print; writing words and stories; translating units of print into units of sound; translating units of sound into units of print
Phonological Awareness	Understanding of different ways that oral language can be broken down into smaller components and manipulated.	Listening to and generating nursery rhymes; word play; moving sounds around to create new words
Prosody	The "music" and rhythmic sounds of one's own primary language	Participating in songs, finger play, poetry; listening to the reading of narrative picture books

most sophisticated substrate at the end of a continuum of phonological awareness, that of **phonemic awareness.** This requires the understanding that the speech stream consists of a sequence of individual sounds or **phonemes** and that we can create new words segmenting, blending, or changing them (Chard and Dickson, 1999).

Phonemic awareness is a critical skill that must be addressed with young children because it becomes the most powerful influence on their eventual success in learning to decode unfamiliar words and learning to spell. Those with little phonological awareness before elementary school become severely disadvantaged and perform significantly more poorly in reading, even through the third grade. They may learn letter–sound associations but be unable to read or spell unfamiliar words. Evidence indicates that children with well developed phonological awareness eventually develop greater *automaticity*, which allows reading to become much more fluent (Gray & McCutchen, 2006; Snow & Kang 2006).

As children move through the preschool period and into kindergarten, they benefit enormously from activities that teach the following eight skills (Bennett-Armistead, Duke, & Moses, 2007).

1. Separate words into syllables or beats
2. Recognize rhyming words
3. Generate rhyming words
4. Recognize words that start or end with the same sound
5. Generate words that start or end with the same sounds
6. Blend sounds into words
7. Segment words into sounds
8. Move sounds around to create new words

The skill of detecting sounds in language depends wholly on the child's developing good listening skills. It is supported when children have ample opportunities to engage in meaningful conversations with adults, have interesting books read to them to enlarge their vocabularies, and play with other children in ways that require speech to be used to express their ideas. **Alliteration** activities, in which all the words used begin with the same sound, and rhyming activities that involve **onsets** (beginning sounds of words) and **rimes** (word families that begin with a vowel and share the same spelling ending) help children develop phonological awareness. For instance, when Ellis is listening to his mother read his favorite nursery rhymes and rhyming picture books—and when he and the other children are participating in songs and finger plays in the classroom—his ears and brain are being trained to pick up the individual sounds in spoken words.

Adults can further enhance children's listening skills and build phonological awareness when they do the following:

1. Include activities in which children hear, say, and see language simultaneously. This can help children at all stages of literacy development to see some of the connections between oral and written language. For example, when Ms. Gregory chooses Big Books that have rhymes in them, points to the words as she reads, and invites children to clap or snap each time they hear the rhyming, and to tell her the rhyming pair, she is building their phonological awareness.
2. Encourage word play by planning for rhyming activities using stories, games, and songs so that children can hear the sounds of language and manipulate them orally.
3. Design segmentation activities. With very young children, teachers can have them count the number of words in a single sentence. For older children, a teacher can segment the words into discrete sounds.
4. Use alliteration activities often, by making up or writing silly poems and reading alliteration books.
5. Encourage children to use temporary spelling (writing the sounds they hear, which may or may not include all the letters in the conventional spelling of the word) (Soderman, Gregory, & McCarty, 2005).

Given the tremendous impact that phonological awareness has on later reading and spelling abilities, waiting for it to happen "naturally" would be unfair. Purposeful activities belong in every classroom, preschool through third grade, and children who respond poorly to them should be assessed to determine risk for not acquiring beginning reading skills. This may be done as early as the second semester of kindergarten, using a psychometrically sound test such as one of the following (Stone, Silliman, Ehren, & Apel, 2004):

Test of Phonological Awareness—Kindergarten (TOPA-K)
Yopp–Singer Test of Phonemes
Bruce Test of Phoneme Deletion

When a child is having trouble isolating individual sounds in words, adults should also investigate the possibility of speech perception difficulty. There may be impaired sensitivity to speech rhythms and the ability to identify words spoken quickly (Holleman, Wood, & Sheehy, 2008).

We know that children's knowledge about the alphabet as they enter kindergarten is also one of the best predictors of eventual reading achievement. **Alphabetic awareness** includes children learning letter shapes, letter names, letter sounds, and letter writing. They also need to learn about upper- and lowercase letters, be able to distinguish between letters, and connect them to the sounds they make (Neuharth-Pritchett, Hamilton, & Schwanenflugel, 2005). This is where **phonics** becomes helpful. It is a systematic approach focused on helping children associate letters and their sounds and to understand connections between letter patterns and the sounds they represent.

Initially, children may find the alphabet confusing, because letter groups such as *b, d, p,* and *q* are rotations of the same visual pattern in different positions. Similarities of other combinations such as *v* and *n,* or *m* and *w,* are also a challenge; *s* is a letter in one position, but the rotated symbol is not a letter. This is a stage at which playfulness with language can enhance early literacy learning. Many games and songs, as well as a treasure trove of lovely alphabet books, can introduce children to letters.

Enhancing and Scaffolding Children's Emergent Literacy

So far, we have discussed a number of factors that predict or, when undeveloped, may deter literacy success. Many of these factors emerge naturally in the preschool years but can also be enhanced by activities structured for the early childhood classroom. **Emergent literacy**, or the development and association of print with meaning, begins early in a child's life and continues until the child reaches the stage of conventional reading and writing (IRA & NCTE, 1996).

The development of many literacy skills seems to follow definite sequences, and these are highly interactive, social processes. The child first begins to attend to and copy certain behaviors and then, with the continued help of adults or older children and additional experiences, begins to remember how to replicate them more and more independently and conventionally. For example, when parents or teachers take young children on a shape hunt to find as many triangles, squares, circles, and rectangles as they can, children develop the following:

Visual discrimination
Awareness of whole-part relations
Memory to recall images and configuration
The ability to differentiate and discriminate
The ability to follow directions
Receptive and expressive vocabulary

With block and puzzle play, children increase the following:

Visual discrimination
Eye coordination
Awareness of whole-part relations
Awareness of spatial relations
Memory to recall sequences and placement
The ability to attend to detail

Listening games in which children must attend closely to discover the "secret object" do the following:

Enhance memory
Build auditory discrimination
Increase the ability to attend to detail and vocabulary

Watching Big Books as the stories are read or sitting in an adult's lap to listen to a favorite book aids in the following:

Heightens children's awareness of literacy conventions (left to right; top to bottom, page-to-page)
Builds vocabulary
Reinforces the concept of reading for meaning
Increases eye coordination

As children play games with familiar text, they increase sight knowledge of words and growing knowledge of the following internal structures of words.

Syllables
Orthographic shapes of graphemes
Grapheme–phoneme connections
Visual discrimination
Memory of configuration
Speed in differentiating between mirror images such as b/d, p/q, m/w, 91/19

All of these skills serve as precursors for and enhance emergent literacy.

For adults to be most effective at scaffolding literacy tasks with young children, they must have expertise with respect to child development and knowledge about the sequence in which literacy skills emerge. For example, in emerging writing, children progress through the following stages.

FIGURE 12.3 Stage 1 in Emerging Writing

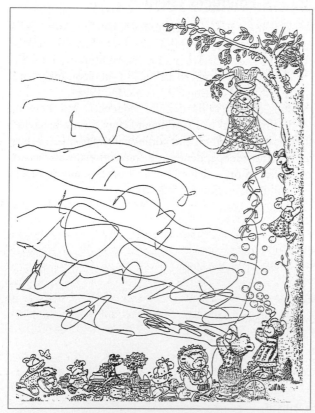

Lauren, age 4, trying to write a thank-you note to her grandmother, complained to her mother, "I don't know grown-up writing!" "Just write like a 4-year-old," suggested her mother. Lauren drew lines on the page to make it "writing paper" and scribbled her message. When asked to read it back, she said, "I don't know what it says. I wrote it in French!"

Stage 1—Emerging

Writes pre-letter marks, followed by differentiation of marks (see Figure 12.3)
Uses letterlike forms
Writes letters and letter strings: *BuTERToWGlpR*
Writes words with fixed quantities (e.g., uses three to five letters, no matter how long or short the word is)
Uses single letters for words
Enters consonant stage: Initial consonants appear (e.g., *VKn* for *vacation*)
Skips endings
Does not use spaces between words
Uses correct directional movement
Learns letter names and letter sounds
Uses approximations and invented spelling
Uses some known words in correct positions
Can select own topic to write about

Stage 2—Early

Uses end sounds of most words correctly
Knows letter names and letter sounds
Enters alphabetic stage: vowels appear (e.g., *vacashun* for *vacation*)
Overcompensates for vowels (e.g., *moashun* for *motion*; *ideeus* for *ideas*)
Can spell many difficult words correctly
Uses more correct spellings than approximations
Uses initial blends
Uses editing skills
Underlines approximations
Uses word sources to correct approximations
Uses capital letters in correct places

Writes a title

Varies topic choice

Stage 3—Fluency

Uses final blends

Uses suffixes correctly (e.g., *-s, -ing, -ed, -ly*)

Uses syllables

Uses editing skills

Compares own work with print in books and elsewhere

Correctly places quotation marks, question marks, apostrophes, and commas

Correctly divides story into paragraphs

Publishes correct articles of work

Varies sentence beginnings

Can sequence ideas

Writes in a variety of styles: friendly letters, factual reports, imaginative pieces, retellings, and poems

Highly effective teachers clearly use an interactive approach in their teaching, scaffolding children from lower level to higher level skills when they have had adequate practice and are ready to move to more sophisticated skill attainment. Recognizing that one of the children was doing a fair amount of early writing and was ready for the next step—leaving spaces between his words—Kay Clevenger, a superb teacher in Brighton, Michigan, challenged a child to find a strategy. "What could you use to separate those words more clearly," she asked him. He decided he would put dots between each word to help him remember (see Figure 12.4). Before long, he recognized that putting dots between the words took longer than just leaving spaces, and he quickly moved to a new level of understanding and capability in his writing. Kay knows that for the children to internalize important principles about their early reading and writing, she must remind them again and again in meaningful ways, provide the daily practice they need, and celebrate with them when they demonstrate they are getting it. She finds all kinds of clever ways to draw their attention to the "big ideas" she wants them to learn about writing:

Letters must be in a certain order to spell a word.

In English, writing goes from left to right, and top to bottom.

Capitalization rules require changes in the size and the shape of letters.

Spaces are used to denote words and ends of sentences.

In another setting, Mr. Hewlett scaffolds a small-group reading experience. Prior to beginning an unfamiliar story with new vocabulary, he leafs through the book, showing the children the pictures and challenging them to guess what the story is about. Mr. Hewlett usually takes time to ask the children about their experiences with the subject matter. Then, after writing some of the vocabulary words (which he calls "juicy words") on a white board and asking the children to watch for the words in the story, he leads into the book, saying, "Let's find out how this situation turned out differently!"

The emotional climate in any scaffolding situation should not only be warm and supportive, but also one in which the mentor constantly adjusts the amount of intervention to the child's needs and abilities. Most of all, the instructional nature of scaffolding should not be allowed to overtake the active engagement of the child in moving to a higher level of understanding.

In 2001, a National Reading Panel report identified five pillars of scientific reading instruction. Critical aspects of development

FIGURE 12.4 Scaffolding to a Higher Level of Emerging Writing

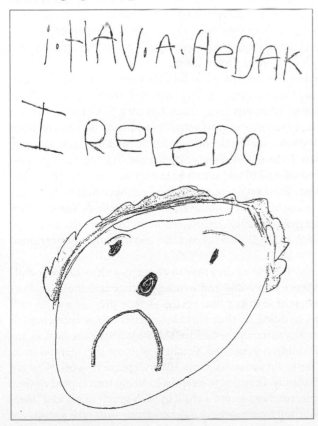

No spaces between words to placing dots between words as a reminder.

leading to a child's ability to read were phonological awareness, phonics, fluency, vocabulary, and comprehension. University of Tennessee Professor Richard Allington (2004) agreed but added an additional five equally important pillars that must be addressed in effective instruction (pp. 22–25):

1. Access to interesting texts and choice to increase motivation and achievement
2. Matching kids with appropriate texts, since children cannot learn from difficult texts or texts they cannot read. Struggling readers need "appropriately difficult books in their hands all day long."
3. Writing and reading have reciprocal positive effects. Reading and writing, composing and comprehension, decoding and spelling should all be well linked.
4. Classroom organization: Balance whole-class teaching with small-group and side-by-side instruction. This provides the differentiation that is an effective alternative to "unscientific" whole-group instruction.
5. Availability of expert tutoring. This will be essential if struggling readers are to catch up with peers and should take place with no more than five children in a group and preferably only two to three.

A Balanced Literacy Program

In years past, teachers focused primarily on developing children's reading skills, often through whole-group teaching. Today, early childhood educators are expected to include daily components of oral language, reading strategies, and writing experiences in preprimary and primary classrooms. Doing so effectively calls for what is known as **balanced literacy** (Rief & Heimberge, 2007). This means including activities that are sometimes teacher directed and modeled, sometimes wholly exploratory and independent on the child's part, and sometimes interactive between child and teacher. For example, an oral language component would include speaking *with* the child and *to* the child and providing opportunities for children to do the talking. Similarly, daily reading and writing activities must be provided that involve children's watching others read and write, interacting with a more experienced person (teacher, parent, peer) in literacy activities, and working alone to practice skill building. Teachers today are also more likely to have children who are nonnative speakers in their classrooms and must design and include literacy activities that work equally well with English speakers and English language learners alike (Chen & Mara-Flores, 2006).

A frequent concern of many professionals is how they can find the time to address the many emergent literacy skills young children must learn, along with so many other teaching expectations during a school day. A system called **literacy rotations** (Soderman, Gregory, & McCarty, 2005) is one example of how to structure adequate time for a range of activities within an 80-minute block (see Table 12.2 for an example). Twenty minutes are usually designated for an initial large group to explain activities that will then take place in three subsequent 20-minute, rotated mini-groups. The procedure can also be adapted to a 60-minute block, allowing 15 minutes for large group and 15 minutes for each of the rotated groups. The small groups may be heterogeneous or homogeneous, depending on the learning tasks or teacher's goals; however, they should be dynamic, rather than static. To gauge whether children are making sufficient progress in each of the three areas, the teacher must use coordinated assessment strategies and guard the consistently uninterrupted blocks of time.

Teachers find this approach especially effective so they may work intensively with fewer children while other children gain independence in reading and writing practice activities. Teachers are better able to observe the transmission of learning that occurs as they provide a mini skill workshop to children in a smaller group. In doing so, they are able to better assess differences in children's understanding, skills, and concepts and may then address those learning needs more intensively during the day with individual children as needed. Teachers who use this method indicate that children *can and do* become fairly autonomous about the independent work they are given to do if the tasks are designed effectively. In order to keep from being interrupted as they work with one of the smaller groups, some teachers assign a child in each group to act as a "traveler" to identify any issues that deter the group from working independently. After the groups are rotated and children begin their work, the teacher takes time from her work with one of the groups, asking "Do any of the travelers have a question that cannot be handled in your group? Is everyone on task?" Children learn to assist one another or to wait briefly with any unresolved

TABLE 12.2   Example of Literacy Rotations

Large Group	Green Group—Teacher Mini-Workshop	Red Group—Independent Writing Group	Blue Group—Independent Reading Group
Teacher begins with a secret message that children decode with her help. She then launches into a brief morning message, in which she works interactively with them on both reading and writing skills. After reading them a familiar poem they have read at the start of each day's session that week, she does a quick activity with phonics work connected to the poem. She reminds them about ways they can take responsibility for their independent learning and designates today's groups and the travelers. She explains carefully the focused work of each group and demonstrates any needed processes or use of materials. She then dismisses them to begin their work in each of the groups, reminding them of the time they have to complete their tasks	Teacher begins a shared reading experience with a book they have already enjoyed, Dr. Seuss's *Oh, The Places You Will Go!* She challenges them to hold up their index fingers silently anytime they spot a contraction during the reading. Before beginning the reading, she asks the travelers in the other small groups if they have any questions. After the reading, she does some additional work with the text for phonological and print awareness. A follow-up activity for comprehension completes the session. She provides the group with copied pages of the text and invites them to work together to order them in the way they appeared in the book, using the book as a check.	The group will be using the materials provided on the table to form as many contractions as they can and to write the contractions in their journals, listing the two separate words and then the contraction that can be made. They may work with a partner or independently, and if they have additional time, they may make up other contractions they can think of.	The group begins with silent or buddy reading work, choosing from a selection of books provided by the teacher. After reading one of the books independently or with a partner, children are then to go back, looking for all the contractions they can find, listing them in their journals.

issues until the teacher interacts briefly with each group at the beginning of each new rotation. While it is helpful to have a classroom aide who can float between the two self-sustaining groups, children demonstrate the ability to take responsibility for getting to work without the teacher directly overseeing the task.

INTEGRATION OF LANGUAGE EXPERIENCES ACROSS THE CURRICULUM

Remember some of your favorite activities when you were a young child?

Playing jump rope to chants: "Teddy Bear, Teddy Bear, turn around. Teddy Bear, Teddy Bear, touch the ground"
Creating a science report in elementary school about different trees (complete with leaf samples pasted to the pages)
Constructing and carefully labeling a globe made from a balloon and collage for social studies

Such activities served multiple purposes relative to skill development—and all of them enhanced your language development. The strength of the language domain is that it reaches naturally across the curriculum into every other domain.

Literature of all kinds should be used to introduce children to information and ideas in science, mathematics, history, and social studies. Also, given the current trend toward using **basal readers** and leveled books with young children, it is critical that teachers include high-quality narrative picture books daily. These texts offer familiarity with more sophisticated vocabulary than is offered in basal anthologies, leveled books, or everyday conversation. Accumulated research indicates that when children's literature is used, there is increased interest in reading and awareness of story structure.

When choosing which books to read to children or include in the classroom library, teachers should consider subject content, language complexity, and quality of illustrations (Otto, 2009). The picture books that are selected should appeal to children, relating to their interests, receptive language abilities, and concepts about their world. As children's conceptual and language abilities increase, teachers will want to choose books that are purposely more complex with respect to syntax, vocabulary, and structure. A conversational tone of voice should be used, and connections with children made prior to reading the text, during the reading, and afterwards to monitor comprehension and the children's level of understanding of concepts and vocabulary. It is also useful to watch which books are chosen by particular children during leisure time in the classroom or to check out and take home.

Children should become as familiar with expository text (factual or informative literature) as they are with narrative text (fictional stories), and they should be encouraged after the reading of a narrative text to do some follow-up work from expository texts when they have questions. For example, Ms. Rinker was sharing Eric Carle's *The Very Hungry Caterpillar* with her class when DeMarco questioned the author's use of the term *cocoon.* "My dad says that should be called a *chrystal,*" he challenged.

Knowing that DeMarco's father had probably used the term *chrysalis,* Ms. Rinker said, "I think DeMarco's father is correct. How do you think your father knew that, DeMarco? Where do you think *we* can find out about that word?" An ensuing and very appealing "science lesson" took place, with a group of interested children taking a trip to the school library on a fact-finding mission. Later, they looked at differences between varieties of moths and butterflies, which led to their classifying, labeling, painting, and drawing a number of them. Along with an interested parent, another group of children looked on the Internet and discovered that Eric Carle had addressed the discrepancy and had provided an explanation about continuing to use the word *cocoon.* A discussion followed about whether Mr. Carle should change the word, and the children wrote a class letter to Mr. Carle, letting him know that they agreed with his decision and why they did so.

To reach across the curriculum, many teachers create what they call *literacy spin-offs,* that is, activities in other curricular domains that seem to evolve naturally from reading a favorite narrative text (Soderman, Gregory, and McCarty, 2005). The book provides the children with a shared basis of understanding for the subsequent activities, which may occur during the span of a day, a week, or longer, and the teacher makes an effort to structure activities in all developmental domains. An example of a set of spin-off activities that could be used with the text *This Is My House,* by Arthur Dorros, a favorite book for many of the children in their classrooms, is provided in Figure 12.5.

When teachers include print materials throughout the room, not just in the library corner, it increases children's attention to written language while relating to learning in other domains (McGee & Richgels, 2007). For example, pictures and books on machines, transportation, and building can be positioned strategically in the block area, along with street signs, exit and enter signs; cookbooks, telephone books, menus, TV guides, cereal boxes, magazines, address books, dictionaries, and home construction books are meaninful in the housekeeping area; books about artists, color, and design can be placed in the art area; and narrative and information books about nature, animals, addition/subtraction, and weather add greatly to the math and science area.

Using literature to reach across the curriculum is natural, and many ways exist for doing so. However, to do so in the most effective way, professionals must (a) discard rigid ideas about time blocks that segment the day or week; (b) think creatively about how all curricular components relate to one another; and (c) involve the children, their families, and the community in the activities that take place inside and outside the classroom. Good planning is required to ensure a balance of activities, and thoughtful evaluation strategies are necessary to provide the documentation needed to ensure that children are making progress.

A number of publishers have developed resources specifically for integrating emergent literacy with dramatic play, science, math, art, music, motor skills, and social studies. Good sources include McGraw-Hill/Good Apple, Scholastic, Pearson Learning, Dale Seymour, Carson-Dellosa, Evan-Moor/Monday Morning, Creative Teaching Press, Milliken, and The Education Center/Mailbox. Web sites for these publishers and the titles they offer are easily accessible.

Teaching Children Who Have Limited English Proficiency

Children enrolled in educational programs who are English language learners (ELLs), non–English proficient (NEP), or limited-English proficient (LEP) need the respect and active support of professionals and peers who will be helping them add English to their primary language. However, more than this,

FIGURE 12.5   Example of a Literacy Spin-off Unit

Narrative Text: *This is My House* by Arthur Durros

Targeted Grade: 2

Synopsis: Children from many countries tell about their houses, which are typical of the kind found in their country. The diversity of the homes is depicted, as well as how each home is constructed. A sample of the different languages people speak is provided as each child in the book proudly proclaims, "This is my house!"

Terms/Vocabulary: *continent, equator, compass rose, hemisphere, foundation, adobe, thatch, yurt, houseboat, shelter*

Facts:

There are seven continents on which people live in a variety of homes.
Homes are often constructed in certain ways because of climate.
Homes are often equipped with plumbing, electricity, appliances and furniture, but not all of them.
People in homes are usually families.
Not all homes are on land; some are on water.
Some homes have only one floor, while others have upper levels.
Not all homes have windows.

Potential Spin-off Activities into Other Areas of the Curriculum:

Create a classroom home from a refrigerator box.
Take a walk around 2 blocks nearby the school to view homes in which people live. Which is your favorite? Why?
Explain why homes are numbered. What is the number of your home? How are the numbers sequenced on your block?
Interview an older family member or friend to discover what that person's home looked like when he or she was young.
Construct a salt-dough globe and label it to show the seven continents that were connected with the homes depicted in the book.
Construct a diorama of one of the homes in the book to depict the climate and living conditions particular to that home.
Graph the kinds of dwellings classmates and their friends live in (e.g., apartment, ranch, condominium).
With a parent's help, develop a scaled floor map of your home's layout.
Find out how many kinds of materials (e.g., wood, glass) were used in constructing your home.
Write a math story problem about the cost of building a home.
In a small group or with a partner, construct a "dream house." What would it look like? What would the contents consist of? Take a field trip to a plumbing shop, a lighting shop, or a furniture store. Estimate the cost of equipping and furnishing your dream home.
What are the names of the trees and bushes that surround your home? Bring in and label leaf specimens.
Make up a poem about what you like best about your own home.
Write a story about what your home might say if it could talk.
Make a rubbing from the outside of your home and compare with classmates.
Learn the song, "There was a crooked man who bought a crooked house" and perform it for the kindergarten and first-grade classes.

Possible Subsequent Units: Animal habitats; everyday lives in other cultures

these children need a teacher who considers bilingualism a positive attribute rather than a linguistic, cognitive, and academic liability. Realistically, this calls for understanding the challenges that second language learners face as they are thrown into educational situations where they must interact with others whose values, beliefs, and backgrounds may be very different (Barrera, Corso, & Macpherson, 2003).

Second-language learners come into the classroom already knowing a lot about language (their own) and, while acquiring a second language, will be driven to higher levels of cognitive flexibility, metalinguistic awareness, concept formation, and creativity than is required of unilinguistic children in the setting. Until they become somewhat functional in the new language, stress can be enormously high for these children, and they need supportive, sensitive adults who will work to find ways to increase their comfort levels.

When creating activities for ELLs, teachers will want to keep in mind the following criteria (Soderman, Wescott, & Shen, 2007).

1. **Activities should help children develop pride and cultural identity in the new languages being learned as well as in their home languages.** Remind them that they now have two languages that they can use, because of their hard work. Keep products in a portfolio to show children occasionally how they are making progress in the new language. Record conversations and play them back to help them recognize that daily participation is moving them forward in the new language, something they can be proud of.

2. **Children will be more willing to engage in classroom activities that are personally meaningful and useful.** Take your cues from the children. How can you take advantage of their interests to motivate them toward second-language development? One teacher captured a German child's interest in replicating the computer keyboard. He put a German flag on one key and an American flag on another. He said, "When you press this key, you get German words. When you press that key, you get American words." The teacher helped him develop pairs of words that he could display on his laminated computer "screen."

3. **Activities that elicit and encourage peer interactions are most highly effective.** In the above example, where a German child was building a "computer" to display German and English words, the teacher paired the child with an American child who showed interest in not only the computer creation but also in what the German words meant. Taking advantage of these common interests led to a friendship between the two children and secondary language development in both of them.

4. **Teacher collaboration in bridging and sharing activities across classrooms helps children make meaningful connections between languages.** Teachers who are working in dual-immersion programs foster deeper understandings and speedier vocabulary production when they implement activities that replicate words in the two languages. For example, at 3e International School in Beijing, China, where children are immersed for 3 hours of Mandarin and 3 hours of English per day, the teachers often use concept charts at the beginning of the thematic units which are played out in both classrooms at the same time. When beginning a unit on undersea life, teachers begin by putting the same picture of a fish in the middle of an easel and then ask children to name attributes of the fish in the language of that particular classroom. Children are excited to learn both the English and the Mandarin words for fish, eye, gill, fin, water, mouth, swim, and sea, and could use them in their journal writing in the Chinese classroom as easily as they could write them in their journal writing in the English classroom.

5. **Teachers need to carefully sequence activities, step-by-step, to build on children's previous knowledge and to advance skills and concepts.** Here, it is particularly important to consider language facility of a child and to think ahead about simplification of an activity so that English learners can still participate in what other children are doing. Children learn a great deal by watching what other children are doing, even when they do not fully understand all that is being said.

Professionals will want to examine the entire classroom structure: Is it a community of learners with an environment that promotes children's interaction with adults and peers? Are the opportunities for all children to speak, listen, read, and write (even in their native language) rich and varied? Are *learning goals* ("Let's see how much we can find out about this!") rather than *performance goals* and drill ("How much do you know about this?") emphasized? Is the active role the student brings to learning recognized and valued? How creative are instructional strategies? Is there sufficient repetition of activities and predictability so that the child can begin to develop a comfort level? Are visual aids, toys, photographs, and books from the child's culture included, as well as tapes, stories, rhymes, and songs? Do opportunities exist for the child or the child's family members to share with others experiences such as a song, counting from the primary language, or how to write children's names in the other language? Are authentic strategies being used for evaluating the child's progress?

Because the rate of acquisition of a second language (including reading and writing abilities) is highly related to proficiency levels in the child's primary language, every effort should be made to have the child continue gaining proficiency in his or her home language. Doing so calls for encouraging parents to continue speaking and reading frequently to the child in their native language. There may be parents who cannot read or write fluently in either their primary language or English, but we should not underestimate the powerful role of oral language development as a strong precursor to a child's early literacy. Wordless picture books can be used in the classroom in English and then provided to a family whose child is learning English so that they can be used at home also to promote a shared literacy experience between parent and child and also connect home and school (Ordonez-Jasis & Ortiz, 2006). It's helpful, too, to recruit someone familiar with the child's home language to participate in the classroom for at least a portion of the day if possible. This person can be a parent, family member (perhaps a sibling), or person in the community who not only can translate in "sticky" situations, but also can scaffold language and literacy experiences for the child both in the home language and in the language being acquired. *Code switching* (the child's switching from one language to the other even within the same sentence) should be accepted without comment.

Within about 3 months in a supportive, secure environment, and with observant and responsive teachers, most ELLs will begin to demonstrate gains in second-language acquisition. However, it will take a great deal longer to develop the academic language required of children in formal learning contexts and continued patience and support from the classroom teacher.

CURRENT EDUCATIONAL ISSUES

As many new teachers enter the field of early childhood education, they are often confused when they discover that colleagues in the same learning community are at opposite ends of a philosophical continuum about guiding young children's emerging literacy. Some educators have no established philosophy, which leaves them at the whim of any new idea that comes along or believing that "nothing is ever new . . . only recycled." When such individuals discuss issues related to curriculum, literacy instruction, or assessment, they have difficulty agreeing about a consolidated direction and, as a result, rarely effect productive change that supports a strong language arts approach for young children.

In other learning communities, staff form ongoing study groups around targeted issues to determine whether existing programmatic practice is still the best practice or whether change is warranted because of new understandings in the field. Following a recent in-service workshop to talk about new directions in early literacy, the early childhood professionals attending were invited to develop a list of questions that continued to bother them. The following questions represent the issues that surfaced quickly and seemed to arouse the most heated discussion.

Scripted Reading Instruction

> *I teach in a school where we are mandated to teach reading by using scripted reading lessons. Are scripted reading programs DAP? Where do they fit into the overall literacy picture?*

Scripted reading instruction involves programs being adopted by increasing numbers of schools, mostly in response to Reading First projects funded by the U.S. Department of Education. There is a continuum of approaches to reading instruction (see Table 12.3), ranging from highly scripted to teacher-produced activities. Many early childhood educators have long been wary of tightly scripted

TABLE 12.3   Reading Instruction Approaches, Most Formal to Least Formal

Type of Instruction	Example of Published Programs	Features
Scripted reading instruction	Reading Mastery Reading for Success Voyager	Provides reading lessons where teachers are expected to follow step-by-step teaching scripts
Guided-reading lessons	*Guided Reading: Good First Children* (Fountas and Pinnell, 1996)	Groups students on the basis of strengths and limitations; uses leveled books
Basal readers	*Trophies* (Houghton Mifflin-Harcourt) *Open Court* (McGraw-Hill SRA)	Published anthologies of stories chosen to illustrate and develop certain skills; accompanying workbooks/worksheets
Teacher-developed literacy lessons	Teacher-selected materials and improvised activities	Teacher relies on trade books rather than text books, while teaching phonemic awareness, phonics, fluency, vocabulary, and comprehension

programs, concerned that they leave nothing to the teacher's imagination, look for "right answers" only from children, and discourage spontaneity and animation during the teaching process.

Michelle Commeyras (2007), professor of language and literacy education at the University of Georgia, states that she has become more open minded in her observations of teachers using scripted programs. She believes they can work and that there is room for teachers to modify them in order to differentiate for certain students—if the school district allows it. Pragmatically, she says, teaching programs and requirements come and go. Preservice teachers and new teachers need foundational knowledge about how to teach a child to read, scripted programs or not, and the ability to do so within the mandates or choices allowed them in schools where they will be working. This requires a solid basis about what it is children must learn in order to become proficient readers and writers, knowledge about how to design lessons related to instructional goals related to the five components of scientific reading (phonemic awareness, phonics, fluency, vocabulary, and comprehension), and the ability to move children confidently from one level to the next in emergent literacy.

Correcting Children's Journal Writing

Should we be correcting children's writing in their journals?

It's best to avoid correcting children's writing in their journals, but you may have them edit their own writing. On an individual basis and after children have begun to write a number of words and sentences by using invented spelling, have them begin to edit for targeted errors. For example, prior to their making a journal entry on Tuesday, ask them to go back to Monday's entry and underline just one word that was difficult to spell or reread and then look it up on the word wall, a large-print children's dictionary, or in the classroom dictionary. Children who still do not know the alphabetic sequence or are unfamiliar with the use of reference materials will need scaffolded assistance until they can use them independently. Another day, you can have children go back for two or three entries and make sure they have a capital letter on each of their sentences. This approach is an effective way of teaching composition with a contextual approach, as long as the child is developmentally ready for this next step. *Remember:* The more *you* do the correcting, the slower the child will be in internalizing the error.

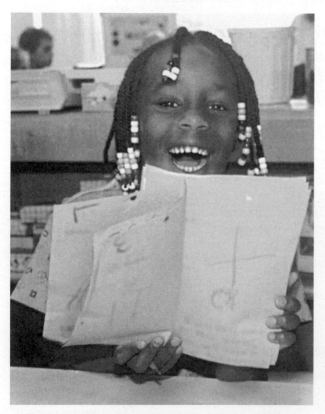

Developmentally appropriate classrooms are joyful places in which children commit their ideas to paper with confidence.

Taking Dictation from Children

What about the child who is not yet writing? Should I take dictation from individual children?

Dictation may be the answer, but it depends on your objective. If the child is still at a stage in which he or she does not yet know that speech can be captured with symbols on a page, then writing what the child dictates, reading it back to the child, and having the child read it back again is a valuable learning experience for the child. Once the child knows that combinations of letters represent words, that spaces must be left between words, and that print communicates to others what we want to tell them, we need to back away from taking dictation from individual children so that their motivation to learn is not hampered. However, you do need to write in front of children daily, taking time to name the letters for emerging readers and writers and to point out configurations of particular words. Words that children need to use frequently in their writing can be placed on the classroom word wall and walked through daily so that they become internalized. Once words are put on the word wall, children should be encouraged to refer to them and expected to spell the words correctly. Classroom dictionaries can be made for each child, with copies updated regularly with the children's help. Concept charts on display in the classroom that contain a number of words that the children have dictated to the teacher about an ongoing theme or project are also helpful as children write about their experiences.

Purpose and Goals

The following purposes and goals are consistent with the standards of the International Reading Association and the National Council of Teachers of English.

Purpose

For children to communicate their ideas and feelings and to accurately interpret the communications they receive.

Goals

Listening and Viewing. As children progress, they will:

1. Interpret unspoken messages, including tone of voice, facial expression, and body language
2. Identify sounds in their environment
3. Listen and view for pleasure
4. Demonstrate courteous listening behaviors
5. Increase their receptive vocabulary
6. Demonstrate auditory memory, comprehension, and critical listening by repeating in correct detail and sequence the messages they hear
7. Develop their understanding of contemporary media (e.g., television, videos, CDs, DVDs, and computer technology); discriminate which aspects are likely true and which are fantasy

Speaking. As children progress, they will:

8. Articulate their ideas, intents, emotions, and desires
9. Ask and answer questions
10. Create and describe imaginative situations
11. Use correct pronunciation, grammar, and appropriate body language (eye contact, body position, and gestures) to alert a listener to their intent and to convey meaning
12. Increase their expressive vocabulary over time
13. Use increasingly complex sentence structure
14. Adapt their language to the audience and situation
15. Demonstrate self-confidence and poise during group speaking and creative dramatics activities

Writing. As children progress, they will:

16. Recognize that they can convey messages to others through written symbols (drawing and writing)
17. Understand that speech can be preserved through writing
18. Observe and imitate writing
19. Connect letter sounds to graphemes
20. Generate graphemes
21. Put their thoughts on paper, first through simple pictures and then incorporating print into their drawings
22. Use their own temporary versions of writing, working gradually toward conventional spelling, punctuation, and format (left to right, top to bottom, spacing)
23. Expand their writing vocabulary
24. Select topics to write about
25. Organize their ideas in a logical sequence
26. Use writing strategies such as mapping, webbing, and clustering to organize and plan writing
27. Express their ideas in complete sentences
28. Improve their ability to evaluate and edit their writing, preparing rough and final drafts
29. Use reference materials, including electronic sources, to help them improve their writing

30. Write original stories, poems, and informational pieces
31. Use word-processing programs on the computer

Reading. As children progress, they will:

32. Recognize graphemes—the letters of the alphabet
33. Recognize they can get meaning from print
34. Enjoy shared reading experiences with varied genres of literature, including classic and contemporary literature
35. Practice reading-like behavior, moving from "pretend" reading to attempting to match the flow of their language with book illustrations and with print
36. Increase their receptive and expressive reading vocabularies
37. Respond to written symbols in the environment (e.g., their name and others' names, signs, advertisements, labels)
38. Predict, on the basis of the information in the text and their personal life experiences, what will come next in stories that are being read
39. Read familiar text (e.g., nursery rhymes, songs, poems, finger play)
40. Develop general concepts of print (e.g., "Books are read from front to back." "We read words, not pictures." "Spaces are used between words.").
41. Develop an understanding of story elements and structure (e.g., story sequence, main ideas, characters, setting and plot development)
42. Show comprehension of what they have read by retelling or dramatizing
43. Create new endings for stories, drawing on logical elements of the original stories
44. Read their own writing.
45. Expand their phonological and print awareness
46. Expand their alphabetic knowledge
47. Develop a sight vocabulary
48. Read independently, using decoding strategies
49. Apply, to their lives and others' lives, knowledge, ideas, and issues drawn from texts
50. Become familiar with libraries as interesting places to find books and other materials for entertainment and information
51. Evaluate their developing literacy skills, identifying their strengths and needs
52. Comprehend what they are reading and use information to compare and contrast, analyze, infer, express ideas, and solve problems

MAKING GOALS FIT

How do we use the same goal with different age groups of children or with children of varying learning capacities and at different places in emergent literacy? Table 12.4 shows an example of how the goal of having children develop an understanding of story elements and structures (Goal #41) can be adapted to three different age groups.

TABLE 12.4 Differentiating with Curriculum Goals

Goal #41	Example of Activity for 3- and 4-Year-Olds	Example of Activity for 5- and 6-Year-Olds	Example of Activity for 7- and 8-Year-Olds
Develop an understanding of story elements and structure	Teacher reads story of Red Riding Hood. Children differentiate among flannel board characters and then watch as the teacher uses them to retell the story. Teacher puts flannel board materials in reading corner for children to use.	Teacher reads story of Red Riding Hood. Children take turns playing characters and identify simple props to act out the story sequence.	Teacher reads two culturally different versions of Red Riding Hood. Children complete Venn diagram, identifying similarities and differences involving main idea, characters, setting, and plot development.

TEACHING STRATEGIES

To optimize the language and literacy acquisition of the children in your classroom, use the following eight strategies:

1. **Structure a communication-rich environment:**
   a. *Model appropriate, rich language usage.*   Although you cannot expect standard English usage from all children, you must have a good command of it yourself. In addition, your diction needs to be clear and understandable to the children, with interesting vocabulary that stretches the children's understanding of and interest in the language.
   b. *Listen to and talk with each child daily.*   The school day is busy from beginning to end, and neglecting children who do not expect or demand attention is far too easy. Make having a personal conversation with every child each day a habit.
   c. *Take advantage of spontaneous events to promote children's language development through discussion.*   Use these events to start conversations with children and to encourage children to talk with one another. Some of the richest teaching moments occur unplanned. If you are too "scripted" by your teaching plans, you may not notice how something a child brings to the class, a change in the weather, or a serendipitous event can be used more effectively to attain your immediate or long-range teaching goals.
   d. *When a child states something, enhance language by repeating it and using a new term or adding an appropriate clause.*   Use an interesting synonym for a word or two or add a related idea. Use open-ended questions and paraphrases as described in chapter 3 to accomplish this.
   e. *Plan the learning environment and the curriculum to provide opportunities for children to communicate informally with one another.*   Centers in the activity-oriented classroom provide a natural environment for peer interaction.
   f. *Plan activities each day in which the primary goal is for children to use language to describe events, make predictions, or evaluate phenomena.*   Not all your goals for children's language development will be attained through activity centers. Plan particular small- and large-group experiences that stretch children's abilities to express themselves in particular ways. Ensure that each child in the group has sufficient opportunities to speak and is developing the confidence and skill to do so.
   g. *Purposely build enjoyable listening activities into the day to enhance auditory skills through listening and response interactions* (Machado, 2005).   Such activities include the following:
      ❑ Oral or musical signals given to children to alert them to a change in activities
      ❑ Auditory memory games
      ❑ Sound cans from which children match similar sounds
      ❑ Activities to determine whether children can follow one-, two-, and three-step directions or oral commands
      ❑ Helping children to hear sounds in words by stretching them out and purposefully slowing down pronunciation
      ❑ Games that challenge children to imitate sounds (such as imitating the teacher's changes in voice [loud–soft], speed, and pitch [high–low]; holding their nose)
      ❑ Times when children listen to the sounds of crunchy foods that are chewed or broken in half
      ❑ Songs, such as "Pop Goes the Weasel," or games, such as Simon Says, in which children must listen to and respond to a signal
      ❑ Matching games in which pictures of animals must be matched to the sounds they make
      ❑ Hidden-sound activities in which children must identify and discriminate certain sounds (e.g., baby rattle, tambourine, toilet flushing, stapler) that are made behind a screen or on a recorded message
      ❑ Play telephone activities

Take advantage of spontaneous opportunities to promote language development. "You're leaping in the air!"

❏ Sound stories—stories during which children make a related sound every time a particular word is mentioned in the story (e.g., making the sound "yum-yum" whenever the word *spinach* appears)

❏ Games that provide clues that children must listen to so that they can identify a particular object in the room

2. **Create a print-rich visual environment.** Integrate language development activities and quality literature throughout all areas of the early childhood curriculum. Because all subjects require language for learning, plan content around the language forms of listening and viewing, speaking, reading, and writing. Make a variety of literature central in your classroom. The literature will have important meanings for the children when you help them explore its relationships to, or its contrasts with, their lives.

Consciously create a visual environment that highlights print in every area of the room. Some examples are word walls charts, predictable charts (see Figure 12.6), book-making materials, labels, names, directions, recipes, menus, and children's writing. The print that children see around them becomes their primary resource for their reading and writing *if* you draw their attention to it and involve them in it in interesting ways. Make the environmental print serve real uses in your classroom. Place print materials at the children's eye level. Draw attention to print messages, pointing to letters or words and asking why the messages are important; refer to them at appropriate times. Model print concepts often, by cuing left to right, top to bottom, and page turning and by noting word and sentence formations (e.g., spaces between words, types of punctuation).

3. **Model and teach the importance of developing and using good listening and viewing skills as follows:**

   a. *Model good listening behavior* by attending to the children and responding to their comments and questions. Stop; look at each child when he or she speaks. Ask relevant questions. Ask other children to respond to what a child has said.

   b. *Give children appropriate cues* to help them listen better. Say, "Look up here" or "Watch me"; use voice inflections; change your volume appropriately for the small- or large-group setting. Prepare children for viewing experiences prior to having them watch a video or take a field trip by providing information about what they will be seeing and what you want them to look for. You cannot expect children to know how to listen or observe well, although they often are more attentive listeners and observers than adults are. Clues to listening and viewing behavior will be useful for them and lessen your frustration over inattentive behaviors.

   c. *Introduce sound discrimination by using common environmental sounds* (e.g., telephone or doorbell). Alert children to interesting sound–symbol relations in written language. Alerting children to the sounds in their environment calls attention to common experiences that are easily overlooked and creates understanding about hearing and sounds. When parents helped these children to learn to speak, the children did not focus their attention on the individual sounds that made up the words they were learning. Sounds and the letters that represent them on paper are more readily understood when they are examined in the context of a song, poem, or story the children enjoy. Early, brief, and natural encounters with phonics, usually on a class chart or a white board, ensures that sound–symbol relations will not be overwhelming or confusing.

FIGURE 12.6 Shared Reading and Writing on a Predictable Chart

My favorite thing to play with is my *tennis racket*.	(Mr. Landon)
My favorite thing to play with is my *steam shovel*.	(Jamel)
My favorite thing to play with is my *Barbie doll*.	(Abby)
My favorite thing to play with is my *bike*.	(Robert)
My favorite thing to play with is my *video game*.	(Demond)
My favorite thing to play with is my *Lego blocks*.	(Andrew)
My favorite thing to play with is my *little sister*.	(Lily)
My favorite thing to play with is my *board games*.	(Gavin)

   d. *Maintain children's attention* by using props, gestures, proximity, and particular facial and vocal expressions, but also gradually help children maintain attention without extra elements. A book, puppet, picture, or your special action is a useful attention getter; often, it visualizes for the children a concept that is difficult for them to conceive. However, children must also learn to create their own mind pictures about the words they hear. Plan listening experiences that develop the children's imaginations from oral stimuli alone as well as with aids.

4. **Involve children every day in engaging reading experiences.**
   a. *Read to the children* at least once every day, more when possible. Model expression, phrasing, and fluency. Employ dialogic reading, having them read interactively with you. Use Big Books and have them echo back sentences you have just read as you run your hand underneath the print. Remember that children who may come from literacy-impoverished homes are in even greater need of read-aloud opportunities, including sitting on the teacher's lap during reading. Provide cues as to what to listen to before you read aloud. Pose one to three questions that can be addressed at the end of a story.
   b. *Choose books* that are developmentally appropriate in terms of age, interest, and culture. Select those with rich language and illustrations. With younger children, choose durable books with fewer words, lots of white space, and larger illustrations (approximately one line of print per age of child). Include those that portray diversity in positive ways. Ranweiler (2004) provides a number of helpful suggestions for selecting books to read aloud to young children.
      - ❏ Books that contain rhyme and alliteration, allowing you to draw attention to the fact that words are made up of various sounds and helping children to develop phonemic awareness
      - ❏ Predictable books, which help children think of themselves as readers
      - ❏ Books with easily remembered phrases or lines for the children to chant
      - ❏ Books that invite physical as well as verbal participation
      - ❏ Books that reflect the identities, home languages, family structures, and cultures of the children in your class
      - ❏ Wordless books that demonstrate to children how they can make up the story as they view the pictures
      - ❏ Big Books of familiar stories or poems
      - ❏ Alphabet books that invite the response of involvement of the child in the read-aloud experience
   c. *Use a variety of literary forms* when you are reading to children (picture books, poetry, folk and fairy tales, and factual books). Plan your oral reading time carefully so that you "tune your children's ears" to the ideas presented in a variety of genres and to the vocabulary and sentence structures typical of different forms of writing.
   d. *Draw attention* to story sequence and development, characters, cause and effect, main ideas, and details, but only when these discussions will not interfere with the children's enjoyment of the story. On appropriate occasions, take advantage of opportunities when you are reading to children to teach them these important concepts. Remember that preserving the continuity of what the children are listening to and the integrity of the overall meaning is also important.
   e. *Involve children* in songs, chants, poems, finger plays, rhymes, choral readings, and dramatic play. Dramatic activity is a natural learning mode for children. Plan for the overt involvement of all the children as much as possible. Combine speaking or singing with reading the lyrics of these favorite songs or poems to lead children into intuitively learning about reading.

5. **Involve children every day in enjoyable writing experiences.**
   a. *Write in front of them every day.* Daily, in large group, have children take turns dictating a message. The messages can be centered on the children's experiences and observations or even brief stories developed by the entire group. This approach allows the children to hear and see their words in print, written in "adult language." By watching you write, they learn so many things: the names of letters, that spoken words have counterparts, that words are made of rows of letters and that writing goes from left to right, that words are

separated from each other by a wider space than the space between letters, that words that begin sentences and words that are someone's name are capitalized, that sentences are made up of words, and how and where to place punctuation (Seefeldt, 2005). As they dictate, they can concentrate on what they want to say without struggling with writing these ideas and words. In this kind of activity, they can dictate longer, more complex pieces than they can write on paper by themselves, and this activity models how messages are composed. Be sure to write what the children say; they need to know that you value what is said and how it is said. Ask questions to encourage more complex sentence structure, adjectives, and adverbs, and insert suggestions appropriately as children offer them. Also use questions to help them think of more complex story lines and to consider cause and effect. Ideas can come from the group about how something might be "fixed" until everyone is satisfied with the message.

b. *Provide daily opportunities for children to draw and write* and then to share their pictorial and written representations with their peers and families, reinforcing the idea that writing is for a purpose. Include ample writing activities and writing suggestions in daily play-based experiences. Provide access to a variety of materials for children to make their own print. Place writing materials in all centers of the room: order blanks for the pretend restaurant, sticks for making words in the sandbox, and so forth. Provide reference materials, such as a simplified dictionary, in some centers so that children can readily use them.

c. *Allow invented spelling,* introducing editing as appropriate on an individual basis. Rather than telling children how to spell a word, ask, "Do you hear any sounds? What letters do you think make those sounds? Stretch it out. Write the first one you hear and then the next one. Tell me what word you've just written." Each child's level of performance in writing will depend on the opportunities he or she has had to write at home and in previous grades at school, his or her understanding of the purposes of printed language, and the degree to which his or her efforts have been accepted by others. Avoid drawing attention to words and letters as the children write so that they can concentrate on the meanings they are trying to express. Avoid the common school practice of spelling words for children as they write because these "helps" turn children's attention away from the ideas they are trying to express. At other, more appropriate times (such as Morning Message or Daily News time), point out similarities and differences in words, correct or unusual spellings, rhyming words, use of capital letters, and punctuation. Because their enthusiasm for writing grows as children hear responses to their efforts, display all children's writing on bulletin boards or in "published" books. Encourage children to share their pictures and writing by taking a turn in the author's chair.

d. *Provide writers' workshops or minilessons* for teaching the elements of the writing process that are developmentally appropriate for the children with whom you are working: topic selection, creation of drafts, and draft sharing. In earlier stages of emerging writing, children write best and write most about the topics they know and care about. Discuss places at which additional words and sentences could be added to their pieces. Show them ways to correct errors but allow them to make the corrections; expect older children to begin higher level revision strategies as they take increasing pride in what they have produced. Do not push the children into revising or editing too soon, or you may diminish their initial writing efforts. Asking the child to read a piece to you or the other children often helps him or her see changes that need to be made.

6. **Plan literacy games, songs, and other play-oriented activities to enhance children's phonological and print awareness.** Help children to develop the letter–sound associations and the phoneme–grapheme knowledge that they need to have by carefully embedding these activities in meaningful experiences. Call attention to letters individually and in words when you are reading charts of familiar poems, dictated writing, and so forth. Highlight the configuration of letters and familiar words by drawing around them and pointing out unique features of a particular letter or word. Also draw children's attention to various writing forms by providing examples (upper- and lowercase letters; manuscript, cursive, boldface, and italic forms; contractions; etc.) when they appear in contexts interesting to children. Model strategies for determining how to read unfamiliar words.

7. **Accept children's risk taking in their listening, speaking, writing, and reading,** even when their efforts do not result in correct or useful production. Be careful about "taking over" too

quickly to provide the correct answer. So that you do not destroy motivation or shortcut the thinking that children must do to internalize a concept, think about what the next small step is in the scaffolding process to help children become more independent and less reliant.

8. **Structure useful assessment strategies** to ensure that children are making progress in every area of the language domain. Observe, record children's developing strengths and needs, save work samples that indicate progress, and involve children in the evaluation process (see chapter 7 for specific suggestions).

ACTIVITY SUGGESTIONS

The following activities are structured to support children's growth in the language domain. Included are ideas for enhancing skills, processes, and concepts in each of the subareas of listening and viewing, speaking, writing, and reading. Clearly, more than one language objective is supported in any of the suggested activities, which is the hallmark of a well-designed activity. However, the primary purpose of each activity is to focus on the goal specifically cited. Doing so allows professionals to determine whether they are offering growth-producing experiences in each of the subareas and across the curriculum.

Because you may be working with children in any or all stages of emergent through fluent literacy and from 3 to 8 years of age, you will need to adapt these ideas to the developmental and experiential levels of the individual children with whom you are working (see Making Goals Fit). To aid this transition, we provide suggestions for simplifying or extending each activity. Also, each activity has been labeled for a specific group: younger and less experienced children, older and more experienced children, or children of all ages.

Listen and Dismiss (For Younger or Less Experienced Children)

Goal 2 Identify sounds in their environment.

Materials None

Procedure Once children have been together in a learning setting for several months, they begin to know one another's voices. This natural development can be used to help them focus their auditory senses to discover who is speaking to them without seeing the person. Model the listening game during large group by turning your chair around just before dismissing the children and having one child at a time say, "Good morning, Mr. (Ms.) _____. How are you?" As you recognize the child's voice, respond by saying, "Very well, thank you, (Child's Name)," and excuse the child from the large group. As children listen carefully, they pick up on the nuances of the other children's voices. They can then participate by closing their eyes during dismissal and trying to guess who is speaking to the teacher.

To Simplify Significantly reduce the number of voices that must be discriminated by designating only four or five speakers from the large group before beginning the game; have the remainder of the children be the listeners. The game may also be played in a small group of only four or five children, which also reduces the discrimination difficulty.

To Extend Choose individual children each day to play the role of teacher and be the dismisser.

Imitating Clapping Patterns (For Younger or Less Experienced Children)

Goal 6 Demonstrate auditory memory, comprehension, and critical listening by repeating in correct detail and sequence the messages they hear.

Materials None.

Procedure Ask children to listen carefully while you clap a pattern (clap-pause-clap-clap-pause) and ask them to try to repeat it. Move on to more complex and longer patterns as the children gain experience. Eventually, have the children clap one another's patterns.

To Simplify Begin with simple patterns.

To Extend Move on to having them clapping the syllables in their names and other words.

Viewing a Story Through Different Lenses (For Older or More Experienced Children)

Goal 7 Develop an understanding of contemporary media (e.g., television, videos, CDs, DVDs, and computer technology); discriminate which aspects are likely true and which are fantasy.

Materials Copy of *Charlie and the Chocolate Factory,* by Roald Dahl (Puffin Books); DVD or video of *Willy Wonka and the Chocolate Factory* (available from Films Incorporated, 440 Park Ave. S., New York, NY 10016; 1-800-323-4222, ext. 234); VCR or DVD player and monitor.

Procedure Using Dahl's book (or any other for which a video is available), read the story to the children (or have them read it independently), providing time for discussion after each section to talk about the way characters are portrayed and the plot is developed. Following completion of the written story, have children view the story on video. Develop a Venn diagram with the children, looking at ways the book and video are similar and different. For example, are the characters depicted differently? Is the story line the same or different? Which did they enjoy most and why?

To Simplify Choose a highly familiar text for emerging readers, such as *Goldilocks and the Three Bears,* so that children have a good sense of the characters and plot. Eliminate use of the Venn diagram in the activity.

To Extend Have the children role-play a familiar story and create a video of it.

Morning Message (For Children of All Ages)

Goal 16 Recognize that they can convey messages to others through written symbols (drawing and writing).

Materials White board or easel paper, markers.

Procedure Using a white board or easel paper, write one to three sentences dictated by the children. Then ask the children to read the sentences back. As children become more familiar with the process, put some "question word" reminders in the upper left-hand corner of the paper (e.g., *how, what, who, why, when,* and *where*). Select a child to dictate a story about a personal experience while you write, purposely making some errors for the children to catch (e.g., ignoring some punctuation or misspelling some words). After each sentence is written, have the children go back to the beginning to read what has been written so far. When the story is finished, work with the children to correct any errors they see in the text or to make changes in the text to clarify or extend some points.

To Simplify Start with only one sentence. As children's writing skills increase, make errors that should be apparent to most of the children. As you correct the errors on the advice of the children, children at a less sophisticated level are picking up skills by watching what the other children are catching and you are correcting.

To Extend Take dictation (about three or four sentences) from the group and then go back through each line of the text, asking if there are any errors that should be circled. As children call them out, circle them and then ask the children to write the message in their journals, individually making their own corrections where they believe corrections are needed.

Book Making (For Younger or Less Experienced Children)

Goal 21 Put their thoughts on paper, first through simple pictures and then incorporating print into their drawings.

Materials Various kinds and colors of paper, markers, scissors, glue.

Procedure Having very young children create their own books is one of the best activities to encourage them to write. A variety of books can be made, including "peek-a-boo" books, pop-up books, shape books (cover is in the outline of a particular animal or other theme), accordion books (paper is folded accordion-style, with each section illustrating separate parts of the story), and flip books (cut into three sections, with head of person or animal on top section, torso on middle section, legs and feet on bottom section). Provide examples of differently constructed books. Explain the tools and techniques needed to construct them. Provide help as needed. Encourage children to draw different pictures on each page.

Have them dictate their thoughts about the picture, and encourage them to write as much as they can under each illustration. Remember that a picture book with no words is still a book in which ideas and a story can be expressed.

To Simplify Provide very young children with a blank book that has been constructed, having them complete the book as appropriate, given their fine-motor and literacy capabilities. Focus on only one type of construction at a time.

To Extend Challenge the children to devise their own themes and shapes relevant to the content of the particular story they have written.

Putting Humpty Together Again . . . and Again . . . and Again (For Children of All Ages)

Goal 22 Use their own temporary versions of writing, working gradually toward conventional spelling, punctuation, and format (left to right, top to bottom, spacing).

Materials Paper, pencils, or markers.

Procedure As an assessment and evaluation procedure, periodically have children illustrate and write the rhyme "Humpty Dumpty." Standardize the assessment by having the children spend only 15 minutes on the task. Have them use a date stamp to date their work sample, put their name on it, and place it in their portfolio for future comparisons. When the work samples are dated and saved, they become an excellent vehicle through which the children can compare their earlier and later versions. Such comparison will reveal to you and them how they are growing in their ability to represent detail through their drawing and in qualitative movement toward conventional spelling, handwriting, punctuation, and format.

To Simplify At first, very young children may be able to only illustrate the rhyme and later add their first name. Later, they may use temporary spelling to reproduce some of the words. Do not point out children's errors at this time. Simply encourage them to do their best.

To Extend Once children can write all of the rhyme and spell many of the words correctly, have them begin to compare their samples with the original rhyme and make the corrections needed. Have them add an original story about why Humpty Dumpty could not be put back together and how it might be done.

What's the Question? (For Children of All Ages)

Goal 30 Write original stories, poems, and informational pieces.

Materials Journals, markers, pencils, easel, easel paper.

Procedure After reading or telling a story, stimulate the children to imagine what something looks like that cannot be seen, such as a leprechaun. Have them take out their journals and draw a picture of the thing on the left-hand page of the journal. Afterward, have younger children dictate a question they have (e.g., "How big is the leprechaun?" "Where does he live?"); older children can write a question they would like to ask. Tell the children to leave their journals open to that page, and sometime after they leave the classroom and before they return the next morning, an answer appears on the right-hand page of the journal. Although children know that the teacher is providing the answer, they love the fun of imagining that the answer has come from the leprechaun. Some teachers add to the fun by making small footprints across the page to accompany the answer.

To Simplify Children at the prewriting stage may act as a group to dictate some of their questions, which you write on the left-hand side of a piece of easel paper. That evening, the questions are answered on the right-hand side. The next day, in large group, ask the children to help you read each question and answer.

To Extend Challenge the children to illustrate and write to other imaginary or mythical characters (e.g., unicorn, fairy, or man in the moon) or real objects that are difficult to see (e.g., germs or a mouse that hides). When answering the question they have written, add a question they must answer in turn.

What's in a Name? (For Older and More Experienced Children)

Goal 40 Develop general concept of print (e.g., "Books are read from front to back." "We read words, not pictures." "Spaces are used between words.").

Materials Magnetic or movable letters, paper, pencils or markers.

Procedure Have children work in dyads. Supply magnetic or movable letters that are in each of their names. Challenge them to use the letters to make as many words as they can. Have them record the words as they find them and total the number at the end of the time provided for the activity.

To Simplify Provide the 26 individual letters of the alphabet and encourage children to form any words they can from these letters.

To Extend Have older children work in groups of three or four and write as many words as they can during a certain time period. Use as a math exercise as well by having them assign 1 point to two- or three-letter words, 2 points to four- or five-letter words, and 10 points to words of six or more letters. Have them write the words they are able to make and total the number of points they have earned at the end of the time period. Second and third graders enjoy the competition of comparing their group results with those of other groups. Remember that individual competition is not appropriate; nor is group competition appropriate for children in first grade or kindergarten.

Puppet Drama (For Younger and Less Experienced Children)

Goal 42 Show comprehension of what they have read by retelling or dramatizing.

Materials Children's storybook *The Little Red Hen* (or another familiar story), stick puppets of characters in the story, supplies to make puppets.

Procedure Read the story to the children several times during a number of days, having brief discussions afterward to learn whether the children have a good sense of the characters and plot. Select a story narrator and supply other children with stick puppets of the characters. Have the remainder of the children act as the audience. Have the players reenact the story, encouraging those in the audience to listen carefully and applaud at the end. Switch roles so that all children have a chance to be either an actor or a participant in the audience.

To Simplify In large group, supply each child with a stick puppet. Have the appropriate child stand when you come to that character and put his or her puppet in the air and say the character's line.

To Extend Have the children make the puppets from materials you provide. Choose other familiar stories and have them play with puppets provided to them or created by them.

Secret Message (For Older or More Experienced Children)

Goal 45 Expand their phonological and print awareness.

Materials White board or easel paper, marker.

Procedure Using a *Wheel of Fortune* approach, print out dashes where the letters for words in a "secret message" would be (e.g., _____ _____ _____ _____ _____!). Have children guess a letter, and if it appears in the message, write it in. If the letter appears more than once in the message, print it in all the places that it appears. As letters are guessed, write them on the right-hand side of the board so that children can see which have been guessed. This exercise is valuable because it is so engaging for children. They learn letter–sound associations and sight vocabulary as they see words produced from the letters (in this case, the message is "This is a secret message!").

To Simplify Limit the number and complexity of the words. Put in the vowels and have children fill in only the consonants, which are easier for them.

To Extend Extend the complexity of the message, using words that have letters less often seen (e.g., *x* and *z*). Do not put the guessed letters on the side of the board, so that memory must be relied on more.

> *It's a Fact! (For Older and More Experienced Children)*
>
> **Goal 48** Read independently, using decoding strategies.
>
> **Materials** Expository texts containing facts and information about famous persons, 3 × 5 inch cards, pencils
>
> **Procedure** Have children choose a famous person they would like to learn more about. Making available a number of expository texts at an appropriate reading level, have them search the books to find at least 10 facts of interest about the person. Have them record one fact on each card. Have children report what they found out about the person to the rest of the class.
>
> **To Simplify** Have children work with a partner to find three or more facts about a particular person.
>
> **To Extend** Have children convert their facts into a set of questions and answers. These can be used by the children to set up a Trivial Pursuit or Jeopardy game to challenge one another about the facts. Some children may enjoy making up and illustrating a board game using the facts they gathered.

SUMMARY

myeducationlab

To check your comprehension on the content covered in Chapter 12, go to the Book Specific Resources in the MyEducationLab for your course, select your text, and complete the Study Plan. Here you will be able to take a chapter quiz, receive feedback on your answers, and then access review, practice, and enrichment activities to enhance your understanding of chapter content.

A child's first word is a joyous experience for any family, signaling a lifetime of communication with others. Additional markers in language development are the child's first indications of interest in and emerging facility with symbolic language.

Although innate drives help children to develop linguistic abilities, the environment plays a critical role in the quality of children's developing capabilities to use language effectively, imaginatively, and confidently. Adults are important players in this unfolding process. Their role is to model listening and viewing, speaking, reading, and writing skills and to help the child gain access to a balanced variety of well-designed experiences to enhance understanding and independent use of the language.

To be as effective as possible, early childhood educators must have expertise related to the emergence of language and literacy skills. Because of the many ongoing controversies surrounding the teaching of reading and writing skills, they must also have a well-researched theoretical perspective about the best practices for guiding children's progress and the capability of articulating it to others. They need to have practical knowledge about structuring optimal learning environments that promote communication capabilities, an ability to draw the child's attention toward print in a variety of ways, and skill in providing the scaffolded experiences that children need to move to new levels of understanding and language usage.

If we want children to be competent readers and writers, they must be involved in quality writing and reading activities daily. Their phonological and print awareness can be fostered and extended through well-designed, meaningful activities that support their individual acquisition of skills and concepts. All this can occur most easily in a developmentally appropriate program in which educators appreciate the complexity of factors affecting language and literacy development; in which language can be naturally integrated across other developmental domains; and in which children's unique interests, strengths, and needs are considered.

Key Words

alliteration	guided reading	phonological awareness
alphabetic awareness	literacy rotations	prosody
balanced literacy	onsets	rimes
basal readers	phonemes	scripted reading instruction
emergent literacy	phonemic awareness	
graphemes	phonics	

Applying What You've Read in This Chapter

1. **Discuss**
   a. Adding the information gained in this chapter to your experience with young children, reexamine the five questions that open this chapter.
   b. If you were interviewing for a position in a school district as a first-grade teacher and a search committee member asked you to talk about your philosophy for teaching young children to read and write, how would you respond?
   c. Name one of the strategies in this chapter that you feel confident about and another that seems more difficult to implement. Discuss why the second would be more difficult and what it would take to remove the barrier(s).

2. **Observe**
   a. Observe a classroom of children who are 3 years old or younger, listening for examples of oral language. Notice whether any children appear to have significantly less advanced or more advanced skills relative to vocabulary, syntax, and ability to elaborate. Discuss your findings with the classroom professional.
   b. Observe the classroom of an experienced early childhood teacher. What evidence do you see that supports a print-rich environment or the need for enhancing this aspect of the learning environment? What strategies do you see that match or disagree with the philosophical underpinnings about emerging literacy presented in this chapter?

3. **Carry out an activity**
   a. Look at three basal texts for a specific grade level. Is a common vocabulary used among the three? What approaches do the authors support for making the reading experience developmentally appropriate? How viable are these suggestions on the basis of your understanding of differences in young children at this age? Can you suggest two or three additional ideas that would enhance the use of a basal text for children in this age group?
   b. Identify one issue presented in this chapter that you continue to be unsure about. Refer to the latest issues of several professional journals such as *Phi Delta Kappan, Educational Leadership, Young Children,* and *Reading Teacher* to determine whether you can learn more about resolving the issue. Write a one- or two-page position paper following your investigation.

4. **Create something for your portfolio**
   a. Develop a language-based lesson plan based on the format provided in chapter 3.

5. **Add to your journal**
   a. Think about your earliest experiences with reading and writing. Which books were your favorites? What can you remember about the process of learning to read? How much do you think your earliest experiences are related to your leisure-time literature choices as an adult?
   b. Identify one goal you have for either extending your expertise relative to understanding children's emerging literacy or planning for more effective application of teaching strategies. What steps do you plan to take to reach this goal?

6. ✋ **Consult the standards**
   Standards for early literacy should include expanding children's phonemic awareness because it is the most important predictor of a child's later fluency in reading.
   a. See if this is included in your state standards.
   b. Think of a phonemic awareness activity that would be appropriate for a 4-year-old.
   c. Think of another one that would be appropriate for a second grader. In what ways do they differ? Why?

PRACTICE FOR YOUR CERTIFICATION OR LICENSURE EXAM

The following items will help you practice applying what you have learned in this chapter. They can help to prepare you for your course exam, the PRAXIS II exam, your state licensure or certification exam, and for working in developmentally appropriate ways with young children.

Kendra Wayland, a kindergarten teacher, has just attended a workshop about the importance of oral language development at a professional conference. It has caused her to think about how the children in her classroom behave during the show-and-tell activity time that she has during large group on Fridays. Despite her reminding the children to be a "good audience" for one another, it hasn't been working very well. They quickly become restless and inattentive while other children are speaking.

1. **Constructed-response question**
   a. What steps could Ms. Wayland take to increase children's ability to listen while their peers are speaking?

   b. Are there other activities that Ms. Wayland can include in her kindergarten classroom to enhance children's oral language?

2. **Multiple-choice question**

   Oral language development includes components of both receptive and expressive language. Which of the following centers mostly on receptive language?

   a. Carlos is an English language learner (ELL).
   b. Carlos enjoys the musical tape that Ms. Wayland has on this morning.
   c. Carlos is proud that he can say good-bye in English to his classmates and teacher.
   d. Carlos knows what his teacher means when she announces "cleanup time" and readily responds.

Chapter

13

The Physical Domain

You may wonder:

Is sending young children outdoors to play sufficient to support their physical development?

How do children develop the fine-motor skills necessary for writing?

What kinds of motor skills are appropriate for children to learn?

What information do young children need so that they can practice safety measures and make healthy choices?

In this chapter we present information to help answer your questions about the physical domain.

PHYSICAL ACTIVITY

◆ ◆ *Mrs. Runningdeer scanned the room, where small groups of 3- to 5-year-olds were engaging in gross-motor activities. Smiling, she watched two girls swinging foam mallets at soft foam balls suspended by strings from the dropped ceiling.*

Carrie, who was not quite 3 years old, held her mallet up and twirled it around and around. Sometimes the ball went swinging as her mallet made contact with it from the front or the back. Her arm and wrist did not appear to move. Each hit appeared to be entirely accidental. She was grinning joyously.

Tabby, at age 4 years, was also focused on her ball as she swung the mallet from her right shoulder with her forearm partially extended, moving her right foot with a half rotation of her whole body. When she connected, the force was great, sending the ball swinging out fast in the full arc of the string. Sometimes Tabby did not move back fast enough, and the soft ball hit her. She struck the ball about once every three or four swings.

Carrie was just exploring the mallet and hanging ball and that Tabby was further along in learning to strike the ball but was by no means at a mature skill level. Mrs. Runningdeer moved forward to suggest that Tabby step into the strike using the other foot.

Having arranged the equipment in the environment, Mrs Runningdeer is providing encouragement and instruction as children play, with an understanding of each child's competence and which steps come next as the child increases in skill.

Importance of Physical Activity

Children benefit in many ways from regular physical activity, some of which are listed next. Physical activity does the following (Copple & Bredekamp, 2009; Hirsh, 2004; Pica, 2006; Sanders, 2002; Seefeldt & Vogel, 1986):

❑ Promotes changes in brain structure and function. Increases capacity for learning.
❑ Assists in the refinement of perceptual abilities involving vision, balance, and tactile sensations.
❑ Builds the skeleton and promotes the maintenance of muscles while reducing fat.
❑ Leads to proficiency in the skills that are the basis for successful participation in games, dance, sports, and leisure activities.
❑ Improves aerobic fitness, muscle endurance, muscle power, muscle strength and feelings of wellness.
❑ Contributes to social adjustment and is associated with positive mental health.

Children obtain these benefits when they are able to participate in a variety of motor activities and are motivated to engage in regular, vigorous play (Pica, 2006; Sanders, 2002; Leppo, Davis, & Crim, 2000). In addition, because physical play is an important part of children's social life, competence as a participant enables children to interact with others, solve problems as they arise during play, and develop concepts of fairness.

With time, children also establish lifestyle patterns of safety, fitness, and healthy daily life practices that many individuals will maintain throughout their lifetime. Meanwhile, adults remain substantially responsible for maintaining a safe and sanitary environment and teaching young children how to move efficiently and to independently make healty decisions and avoid injury.

Principles of Motor Development

The principles of motor development, maturation, and learning apply to all aspects of physical activity: gross-motor, perceptual-motor, and fine-motor skills. Physical skills develop from head to toe and from the center of the body outward. Thus, children will be able to move their upper arms and hands before they will be able to engage in complex dance steps. In addition, youngsters scoop a ball with their arms and body before being able to catch it with their hands. We generally recognize that **locomotor movements** (going from one place to another) require the use of the large muscles in the trunk, legs, and arms, whereas **manipulative movements** require the use of the many small muscles of the hands or feet for children participating in dance and soccer.

Growth also influences performance because taller children usually run faster and are generally stronger than shorter children. Children learn the specifics of each motor skill once their bodies are sufficiently mature. Children may be advanced in one skill and just beginning the developmental sequence for other skills.

The principle of developmental direction is very apparent in motor skills. Children move from awkward movement to mechanical efficiency in sequential steps. Many fundamental motor skills progress from the following positions: *bilateral*—usually forward facing, both hands at body midline; *unilateral*—one-sided, shift of body; *ipsilateral*—the foot, arm, and body move from the same side, some rotation; and *contralateral*—across the body, the movement is diagonal, involving both sides of the body and body rotation with stepping. Activity that requires crossing the midline and contralateral movement also requires that both sides of the brain are used, strengthemig these connections.

Fundamental Motor Skills

After the first year of life, children learn to walk on their own, exploring their environment, manipulating objects, climbing on furniture, and moving around their near environments with curiosity and interest. Gradually, these skills improve qualitatively in a predictable sequence so that movement is more automatic and fluid. Some gross-motor skills such as walking and striking are **fundamental motor skills**, which form the basis for games or other more complex movements. Between ages 3 and 8, children become mature enough to acquire these movement competencies on their own or with adult guidance. Unfortunately, not all children experience optimal conditions. Some children in Head Start (41%) demonstrate delays in fundamental motor skills, whereas others (16%) exhibit substantial deficiencies (Woodard & Yun, 2001). If children do not acquire proficiency by age 6 or 7 years, they may never acquire it during the elementary years (Gallahue, 1993). In Figure 13.1, we provide a summary of selected gross-motor skills that most youngsters can achieve (Gallahue, 1995; Ignico, 1994; Payne & Isaacs, 2007).

FIGURE 13.1   Select Gross-Motor Skills Usually Learned Between 3 and 7 Years of Age

Locomotor Skills

Walk	Run	Leap	Jump	Hop	Creep	Roll
Stop	Start	Dodge	Slide	Start	Skip	Gallop
Climb						

Manipulative Skills (Projecting and Receiving Objects)

Throw	Kick	Punt	Strike	Volley	Bounce	Roll
Dribble	Catch	Trap	Hug			

Nonlocomotor Skills

Bend	Stretch	Twist	Turn	Swing	Curl	Swivel
Whirl	Spin	Rock	Bend	Hang	Pull	Push
Lift	Sway					

Most of the locomotor and manipulative skills listed in Figure 13.1 have inherent sequences that begin as exploratory movements and gradually evolve into more mature forms of movement. The throwing sequence is presented in more detail in Figure 13.2 to illustrate the predictable steps that children go through while achieving competence. Additional skills are described in Table 13.1. Youngsters move through these sequences at different rates and that ultimate performance at the end of the early childhood period is determined by maturation, learning, and practice during this time. Adults may or may not observe each of the stages, as a child may move through a specific step in the sequence either very quickly or very slowly (Sanders, 2002).

Summary of Fundamental Motor Skill Stage Characteristics. The number of stages that a particular skill appears to involve varies; throwing and catching have five distinct stages, and galloping and skipping only three. There does not appear to be carryover from one fundamental motor skill to

FIGURE 13.2 Developmental Sequence for Throwing

Stage 1
Vertical (upward–backward) windup
Little or no weight transfer
No spinal rotation
"Chop" throw

Stage 2
Windup in horizontal or oblique plane
Straight-arm throw (sling) in horizontal or oblique plane
Block rotation with weight shift to opposite foot
Follow-through across body

Stage 3
High (upward–backward) windup
Forward stride with ipsilateral foot
Hip flexion, arm movement in vertical plane
Little trunk rotation
Follow-through across body

Stage 4
High (upward–backward) windup
Forward stride with contralateral foot
Trunk–hip flexion, arm movement forward, elbow extension
Limited trunk rotation
Follow-through across body

Stage 5
Low (downward–backward) windup
Body (hip–shoulder) rotation
Forward stride with contralateral foot
Sequential derotation for force production
Arm–leg follow-through

Source: Haubenstricker, J. (1991, May). *Gross Motor Development in Preschoolers.* Paper presented to Michigan Council of Cooperative Nurseries, East Lansing, MI.

TABLE 13.1 Summary of Fundamental Motor Skill Characteristics by Stage

Fundamental Motor Skill	Stage 1	Stage 2	Stage 3	Stage 4	Stage 5
Throw	Vertical windup "Chop" throw Feet stationary No spinal rotation	Horizontal windup "Sling throw" Block rotation Follow-through across body	High windup Ipsilateral step Little spinal rotation Follow-through across body	High windup Contralateral step Little spinal rotation Follow-through across body	Downward arc windup Contralateral step Segmented body rotation Arm–leg follow-through
Catch	Delayed arm action Arms straight in front until ball contact, then scooping action to chest Feet stationary	Arms encircle ball as it approaches Ball is "hugged" to chest Feet stationary or may take one step	"To chest" catch Arms "scoop" under ball to trap it to chest Single step may be used to approach ball	Catch with hands only Feet stationary or limited to one step	Catch with hands only Whole body moves through space
Kick	Little or no leg windup Stationary position Foot "pushes" ball Step backward after kick (usually)	Leg wincup to the rear Stationary position Opposition of arms and legs	Moving approach Foot travels in a low arc Arm–leg opposition Forward or sideward step on follow-through	Rapid approach Backward trunk lean during windup Leap before kick Hop after kick	
Punt	No leg windup Ball toss erratic Body stationary Push ball and step back	Leg windup to the rear Ball toss still erratic Body stationary Forceful kick attempt	Preparatory step(s) Some arm–leg yoking Ball toss or drop	Rapid approach Controlled drop Leap before ball contact Hop after ball contact	
Strike	"Chop" strike Feet stationary	Horizontal push or swing Block rotation Feet stationary or stepping	Ipsilateral step Diagonal downward swing	Contralateral step Segmented body rotation Wrist rollover on follow-through	
Long jump	Arms act as "brakes" Large vertical component Legs not extended	Arms act as "wings" Vertical component still great Legs near full extension	Arms move forward, elbows in front of trunk at takeoff Hands to head height Takeoff angle still greater than 45 degrees Legs often fully extended	Complete arm and leg extension at takeoff Takeoff near 45-degree angle Thighs parallel to surface when feet contact for landing	
Run	Arms—high guard Flat-footed contact Short stride Wide stride, shoulder width	Arms—middle guard Vertical component still great Legs near full extension	Arms—low guard Arm opposition—elbows nearly extended Heel–toe contact	Heel–toe contact (toe–heel when sprinting) Arm–leg opposition High heel recovery Elbow flexion	
Hop	Nonsupport foot in front with thigh parallel to floor Body erect Hands shoulder height	Nonsupport knee flexed with knee in front and foot behind support leg Slight body lean forward Bilateral arm action	Nonsupport thigh vertical with foot behind support leg—knee flexed More body lean forward Bilateral arm action	Pendular action on nonsupport leg Forward body lean Arm opposition with leg swing	
Gallop	Resembles rhythmically uneven run Trail leg crosses in front of lead leg during airborne phase, remains in front at contact	Slow–moderate tempo, choppy rhythm Trail leg stiff Hips often oriented sideways Vertical component exaggerated	Smooth, rhythmical pattern, moderate tempo Feet remain close to ground Hips oriented forward		
Skip	Broken skip pattern or irregular rhythm Slow, deliberate movement Ineffective arm action	Rhythmical skip pattern Arms provide body lift Excessive vertical component	Arm action reduced, hands below shoulders Easy, rhythmical movement Support foot near surface on hop		

Source: Haubenstricker, J. (1990). *Summary of Fundamental Motor Skill Characteristics: Motor Performance Study.* Unpublished document, Michigan State University, East Lansing, MI.

another except for skipping, which is a combination of running and hopping. However, children who can strike a ball at Stage 3 may be able to throw it only at Stage 2. and may function at Stage 1 of the long jump at age 7 years if the opportunity to learn the skill has not occurred. Once the final stage of each fundamental skill is reached, children continue to eliminate extraneous movement and increase in power and strength, and they may incorporate elements of style exhibited by skilled players. **Coordination** (the use of more than one set of muscles) of body parts and sensory information generally increases as the skills of typically developing children increase. Children may develop additional or complex skills as a part of ballet, horseback riding, or sports.

With thorough reading of Table 13.1, you can identify fine distinctions between stages. Children seem to need time to explore and practice movements in each stage before moving forward to the next. The level of detail allows classroom teachers to determine which actions to encourage. Adults may provide cues that enable children to advance if they need this level of support. Often, more-skilled children provide such support for less-skilled youngsters during informal play.

Children also begin developmental sequences at different times, and the amount of time that they need to perform at mature levels also varies considerably. Throwing begins at age 1 year for both boys and girls, and 60% of all boys demonstrate a mature technique by age 5 years. Girls do not show this level of performance until much later. Catching does not begin until around age 2 years, and both boys and girls show a mature form by about age 7 years. Nevertheless, substantial individual differences can be seen in children at any age.

Perceptual–Motor Skills

Children always use all their sensory capacities as they engage with the environment, explore, move, or handle objects. When professionals speak of perceptual-motor development, they are usually referring to movement activities that will lead to academic or cognitive outcomes (Payne & Isaacs, 2007). In the following discussion, we focus on a few skills that appear to be distinctive and particularly useful.

The perceptual process improves with practice during the early childhood period. All modes of receiving sensation from the environment are involved: sight, hearing, scent, taste, and touch. Frequently, multiple modes of sensation come from one source at the same instant, which requires **sensory integration**. For example, if a dog approaches a child, the child is likely to see (color, size, conformation, and demeanor), hear (footsteps, panting, or barking), and possibly smell (breath or fur) the dog. These sensations are transmitted to the brain through the nervous system. The brain uses the current information, organizes it, and integrates it into previously learned concepts such as *animals, brown things,* or *things that move with four feet.* After a decision is made about a course of action, the brain transmits signals through the nervous system to initiate the desired movement. Finally, the movement is performed. A very young child may decide to run to an adult from fear, approach the dog cautiously, or even approach joyfully, depending on the decision he or she makes. Last, relevant information is stored in the child's memory, which will ultimately affect similar future experiences.

The perceptual process is rapid, continuous, and ongoing. The same set of events might constitute vastly dissimilar experiences for children. For example, if two children observe a large, inflated ball in the yard, one child might classify the ball as something to kick, whereas the other might perceive it as something to roll. Both children will enhance their concepts and skills as they learn to play successfully, using either or both responses. To the extent that perception of the environment is a steady component of living, all movement uses this capacity. Five aspects of perceptual-motor development are of particular importance: balance, spatial awareness, figure–ground perception, temporal awareness, and body and directional awareness.

Balance. **Static balance** is the ability to maintain a posture while holding still. Standing on one foot, leaning forward with one foot in front of the other, and teetering on the edge of a stair with the toes only on the tread are examples of static balance. **Dynamic balance** is the ability to remain in a desired posture while moving. Walking on a balance beam, hopping on one foot, running, and turning rapidly are all examples of dynamic balance. Balance is a component of most movements but is particularly important for complex movements in games or dance. Visual information is helpful in maintaining dynamic balance. Because children's center of gravity changes as they grow, youngsters require ongoing practice to adjust for changes in height and weight.

Spatial Awareness. Young children understand their surroundings in relation to their bodies or body parts (Epstein, 2007; Sanders, 2002). Children may move on a high, medium, or low level in a direction that might be forward, backward, or sideways. They may move under or over or around objects in a pathway that is straight, curved, or zig-zagged. Location such as **self space** or **shared space** are concepts acquired as groups of children work together. Additionally, spacial awareness ideas are used in fine-motor activity as children begin to control the direction of cutting, the position of paper when writing, and as they arrange materials on shelves in front of, behind, or near other objects.

In practical terms, youngsters may bump into each other during play because they misjudge the distance between themselves and another. Beginning writers often run out of space on a piece of paper because they misjudge the amount of space they will need for all the letters. Experienced teachers learn that children are likely to be more appropriately separated for a dance experience if they stand with arms and legs outstretched and cannot touch another person than if the teacher simply asks the children to disperse so that they will have enough room to move. The space in the former strategy is defined by the child's body; in the latter, their strategy depends on a more abstract concept of their own and others' space.

Figure–Ground Perception. Determining what is in the foreground and in the background usually involves auditory or visual perception skills. The task in the visual modality is to find a specific object within a group. Three- to 5-year-olds have difficulty selecting toys from crowded cupboards, instead choosing to play with a toy on the table or a toy that someone else is using. They will also find locating a particular letter within a word challenging.

Separating the foreground from the background develops with time and experience, so that primary-age children can "find" animals in drawings in which the lines form other, more obvious shapes, identify a phonetic sound in the middle of a word or the voice of an instrument in an orchestra, or discern directions spoken in an open classroom in which several muted conversations are ongoing during the primary grades. Memory plays an important part in these skills as well (Puckett & Black, 2005).

Temporal Awareness. Time relations are not fully developed until late in the early childhood period or even into adolescence. However, the beginnings of the notions of speed and timing do begin to emerge. Rhythm is one aspect of organized time that most young children enjoy. Toddlers between the ages of 12 and 18 months will bob, bounce, or bend in time to music as an expression of their involvement. With guided practice, 2- to 5-year-olds may clap complex patterns and engage in increasingly challenging rhythmic activity. Sequence of movements or dance steps is another aspect of temporal awareness (Frost, Wortham, & Reifel, 2008). Moving to a steady beat in a simple pattern or sequence helps the child develop inner control and coordinated competence and requires focused attention. When young children are engaged in dance experiences, they learn to explore time, space, and energy as they learn to express themselves and move their bodies (Koff, 2000).

Because young children's spatial awareness is not fully developed, and their senses of time and cause and effect are still immature (Frost & Sweeney, 1995), estimating the speed of an object is extremely difficult for 3- to 5-year-olds and challenging for 5- to 8-year-olds. You might observe that these youngsters close their arms after the ball has passed them. Many accidents occur on playgrounds because children do not accurately judge the speed of objects and other people. Children improve with practice, but an approximate estimation of an object's trajectory and speed emerges only during the primary years; some 8-year-olds become adept at catching balls thrown at different speeds (Payne & Isaacs, 2007).

Children who learn to assess their speed as slower or faster than their previous performance experience pride and pleasure in their accomplishments. However, premature competition is generally discouraging to all but the one child who is recognized as the winner. During the early childhood years, the feeling of moving rapidly through space is exciting on its own. As children move into primary grades, noncompetitive running games are most appropriate because children are developing their competence in efficient running (Pica, 2009; Sanders, 2002).

Body and Directional Awareness. **Body awareness** is a part of the social-conventional knowledge about the names and functions of the various body parts. For most children, naming external body parts is primarily complete during the preschool years. Finger plays such as "Head, Shoulders,

Knees, and Toes" or "Where Is Thumbkin?" can help familiarize children with the vocabulary. This vocabulary is most helpful to children when teachers give them cues such as "Billy, bend your knees when you land" while they are engaged in motor activity. **Body relationship awareness** also incudes roles that children create with their bodies, such as copying, leading/following, meeting/parting, passing, mirroring, acting in unison, alternately solo partner and group. These concepts and vocabulary require active adult intervention and instruction (Epstein, 2007).

Directional awareness is a combination of the understanding of concepts such as *up* and *down*, *front* and *back, side by side, on/off, near to* and *far away,* and other descriptions of location and the application of this information during a physical activity. Ideas such as *left* and *right* are related to a specific speaker and are much more difficult to understand than other concepts of direction or spatial relations. For example, if two children are facing each other at a table and an adult asks them to point up, the children would be pointing in the same direction, yet if the direction were to point to the left, they would point in opposite directions. Most children master this idea by the end of the early childhood years.

Children whose spatial and directional awareness is immature may confuse *3, m, w,* and *E* and other combinations of handwritten letters because the main difference in this script is the direction of the lines. Reversals and inversions are common during the primary years, although with practice and support, children develop the necessary discrimination. Practice in perceptual-motor learning continues throughout everyday life and play. Adults support learning through instruction and the provision of materials and equipment. Skilled coordination between perceptual information and muscle groups requires learning the movements until sequences are almost habitual.

Fine-Motor Skills

Using the hands to move objects precisely and accurately is the task referred to as **fine-motor skill**. As with gross-motor skills, maturity, instruction, and practice are necessary for optimal development. Coordination of sensory information with the motoric action is also necessary.

Throughout the preschool period, children become fatigued easily, often feeling frustrated at their inability to accomplish tasks. Because of the variation in rates of maturation and experience, early-primary-aged children may also experience fatigue and stress as they try to perform fine-motor tasks such as precision coloring or writing. Adult support and encouragement without pressure to perform to an external standard is helpful. Adults should provide information, demonstration, and encouragement, as well as opportunities for practice.

Six- to 8-year-olds can make simple crafts, such as those involving straight sewing, cutting objects reasonably skillfully with scissors, and stringing fine beads into simple patterns independently. These children move to greater control, precision, and accuracy while refining earlier accomplishments. Girls tend to be more skillful at fine-motor tasks earlier than boys, who appear to excel earlier at tasks requiring strength or power (Berk, 2007). Many boys find penmanship challenging but may draw objects of interest in greater detail. Fine-motor skills are fostered in settings in which the tools, children's experiences, and cultural expectations are supportive (Bredekamp & Copple, 2009).

Children who have the maturity to perform the tasks illustrated in Table 13.2 but not the experience using the tools or engaging in the activities will begin their skills as much younger children do. For example, 4-year-old Emily had never been given writing implements of any kind at home. When she entered the children's program, she first used a fist grasp on crayons and pencils, learning quickly and with practice to use a more mature grasp. At age 3 years, Vivian had always been fed by her parents to avoid a mess. Her use of a spoon and a cup in a childcare program was immature for her age, but, in a climate of encouragement and support, she progressed rapidly. Healthy children seem to catch up when their earlier experiences have not been conducive to the acquisition of skill. However, such situations require time, patience, support, and instruction. Adult expectations must be adjusted accordingly. Youngsters whose skills are first attempted between 2 and 3 years of age and are brought to greater control and accuracy by age 7 years are more likely to be more physically advanced than children who do not begin this process until age 4 or 5 years.

Handwriting as a Fine-Motor Skill. Children learn about the written language much as they learn oral language: They first observe it and then imitate it. Beginning attempts are so rudimentary that adults may fail to recognize that the child is beginning the process of handwriting. In environments

TABLE 13.2 Expected Timing and Sequence of Fine-Motor Skills for Children in Supportive Environments

Age (yr)	General	Targeting	Cut and Paste	Self-Help	Graphic Tools
2–3	Fatigues easily Undresses Carries small objects easily Precisely picks up small objects Uses doorknob	Places one-piece knob puzzles accurately Puts shapes in appropriate holes Strings large beads on plastic tubing	Tears paper May put large globs of paste on top of the piece to be pasted instead of between the pieces of paper Snips with scissors Holds paper and scissors incorrectly Likely uses both hands with scissors	Eats with a spoon Drinks from a cup Undresses if fasteners are simple	Scribbles with pleasure Copies a cross or a circle May attempt simple capital letters such as *H, V,* and *T* May hold implement in fist
3–4	Opens doors, manages most latches Builds block towers Uses keyboard for simple programs Pounds, rolls, squeezes clay Turns pages of a book one at a time Exibits hand preference	Inserts large pegs into pegboards Strings large beads with a string Puts together simple puzzles with objects representing an object or a clear segment of an object (e.g., tail of a dog) Manipulates pegs and puzzle pieces with accuracy	Uses large globs of paste Pours on lots of glue Uses index finger or paste brush to spread Cuts full length of scissors, may do two lengths Has little directional control May not use correct grasp of scissors	Pours liquid from a pitcher into a container with increasing accuracy and control Handles Velcro fasteners easily Puts on outdoor clothing but usually needs help zipping or buttoning Eats most foods independently	Tries three-point grasp of writing implement Is inconsistent and may grasp implement far from the point Uses circles, crosses, and horizontal and vertical lines in drawings May outline a scribbled shape of a rectangle
4–5	Builds complex structures with various construction materials May have problems with spatial judgments and directionality Practices to attain mastery of fine-motor tasks With practice may become adept at computer programs or video games Coordinates hand and arm movements with vision, hearing, touch, and other senses	Uses pattern cards skillfully in placing small pegs in pegboards Laces Sews May master multipiece puzzles if they have color and shape cues Threads large needle with help Threads small beads on a string	Holds scissors and paper correctly Cuts straight lines and turns corners Places appropriate amounts of glue or paste in correct spot and spreads with control	Dresses and undresses, buttons and unbuttons, zips haltingly Needs help starting coat zipper Uses a hanger if reachable Usually has complete toileting independence Eats with a fork Spills infrequently Washes and dries hands	Uses tripod grip on writing implement, although position may still be high Draws sun and tadpole people and scribbles Paints with deliberateness Writes letters anyplace on the paper May write name or initials or portions of their names on their drawings

(continued)

TABLE 13.2   Expected Timing and Sequence of Fine-Motor Skills for Children in Supportive Environments *(continued)*

Age (yr)	General	Targeting	Cut and Paste	Self-Help	Graphic Tools
5–6	Sculpts with dough, able to do a pinch or coil pot Shows increased precision and control Has few if any false starts Pounds nails with accuracy Uses keyboard with increasing skill	Inserts increasingly small objects with ease Manages a 12- to 15-piece puzzle without dependence on color	Usually can cut on a curve, cut out interior shapes, geometric shapes, or magazine pictures Uses scissors easily and accurately Uses glue and paste skillfully	Organizes and takes care of own materials Combs and brushes hair, washes face and hands without getting wet Manages own clothing fasteners and ties shoelaces Spreads with a knife and can do simple cutting with a table knife	Exhibits good control of pencil or marker Makes letters, both upper- and lowercase, crudely but recognizable Makes inversions and reversals often Writes letters of name but not necessarily on a line or correctly spaced Draws cars, boats, houses, trees, and flowers with increasing detail Writes numerals
6–8	Has good basic skill Shows improvement in precision and accuracy Makes simple crafts, depending on interest Good prehension and dexterity	Does multipiece puzzles Uses shape and size to place pieces Places small objects more precisely Good overall eye–hand coordination	Shows good control and improvement in precision	Demonstrates mastery	Ninety-seven percent of children make acceptable letters Spacing and placement of letters on page acceptable Word, letter, and numeral reversals common, often self-corrected Drawings made with many media, increasing details

Sources: Adapted from *Developmental Profiles: Pre-birth Through Twelve,* by K. E. Allen and Marotz, 2007, Clifton Park, NY: Delmar Learning; *Developmentally Appropriate Practice in Early Childhood Programs,* by S. Bredekamp and C. Copple, 2009, Washington, DC: National Association for the Education of Young Children; *The Developmental Resource: Behavioral Sequence for Assessment and Program Planning* (vol. 2), by M. Cohen and P. Gross, 1979, New York: Grune & Stratton; "Early Childhood Education: Providing the Foundation," by A. Ignico, 1994, *Journal of Physical Education, 65*(6), pp. 25–56; *Assessing and Guiding Young Children's Development and Learning* (3rd ed.), by O. McAfee and D. J. Leong, 2006, Boston: Allyn & Bacon; *Early Childhood Development* (vol. 5), by J. Trawick-Smith, 2010, Upper Saddle River, NJ: Pearson; *The Young Child: Development from Prebirth through Age Eight* (4th ed.), by M. B. Puckett & J.K. Black, Upper Saddle River, NJ: Pearson.

in which children see adults write grocery lists, letters, holiday greetings, or notes to family members, toddlers will attempt to participate in the activity as soon as they obtain access to a writing implement.

> *Gwen, about 18 months old, played near her mother's chair as her mother graded papers. When her mother left the room for a few minutes, Gwen climbed on the chair, picked up a red pen, and marked every page of a stack of papers with a large mark. With mother's return, she smiled, pleased with herself for having completed this task so promptly!*

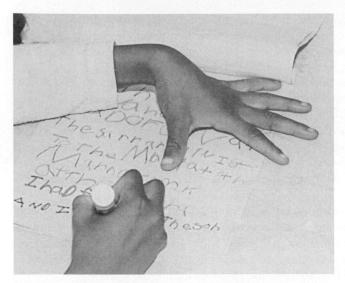

Early attempts at writing involve using large-muscle groups and result in the formation of large, skewed letters.

The concept that meaningful messages may be written is discussed in chapter 12. However, handwriting involves a progression of fine-motor skills that entails maturation, learning, and practice.

Using Writing and Drawing Implements. Children use tools to write. At first, fingers are useful for drawing and writing in finger paint and sand, and these techniques remain the easiest method of leaving a mark on something. However, even very young toddlers use a variety of tools to write or make graphic designs. Paintbrushes vary in diameter and length. Crayons vary in diameter and are available with and without paper wrapping. Pencils vary in hardness, diameter, and shape (round to many sided). Pens vary in texture and materials, in the point size, and in diameter. Markers vary in diameter and in point shape. All tools are available in many colors.

The least mature, least experienced child will more likely maintain interest in and explore the use of writing implements such as markers, nylon-tipped pens, or No. 2 pencils. These implements create clear, colorful marks with little effort by the child. Children enjoy causing something to happen, and early success is encouraging. With older, more experienced writers, pencils offer greater control. The general guideline suggested by experienced teachers is to move from larger to smaller diameter as the child matures and from implements that more easily make a mark to those that require more control.

Holding the Writing Implement. The mature finger tripod associated with adult writing is usually present in children by age 7 years. In addition, writing posture improves with age, although visible tension increases with age as well. In the earliest phases of writing, the muscles of the head, neck, trunk, and shoulder are primarily engaged. Later, the muscles of the elbow, wrist, and fingers are brought into use as the child attains greater control. A relaxed grip about 1 inch from the point with the index finger on top and thumb and middle finger holding the two sides is the most efficient position. The progression from the earliest pattern to more mature patterns is as follows (Payne & Isaacs, 2007):

❑ All four fingers and the thumb are wrapped around the implement, with the thumb up (away from the point).
❑ The palm is engaged with a full-hand grasp, with the thumb toward the point of the implement. The implement is often grasped well away from the point. The arm and shoulder control the movement, which is usually large.
❑ The hand moves closer to the point of the implement. Control of the movement of the pencil shifts from shoulder to elbow to fingers as the grasp moves toward the tip.
❑ Tripod positioning of the fingers with noticeable wrist movement and minimal finger control is often combined with the fingers bent and the fingertips on the implement. (Children using this grip can tire easily, and their fingers may cramp.)
❑ The mature tripod, with the implement resting on the middle finger, allows rapid finger control of movements and is seen at about age 7 years for most children.
❑ Refinement of the dynamic tripod occurs between age 6 and 14 years, with the writing implement resting on the side of the middle finger and infrequent use of the fingertips to hold the implement.

The age at which children achieve a mature tripod grip varies widely; some youngsters achieve this milestone as early as age 3 years (48%) and 90% achieve it by age 6 years (Payne & Isaacs, 2007). The remainder may not achieve it until middle childhood. Parental expectations and opportunities for children to practice writing at home and in programs may account for such differences (Huntsinger et al., 1994).

Children need extensive practice with their hands before beginning to print letters, and they require opportunities to practice letter formation to develop the necessary motor skills. They learn to print from everyday experiences: observing adults print, observing letters and words in the environment, and "writing notes" of one type or another during pretend play. One group of 3- and 4-year-olds were provided a writing table, unlined paper, and each of their names printed on a note card; the children were *invited* to "sign in" as they entered their preschool classroom. Their teacher observed carefully and made notes of their progress as they moved from controlled scribbles to scribbles and mock letters, to one or two letters of their names, to their first name with the letters placed randomly, to writing their first name. At the end of 7 months, none of the children wrote with only controlled scribbles, but their writing skills ranged across the various achievement levels (Green, 1998). The teacher's strategies were exploratory, with demonstration and paraphrased reflections used as each child progressed. Very little research is available about letter formation for children younger than 5, although children between 3 and 4 years understand the difference between drawing and writing and can produce a letter on request. Between ages 4 and 6, children learn to produce their own names, make linear expansions (wavy lines to represent print), label drawings, and produce some letters or numerals without regard to phonetics (Baghban, 2007).

Research on handwriting for kindergarteners suggests that fluent transcription (letter drawing) contributes to written expression, spelling, and phonemic awareness among first graders (Edwards, 2003). Such fluency is the result of maturation, instruction, and practice as are all motor skills. Five- and 6-year-olds benefit from direct instruction and guided practice. To summarize, in addition to attention to the grip and posture of the child, effective strategies include the following:

- ❏ Attending to similarities and differences in letter forms when copying or viewing environmental print
- ❏ Tracing both upper- and lowercase letters while the letter name is announced
- ❏ Copying modeled lowercase letters that are marked with arrow cues or dashes while letter names are said aloud
- ❏ Writing letters from memory (This means drawing the letter on command. Older children are able to draw the letter that comes before or after a sequence in the alphabet, such as *l m n o _.*)
- ❏ Using letter names when children copy or write letters (or words) in all contexts

Handwriting is one example of a fine-motor skill that has been closely examined. Other skills such as keyboarding, piano playing, sewing, and paper folding have not been sufficiently researched to merit a similar discussion. In summary, these general principles might still be applied.

- ❏ The proximal–distal principle, in which the shoulder, arm, wrist, and then finger muscles are used in succession as children move on to greater control, is applicable in most instances.
- ❏ Maturation, learning, and practice are all significant factors in a child's ultimate success; maturation alone does not lead to skillful performance.
- ❏ Children acquire knowledge and skill gradually and are heavily influenced by the presence of models in the environment.
- ❏ Mature performance is the result of years of practice.
- ❏ Growth, or the increase of the size of the hands, may contribute to children's learning some skills, such as keyboarding and piano playing, because of the reach that is required to use the correct form.
- ❏ Children progress through the same developmental sequences, although considerable variation in rates can be seen.

Movement Concepts

Children use all the fundamental motor skills and perceptual-motor competencies together to produce movements of different qualities such as when variations of time, space, effort, or flow are explored (see Figure 13.3). As children build their ideas and meanings, they must also learn the vocabulary of movement. Music may also support children's understanding of qualitative distinctions of movement. The teacher should select combinations of these movement ideas and incorporate them into an activity. An obstacle course in which children move through, around, under, and on top of objects at a slow pace until they reach a rug where they stop to rest is an example of a gross-motor array of movements. Similar combinations may be made by moving smaller items with the hands. For example, Mr. Towl asked a few kindergarten children to draw diagonal lines on tissue paper that they would later use to wrap around a shoe box to cover the inside and the outside of the box. Clearly, movement concepts apply to fine- and gross-motor skills and require the use of perceptual-motor skills as well.

FIGURE 13.3   Selected Movement Concepts

Effort: Strong   Firm   Light   Fine

Space: High (head and shoulders)
Medium (waist)   Low (below the knees)

Time: Accelerate   Fast   Decelerate
Slow   Sudden   Sustained

Direction: Forward/Backward
Diagonal/Sideways   Up/Down
Lift/Lower   Rise/Fall   Reach/Collapse

Flow: Free (outward from the body)
Bound (close to the body)   Smooth
(continuous)   Jerky (starts and stops)

Pathways: Straight   Curved   Zigzag
Twisted

Percussive/Vibrate: Stamp   Pound
Punch   Shiver   Wobble   Shake   Flutter
Swing   Shudder   Shake   Tremble

Stops: Freeze   Pause   Hold   Grip
Brake   Pull up   Rest

Spatial relations: Over/Under   In/Out
Between/Among   In front/Behind
Above/Below   Through/Around   Near/Far
Meeting/Parting   Expand/Contract

FIGURE 13.4   Physical Activity of Children with Special Needs

Bettina
Bettina smiled as she ran into the playground. Her large hearing aid bumped on her chest as she moved, although she did not pay any attention to it. With some other children, she climbed the ladder and went down the slide, watching what the others did before trying it. Playing in the sand, she alternated between watching others and digging, filling a container, and tipping it over. Dusting off the sand that seemed to cling to her, she approached another pair of girls who were kicking a ball, watching first, then joining the play. Ms. Goldbeck blew her whistle, which Bettina did not appear to hear, and walked toward her, moving in front of her, saying, "It is time to go inside."

Physical Activity of Children Who Have Special Needs

For children who experience challenges in language and learning, physical play is often an opportunity for more typical participation. Youngsters who have a disability may require more repetition to achieve success and often show delayed achievement. However, for many children, vigorous play is one arena in which they may participate successfully with their peers (Figure 13.4).

Safety may require particular attention when children do not hear or see well. The arrangement of equipment, the structuring of activities, and the cooperation of other children usually are adequate to enable most children to participate in large- and small-muscle activities.

Usually, modifications in instruction are successful, such as gaining attention in the sensory modality that the child uses more typically to accommodate particular limitations. Clearly, children who do not see cannot develop visual discrimination tasks. However, touching a youngster with a hearing impairment and then demonstrating a skill, followed by pointing to the child is usually sufficient to give such a child instructions. The physical domain is unique in that language may be optional in teaching.

Children with serious visual impairments are usually hesitant initially. In particular, balance seems to rely heavily on visual information. Continuous physical contact, oral encouragement, and spoken direction may provide sufficient security for the child to try new motor tasks.

Some children have impairments in the physical domain. A report from the physical or occupational therapist is useful for identifying the child's strengths and should be used as a guide by the general practitioner. If a child does not walk independently, walkers, wagons, or wheelchairs may enable the child to move and even engage in some games as wheelchair control improves.

Heidi, a 7-year-old with leg braces, had sessions with the physical therapist once a week. She also went outdoors with the other children, one of whom was assigned to push open a

Teachers adapt their methods and activities to include all children.

day, even in winter. Cold weather does not cause colds and flu; rather, close contact with people carrying the contagion is the cause. Children are less likely to catch a cold outdoors than inside.

Other considerations for health and safety are addressed through the health curriculum. This curriculum is discussed next.

Comprehensive Health Curriculum

Even the youngest children participating in programs learn basic ideas about health, safety, and nutrition every day as a consequence of living and learning in an environment in which these issues are addressed and adults model the healthy behavior. In addition, educators teach specific knowledge that they know will help children to make safe and healthy choices. With the exception of mental health, which is covered in the affective domain, a broad range of health topics is listed in Table 13.3. Generally speaking, the younger children's curriculum should focus first on the most immediate

TABLE 13.3 Sample Health Topics

Category	Topic	Examples
Safety and First Aid	Body rights, touch awareness, and personal safety	How to seek help
	Strategies to use when lost	Learning address and phone number
	Fire/water safety	Stop-drop-and-roll
	Recognition of poisons	Using helmets, goggles
	School rules	Bike and trike safety
	Traffic signs and seat belts	
	Transportation safety	
	Injury prevention	
Nutrition	Identification of foods and nonfoods	Names of vegetables
	Food sources	How food is marketed and sold
	Body using food	Vegetable soups from around the world
	Culture and food	Food groups
	Food groups	Need for healthy eating habits
	Healthy snacks	
Family Health	Family structure and diversity	Similarities and differences
	Family roles, responsibilities, abilities	Listening skills
	Changes that affect families	New babies, moving houses
	Family members as health helpers	
Consumer Health	Health helpers and their roles	Nurses, doctors, paramedics
	Health products and their function	Soap and water, bandages, etc.
	Aids for visual or hearing impairment	
	When to tell an adult	
Community Health	Emergencies	When and how to call 911
	Fire and police	Trash as health hazard
	Immunizations	Noise and air pollution
	Recycling and conservation	
	Pollution	
Growth and Development	Senses	Sight, sound texture
	Body parts	Names of parts
	Body functions	Muscles, bones
	Living and nonliving	Criteria for life/death
	Abilities of differently abled people	Moving without sight
	Functions of eyes and ears	

TABLE 13.3   Sample Health Topics *(continued)*

Substance Use and Abuse	Definition of drugs	How to say no to drugs
	Contrast with medicine	Effects of smoke on lungs
	Identifying alcohol and cigarettes as drugs	
	Identifying other drugs	
Personal Health Practices	Protective equipment	Helmet wearing
	Care of teeth, skin, hair	Tooth brushing
	Care of handling body wastes,	Nose blowing
	Sleep, rest, and exercise	Getting enough sleep
	Seat belt use	How others get sick
	Protection of self and others when ill	
	Eye and ear protection	
	Grooming tools and their uses	
	Exercise	
Disease Prevention and Control	Prevention of spread of germs	Cleanliness
	How and when to get adult help	When mom is really sick
	Food choice and disease control	Wise food choices and exercise

topics related to daily life, especially those related to the routines and rules in the school that are learned experientially, such as how to blow one's nose and what to do with the tissue. As children get older, additional information, projects, and themes should be devloped related to new health topics.

Selected Health Topics

Do you recall if you washed your hands before and after the last meal you ate? Do you routinely wash your hands before you enter into an interaction with children in the classroom and again as you leave? How often do you eat fast foods, which are high in salt and fat, instead of a well-balanced meal with fruits and vegetables? Do you select fruit instead of another dessert? Think about these questions as you read the following section.

Hand Washing. The single most effective deterrent to contagious disease is the frequent and proper washing of hands. To help you teach children an effective strategy, the directions are listed next (Kendrick, Kaufmann, & Messenger, 1988):

Washing Your Hands
❏ Use soap and running water.
❏ Rub your hands vigorously.
❏ Wash all surfaces including wrists, backs of hands, between fingers, under fingernails.
❏ Rinse well from wrists to fingertips.
❏ Dry hands with paper towel.
❏ Turn off the water with the towel.
❏ Throw the paper towel in the basket. (p. 27)

Food Selection. Opportunities to influence eating practices and food choices abound in full-day programs, Head Start, and elementary schools in which children eat together. Young children tend to eat foods with which they are familiar and reject foods that are new to them. It takes several (8 to 12) experiences with a new food for a child to try and then accept it (Bellows & Anderson, 2006). When new foods are introduced slowly and along with other, more familiar choices, children become interested and learn to enjoy a greater variety. For example, every culture has a variation on vegetable soup. Pea pods are an ingredient in Chinese vegetable soup but not in minestrone. A child familiar with one might be inclined to try the other, especially when it is served with a familiar sandwich.

The following strategies help children relax and eat appropriately (Bellows & Anderson, 2006; Lumeng, 2005).

❑ Teach children the behavior expected during meals as a very early topic.
❑ Demonstrate eating a variety of foods.
❑ Encourage a picky eater to sit next to a child with good selection strategies.
❑ Let children choose to try new foods; avoid forcing them to do so.
❑ Accept children's contribution to discussion describing various culturally specific food selections.

CURRENT EDUCATIONAL ISSUES

For each domain, educators must address some recurring issues in their practice. The physical domain is no exception. Following are discussions about the three most common issues raised about the physical domain.

1. **How can I teach gross-motor skills when I have neither a playground nor a gym. Won't teaching motor skills take time away from the "real" school subjects?** A child develops holistically. In addition, physical fitness is a component of healthy functioning, mental well-being, and longevity. Moderate physical activity is associated with academic achievement because it improves the children's ability to focus their attention after participation (Fox News.com, 2009; Pellegrini & Bjorklund, 2002) and the amout of time spent in physical activity does not have a negative effect on achievement (Carlson, Fulton, Lee & Maynard, 2008). A study by the California Department of Education (2002) found that the number of fitness standards that children met was correlated closely with the SAT in Grades 5, 7, and 9. Several 8- to 10-minute activity breaks using a variety of skills during the day are appropriate and effective (Sanders, 2006).

    Gyms and playgrounds with developmentally appropriate equipment and a variety of other materials such as cones, riding toys, balls, and jump ropes are ideal but not required to incorporate physical activity into the program. Committed adults work to ensure the following:
    ❑ Reduce the time that children wait for routine events
    ❑ Incorporate exercises into opening and closing routines
    ❑ Use yoga stretches and breath control during brain breaks
    ❑ Plan for locomotor activities outdoors
    ❑ Incorporate short bouts of activity in transition times using movement concepts

    Ms. Rodd swept the broken glass off the square of asphalt behind the mobile classroom where her group was housed, picked up the trash, and planned interesting and vigorous activities that she supervised herself. She was always mindful of the risk of falls, but she carried out activities there all year long.

    Mrs. Bronson placed orange cones in the church parking lot where the child-care center rented space to keep cars away from a play area where she brought a mobile climber, mats to place under the climber, and assorted riding toys.

    Ms. Stein set up a "bowling alley" in the hallway of an early childhood program that was used at various times of the day by different classrooms. In addition, she alternated physical activities and block play in a large-group area of her small classroom.

    Perhaps it is time for classroom teachers to reorient this question to, "What is more important than the health and well-being of the children now and in the future?"

2. **When should children begin to learn formal penmanship?** Children draw letters after they have learned to grip a writing implement and when they want to communicate across distance or time. Young children may be given crayons in restaurants, in early childhood programs, and at home when they are seated at a table. When children are scribbling and making large shapes, adults generally refer to the child's activities as "drawing." As children gain practice and observe adults write, their pretend writing becomes linear, with left-to-right progression, and they randomly place a few letter shapes on the page. Children begin to distinguish between the "writing" and the drawing early in their experiences.

    If children have appropriate samples of manuscript print available, they will try drawing some of the shapes on paper. This attempt usually occurs sometime between age 3 and 4 years. The letters most often available to children are their names. Because children may scatter the letters in random order, tilted on the side, or otherwise distorted, adults may or may not recognize them. They are very large and frequently misshapen. The form of the letters appears to be jagged because the children are using muscles in the shoulder, elbow, or wrist instead of their fingers to shape the letters. Providing writing implements and paper and displaying as much manuscript printing as possible is sufficient to encourage children to explore drawing letters. Tracing and copying upper- and lowercase letters may follow the child's initial self-generated writing. Imposing premature adult standards for letter drawing is inappropriate until children have demonstrated a tripod grip and wrist and finger control during exploratory handwriting and drawing. However, usually by the end of first grade, children will produce letters on lined paper rapidly and fluidly, if they have had the instruction and practice necessary.

Informal instruction in short bursts when children ask, "How do I make a *k*?" is always appropriate as the adult draws the letter. Asking children if they want to write their name or if the adult should write it on a painting is also always appropriate as long as the adult accepts the child's approximation. The more modeling, exploration, and practice the child has, the more probable that the skill will emerge.

Age alone is not the best criterion for skill emergence. Youngsters who enter kindergarten and have never held a writing implement need a lot of time using crayons, painting, and drawing with pencils before they have sufficient practice with finger and wrist muscles to produce credible approximations, whereas children with more experience may enter school drawing the letters of their name in a recognizable but imperfect form. Once children's printing is decipherable, the focus of instruction should be on the message, not the mechanics. However, second- and third-grade children who tire easily and whose handwriting is indecipherable may need individualized strategies that focus on posture, trunk, and shoulder stability; pencil grip; and correct form to improve.

Historically, beautiful cursive writing was the hallmark of the educated person and was viewed as an art form. Such refined skills take much time and practice during many years to perfect. Educators are questioning the value of the time spent on penmanship as the range and depth of other content has increased with the years. Some children are taught to print, and cursive writing is omitted. Instead, children learn to print more accurately, smaller, and faster. Other children are given minimal instruction in penmanship, with print formation in kindergarten and first grade, followed by cursive instruction in second grade only. Except for the children who have not achieved basic letter formation, penmanship is not addressed again. Children are left to cultivate their own personalized form thereafter.

3. Will I offend parents if I teach personal safety or talk to them about the child's obesity? Early childhood educators may feel uncomfortable about addressing both these topics and may have assumed that such topics are within the family realm or are not appropriate subject matter for young children. However, a multilevel approach in which parents, teachers, and children cooperate is probably necessary to achieve the most desirable outcome. Preparing parents and involving them in discussions about personal safety, the nutritional needs of young children, and the importance of physical activity are always sound practice. When families are treated with respect and early childhood professionals are culturally sensitive, families rarely become angry, especially if they believe that the professional is working with them toward a common goal. Professionals have access to accurate information and can ensure that the learning setting is consistently supportive of optimal health knowledge, attitudes, and practices. Family instruction on child sexual abuse is relatively rare (Finkelhor, 1984), and childhood obesity is related to many variables ingrained in family culture such as lifestyle patterns, the amount of sedentary activity at home, and the family's understanding of the relationship between health and obesity, so both issues are challenging (Huettig, Sanborn, DiMarco, Popejoy, & Rich, 2004).

Childhood sexual abuse is a serious health problem and is widespread with 20% of women and 10% of men having reported incidents (Freyd, J. Putnam, F.W., Lyon, T.D., Becker-Blease, K.A et. al, 2005). Sexual abuse is more likely to begin during the preschool years than at any other time though during the past decade there appears to be a shift to older children; (Finkelhor & Baron, 1986; Casey & Nurius, 2006). Professionals have had mixed success with teaching personal safety at the preschool level, although older children appear to understand the concepts and can describe a course of action that should be taken. Either teachers or parents may be effective in teaching the basic concepts of personal safety so that children can do the following (Wurtele, Gissispie, Currier, & Franklin, 1992):

- ❑ Know that they are the bosses of their bodies
- ❑ Locate their private body parts

❑ Distinguish between touching that is appropriate and touching that is not
❑ Understand that touching an adult's private body parts is not appropriate
❑ Say "no!" and then run away and tell someone what happened if a person tries to touch them inappropriately
❑ Understand that they are not at fault nor are they bad if someone does touch them inappropriately

A combination of physical exercise and sensible, balanced food intake is most likely to be effective in controlling obesity. Such a plan must occur consistently in all regular settings in which children live and work: homes, schools, after-school programs, and child-care settings (Sorte & Daeschel, 2006).

All adults can do the following (Eastman, 2002):

❑ Plan for daily physical activity
❑ Serve child-size meals (one half to two thirds of the adult size in each food group)
❑ Serve low-calorie foods, such as fruits, for second helpings
❑ Serve low-fat snacks (fruit instead of a cookie)
❑ Minimize the amount of sugar-laden treats (foods and beverages) eaten
❑ Most important, encourage obese children to participate in sensible eating patterns

Young children can learn to do the following:

❑ Eat slowly and chew well
❑ Drink lots of water
❑ Try new fruits and vegetables in small quantities
❑ Stop eating when full
❑ Join in the fun of movement activities

Educational Standards

The following goals are consistent with the health education content standards (National Health Education Standards, 2009) and benchmarks and similar standards in physical education for young children. Standards related to mental health and social relationships are addressed in the affective and social domains.

PURPOSE AND GOALS

Purpose

For children to develop confidence and competence in the control and movement of their bodies and to develop the attitudes, knowledge, skills, and practices that lead to maintaining, respecting, and protecting their bodies.

Goals

Movement. As children progress they will:

1. Gain confidence in using their bodies
2. Identify body parts by name and location
3. Develop spatial awareness (understanding of personal and general space, direction, and spatial relations)
4. Develop temporal awareness (awareness of speed, timing, duration, and rhythm)
5. Improve total sensory awareness and integrate sensory information to solve movement problems
6. Distinguish the foreground from the background visually and auditorily
7. Engage in a variety of activities that require static and dynamic balance
8. Engage in a variety of activities that require coordinated movements with large- and small-muscle systems
9. Sustain vigorous motor activity with time to develop endurance
10. Engage in activities to develop muscular strength in all parts of the body (climbing, hanging, etc.)

11. Engage in a variety of activities that require flexibility, agility, and stretching
12. Move the major joints of the arms, legs, and trunk through a full range of motion
13. Use their whole bodies in appropriate activities to strengthen muscles and muscle groups
14. Demonstrate appropriate form in the fundamental motor skills such as jumping, hopping, running, skipping, leaping, galloping, sliding, and climbing
15. Demonstrate appropriate form in the control of objects: throwing, catching, kicking, and striking
16. Demonstrate competence in nonlocomotor skills: bending, twisting, pushing, pulling, swinging, etc.
17. Demonstrate good posture while walking, sitting, or standing
18. Demonstrate, imitate, or create movement in response to selected rhythms
19. Demonstrate locomotor skills in time to rhythmic patterns using a variety of movement concepts
20. Demonstrate control of speed, direction, and force of movement through space
21. Coordinate wrist, hand, finger, finger–thumb, and eye–hand movements
22. Control the movement of their bodies in relation to objects
23. Use tools skillfully, including implements for eating, writing, dressing, and playing
24. Develop a positive attitude toward their bodies; appreciate their competence and that of others

Health and Safety.   As children progress they will:

25. Learn practices that keep their bodies and their environments clean and sanitary
26. Acquire attitudes, knowledge, and skills about physical activity that predispose them to maintaining physically fit lifestyles
27. Acquire and practice sound nutritional habits and healthy, polite eating behaviors
28. Demonstrate self-help skills such as nose blowing, hand washing, using the toilet independently, tooth brushing, and grooming and other behaviors that reduce health risks to themselves or others
29. Identify and practice appropriate safety procedures for school, playgrounds, home, and the neighborhood
30. Discriminate good and poor health, nutrition, and safety practices
31. Learn how to apply health, nutritional, and safety knowledge when making choices in daily life
32. Describe how media influence health behaviors
33. Identify trusted adults and professionals who help promote health and safety (community health helpers)

MAKING GOALS FIT

As in other domains, we can use the same goal with different age groups of children. Table 13.4 is an example of how one goal can be adapted to three different age groups.

TABLE 13.4   Identify Trusted Adults and Professionals Who Help Promote Health

Goal #33	Example of Activity for 3- and 4-Year-Olds	Example of Activity for 5- and 6-Year-Olds	Example of Activity for 7- and 8-Year-Olds
Identify trusted adults and professionals who help promote health	Discuss the roles of adults in the family, childcare center or school who assist in promoting health by: cleaning and bandaging scrapes and cuts, removing splinters, taking temperatures, etc.	Identify uniformed men and women helpers and describe how they promote health and safety and discuss some of the tools that they use. Examples are police, nurses, emergency medical technicians, sanitation workers, school janitors	Discuss the roles of non-uniformed persons who promote health and some of the tools they use. Examples: nutritionist, health educator or teacher, counselor, therapist, housing inspectors

34. Differentiate between situations when a health-related decision can be made individually or when assistance is needed

35. Demonstrate how to tell a trusted adult if threatened or harmed and how to ask for help (call 911).

TEACHING STRATEGIES

The two major components of the physical domain—skills and knowledge—utilize the strategies for teaching skills and those for teaching social-conventional knowledge. Both types of learning are addressed in chapters 3 and 4. Following are discussions of 24 specific strategies useful for this content.

Gross- and Fine-Motor Skills

1. **Use learning centers to teach skills.** Young children have short attention spans, so movement from one activity to another allows them to participate in a variety of activities and maintain interest in as well as acquire and practice new skills. Depending on the facility, a motor skill may be the basis for a center in a classroom, with other centers representing other domains, or, if a gym is available, four to five motor-skill centers may be set up at the same time. Usually classrooms are not large enough to contain more than one gross-motor center and one writing center. Often, several motor activities can be set up outdoors.

2. **Provide opportunities for children to explore equipment and try out physical behaviors suggested by the equipment or materials.** Children should have time to explore equipment and materials before instruction begins. In addition, adults have opportunities to observe what the children can do on their own. For example, in a preschool classroom, place pencils on a table with paper and watch how the children pick them up and hold them. Provide pencils of varying lengths and diameters. Place several large balls outside where they are convenient for children to use, and watch what the children do. Younger children may need a lot of exploration time, but by the time youngsters reach age 6 or 7 years, only a few minutes may be necessary.

3. **Observe children's performance of each skill of interest.** To be effective and efficient, teachers must know children's current developmental level to know what to do next. Just how does the child throw, kick, or catch? What new information will help the child to move toward the next level? Patience is always required because skills are acquired slowly. Most children will use the next stage of a skill and then revert to more comfortable levels before they move forward more or less consistently. Establish specific objectives that move just ahead of the children and that are attainable challenges.

4. **Demonstrate the skill to be mastered and incorporate do-it signals.** The child may or may not be able to imitate your behavior. Let the child continue with the approximation of the motion. Repeat demonstrations as often as necessary to support the child's learning. Demonstrate in silence, then provide verbal direction, and finally do them both together.

5. **Provide suggestions and strategies to support the child's learning.** Scaffolding for a large-motor task might be as simple as placing a silhouette of feet on the floor where the child is supposed to stand to be in position to strike a ball. Likewise, a piece of tape on a paintbrush indicating where to hold it may be helpful. Keep in mind that children must practice for long periods before moving on to greater control or efficiency, but not long in any one session (Sanders, 2002).

6. **Give oral cues, presented one at a time, to help the child attain greater control or efficiency** (Sanders, 2002, 2006). Break down the movement into its component parts to help develop the oral cues. The stages of fundamental skills presented in Table 13.5 will help you in this task analysis.

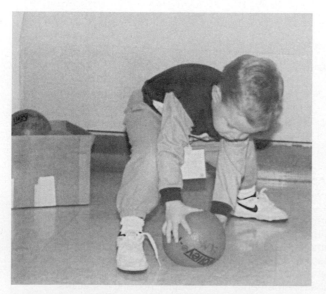

Large, soft balls rolled along the floor help this preschool child learn to secure the ball by using only his hands.

TABLE 13.5   Sample Oral Cues

Activity	Verbal Cue
Catching	❏ Watch the object.
	❏ Get hands and arms in position to catch.
	❏ Reach for the object.
Jumping	❏ (At take-off) Bend knees and crouch.
	❏ Swing arms forward and upward to take off from the ground.
	❏ (In flight) Extend arms into the air as feet leave the floor.
	❏ (On landing) Land with feet apart and body over feet.
Galloping	❏ Keep the same foot in front when you run.

7. **Emphasize qualitative movement over quantitative outcomes.** Form is important. When you are teaching the formation of letters to 5- or 6-year-olds, the position of the paper and the student's posture become important to the eventual speed and quality of handwriting. With throwing, the orientation of the body, the step on the foot opposite the throwing arm, the rotation of the body, and the follow-through are extremely important to eventual success. The distance thrown or the speed of the ball will improve with time. In the early childhood years, basic skills and habits are established that last, skills become more refined, power and accuracy increase, and their movement becomes more complex.

8. **Provide encouragement and feedback to children about their performance.** As discussed in chapter 3, praise children by using specific descriptions when they are successful: "You took a step that time when you threw the ball!" Focus on the progress each child makes so that each experience is a success. Intersperse cues and demonstrations as children engage in guided practice.

9. **Use problem-solving strategies and challenges to explore movement concepts.** After demonstrating high, medium, and low levels (see the Exploring Vertical Space activity at the end of this chapter), ask children to show how they could move across the floor on the low level. Then ask them to find another way to do so. Use reflections to support individual children and to encourage creative movements. Vary the problems so that children explore the space near their bodies without moving their feet. Generally, this strategy works well with whole-group instruction because of the amount of space required. Music and rhythm may be added but are not necessary as youngsters begin to understand the movements.

10. **Encourage suggestions from the children.** You will be able to assess children's movement vocabulary and concepts when you hear their suggestions. Ask children to assist in constructing an obstacle course that includes a variety of object–person relations: *under, through, behind,* and *on top of.* Remind the children of safety considerations if necessary.

11. **Establish guidelines for safety, level of participation, and respect for others.** Children must learn to be safe during physical play and must develop a concern for others' safety. Supervise very young children closely, standing close to children who are climbing or hanging from higher equipment. Teach safety directly and provide practice so that each child knows what to do. Remember that the youngest children have difficulty stopping. In addition, because physical competence varies considerably across the group, each child should focus on his or her competencies and offer encouragement to others. Following are a few suggested guidelines (Sullivan, 1982).

❏ Hard or sharp objects must be left in lockers or on the sidelines. Dangerous items should not be worn or carried.

❏ Children should be aware of their personal space and avoid collisions or pushing if possible. They may not hurt one another deliberately.

❏ Words of self-praise and encouragement of or appreciation for others are appropriate. Children may not tease or ridicule one another.

❏ Children must come to the adult promptly when they hear a prearranged signal.

❏ Children should engage in the activities that are developmentally appropriate for them with some level of commitment. The "couch potato" pattern and the "I can't do it" pattern are unacceptable. (Adults must distinguish between real fatigue and a general pattern of no participation.)

❏ Children will "freeze" when called on to do so. Such freezing allows the adult to call attention to competencies and interesting or creative postures. Freezing is also a safety strategy.

Perceptual–Motor Skills

12. **Provide opportunities to practice balance that are simple at first, then move on to more challenging opportunities, such as the following:**
   ❏ Walk on a taped line on the floor.
   ❏ Use a wide, low balance beam and then move to balance beams progressively higher from the floor.
   ❏ Incorporate a variety of movement skills, such as sliding, jumping, and hopping, on the balance beam.

   Be sure to place mats under the beams to absorb the force of falls. Always remain near the children so that you can support or catch them as they attempt new challenges.

13. **Incorporate concepts of spatial and time awareness into other domains as opportunities arise.** Various strategies using small- and whole-group instruction are effective for helping children become more aware of space and time. However, only as these concepts are embedded in other ongoing activities do young children probably begin to understand the breadth of these concepts. All objects occupy space. Problems with space occur in the block area as a youngster shoves a long board along the floor, unintentionally interfering with another child's play. Sometimes adults and other children misinterpret a misunderstanding of the spatial concept as disregard for another child's rights. Make every effort to use time and space concepts accurately. A 5-minute warning should be given as close to 5 minutes before the children put away materials as is possible. Young children have sufficient difficulty estimating time that the intervals labeled as 5 minutes should not be between 2 and 15 minutes.

14. **Select noncompetitive group games or modify familiar games to reduce or eliminate competitiveness.** Try to provide games in which all the children play all the time. For example, assist children to stand in a circle. Give the group one to three pillow balls (large, soft cloth balls) and ask them to throw the ball to someone across the circle. Instead of having an "out" as in dodge ball, tell children to catch or pick up the ball and throw it to another person. The fun is in the throwing and catching. Children will have many opportunities to play competitively later.

15. **Use directional language in context daily, including "left" and "right" for the older children.** For preschool, modify dances such as "The Hokey Pokey" so that you sing "Put one hand in" instead of "your left hand." This approach allows the children to enjoy the dance and song and to participate in it fully. Put a piece of yarn on the left hand of kindergarten children and other primary children whenever they need it, and label it appropriately. Remember that some people have difficulty with the meaning of left and right into adulthood.

16. **Use accurate language for naming body parts.** Most 2-year-olds know *head, knees, hands, arms,* and *legs* because caregivers use these terms when they are dressing children. Other body parts such as the chest, thigh, and forefinger are less frequently discussed and can easily be introduced. The genitals should be labeled with correct terminology: penis and testicles for males, labia and vulva for females. Sometimes children will surprise you with questions or comments. When an infant was being bathed by his mother during group time, one 3-year-old commented, "He's a boy 'cause he got balls." The teacher paraphrased the child's comment and responded by using accurate language: "You noticed that he has testicles. All boys do."

   Joking and laughing about private body parts is normal in informal settings for 6- to 8-year-olds even though their understanding may be inaccurate or incomplete, just as 3- to 5-year-olds find comments related to elimination hilarious. Less appropriate behaviors generally diminish as children are provided with straightforward, factual information with accurate vocabulary.

17. **Provide safety information and guidance to prevent hazards as children explore their bodies' functions and capabilities.** Body awareness includes notions of what the body does. Body functions such as eating, drinking, eliminating, and sleeping are of interest, as are the internal body parts (Fleer & Careen, 1995). Include appropriate information within meaningful contexts or through direct instruction.

Delighted by their strength and increasing competence, young children explore the environment. As a result of less-than-accurate estimates of space, youngsters stick arms, legs, fingers, toes, and heads into amazingly small apertures and cannot get out again. For this reason, adults must always supervise children in this age group, pointing out hazards in matter-of-fact ways as children use equipment. Children also experiment with stuffing objects into the orifices of their bodies. One teacher extracted five dried peas from a youngster's ear. The general rule is that food and water go into the mouth, but nothing is to be put into any other part of the body.

18. **With younger children, provide an uncluttered background for objects you want them to see.** High contrast in line, pattern, and color is easier to perceive than low contrast. Place play and work materials on uncrowded shelves so that children can find them. As children get older, they become better able to distinguish figure–ground relations. For example, when teaching children about handwriting, use one letter or just a few letters on a whole page. Then the child can find and copy them. Usually the child's name is recognized first, but many youngsters focus on "their" letter—the initial of their first name. They are also aware of letters from the community, such as the *M* in the McDonald's sign. Using decorated or cute letters on the wall to stimulate interest in handwriting is not recommended because such decorations are too cluttered for the child to perceive the letter easily. Children often find it easier to see letters on the same plane as that on which they are drawing them.

Similarly, children hear rhythm and melody from instrumental music more easily than from a combination of instrument and voice. The tune of the music line is less complex and easier to imitate. Children need guidance in learning what to attend to and what to ignore. More information on this topic can be found in chapter 9.

Health, Nutrition, and Safety

19. **Plan vigorous physical activity every day.** Provide breaks in sedentary activity to stretch and bend on one occasion and to move actively on another. Incorporate physical action as a part of group time and prolonged active play during outdoor time. Include motor skills instruction in daily schedules. Use balloons for tossing in the air, catching, and hitting upward with the hands or feet as a 10-minute break in the day. Exercise tapes for children are widely available and can be used when weather inhibits outdoor activity.

20. **Demonstrate a concern for your fitness and health so that children can imitate what you do.** Teachers who have some difficulty with flexibility and stamina should tell the children about this and do as much as they can.

21. **Incorporate health and safety education when applicable.** Do not assume that children know such information. Statements such as "Use a tissue once; then throw it away" provide children with straightforward guides for functioning with greater safety and healthier practices. Place hand-washing pictograms or a sequence of photos near the sinks. Straightforward instruction on toileting, hand washing, and other self-help skills is essential for young children and older ones who have not learned from previous experiences.

22. **Communicate regularly with families.** Give them the health and safety information you are teaching children. When families and teachers speak the same language about the same topics, children learn better and remember more. In addition, you will be reminding families of the basic concepts. For example, when you teach what to do in case of a fire, send home directions for family fire safety inspections and evacuations. When you attempt to expose children to a greater variety of vegetables in a tasting experience, send the list of selections home so that the children can tell parents which vegetables they liked. Collaborate with family members about strategies to help youngsters maintain an appropriate weight.

23. **Use mealtimes to teach nutrition and proper eating habits.** Children should learn to chew food slowly and to eat a variety of foods. Each child can taste a tiny portion (about 1 teaspoon) of the foods that are unfamiliar or disliked. Do not expect children to clean their plates every day. Meal and snack time should be relaxing conversation time, not hurried. Teach socially polite behavior

Mealtime should be a pleasant learning experience for children.

such as eating with the mouth closed and listening while chewing. Encourage children to drink plenty of fluids every day. When discussing what to eat for meals and snacks, focus on foods lower in fats and sugar and higher in other nutrients. For example, choose pretzels instead of potato chips. For the same volume of food, the child is better nourished with pretzels.

When children begin to participate in a school lunch program, rehearse the appropriate behavior with them at another time of day and then eat with them during the first few weeks and sporadically throughout the year. Many children do not know how to negotiate a cafeteria line or where to sit and are unfamiliar with the food. Children with free or subsidized lunches should always be indistinguishable from others. Help children to develop patterns of support and consideration by teaching them not to comment negatively on a child's food from home. Be alert to problems such as older children's taking lunch money away from younger children, and ensure supervision as necessary. Children should not be denied their food for behavioral transgressions; instead they should have a supervised eating area where they may learn more appropriate behavior.

24. **When talking about food choices, use the phrase** *a better choice* **rather than** *good foods* **and** *bad foods.* The term *bad food* is best reserved for decayed, moldy, or otherwise unsafe food. Care should be taken not to undermine parents and cultural patterns. For example, a quarter cup of salted peanuts is not the best choice for a snack but is an excellent meat substitute in many main dishes such as curries or stir-fried mixtures.

ACTIVITY SUGGESTIONS

Most of the following activities are taught in small groups of children and become self-sustaining with intermittent supervision as children practice the skills. Some activities may be incorporated into whole-group sessions as a means for increasing physical activity in an otherwise sedentary experience. A few are for whole-group activities. Keep in mind that the typical patterns of motor-skill acquisition range across the entire early childhood period and that children who do not have opportunities for instruction and practice are likely to perform as younger children do.

Moving While Standing Still (For Older or More Experienced Children)

Goal 3 Develop spatial awareness (understanding of personal and general space and direction).

Materials A list of instructions

Procedure Children need only their personal space—the amount of space they can take up within kicking or stretched-arm distance. Vary the movements, the body parts involved, and the tempo of the movements in the various directions. Ask children to stay standing on the same spot throughout the experience. Sample directions are as follows:

Bend one part of your body while stretching another part.
Stretch as many parts of your body as you can all at the same time.
Keeping your feet still, twist around as far as you can.
Discover how many directions in which you can push. Think of all the body parts that can be used to push.
While standing, show all the body parts that can swing.
Swing fast. Swing slow.
Collapse to the floor slowly.
Pull something heavy as you rise.

To Simplify Demonstrate so that children can imitate, and gradually repeat directions so that they learn to follow the instructions without imitation. Use only a few directions.

To Extend Increase the difficulty of the movements or the speed of transition from one movement to another or both.

Exploring Vertical Space (For Older or More Experienced Children)

Goal 4 Develop temporal awareness (awareness of speed, timing, duration, and rhythm).

Materials Tambourine, large balls

Procedure Ask the children to spread out so that they cannot touch anyone else. Tell them to put their hands on their shoulders and then raise their arms overhead and say, "This is your high space." Then ask them to touch their shoulders and then the area joining the leg to hip and say, "This is your middle space." Finally, ask them to touch the floor and then their hip joint and say, "This is your low space." Demonstrate, using your own body, while providing directions and defining the meanings of *high, middle,* and *low* spaces.

Making a slow walking beat on a tambourine, ask the children to start at their high space and move their bodies to their low space. Using words such as *smooth, jerky, bent,* or *twisted,* and denoting speeds such as *very slow* or *fast,* continue giving children movement directions. Alter the rhythm on the tambourine to match your directions. Intersperse "Freeze" or "Stop" directions when children make interesting forms with their bodies, then praise the performance.

To Simplify Demonstrate most of the specific moves with the language cues if the children do not know the vocabulary.

To Extend First, give the children large balls to hold as they move through vertical space. Next, provide simple music and then ask children to suggest ways to move. Last, include locomotor directions. Remember that the more directions the child must include, the more difficult the activity becomes; thus, leaping smoothly while holding a ball in high space is extremely challenging.

Fun on the Balance Beam (For Younger or Less Experienced Children)

Goal 7 Engage in a variety of activities that require static and dynamic balance.

Materials A steady 2 × 4 inch balance beam with fall-absorbent mats for indoor activity or a similar balance beam surrounded by fall-absorbent material outdoors; floor tape

Procedure Demonstrate a walk across the balance beam at a slow, comfortable speed. Invite children to walk across the beam. If they are successful, suggest that they find another way to cross the beam. Stand nearby to support children if necessary. If they cannot think of any ways that are challenging, try some from this list: forward; backward; sliding; step sideways, step together; forward, turn around, then go backward; forward, bend knees, collapse, stand, then move forward; forward, hop, forward. (Suggestions are in order of difficulty.)

Safety Allow only one person on the balance beam at a time. Children must be careful not to push or bump one another when they are on the beam.

To Simplify Tape two lines (2–4 in. wide) on the floor and have the children walk between them with the suggested movements.

To Extend Use a narrower balance beam or a higher one. Some extensions to easy levels are suggested in the preceding list of movements.

Mother/Father, May I? (For Older or More Experienced Children)

Goal 11 Engage in a variety of activities that require flexibility, agility, and stretching.

Materials None

Procedures This game is fun to play outside. Invite children to arrange themselves in a horizontal line so that they cannot touch anyone else as they move. The leader—Mother/Father—stands in front, facing the line of children. The starting line may be real, drawn in the dirt or grass, or imaginary. The leader presents the children with tasks that require flexibility as they move forward. The leader may say, "Israel, bend down and put your hands on the ground and walk them forward."

Israel must respond, "Mother/Father, may I?"

If the leader says, "You may," Israel may carry out the movement. If the leader says, "No, you may not," Israel should remain in place. If a child is caught moving without permission, he or she returns to the starting line. The object of the game is to reach Mother/Father first.

Some moves requiring flexibility are the following:

Put your hands behind your neck and take two steps forward.
Squat and waddle four times.
Turn your body sideways and step sideways twice.
Swing your arms around and around and take three giant steps.
Sit down with your feet tucked under you and stretch your arms forward as far as possible, then move to where your arms reach.

To Simplify Use only with a small group so that each child must not wait long for a turn. Younger children may need to practice the traditional steps before attempting the actions requiring flexibility. Doing so alters objectives 11 to 14 (develop fundamental motor skills such as jumping, hopping, skipping, leaping, galloping, running, sliding, and climbing), although children do learn the rules of the game, which are as follows:

Baby step: Place toe to heel.
Giant step: Make the step as big as possible.
Banana split: Slide one foot forward as far as possible.
Umbrella step: Place your forefinger on top of your head and spin around once.
Frog leap: Do a two-footed jump.
Bunny step: Do a one-footed hop.
Fire engine: Run until Mother/Father says "Stop."

To Simplify Further Use only forward and backward variations of *step* and *jump*.

To Extend Older children may enjoy adding a game of tag at the end. The child tags the leader, who then chases the child back to the starting line. If the leader tags the child, that person becomes the next leader.

Encourage children to become the leader and invent twisty ways to move. Make suggestions to encourage flexibility.

Pull a Friend (For Older or More Experienced Children)

Goal 13 Use their whole bodies in appropriate activities to strengthen muscles and muscle groups.

Materials Wagons, sleds, cardboard sheets with ropes making long bails, or tricycles that will carry passengers, blocks

Procedure Outdoors, suggest that one child pull or push another in the conveyance. Demonstrate and then suggest that another child take your place.

To Simplify Provide blocks or other lighter objects for the children to transport.

To Extend Increase the weight being transported, or suggest that the children try the cardboard-and-rope combination. Because of friction, this task is much more difficult, but it will work.

Indoor Striking (For Younger or Less Experienced Children)

Goal 14 Demonstrate appropriate form in the fundamental motor skills such as jumping, hopping, running, skipping, leaping, galloping, sliding, and climbing.

Materials Four moderate-sized Nerf balls, heavy cord, large paper clips, foam mallets the size and shape of ping-pong paddles

Procedure Hang three or more Nerf balls from the ceiling with string so that the balls hang at approximately child waist height. Adjust the balls for the various heights of the children. The balls should be hung 3 or more feet apart and be well out of the pathway of other people. (They can be clipped up when not in use.) Give each of three children foam mallets and demonstrate how to hit the ball.

Safety A hard strike will send the ball the full radius of the string. Soft balls will not injure a child, but being hit by a mallet during the striker's follow-through may sting. Young children are not skilled at stopping in the midst of an action like this. For this reason, other players should remain outside the radius of the balls.

To Simplify Ask the children to strike the balls with their hands. Encourage striking the moving ball as well as the stationary ball.

To Extend After observing a child's exploratory hits, make suggestions about form so that the child moves from a straight approach with a chop to standing sideways to the ball to swing the mallet. If there appears to be any movement of the foot associated with the striking hand, encourage the child to move the foot and rotate the body. If the child is in the appropriate stage of striking, demonstrate the step, strike, and follow-through typical of more mature form. (See the description of stages for striking in Table 13.1.)

Puzzles (For Children of All Ages)

Goal 21 Coordinate wrist, hand, finger, finger–thumb, and eye–hand movements.

Materials Puzzles, puzzle rack

Procedure Place a variety of puzzles in a puzzle rack or on the table where children can see them. Demonstrate how to take puzzles out by pouring puzzles of 50 to 100 pieces into a large tray or laying them out on a surface with the picture side up. Puzzles in frames should be removed one piece at a time and placed on a table. Do not flip them over because the pieces will slide and get lost on the floor or under furniture. Ask a child to look carefully at the picture, noting distinctive features. Guide the child as necessary to solve the problem. Point out curved and straight lines. Suggest tracing the edges of the shapes with a finger. Suggest looking for corner or edge pieces first because they usually have distinctive features.

To Simplify Select easier puzzles: puzzles with one hole for each puzzle piece; 3- to 5-piece puzzles; 5- to 10-piece puzzles with the cuts in logical places such as a tail or a foot; 11- to 15-piece puzzles.

To Extend Increase the number of pieces or the complexity of the picture. Three-dimensional puzzles are available and require a long time to complete but provide great challenge for older children.

Exploration with Balls (For Children of All Ages)

Goal 22 Control the movement of their bodies in relation to objects.

Materials 4–10 cardboard boxes of moderate size, several balls ranging in diameter from 2 to 10 inches

Procedure Outdoors, randomly place several mid-size cardboard boxes on the ground. Put several balls ranging in diameter from 2 to 10 inches nearby. Observe as children play. Refrain from directing the play. The way in which children use the materials will vary with their age and experience.

Mastering Cutting Techniques (For Children of All Ages)

Goal 23 Use tools skillfully, including implements for eating, writing, dressing, and playing.

Materials Magazines, pieces of scrap paper of various colors and textures, paste or glue, old sacks, classified-ad pages, wallpaper scraps, scissors

Procedure Intersperse guided practice with demonstrations about how to use the scissors and encourage children to attempt more challenging cutting tasks.

Draw lines on some of the scraps so that children cut increasingly difficult pieces:

Younger and Less Experienced Children	Older and More Experienced Children
No lines	Sharply curved lines
Straight lines	Corners
Long, wavy lines	Zigzag lines

Children may paste pieces on other reused products such as newspaper or paper bags.

To Simplify Use small pieces of unlined paper of moderate weight or tear the paper.

To Extend Ask children who can cut all the lines listed in the preceding table to cut on the line simple shapes that they draw themselves or to cut out the inside space of two concentric circles or two concentric squares or pictures from magazines.

Snowperson Walk or Run (For Older or More Experienced Children)

Goal 26 Acquire attitudes, knowledge, and skills about physical activity that predispose them to maintaining physically fit lifestyles.

Materials None

Procedure On brisk winter days, take the children outdoors and walk rapidly or run around the building. This activity is particularly effective after prolonged work at tables or quiet activities. Tell children that they are snowpersons in a hurry.

To Simplify Select a closer destination.

To Extend Gradually increase the length and speed of the walk. When returning inside, indicate how good you feel after you get out and really move.

✎   *Vegetable Tasting (For Younger or Less Experienced Children)*

Goal 27 Acquire and practice sound nutritional habits and healthy, polite eating behaviors.

Materials Variety of cooked and raw vegetables, serving spoon, tray, tasting spoons or toothpicks, small soufflé cups

Procedure Place a tray containing tasting spoons and a selection of vegetables where children can see it. Include small samples that you use to talk about and others that are used for tasting. Select combinations of common and less common vegetables so that children are familiar with some and not with others. Keep the portions tiny; one slender carrot coin or a kernel of corn is sufficient for children to explore the taste. To prevent children from dipping used spoons into a serving dish, use small soufflé cups. Put a little food in a cup and then allow the child to eat it. Name the vegetables and encourage children to comment. Within the context of this taste exploration, provide children with additional information such as "Raw, crisp vegetables help keep your teeth clean" or "Children should have several servings of vegetables every day to stay healthy." Maintain normal sanitary practices: clean hands, wash vegetables, and so forth.

To Simplify Use fewer vegetables, and repeat the process several times. Deliberately include vegetables common to all cultural groups represented in the classroom.

To Extend Increase the variety of vegetables to include those not commonly eaten by the children in the ethnic group being taught. Increase the information given so that children learn that some vegetables are really good or energy producing: potatoes of all kinds, corn, and peas. Tell the children that groups of vegetables such as leafy green and yellow vegetables have specific vitamins (particularly vitamin A) that people need, and some are mostly fiber and are also necessary for good health.

SUMMARY

PEARSON
myeducationlab

To check your comprehension on the content covered in Chapter 13, go to the Book Specific Resources in the MyEducationLab for your course, select your text, and complete the Study Plan. Here you will be able to take a chapter quiz, receive feedback on your answers, and then access review, practice, and enrichment activities to enhance your understanding of chapter content.

The focus of education in the physical domain is the development of motor skills, physical fitness, and health. The ultimate goal is to provide the knowledge and skills that children need to engage in developmentally appropriate activity safely and to maintain a healthy lifestyle. All physical skills are based on the maturation of the individual, instruction or the child's imitation of a model, and the opportunities to practice movements until efficiency and style are developed. Instruction without corresponding maturation of the body is ineffective, as is simply waiting until a skill emerges once appropriate maturation is attained. Skill increases in efficiency and refinement during the early childhood period.

Children acquire information and develop health and safety habits early in life. The teacher's role is to provide instruction when new information or new skills are needed and to provide an environment that supports healthy eating and safe playing. Direct instruction is sometimes needed, but concepts are also learned informally as children play, rest, and eat. Often, children who have disabilities in other domains can successfully engage in the physical domain once some adaptations are made.

Parents and teachers working together are better able than either working alone to be more successful at teaching children to have a healthy lifestyle. Children gradually learn to engage in play safely, eat sensibly, and use ordinary health habits such as hand washing and toothbrushing regularly as they begin to take some responsibility for their own health and safety.

Key Words

body awareness	fine-motor skills	sedentary
body relationship awareness	fundamental motor skills	self space
coordination	locomotor movements	sensory integration
directional awareness	manipulative movements	shared space
dynamic balance	physical fitness	static balance

Applying What You've Read in This Chapter

1. **Discuss**
   a. If children are allowed to play on a playground daily, will all of them develop the fundamental motor skills by the end of the early childhood period? Explain your answer.
   b. Ms. Cunningham wanted 2-year-old Phillip to be an athlete, so she showed him videos of tennis players and golfers; did infant massage; and engaged him in many bouts of training in jumping, kicking, striking, and throwing. What do you think was the outcome of all this effort and why?
   c. Describe how a dance experience for 5-year-olds that would enhance their nonlocomotor movement skills might be organized.

2. **Observe**
   a. Carefully watch two to five children engaging in gross-motor activity. Using the information in Table 13.1, try to determine each child's competence level for one of the fundamental motor skills. Record your findings as best you can. List the difficulties you had in doing this.
   b. Observe the fine-motor skills of two children at least 12 months apart in age. Compare your observations with the descriptions in Table 13.3 Explore why differences exist between the description and the individuals you observed.

3. **Carry out an activity**
   a. In pairs, try out the stages of each of the fundamental motor skills described in Table 13.1. One adult student should read the description while the other tries to do it. If you can do it yourself, you will understand which muscles are involved for the children.
   b. Give a felt- or nylon-tip pen and paper to a preschool child and suggest that he or she write you a letter. If the child informs you that he or she cannot write, tell the child that it is not necessary to do grown-up writing, only children's writing or pretend writing. Describe how the child gripped the writing implement. Compare this with the description in the text. Was there any apparent understanding of letters, left-to-right progression, or other aspects of written language?
   c. Select a fine-motor task such as sewing on a button, eating with chopsticks, or tying a fish lure, and write out step-by-step directions on how to perform the task. Teach this task to another adult who is a novice and evaluate your effectiveness. Reflect on the strategies you used. What scaffolding was necessary, if any?

4. **Create something for your portfolio**
   a. Write a lesson plan using the suggested strategies for any skill or movement concept. Prepare any visual aids that are necessary. Implement the plan if possible, and photograph a youngster carrying out the skill. Place these materials in your portfolio.
   b. Snap fast, multiple photographs of two children engaging in a fundamental motor skill to catch the action. Write a short analysis of the stage that each child is in, and identify the next step necessary to advance the skill attempted.

5. **Add to your journal**
   a. You are a teacher in a child-care program. Your assistant is a picky eater and does not want to sit down with the children at lunch. When she does, she complains about the food selections and preparations, and she stirs the food around indifferently. What are the health implications for the children in the group? What is your responsibility in this situation, and what actions should you take, if any?
   b. Examine the curriculum suggested for substance use and abuse. Think about the choices you have made. Considering the young children who will respect and emulate you, do you think you might reconsider some of your choices? Where does your personal freedom impinge on your professional responsibility? What will you say when they ask, "Do you . . . ?" or "Did you ever . . . ?"

6. **Consult the standards**
   a. Use the standards for your state or a neighboring state. Select one standard in physical education and one in health education. Identify the information you would need to address the standard. How would you adapt the standard for younger children?

PRACTICE FOR YOUR CERTIFICATION OR LICENSURE EXAM

Physical Development and the Curriculum

The following items will help you practice applying what you have learned in this chapter. They can help to prepare you for your course exam, the PRAXIS II exam, your state licensure or certification exam, and for working in developmentally appropriate ways with young children.

The gymnasium for the Oakwood Elementary School is under reconstruction. This early childhood center serves children from 3 to 8 years of age. Due to the remodeling, both the gym and the playground are inaccessible to children and teachers for at least 3 months. Teachers are talking about what to do. Various opinions are expressed. Some teachers think that the school should have regular field trips to a playground several blocks away. Another group recommends hiring someone to lead aerobics in the classrooms every few weeks. Other teachers wonder how they might integrate the physical domain into their daily schedules even though they do not have access to large open spaces or sports equipment beyond balls and jump ropes.

1. Constructed-response question
   a. How might each of the solutions to this problem address the minimum needs of children to attain and maintain physical fitness?

   b. If the teachers chose to integrate physical activities, how should they proceed? What do they need to be thinking about? Offer examples of two strategies that they might use.

2. Multiple-choice question

   You are in a child-care center classroom with children ages 3 to 5 years. You have observed that multiple children are contracting colds or flulike symptoms on a regular basis over several weeks. What strategy is the best one to reduce the infectious illnesses?

   a. Make sure that all children and adults are up to date on their immunizations.
   b. Ask that adult assistants be paid for sick days so that they will stay home when ill.
   c. Send home a note to parents reminding them of the conditions when they should keep the children home.
   d. Ensure that everyone washes their hands as they enter and leave the classroom, after nose blowing, before meals, and after toileting.

Chapter

14

The Social Domain

You may wonder:

How do children develop social skills? What is my role in this process?
In what ways do children's friendships contribute to their developing social skills?
What can I do to help children resolve conflicts peacefully?
How can I help children feel comfortable with and appreciate differences among
    people?
What roles do the social studies play in young children's learning?

In this chapter, we present information to help answer questions like these about the social domain.

◆ ◆ *Parents of the 4-year-olds are meeting prior to the opening of school. The director, Ms. Reyes, greets them: "Welcome to the Sandstone Community Preschool. As our name suggests, we are indeed a community of learners as we work and play together. Our goal is to create a participatory environment to which both children and adults contribute. We view our school as a learning laboratory in which children learn about the world they live in and how to get along with the other people in that world."*

◆ ◆ *The children in the kindergarten classroom have been squabbling in the block area. Some children have been pushing down other's buildings; some boys have told the girls they can't play. Mrs. Newton, their teacher, presents the problem at group time and asks the children to make rules for the block area. With her help in phrasing the rules in positive language, the children come up with the following set of guidelines:*

> *Only knock down your own buildings.*
> *Girls AND boys can play in the block area.*
> *Block buildings can be tall.*
> *Tell people when you are finished with the blocks.*

Mrs. Newton posts the list in the area and notices that the children are reminding each other about the rules.

◆ ◆ *Ms. Roth's first graders are on their way to visit the local fire station. Their mission is to find out how the firefighters work and live and the ways in which they protect the community. The children have generated a list of questions they will try to answer through observations and discussion. One of their aims is to note gender diversity among the staff at the station. The children have brought paper, pencils, and markers so that they can record, in any way they are able, what they discover.*

◆ ◆ *It is late October, and Mr. Hwang's second graders have been learning about the upcoming elections in their city, county, and state. The youngsters have demonstrated a great interest in voting, and lively discussions have arisen about issues of "fairness." When a guinea pig is offered as a class pet, the children hold an election to choose a name for it.*

Although these scenarios depict a variety of situations, they all describe the social domain. This domain encompasses four essential facets of children's development and education.

1. **Social skills**: children learning to interact with others
2. **Socialization**: children learning the values, beliefs, customs, and rules of society
3. **Social responsibility**: children developing respect for individual differences and functioning as contributing members of the communities in which they live
4. **Social studies**: children exploring people's interactions in and with their social and physical environments, now and in the past

Each of these facets is different and important in its own right, yet inextricably linked. Early childhood teachers therefore address all four components separately and together. They do this by creating a sense of community in the classroom and by helping children gain new knowledge and skills through naturally occurring interactions with others as well as through planned lessons and relevant projects (Chapin, 2009; Epstein, 2009).

THE IMPORTANCE OF THE SOCIAL DOMAIN

Teaching within the social domain provides children with opportunities to develop knowledge and skills pertaining to themselves in relation to the people in their near environment. Gradually, children extend this information to understanding human relationships in the larger world. The family provides the foundation for such learning, establishing the social lens through which children initially view the world. As young children enter early childhood classrooms, they are confronted with ideas and people both similar to and different from themselves. These circumstances set the stage for further learning in the social domain.

From birth through age 8 years, children are discovering how to establish and maintain relationships with members of the group. As time passes, they also explore their contributions to the well-being of the social communities in which they participate (Epstein, 2009). Throughout this period, they continually work out how to value others and how to understand and cope with the differences they encounter. Thus, the classroom functions as a "human relations laboratory" in which children explore social knowledge, concepts, and skills through daily interactions, routines, activities, and on-the-spot instruction. It is the place where they assimilate values and attitudes about other people from listening to and watching the adults around them. It is also the arena in which they practice citizenship in its most basic forms. Through their social encounters and activities, children build their understanding of democracy, history, sociology, economics, and culture. These are by no means the only issues they face, but these are so important that teachers must know how to address them purposefully (Seefeldt, Castle, & Falconer, 2010; Neuman & Roskos, 2007).

To derive a greater understanding of the social domain, we will first look at its individual components. Let's begin with a discussion of social skill development, particularly children's friendships and prosocial behavior, with an emphasis on the roles adults play.

SOCIAL SKILL DEVELOPMENT

Establishing relationships with others, learning to live within the bounds of societal expectations, and discovering your place in the group are all major tasks of children in early childhood and reflect aspects of children's social development. In fact, as children mature, more and more of their time and energy becomes devoted to this area of development. This is especially true as they move beyond their family and neighborhood and come into greater contact with community institutions such as early childhood centers and elementary schools. In these circumstances, children encounter new sets of expectations to which they must adapt.

Social Competence

How well children perceive, interpret, and respond to the variety of social situations they encounter is a measure of their social competence. A high level of social competence in our society means that a person exhibits responsible, independent, friendly, cooperative, purposeful, and self-controlled behavior (McClellan & Katz, 2001; Goleman, 2006). Such children are perceived positively by peers and adults and generally experience satisfying interpersonal interactions with others. In contrast, youngsters who act irresponsibly, timidly, hostilely, uncooperatively, or impulsively are considered low in social competence. They tend to be less successful socially and not as happy as their more adept counterparts. Research demonstrates that social competence influences children's academic performance, too. Children who have better social skills and more positive social attitudes tend to do better academically than less socially skilled children (Berndt & Murphy, 2002; Payton et al., 2008). As a result of such outcomes, socially competent children often experience high self-esteem, viewing themselves as worthwhile, capable people. The same is not true for children whose social skills are poor.

The classroom functions as a "human relations laboratory" where children interact with one another.

Early Social Development

Children are not born knowing how to make friends and influence people, nor do they automatically understand the rules of society. Time and many varied experiences are necessary for them to master the skills required for successful social functioning (Kostelnik, Whiren, Soderman, & Gregory, 2009). For these reasons, children spend much of their early lives trying out various strategies to make sense of the social world. Through experimentation, they begin to discover what works and what does not and under which circumstances certain behaviors are effective or acceptable. This requires practice and support from adults.

Children's social development can be looked at as the foundation on which other types of learning are built. Apart from nutrition and physical comfort, the need for human association is basic (Berk, 2009). This finding further implies that until individuals' essential needs, including positive association with others, have been met, they are unable to move beyond those realms into other areas of learning (i.e., academic, cognitive). Therefore, instructional time spent on social development is not simply "icing on the cake," but an essential ingredient for learning of all kinds.

Three critical aspects of children's social development directly affect their lives in early childhood programs. The first of these involves children's relationships with peers, that is, making and keeping friends as well as engaging in prosocial behaviors such as helping and cooperating. A second aspect centers on children's interactions with adults, as they begin to determine how to fit their behavior to adult expectations and rules. Finally, learning to understand and appreciate differences in a diverse society and responding as a community member is a critical focus of youngsters' associations with both grown-ups and children as they develop. In this section, we address the first issue. The other two issues are addressed subsequently.

Children's Friendships

Five-year-olds Brian and Casey are playing with dinosaur models in the dinosaur habitat. They are deeply engrossed in their activity, moving the figures from place to place and actively communicating their ideas for the scenario with each other. Jimmy walks over, picks up a dinosaur, and tosses it into the middle of the play area.

"Hey," says Brian, "you can't put it there. That's the water hole."

"Yeah," adds Casey. "Besides you're not on our team!"

"I am so, if I wanna be," Jimmy asserts, angrily standing up with his hands on his hips.

"No, you can't," Brian responds.

"Teacher, they won't let me be on their team!" wails Jimmy.

Until fairly recently, it was assumed that making friends and keeping friends were aspects of life that some children were better at than others, but that nothing much could or should be done about it at school. People reasoned that the most appropriate place for children to deal with this issue was on the playground or before and after school, not during instructional time. Youngsters having persistent difficulty interacting with peers were referred to the school counselor or administrator. We are now more aware of the negative impact that disharmony in social relations has on children's abilities to concentrate on school subjects and, as a consequence, their school achievement. Furthermore, we also know that teachers and classroom aides can accomplish much by helping children become more successful with their friendship strategies (Myers & Pianta, 2008; Wilson, Pianta, & Stuhlman, 2007). To effectively assist children in improving their friendship skills, adults must understand the role that friendship plays in children's lives.

Why Friends Are Important. As they mature, children become increasingly interested in establishing friendships (Rubin, Bukowski, & Parker, 2006; Bronson, 2006). Among other benefits, friends provide stimulation, assistance, companionship, social comparison, and affection. Furthermore, within a friendship, children can experiment with a number of social roles such as leader, follower, risk taker, and comforter. In essence, children develop a sense of belonging and security through the special relationship they have with a friend.

Life without friends can be fairly bleak. Although truly friendless children are few, evidence exists that poor peer relationships in childhood lead to difficulties in later life (Hendrick & Weissman, 2010; Guralnik, Neville, Hammond, & Conner, 2007). For instance, adolescent delinquency and emotional instability have been linked to friendlessness in the early years. Naturally, as in the case of adults, children vary as to how many friends they want to have. Some are content with one "best" friend, whereas others seek a wide circle of friends. The quality of these relationships counts more than the quantity (Berk, 2009).

Children's Changing Ideas About Friendship. Children's ideas of what constitutes a friend change as they grow older (Selman, Levitt, & Schultz, 1997; Ladd, 2005). Significantly, children at various stages of development view friends differently than adults do. Consequently, adults should look at this developmental process to assess and facilitate children's relationships with one another more constructively.

In the early stages of friendship, children are preoccupied with their own needs and emotions. They concentrate on other youngsters on the basis of who is available, as well as on their physical attractiveness or other outward characteristics and their material possessions. As part of their focus on the here and now, children between the ages of 3 and 7 years are better at initiating relationships than sustaining them, and they may also inadvertently rebuff others' advances because they are simply not good at picking up friendship cues. They sometimes have difficulty entering an ongoing play situation or accepting others who want to join, as illustrated by Brian and Casey in the previous example (Kostelnik et al., 2009). Adults who observe these difficulties sometimes view children as being unkind instead of recognizing that they are actually experiencing a cognitive dilemma—that of centering on only one way to carry out the play episode.

Somewhat later in their understanding of friends, between the ages of 4 and 9 years, children begin to look for pleasing behaviors from others, such as giving one another turns, sharing toys, or deliberately choosing to sit together. Although children seem content with their choices, some of these relationships may not always appear equal in the eyes of an adult. Adults worry when children select friends that seem to be uncongenial companions—those who are bossy or overly compliant, for instance. Teachers and others have difficulty standing by when children persist in these types of friendships. Parents and educators are often tempted to separate youngsters forcibly. However, they must remember that children are deriving benefits from these relationships that are not always apparent to adults. For example, children may use their companion as a model for future behavior. Thus, the shy child may observe the bossy child achieve his or her aims through assertiveness and may ultimately try a few of these strategies. Similarly, the bossy child may admire the more modest approach of his or her peer. If, as the children assume different behaviors within the friendship, their relationship flexes to accommodate these new variables, youngsters may continue to remain close companions. If it does not, they will lose interest in each other and try out new relationships. Adults must allow children to decide for themselves when and if this change is to occur.

Children in this phase of friendship desire so much to have a friend that they often resort to bribery or threats. Furthermore, they still have difficulty having more than one close relationship at a time and are often heard to remark, "You can't be my friend—José is my friend." Adults are sometimes appalled at the tactics the children use toward one another. However, adults must recognize that children are merely trying out strategies to get what they want and will soon learn from their peers how well such strategies work; their aim is not to be deliberately mean or hurtful (Ladd, 2005).

Because children at this stage actively seek friends that are like them, they are busy comparing themselves with others to determine likenesses and differences. They begin to choose same-sex and same-race playmates. This behavior becomes even more pronounced in the next phase, which describes children between the ages of 6 and 12 years. In this stage, children are finally beginning to understand that their behavior must please another person, not simply the reverse. They are deeply involved in what is fair and not fair (as viewed from their special viewpoint). In this stage children want to be most like their friends, and so conformity in dress, speech, and actions reaches a peak.

Furthermore, friendships at this stage tend to come in twos; girls especially form close-knit dyads, whereas boys travel in looser packs (Fabes, Martin, & Havish, 2003). Both boys and girls are extremely possessive of their relationships, and conflicts and hard feelings often result. Adults express concern about the extremes of self-segregation by sex, race, and differing physical abilities that frequently occur at this stage. Although adults cannot mandate friendships, they can do much to help children recognize similarities between themselves and others despite certain obvious physical differences. Some common ground between children might include cognitive skills, degree of sociability, interests, and attitudes (Rubin et al., 2006). These issues are especially relevant when adults are helping children develop non-prejudicial attitudes and behaviors. To promote these values, adults must think of ways to take advantage of children's growing abilities to observe and reason (Epstein, 2009). (Lessons for helping children achieve a heightened awareness of similarity among people while recognizing and appreciating differences are presented in the Activity Suggestions section of this chapter.)

How children look at interpersonal relationships with peers across time is an important aspect of their growing capacity for friendships. Other crucial factors in their ability to make and keep friends are the skills they bring to the process. These skills can be divided into three distinct categories: establishing contact, maintaining positive relationships, and resolving conflicts (Kostelnik et al., 2009).

Friendship Skill: Establishing Contact. To start a potential friendship, one child must first approach another. If the friendship has any chance of success, the second person must respond positively. How this contact is carried out influences each child's perception of the other. If both have a good impression, the interaction will continue; if they do not, it will terminate at this point. Children who are cordial—that is, who smile, speak pleasantly, offer greetings, and seek information—tend to elicit positive responses from others (Goleman, 2006; Willis, 2009). These replies can be cast in the form of responding to others' greetings and questions, offering information, and inviting participation. Another successful strategy for breaking the ice is imitation. Very young children feel flattered when others mimic their actions by playing nearby or using the same materials, and they tend to welcome more direct involvement by the imitator. Older children are more leery of this tactic and may become irritated at someone who is "copying." Some finesse may be required on the part of the approaching youngster to recognize when he or she has breached the boundaries.

This kind of judgment may seem natural for all children to develop, yet many fail to recognize that even the seemingly simple strategy of "acting friendly" will gain friends. They may have the correct idea, but their timing may be off, or their actions may be misapplied. They may miss social cues, such as failing to recognize a smile or a greeting directed at them. While this may be the case for many children, children with special needs often struggle in this regard. For instance, they may not perceive that children are talking to them, or know how to ask for a toy or how to join a playgroup in progress (Willis, 2009). All such children benefit greatly from friendship coaching (Kostelnik et al., 2009). This strategy involves pointing out the child's behavior and its effect on other children by using specific, observable terms rather than generalizations (e.g., "Conner, listen. Darrel said hi to you. You didn't say hi back. He thinks you don't want to play."). Then the adult demonstrates the appropriate skill and explains the rationale for why it is effective ("Hi, Darrel. You see, Conner, when I say hi, Darrel knows I am friendly."). The next step is for Conner to practice the skill and participate in an evaluation of how well it worked. Naturally, a great deal of time and practice is required for children to learn to make themselves more appealing to others. In this situation, Darrel may also need some coaching to remain persistent in his attempts to attract Conner's attention ("Darrel, say hi again. Conner didn't know you were talking to him.").

Friendship Skill: Maintaining Positive Relationships. The second level of friendship skills is to maintain positive relationships once they have been initiated. Children who speak directly to one another, are attentive to others in particular interactions, respond in an interested fashion, and offer suggestions are popular with others (Rubin et al., 2006; Willis, 2009). In addition, these youngsters demonstrate cooperation and helpfulness and are comfortable expressing emotions such as affection, empathy, and joy at their pals' accomplishments.

These children are able to sustain relationships because their behavior makes them fun and satisfying companions. Children who lack these skills are far less successful in their abilities to sustain friendships with time. They annoy and antagonize their peers by showing off, being insensitive to people's reactions, becoming overly exuberant in their displays of affection, or taking over rather than being helpful or cooperative.

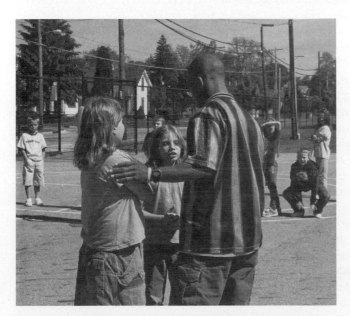

Educators play an important role in helping children learn how to resolve disputes.

TABLE 14.1 Negotiating Conflicts

Strategy	Example
Expressing your rights, needs, or feelings	"It's my turn to use the stapler."
Listening to and acknowledging others' rights, opinions, and feelings	"Oh, you haven't finished yet."
Suggesting nonviolent solutions to conflict	"How about giving it to me in 2 minutes?"
Explaining the reasons behind the solution suggested	"That way we'll both get to use it before lunch."
Standing up against unreasonable demands	"No, it's not fair if you use it the whole time. I want it, too."
Accepting reasonable disagreement	"OK, I hadn't thought of that."
Compromising on a solution	"I can use tape now, and you can use tape later when I'm using the stapler."

Even though their intentions may be positive, their actions make viewing these youngsters as potential friends difficult.

Friendship Skill: Resolving Conflicts. The most complex aspect of peer relationships is handling conflicts. Children's ability to deal with disputes in democratic ways such as recognizing and taking into account differences in another's viewpoint, compromising, bargaining, or suggesting nonviolent solutions to the problem is highly indicative of the future success of a relationship (Ladd, 2005; Epstein, 2009). Children who forcibly demand that issues be decided their way or, conversely, who back down from establishing their legitimate rights lose their peers' respect and are often rejected by them. On the other hand, children who use constructive means of resolving disputes while also satisfying their own needs are most successful in forming lasting relationships. The facets of this process are illustrated in Table 14.1 (Stocking et al., 1980; Wheeler, 2004; Gartrell, 2006).

Educators play an important role in helping children learn how to use these strategies. One way teachers can do this is by modeling the role of a conflict mediator in disputes between children. Doing so involves being a nonjudgmental facilitator so that children learn to find peaceful solutions that are mutually satisfying.

The conflict mediation process consists of seven steps, summarized in Table 14.2. How to present this process so that children can practice the specific skills is discussed in the Activity Suggestions section of this chapter.

Children vary widely in their abilities to engage in this form of resolving conflicts. Success depends on their age, understanding of relationships, communication skills, and experiences. The technique has been used productively with children as young as age 3 years who could communicate their wants. As children mature, refine their abilities to express themselves, and become more familiar with how the process works, their capacity for staying with the process increases. They shift from the belief that disputes are caused by one person against another to a more balanced view of shared responsibility. The mediation model presented in Table 14.2 helps children move in this direction. They have opportunities to observe problem solving firsthand and experience the benefits of nonviolent solutions.

In addition, as the negotiation process becomes more familiar, the number of participating onlookers grows, which increases the involvement of more children. Promising evidence also indicates that not only does aggression diminish, but positive prosocial behaviors also increase in groups in which mediation is commonly used (Wheeler, 2004). Furthermore, when adults take on the mediator role, the number and duration of children's conflicts decline with time and children take over the peaceful management of their disputes (Gartrell, 2006).

As stated previously, the give-and-take of children's relationships with their peers has a profound effect on their success at school. Also important is their understanding of how groups of

TABLE 14.2 Conflict Mediation

Step in the Process	Adult's Role
1. Initiating the mediation process	Assumes mediator role
	Stops aggressive behavior
	Neutralizes object or territory
2. Clarifying perspectives	Solicits statements from each party
	Paraphrases perspectives
	Establishes own neutrality
3. Summing up	Defines problem in mutual terms
4. Generating alternatives	Solicits ideas from combatants and bystanders
	Suggests possibilities, if necessary
5. Agreeing on a solution	Summarizes points of agreement
	Identifies resolution
6. Reinforcing the problem-solving process	Praises children for developing solution
7. Following through	Helps children carry out terms of agreement

people can live and work comfortably and productively together. Being kind toward one another by behaving helpfully and cooperatively makes group living a more positive experience for all.

Prosocial Behavior: Acting Positively Toward Others

Prosocial behavior represents the most positive attributes of society. Acts of kindness such as helping, sharing, sympathizing, rescuing, defending, cooperating, and comforting benefit all persons, the givers and the receivers. When children and adults cooperate with one another by working toward a common goal or help someone by alleviating his or her distress or facilitating work or play, they contribute to an environment in which friendly interactions and productive group efforts abound (Gazda, Balzer, Childers, Nealy, Phelps, & Walters, 2006; Willis, 2009). Furthermore, in such an atmosphere, routine or uninteresting tasks are easily handled because no single person is burdened with them. In essence, then, a classroom in which prosocial values and behaviors are transmitted and encouraged tends to produce participants with a positive self-image and group image. Further, they are likely to view themselves and others as competent and congenial (Kostelnik et al., 2009). Finally, children who learn to be kind tend not to be selfish or aggressive. Thus, providing instruction in prosocial behaviors within the classroom creates the kind of setting in which all learning is enhanced.

Once, researchers believed that if people were taught to think prosocially, corresponding prosocial behaviors would follow automatically. Unfortunately, this correlation does not hold true. Good thoughts do not necessarily lead to good deeds. Although children can, on cue, proclaim, "We're supposed to share," all reason may go out the window in the midst of a race to get the red marker. Children must be helped to go beyond thinking and saying what is appropriate to doing what is right. To accomplish this, they must go through a series of steps. First, they need to recognize that help or cooperation is required; second, they must decide whether or not to do something. Third, they must perform a prosocial action that is appropriate for the situation at hand.

Prosocial Skills: Recognition, Decision, Action. Sensitivity to someone's cues for help or cooperation is the initial skill children must acquire to learn to be prosocial. The messages sent by others can be nonspoken (panting, crying, or sighing) or the more obvious strategies of complaining or requesting assistance. Surprisingly, although these signals seem clear to most adults, some children appear to ignore them. Either these children misunderstand their meaning, or they do not think the signs are meant for them. Thus, adults cannot assume that just because children are in the presence of such cues they necessarily recognize them.

Once children realize a person is in need, they must decide whether to act. In early childhood at least two factors play a role in their decision. First, youngsters are most likely to respond to people they know, like, or admire. They also react more positively to people who have been kind to them in the past (e.g., shared a toy or cooperated in taking turns). In either case, children's decisions to act are guided by their sense of fairness and reciprocity (Eisenberg, Fabes, & Spinrad, 2006). Second, children who frequently hear themselves described as helpful or cooperative believe their actions matter. As a result they often choose to act in ways that support a "kind" self-image (Paley, 1993).

Finally, children must perform an action. The suitability of that action is influenced by their ability to take another person's perspective into account: What does this person need or want? It is also determined by their instrumental know-how (e.g., knowing how to fix the stapler, knowing where to find the bunny food, or knowing how to turn off the alarm) (Berk, 2009; Ladd, 2005).

At any stage of this process, children may experience difficulties. They may misinterpret cues or overlook them, they may miscalculate which behaviors would be effective, or they may act hastily or incompletely. They may also lack knowledge and skills that fit the situation appropriately. As children mature and gain experience, their efforts will more likely meet with greater success.

Promotion of Prosocial Behavior. As the primary conveyors of social values outside the family, early childhood educators play a key role in influencing children's prosocial behavior. Furthermore, they have a profound effect on the degree to which children demonstrate prosocial behaviors in the classroom. Adults can increase children's kindness by creating an environment in which they model the behaviors they expect of children, look for instances of prosocial behaviors and reward them, and teach children directly to think and act prosocially (Epstein, 2009).

In addition, children can be given many planned opportunities to participate in tasks and situations that allow them to rehearse prosocial skills. Children benefit greatly from these occasions and demonstrate a greater frequency of such positive behaviors in similar circumstances (Eisenberg et al., 2006). This increase in positive behaviors occurs because children can better remember both the appropriate behavior and the cues that signal which conditions apply in a given circumstance when they have had a chance to practice. (Specific techniques that combine oral descriptions and explanations with practice are illustrated in the Activity Suggestions section of this chapter.)

The educator's role is significant in influencing children's prosocial actions. In the same vein, how adults teach children about expectations for behavior affects children's ability to understand and follow rules.

SOCIALIZATION: CHILDREN'S BEHAVIOR AND ADULT EXPECTATIONS

Many of children's interactions with teachers and other adults in school revolve around rules. Children are continually learning what the rules are and how to act in accordance with them. This process is not simple for children to master.

Educators often expect children to learn classroom and school rules within a few weeks and then be able to follow them consistently. Failure to do so has frequently been viewed as willfulness or resistance on the child's part, and such youngsters develop reputations that follow them throughout their school career. Although teachers believe that teaching rules is important, they often resent having to take class time to teach children about the rules more than a few times. Furthermore, because following rules is an expected behavior, infractions are often noticed more than compliance. Learning rules and being able to follow them takes time. Just as in other areas, children vary both in the rates at which they acquire the knowledge and skills and in the extent of adult intervention they require.

One major goal of early childhood educators is for children to be able to understand and then follow rules even when adults are not present; in other words, for children to achieve self-discipline. How this can be achieved is such a vital aspect of children's social development that chapter 6 is devoted entirely to how children develop self-control and what the adult role is in the process.

SOCIAL RESPONSIBILITY

Many changes have occurred in the world during the past few decades, and more changes are to come. Families have become more mobile, youngsters with special needs are being integrated in ever-increasing numbers into classrooms, neighborhood boundaries are more permeable, and so children are exposed to a wider variety of people. In addition, the health of our planet has been brought into question. Furthermore, as a consequence of the impact of world events, we realize that we truly live in a global village. At the same time, educators have become aware that social attitudes are formed when children are young. Given these facts, the question becomes how to prepare our young people to live in a diverse, multicultural, multilingual society in ways that uphold the democratic principles of fairness, equal opportunity, and justice (Seefeldt et al., 2010). Thus, we have come to understand that we must teach children about their responsibility to the world beyond their doorstep. Doing so is the essence of encouraging children to become good citizens of their classroom, their neighborhood, and the larger society they will encounter as they mature. Through attention to social issues that are important to children's lives now, we are teaching them the attitudes and skills they will need to make reasoned decisions now and in the future. By teaching them specific social strategies such as how to work cooperatively in diverse groups, how to confront bias, or how to recycle and reuse materials, we are giving them the tools.

Celebrating Diversity

Dictionary definitions of *diversity* include "different" and "variety." How one approaches the concept of diversity relates to one's attitude toward, knowledge of, and experiences with people who are different from oneself. This creates both challenges and opportunities for educators who are charged with the responsibility of offering appropriate programs for all children.

What are the ways in which people differ from one another? There are obvious attributes, such as appearance or dress; there are less visible differences as well. Consider the wide variety of possibilities listed below.

religion	ethnicity	gender role	culture
race	age	family composition	child-rearing practices
language	abilities	lifestyle	music
interests	values	skin color	social class

This list represents only a fraction of the variations children encounter among people in early childhood settings. Some of these differences are immediately apparent to children, whereas others take longer for them to discover. Children's attitudes about diversity have their roots in childhood. Even before they are 3 years of age, children notice others' physical attributes and begin to compare these features with their own. As their experiences broaden and their cognitive and language abilities develop, young people also become aware of and comment on more subtle distinctions (York, 2003; Willis, 2009).

The development of valid concepts of race, gender, and differing physical abilities appears to be age and stage specific, with older children displaying more accurate understandings than those of younger children (Trawick-Smith, 2009). As an example, until about age 8 years or older, children are not sure which physical attributes are constant and which will change with time. Furthermore, their rudimentary notions of causal relationships make determining what the process of change entails difficult for them. For instance, they may conclude that dark skin is dirty and, if washed, will turn white; that they may lose the function of their legs if they play with a child in a wheelchair; or that if a girl gets a short haircut she turns into a boy. Although exactly when children understand these issues is unclear, what is clear is that such understanding is gained during childhood.

Another developmental issue that comes into play is children's continuing efforts to sort out likenesses and differences. In their attempts to determine who is like them and who is not, their criteria may be based on obvious physical characteristics alone. At certain friendship stages, when children are seeking others who are like them, they may exclude children on the basis of these external attributes unless other similarities are brought to their attention.

In addition to developmental considerations, how children evaluate differences and how they consequently behave are highly influenced by the adults around them, their peers, and societal values as expressed in the media and other outside sources. Children's opinions of both their worth and others' worth are affected by these forces (Ramsey, 2006). Therefore, early childhood professionals must pay attention to the messages they convey about diversity in the settings they create, the teaching materials they use, and the manner in which they respond to children's behavior and words.

Creating Inclusive Early Learning Environments. **Inclusive environments** and teaching practices are those in which all forms of diversity are fairly and consistently represented. By virtue of the interpersonal interactions and planned activities that occur, the physical structure of the space, and the materials on walls and shelves, communities are created in which all people, adults and children alike, feel acknowledged, accepted, and valued (Bredekamp & Copple, 2009; Epstein, 2009).

One strategy for ensuring that diversity is valued is to make sure that classroom activities and materials represent different cultures, different ages, different lifestyles, people with differing abilities, and men and women in nongender, nonstereotypic roles. Diverse people should be deliberately introduced and integrated into programs on an ongoing basis rather than on a special basis. Furthermore, all materials used in the educational setting must be examined so that stereotypical portrayals of groups are not unconsciously displayed or categories of people are not left out. In addition to the obvious (e.g., Native Americans shown with feathers in their hair or only at Thanksgiving), more subtle cues should be explored. For instance, classrooms and school hallways that feature only Christmas trees in December send the message to non-Christians that their holidays and traditional practices are not important. Furthermore, cultural awareness should focus on how people live today in the United States, not only on cultures and people in other nations (Derman-Sparks & Edwards, 2010; Gronlund, 2006).

Adults have a responsibility to help children sort out valid conclusions from those based on incomplete or erroneous information. Educators can do this by providing accurate data for children to work with as well as deliberately setting up experiences that confound children's stereotypical assumptions. Answering children's questions honestly and carrying out frank and open discussions about the differences children observe is another way to help them gain important knowledge about others.

One additional strategy is to help children recognize the effects of their actions and words on others (Kostelnik et al., 2009). Pointing out instances of kindness and explaining how they made another child feel encourages further prosocial behaviors. In addition, children should be confronted directly when they show evidence of overtly biased behavior or opinions. Letting children know that insensitive remarks made someone feel hurt or angry is the first step in changing their behavior in a more socially responsible direction (Derman-Sparks & Edwards, 2010; Teaching Tolerance Project, 1997). The adult must be sure to indicate a positive alternative to the child and determine any appropriate acts of restitution.

Changing the Curriculum. Four stages of curricular reform have been identified as early childhood educators strive to create truly inclusive programs (Banks, 2007). Although these approaches were originally designed to address ethnic content, they can be generalized to encompass all areas of diversity.

❑ The first stage that teachers often go through is called the contribution approach. This approach focuses on heroes, holidays, and discrete cultural elements. For example, teachers introduce heroes into the program, treating their lives as exemplars with special abilities. They are not integrated into the curriculum, nor are the issues they confront as members of minority groups, such as discrimination, truly explored. Rather, their successes are promoted, and they are treated as exotic, exceptional human beings, not representative of their group.

Mr. Raymond used a popular first step to introduce concepts of racial diversity by presenting the life and work of Dr. Martin Luther King, Jr., during a week in which African American history was celebrated. Pictures of Dr. King were prominently displayed in the classroom, his "I Have a Dream" speech was read to the second graders, and Dr. King was depicted as a singular human being. Once the week ended, the pictures were taken down, and no mention was made of voting rights or Dr. King for the remainder of the year. On reflection, Mr. Raymond concluded that the children had not learned much. He realized further that he had not given children information about what the absence of voting rights would mean to people within the fabric of a democracy and that, although introducing Dr. Martin Luther King, Jr., to the children represented a step for him as an educator, his method had made little impact on the children.

❑ The ethnic-added approach is a second means teachers use to introduce content related to diversity into their programs (Banks, 2007). At this level, content, concepts, and themes are added without changing the curricular structure. That is, although important steps have been taken to integrate diversity, the curriculum is still based on a majority-centered view.

> Ms. Somerset enjoyed a first-grade class that included children of several ethnic backgrounds. As the winter holidays approached, she made a special effort to encourage parents to demonstrate holiday celebrations representative of their cultures. Parents brought in special songs, stories, and foods, and demonstrated lighting candles as befit their specific holiday. Children and families enjoyed the celebrations. However, when the youngsters returned to school after winter break, all evidence of the diverse cultural artifacts that had been collected were gone, none of the songs were included in the classroom repertoire, none of the stories were added to the library, and the classroom had reverted to its "normal" state. Ms. Somerset was pleased to have involved so many families in the preholiday experience but decided that next time she would incorporate the activities on an ongoing basis.

❑ The third stage is called the transformational approach (Banks, 2007). At this level, teachers have infused various perspectives, frames of reference, and content into their curricula. The result is that students will come away with a greater understanding of the complexities of our society and how society is a result of a synthesis and interaction among the diverse elements that compose it.

> Mrs. Sterns often used literature to integrate diversity into the curriculum. For her kindergarten students this year, she focused on common themes, such as stories of origins—how the earth was formed, how the sun and moon got in the sky, how people and animals came onto the earth, and so on. She found tales from Native American, African, and European sources. She read these to the children. They discussed the similarities and differences among the various versions and wrote their own origin myths. In addition, children used art media to illustrate their ideas, created props to dramatize their stories, and struggled to understand why people might develop stories to make sense out of what might otherwise seem impossible to comprehend. In addition, Mrs. Sterns used parents as resources for both scientific and fanciful explanations. Acceptance of divergent thinking was a hallmark of the study, as no one person had the "correct" answers.

❑ The final stage is called the decision-making and social action approach (Banks, 2007). The most sophisticated of all, this approach includes all elements of the previous stage but requires children to make complex decisions related to their study and to take some action.

> The year following his initial inclusion of Dr. Martin Luther King, Jr., in the second-grade curriculum, Mr. Raymond expanded his and the children's horizons. He helped children understand the context in which Dr. King and others worked by giving them background on the struggle for voting rights that had occurred in the communities in the South for many years before it became recognized nationwide. Then he tried an experiment to help children understand what not having the same right to vote as your neighbor would be like. Arbitrarily, he chose a physical characteristic, blue eyes, and declared that all children possessing this trait were ineligible to vote on a choice for a class treat on Friday. He separated the blue-eyed children from the rest, seating them at the back of the class, and proceeded with the election. After it was over, he monitored a heated discussion by the voters and the nonvoters about bias, discrimination, fairness, equality, and the like. As they discussed, they speculated on various options that might be available for remedying the situation. They found that no solution was simple. In this experiment, children were exposed to a taste of some of the issues that disenfranchised individuals face. This experience was the first of many hands-on strategies Mr. Raymond used to bring what might seem abstract and out of children's realm of experience into the focus of their lives.

Changing Adults' Thinking.   The paradigm set forth by Banks (2007) offers much information for the teacher. A blending of the approaches just described seems a reasonable way to tackle the difficult task of changing your thinking and practices to be more inclusive. Professionals must examine their attitudes and practices for evidence of prejudice. This task is not easy, because bias may rear its head in numerous subtle ways and emanate from sources that relate to early life experiences and learnings. Thus, by monitoring one's own behavior, as well as confronting children's stereotypical

The beginnings of social responsibility develop as children contribute to their community.

beliefs, reinforcing positive behaviors, and proactively teaching about the similarities and differences that make us all part of the human family, educators can help children make strides toward a bias-free society. See Figure 14.1 for a guide to reflecting on this facet of social learning.

Becoming Environmentally Aware

Every individual, beginning with children, must learn to care for the place we live in—our earth.
— Seefeldt et al., 2010, p. 229

The most obvious thing schools can do (to promote environmental awareness) is give children experiences with real things . . . A picture may be worth a thousand words, but to a second grader who has held a squiggly night crawler in her hand, even the printed symbol "worm" resonates with far deeper meaning than a thousand pictures or a dozen Discovery Channel videos.
— Monke, 2007, p. 20

As noted in chapter 5, there is a growing national movement to encourage young children, many of whom spend long hours indoors, to become more connected to the natural world (Louv, 2005). Promoting environmental awareness among children is one facet of this movement. Individuals on almost every side of every issue use a popular saying: "Think globally; act locally." In no area is this more apt than when we are teaching children about assuming responsibility for the indoor and outdoor environments in which they live and play.

Environmental awareness deals with the complex interrelationships among all living things and their surroundings. Like most areas of study, caring about and for the environment spans more than one domain. It involves aesthetic appreciation, principles from science, and many goals of the social domain, including social consciousness (Seefeldt et al., 2010). Attention to the environment has far-reaching consequences in the lives of young children. Just as attitudes about human differences are established at an early age, so, too, are attitudes toward the world. As we know, adults exert a powerful influence on children, and the behaviors that adults display are more significant in proclaiming their values than any words they

---

FIGURE 14.1 **Questions for the Reflective Practitioner Interested in Promoting Diversity**

1. How do I model valuing of and respect for each child's gender, ethnicity, age, religion, family structure, ability levels, physical traits, culture, and language?
   - How do I treat each child as a valuable contributor?
   - How do I plan activities that include all children, adapting as necessary so every child can participate in some way?
   - Do I answer children's questions about diversity issues honestly and openly?
   - How careful am I to use people-first language, referring to the child first and characteristics of diversity second? ("Callie is a child with a hearing loss." Not, "Callie is our hearing loss child.")
   - How do I remind children that we all have strengths and areas in which we are still growing?

- How do I intervene when children tease or exclude children because of diversity issues?
2. How do the books, pictures, and other classroom materials in my room reflect the diversity of the children in my class? What about all groups in the community?
3. How does the curriculum I provide systematically and intentionally address diversity every day?
4. How do I treat diversity as routine, not exceptional?
5. How do I integrate various traditions, values, histories, interests, games, music, art, languages, and families into the program?
6. How do I create opportunities for children with varying backgrounds to cooperate, help one another, and problem solve constructively?

Sources: Based on "Social Studies in Kindergarten," by G. Mindes, 2006, in D. F. Gullo (Ed.), *K Today: Teaching and Learning in the Kindergarten Year*, Washington, DC: NAEYC, pp. 107–115; *A Practical Guide to Early Childhood Curriculum* (7th ed.), by C. Eliason & L. T. Jenkins, 2008, Upper Saddle River, NJ: Merrill/Prentice Hall; *Creating Inclusive Learning Environments for Young Children*, by C. Willis, 2009, Thousand Oaks, CA: Corwin Press.

profess. Thus, for children to become sensitive to the needs of the global community, adults must demonstrate their concern through their actions (Anderson, Corr, Egertson, & Fichter, 2008).

Specific planning within the classroom in terms of activities and routines is an effective way of conveying children's responsibility for their setting. The simple three Rs of environmental responsibility—recycle, reduce, reuse—can be incorporated into daily activities and serve as the source of group projects. Children can recycle cards in the art area, use paper on both sides for writing, and incorporate food scraps into a compost pile. They can be taught to clean up their messes, either individually or with help from others. They also can be shown how to generate less waste in school and at home. Something as simple as planting, caring for, and harvesting plants or creating a classroom recycling center can illustrate environmental concepts as well. Activities and routines like these reveal important causal relationships to children because children experience directly the results of their actions. It is never too early to begin such lessons. At the same time, it is important to note that these lessons have the most meaning when they revolve around environmental issues close at hand. Young children need firsthand experiences with environmental awareness, as with other concepts. Thus, it is more meaningful for young children to pick up the trash around their schoolyard than to rally around the notion of saving the rainforest.

SOCIAL STUDIES

Who am I?
In what ways are people the same? In what ways are they different?
Where do I live?
How does my community work?
What role do I play as a community member?

Go to the Assignments and Activities section of Topic 9: Content Areas/ Lessons and Activities in the MyEducationLab for your course and complete the activity entitled *Teaching Social Studies.* Note the wide range of experiences and props teachers use to introduce the Social Studies to young children. Identify at least 3 of the 10 Social Studies themes listed in your text that are evident in these classrooms.

These are questions young children explore every day within the community of their families, classrooms, and neighborhoods. In doing so, they are learning about people, past and present, and their relations with each other and the world around them (National Council for the Social Studies [NCSS], 2009). This is the content of the social studies. The social studies are derived from a variety of disciplines, such as anthropology, history, geography, sociology, economics, and political science. These disciplines focus on understanding human behavior; however, the key concepts of each make unique contributions to children's knowledge (Seefeldt et al., 2010). Ultimately, learning about social studies helps children learn more about themselves as members of a community and encourages them to "develop the ability to make informed and reasoned decisions as citizens of a culturally diverse, democratic society in an interdependent world" (NCSS, 2009).

Standards and Goals for Social Studies

As with other curricular domains, the goals for social studies can be grouped by knowledge goals, skill goals, and attitude goals (NCSS, 2009). **Knowledge goals** focus on concepts that reflect the content of social studies, such as the uniqueness of all people, the interdependence of people, the influence of environment on people's choices of habitats and work, and the function and operation of social groups. Other knowledge goals deal with the structure of the social science disciplines, such as what and how we learn about human history and how people make decisions. Additional knowledge goals reflect similarities and differences among individuals and groups and how people learn to live together. **Skill goals** focus on children's mastery of techniques related to gathering information, improving their interpersonal interactions within their group, and problem solving, both in terms of content and social relations. **Attitude goals** relevant to social studies emphasize respecting individuals both similar to and different from themselves, understanding and appreciating their own and others' culture and traditions, and caring for the world around them. These goals and their implementation across the early childhood age range clearly encompass the entire range of the social domain.

During the past few decades, our nation has attempted to equalize educational opportunities for all its youngsters by developing standards in all academic disciplines. Academic standards relate to quality of instruction, content, and assessment, as well as the quality of teacher preparation. The assumption is that with national standards, children nationwide will receive improved educational experiences (Isaacson, 2009). The social studies standards have been developed around 10 themes that encompass the range of subject matter disciplines (NCSS, 2009).

1. Culture
2. Time, continuity, and change
3. People, places, and environments
4. Individual development and identity
5. Individuals, groups, and institutions
6. Power, authority, and governance
7. Production, distribution, and consumption
8. Science, technology, and society
9. Global connections
10. Civic ideals and practices

Although this may seem a lot for young children to absorb, research has shown that early experiences form the foundation of future learning (Mindes, 2006). Furthermore, as they become more aware of the world outside themselves, children spend much of their time and energy learning who they are in relation to others (Schmidt, Burts, Durham, Charlesworth, & Hart, 2007). Because the social studies standards span the years to Grade 12, we will focus on those standards and themes most relevant for preschool and early-primary-age children. The themes of science, technology, and society; global connections; and power, authority, and governance are more appropriate to the older grades. In addition, the theme of individual development and identity is explored in chapter 10.

The Relationship Between Social Studies Standards/Themes and Traditional Subject Matter

Culture. Whether aware of it or not, every person and every group has a culture (Nieto, 2007). The study of culture addresses the art, language, history, customs, beliefs, and geography of different people in the United States and throughout the world (Seefeldt et al., 2010). Through activities in the classroom, children develop knowledge of their own culture and the culture of others. They begin to understand that people represent many cultures as they come in contact with others in their school and community. Even people who look the same may have different beliefs, different ways of celebrating holidays and festivals, and different family structures. Children also learn that people who seem unlike them may share similar ideas and values. Finally, children are made aware of bias and injustice and helped to stand firm in relation to such in their daily lives (Williams & Cooney, 2006). *Anthropology* is the study of human beings and their diverse cultures and lifestyles.

Time, Continuity, and Change. Important to the lives of young children is their personal history and that of their family. Every child has an ancestry, and becoming aware of their forebears helps children develop a sense of belonging and pride. In the early childhood setting, these elements are built into the structure of daily living. Bringing them to children's consciousness is the first step in their understanding of temporal relationships (National Center for History in the Schools, 1994; Neuman & Roskos, 2007). *History* deals with the past, the concept of change, and the forces that influence it. History also deals with the passage of time and the sequence of events.

People, Places, and Environments. Where things are in children's near environment is important information for them to have as they move farther from their home. In addition, children develop a better appreciation for the natural world and its resources when they learn to be responsible for the waste they generate and the ways in which they dispose of this waste (NCSS, 2009). *Geography* illuminates the characteristics of the earth's environment and the relation of this environment to the people who live in it. Geography also relates to how people get from one place to another and the reasons they choose to move.

Individuals, Groups, and Institutions. Like adults, children belong to many social groups, such as their family, class, after-school activity group, and congregation. How people function within these different settings—as leaders or followers, initiators or passive observers, dependent or independent thinkers—provides a focus for discussion among children. Specific activities can be planned so that children will sharpen their awareness of the roles they and others assume in their work and play. *Sociology* helps us understand the social groups in which we live.

Production, Distribution, and Consumption. Children can be made aware of the diverse kinds of work adults engage in by talking with and observing persons who fight fires, care for people, buy and sell goods, grow produce and livestock, work in factories to build useful products, and perform services for pay. Money exchange and the value of money is a topic that can be introduced to children at a young age. Consumer education, such as learning how to evaluate advertising, is critical for children to understand. One component of such education is for children to be able to distinguish their needs from their wants and to make informed decisions on the basis of the difference (Seefeldt et al., 2010). *Economics* informs us about how people produce, distribute, and consume goods and services (National Council on Economic Education, 2002.)

Civic Ideals and Practices. Children have opportunities to practice aspects of democratic living when they learn to understand the rules that govern the classroom and when they become involved in making some of these rules themselves (Neuman & Roskos, 2007). Within the social studies curriculum, children learn that everyone has rights and responsibilities and that sometimes they must negotiate and bargain for the things they need. Furthermore, they participate in group problem solving about issues that are important to them. Underlying is the concept that people learn to give up some of their desires and wishes for the good of the group. All these experiences teach them how societies function for the benefit of all members. *Political science* relates to the management and governance of social units in a democracy.

Social Studies in the Classroom

How might a social studies curriculum look in practice for children of different ages? Table 14.3 includes sample experiences appropriate for the youngest children (3- to 5-year-olds), somewhat older children (5- to 7-year-olds), and the oldest children (6- to 8-year-olds). Children's maturity and prior access to the materials and activities will affect which experiences are best suited to their needs. Therefore, the age range should be viewed as a guide.

Clearly, teachers have the responsibility of teaching social studies directly, as well as helping children learn to have positive interpersonal interactions. This learning must take place in the context of the child's daily experience in the classroom. This is best accomplished when teachers carefully plan activities that relate to children's lives and take advantage of the spontaneous occurrences that are a natural part of group dynamics to teach important lessons. Active participation by children in the exploration of these issues ensures that they will derive the meaningful knowledge, skills, and attitudes that are the foundations of a social studies curriculum. As a result, these children will demonstrate good citizenship in their school, their communities, and, ultimately, their world.

From the earliest inclusion of social studies in the early childhood curriculum, real experiences have been the appropriate vehicles for teaching social studies content and concepts. Children's active and direct participation in projects and activities is the necessary means of instruction because it is congruent with what we know about children's development (Copple & Bredekamp, 2009). The classroom is an ideal arena within which children learn the social skills, values, and rules required for living in society. Therefore, for young children, social studies is viewed as an extension of their social development. Understanding that children learn best that which is most important to them, educators can logically translate children's natural concerns about their relationships with others and the world around them into studies of the self, the family, the school, and the community (NCSS, 2009). Thus, the integrative nature of social studies promotes children's understanding of the society in which they live.

THE RELATIONSHIP BETWEEN THE SOCIAL DOMAIN AND COGNITION

Even as children are engaged in social pursuits, they are exploring and sharpening their physical knowledge, intuitive knowledge, representational thinking, social-conventional knowledge, language, and critical-thinking skills. Let us use as an example an activity outlined toward the end of this chapter: The People's Choice. To summarize, children are offered an opportunity to negotiate a conflict or a difference of opinion in a democratic way by voting. In the activity, the adult poses a problem for the children to solve—naming a classroom pet, for instance. Children examine the animal in an effort to understand its physical characteristics (physical knowledge). They may discuss its characteristics and thus learn the appropriate descriptive vocabulary (language). Names are

TABLE 14.3   Implementing the Social Studies Curriculum in the Classroom

Discipline	Experiences for		
	3- to 5-Year-Olds	5- to 7-Year-Olds	6- to 8-Year-Olds
Culture	Children are provided with a wok, chopsticks, plastic models of sushi, and plastic plates with Asian designs as normal props in the Family Living Center.	Children are taught two versions of a similar singing game, each with a different ethnic origin.	Children interview family members about their cultural heritage. They make an i-movie or record on paper a story that represents their heritage and share it with the class.
Time, Continuity, and Change	Children bring in pictures of themselves as babies and dictate stories.	Children bring in pictures of their parent(s) as youngsters. They write or dictate descriptions comparing their parents' past and present appearances.	Children create their individual family trees. They obtain the information by interviewing family members.
People, Places, and Environments	After a walk in the neighborhood, children are encouraged to use blocks to reconstruct their experience.	After a walk through the neighborhood, children arrange photographs of features in the area in the order in which they observed them. Later, they make a return trip to check out their recollections.	After a walk in the neighborhood, children create a map representing the buildings and other landmarks near the school.
Individuals, Groups, and Institutions	Children take turns conducting a rhythm instrument band.	Children participate in a theme on friends and friendships, during which they identify and practice friendship-making skills.	Small groups of children work on solving a designated classroom problem (e.g., determining how to make sure children's possessions remain undisturbed). The groups present their solutions to the class, where these solutions are discussed and evaluated.
Production, Distribution, and Consumption	Children participate in a theme entitled "The Work People Do."	Children set up a store in the classroom. Classmates are allotted a limited amount of money with which to buy goods. They are encouraged to bargain or to barter other goods and services to get what they want.	Children develop a plan for a class project to earn money for a special field trip.
Civic Ideals and Practices	During interpersonal disputes, children participate in conflict negotiation, with the teacher as mediator.	Children establish classroom rules for the safe use of a microscope on loan from the museum.	Children hold a mock election for a town council seat. A campaign gives children the opportunity to influence their "constituency."

solicited from children, which requires them to link the physical object to an abstract idea (representational thinking) and to recognize that the names written on the chart represent the animal. Each child has the opportunity to vote for his or her favorite (critical thinking and decision making). Finally, children determine which name has the most number of advocates—first by viewing the groups of children and guessing; second by using one-to-one correspondence, as the groups line up next to each other (logical-mathematical knowledge); and finally by counting (social-conventional knowledge). Throughout the decision-making process, children must separate what they want from what they think. Doing so requires a high level of cognitive functioning. This brief examination of the relation between cognition and the social domain illustrates that the two are inextricably linked and that we cannot delve into social issues and skills without engaging children's minds.

CURRENT EDUCATIONAL ISSUES

Teachers working with young children confront several issues in relation to social development and social studies. These issues represent key topics regarding the social domain and the early childhood curriculum.

Teaching Peace Through Conflict Mediation

In our program, the rule is "No fighting allowed." When a conflict erupts I remind children of the rule and then direct them to other things.

When children get into an argument, I seldom intervene. They need to figure out how to solve problems on their own.

Go to the Assignments and Activities section of Topic 12: Guiding Children in the MyEducationLab for your course and complete the activity entitled *Peaceful Conflict Resolution*. Observe as a teacher guides three young girls through the connflict mediation process.

Conflict is a natural outgrowth of human behavior in social groups. However, conflict resolution is not intuitive. Just as with other social content, children must be taught how to generate and carry out peaceful solutions to disagreements. When teachers (like those quoted above) ignore conflict, simply distract children, or mandate a solution to every dispute, they deprive children of valuable lessons and skills they need to become effective problem solvers (Williams & Cooney, 2006). To provide such lessons, many teachers adopt a conflict resolution model like the one illustrated in this chapter as they work with young children. In each case, the teacher serves as a neutral mediator guiding children through a step-by-step problem-solving process until children can agree on a mutually satisfying solution. As they engage in conflict resolution at different times and in different situations, young children begin to develop the basic skills they need to live peaceably within the classroom community.

Embracing Diversity: Interpretations and Misinterpretations

Some people in our program think that to promote harmony we need to emphasize our similarities, not our differences. How does this fit in with the notion of celebrating diversity?

An essential premise of developmentally appropriate practice is that children of all races, religions, home languages, family backgrounds, economic circumstances, and cultures be treated with understanding and consideration. These values of equality and respect reinforce the democratic foundations of pluralistic societies. How these ideas are implemented in daily practice varies enormously across programs. Some educators interpret these guidelines to mean that differences among children are to be acknowledged if they arise in the normal course of play or conversation; others prefer to be proactive and to seek out and introduce the variations in children's lives to them and to plan discussions and activities that emphasize the uniqueness of individuals and social groups. A different interpretation is to practice democratic principles in the classroom by involving children in making choices about what they learn. Others extend this idea to include classroom governance as a mutual agreement between adults and children. Wherever such interpretations fall within the spectrum, they are consistent with the values and goals of a democratic society.

During the past several years, criticisms of these ideas and practices have surfaced from a number of sources. Some educators interpret the notion of embracing diversity as eliminating standards and values. They believe it is wrong to teach youngsters that differences are real and that no one culture is superior to another. Others misinterpret acceptance of each child's family structure as active promotion of gay lifestyles. Still others misinterpret the practices of offering choices to children and of democratic governance in the classroom to mean that children are being taught to flout authority, which, they believe, will lead to acceptance of inappropriate behavior. Still others object to including diverse ethnic festivities in schools, claiming they dilute traditional Christmas and Thanksgiving practices. Such interpretations claim to uphold family values and the "American Way."

Misinterpretations of the goals and attributes of diversity education for young children may be addressed by examining the practical outcomes for individuals and society. Building self-esteem in youngsters through acceptance of who they are and whence they come enables them to overcome adversity because they have the confidence to try again. Offering numerous opportunities to attempt solutions to problems, evaluate these solutions, and seek other pathways if those routes are not fruitful develops perseverance and creative thinking. This quality leads to the ability to hold a job later in life and to be responsible to one's family. In the same vein, practicing decision making as a child allows one to more easily make productive decisions when the stakes are higher. Exploring

Children cooperate in planning and carrying out projects to benefit their school and community.

ideas creatively, taking risks, not assuming there is a "right" answer, and understanding that a "right" answer may not exist has led, for instance, to technological innovation. Practice in decision making, reaching compromises, and experiencing the consequences of decisions fosters increased involvement in governance on every level. Thus, expanding the possibilities for children to participate actively in their school lives is to be welcomed rather than feared and avoided. Finally, exposure to a wide variety of people, ideas, and customs enriches the individual as well as society. Learning to recognize and appreciate differences among people by embracing diversity is a key to more harmonious living for all.

Determining How the Social Domain Fits into the Daily Routine

How can I fit the social domain into a day already packed with academic content?

Teachers have numerous demands on their time and resources during school. They are expected to plan for instruction in all the domains and to fulfill many other responsibilities. Where, then, does teaching about the social domain fit?

Unfortunately, time devoted to the social domain is diminishing in early childhood education and in the upper grades (Kostelnik & Grady, 2009). Attention to social knowledge and skills is being "squeezed out" of the day by increased time spent on literacy and mathematics. We suggest that rather than seeing this as an issue of social development versus other areas of the curriculum, it is important to remember that social development is integral to every part of school life. It appears in both implicit and explicit forms. Fundamentally, teachers are conveying information and values related to social development in everything they do in the classroom. How they treat children both individually and in groups; how they interact with aides, volunteers, and parents; which disciplinary strategies they employ; and how they respond to diversity of all sorts within their school community directly affect children's social development. In addition, teachers influence children when they take advantage of spontaneous opportunities to make children aware of the effect of their behavior toward others and when teachers model, encourage, and promote helpful and cooperative behavior. Other ways in which implicit instruction is conveyed are when teachers set up routines and practices during which children are expected to care for their immediate environment and the school environment. In all these areas, teachers are addressing important aspects of children's social development.

In addition to pervasive incidental attention to the social domain, teachers can deliberately plan for the inclusion of social learning in their program (Epstein, 2007). Social content can be integrated in daily lesson plans for learning centers in every part of the room. It can also be imbedded in small-group work and in large-group times (Gronlund, 2006). Planning thematic units or projects that revolve around social studies content, such as "Families," "People in Our Community," and "The Work People Do," is another way teachers can underscore these significant understandings and help children comprehend the relationship between what they are experiencing and the processes in the world outside themselves.

PURPOSE AND GOALS

The following purpose and goals are based on content standards developed by the National Council for the Social Studies (2009) as well as various state standards (PreK–3) associated with social development and the social studies.

Purpose

For children to develop social awareness and social competence in a culturally diverse, democratic society, in an interdependent world.

Goals

As children progress they will:

1. Develop play skills:
   Initiate play
   Join a group at play
   Make suggestions
   Take suggestions
   Recognize ways to deal with unpleasant social situations and the emotions associated
     with them
   Learn to play productively alone
2. Develop friendship skills, that is, how to initiate, maintain, and terminate interactions and relationships constructively
3. Develop awareness of other people's opinions, viewpoints, and attitudes
4. Negotiate conflicts in peaceful ways by compromising, bargaining, and standing up for one's rights.
5. Develop empathy for others (recognize others' emotions, respect others' emotional responses)
6. Perceive adults as sources of gratification, approval, and modeling
7. Conform to reasonable limits set on behavior, play space, use of materials, or the types of activities in which they are involved
8. Identify the reasons for classroom rules
9. Distinguish acceptable from unacceptable classroom behavior
10. Use their knowledge of appropriate behavior in one circumstance to determine appropriate conduct in another
11. Develop skills related to self-control, such as impulse control, resistance to temptation, delay of gratification, and how to carry out positive social actions
12. Cooperate (work with others toward a common goal)
13. Help (share information or materials, give physical assistance, offer emotional support)
14. Recognize their own and others' cultural values and practices
15. Develop understanding and respect for the similarities and differences among people
16. Demonstrate approved behaviors related to social and ethnic customs (e.g., manners and other respectful behaviors)
17. Acquire rudimentary ideas of how goods and services are produced, exchanged, and consumed
18. Recognize their place in the physical environment and how they and others orient themselves
19. Display responsibility for the environment
20. Develop an understanding of time, continuity, and change in relation to past and present events
21. Understand and act on democratic principles and practices
22. Show awareness of and concern for the rights and well-being of others
23. Describe how people live together in families, neighborhoods, and communities
24. Develop positive attitudes about belonging to a group beyond the family
25. Exhibit skills related to social studies content, such as collecting and analyzing data, mapping, and making decisions
26. Use social studies vocabulary and facts

Teaching Strategies

Following are 12 strategies that educators can use to teach children skills in the social domain.

1. Help children make friends at school by using their names. Children feel most comfortable interacting with people whose names they know. Thus, acquainting children with one another's names is a basic strategy for facilitating children's friendships. To accomplish this, use children's names frequently. Identify by name youngsters who are sitting near one another, working together, and playing with one another. Unfamiliar or uncommon names will seem less strange with frequent repetition. Be sure you know how to pronounce every child's name correctly.

MAKING GOALS FIT

Table 14.4 illustrates how the same goal can be implemented with children of different ages or abilities. These variations demonstrate the DAP concept of age-appropriate practice. They also illustrate how the same goal can remain relevant throughout early childhood.

TABLE 14.4 Teaching Children Essential Friendship Skills

Goal #5	Example of Activity for 3- and 4-Year-Olds	Example of Activity for 5- and 6-Year-Olds	Example of Activity for 7- and 8-Year-Olds
Develop friendship skills: how to initiate, maintain, or terminate interactions constructively	Sing songs at group time that use children's names. Have children identify who is present and who is missing each day during group time.	Make a class book about all of the children with photos, interests, likes, and dislikes. Have children add to their own pages and the pages of classmates throughout the year.	Have each child interview another child in the class and then create a page in his or her journal about the interview. Invite one or two children to report on their interviews at group time.

2. **Help children make friends at school by promoting social interactions.** To help children become more aware of others in their group, deliberately pair children to work on projects. Choose children who have something in common. Remember to point out these common attributes, attitudes, preferences, or shared experiences so they will become more aware of them. Shy children, in particular, benefit from this technique, but it is effective with others as well, such as children for whom English is not their home language, or children with disabilities that make social interaction more difficult. For the benefit of all children, remember to provide numerous opportunities during the day for children to interact with one another informally. Also, plan activities that require more than one child's participation. Observe how children behave with one another and use this information in future planning.

3. **Provide activities that encourage children to practice social skills.** Use the suggestions following this section to create activities that focus on specific social skills. For instance, use skits to teach children numerous ways to let others know that they want to play. Carry out discussions during which children generate alternatives and explore the effectiveness of different solutions. As a follow-up, create opportunities for children to practice the strategies in real-life situations. Then, provide them with on-the-spot information regarding their progress in applying their knowledge. This approach will help them determine which techniques are successful and encourage them to eliminate those that are not. Other examples include deliberately setting out materials in such a way that children must ask, bargain, or trade to get what they want. Always make sure to provide additional support for any child who does not easily interpret social cues (e.g., how to interpret another person's facial expressions, how to exit a group constructively, or how to negotiate a turn). Do not assume all children can do these things readily. Provide coaching and reinforcement as needed.

4. **Help children become more helpful and cooperative.** A necessary first step in this process is to recognize and acknowledge the times when children behave in positive or prosocial ways. Pointing out such instances increases the chances that children will repeat the acts of kindness. Another strategy is to plan activities in which children have opportunities to practice helping or cooperating. For instance, activities in which children must work together cooperatively to reach a common goal are far more supportive of children's prosocial behavior than those that pit child against child or group against group.

Indira's horizons have expanded through her relationship with Mrs. Anna, a classroom volunteer.

5. **Help children develop empathy for others.** Empathy contributes to children's development of self-regulation (see chapter 6), friendly behavior, prosocial actions, and respect for diversity. Use interactions in the classroom as a vehicle for drawing children's attention to other people's feelings ("Look at Rodney. He is excited to get a turn." "Sara is sad. She is missing her mom."). Invite children to talk about their feelings with one another throughout the day. Also, ask children questions that prompt them to describe how they feel or provide scripts as necessary (e.g., "Did you like it when she took the hammer? Tell her what you were feeling." Or, "You can tell Kathy you don't like when she takes your things."). Integrate discussions about emotions into the daily routine (e.g., use storybooks or artwork to initiate feeling-related conversations or refer to incidents that occurred during the day to spark discussion). Help children figure out how another person is feeling based on that person's actions. These conversations could be around real incidents as they occur or part of a planned lesson using books or other props such as puppets.

6. **Help children develop positive attitudes toward diversity.** As is well known, familiarity with a wide range of people helps children be more accepting of differences. Therefore, one valuable strategy is to present children with opportunities to interact with adult members of their own and other cultural groups, individuals who display varying physical abilities, older people, and younger people. For example, invite grandparents into the classroom to talk with children about what life was like when they were growing up. Ask them to talk also about the activities that they engage in at present to dispel stereotypical attitudes about old people's being helpless. Ask parents in the group to come in to tell stories remembered from their childhood and, if possible, bring books in their language of origin. Send home a request to families for recipes from their culture. Finally, use neighborhood resources to acquaint children with people who are different from themselves. In sum, introduce and celebrate diversity by connecting it to children's common experience in the classroom.

7. **Provide children with classroom activities, materials, and discussions that address the wide range of diversity.** Ensure that diversity education and awareness is an ongoing part of your classroom by planning multicultural activities that are integrated into the daily routines of the program rather than reserving them only for holidays or special occasions. Check the pictures, books, learning materials, and other classroom props for evidence of stereotypical portrayals of any group. In some cases, remove them; in others, use the biased depictions as springboards for discussions with the children. When appropriate, create new pictures that more justly represent the true diversity in the world and, if relevant, in the classroom. Finally, engage children in sending letters of criticism and concern to manufacturers who are producing and marketing toys and games that undermine a fair portrayal of an ethnic, racial, gender, or ability issue.

8. **Help children deal with stereotypical ideas.** The first part of this process is to provide accurate information about the differences and similarities that children perceive. This means that you should respond openly and honestly to children's observations and to the questions they ask. Giving them chances to explore differences by providing direct experiences is an important component. For example, activities during which children compare and graph skin color or hair texture sharpens children's awareness while presenting variety in a positive light. Another aspect of this strategy is to build children's critical-thinking skills so that they will become more attuned to evidence of prejudice—within themselves, in others, and as portrayed in the media. Increasing their prosocial attitudes will allow them to respond to these situations in positive ways. Furthermore, the more prosocial the child, the more likely that he or she can come to the aid of a friend. The final step is to assist children in defending themselves against bias directed toward them. School personnel are an important influence on how children view themselves and can therefore be effective in teaching children coping skills. Work with youngsters in designing spoken responses to name-calling. Allow them time to practice with their peers in the haven of the classroom. Give them opportunities to talk about their experiences during school time.

9. **Help children learn to care for their near and far environments.** Give children practical experiences in cleaning up the classroom, the school hallways, the playground, and other areas in which they work. Use activities such as those suggested in this chapter to alert children to the uses of materials they would otherwise discard. When engaged in picking up litter, readying the classroom for the next day, and so on, use music to lighten the burden. Have children perform these

tasks in groups so that they feel a sense of group participation and camaraderie and further develop their repertoire of shared experiences. Base themes around the issue of recycling. For example, prepare projects for children to ascertain the recycling efforts of their community, and invite local groups with interests in these matters to give presentations to the class. Assist children in assessing what actions they, as young people, can reasonably take.

10. **Help children build social studies concepts by practicing democracy in the classroom.** Plan activities in which children have opportunities to identify, generate solutions for, and carry out solutions for problems inherent in group living. One way to do this is for children to create some of their own classroom rules and designate the appropriate consequences for infractions of these rules. When work is to be done in caring for the classroom, let children decide the means for handling it. In addition, promote children's abilities to evaluate the techniques they choose and to redesign the strategies as needed. Introduce vocabulary associated with democratic principles, such as *fair, more, less,* and *majority rule.* Encourage children to use these words and concepts in relation to their activities. Practice democratic problem solving by modeling strategies for helping children solve interpersonal conflict peacefully. Take on the role of mediator in the conflicts that arise in the classroom or outdoors.

11. **Help children build social studies concepts through theme/project choices.** When deciding on themes or projects for teaching in the classroom, choose some that focus on social studies content. Such topics as self, family, community, interdependence of people, and care for the environment are subjects in which children are naturally interested because they are directly related to youngsters' lives and activities. They also are ones that lend themselves to tangible, firsthand content and experiences. Other aspects of social studies can be addressed, for example, when you teach children that people learn about the past from evidence left by others and that they, too, can leave records for others to study.

12. **Help children build social studies concepts and skills across the curriculum.** Social studies is truly an integrative area of focus. For example, teach historical understanding and literature comprehension through the use of modern and old versions of the same story. Another idea is to compare the ways of living of two families during different periods in history, assessing both similarities and contrasts (e.g., *Little House on the Prairie* books can be read alongside a modern story by Judy Blume). Assist children in relating mapping skills both to geography and to mathematics by creating a map of the play yard or representing an area of the school in a diorama. Combine political understanding with increased self-esteem as you aid children in expressing their needs and wants during a conflict negotiation session. These suggestions are only a few examples of how social studies can pervade daily life in the classroom.

ACTIVITY SUGGESTIONS

Following is a set of activities designed to encourage children to practice the social strategies outlined in this chapter. Each subarea of social development has been addressed by at least one activity. Thus, plans are offered that touch on developing play and friendship skills, negotiating conflict, recognizing other viewpoints, establishing rules, cooperating, helping, recognizing similarities and differences between self and others, and solving problems of group living. These lesson plans are aimed initially at 5-year-olds, with suggestions for simplification and extension so that they can be used successfully with children 3 to 8 years of age. Easily obtained materials are listed for each plan, when appropriate.

*Using Skits to Teach Social Skills * (For Children of All Ages)*

Goal 1 Develop play skills.

Materials Two dolls, puppets, or pictures of children; several small blocks or other objects

General information An effective strategy for introducing and reinforcing particular play skills is to use skits or short scenarios. Children enjoy watching these presentations and can learn a great deal about ways to interact with others. However, simply viewing them is not sufficient. Adults must point out the pertinent features of the interplay and pose questions that help children clarify their understanding. Older children benefit from opportunities to reenact the scenes and to generate their own. Following are general guidelines for developing and presenting skits to children.

Procedure

1. Select one play skill as a focus.
2. Decide on the medium of presentation. Use realistic props such as dolls, puppets, or photographs that look like children rather than animals or cartoon characters. Be sure the dolls or puppets represent both genders (or are androgynous) and depict a variety of racial and ethnic groups and differing physical abilities.
3. Outline a script that is succinct but consists of five parts:
      Demonstration of a skill
      Demonstration of lack of the skill
      Explanation by the adult
      Discussion by the children
      Opportunity for children to use the props
4. Write out the statements and questions you will use to facilitate discussion: Which characters demonstrated the skill, which showed lack of skill, the reaction of each character, how viewers evaluated the behaviors and why, and what they think the characters could do to improve their situation. Be sure to include both effective strategies and ineffective strategies. Doing so is important for helping children distinguish appropriate from inappropriate behaviors in a variety of situations.
5. Before introducing the skit to children, rehearse it until you feel confident. Write the questions you want to ask on cue cards, if needed.
6. Present the skit. Seat children in a semicircle, facing so that everyone can see your face and hands and the space directly in front of you. Use a low bench or table to display the props.
7. Say, "Today we are going to talk about friends. Here are two dolls. We are going to pretend that these dolls are real children just like you. Their names are Sarvesh and Cathy. They are 5 years old and go to a school just like ours. Watch carefully and see what happens."
8. After you present the skit, ask the questions you prepared, adapting them to situations that arise. Paraphrase children's ideas. If children have difficulty thinking of ideas, prompt them by providing suggestions.
9. Once children suggest their ideas, replay the scene, using each suggestion, one at a time. Ask the children to predict how Sarvesh will react in each case. Play out the scene as they suggest. Provide further information as appropriate. "John, you said Cathy could help Sarvesh build. Let's try that." (Maneuver the dolls and provide appropriate dialogue.) "Tell me what you think Sarvesh will do now."
10. Help children evaluate how well their solution worked. For example, "Sarvesh still doesn't know that Cathy wants to be friends. Tell us another way that Sarvesh could ask Cathy to play." Continue trying out their ideas. As children find solutions, praise them for thinking of ways to help the friends determine what to do. Summarize for them the ways that were tried and which proved more successful. As unfriendly solutions are suggested and role-played, point out that the results may be confusion, hurt feelings, sadness, and anger.
11. Remember that children learn from repetition, so you should present each social skill numerous times and in several ways across time. Each time you do a new skit or repeat an old one, change the roles that the characters play so that in children's minds particular behaviors will not be associated with a specific figure.

To simplify Carry out the activity with a very small group of children. Keep the scenarios short and simple. As children suggest solutions, act them out and point out the results.

To extend Encourage the children to reenact on their own the scenario you demonstrated. Introduce open-ended scenarios in which a problem is posed but no solution (effective or ineffective) is modeled. Invite the children to create a solution and then evaluate it. Make dolls available to the children so that they can role-play other scenarios of their invention.

---

*Many of these ideas are based on skits developed for *Teaching Young Children Using Themes*, M. J. Kostelnik (Ed.), Glenview, IL: Good Year Books, 1991.

Conflict Mediation* (For Children of All Ages)

Goal 4 Negotiate conflicts in peaceful ways by compromising, bargaining, and standing up for one's rights.

Materials None

General information This activity is to be carried out during a naturally occurring conflict between two children in the classroom or on the playground. The exact nature of the conflict will influence the specific words and phrases used by the adult. Be sure to follow the steps of the mediation process exactly.

Step 1: Initiating the mediation process The adult in charge observes signs of a conflict taking place. He or she moves to the site and watches carefully. The adult takes action if children seem unable to resolve the dispute or if they behave aggressively toward one another. The teacher stops any aggressive behavior and separates the combatants, saying, for example, "Sookyong and Alonzo, you are both pulling the toy. It looks as if you both want it. You have different ideas about how to use it. I'll hold it while we're deciding what to do. I'll give it back when we've figured it out." The adult then removes the toy; if territory is at issue, he or she safeguards it from being taken over by other children by declaring it out of bounds. This procedure stops the children from continuing to hit or grab, helps them to listen, and assists them in approaching a highly emotional situation more calmly and objectively.

Step 2: Clarifying each child's point of view Ascertaining and paraphrasing each child's perspective vis-à-vis the conflict is the second part of the process. The adult asks each one, in turn, to tell his or her side of the story without interruption: "Alonzo, you think . . . ," "Sookyong, you wanted . . . ." Then the adult paraphrases every statement as it is made. This step is critical. For the adult to be trusted not to make an arbitrary decision, he or she must establish neutrality. Thus, he or she must not make any evaluation or comment on the merits of either position. This step in the process may take considerable time; do not expect inexperienced children to complete it quickly because they may require repeated chances to fully express their viewpoints.

Step 3: Summing up The adult should state the problem in mutual terms: "You each want. . . . We have a problem. It is important that we figure out what to do so that each of you will be satisfied and no one will get hurt." The problem thus defined implies that both youngsters have responsibility for the problem and its solution.

Step 4: Generating alternatives The focus of the fourth step is for children to think of a number of possible solutions to the problem. At this point bystanders as well as the combatants can have their say. Every time a solution is offered, the mediator paraphrases it to the youngsters directly involved. Each is then asked for an opinion. Children often initially reject a solution they later find acceptable, so even repeat suggestions should be brought to the table. The mediator can make suggestions such as "Sometimes when people have this problem, they can decide to share or take turns" if children seem unable to devise their own ideas. However, to truly leave the solution up to the children, the adult must not indicate by words or tone of voice that any one plan is best.

Step 5: Agreeing on a solution The ultimate aim of this step is for individuals to agree on a plan of action that is mutually satisfying. The mediator should help children explore the possibilities and find one idea or a combination of ideas that is acceptable. The final agreement should generally involve some compromise on the part of the children and may not represent anyone's ideal. The mediator then states the result: "You've agreed that you can take turns. First, Sookyong will have it for 2 minutes, then Alonzo. It sounds as if you solved the problem!"

Step 6: Reinforcing the problem-solving process The adult must praise children for their hard work in reaching a solution. The goal is to demonstrate that the ultimate solution is not as important as the process for reaching it. Thus, children's emotional investment in the problem and the compromises that were made should be acknowledged as well.

Step 7: Following through The mediator should help the children carry out the terms of the agreement. This step is especially important so that they will learn to trust that the mediation process is worth the time and effort they have put into it.

To simplify Shorten some of the procedural steps if you see signs of boredom or fatigue, such as extreme restlessness, turning away, or yawning. Keep the dialogue short and simple.

To extend Teach children the mediator role.

---

*For a more detailed discussion of this strategy, see Kostelnik et al. (2009).

We Are a Family (For Older or More Experienced Children)

Goal 14 Recognize their own and others' cultural values and practices.

Materials Photographs of children and adults in the classroom and members of their families, a display board, pen, paper

General guidelines Request photographs from each child's family well in advance (2 to 3 weeks may be necessary). Assure the families that their photos will be returned. Label the pictures with names and relationships of each person. When you have secured the pictures, mount them temporarily on a bulletin board or oaktag, taking care not to mar them. Label the pictures with names and relationships of each person. Numerous activities using these family pictures can then be planned.

Procedure

1. During a period of time, allow each person in the class an opportunity to talk about his or her family. Respond positively to children's comments about any similarities or differences they notice in family structures. Avoid using terms like *only* when describing a child's family, as in "Judith has only a grandma in her family." Talk with children about the range of possible family compositions.
2. Encourage children to write or dictate stories about their family, telling what they like to do together, how each person in the family works to help the family, how they celebrate special holidays or occasions, and so on. Tell children to read these stories to the other children. Elicit comments from children about these practices. Reinforce the idea that each family does things in ways that are meaningful to its members.
3. Instruct children to graph independently the various families in the group. These graphs can be compared with those of one another as children identify which families are composed of many people, which fewer; which families include pets, which do not; which family members look like other members, which do not.
4. Put the pictures in a book called *The Families in Our Class*. Include stories and other descriptions that children have written or dictated. Make the book available for children to "read."

To simplify Focus on what children can see depicted in the photographs, such as family composition.

To extend Delve more deeply into family traditions by asking children to bring in and talk about important family artifacts. Elicit information from families about favorite stories, jokes, and so forth. Write this information out for children to see. Compare it with other versions.

Alike and Different (For Children of All Ages)

Goal 15 Develop understanding and respect for the similarities and differences among people.

Materials Standing mirror, paper and pencil for recording children's observations

Procedure

1. Invite children two at a time to look into a mirror at themselves and each other. Help them discover characteristics they have in common and things that are different. This opportunity is ideal for pairing children who may be different in physical ableness, sex, and appearance to help them discover similarities beyond the obvious.
2. Make two lists, one in which likenesses are indicated ("We are alike") and another on which differences ("We are different") are recorded. Urge the children to begin with physical appearance and to move on to other attributes, such as interests, ideas, preferences, skills, handedness, number of siblings, letters in their names, and so on.
3. Tell the partners that as they observe more things about themselves and each other, they can add to the list throughout the day. At this point, allow the children to continue the activity without interference.
4. At the end of the day, suggest that children review the list and count all the things they discovered. Let them find out if they discovered more similarities or differences.
5. Repeat this activity, mixing up pairs until all the children have had a chance to be paired with each other. If ample time exists, repeat the activity later in the year and compare the new lists with the original lists. Determine whether the categories increase as children learn more about each other with time.

To simplify Focus only on physical attributes, adding other dimensions as children mature.

To extend Without naming the children involved, read some lists to the class and have them guess the pairs in question.

Stores (For Children of All Ages)

Goal 17 Acquire rudimentary ideas of how goods and services are produced, exchanged, and consumed.

Materials Set up a store in the classroom. Stock it using materials gathered from shops, families, and other sources. This may be general merchandise, as in a department store or super market, or specialty shop, such as a shoe store. Include cash registers, bags for packing, order forms, pencils, chalk boards on which to list "specials," and plastic grocery carts.

Procedure

1. Initiate the study with a trip to a local store. Prime children to look for what is sold, how items are displayed, how money is exchanged, and who works in the establishment. This field trip can be repeated at the end of the unit as a culmination and review activity.
2. Back at school, hold a discussion focusing on the issues outlined above. Help children figure out the roles of seller, customer, restocker, and so on. Decide as a group what the medium of exchange will be (e.g., "paper" money, barter for other goods or services, "play money"). As appropriate, children can create the money at the art table for use in the store and, when able, make signs for various "specials."
3. Help children make shopping lists.
4. Occasionally, introduce real food items (if children are working in a food store) or a variety of sizes and styles of clothing, making sure that in each case you are fairly representing children's experiences in their home or neighborhood.

To simplify Set up a grocery store or neighborhood bodega, whichever one the children are most familiar with.

To extend After several days, pose questions such as where the items might come from, how they are produced or manufactured, and how they get to the store. In addition, discussions can be held regarding how people get the money they spend in stores. These issues can lead to future themes or projects. A further extension is for older children to offer a store to the rest of the school to raise money for charity or a class trip.

Recycle-Ikles (For Children of All Ages)

Goal 19 Display responsibility for the environment.

Materials Medium-size plastic bags labeled with each child's name, safety pins to secure them to children's clothing

Procedure

1. Carry out a discussion with children about trash—what it is, how it is generated, what the effect is on the environment, and what people can do to recycle materials that are no longer wanted. Explain that each child will collect the trash he or she produces during a day and place it in the plastic bag. Tell children that at the end of the day they will examine their trash and make determinations about how to reuse it. Then allow children to proceed independently.
2. Plan a time at the end of the day for children to examine the things they have collected in their bags. Ask each individual to state one way he or she can recycle the materials (include the collection bag as well). Tell children that they are now "Recycle-Ikles." Provide each child with a badge that says, "I am a Recycle-Ikle. I reduce, recycle, and reuse my trash."
3. Set aside a recycling center in which to store the materials they have collected and encourage children to reuse them on the following day.

To simplify Use a classroom collection bag rather than individual bags.

To extend Carry out the activity during an extended period. Evaluate whether children are able to generate less trash as time goes on. Set this as a goal for the school year. Extend the activity to include a collection of schoolwide trash. Follow a similar procedure and acknowledge the efforts of each classroom as they cut down on the trash they generate with time.

The People's Choice* (Figure 14.2) (For Older or More Experienced Children)

Goal 21 Understand and act on democratic principles and practices.

Materials Whiteboard and marker, or large piece of writing paper and marking pen; three to five 3" × 12" pieces of oaktag or sentence strips

Procedure

1. Introduce the activity by explaining that the whole group will select a name for a class pet, their favorite story, or whatever. Tell them they are going to vote, which means that each person will have a chance to choose a favorite name or story, and at the end they will determine which choice most people liked best. This choice will be the most popular because the most people liked it best, and it will be the one that wins.

2. Begin the process of choosing the alternatives. Limit the number of possibilities to three to five, enough so that children can have a real option but not so many that the cluster of children for each group is too small. Explain the limit to the children. Solicit suggestions and write down the first ideas on the whiteboard or paper, reading each aloud. When the list is complete, read each entry, running your hand under the word as you say it so that children can "read" it.

3. Write each option on a piece of oaktag and place it in a corner of the group area, separate from one another. For younger children, place an adult with each tag.

4. Tell children they are going to vote. Explain that they will choose only one of the options and will then stand by the corresponding name. Say that they may not change their minds once they are in place, but assure them that they will have many opportunities to vote throughout the year. Ask each child in turn to pick a favorite from the list. You should read the list before each child chooses, to remind him or her of the options and to minimize the likelihood that children will simply repeat the last person's selection. Write the child's name on the whiteboard next to the appropriate station. Children may abstain from voting. In this case, direct the individual to remain seated and offer another chance when everyone is finished.

5. Once the group has divided into areas, instruct children to look at the groups and estimate which has the most people (which choice is the most popular). Make sure everyone who wants to has a chance to speak. Paraphrase and then summarize their ideas.

6. Tell children that there are several ways to find out which is most popular. Line up two groups and ask the children which line is longer.

7. Paraphrase children's responses. Compare another group's line with the longer line. Continue comparing until the longest line is determined. Then ask children which line has the most people.

8. With the children assisting, count the members of each group and record the number on the board or chart. Ask children which number is largest.

9. Explain again that the group with the most members represents the most popular choice. Ask children to tell which entry won the voting. Announce the result and mark it on the chart or board.

A child may insist that the name he or she has chosen is the most popular (even if this is not the case). Differentiate what the child *wants* to be true from what he or she *thinks* is true. Carefully review the evidence (counting again if necessary) until the child can accept the answer. Be patient. The child's response is evidence of egocentric thinking, not stubbornness.

To simplify Younger children may tire of the process before the final decision. If you detect signs of restlessness, move to the final step quickly (you may have to condense a few steps) so that the children experience closure to the activity. Limit the children's choices to two or three.

To extend In the step in which children "vote with their feet," substitute using their names on the whiteboard to represent them. Ask youngsters to count these names and compare quantities. If this is your plan, print the names clearly enough for children to see them easily. If children are having difficulty, quickly move to the original procedure. At a later time, ask children to recap the decision-making procedure that occurred and discuss the results. After a period of days or weeks, revote and compare the results with the original outcome.

---

*Many of these ideas are based on skits developed for *Teaching Young Children Using Themes*, M. J. Kostelnik (Ed.), Glenview, IL: Good Year Books, 1991.

FIGURE 14.2   How One Teacher Adapted the People's Choice Activity for a Child with Down Syndrome

Ronna

Ronna, a child in Mrs. Scarpetta's kindergarten class, has Down syndrome. Down syndrome is a common genetic disorder, affecting 1 in every 800 to 1,000 newborns. As a result of her disorder, Ronna shows moderate mental disability and exhibits a range of medical problems, such as low muscle tone, some delayed speech, and vision problems. To help Ronna be successful in school, Mrs. Scarpetta adapted activities for her special needs. One example was The People's Choice activity. First, Mrs. Scarpetta paid particular attention to where Ronna was seated—ensuring that Ronna had an unobstructed view of the board or paper on which she (the teacher) wrote and making sure that Ronna was near it. Second, Mrs. Scarpetta limited Ronna's choices to two, instead of the four or five she offered other children. Doing so lessened Ronna's potential confusion. In addition, Mrs. Scarpetta paired Ronna with Damian, a more skilled partner, someone with whom Ronna played, and a potential "coach" in the choosing process. Mrs. Scarpetta was prepared to take on this role if Damian could not or did not want to do so. Finally, because Ronna's speech was limited and Ronna was not yet comfortable speaking in front of other children, Mrs. Scarpetta encouraged her to indicate a choice through gesture.

SUMMARY

The social domain encompasses four essential aspects of children's development and education: social skills, socialization, social responsibility, and social studies. The most effective paradigm for integrating this body of knowledge and skills is through children's personal experiences at home, at school, and in the broader community in which they live.

Learning to get along with others, both children and adults, is a major task of children and is one on which they spend an increasing portion of their time and energy. Some children make friends easily, and some do not. Friendships are so vital to human beings that friendless children and those whose interpersonal relationships with peers are unsatisfactory lead unhappy lives. The development of friendship skills, such as establishing contact, maintaining positive relationships, and resolving conflicts, and how they view friendships with time are important aspects of children's ability to make and keep friends. Youngsters who behave prosocially (e.g., helping, cooperating, comforting, and sharing) develop feelings of competence, enjoy many successful personal encounters, and respond positively to offers of prosocial actions from others. Being sensitive to someone else's cues, deciding to help, and taking appropriate actions are the facets of successful prosocial behavior.

How well children understand and enact the rules and customs of society is a measure of their socialization. Chapter 6 is devoted entirely to this topic.

Societal factors in our modern world mandate that children become aware of and share responsibility for the world beyond themselves—become good citizens in their homes, schools, and communities. Doing so requires that children learn to recognize and embrace diversity in all its forms and that they learn about and care for their immediate environment.

Social studies is the study of people in society, past and present, and their relations with one another, both near and far. Thus, the social studies encompass anthropology, economics, geography, history, political science, and sociology. Knowledge goals for social studies reflect the similarities and differences among people and groups and their interdependence; how people fit into and use their environment; the ways in which people have learned with time to live together in democratic ways; how people view themselves in and over time; and an understanding of how goods and services are produced, distributed, and consumed. In addition, skill goals focus on children's mastery of tools and techniques, whereas attitude goals emphasize respect for all people and efforts to make the world a healthier and safer place to live. Thus, social studies is the framework within which all the areas of social development are integrated.

Key Words

attitude goals	skill goals	social studies
inclusive environments	social competence	socialization
knowledge goals	social responsibility	
prosocial behavior	social skills	

Applying What You've Read in This Chapter

1. **Discuss**
   a. On the basis of your reading and your experiences with children, discuss each of the questions that open this chapter.
   b. Discuss the educational issue "Embracing Diversity: Interpretations and Misinterpretations" raised in this chapter. Do you agree with the positions taken in the text? Explain your reasons. Include personal experiences you may have had.
   c. Using Table 14.3, create an additional activity in each category that is appropriate for the children with whom you work.

2. **Observe**
   a. Observe a group of children for signs of prosocial and antisocial behavior. Tally the incidents of each and summarize the results. Be sure to include the ages of the children in your report.
   b. Watch a group of children at play. Determine who is friends with whom. Give a detailed description of their relationship. Using the information about the characteristics of friendship in this chapter and your observations, determine the children's level of friendship.
   c. Observe an early childhood classroom. Determine the degree to which children have decision-making opportunities by recording the number and types of choices that are offered or group problem-solving experiences in which children participate.

3. **Carry out an activity**
   a. Write a script using the guidelines in the activity section of this chapter. Choose a prosocial or a skill on which to focus your teaching. Practice the skit at home or with friends. Present the skit to the group, using dolls or puppets to create the characters and the situation. Hold a follow-up discussion with the children and, if appropriate, replay the skit using information gleaned from them.
   b. Set up a recycling center in the classroom. Collect all scrap paper and paper products during a single day and plan for children to use the paper on the following day for an art project.
   c. Carry out one or more of the activities you developed for the social studies chart. Evaluate results.
   d. Carry out one or more of the activities listed at the end of the chapter. Evaluate the results in of your preparation and the children's responses.

4. **Create something for your portfolio**
   a. Make a video of your presentation of a skit in which you focus on prosocial or friendship skills. Include the script with the video. Limit the video to no more than 10 or 15 minutes.
   b. Write a summary of the skit, focusing on prosocial or friendship skills. Give a synopsis of the discussion that followed the skit and note any changes in children's behavior that you as a direct or an indirect result of the ideas presented in the script.
   c. Keep a weekly or monthly record of children's friendships. Compare their relationships after you present specific information to them by means of skits, discussions, or literature.
   d. Document ways in which you have integrated social studies and social development into your curriculum. Use photographs, examples of children's writing or drawing, and anecdotal records you have kept with time.

5. **Add to your journal**
   a. What is the most significant concept that you have learned about the social domain on the basis of your reading and with your children?
   b. Does the information presented in this chapter correspond to your personal and professional experiences in the field? What are consistencies and inconsistencies you perceive?
   c. Think about ways in which you will integrate social skill acquisition and instruction in prosocial behavior into your program.
   d. On the basis of what you have read, would you like to see changes made in the social studies curriculum used in your program? What are they, and how might they be implemented?

6. **✋ Consult the standards**
   a. Look up the social studies standards for your school district or program. Compare them to the national social studies standards, which can be accessed through the NCSS website, www.ncss.org. Find similarities and also ways in which your state has adapted the national standards to take account of geographic, historic, economic, or cultural factors particular to your state.
   b. Choose one of the national social studies standards, which can be accessed through the NCSS website, www.ncss.org, and discuss how the program with which you are involved implements the standard. Give specific examples of activities.

PRACTICE FOR YOUR CERTIFICATION OR LICENSURE EXAM

The following items will help you practice applying what you have learned in this chapter. They can help to prepare you for your course exam, the PRAXIS II exam, your state licensure or certification exam, and for working in developmentally appropriate ways with young children.

Social Development and the Curriculum

A common criticism of American education is that young children do not know very much about geography and history.

1. **Constructed-response question**

   a. Describe an activity that you would create to help a group of 4-year-olds become interested in one of these subjects. Discuss in detail what the activity would look like and what you would expect children to learn from it.

   b. Describe what you would plan for a group of second graders. Discuss in detail what the activity would look like and what you would expect children to learn from it.

2. **Multiple-choice question**

   Mrs. Feeney is a first-grade teacher who is concerned about the increased conflict she is seeing among the children during free choice activity times. Which of the following strategies should Mrs. Feeney first carry out when conflicts arise?

   a. Separate the children who are arguing and send them to opposite parts of the room to cool off for a while.

   b. End free choice early and substitute a more teacher-directed form of activity.

   c. Intervene and help the children define the problem.

   d. Intervene and tell the children how to resolve the conflict.

PART 4

INTEGRATING CURRICULUM

Integrating Curriculum Through Pretend and Construction Play

You may wonder:

Isn't play just natural for children?

How can I convince parents or colleagues that play is important?

How do we account for the differences in the way children approach pretend and
construction play?

How do children use pretend and construction play to represent experiences
or objects?

How do pretend and construction play contribute to all other domains of learning
and development?

In this chapter on pretend and construction play, we present information to help you answer
the preceding questions.

◆ ◆ *Four first graders were talking intently in the bushes near the corner of the playground. "Let's
pretend we're lost and all alone and have to build our house," suggested Alice.*

"Yeah, we'll have to build it here. This could be a place to sleep," contributed Diane.

*"And nobody knows where we are. No grown-ups. And no boys can come in here. Right?" Joan
queried. "Shari, you get started on the kitchen. We gotta have a kitchen. Tomorrow we can bring
some food."*

All play is a delight to the young children engaged in it. In fact, pretend and construction play
are the hallmarks of the early childhood period (Piaget, 1962). Some believe that block constructions and the little things children make to support their play are simply amusements. More recently, scholars have recognized that play has not only a formative function that enables children
to adapt to the social and physical environment, but also an expressive function that facilitates
children's communication with others about their thinking and feelings related to their understanding of the world (Frost, Wortham, & Reifel, 2008). Early childhood educators have long perceived pretend play as a vehicle for integrating various developmental capacities. Growing
increasingly complex during this period, children's pretend play allows for some skills to be practiced and new challenges to be mastered.

CHARACTERISTICS OF PLAY

Play is fun, carried out for the pleasure of doing it, free of externally imposed rules, spontaneous, and voluntary. It requires the player's active involvement and the suspension of reality.
It is symbolic behavior that allows the player to treat objects as though they were something
else. The spoon becomes the musician's baton; a block structure becomes a spaceship. Players
assume roles as though they were performers or explorers and sometimes machines. Players
establish rules consistent with the play theme and roles requiring one another to perform in
patterns that fit the narrative. For example, any contribution to the establishment of a household, the protection of the group, or other survival topics would be appropriate to the scenario
described at the beginning of this chapter. Extraneous events, comments, or behavior would
be either rejected or ignored by the players or would cause the play to disintegrate. Reality is
suspended, but the play is governed by internal rules; thus the play event has internal coherence. Children function in the enactive mode (use gestures to convey meaning or to substitute
for objects) as they engage in simple make-believe, shift to the iconic mode (use of drawings,
sculpture or objects to convey meaning) when they need to construct an object to further their
play, and use the symbolic mode (use of narrative to convey meaning) in complex play scenarios. Thus, imaginative, abstract thinking, composed of sequences of action events, narrative, and objects is typical.

The Play Frame

The **play frame** defines the scope of the pretend-play event. Inside the play frame are all the people and objects that are engaged in the episode. The people, objects, and pretend narrative are all relevant to one another and to the progress of the play. If a photograph were taken of the pretend-play episode described at the beginning of the chapter, the photographer would automatically move back to include all the players and relevant objects, even though other persons might be in either the foreground or the background of the photograph. Players within the frame are those who have a communication link and share a common pretense. Everyone and everything else not involved in the narrative in progress are not in the play frame. Thus, a child who just wanders by and does not engage in the play is not in the play frame, though she may be within the space momentarily.

The frames of play may be established by a variety of modes (Sutton-Smith, 1992). Establishing the frame of the play allows children to communicate the theme, roles, and specific story to be enacted. Children might establish the frame by announcing it ("This is the house."), by announcing a play role ("I'm the policeman."), or simply by acting on objects such as putting the train track together and running the train on it. Sometimes a smile and a gesture are sufficient between familiar players revisiting a common action sequence.

Recognition of play frames is important to educators because, although pretend play has its own internal logic with a unique imaginative quality, the players' behavior must be understood from this perspective. However, usually, the "reality" described in the pretend play reflects the level of understanding shared by the children. For example, if children are pretending to be firefighters and they assign one of the players to set fires, they lack information about the causes of fires and the true functions of firefighters. Play breaks down if there is not common agreement among the players, so the development of the play frame is a key tool for social interaction. In addition, the play frame communicates that the scenario is not a reality to all of the players.

Elements of Pretend Play

Pretend play is composed of a set of skills or elements that may be used singly (by less-skilled players) or in combination (by players with greater skill). All players must be able to participate in **make-believe**; that is, they must be able to suspend reality, even momentarily, to engage in the simplest form of pretend play. When the needed object is not at hand, children engage in **object substitution**. This is straightforward representational thinking in which the child represents one object with another closer at hand. Primary-age youngsters may not need an object for the substitution. Instead, they use **object invention** and represent the needed objects solely through pantomime. All children have difficulty, when they are playing in groups, with more than one imaginary person or object. They appear to need something as a placeholder so that they can engage in sharing imaginary objects. Frequently, when several players are involved, iconic representations of objects are used as placeholders to avoid the confusion. Children "take on roles" of others, which may be based on TV or movie characters (Bolt), functional roles (someone who uses a computer), familial or relational roles (husband–father, wife–mother), or occupational roles (nurse, firefighter). Family roles predominate during the preschool period, with presentations of primary caregivers portrayed with emotional meanings as youngsters begin to understand that other people think and feel, and become elaborate over time. Occupational roles emerge slowly in older preschool children and are heavily influenced by children's experiences and their school curriculum. School-age children elaborate on earlier roles and include frightening fantasies and themes of victim and

These girls have transformed the shaving cream into fluffy clouds on their hands and on the paper!

aggressor. Fictional roles—those developed for television, the movies, or literature—generate high-action, powerful characters. Sometimes these portrayals lack the personal creativity that the children are otherwise capable of demonstrating. Children's **transformations** of time, place, and setting enable them to pretend to be pioneers or space adventurers. The beach, stores, the circus, or the market might be a place "visited" in the classroom play space. Time and place are limited only by the information available to the players. The definitions and variations by age of the elements of pretend play are displayed in Figure 15.1.

Go to the Video Examples section of Topic 4: Play in the MyEducation-Lab for your course and watch the video entitled *The Restaurant*. Note how the leadership in this pretend play sequence changes within just a few minutes. What strategies do the children use to organize their play?

Communications That Enable Play to Work.   When children play make-believe together, they must engage in complex communications called **metacommunication**, which means a communication about a communication (Bateson, 1971). Metacommunications allow children to coordinate their activity knowledgeably and develop complex play scenarios where each player understands what the roles are and how the story is enacted. Metacommunications have the following functions:

- ❑ Describe what is "play" and what is not
- ❑ Construct the play frame ("Let's pretend to be hunters.")
- ❑ Define roles ("We can be neighbors who don't like each other.")
- ❑ Transform objects and settings ("This [puppet stage] is the post office window.")
- ❑ Begin the narrative ("I'm in a dark forest and lost.")
- ❑ Extend play and elaborate on characters' feelings or actions ("This is a very dark forest, and I hope there are no monsters here." or "Pretend that you are a really mean bad guy.")
- ❑ End the framed sequence by denying the role ("I'm not the bad guy anymore.")
- ❑ Change the meaning of the props ("This window [puppet theater] is really a window out of a spaceship.")
- ❑ Redefine the setting ("Why don't we pretend we were rescued and put in the hospital?")

Applications of Pretend Play

The following list of pretend-play applications is not intended to be definitive. The quality and complexity of the play and the setting are important variables, as is the number of players.

Make-Believe.   Simple pretend is when a child takes on the characteristics of an object or a person and acts out a sequence. For example, 3-year-olds might pretend to be balloons that are being blown up by another child. Five-year-olds might walk down the hallway connected to one another to form a train and say, "Chug-chug-chug" as they move. Eight-year-olds might pretend to be an airplane or a cloud moving over the mountains. Such episodes may be encouraged deliberately by the teacher or developed spontaneously by the children.

Pretend with Objects.   Exploration of an object or any new material always precedes well-developed play sequences, regardless of the children's age, skills, or familiarity with the material. In exploration, a child asks, "What is the nature of this object?" whereas in pretend the child wonders, "What can I do with this?" Unskilled players may vacillate between pretend play and exploration while learning how to pretend with an object. For example, Rico, age 4 years, picked up a stethoscope and correctly identified it as a "doctor thing." He swung it around, talked into it, hung it on his neck, and used it to hit at Maria. Mark told him to put the earplugs in his ears and listen to his heart. Rico tried this. He listened to tables, a window, and a radiator before attempting to listen to another child. Then he engaged in a brief "doctor" episode while listening to a doll's chest. Alternating between listening to dolls, children, and other objects in the environment, Rico's play vacillated between pretending with an object and exploration. Older children may also pretend by themselves and focus on the object they are using. Children who have few playmates may be very skilled in developing a variety of pretend scenarios based on a single object. During several play episodes, Allison used an old-fashioned washbasin variably for a doll bath, a helmet, and a cooking pot. Even in the most traditional classrooms, teachers are familiar with children's tendency to use anything for play: bits of paper, pencils, articles of clothing, science equipment, and so forth.

FIGURE 15.1 Elements of Pretend Play

Element	Definition	Younger Children	Older Children	Examples
Make-believe or pretend with an object	Suspension of reality, imaginary situation or objects.	Short episodes where children incorporate imaginative behavior into any activity.	May be elaborate scenarios with multiple players.	Making the sounds of an engine while moving a car. Enacting a complete sequence of caregiving with a doll, including eating, sleeping, dressing, and visiting.
Object substitution	Replacing an object that is needed for a pretend sequence with a different object.	One object substitution during play. The object must in some way be similar to the object desired	Multiple objects substituted; may substitute objects with more than one player.	Child uses a shell for a horse trough. Child uses the palm of hand for paper and a finger for a pencil to take an order and serves small blocks as food.
Object invention	Objects that are needed for pretend play are represented through pantomime.	Youngest children seem to need a placeholder and find this difficult to do. Objects invented often have other objects in association so that it is clear what is invented.	Older children may invent several objects when playing alone, rarely more than one or two when playing with others.	Child lies down on the floor (where there is no bed) and puts a doll blanket over herself. Child opens a cupboard door (that does not exist) removes a bowl (that is not there), places it on a real table and begins to stir with an imaginary spoon.
Taking on a role	Children enact roles of others based on family roles (baby, mother, etc.), occupational roles (nurse, firefighter, construction worker), functional roles (someone who eats) or character roles (Papa Bear of the three bears or a superhero from television).	Functional and family roles appear first. Children must have opportunities to learn the roles prior to trying them out.	Children are more likely to engage in occupational roles and character roles though family roles remain strong favorites.	Child pretends to be a father, going to work, helping with the baby, eating, and doing chores. Child pretends to be a doctor, putting on bandages or giving shots.
Transforming time, place, and setting	Children may pretend to live in the present, the past, or the future. Usually, they pretend adult roles. They can be in a forest, a city, or in space. Usually, the time and place are defined by narratives of the children, and all players must act as though they were indeed in that place.	Younger children may pretend to be in a grocery store or other familiar location. Usually take on "adult" time framework but may choose to be a "baby."	Older children may select settings related to instruction, such as spaceships, banks, airplanes, or post offices. Children must have information about the setting to play it.	Child takes the doll in a grocery cart and selects cartons from the shelves, then pays to leave area. Child or group of children build a spaceship, pretend to take off, and have adventures in faraway places.

Pretend with Art Materials. Some 3- to 5-year-olds are primarily concerned about the pattern, color, or form of their visual art experiences, whereas others typically have a story that the graphic portion represents. Children may orally express the pretend story component as the child produces the graphic: "And the scary spider dropped down . . . to the ground. And he moved around. He went up and the wind blew him. Almost hit the boy." Thus, they use the "movements of play, the lines of drawing, and the sounds of language to represent the people, objects, and events that comprise their world" (Dyson, 1990, p. 50). Children may even share a pretend-play sequence, talking and drawing at the same time. Five- and 6-year-olds draw, pretend, and converse while labeling real or imaginary events or objects as they stimulate one another (Coates, 2002).

myeducationlab

Go to the Assignments and Activities section of Topic 4: Play in the MyEducationLab for your course and complete the activity entitled *Building with Blocks*. Observe how the children use construction objects and pretend in an integrated way. Notice which children engage and disengage.

Pretend with Construction Materials. Probably the most complex of all play episodes are those in which children construct the necessary play props to support their pretend theme or action sequence. In this case, the play shifts back and forth from construction to pretend play. With younger children, this shifting is seen most frequently during block play, in which a child might build a house or a barn and then use cars and small dolls to enact a scene. Older children may continue the same play action sequence for several days, building additional components as they go. In one Indiana kindergarten, children reconstructed their small town during several weeks by using clay, small cardboard boxes, and other discarded materials. Throughout the elementary school period, children build snow forts, tree houses, stores, and homes in which to engage in increasingly elaborate pretend-play sequences.

Pretend with Miniature Buildings and People. Dollhouses, barns and animals, vehicles with passengers, and other miniature pretend settings stimulate pretend play. Children imagine the story and manipulate the figures. Unlike basic dramatic play, children cannot use facial expression or body action to convey ideas and feelings. They become the narrator; although they might portray many parts, they are not actors with their own bodies. Children aged 5 to 8 years usually have the capacity to use their voices to portray a variety of emotions and characters. Younger children are likely to find some way to include larger movements, such as transporting farm animals in a truck.

Dramatic Play. During dramatic play, the child carries out a sequence of events or actions that are related to one another. It is make-believe with a story line developed by the players. The play may be solitary or in the company of other children but not necessarily interacting with them except through observation or shared space. Six- and 7-year-olds can pick up the play theme from day to day and continue, whereas 3- to 5-year-olds are more likely to start over. Such differences in skill and maturity influence the selection of the play topic and the duration and complexity of the play enactment.

Sociodramatic Play. Several children who are playing together for at least 10 minutes and sharing the same narrative sequence are involved in **sociodramatic play**. The story is negotiated and the roles are established. The play is usually pretend, with time, setting, and place agreed on by the players as the play progresses and may be completely embedded in the script. "Gee, it's getting dark now" automatically calls for an evening sequence of actions by other players. A second child might respond, "Where will we sleep?" which draws the play into a housing or furnishing problem. All the players share the story line, with individual children both following others' leads and contributing new ideas. Children frequently prompt one another when factual errors are made in the play, such as one child's whispering loudly, "The store man collects the money for the stuff. Doesn't pay someone to take it."

Theme-Related Play. A variation of dramatic and sociodramatic play, theme-related play is goal directed and may center on a number of occupational themes: beauty shop, school, camping, hospital, restaurant, or fire station. When children are engaged in thematic instruction, some aspect of the theme is available for pretend play. Children may initiate it or adults may instigate the play by providing the props, time, space, and information necessary. Sometimes even the action is suggested by supervising adults. However, once initiated, children should take it over or develop it themselves. Children who rarely participate in house play may readily engage in occupational or adventure roles that are more typical of theme-related play.

The detail and accuracy of portrayals increase with practice and maturity. In addition, children add problems that must be solved within the play. These problems are frequently reasonable for the setting, such as having a fire drill while playing school, running out of permanent solution in a beauty shop, or having a fire in a garage. Primary-age children may successfully incorporate themes from television, video stories, or literature within their play. Preschool children's most complex sociodramatic scenarios are based on settings with which they are the most familiar (e.g., home setting, including babies, families, and neighbors), although they sometimes also attempt fantasy characters.

Story Reenactment. Variously called *creative dramatics, thematic play, fantasy play,* or *story reenactment,* story reenactment involves children's developing the skills of taking on a role and recreating a plot they have heard in a myth, legend, poem, or story. Through story reenactment, children can assume a variety of roles they otherwise would have no way of experiencing, such as a princess or a space traveler. The scope of mood, setting, and plot structures in literature far exceeds what a small group of children can imagine without additional sources. Older children may read–play–read again as they engage in the story enactment. Discussions about character and other elements of literature are possible and comprehensible as children dramatize a written or traditional story.

Write and Play, or Writer's Theater. In writer's theater, children dictate or write a story and then enact it. Unlike reader's theater, children create and write the story. Sometimes the story arises from a pretend-play episode, story dictation, or a story that a child has written. This form of pretend play builds on the skills of 6- and 7-year-olds to develop pretend-play story plots and characterization. The additional transformation to word stories connects this form of play to learning in the language domain. Children also face the dilemma of written dialogue and begin to use grammar rules they otherwise would never attempt.

Fundamentally, children's story writing and their pretend play are blended so that the strength of one can foster the other. For example, a simple story written by a 6-year-old was only two sentences: "My baby brother got in my room. He made a mess." Several first graders were asked to think about this basic plot and to pretend play it. The author was in the group and watched as various children played the roles of baby, older brother, and parents. Children tried more than one pretend sequence and explored several solutions to the problem as they acted out their roles. The author had the choice of incorporating some details, problems, and solutions into the story or leaving it alone. The advantage of this play form is that the connection between the familiar play and the new tasks of writing are clear, meaningful, and obvious. Table 15.1 lists applications of pretend play.

Pretend play is the symbolic representation of ideas through the enactive mode. Children portray their ideas about events by what they do and say and use props to support their scenarios. They also use the iconic mode when they symbolically represent their ideas through what they make. Objects that children construct represent processes, events, or other objects. By constructing a concrete representation, they gain greater understanding of their experiences. Construction play, although similar to pretend play in that it represents children's interpretation of the world around them, has distinctive characteristics. Both pretend play and construction play include symbolic modes of representation.

CONSTRUCTION PLAY

Four-year-old Kate spent several minutes studying a spiderweb in the fence of the play yard. When she returned to the classroom, she used Wikki Stix, which are flexible colored-wax strips that stick to many surfaces, to reconstruct the spiderweb in three-dimensional form. Then she drew the spiderweb on paper with crayons and announced, "I can make a spiderweb, too!" She was completely engrossed in her activity.

Aida was playing store with other kindergarten children. She seemed dissatisfied with simply pretending to offer money to the clerk and said, "I gotta get some real money to buy this stuff." Looking around the room, Aida walked to the paper supply shelf, selected a few sheets of

TABLE 15.1   Activity Ideas to Support Pretend Play

Type of Pretend Play	Sample Activities
Make-believe	Imagine what the clouds might be
	Pretend to be animals, automobiles, or simple machines
	Portray how a character in a story feels
Pretend with objects	Use props to support child-initiated activity
	Imagine an object if no placeholder is at hand
Pretend with art materials	Create stories as part of the drawing experience
	Illustrate told or written stories
	Listen to "pictorial" music selections while painting
Pretend with construction materials	Build or make a prop for pretend play
	Use blocks to build a setting for a pretend episode
	Use leaves, sticks, and other natural materials to build boats or houses
Pretend with miniatures	Use models or replicas in enactments
	Engage in dollhouse play
	Use toy farm animals or miniature people with blocks
Dramatic, sociodramatic, and thematic play	Enact occupational roles related to class themes
	Enact house, neighbors, and school play
Story reenactment	Perform a simple ballad with a clear story line
	Select and act out a traditional folk tale or folk song
	Dramatize a more modern story such as *Ask Mr. Bear* or *Caps for Sale*
Write and play	Pretend they are the characters in a story that a classmate has written
	Write a story based on their own sociodramatic play

green paper, carefully tore it into rectangles, wrote numerals on each piece, and returned to complete her purchases in the pretend store.

Mark, who had been participating in a unit on trees in his third-grade classroom, spent several days accumulating leaves from the trees in his neighborhood on his own. Each leaf was mounted on a sheet of paper and labeled with its name. He carefully drew several trees with some details of the surrounding environment and labeled them "Tree in front," "Mr. McDirmid's tree," and "On the corner." Then he arranged them into a book of leaves in his neighborhood.

These children have demonstrated their ability to bring together a variety of skills and concepts to represent objects, events, or groups of objects that are meaningful to them in a concrete, physical way. For example, Kate demonstrated memory skills, imagination, perseverance, planning, and fine-motor skills. She used her knowledge of materials; whole–part relations; and concepts of line, direction, and space in addition to her obvious understandings of the spiderweb. Her emotional satisfaction was expressed in her comment. Aida, who could not pretend play comfortably without a placeholder for the symbolic money she needed, used her knowledge about money and good problem-solving skills to make "money." Mark, who is much older, represented a group of trees, their location and environment, and their relationship to people and places familiar to him. He incorporated information that he had learned at school and used the skills of observing, recording, and communicating his experience.

Construction play is the transformation of an experience or object into a concrete representation of this experience or object. Children use materials to make a product. Often these are symbolic products, such as drawings, paintings, and three-dimensional creations, that represent objects (e.g., house), ideas (e.g., friendship), or processes (e.g., war). Constructive and symbolic play can also be combined to create a poem, a dramatic production, a tape recording, or other visual or technological products (Bergen, 1988a, p. 247).

TABLE 15.2 Applications of Construction Play

Type of Construction Play	Sample Activities
Projects stemming from natural encounters	Use tissue paper, adhesives, egg cartons, scissors, and so forth to make worms, flowers, or bugs
	Build houses from hollow blocks
	Construct a village using unit blocks and miniatures
Projects stemming from mutual interests of teacher and children	Make something of interest using found materials
	Draw something seen on a field trip and use it to report about the activity
	Make a diorama related to a thematic unit
Projects stemming from teacher concerns	Transportation unit: Build paper airplanes, boats from assorted materials, or cars using wood, saws, and nails
	Energy unit: Build a circuit board with batteries, bells, lights, and so on; make a magnet using a nail and another magnet
	Holiday unit: Create a collage depicting the many ways people celebrate
	Nutrition unit: Make and paint papier-mâché "food" to be used in pretend play

When a child constructs an object in many different ways such as in a report, in a drawing, with cardboard, or as a clay or wood model, the child must take into account previous representations as new ones are created. Each rendition takes a perspective that when passed on to the next medium generates conflict, challenge, and change (Forman, 1996). Such multiple perspectives can be considered variations on the same system.

Most physical products are accompanied by children's commentaries. These comments complete the representation. For example, a child might name a particular block a "car," although it does not differ greatly from the block next to it. When children build machines, an adult may be able to identify them by the associated sound effects. Thus, auditory information may supplement the physical to represent the child's idea more adequately. Among the patterns of developmentally appropriate curriculum, perhaps construction play is the easiest for experienced traditional teachers to understand and emulate. To many educators, it appears to be related to both play and work, and the outcomes are observable and understandable (Chaillé & Silvern, 1996).

Types of Construction Projects

Three broadly defined types of construction projects are "1) those resulting from a child's natural encounter with the environment, 2) those reflecting mutual interests on the part of the teacher and children, and 3) those based on teacher concerns regarding specific cognitive and/or social concepts" (New, 1990, p. 7). In all three types, the products emerge from an intense interest, an acute investigation, or a hands-on exploration of an object or event that appeals to the children. Specific examples of each are presented in Table 15.2. Constructions are children's attempts to solidify their ideas or to communicate ideas to others through imagery.

Projects Stemming from Natural Encounters. All young children are in the process of trying to understand their world. It can be as simple as encouraging children to come and explore potter's clay often enough so that they begin to impress their ideas on the material (Rogers & Steffan, 2009). Often an ordinary object or some aspect of nature will capture a young child's interest. Drawings of people, houses, and animals are typical, as are modeling dough constructions of cakes, cookies, snakes, and bowls. Some constructions may be extremely simple, as when Sasha, age 3 years, watched raindrops flow down the pane and then painted the irregular vertical lines at the easel. At other times, children's constructions are more elaborate. For example, when three children noticed the movement and seemingly purposeful activity of ants on the playground, their teacher suggested that they make something to help them remember what they saw. Other children joined the discussion about the ants' behavior and were encouraged by their teacher to elaborate on their comments by making something with clay or illustrating their understanding of the ants by using paper and chalk. This group of children continued to observe the ants and document what they saw.

Projects Stemming from Mutual Interests of Teacher and Children.   Teachers often stimulate a construction experience based on common events in children's lives. For example, many young children are concerned about having a friend. Discussions of friendship enhanced with constructions of modeling dough or collages of magazine pictures representing children's ideas about friendship further mutual communication and understanding. Sometimes current events discussed at home or on television may stimulate both children and adults to read, discuss, and construct images related to the topic. For example, 4-year-old Emma filled a large paper with black, brown, yellow, and red tempera paint and then clawed strips out of it with her fingernails from top to bottom, commenting, "It's the New York fire" (Gross & Clemens, 2002). Teachers listen and respond to children's ideas and concerns. Teachers also provide accurate information, ignite the children's creative thinking and questions, and support further examination of ideas. Often children's constructions provide clues that suggest children have misinformation and misconceptions, to which the teacher then responds. For example, Issac drew a tree with a humanlike figure under it with arms extended upward. When Miss Gable asked him to tell her about his drawing, he explained that the man was holding the tree so it would not fall over because the top was larger than the bottom. This led to a series of activities where children examined roots of plants.

Projects Stemming from Teacher Concerns Regarding Specific Concepts.   Another type of construction focuses on ideas or concepts initially unfamiliar to children but perceived by adults as valuable for children to explore. Such construction activities are embedded in a theme or unit in which children learn about other aspects of the social and natural world by using various strategies described in previous chapters. For instance, children living in forested areas of the United States are exposed to ideas related to oceans and deserts. Children living in a homogeneous community may explore ideas about people of various ethnic and racial backgrounds. Children may generate construction activities that emerge from topics in science, social studies, mathematics, health, literature, or music. Children listen or read, discuss, and then construct a representation of their understanding. Both the children and the teacher have opportunities to share insights into others' thinking as the projects are examined and classmates communicate their interpretations (Gandini & Edwards, 1988). Constructions of this type are more typically products of the primary child, although some 4- and 5-year-olds may attempt them.

Comparison of Construction and Other Related Activities

Object exploration, practice in fine-motor skills, and craft projects are related to children's construction activities but are not the same. Each of these three activities involves knowledge or skills children use when constructing, but they do not require the level of representational thought and creativity associated with construction.

Construction Is Not Simply Object Play.   Object play is exploration and investigation. A child attempts to discover the properties of an object or to answer the questions "What is this object like?" and "How does it work?" The novelty of the object attracts the child's attention, and its complexity sustains interest. Repetitive actions, systematic examination, and attempts to use the object in a variety of ways are typical of object play. Thus, object play with materials usually occurs before construction becomes possible.

When children stop investigating the nature of objects and begin using them to build something, they shift into construction. The contrast between object play and construction can be seen in the behaviors of two 3-year-olds. Jerry John arranged several blocks in front of him and engaged in snapping them together in various combinations. He seemed most interested in determining whether any combination could be snapped and unsnapped readily and answering the question "How does this work?" In contrast, Alexi selected only the units that could be fastened in a linear pattern and commented, "See my snake."

Three- and 4-year-old children may spend substantial time exploring a material, creating a combination that reminds them of a familiar object, and naming it, as Billy did in one of his rearrangements of the blocks: "Look here, I got this house." Sometimes youngsters are aware of this, as Dimitri was when he told an inquiring adult, "I'll know what this painting is when I've finished it." Regardless of age, all children move between object play and construction when they encounter new media or materials or those that they have not used in a long time. However, in general, as children mature, they spend less time exploring and more time using the materials to construct.

Construction Is Not Simply Fine-Motor Practice. The imitation of hand skills such as holding a writing implement, cutting with scissors, sewing, weaving, and using various tools develops fine-motor skill. Something may be produced, but it is a by-product of the process and not intended to represent a child's idea or concept. Instead, it is the natural outcome of the process, such as fringe produced while snipping paper or a cutout of a pattern given to the child to practice cutting. Occasionally, preschoolers will name their by-products if they resemble a familiar object, such as labeling a spiral-cut paper "snake" when they pull the ends apart. Primary-age children may have the basic skills and refine them during the construction process as the need arises. Clearly, children must control the materials and tools used for construction and apply their knowledge to tasks skillfully.

Construction requires that the child have an image in mind that he or she then represents by using familiar processes. For example, Rebecca carefully cut along the lines of a pattern drawn for her. She focused her entire attention on the process of producing a smooth curve and turning corners neatly. In contrast, Marietta left a group of children looking at the visiting cat, walked to the center where materials were stored, and created a cat face by cutting into a paper plate to form eyes and ears and adding whiskers with a marker. Rebecca and Marietta both produced products, but only Marietta had a specific idea in mind when she engaged in the activity. The child's imagination is central to the reasoning process, and no activity is undertaken without some image of the result, whether his or her conception is accurate or not (Smith, 1990). As with object play, the skills with which to control the processes of construction are necessary but insufficient.

Construction Is Not Simply the Demonstration of Technique. Children must also learn techniques. For example, a child who wants to adhere two pieces of paper must learn where to put the paste. Children also learn which adhesive (e.g., white liquid glue, school paste, rubber cement, or a mixture of white glue and paste) will adhere pieces of wood or cardboard. Skill in the use of tools and techniques generally precedes construction activities or is learned in the context of a construction project as the need arises. As children shift from one medium to another, the demands for technical knowledge and skills increase.

Construction Is Not Simply Following Directions for a Project. In her kindergarten class, Diedra listened carefully as the teacher gave directions and demonstrated how to make a rabbit. Each piece had been reproduced on paper, and the rabbit would have movable legs. She cut, colored, and assembled the rabbit as directed, even though it did not quite look the same as her teacher's. Diedra used her language, memory, and motor skills to perform this task. In the kindergarten at another school, Fredrico had listened to the story of Peter Rabbit and studied several photographs of real rabbits. He constructed a rabbit from materials that he selected from the supply shelves. Fredrico also used language, memory, and motor skills to produce a rabbit. In addition, he made decisions about materials and used imagination and representational thinking to form his image of the rabbit. Both children created products, but only Fredrico was involved in the representational thought necessary for construction. However, Diedra might have produced a rabbit more appealing to adults by copying her teacher's image rather than creating her own.

Knowledge of necessary processes or step-by-step operations necessary to achieve a specific end is useful to the construction process but not a substitute for it. Does the child-drawn image of the human figure with a very large mouth and exaggerated hands mean that the child is unable to perceive the difference in length between fingers, arms, and legs? No, but adults sometimes mistakenly behave as though children are functioning without sufficient information. The copyist theory of knowledge is that if children only followed the directions with care, then the product, and incidentally the idea, would be replicated. Children during the early childhood period develop their abilities to perceive with accuracy, follow directions, imitate, and copy processes thereby acquiring the techniques that provide them with the skills for carrying out their construction projects.

For example, two 5-year-olds recreated their experiences with vehicles in the snow, using different media. One child drew a rectangle with circles on the side with a red crayon on blue paper and neatly glued cotton balls around it. The second child used two paintbrushes held side by side and made parallel wavy lines across white paper to illustrate car tracks in the snow. Both youngsters demonstrated their abilities to use materials and fashion a concrete representation of an idea. Both used appropriate techniques for the medium selected and worked with care and deliberation. Imitation of the technique might be important, but once the technique is mastered, children construct the product according to their own ideas and interpretation. Children increase in confidence as their sense of competence evolves as a result of successfully constructing.

A second-grade teacher who had provided models and detailed directions for products in the past commented about a marked change in children's behavior when she altered her approach. "I have been really surprised," she said. "The children used to be concerned that their pictures looked 'just like their friends' pictures'; now they are trying to be unique in what they do."

Arts and crafts are favorites of young children and their teachers. When children make holiday ornaments from printed fabric and canning lids, decorate orange juice cans with macaroni and paint, or weave potholders, they are participating in activities that have become traditional in some communities. These activities are legitimate exercises in fine-motor control and may be useful in promoting perceptual development or listening skills. They have a place in the curriculum but do not substitute for genuine opportunities for children to construct something on their own. They have independent value but do not require the transformation of an idea into a product.

Construction and Materials of Choice

Construction opportunities are facilitated when children have access to a large array of materials. For example, one 4-year-old wanted a "cape." He examined butcher paper that was stiff but could be wrapped around and taped. He tried some lightweight tissue paper. Then he discovered some yarn and a piece of fabric. The texture of the fabric made this his best choice for the purpose. Only the materials were necessary to provide for this problem solving.

Various Blocks. Blocks abound in sizes, colors, and textures. Some fasten together and have pieces designed for wheels and axles. Others, such as unit blocks, are cut in regular, predictable intervals. Some sets have a color for each shape and provide a variety of angles in wedge-shaped pieces. Large, hollow blocks may be used to build structures that children may enter.

Commercial Construction Sets. Numerous commercial construction sets have sections that children can fasten together with nuts and bolts or pieces that fit together when laid in place. These sets often have extender sets that include more complicated pieces and may even come with electric motors so that children can make more complex machines that run. Products that have many pieces and can be assembled in different ways provide for more diversity than those with fewer pieces or that are limited to a predetermined outcome. Older children frequently want their constructions "to work."

Carpentry Supplies and Tools. Woodworking benches with real hammers, nails, saws, drills, screws, screwdrivers, safety goggles, and other tools to enable a child to construct with real wood are an alternative in many programs for young children. Good-quality tools may be costly, but they have the potential for lasting a long time (Huber, 1999). Most toy tools do not work. Soft woods are easier for children to use than hard woods. They are also less expensive and can be obtained as discards from local businesses.

Art Materials, Paper, and Common Discards. A multitude of papers that differ in color, texture, and size are available for purchase and as discards from businesses or families, such as old wrapping paper, commercial sacks, forms, and packing materials. The numbers and colors of available paint and writing implements are considerable as well. In addition, a variety of three-dimensional materials such as egg cartons, packing material, meat trays, and other throwaway objects with interesting patterns, colors, or textures can be obtained for children to use in their symbolic representations.

Open-Ended Materials. Flexible materials such as sand, clay, and play-doh can be used to represent a variety of ideas. Once children understand the properties of the materials, they can create a wide array of representations with the appropriate tools. The advantage of these materials is that they are three dimensional, with an undetermined shape in the beginning. With sand, children can try out their ideas and erase them without fear of making mistakes. Children can have better control over such media at younger ages.

Natural Materials. Children have long used stones, mud, sticks, leaves, and other plant materials to create little worlds in which pretend people carry out their lives. Snow is another excellent building material. These natural resources may be used outdoors or brought into the classroom as the occasion demands.

Materials Assembled with Specific Teacher Goals in Mind. Older children can create board games from file folders, poster board, or shirt boxes with assorted stickers, markers, and pieces to move (Castle, 1991). The child is required not only to construct a product but also to establish the rules of the game. The problems they encounter, such as how to have moving pieces that can be distinguished from one another or how to make the game challenging and fun, engage their creative interest and require access to an array of materials.

Independence of Materials from the Ideas They Represent

At times, children use the same materials to represent a variety of ideas. Paint and play-doh are particularly versatile. In one small group, children used play-doh to make nests and eggs, dishes, cups with handles, a ring, a long snake, and a cake. The diversity of ideas that individual children expressed expanded the entire group's vision. Children see more and more possibilities as they practice with the materials and tools. In another group, children used paint to represent abstract ideas such as *friends, conflicts,* or *feelings* in more concrete terms. Nevertheless, paint is also used to represent some of the first identifiable drawings of people, vehicles, and houses (Kellogg, 1969). Whether children depict their ideas in realistic or abstract constructions, they tend to become more versatile when they are thoroughly familiar with the material and are in control of the process. Yet, to some extent each material also limits the content of expression and the approach used (Forman, 1996). For example, representing the ocean would be easier using paints and paper or a paper collage than using blocks.

Children often depict the same idea by using a variety of materials. Children must use their problem-solving skills when they have a choice of materials for representing the same general idea. Different materials give different results, so the character, mood, or level of detail may vary from one depiction to another. Children must also solve a variety of problems relating to technique when materials are varied. Developing the theme of "houses," the same child made houses from sticks, straw, and string; sugar cubes; blocks; crayons and paper; paints; and small boxes. The child experienced the gravest technical difficulties when he tried to use the straw and finally tied it at the top and stuck a finger in to make an interior. Children tried various adhesives, and the sizes of the houses differed considerably. The block house had an interior and an exterior. When given crayons, the child drew only the face of the house. These activities, extended across several days, involved much peer cooperation and prosocial behavior. Children also compared their work on the same idea from one medium to the next.

As children increase in their ability to represent objects and events, they can also better select the appropriate material with which to achieve their desired end. With practice, they become more confident, skillful, and often more creative.

Individual Differences in Children's Pretend and Construction Play

Preferred level of social involvement, maturity, family life experiences, style preferences, classroom context, practice, cultural background, and play quality all influence the content of pretend and construction play as well as the players' performance (Mellou, 1994).

The "house" built by these 3-year-olds is a typical Stage 2 block construction.

Social Involvement. Children engage each other at differing levels during play (Parten, 1932; Kostelnik, Whiren, Soderman, & Gregory, 2009). They learn how to do this gradually over time but eventually make choices as to the level of participation in the following order:

❏ *Onlooker* The child watches others play with focused attention.

❏ *Solitary Play* The child plays with toys or materials without interacting with others. This child uses problem-solving abilities and intelligence to play alone (Bornstein, 2007).

❏ *Parallel Play* The child plays independently near other children doing the same activity such as putting puzzles together at the same table. There may be shared visual regard, but they are not coordinating their actions.

TABLE 15.3   Developmental Stages of Block Play

Stage	Description
1. Object exploration	*Carrying blocks*—Children move blocks around and discover properties of the material.
2. Learning techniques	*Piling and laying blocks on the floor*—Children arrange both horizontal and vertical sets of blocks. Sometimes completed arrangements suggest a use, such as a "road."
3. Construction	*Connecting blocks to create structures*—Children make enclosures, build bridges, and design decorative patterns and layouts.
4. Advanced construction	*Making elaborate constructions*—Children create complex buildings, often with many parts, using curved and straight lines, around or over obstacles. This stage is frequently associated with pretend play.

❏ *Associative Play* A child plays with other children and interacts with them intermittently around similar materials. For example, Janet may deliver blocks to Theodora and Penny occasionally but is mostly engaged in filling and emptying her truck with blocks while they are building an enclosure.

❏ *Cooperative or Organized Supplementary Play* The child engages in sharing a goal with others during play as well as materials. There is discussion and mutual cooperation in making the object or in enacting a pretend sequence with more than one player. Theodora and Penny are engaged with building a structure together in this way.

Maturity. Three-year-olds do not possess the vocabulary, life experience, or level of abstract thinking that older children demonstrate. Their play is usually solitary, beside another player who is playing similarly, or in short episodes of cooperative play. Frequently, they cannot express the metacommunication messages necessary for more elaborate pretend play.

A few children will begin true construction with regular materials as early as age 3 years. If the structure is not named, the adult may have difficulty discerning whether the child is involved in object play or simple construction. As children mature, their structures become more complex (Gregory, Kim, & Whiren, 2003). Details of interest become elaborated and are often the subject of conversation among children. In addition, the child's intent is much clearer, being either announced in advance or obvious from the context of the ongoing play. Four- and 5-year-olds regularly engage in pretend play during the construction process. Six- and 7-year-olds may discuss in detail what they plan to construct and even determine the relation among the structures before they begin. At any point in time, children produce constructions that are more recognizable (drawing of a person) or abstract (whirling leaves in the wind). They may do so independently or as part of a larger, more complex play frame. The developmental stages of block play are presented in Table 15.3, because blocks are a familiar and typical construction material. A more elaborate and complete description of block play can be found in *The Block Book* (Hirsch, 1996) and in *A Constructivist Approach to Block Play in Early Childhood* (Wellhousen & Kieff, 2001).

Family Life Experience. The general life experience of 3- to 8-year-olds varies considerably. Children from rural areas know more about farming than urban children do and can pretend appropriate roles much earlier than their city counterparts of similar maturity. Some children have experienced police raids in their neighborhoods and have a working knowledge of street gangs by the time they are 5 years old, whereas other children of similar ages are completely ignorant of such occurrences. Ordinary factors

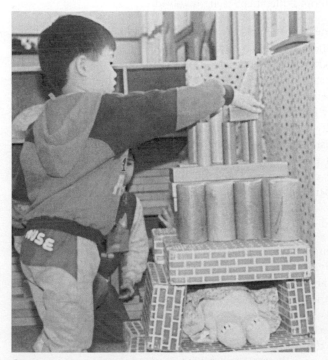

Stage 3 constructions such as this "skyscraper" are common in kindergarten.

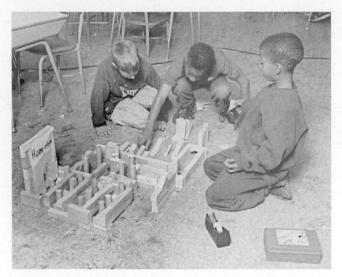

These second graders have constructed an elaborate Stage 4 movie theater, complete with screen, seating, concession stand, and parking.

such as family composition, presence of pets, modes of typical transportation, and occupations of adults in the home provide some children with information that others do not have. Children tend to play out the scenes and scenarios with which they are most familiar. In addition, the child's language and the caregiver's support of symbolic play positively influence children's cooperative play (Bornstein, Haynes, O'Reilly, & Painter, 1996).

Cultural Differences. Many classrooms are composed of children from various cultural backgrounds. The roles of mother and father differ from one family to another. This is true of the individual family culture as well as of nationality, such as Arabic, Japanese, or Spanish. Thematic content, communicative strategies used to structure and maintain play, and the choice of play types are influenced by family culture, which should be respected (Kuschner, 2007; Farver & Shinn, 1997). Players often need help in negotiating their play. Younger children do not usually realize that different people may come to the play with perspectives vastly dissimilar from theirs.

Practice or Skill Differences. Children who do not have access to a wide variety of materials will not be as skillful as those who do, regardless of age. For example, although many 3-year-olds can cut simple straight lines, 5-year-olds who have just acquired access to scissors may still be discovering how they work. High-quality construction play depends on the skillful use of the tools and materials used in the process. Construction with blocks requires skillful placement and organization; with graphic materials, construction requires control of implements.

Because pretend play begins very early, children often exhibit differences in learned skills. Smilansky (1968) was the first researcher to note that skill development in the elements of pretend play was limited or absent in lower socioeconomic groups. This finding was modified to indicate that the deficiency was a function of opportunity, not inability. Some kindergarteners may not possess the rudimentary pretend skills that other children exhibit at age 3 years. However, children can and do learn the elements of pretend play with appropriate adult instruction and support in educational settings especially when more skilled players are involved.

Classroom Context. The context of the classroom also accounts for individual differences among children in play performance. First, the materials, the equipment, and the organization of classroom space influence whether or not children play and the number of players engaged at one time (Wellhousen & Kieff, 2001). Even the subtle differences in play with hollow and unit blocks affect play content and social structure. Theme-related play is unlikely to occur without the necessary theme-related objects and sources of information (Fayden, 1997). The presence of peers with whom to play and the level of creativity and flexibility other players bring to the pretend-play situation often influence not only the existence of play, but also its quality (Monighan-Nourot, 1998). The presence of one or two "master players" capable of sustaining the play by adjusting play scripts, imaginative problem solving, compromising, negotiating, and suggesting play elaborations influences the other children's performance. An integrated classroom of 6- and 7-year-olds who have been in a mixed-age group for at least a year will play more skillfully together than an age-graded group that has just formed.

Play Style. Some youngsters focus on form, line, color, design, and the general aesthetics of the construction. A 5-year-old with this style builds more elaborate block structures, with turrets, corners, and arches, using lots of blocks and space. These *patterners* may show interest in maintaining structures for several days. In contrast, *dramatists* tend to focus on the narrative of the pretend play and might use only a few blocks as long as they represent the idea they have in mind. For a dramatist, the form is much less important than the function. As soon as the pretend sequence is complete, this child is finished with the materials and more readily returns them to the shelf. A youngster's characteristic style applies to all materials. Children can and should be encouraged to extend their constructions beyond the limits of their preferred styles. More than one third of all children use either style with equal ease (Shotwell, Wolf, & Gardner, 1979).

Differences in style also appear in pretend play: Some children are extremely focused on the materials being used, and others, on fantasy (Grollman, 1994). One child may be very careful about the arrangements of the house, the neatness of the dishes, or the clothes the doll has on. However, another may use words and gestures to create a fantasy in the same setting that is stimulated by, but not limited to, the objects therein. Both children might be imaginative and creative, but in different ways.

Quality of Play.   Finally, the quality of play differs. This difference centers on the ability to maintain a group-play theme with time and the inclusion of problems to be solved by the players (Roskos, 1990). Children enact roles relevant to settings such as a bakery, hospital, beach, school, or library. When they include a problem such as a fire starting in the library basement or an emergency patient entering the hospital, the narrative and enactment of the pretend play has more storylike qualities: (a) beginning, (b) problem identification, (c) plot development, (d) problem resolution, and (e) ending.

Increased complexity of play is possible for 4- and 5-year-olds in supportive environments if they are skilled in all the play elements. Maturity is necessary but not sufficient to enable children to engage in high-quality play. Skill, supportive environments, practice, and time are essential to achieve the most advanced levels of pretend play. Complex sociodramatic play is predictive of self-regulation during cleanup, whereas solitary dramatic play is not. The beneficial effect of complex sociodramatic play is particularly strong for high-impulse children (Elias & Berk, 2002).

The complexity of constructions and the degree to which they are deliberately built, as representations of children's concepts and ideas, are indicators of quality in block play. In addition, when pretend play and construction play are integrated into the same scenario, higher quality play is achieved.

What strategies do teachers use to support all of the children in their play? A few suggestions are as follows:

- ❏ Assess the play and construction skills for each child.
- ❏ Help children improve their skills or the quality of their play, taking individual differences into account.
- ❏ Encourage less-skilled players to play with other, slightly more skillful children.
- ❏ Provide the time, props, and materials for pretend play and construction practice on a regular basis. As with other learning, children improve the quality of their play with practice.
- ❏ Demonstrate skills by playing yourself or offer verbal cues to children having difficulty while they are playing.
- ❏ Describe the problem or situation so that children can cope with cultural or familial differences such as when there is confusion between youngsters who understand the role of women differently.
- ❏ Support individual preferences for play style by describing what another child is doing (if it is apparent) and by showing respect for stylistic differences.
- ❏ Challenge children by asking questions such as "What would happen if. . . . ?" to extend or adapt their play.
- ❏ Adapt play experiences for children with special needs by simplifying activities, encouraging peer support, and providing high interest material and opportunities for repetition (Kostelnik et al., 2009).

PRETEND AND CONSTRUCTION PLAY ACROSS THE CURRICULUM AND IN DEVELOPMENT

Although studies of construction and pretend play have been conducted independently of each other, both tend to show that they are systematically related to positive developmental and learning outcomes. Understanding the physical and social world is the result of high-quality play in which children demonstrate focused interest, attention, experimentation, and cooperation (Frost et al., 2008; Chaillé & Silvern, 1996). It requires considerable mental activity rather than the simple manipulation of materials. Play has the significant attribute of "uniting and integrating cognitive, language, socioemotional and motor aspects of learning and development" while "supporting children's positive beliefs in their own competency" (Kieff & Casbergue, 2006, pp. 8–9). The skills supported by pretend play and construction are presented next as they apply to all the curricular domains.

Cognitive Domain

Play may serve to consolidate children's constructs (Piaget, 1962) or stimulate the emergence of abstract thought (Van Hoorn, Monighan-Nourot, Scales, & Alward, 2007); Vygotsky, 1967). Whether play mirrors children's cognitive processes or causes them is yet unclear. However, ample evidence exists that pretend play is a significant factor in children's intellectual functioning (Fromberg, 2002; Frost et al., 2008). There is substantial evidence that logical-mathematical thinking is evidenced in play related to science and mathematical standards (Eisenhauer & Feikes, 2009; Van Hoorn et al., 2007). For example, when a 4-year-old weighs a doll during pretend play, he is demonstrating that he can use scientific tools and methods to learn about the world. When Meg counts out pretend money in a store, she is demonstrating her understanding of number and simple operations.

Children may also acquire new information, although such acquisition is not the primary function of pretend play. It is most likely to occur when children of differing backgrounds and experience confront one another in the play setting. Players tend to require their peers to play consistently within the theme and behave appropriately for their roles. To this end, they may inform, coach, or direct other players and teach one another, which is consistent with Vygotsky's (1979) ideas that one child can assist the processes of learning in another. Investigative play with blocks leads children to discover interrelations among concepts such as balance; cause and effect; classification; counting; estimation; whole–part relations; geometric solids; serration; predictions; and the understanding of simple machines such as ramps, fulcrums, and levers (Wellhousen & Kieff, 2001). It is not surprising then that in one study young children's block play reliably predicted mathematics achievement at the seventh-grade and high school levels (Wolfgang, Stannard, & Jones, 2001). Play also contributes to increasing concentration skills and the expansion of imagination, creativity, and curiosity as well as developing the capacity to be flexible (Oliver & Klugman, 2002) and develop internal imagery (Singer & Singer, 2005).

Aesthetic Domain

Construction activities provide opportunities for children to apply creative-thinking skills. All creative efforts require two familiar elements of the active imagination: the generation of alternatives and a selection among these alternatives (Smith, 1990). Children must choose among a variety of materials that may be suitable for their project. Additionally, the materials may provide ideas for constructions. Given encouragement and time to think, children will propose many uses beyond the obvious for common materials such as paper (Tegano, Sawyers, & Moran, 1991). Even properly identifying the problem is a challenge for the very young, and the teachers' support and guidance of even older children may be necessary (Tegano et al., 1991).

Children also plan what they are doing (Casey & Lippman, 1991). They may do so briefly and casually at first, beginning with an idea or a goal. Once materials are assembled and implementation begins, children often start over or add and delete as they alter the direction of their work. Sometimes they comment on the criteria with which they judge their products. For instance, when Janet and Lanna, age 4 years, were building a house of blocks, Janet said, "We gotta get the bigger ones. These won't fit [across the roof]." Lanna replied, "Yeah, and get some little red and blue ones from the table to be flowers."

More mature creative efforts are never haphazard. Older primary children may plan a "fort" or "clubhouse" for several days before beginning construction. If allowed to continue, such constructions may be transformed repeatedly as children think of new alternatives.

Children demonstrate their grasp of the standard of responding to the elements of graphic art when they use information about texture, size, shape, weight, flexibility, and translucency of materials to carry out their projects. They also learn about part–whole relations as they construct complex forms having many components (Reifel & Greenfield, 1983). Position in space and placement of objects in relation to one another are typical concepts developed during the construction process. Children may use their drawing constructions to facilitate memory of an important experience (Raines, 1990). Anne Janette's picture is the painting of an 8-year-old child with disabilities that was produced shortly after she and her father built a snowman. The most complex construction that this child produced during the early years, this painting provided a source of

Anne Janette created this iconic construction to represent the snowman she had built the evening before.

many good memories as she grew. Construction is inevitably an outcome of children's need to understand their social and physical world in their own very active terms by making things (Franklin, 1994).

Similarly, children create music. They use rhythm, pitch, the voices of simple instruments, and their own voices to generate simple tunes within the context of play. They explore the concepts of duration and pattern and the use of repeated phrases in their chants. When Patti sang a lullaby to her doll, using the elements of music as well as clearly demonstrating the standard of recognizing music as a form of communication, she demonstrated two standards of aesthetic curriculum. Often such chants are used to denote special effects during their pretend play or "magical" transformations such as when Sara chanted, "Grow, gro . . . ow gro . . . ow," to alter her pretend role from baby to someone who could iron clothes.

Affective Domain

Pretend play has long been recognized as a vehicle for children to express their innermost thoughts and feelings, an affective domain goal. Although most play episodes either are based on immediate past observations and experiences or occur in response to cues from the physical environment of the school, children can and do enact play sequences that express their concerns. Increasing evidence indicates that children's pretend play fosters their ability to simulate feelings and desires not currently held, which allows the child to understand that other people may hold different beliefs about the world and to perform correctly from that viewpoint (Jenkins, 2000). Sometimes the experiences they view on television may be so emotionally overwhelming that such tragedies are expressed only through their constructions (Gross & Clemens, 2002). Children achieve mastery of their feelings when they rework a scene to a happier conclusion, can express repressed feelings, and can try out solutions to normal daily crises. Play is also one of the most powerful and effective means of reducing children's ordinary stress (Jesse, Wilson, & Morgan, 2000), demonstrating the standard of learning strategies for coping with emotions. All children experience fears about being accepted (and may be temporarily rejected by their peers) or may have concerns about family members. For example, two 8-year-olds played out marriage, separation, divorce, courtship, and remarriage during a period of several weeks. One child came from a stable two-parent family, and her best friend had already lived through the divorce process, with her father remarrying and a mother contemplating a second marriage. Through multiple play sequences, the inevitable uncertainties that one child was experiencing were portrayed while the other learned about the social and emotional realities experienced by another. Pretend play is a normal process by which healthy children learn to cope with the problems of daily life.

Children gain self-confidence and demonstrate pride in their creations: "I did it!" "Look at mine!" "This, here, is my house!" Children have a sense of mastery as they work hard, solve problems, test their skills, and demonstrate patience and perseverance in the construction process. Construction play leads to a sense of confidence and competence as children have concrete evidence of their endeavors.

During play, children communicate their anxieties that cannot be simply explained to an adult that relate to and predict the status of their mental health (Warren, Emde, & Sroufe, 2000). Similarly, children develop their skills in expressing, controlling, and modeling emotional behavior through play as they come to better understand the contextual situations in which modulating emotional responsiveness is appropriate (Kwon & Yawkey, 2000). This skills set is generally termed *emotional intelligence*.

Language Domain

Research on the effect of pretend play on language development is extensive, and the results of most studies indicate positive relationships (Frost, 1991). In a detailed review of the literature, play was found to have specific effects all related to learning standards (Levy, 1984, p. 167).

- ❑ Stimulates innovation in language
- ❑ Introduces and clarifies new words and concepts
- ❑ Motivates language use and practice
- ❑ Encourages verbal thinking

Apparently, the relation between symbolic play and language increases with age, because the play becomes more abstract and independent of real objects as a source of shared meaning. Good players are more verbal during play. In fact, examples of kindergartners' language at play were found to be better indicators of language ability than formal assessments such as the Illinois Test of Psycholinguistic Abilities (Levy, 1984). Language fluency and the variety of language structures were even greater during block play than during housekeeping play (Isbell & Raines, 1991). Pretend play also enhances short- and long-term recall and the ability to comprehend stories (Kim, 1999).

When pretend or construction play is enhanced with appropriate materials, children incorporate literacy acts, such as looking at a cookbook while preparing a pretend meal or writing labels on their constructions (Goldhaber, Lipson, Sortino, & Daniels, 1996–1997). When appropriate teacher guidance is added, the variety and frequency of such acts increases (Morrow, 1990). The free use of open-ended materials enables children to play with the forms of written language as a part of their constructions, supporting emergent literacy (Miller, Fernie, & Kantor, 1992). An even greater effect was observed as teachers played beside children in a literacy-enriched environment, informally modeling the use of books and helping children to produce signs (Pickett, 1998). In a mixed-age primary group (K–Grade 2) of children, youngsters incorporated reading environmental print, functional reading, reading for pleasure, academic reading (practicing letter recognition, etc.), reading aloud, engaging in other book-related activities with art or drama, and both recreational writing (self-expression) and academic writing (penmanship and spelling) during sociodramatic play with mixed-age classmates (Stone & Christie, 1996). Children also produce a variety of written language that is functional. They write to (a) serve instrumental purposes (making a list of things to get), (b) regulate the behavior of others (preparing a "Keep Out" sign), (c) meet interaction needs (writing a telephone number for a friend), (d) fill personal needs (putting their name on paper), and (e) relay information (making a "Telephone Broken" sign; Stroud, 1995). Children also engage in conversations about literacy within the play context, which might include using literacy conventions, naming literacy-related objects, or even coaching one another in some literacy task to achieve a play goal (Neuman & Roskos, 1990).

Second language learners follow a pattern that parallels the development of their first language in a playful context (Seefeldt & Galper, 2007), in way of the following:

❑ Having a silent period where English is not used but rather their home language (onlooker play and parallel play)
❑ Speaking in very short sentences with simple syntax and grammar ("I mama.")
❑ Gradually increasing language structures including present, past, and future tenses ("I will go to the store.")
❑ Using short, fully developed sentences to move the play forward

Primary-age children from low socioeconomic families are far more likely to benefit by attaining literacy competence from drama instruction than are students from average populations (Podlozny, 2000). This finding is particularly true for helping children learn the elements of a story (Creech & Bhavnagri, 2002). The linkages between aesthetics and pretence enhance children's ability to write stories.

Physical Domain

Motor development is perhaps the skill most obviously affected by pretend play and construction and therefore not typically the focus of research. Children manipulate fasteners when they dress up, develop the tripod grip and increase their control over writing instruments as they pretend to be writers, and coordinate eyes and hands with the rest of the body when moving objects as they engage in play. Three-year-olds build with great concentration, but their blocks are haphazardly stacked, which leads to imbalance. Four-year-olds are more precise and straighten blocks that are not aligned. By five, these skills have become so refined and controlled that children can place blocks with precision and move more rapidly, making increasingly complex structures (Santrock, 2010). Older youngsters can achieve similar results with smaller blocks and less uniform materials. Construction with large blocks in particular strengthens muscles. Body awareness in relation to specific spaces as they stand, sit, crouch, or reach across other blocks contributes to understanding spatial relations as they maneuver during construction activities (Wellhousen & Kieff, 2001).

Social Domain

Social competence, or the ability to function effectively in society appropriate to your age, comprises several aspects. Perspective taking, conceptions of friendship, interpersonal strategies, problem solving, moral judgment, and communication skills are all components of social behavior. Participation in sociodramatic play requires a high level of both social and cognitive abilities, including sharing and cooperation, appreciation of role reciprocity, self-regulation, stress management, the ability to delay gratification, negotiation, conflict resolution, and nonviolence (Spiegel, 2008; Stephens, 2009). Generally, increases in pretend-play skills are associated with corresponding increases in all three aspects of social cognition.

❏ Visual or perceptual perspective taking—How does another person see the world?
❏ Cognitive perspective taking—What are other people thinking? What are other people like?
❏ Affective perspective taking—What kind of emotional experiences is another person having?
   (Johnsen & Christie, 1984, p. 109)

The spontaneous play of pretend scripts provides the context and the practice for children to learn negotiation skills and achieve social acceptance. Children continually engage in social comparison as they encounter differing perceptions of a given situation. These checks are frequently in the form of tag questions ("You're not going to her house, right?") as a request for information. Correspondingly, they make requests for agreement ("Let's not play house today, okay?"), permission ("I need to make this street longer, right?" [moving into another's play space]), compliance ("You can put those babies to bed now, huh?"), verbal response ("You like to play cars, right?"), and attention ("This is a bridge; see?"; Chafel, 1986). As children initiate and respond to verbalizations that are essential to social play, they develop leadership skills (Trawick-Smith, 1988). In early childhood, children who rank high in leadership skills also rank high in following skills. They can contribute to the direction of play but do not dominate it. Kindergartners and primary-grade children use richer texts, more contoured scripts, and more elaborate plots than those used by preschool children. There is also more directing and stage-managing of the play at this age (Johnson, Christie, & Yawkey, 2005). Friendship grouping in play and construction is stronger and flows across activities.

The social skills practiced during pretend play are also used in construction play. Cooperation and teamwork are required in a variety of construction activities: building with blocks, painting murals, making a bus from a big box. Children negotiate ideas, share information, cooperate, share space and materials, and compare their performance with that of others (Chafel, 1986). For example, because large, hollow blocks are difficult to handle alone, they challenge 3- to 5-year-olds physically. Such blocks also afford opportunities for immediate holistic experiences requiring social organization and cooperation as youngsters build and later engage in pretend play.

INTEGRATION OF MULTIPLE DOMAINS

Construction and pretend play are integrative, requiring that children use all the information at their disposal, share it with others, and apply it in ways that reflect their understanding (Kostelnik, Whiren, Soderman, & Gregory, 2009; Cooper & Dever, 2001; Phelps & Hanline, 1999). Children must synthesize ideas to enact or plans to build in this experience and utilize a variety of skills and abilities (Adams & Nesmith, 1996). The child is a meaning maker, the embodiment of knowledge rather than a passive recipient of it. One of the most salient characteristics of this type of play is that it facilitates the cross-fertilization of ideas and connections across traditional content areas (Chaillé & Silvern, 1996). Children must use logical-mathematical thinking about space relations, oral language skills, and techniques for negotiation and cooperation to build a fort and play in it. Like pretend play, construction play challenges children to use all that they know and can do to be successful.

> *Berry, Stan, Chico, and William labored with the large blocks. "We have to make this longer so everyone can get to Mars," noted William. His teacher had just shown this group of youngsters pictures of the space shuttle as a result of their interest expressed as the class studied the night sky.*
>
> *"And wear space suits to build it," commented Stan who had interestingly watched a space walk recently on television. The boys collected some large boxes and used masking tape to make appropriate space suits.*

These children are combining mathematics, language, and social skills as they pretend "store."

Once the space-going vessel was built, Berry took the role of steering it. When Chico, who had removed his costume, stepped out of the structure, William cried, "Man lost!" as Stan commented, "You're going to just pop out there. You have to wait till we land!"

Chico entered the vessel and waited for the slow process of landing before heading off to another activity.

To illustrate the amalgamation of curriculum goals more completely through pretend play and construction, Table 15.4 has been compiled to analyze the relation of specific goals to a particular scenario in a primary-classroom post office. The opportunity to learn does not guarantee that all children will learn the same things. Participants must actively engage in the activity and take advantage of the opportunities provided.

Many goals within the domains may be addressed during pretend play or construction; objectives may be combined as described in Table 15.4. The children's maturity, their skills in pretend play and construction, their experience in playing with one another, and the topic of the pretend play are all relevant. For example, the goals addressed in the cognitive and language domains would not be as appropriate for 3- and 4-year-olds. In addition, the degree of the teacher's guidance and support would have to be adjusted for children of varying ages and abilities.

TEACHERS' QUESTIONS REGARDING PRETEND AND CONSTRUCTION PLAY

1. Don't children get enough play at home? For children who enter a program without play skills, the school is the only source for learning. For children who enter programs having some skills, often their parents do not have the materials, information, and guidance techniques for developing a variety of play opportunities such as archaeologist, scientist, or space explorer that will lead them to more complex levels. As with other strategies that support learning, families generally are supportive and willing within the limitations of time, skill, and their resources especially if early childhood programs provide them with information and suggestions. In addition, television and other technologies compete with play time (Hirsh-Pasek & Golinkoff, 2004) Time outdoors in the natural environment may be limited by concerns for safety and the absence of natural spaces near where children live. In addition, there is the trend of increasing scheduled activities and lessons, particularly of older children and reducing play time even more.

2. What can I do without the proper equipment and materials? Because pretend play for 3- to 5-year-olds is a priority, programs should allocate resources to this domain first. Quality equipment and furnishings that support pretend and construction last for 30 to 40 years and require minimal upkeep, which children can undertake themselves, so such items are a relatively low-cost investment in the long run. Unit and large blocks, as well as pretend furnishings, are flexible in supporting all the domains of learning and have the unique capacity for integrating children's experiences.

Many of the materials for pretend play and construction are found rather than purchased. The task of adding to and replacing materials in teacher-developed pretend-play kits (Figure 15.2) may be shared. Garage sales, flea markets, donations from parents, and discards from industry are sources of pretend-play props. File boxes are often useful for storage, and schools may install near-ceiling shelving to hold them. Industrial and household discards make excellent resources for construction projects. Figures and vehicles used in construction are inexpensive and may also be donated by families whose children have outgrown them.

3. What do I do about superhero play and other play themes that make me uncomfortable? Teachers are legitimately concerned about the level of violence in children's play. Each of the sources of violence or aggression that might appear in pretend play should be treated separately. A child may do the following:

❑ Imitate observed adult behavior at home and in the community
❑ Portray events such as earthquakes, war, car accidents, and other catastrophes

TABLE 15.4   Analysis of an Experience of Primary-Age Children Creating a Postal Center

Domain	Goals	Objectives	Pretend Play	Construction
Aesthetic	Reflect on and discuss aesthetic experiences Appreciate art as a means of nonverbal communication	❑ Collect a variety of used postage stamps ❑ Discuss the images on the stamps ❑ Select stamps to use for pretend mail	Children contribute stamps for the post office. Customers select stamps for their letters.	Use postage stamp designs as a part of the display in the post office. Place as appropriate to the structure.
Affective	Gain experience and demonstrate independence in using age-appropriate materials and tools Assume responsibility for caring for classroom materials	❑ Use pretend money with the cash register and scales ❑ Put away materials at the end of the daily play session ❑ Use hollow blocks and long boards appropriately	Children will have scales to weigh the letters and packages, pretend money to purchase stamps, calculators to compute totals for multiple purchases, and writing materials for receipts.	Children build the postal center with blocks, boards, and furnishings.
Cognitive	Discover measurement relationships by using standard unit tools Add and subtract Identify numbers	❑ Base charges on actual weights and using current postal rates ❑ Use a rate chart ❑ Calculate charges either by hand or with a calculator	Most primary-age children can read the numerals for the postage stamps and charts. The challenge will be to figure cost per unit.	
Language	Demonstrate courteous listening behaviors Demonstrate comprehension of spoken language Use own version of writing Respond to written symbols in the environment	❑ Engage in polite exchanges between seller and buyer ❑ Ask appropriate questions in the pretend context ❑ Respond to written signs ❑ Write letters to classmates and others in the school; read own letters	Maintain the flow of pretend play through metacommunications. Use enactment to supplement visual symbols and create the narrative that supports the pretend story. Use reading and writing within the play frame.	Make signs, envelopes, or other props using written language or pictographs.
Physical	Coordinate wrist, hand, finger, finger–thumb, and eye–hand movements Maintain adequate levels of physical activity	❑ Use pencils, pens, tape, and other adhesives ❑ Wrap and unwrap packages	Children will be engaged almost continuously in fine-motor activity as they write letters, put stamps on them, organize the post office, and use the tools and props provided. Post office play is active, with postal deliveries and general movement in the setting.	Children will be moving furnishings and blocks, which requires coordination during the construction process.
Social	Learn how to cooperate Develop knowledge related to social studies	❑ Make plans for building the postal station together ❑ Build the station ❑ Collect information about postal services from the community ❑ Use accurate information in play	Many skills in play and social intercourse are required during complex thematic play in addition to those listed. Children must relate to one another in role-appropriate ways, settle disputes, negotiate roles, and use metacommunications to make the play move forward. Exchanges with one another must be mutual and balanced.	Cooperation is required for children to build the postal station with large blocks and furnishings. Work must be organized, jobs assigned, placements agreed to, and then implemented. Objects must also be collected and placed and signs made.

FIGURE 15.2 Pretend-Play Kits with Associated Teaching Themes

---

Unit Theme: Living in Homes

Pretend-Play Theme: Houses
Props: Dolls, doll clothes, kitchen furnishings and utensils, dishes, table and chairs, storage for doll clothes, doll bed and blankets

Camping
Props: Sleeping bags or blankets, wood for pretend fire, dishes, utensils, tent or a shelter made from a blanket and rope or a blanket and a card table.

Unit Theme: Clothing

Pretend-Play Theme: Washing Clothes
Props: Doll clothes, a tub or water table with soap, clothesline and pins, plastic aprons

Dress Up
Props: Scarves, hats, curtains, coats and capes, shoes, mirror, dresses, ties, shirts

Unit Theme: Vehicles

Pretend-Play Theme: Gas Station
Props: Gas pumps with hoses, windshield-washing equipment, tires, tire pump, wrenches, fan belts, screwdrivers, cash register

Vehicle Showroom
Props: Many vehicles arranged, car sales brochures, ads, calculators, pencils, forms, price stickers, balloons

Unit Theme: Insects

Pretend-Play Theme: Entomologist's Laboratory
Props: Insect pictures, specimens, tripod, magnifying glass, white coats, paper, pencil, insect books, dried insects, wasp nests, or other real things

Picnic Partners
Props: Dishes, pretend food, tablecloth, plastic or paper insects

Unit Theme: The Sky

Pretend-Play Theme: It's Raining, It's Pouring
Props: Sand-table village or miniature houses; rocks; seashells; twigs; miniature people for the houses; squirt cans; small drum for thunder; "Cirrus," "Stratus," "Cumulus," and "Nimbus" signs

Outdoor Slumber Party
Props: Sleeping bags or blankets, alarm clock, different phases of the moon to hang, stars, large pajamas (worn over clothes), stuffed animals

Unit Theme: Machines

Pretend-Play Theme: Repair Shop Props
Wrenches, screwdrivers, pliers, old clocks, radios, toasters, pencil, paper, do-it-yourself books, "Repair Anything" sign

Bike Repair
Props: Wrenches, loose spokes, cogs and sprockets (donations from local bike shop, cleaned), rags, telephone, pencil, paper, bikes or tricycles

Unit Theme: Storytelling

Pretend-Play Theme: Storytelling Theater
Props: Chairs for seating, a "stage" marked off with blocks or tape, tickets, playbill, cash register, dolls for audience, dress-up clothes, hats, child-constructed costumes if desired, child-painted backdrops for older children

Bedtime Stories
Props: Dolls, doll beds, picture books, rocking chair, lullaby CDs

---

Source: Adapted from material in *Teaching Young Children Using Themes*, by M. J. Kostelnik (Ed.), 1991, Glenview IL: Good Year Books.

❑ Act on inner needs to handle feelings of aggression and helplessness
❑ Use toys and scripts from television, selecting only the action sequences
❑ Engage in *masked play*, where the child claims to be playing to avoid responsibility for deliberate aggression and its consequences

Youngsters enact events they have observed. Adults in some families have little privacy, so children are likely to incorporate behaviors such as parental arguments, physical fights, and sexual intercourse into play sequences. Young children do not understand what should remain private and what is appropriate for play in school. Teachers who observe inappropriate play have found simple, low-key redirection to be useful. Focusing on other activities that adult men and women engage in is usually sufficient. By first grade, youngsters usually can distinguish between public and private family information and are less likely to enact the latter.

Children who experience a natural disaster (earthquake or a flood) or who witness serious accidents or violence on the street may struggle with feelings of intense fear, anger, and helplessness.

A child can work out a variety of situations and solutions and perhaps master these emotions through play. Such play may require many repetitions before the child feels safe. Teachers may facilitate this process by providing accurate information and reassurance as children play out violent scenes. Listening to the real concerns of children as they depict this type of violence through either their constructions or their pretend play is key to helping them to understand and to cope with their fears (Gross & Clemens, 2002). The content of the play is the fear and violence itself, and other players often take on the roles of nurturer, rescuer, and comforter.

The number of fantasy action heroes portrayed on television has increased with time. Considering that young children are exposed to as much television as schooling, the fact that children reenact media episodes is not surprising (Bergen, 1994). Working with parents to monitor television viewing may be the most practical solution to the least desirable programs (Boyatzis, 1997). Older children are concerned about aggressor and victim roles in a more general sense, as in good guys and bad guys or monsters and victims. This opposing-force pretend play may occur during children's recess without real violence occurring. Frequently the bad guys are imaginary. If no injuries and no real violence occur, dealing with the forces of good and evil as a play theme may allow children to work out their ideas of right and wrong in an acceptable framework (Boyd, 1997). Play around issues of justice, right and wrong, and fairness are important concepts for older children to explore.

Violence masked as play should be treated as inappropriate behavior, as discussed in chapter 6. Violent themes rarely emerge from the carefully planned play opportunities provided by teachers as a part of the curriculum (Boyd, 1997).

As with roles selected from commercial characters, children incorporate rough-and-tumble play into their pretend play. Enactment of fantasy heroes of this type is much more common in casual or illicit play than in teacher-initiated or teacher-guided classroom play. **Rough-and-tumble play**, consisting of laughing, running, smiling, jumping, open-hand beating, wrestling, play fighting, chasing, and fleeing, looks aggressive to many adults. However, children engaging in this type of play do not get hurt or cry, nor are they confused about what is or is not play. Rough-and-tumble play facilitates social cognition (Bjorklund & Brown, 1998). Frequently, rough-and-tumble play is a transitional activity leading to games with rules, especially for popular boys (Pellegrini & Perlmutter, 1988). Teachers become distressed with excited, physically active play more than the children or other objective observers do. Aggression, which includes fixation, frowning, hitting, pushing, taking, and grabbing, is more likely to occur in relation to possessions than in the fast-moving superhero play typically seen on playgrounds.

4. **What do teachers do when children say "You can't play!"** Even preschool-age children judge straightforward exclusion from activities on the basis of gender as wrong (Theimer, Killen, & Stangor, 2001). However, children who are engaged in making a project, who are building a complex structure together, or who are involved in an ongoing pretend scenario are likely to reject new players unless they contribute something unique to the activity. Sometimes the new players would be rejected anyway, or if accepted, the play would disintegrate. In such a case, their inclusion would be similar to adding a fifth player to a partnered card game. However, individual children cannot control the materials from one day to the next. When teachers want particular children to engage in either a construction or a pretend-play episode, these children should begin the activity period in that area as part of the daily plan. When children do not know how to play, planning for moderately skilled players to engage in play with unskilled players is generally effective. As with other scaffolding tasks, the level just above the current level of performance is the goal for the less skilled.

Children may exclude others on the basis of language, social group, race, ability, or gender. When such exclusion occurs, teachers should take the opportunity to help children understand biases better and to develop together several rules based on fairness. Typically, primary-age children prefer to play in single-gender groups, which is both supportive of gender-role socialization and acceptable. However, one first-grade teacher helped her group to develop the rule that space and materials had to be shared fairly but that individuals could choose with whom to play. Children understood the "fairness" issue and were cooperative.

5. **What if the child has worked with blocks or wet sand and has nothing to carry home?** A photograph taken periodically to represent the child's construction is useful and, if computers are available, can be printed out on plain paper. Children who produce music as a creative effort may

consent to tape it if the teacher is unable to write the notation. Older children are often less concerned with carrying something home than they are with saving it from one day to the next. Block or box structures may be saved for a short time to maximize the opportunities for elaboration and expansion typical of these activities. Often the class as a group can establish its own ground rules and propose solutions.

6. **What will the parents think if children are playing in school rather than engaging in real learning?** Parents are very supportive of play in child-centered programs for 3- and 4-year-olds, but believe that the time spent in play should decrease as children get older (Rothlein & Brett, 1987). Parents do not indicate that play should be eliminated for 6- to 8-year-olds, merely that the amount of time dedicated to play should be less. The value of play to the development of a competent child has considerable support in research and can be presented understandably to parents (Van Hoorn et al., 2007). For example, if birds are being studied, young children may pretend to be birds in the nest, and older children, scientists studying birds. In pretend play, children use the information that they have to solve problems. In addition, teachers can assess children's level of understanding about the topic on the basis of their play.

If children are unable to incorporate information into pretend-play sequences, they do not understand it well. Other intellectual skill development is also needed. Guided-theme pretend play and construction play that use ideas from science, social studies, or other domain content are logically coherent components of curriculum. Teachers of primary-age children in rural areas provide more opportunities for play than their counterparts in suburban areas, who in turn provide more time than urban teachers do (Newman, 1996). Teaching is more than telling and setting up drill experiences; it is also more than going through textbooks, as a group of Iowa teachers discovered when they set aside all their textbooks and shifted to unit instruction using developmentally appropriate goals (Barclay, Benelli, Campbell, & Kleine, 1995).

Promotion of Play Skills

Providing an ample supply of materials, organizing them, and presenting them to children is usually sufficient to encourage exploratory, investigative, and testing play in 3- to 8-year-olds. To play productively, youngsters must be rested, free from hunger or other physical discomfort, safe, secure, and comfortable. Thus, adults must let children know in many ways that child-initiated activity is acceptable. When adults show a lack of interest, fail to provide the materials necessary to support play, neglect skills assessment, or criticize processes in play, the climate is not conducive to experimentation, exploration, pretend play, or construction.

Adults responsible for youngsters' development must attend to individual and group characteristics so that if children are not self-sufficient in this area, appropriate support and instruction are provided. The first step is to recognize what these skills are and then to examine how they can be taught. In Figure 15.3, specific behaviors are inventoried that are necessary for pretend play and construction. Strategies for actively supporting play are described in the following section.

Customary Strategies to Enhance Play

Educators can use the following 10 strategies to enhance play.

1. **Set the stage for children's play.** The teacher is responsible for establishing conditions that accept and encourage play. Suggestions for doing so are as follows:
   a. Incorporate make-believe into transitional times such as cleanup, dressing, or moving from one room to another as a group.
   b. Encourage pretend play in other aspects of the curriculum. Ask children to imagine what someone would feel like or how a setting would look, or to pretend that they are the character in the story.
   c. Coordinate the theme of the dramatic play center to match other ongoing themes in your room. Provide theme-related props and materials for construction related to the theme. Add additional materials to the pretend-play setup to expand the play as needed.
   d. Provide adequate space for play. Occasionally furniture may need to be moved, or room made for miniature play sets.

FIGURE 15.3   Skills Children Need to Engage in Pretend Play and Construction

Children must be able to
- Mimic in their play the behaviors that they have seen or experienced.
- Engage in a wide range of experiences from which to draw their interpretations.
- Use their bodies to represent real or imaginary objects or events.
- Assign symbolic meaning to real or imaginary objects using language or gestures.
- Take on the role attributes of beings or objects and act out interpretations of these roles.
- Create play themes and engage in play themes created by others.
- Experiment with a variety of objects, roles (leader, follower, mediator), and characterizations (animal, mother, astronaut, etc.).
- React to and interact with other children in make-believe situations.

- Maintain pretend play for increasing lengths of time.
- Use narratives and metacommunications to structure the play.
- Dramatize familiar stories, songs, poems, and past events.
- Interpret events and reconstruct them in tangible ways.
- Use diverse approaches and materials to represent objects or events by representing a single object or event using different materials or techniques representing different objects and events using one material or technique.
- Collaborate with classmates to construct a representative object.
- Integrate new information into play episodes.
- Integrate construction into pretend-play episodes.

    e. Provide enough time in any one segment for play to get under way.

    f. Pay attention to what children say and do during play. Listen for their appropriate application of concepts or misinformation.

2. **Create conditions of acceptance and safety by what you say and do.** In a psychologically safe environment, children can risk being wrong or having a project not work out as they had hoped. Creativity is the outcome of challenge and risk taking. The strategies described next include behavioral reflections and questions initially described in chapter 6. The concepts apply equally to pretend play and other forms of play, although for clarity, the following specifics related to construction have been selected.

    a. Allow children to engage in their activity without intervention or comment unless they contravene safety, property, or the social cooperation rules of the classroom. Often acceptance, observation, and general support are sufficient.

    b. Ask about a project or pretend event when children are seeking information or assistance; do not assume you know what the intent is (Cassidy, 1989). You might be wrong. "Tell me about your drawing" and "I don't quite understand what you are trying to do here" are general statements letting the child know that you are not able to interpret his or her construction. "Did you have something specific in mind?" is more direct and is responsive to the child's questions or comments when the teacher is unable to respond because the representation is not clear. Avoid taking over the project.

    c. Describe what you observe about the materials or technique being used or other specific characteristics of the project. Such statements should not be judgmental but might be comparative, such as "I see Harry has used all bright primary colors and George chose the pastels." Describing specifically what the child has done models the appropriate language and conveys respect for the unique characteristics of each child's work. Examples of respectful comments on children's block constructions are listed in Table 15.5. Similar statements could relate to other constructions or to pretend-play events. Such observations may assist children in opening conversations so that adults and children alike may understand.

    d. Provide opportunities for children to share their projects with others. Display drawings, paintings, and sculptures regularly. Ask the child who made the construction to talk about his or her ideas at group time. Encourage relevant peer questions and comments. Color, line, mass or volume, pattern, shape or form, space, and texture are appropriate topics for discussion (Moyer, 1990). Demonstrate how to give feedback or ask questions about the construction. "You selected interesting colors for the [purple] cow" and "The size of this

TABLE 15.5 Respectful Commentary on Children's Block Constructions

Observation	Statement
Which blocks were used	"You found out that two of these make a half circle."
Where the blocks were placed	"You used four blocks to make a big square."
How many blocks were used	"You used all the blocks to make the building."
Whether the blocks are all the same	"All the blocks in your tower are exactly the same size."
How the blocks are connected	"All your blocks are touching."
How the blocks are balanced	"Those long blocks are holding up the shorter ones."

Sources: Adapted from *Creative Curriculum for Early Childhood*, by D. Dodge, Colker, Heroman & Bickart, 2008, Washington, DC: Teaching Strategies; "The Effect of Verbal Scaffolding on the Complexity of Preschool Children's Block Structures," by K. Gregory, A. S. Kim, and A. Whiren, in D. Lytle (Ed.), *Play Theory and Practice* (p. 123), 2003, Westport CT: Praeger.

drawing is very small; tell us why you chose to do it that way" are statements based on observations of the construction as well as openings for explanation if the child wants to provide it. Never use sarcasm; the child's feelings will be hurt, and no educational goal can be reached. Do not allow children to provide gratuitous negative comments without making them accountable. For example, if a child says, "That's ugly!" respond by saying, "You think that drawing is not attractive; tell us why you think that." If the child responds with detail, then discuss how the same characteristics that appeal to one person may not be attractive to another.

e. Support children who are feeling frustrated and angry when their work appears unsuccessful to them. Help them define the problem ("Tell me why you think this isn't going to work." "What's wrong?" "What do you think you can do about it?" "Is there anyone else in the class who might be able to assist you?"). Children should be able to achieve their goal by their own actions when they work together. Occasionally offer assistance, but allow the child to make the decisions.

f. Provide display opportunities to everyone. Keep the displays posted for a few days and then dismantle them. Avoid selecting the "best" construction for display. Sometimes the most appealing product does not indicate the most creative thinking.

g. Teach children to respect one another's work. Help them to understand that having respect is why they do not kick down someone's blocks, make noise while someone shares a song, or jeer when someone hangs up a drawing (Kostelnik et al., 2009).

h. Help other children focus on the play potential of the construction. If a child has made a particularly effective supplement to pretend play, recognize his or her contributions. When children are working together on a construction, encourage them to discuss what they plan to do and how the construction will fit into their continuing play plans. Demonstrate respectfulness yourself. Make statements that recognize children's positive contributions to the ongoing play of their peers.

3. **Actively help children improve their level of performance in pretend play.** Table 15.6 lists procedures that increase in the level of intrusion and power exercised by the teacher. Usually, the teacher selects the least intrusive strategy that will accomplish the change. For example, either active observation or nondirective statements may facilitate children becoming more focused or the teacher's starting to develop the theme for skilled children. Inexperienced youngsters may need stronger measures such as modeling and physical intervention (Wolfgang & Sanders, 1986).

Modeling is always done inside the play frame or within the context of the play itself including people, materials, and space. The teacher becomes a player and assumes a role. Physical intervention during the play usually requires that the teacher enter the space of the play frame, if only briefly, to provide or take away materials. Removing materials is usually more effective if the adult assumes a role ("I'm the plumber and I have come to get the sink [full of water] for repair. You will get it back in a day or two."). This would be done only if there were sufficient reason to intervene— say, if children began adding real water to pasta the teacher had provided for pretend cooking. The water would ruin the pasta and make a sticky mess.

TABLE 15.6   Methods of Instruction from Least Intrusive to Most Intrusive

Methods of Instruction	Example
Active onlooking	The teacher intently observes what children are doing and saying as they play.
Nondirective statements	"It looks like you're going to the beach." or "You're a cloud floating in the air."
Questions	"What do heroes really do?" or "When you go to the store, does the customer pay the storekeeper, or the other way around?"
Directive statements	"Tell me about the family that lives in the dollhouse." or "Think about the middle Billy Goat Gruff and show me how he crossed the bridge."
Modeling	"I'm your new next-door neighbor [knocking at the pretend door]," or the teacher picks up a stethoscope and says, "Is your baby sick?"
Physical intervention	The teacher adds or removes props during the play.

Nondirective statements, questions, and directive statements can quickly offer suggestions or assistance from outside the play frame. Usually the teacher watches, makes the verbalization, and listens to the children's response, but does not move into the play directly. These strategies are effective before and after a play sequence for assisting in the planning and evaluation process. Avoid rushing older children. They frequently take 30 minutes to plan a scenario and 10 minutes to enact it. This planning requires both skill and knowledge.

4. **Teach children the technical skills needed to use materials when they are engaged in construction activity.** Showing the child how to use materials appropriately does not impede creativity. On the contrary, lack of skill inhibits children's ability to do construction. For example, show children how much paste to use and where to place it, show them how to cut; demonstrate sewing; model the use of a wire cutter on potter's clay; and deliberately mix paints so that they can see the effect. Then let them use the skills to implement their own goals (Culv, 1990).

Nondirective statements, questions, suggestions, and demonstrations that help the child to do what he or she has in mind are always appropriate. Discrimination between a statement that specifies an outcome and a technique that enables a child to achieve his or her chosen outcome is necessary. As in pretend play, use the least intrusive strategy necessary to support the child's activity.

5. **Encourage children to create their own sociodramatic play independently.** Prepare the environment, provide information and resources, then allow the children to create their own scripts. If intervention is necessary, intervene and withdraw promptly. Most 5-year-olds have all the basic skills and can elaborate on them within an appropriate setting; therefore, the sociodramatic play center may run smoothly for 5- to 8-year-olds and require limited adult intervention. Encourage experimentation and creative problem solving when possible.

6. **Provide information relevant to the play theme.** Use picture books, field trips, videotapes, photographs, and other sources of information so that children know what is supposed to occur in the pretend situation. Themes and topics from social studies, science, and literature support older children's knowledge needs and can be most easily incorporated into related pretend-play themes. Identify information gaps and misunderstanding. If children pretend that firefighters set the fires before putting them out, they need additional information on fire safety and community helpers. Strategies for providing information for pretend play also work for construction.

7. **Provide a solid base of information and experience from which children develop their constructions.** Projects of investigation should be a regular part of the curriculum, not an add-on or an

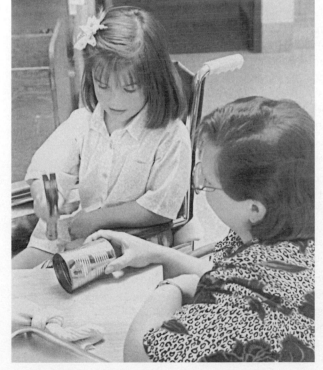

Learning how to use a variety of tools expands children's construction skills.

extra. Build on children's interest, and use the surrounding community as a source of information and assistance. Both field trips and visitors to the classroom enhance the information base established by the teacher. Projects and themes, which are described in the next chapter, are another good avenue to support construction.

8. **Support children in their problem solving, and encourage them to expand the number and diversity of potential solutions (Casey & Lippman, 1991).** (The corollary is that teachers should not arbitrarily announce "That won't work!" before a child has had a chance to think about his or her plan.) The following strategies are useful.

   a. Attempt to grasp the child's intent. Direct observation sometimes works, but you may need to ask ("It seems that you are trying to . . ."). Honestly inquire if necessary ("I don't understand . . . ").

   b. Ask about alternatives children considered ("Tell me what you thought about doing. . . . Anything else?").

   c. Inquire about the possible sources of information ("Has anyone done anything like this before? Might he or she help?"). Encourage the use of reference materials ("Where might you get a picture of the . . . ?" or "Is there anything else you might use to help you figure this out?"). In one instance, a 4-year-old was attempting to build a pair of walkie-talkies. She had already nailed long spikes into the ends of two blocks of wood and was worried that "they won't work just like that." She had never seen a walkie-talkie up close but knew they had more than an antenna to make them receive and transmit. The teacher could have just handed her a walkie-talkie. Instead, she carefully engaged the child in a conversation until the child recognized the scope of the problem and could quickly identify a potential solution.

   d. Encourage children to participate in the general planning and decision-making process. When a child enthusiastically asks, "Can we build a . . . ?" respond, "Yes, and what materials [space, time] will you need?" or "Yes, and how will you do this?" Avoid "Yes, but . . . " Children cannot do everything just when they might like to. Older children are particularly sensitive to the competing needs for time and space. Involve them in making opportunities for carrying out and building projects.

   e. Actively involve children who are less likely to initiate construction projects. Often the more timid child is left out of group constructions or does not initiate construction activities independently. Good ideas may be lost to the group and the timid child's abilities not acknowledged or recognized, even by the individuals involved. Watch for opportunities to suggest that the timid child participate in the group endeavor. Interact with the less forceful students, and encourage them to share their ideas with you and one or two others. Avoid telling them what to do or giving them solutions to problems. Standing by them (literally) when they approach other children is more likely to give them confidence and practice and to help them with the task at hand.

   f. Allow time for children to think about and develop their ideas. Few problems are solved spontaneously. Little creative work happens on the spur of the moment. Sometimes more time is required to think about and plan a project than that required to implement it. Rather than urging a child who is sitting quietly or abstractedly to "Get started on . . . ," offer a listening ear: "Would you like to share what you are thinking about? Maybe that will help."

9. **Encourage the flow among play, construction, and information acquisition.** Given the appropriate circumstances, experiences that are intended as basic information generate construction. Equally often, children's desire to construct something for their play motivates them to seek the information. Topical reference materials are essential to every classroom, even for the youngest children. Older children may look up information for themselves, and younger children can watch teachers who "don't know, but I'll find out."

10. **Evaluate the level of skill development.** Observe all the children and determine whether each child is able to pretend play. If a child can do so, check such qualitative aspects as posing problems to be solved, generating ideas, initiating play, following play, negotiating, allowing new players to enter the play, and creating objects to be used in the play. Check to see whether children are using metacommunication skills to structure pretend play. Because play is often an area of strength, skills developed in this context may be transferred to other areas of developing competence. Recall that the highest level of play has a story structure with a plot and resolution of a problem. Higher levels of construction incorporate artifacts into pretend play or other areas of learning.

Approaches to creating an appropriate climate, interventions for children who lack the skill, methods for combining play and information, procedures for fostering cooperation and respect among the players, patterns of effective adult–child conversation, and recommendations for assessment are essential for achieving desirable skills, yet more remains to be done. Adults must plan for play to occur, provide many opportunities for a variety of construction activities, and foster specific sociodramatic and theme play that enables children to make sense of their world.

One advantage of planning for pretend play daily is that once the basic plan is made and the center is operating, it can continue as long as the unit of instruction continues. The teacher may add props or materials occasionally or encourage children to bring household discards from home to supplement school supplies. The teacher's task is to encourage, guide, and assess children's accomplishments.

Construction activities may be short term for younger children or may involve weeks of work with primary-age children. Various materials representing the same objects and events with different media enhance children's understanding. Often construction and pretend play are a part of the same episode or activity. When children make their own props to enact a story with a problem and a resolution, they are involved in a very complex, intellectually demanding activity.

SUMMARY

At the beginning of this chapter you were asked a number of questions that you should now be able to answer readily. Play has unique characteristics that distinguish this behavior from all others.

Children integrate their understanding of experience through pretend play and construction and learn other things on their own. The relations between specific areas of development and play are illuminated in this chapter, as are the areas in which expectations for individual differences can be anticipated. When teachers understand this, they are better prepared to plan for play experiences.

General strategies to support play and ideas for planning appropriate learning centers and projects are also presented. When themes are incorporated into pretend play and construction, much learning is consolidated in children's minds. As you learn how to develop themes and projects in the next chapter, keep in mind the role that pretend play and construction might play for each theme.

Key Words

construction play	object invention	rough-and-tumble play
make-believe	object substitution	sociodramatic play
metacommunication	play frame	transformations

Applying What You've Read in This Chapter

1. **Discuss**
   a. What makes an activity playful or not playful? How can you tell the difference?
   b. Why does resistance to including play exist in many public school settings, and what role might you play as a member of the teaching team in one of these settings?
   c. Describe what you might expect to see in (1) a classroom in which guided play is a part of the curriculum, and (2) a setting in which the teacher simply lets children play if they want to and treats it as a time filler until dismissal.

2. **Observe**
   a. Observe children at play with materials that can be used for construction and find (1) a child exploring or investigating only, (2) a child who appears invested in the design

(patterner), and (3) a child who appears to be pretending with what he or she has made (dramatist). How is their play similar? What distinguishes these approaches? Do children change in their approach during the observation?
   b. Observe a 3-year-old and a 5-year-old engaged in pretend play. What skills does each child have for pretending with an object; pretending about time, place, or setting; substituting objects; pretending with another child for at least 10 minutes; maintaining an idea or a topic in the play with another; and introducing a problem and resolving it in the pretend-play sequence.
   c. Review Table 15.4. Organize a similar table for analyzing either pretend play or construction. Observe a group of children at play for at least 30 minutes and identify the

specific intermediate objectives in each of the six domains that their play suggests. You should infer the relevant objectives from what the children do and say. You may not recognize all the learning potentials in each domain on any one occasion.

3. **Carry out an activity**

    a. Examine the play ideas presented in Tables 15.1 and 15.2. Select one activity from each and write a long-form lesson plan to implement it.

    b. Participate in the block area of a program. Use the strategies to support block construction suggested in the section on promoting children's play skills.

4. **Create something for your portfolio**

    a. Using the information in this chapter, prepare a checklist to use to assess pretend play and construction play skills.

    b. Write a newsletter for parents, explaining why you will include pretend play in the classroom. Explain briefly how such play will contribute to the children's learning. The newsletter should be well written and no longer than two single-spaced pages.

    c. Review chapter 3 and select four teaching strategies that support pretend play and construction.

5. **Add to your journal**

    a. Describe in detail one memorable play experience from your childhood in a program setting. Include details about what made this experience so memorable. Then review the chapter and reflect on the content in terms of your personal experience.

    b. After interacting with a group of children who have had some opportunity to engage in pretend play or construction, contemplate your performance in terms of the suggestions offered in this chapter. In what areas were you more or less successful? What questions do you still have regarding children's performance?

6. 👋 **Consult the standards**

    a. Read the preamble to the standards in your state for any three domains. Look for key terms such as *hands-on experience, cooperative learning, social cooperation, planning,* and *implementing* as well as obvious words such as *pretend play* and *construction.* Summarize how the preambles refer to play or playlike behaviors, learning dispositions, and child-initiated activity.

    b. Identify one specific standard in each of the three domains that could be assessed, facilitated, or both through pretend play or construction. Explain how this might work.

PRACTICE FOR YOUR CERTIFICATION OR LICENSURE EXAM

The following items will help you practice applying what you have learned in this chapter. They can help to prepare you for your course exam, the PRAXIS II exam, your state licensure or certification exam, and for working in developmentally appropriate ways with young children.

Play and Construction

Some parents have asked you why children are wasting their time in pretend play in the 4-year-old classroom instead of focusing on getting ready for kindergarten.

1. **Constructed-response question**

    a. Describe in detail your rationale for including pretend play in the classroom. Identify three things children are learning as they engage in pretend play.

    b. Identify three ways to document children's learning during their play.

2. **Multiple-choice question**

    What activities require the most intellectual and skillful behavior of the children?

    a. Building a hospital out of blocks and making signs and garments from materials in the creation center

    b. Putting together a 26-piece, precut movable string puppet

    c. Imitating the correct technique for doing watercolor using a full palette of paints

    d. Rolling a long snake out of dough and coiling it

Chapter
16

Integrating Curriculum Through Thematic Planning and Projects

You may wonder:

What is thematic teaching? What is a project?
What are the benefits of using themes and projects in my classroom?
What kinds of themes or projects are most suitable for preschoolers? for school-
    age children?
What steps will I follow to create a theme or project from start to finish?
What are the pitfalls I should avoid in developing themes and projects?

In this chapter, we present information to help answer your questions about themes and projects.

◆ ◆ *The children gather a variety of leaves for their collection. With their teacher's help, they create a graph depicting differences in the color, size, and shape of the leaves.*
◆ ◆ *The children create a classroom book in which they draw, dictate, and write descriptions of trees and leaves seen on a recent nature walk around their school.*
◆ ◆ *The children visit a local nursery to gather information about trees and discover which types of trees are most appropriate to plant on their playground.*
◆ ◆ *A lively discussion takes place when the teacher asks the children to predict what will happen to two large trees as spring arrives. She records the group's predictions, and encourages the children to observe the trees carefully over the next few weeks and record their observations. Children wonder why one tree has sprouted buds while the other has not. Why do some trees have smooth bark and others rough? These questions lead to individual and collective investigations by the children (also known as project work) that lasts several weeks.*

These are typical activities you might see occurring in any early childhood classroom from preschool through the second grade. All involve hands-on experiences for children and support children discovering information about trees. Children are also engaged in observing, comparing, counting, predicting, remembering, role-playing, expressing ideas, and developing fine-motor skills as they participate in such activities.

In one classroom, these activities might be dispersed throughout the year; in another, they might be offered within the framework of a multiweek theme focusing on trees. Children experiencing either approach will probably profit from the activities and increase their knowledge. However, youngsters involved in several tree-related activities concentrated within a month-long theme have the added advantage of being able to make connections among these activities that could be more difficult to make if the lessons were more spread out across time. The creation of such linkages is the essence of teaching with themes and projects (Kostelnik, 1996; Schickedanz, 2008).

DEFINING THEMES AND PROJECTS

Thematic teaching involves creating an array of meaningful activities planned around a central idea or topic. These activities are integrated into all aspects of the curriculum and take place within a concentrated time frame, ranging from several days to several weeks. Such integration creates a common thread among activities that facilitates children's generalization of knowledge and skills from one experience to another (Eliason & Jenkins, 2007; Machado & Meyer, 2008). Thematic teaching is not simply a collection of related activities, but an integrated approach to learning where teachers consider how learning will be supported in all areas of the curriculum. This type of integrated teaching provides powerful instruction to children because it is interesting, meaningful, and engaging to children and allows them to see the connection between experiences (Chaille, 2008).

Themes often evolve into long-term projects. A **project** is an in-depth investigation about a topic that incorporates childrens' questions, interests, and theories about that topic. One key aspect of project work is the active role children take in the selection of the topic and the direction of the project. In project work, children take on significant decision-making responsibility for how the project will unfold and what steps will be utilized next. Teachers must become active listeners and keen observers in order to base curriculum on children's interests and theories about the world.

HOW THEMES AND PROJECTS CONTRIBUTE TO CHILDREN'S CONCEPT DEVELOPMENT

Using themes and projects to organize young children's educational experiences is not a new idea. It has been a popular teaching method since Dewey (see chapter 1) first proposed that curriculum be related to children's real-life experiences. Integrated teaching that utilizes themes and projects continues to gain recognition through the project approach (Bodrova & Leong, 2007; Katz & Chard, 2000) and the schools of Reggio Emilia (Raikes & Edwards, 2009; Wein, 2004; Edwards, Gandini, & Forman, 1998). Thematic teaching supports children in forming connections among individual bits of information. These connections contribute to children's concept development and are the most important reason to use themes/projects as part of your program.

Conceptual Development

Concepts are the fundamental ideas children form about objects and events in the world. They serve as the cognitive categories that allow children to group perceptually distinct information, events, or objects (Eliason & Jenkins, 2007). As such, concepts serve as the building blocks of knowing, thinking, and reasoning.

Children form concepts through firsthand experiences (Bodrova & Leong, 2007). Each time children act on objects or interact with other people, they extract relevant bits of meaning from the encounter. New information is combined with previously acquired knowledge to clarify or modify current understandings and construct new ideas. By mentally cataloging a growing number of experiences and making finer discriminations and more abstract connections among them, children build, adjust, and expand their concepts with time.

Link Between Concepts and Thematic Teaching

The natural process of mentally connecting bits of information into more integrated ideas is enhanced through children's involvement in thematic instruction. As children engage in activities connected by a topic, they can more easily link what they have learned in one activity to what they have learned in another. In this way, thematic teaching provides children with opportunities to assimilate learning across the curriculum (Schickedanz, 2008; Bergstrom & O'Brien, 2001). For instance, participating in related aesthetic, language, and cognitive activities enables children to combine the individual elements of the curriculum into a cohesive whole. Similarly, when children carry out math, science, and social studies activities linked by a topic, they go beyond the bounds of traditional subject matter to form more holistic, comprehensive understandings. These understandings represent increasingly elaborate concepts. Because young children are continuously striving to make sense of their environment, the early childhood years are ones of rapid concept development. Consequently, educators have become increasingly interested in helping young children make conceptual connections through an integrated curriculum such as that used in thematic teaching (Chaille, 2008; Chard, 2001).

Additional Benefits for Children

In addition to enhancing children's concept development, thematic teaching provides other advantages to young learners. First, they offer children a means for learning about a topic through many different avenues. Consideration of individual needs and development is an important part of thematic planning. Teachers plan activities to accommodate the wide range of learning styles and abilities of the children in their classroom so that each child experiences success. If one activity is unappealing or does not match their learning style or fails to fit their abilities, then children have other options for learning about the concept. They may pursue alternative activities instead, gaining similar insights. This is not the case when ideas are presented only once or in only one way.

Second, themes and projects encourage children to immerse themselves in a topic. As children become interested in an idea, they often want to know *all* about it. Children are actively involved in planning and implementing the activities included in thematic teaching. This active involvement increases children's ownership of the experience as well as their own learning. It also enhances children's disposition to become mentally absorbed in pursuing ideas (Katz & Chard, 2000). Because thematic teaching is based on children's interests, children are more likely to be productively engaged than when activities are purely teacher initiated.

Keeping the early childhood curriculum varied and interesting is a third value of thematic teaching. Both children and teachers experience a sense of novelty with each new topic. As themes change, so do props, activities, and materials, which reinvigorates daily routines. Because much attention is given to the individual needs and interests of the specific children investigating the topic, even themes utilized in past years will have new focus. Not only do new themes provoke original activities, but the same or similar activities (such as grouping objects or writing in journals) are given a fresh emphasis when they are used to support different topics.

Fourth, group cohesiveness is promoted when several children focus on a particular topic simultaneously. As children discover classmates whose interests match theirs, their social circles widen. Their perceptions of one another also broaden because with each theme change, different children act as novices and experts; youngsters who are leaders for one topic may be followers for another. Thus, their patterns of interaction vary, allowing each child an opportunity to experience different social roles.

Finally, themes or projects prompted by the interests of some children may pique the curiosity of others. In this way, children broaden their interests over time and find new topics to explore.

TEACHERS' BENEFITS

By acting as a focus around which to plan, themes and projects help practitioners organize their thinking, choose relevant activities and vocabulary to support curricular goals, and locate resources prior to implementing their plans (Brewer, 2007). All these factors increase teachers' confidence.

Another advantage is that thematic teaching enables early childhood educators to address topics in sufficient breadth and depth to ensure that each child has had a chance to learn something new. In designing multiple theme- or project-related activities across domains, teachers structure the presentation of concepts more coherently and devise sequential plans that gradually challenge children's thinking (Eliason & Jenkins, 2007).

Providing integrated instruction through thematic teaching allows teachers to address multiple developmental domains through connected activities. This supports teachers in using their class time wisely and makes learning more meaningful to children (Schickedanz, 2008).

In addition, teachers who approach thematic teaching appropriately research each topic, generating a pool of factual information and identify primary and secondary sources that children can use to learn about the topic. Doing so increases their knowledge base as well as the accuracy of the information they provide to children. Further, it allows practitioners to consider in advance how to handle sensitive issues associated with the topic and prompts them to think of original activities, a process that teachers find intellectually stimulating. The collegiality that sometimes arises when teachers collaborate on developing thematic units or projects is also pleasing. Brainstorming theme-related activities, solving problems in relation to the theme/project, sharing materials, and swapping written plans are timesaving, invigorating activities that teachers find rewarding.

Themes and projects also provide a unifying framework for measuring children's progress. An important teacher responsibility is to continually assess children's grasp of concepts addressed by the curriculum (Bredekamp & Copple, 2009; Donegan, Hong, Trepanier-Street, & Finkelstein, 2005). Teachers do this by observing children and interacting with children individually and in groups. Teachers document these interactions and later reflect carefully on this documentation. This process of revisiting can provide profound insights into children's learning. Attempting to evaluate children's concept development on a child-by-child basis, with no unifying framework within which to make judgments, is extremely difficult because of the fragmentation. Such assessments are more easily accomplished when practitioners have a single concept on which to focus. Seeing and hearing many children within the group demonstrate varying interpretations of the same concept provides a context for the teacher's judgments. For instance, an adult is better able to determine whether children's incomplete or erroneous ideas are universal or particular to an individual. Teachers may also gauge which of several activities will enhance or detract from children's grasp of a particular idea. This is more difficult to accomplish within a totally unrelated set of activities. Thematic teaching allows teachers to integrate curriculum standards in a meaningful way for children; and as children's participation and learning are documented, teachers are able to gather evidence of how state and local education standards have been met (Benson & Miller, 2008; Helm, 2008). For all these reasons, practitioners report that theme teaching and project work are extremely self-satisfying (Hurley & Blake, 1997; Peaslee, Snyder, & Casey, 2007).

PROGRAM EFFECTS

As you can see, thematic teaching enhances both children's and practitioners' educational experiences and also yields programwide benefits. First, themes and projects can be implemented across diverse program structures, among children of all ages, with youngsters whose needs differ greatly, by beginning teachers and more seasoned ones, and by teachers whose philosophies and styles vary (Donegan et al., 2005; Dresden & Lee, 2007). Integrated teaching that utilizes a thematic approach allows for a wide range of learning opportunities, permitting each child to use his or her individual learning strengths (Railsback, 2002). Because educators create themes and facilitate projects with a specific group of children in mind, they are better able to individualize their instruction to accommodate the needs of all the children in the group.

Second, family members who are informed of upcoming themes and projects are better able to contribute their knowledge, expertise, and resources to children's educational experiences. They can more easily envision how to participate in children's education when they have a particular topic in mind than to do so in terms of the more generalized instruction that takes place from day to day. Consequently, family support for the program may go beyond the traditional donations of recycled materials. For instance, knowing that the class is studying birds, a family may send in a bird's nest they found, a photograph of a bird taken at their feeder, or a magazine article about birds. An older sibling may help the children build bird feeders, or a grandparent may show the children how to care for a baby bird fallen from its nest. This kind of family involvement promotes constructive home–school relationships and helps parents and other family members feel more involved in the educational process.

The third and perhaps most important impact of thematic teaching is that it provides a tool by which content learning and process learning can be integrated within the curriculum. Often treated as mutually exclusive categories of knowledge, content and process can be combined through thematic teaching without violating the integrity of either.

Focusing on Content

Content learning encompasses all the factual information relevant to the theme. Learning content requires such mental abilities as attending, listening, observing, remembering, and recounting (Hendrick & Weissman, 2010). Thus, a group of first graders studying wild birds might engage in a variety of experiences to learn the following facts:

❑ Birds live in a variety of places: in the woods, meadows, plains, and deserts; near ponds, lakes, and oceans; and in cities.
❑ Each species of bird builds a nest characteristic of the species.
❑ Birds build nests to protect their eggs, which contain baby birds.
❑ Birds build nests of varying complexities.
❑ Different bird species build their nests in different places: on the ground, above the ground, in the open, or hidden.

As you already know, simple exposure to factual content such as this does not teach in and of itself. Only when children become physically involved in, talk about, and reflect on their experiences do they learn from them. This type of thematic teaching provides hands-on discovery which is highly motivating to children (Henniger, 2009). Children might gain access to factual knowledge about wild birds through firsthand activities such as going outdoors to watch birds fly, observing a nesting bird, recording the numbers and kinds of birds they see, or examining several different abandoned bird nests. Teachers might also give children make-believe wings and straw to use to act like birds caring for their young, or teachers could work with children to construct a replica of a bird's nest. Throughout these activities, teachers and children would

The children's interest in siblings at home led their teacher to introduce a theme on families.

discuss which type of bird might build which type of nest, which would further extend children's content learning. In addition, because the most appropriate themes and projects are based on children's interests and experiences, children are more likely to be intrinsically motivated to learn content to answer their own questions and satisfy their own curiosity. As teachers observe carefully, they are able to see children demonstrate in numerous ways what content they have learned.

Focusing on Process

All the aesthetic, affective, cognitive, language, social, and physical operations and skills that form the basis for children's experiences within the early childhood curriculum constitute process learning. Because they encompass the "whole" child, such processes range from imagining, creating, and performing to grouping, differentiating, inferring, and concluding to pretending, representing, and constructing. Just as with content learning, children gain proficiency in process learning through hands-on activities. In fact, the same bird activities cited in the preceding section could provide the means for children to increase their competence and understanding in any domain.

Integrating Content and Process

Content and process come together in the integrated activities of thematic teaching. These activities form the basis for instruction and offer children an applied means for experiencing the curriculum. Thus, two children acting out the roles of wild birds not only gain factual insight into bird life, but also have opportunities to practice social and cognitive processes such as offering ideas ("You be the baby bird. I'll be the mommy."), reaching compromises ("Okay, I'm the mommy bird first, and then you."), and drawing conclusions ("If we have two mommy birds, we'll need two nests."). In fact, during the early childhood period, often the content included in each activity is simply the medium through which children explore other, more process-oriented operations and skills (Hendrick & Weissman, 2010). Sometimes children may be much more involved in the process learning represented within that experience. In this case, the children may eventually ignore the bird theme to concentrate on the dynamics of their social relationship. Even so, they are continuing to learn and benefit from the activity.

Even though children frequently stray from the goal originally identified by the teacher to explore aspects of the activity related to other domains, it does not mean teachers should simply provide generic activities with no real content-learning or process-learning goals in mind. Teachers must be purposeful in their planning so that they assist children in exploring facts and processes they might not otherwise experience and ensure a coherent, comprehensive set of activities from which children may choose. The integrative nature of such activities is well suited to the holistic manner in which children learn.

PITFALLS IN THEMATIC TEACHING

Considering all these benefits, thematic teaching might appear to automatically translate into DAP. Unfortunately, this is not always true. Themes may be enacted poorly. For instance, some teachers violate the principles of DAP by failing to accommodate children's needs for movement and physical activity, social interaction, and independence. These educators may try to get across the "facts" of the theme by reciting them to children or by creating a mountain of theme-related worksheets for children to complete. Teachers using such approaches ignore the importance of hands-on learning and self-discovery.

Some topics are too narrow or too contrived to make good themes. Examples are weekly plans centered on letters of the alphabet, such as *g*. As children paint with green tempera at the easel, eat grapes for a snack, and growl like lions, the teacher may confidently believe that youngsters are learning all about the letter *g*. In reality, the children may be focusing on the subject of their paintings rather than on the color, they may be thinking of grapes as fruit rather than a *g* word, and they may be more aware of the loudness or mock ferocity of their growling than the consonant sound they are making. Because *g* is not a concept and does not directly relate to children's real-life experiences, it is not a worthy theme.

Another problem occurs when teachers fail to adequately research the theme they are planning. Relying on their personal store of knowledge, they may omit critical aspects of the topic or present erroneous information to children as fact. For instance, assuming she knew enough about opossums to handle the interests of the 3-year-olds in her class, Ms. Miller told the children that opossums are mammals (they are marsupials) and that wild opossums have as many as 20 babies at a time (not so). Such misinformation undermines the conceptual value of theme planning.

Some teachers may use the same themes over and over each year without regard to the individual children in their class. True thematic teaching is rooted in children's interests and focuses on the abilities of the children in the group. Because the abilities and interests of each group of children will be different, it is not likely that the same topics can be completed in the same way or on the same timeline as was done with previous groups. By looking at each topic with fresh eyes and utilizing new ideas, teachers are able to capitalize on teachable moments with children and prevent themselves from feeling stagnant.

Lack of resources may be a pitfall related to some themes. Although a topic may appear appropriate for a theme and even seem to have the potential to lead to a long-term project, it is necessary that you have adequate resources available before you begin. Topics for which there are no **primary sources** of information do not make good themes in early childhood. When teachers choose topics where no firsthand experiences exist for children to investigate their questions and discover new information, true thematic teaching cannot occur. Firsthand experiences could include visiting field sites to learn about the topic, speaking with local experts, or manipulating and investigating real-life objects. **Secondary sources** such as books can certainly be used to supplement the primary sources, but are not adequate for discovery learning.

Another problem is planning themes or projects that are always the same length of time, regardless of the children's interest in the topic. Some topics are better suited to short-term investigations, while others can capture and hold children's interests for an extended period of time. Though teachers may have an idea of how long a theme or project will last, it is better to remain open to the children's ideas and make adjustments to the timeline as necessary.

Finally, some teachers assume they are theme teaching effectively when they simply relate several activities to a central prop, such as "pockets." Children may sing about having a smile in their pocket, hear a story about pockets, eat "pocket bread" for a snack, and decorate paper pockets. Unfortunately, these activities do not challenge children to think, problem solve, expand their literacy skills, or develop their social and physical abilities. Although the activities may keep children busy and entertained, they fail to engage childrens' minds and bodies in the excitement of real learning. This type of theme planning is trivial—it addresses neither content learning nor process learning, and does not fit the definition of the term *thematic teaching* that we espouse. Good theme planning will incorporate meaningful activities and materials that are of high interest to the children and provide real-life opportunities to explore and understand the theme. Any activity planned should be worthy of the children's time and attention.

PRINCIPLES OF EFFECTIVE THEMATIC TEACHING

Effective thematic teaching is much more complex and comprehensive than any of the misdirected approaches just described. Thematic teaching is most likely to be effective when activities and experiences have the following characteristics (Katz & Chard, 2000).

- ❑ Directly relate to children's real-life experiences, building on what children know and what is readily observable in their immediate environments
- ❑ Are age appropriate and culturally sensitive
- ❑ Represent a concept for children to investigate
- ❑ Are supported by a body of factual knowledge that has been adequately researched by the teacher(s), including primary and secondary sources of information

❏ Involve firsthand, direct investigation
❏ Address all six curricular domains and promote their integration
❏ Address thematic content and processes more than once and in different kinds of activities (exploratory play, guided discovery, problem solving, discussions, demonstrations, direct instruction, small-group and whole-group activities)
❏ Integrate content learning with process learning
❏ Give children a chance to practice and apply basic skills appropriate for their age and ability
❏ Expand into projects that are child initiated and child directed
❏ Encourage children to document and reflect on what they are learning
❏ Involve children's families in some way

HOW TO CREATE THEMATIC UNITS

Go to the Assignments and Activities section of Topic 11: DAP/Teaching Strategies in the MyEducationLab for your course and complete the activity entitled *A Theme Is Hatched*. Ideas for themes and projects can come from a variety of sources.

Sources of Ideas

Cats, gardens, art and artists, storytelling, people in our neighborhood, insects, measuring—all these topics are potential themes or subjects of study. As an early childhood educator, you will have to decide which topics are best suited to the particular children in your group. Ideas are available from many sources: the children, special events, unexpected happenings, program-mandated content, and teachers and parents.

The Children.   The best sources for thematic ideas are the children themselves and what they are experiencing day to day. Observe the children carefully to see what things they frequently enact, discuss, or wonder about. Listen carefully to their questions to determine what they are trying to figure out. This will provide a relevant basis for selecting and implementing themes in your program. Keen observations and vigilant listening will provide you with insight into what the children already know, what misconceptions they may have, and what theories guide their actions and beliefs. Challenge yourself to think deeply about questions the children ask or comments they make. Sometimes what appears to be a simple question might actually be the impetus for a new theme or project. You may use more formal means to assess children's interests, such as interviewing children or using the KWHLH brainstorming strategy described in chapter 4. Information from parents regarding upcoming events in children's lives or events at home provide additional clues about concepts that will be important to children in your class throughout the year.

For instance, you might decide to study "machines" because children are curious about the heavy equipment they observed at a nearby construction site. The birth of new siblings to one or more families in the class might prompt an inquiry related to babies or families. Ordinary events like these are important to young children, which is why they provide such a strong foundation for planning and implementing themes in the classroom. No matter what age group you are teaching, child-initiated topics are a valuable source for themes and should be the basis for many of the topics you teach.

Special Events.   Occasionally, out-of-the-ordinary occurrences such as a field trip to the farm, an assembly featuring guide dogs for the blind, or the celebration of Arbor Day also serve as a spark for theme development. Occasions like these, which teachers know about in advance, may be integrated into or serve as the cornerstone for related units of study such as "farm products," "working dogs," or "trees."

Unexpected Happenings.   Sometimes unanticipated events stimulate children's thinking in new directions. This was the case for second graders intrigued by the habits of a grackle whose nest was in the rain gutter above their classroom window. The teacher responded to their curiosity by introducing a unit on wild birds, using the grackle as a firsthand example.

Program-Mandated Content.   In addition to child-inspired content, many school districts require particular subject matter to be addressed at given grade levels. Some programs also require certain topics such as dental care or fire safety be included in the curriculum. Such required content can also serve as a basis for thematic teaching. Social studies, science, health, math, or

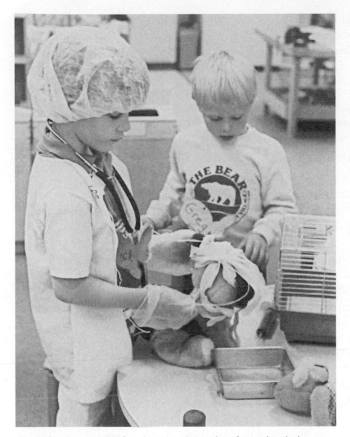

These boys' continuing interest in caring for animals in the pretend play area may signal a good topic for a theme or project.

language arts concepts can be used as the core around which a variety of theme-related activities are created and integrated throughout the day. As teachers plan theme-related activities, they can identify which required content will be addressed by which activity and what evidence will be gathered to document children's learning. This approach has the advantage of ensuring that all important subjects receive adequate attention. Moreover, teachers gain the satisfaction of covering prescribed material in ways that are meaningful to children.

Teachers and Family Members. Theme ideas may also have their source in concepts that teachers and family members find exciting or valuable. A teacher enthralled by gardening may share his or her enthusiasm through a unit on plants. The teacher's desire to teach children constructive ways of working together could be the motivation behind the theme "cooperation."

Considering Essential Theme Criteria

With so many options, the number of potential topics usually exceeds the amount of time available to teach them. Certain additional criteria will narrow your choices and help you pick the most appropriate themes. When finalizing an idea for a theme, consider the following five factors:

1. Relevance
2. Hands-on activities
3. Diversity and balance across the curriculum
4. Availability of primary and secondary resources and materials
5. Potential for projects

Relevance. The most important criterion to consider when selecting a topic is relevance. Themes are relevant when the concepts they represent are directly tied to children's real-life experiences and build on what children know. If relevance has been properly considered, themes are age appropriate, individually appropriate, and socioculturally appropriate. Relevant themes highlight concepts with which children have initial familiarity and provide new insights into their daily experiences. Themes such as "self," "home," "family," "foods," and "plants" are pertinent to young children because they help the children understand their lives and the world around them. In contrast, some themes are inappropriate for this age group. "Life in ancient Rome" and "penguins" are too far removed from most children's day-to-day living to be relevant. Gravity and electricity are too abstract to constitute an entire theme, especially for children younger than 5 years of age.

Naturally, themes are most meaningful when they match the needs and interests of particular groups of children. Locale as well as family and community resources or traditions will influence which aspects of the concept are most relevant. For instance, "plants" has relevance for most children no matter where they live. However, children growing up near a marsh would naturally focus on cattails, marsh grass, and milkweed as examples of plant life, whereas children living in an arid region would find studying desert vegetation such as cacti, sagebrush, and yucca plants more relevant. Moreover, entire topics that are relevant to one group of young children may be irrelevant to others. For example, studying tidal pools could be a significant learning experience for children living in Kennebunk, Maine (which is near the ocean), but not so for those in Lincoln, Nebraska (which is landlocked). Having never seen a tidal pool, the Nebraska group would benefit from studying a more familiar water habitat, such as a pond or a river.

Timeliness is another aspect of relevance to consider when choosing topics. Timely themes build on children's current interests. What are children talking about? What has piqued their interest? The answers to these questions should shape your choice of themes. Consequently, effective theme planners do not plan a year's worth of themes in advance. Instead, they create one theme at a time in response to children's curiosity or concerns. Timeliness may also prompt teachers to substitute one theme for another to take advantage of current events or to respond to shifts in children's needs and interests. The reasoning behind early childhood professionals' decisions to change themes is illustrated in the following situation.

A group of first graders was deeply engrossed in a theme on folktales when construction began on the empty lot next to their school. The construction stimulated much discussion among the children. What were they building? How are all the different types of heavy equipment used? What types of jobs did the different workers have and what were their responsibilities? Capitalizing on their excitement, the teacher substituted a theme on construction for the plant life unit she had originally planned.

In the preceding example, delaying attention to the construction or ignoring children's hypotheses would have resulted in missed learning opportunities. The timeliness of the theme in relation to the children's expressed interest made it relevant to these youngsters.

Hands-On Activities. Another criterion for selecting a theme is how well the content lends itself to the creation of related hands-on activities. Only topics whose content children can experience through the direct manipulation of objects are suitable for children 3 to 8 years old. This hands-on instruction *must* include firsthand experiences, but may also involve some simulations. Both forms of hands-on instruction could be offered through exploratory activities, guided discovery, problem solving, discussions, cooperative learning, demonstrations, and direct-instruction activities. However, the emphasis must be on exploratory play and inquiry if children are to truly expand their concepts with time.

Firsthand experiences are those in which children become directly involved with the actual objects or phenomena under study. These experiences are real, not analogous or imaginary. For instance, youngsters engaged in the theme "pets" would gain firsthand insights into the life and activities of pets by observing and caring for pets in the classroom. A visit to a pet shop to see the variety of pets available and a trip to a veterinarian to see how pet health is maintained are other examples of real-life experiences. These primary sources give children opportunities to derive relevant bits of information from the original source of the concept. Simply looking at pictures or hearing about these things could not replicate the richness or stimulation provided by firsthand involvement. When teachers know that children have had no direct experience with the theme and that related firsthand activities cannot be provided in the program, they should consider the theme inappropriate for their group.

Simulations are another hands-on activity type. They approximate but do not exactly duplicate firsthand experiences. Providing make-believe ears and tails so that children can enact life as a pet and working with children to construct a replica of a veterinarian's office using toy animals are examples of simulations. In each case, children act directly on objects or carry out activities that resemble the real thing. However, for such activities to be meaningful for children they will need to have some firsthand experience with the topic prior to the simulation.

Once you have determined that a topic offers a wealth of potential hands-on activities, consider the *variety* of hands-on experiences children will have. Activities should provide meaningful experiences that promote critical thinking and allow children to develop a deeper and more relevant understanding of the topic. For example, themes that prompt many craft ideas but are not well suited to pretend play, games, or problem-solving activities are best rejected as too limited. A more appropriate topic would encompass a wider range of learning opportunities for children.

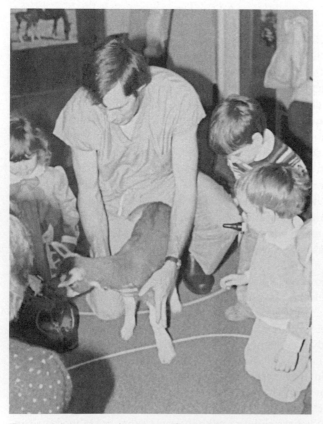

These visitors came because of the children's interest in animals and gave the children firsthand experience with the "real thing."

Diversity and Balance Across the Curriculum. Throughout the year, children should experience a broad array of themes. Thus, diversity and balance across the curriculum is another criterion for consideration. For example, some themes are primarily scientific (seasons, machines, leaves, insects, and fish); others reflect a social studies emphasis (families, friends, occupations, and the neighborhood); and still others highlight language arts content (storytelling, poetry, and writers). Furthermore, many topics can be adapted to fit several foci depending on what intrigues the children and what the teacher chooses to emphasize. For example, a unit on stores could stress the mathematical content of money and counting, the more social aspects of employees' working together toward a common goal, or the health-related focus of safety in the store. Teachers can deal with these ideas separately, sequentially, or in combination.

When selecting themes, teachers should choose a cross section of topics in which all content areas are eventually addressed. With time, children will then have opportunities to expand their concepts and skills across a wide range of subjects, with no one area predominating. For instance, a teacher has both diversity and balance in mind when, in response to second graders' fascination with the space shuttle, he or she plans a natural science unit on the sky to be followed by a theme on space exploration in which social cooperation is the primary focus. In this case, children initiated the original idea for the themes, and the teacher influenced their direction.

Resources and Materials. The availability of support materials is another factor to consider when determining what themes to select (Katz & Chard, 2000). Because children need objects to act on, teachers should choose themes for which several real items are obtainable. Children require access to real-life materials for activities to be meaningful and interesting. Themes for which no real objects are available for children to use should be dropped from consideration. This is also true for themes that depend on one spectacular prop, such as a hang glider or a spinning wheel, which, if suddenly unavailable, would deny children their only access to direct firsthand investigation of the topic. Better topics are those for which a variety of real materials are easily accessible. In addition, consider opportunities for field visits or local experts, which can serve as resources for the children. For example, trips to visit a nearby pond or opportunities to ask questions of a waterfowl specialist would be valuable experiences for children's understanding of ducks.

Project Potential. The best thematic topics are those that have project potential. As mentioned earlier in this chapter, projects are open-ended activities in which youngsters undertake, during a period of days, weeks, or even months, the in-depth study of some facet of the theme. Ideas for projects emerge as children gain experience with a concept and become curious about particular aspects of it (Chard, 1998a). Children need guidance to focus their ideas and identify questions that can be investigated (Worth & Grollman, 2003). As children's interests evolve, individual or small groups of children, in consultation with the teacher, plan and then carry out a relevant project. These projects are primarily child initiated and child directed. For example, children involved in a pet theme might wonder about pets owned by classmates and adults in the group. In response, the children could decide to conduct interviews and create a book of all the different pets represented in the class. They might use the information they gather to create charts, stories, and displays related to their investigation. Later, the children could share what they have learned with family members in a celebration at the conclusion of the unit. Project work requires sustained effort and involves learning processes such as exploring, investigating, hypothesizing, reading, recording, discussing, representing, and evaluating. Consequently, projects give children many chances to plan, select manageable tasks for themselves, apply skills, represent what they have learned, and monitor their personal progress. More structured than spontaneous play and more self-determined than teacher-planned instruction, projects provide a bridge between the two. They offer children strategies for exploring topics in ways that are individualized and therefore more personally meaningful.

Because projects are such a valuable learning tool, we invited Sylvia Chard, a noted expert on the project approach, to offer a brief description of how projects can be implemented in early childhood classrooms.

Although projects could be carried out independent of a theme, we suggest that they serve as an extension of theme planning. In this model, projects evolve after children have had exposure to a thematic concept in the ways described so far. As a result of participating in teacher-planned activities and group discussions, children begin to suggest related topics they would like to further examine. These investigations become their projects. While children carry out projects, the teacher promotes their learning by using many of the teaching strategies found in chapter 3, such as reflections, scaffolding, questions, and silence. Teachers also help children document their work and prompt them to reflect on what they have discovered. Although not every theme will lead to a project, the best themes are those that would allow projects to develop in accord with children's interests.

Let us now turn our attention to the steps necessary to develop a thematic unit from start to finish.

▲ ▲

THE PROJECT APPROACH

Sylvia C. Chard, Ph.D.
University of Alberta, Canada

A *project* is an in-depth study of a real-world topic. Teaching strategies associated with the project approach are designed to help children develop a fuller understanding of the world around them. Through collaborative projects, children carry out investigations and learn many ways to represent new information. As children study topics in depth, they apply language and math skills as they build new understanding in the areas of science and social studies.

Origins

In the 1960s and 1970s there was interest around the world in "infant schools," where young children were educated in Great Britain. These programs featured the "integrated day." Young children experienced no separation of curricular subjects and learned incidentally with the guidance of the teacher as they carried out in-depth studies of local buildings, businesses, services, and features of the natural environment. The book *Engaging Children's Minds: The Project Approach* (1989) was written to rekindle interest in what Katz and Chard believe to have been an important part of early education in mid-20th-century Britain.

Methods

The teacher selects a topic on the basis of the children's interests, curricular goals, and the availability of local resources. The teacher brainstorms his or her experience, knowledge, and ideas, representing them in a topic **web**. The potential scope of the project is assessed. A web of ideas is developed throughout the project and continues to be useful for planning and recording its progress.

Three Phases in the Life of a Project

Projects generally develop through an introductory phase, a research phase, and a review phase. This three-phase structure helps the teacher organize and guide the study in ways that match the children's interests and personal involvement.

Phase 1

The teacher discusses the topic with the children to find out about their previous experiences with the content. The children represent their experiences in a variety of ways and show how well they understand the concepts involved. The teacher helps the children ask questions about what they would like to investigate. A letter is sent to parents about the study, inviting them to talk with their children about the topic and to see if anyone can offer special expertise.

Phase 2

The teacher arranges opportunities for the children to do fieldwork and to speak to experts. Resources are provided to help children with their investigations: real objects, books, and other research materials. The teacher suggests ways for children to carry out a variety of investigations. Children are involved in representing what they learn and in participating in learning centers at their own developmental levels in terms of basic skills, drawing, music, construction, and dramatic play. Different representational possibilities can be suggested and provided for. Children share their work with classmates in class meetings at the beginning and end of project work sessions. The teacher helps children be aware of all the different work being done through class or group discussion and displays of work around the classroom. The topic web developed earlier provides a shorthand means of documenting the progress of the project.

Phase 3

Once the teacher decides that the work of the project is almost complete, he or she arranges for the children to share what they have learned. They feature the highlights of their project for another class, the principal, or the parents. In preparing such an event, the teacher helps the children purposefully review and evaluate the whole project. The teacher also offers the children imaginative ways of personalizing their new knowledge through art, stories, and drama. Finally, the teacher uses children's ideas and interests to make a meaningful transition between the project being concluded and the topic of study for the next theme or project.

Assessment

Assessment is carried out daily as the children plan their work and implement their plans. The teacher notes how well the children understand the information they are learning, how well they can apply the skills they have acquired, and how well they can account for what they have learned, explaining it to other children at class meetings and in the final sharing or celebration of learning. The teacher makes anecdotal notes about dispositional learning and how children approach their work, collaborate with peers, and develop their strengths and interests.

Distinctive Features

Projects involve in-depth investigation. Teachers encourage children to develop interests and work on their strengths. Projects are energized by questions the teacher has helped the children to formulate. Activities are chosen for their representational contribution to the evidence that the whole class group has collaboratively achieved a significant depth of understanding. The project approach offers teachers a powerful way to address many aspects of the early childhood curriculum.

Where Readers Can Find Out More

A comprehensive website about the project approach is www .project-approach.com. In addition, the project approach is described in more detail in Chard (1998a, 1998b, 1999, 2001, 2002) and Katz and Chard (2000).

▲ ▲

Creating an Information Base

The core of every theme is the factual information on which it is founded and that is embodied in a comprehensive list of **terms, facts,** and **principles** (TFPs) relevant to the theme. These TFPs are similar in form to the content you learned about in chapter 3. Although the TFPs embody the theme, adults do not formally recite them to children. Instead, educators provide hands-on activities where discovery learning can take place. Through such activities children derive factual information, learn relevant terminology, and engage in relevant conversations with peers and adults. Through such experiences, children gain meaningful insights that enlarge and refine their concepts.

To be useful, TFPs must be accurate and thorough. Five steps are suggested for creating a suitable listing.

Step 1. Select a topic of study. Keep in mind relevance to children, hands-on activities, diversity and balance across the curriculum, the availability of resources, and project potential.
Step 2. Brainstorm logical subtopics for the theme. You may do this on your own or in conjunction with colleagues or the children. For instance, a unit on cats might include the subtopics depicted in Figure 16.1, which could be relevant to children in preschool through second grade.
Step 3. Use reference books, field guides, textbooks, children's books, or other people as resources to help you thoroughly research the topic. You can then generate a list of TFPs to support the various subtopics in the topic web you created. Begin by writing down every item that seems relevant to the theme. At this point, do not worry about differentiating terms, facts, or principles. (Some teachers reverse steps 2 and 3, beginning with a general list of content and then developing a topic web. Choose the sequence that makes the most sense to you.)
Step 4. On the basis of the children's interests and abilities, decide whether a general overview or a more in-depth study of one of the subtopics is best suited to your class. If the former is true, choose a few TFPs from each of the subcategories; if the latter is your choice, focus primarily on one subset of TFPs.
Step 5. Pick up to 10 TFPs on which to focus directly. Use the others simply as background information or as a guide for responding to children's questions regarding the topic.

Developing Activity Ideas

The steps for developing appropriate theme-related activities are straightforward and not nearly as time consuming as those required to create TFPs.

Step 6. Brainstorm activities for each of the TFPs you selected. Go through the TFPs one at a time, generating at least two or three activities per TFP. Do this with a colleague or in a small group to enhance the richness and variety of the activities generated. For instance, you might want children to learn that "people who own cats are responsible for providing them with food, shelter, attention, and medical care." Sample activities to support this information could include

FIGURE 16.1 Initial Topic Web for "Cats" Theme

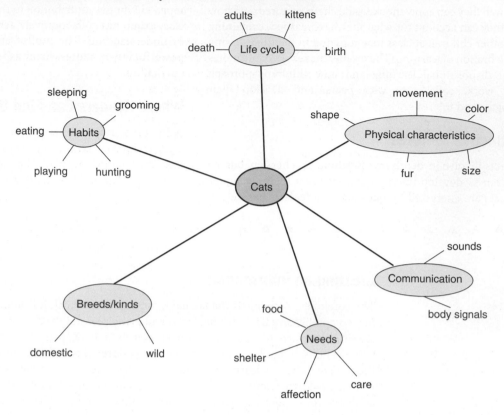

(a) having children take care of a visiting cat for a day or a week, (b) reading books about cat care, (c) visiting a veterinarian's office to witness cat care, (d) inviting a cat owner to visit the class to talk about how he or she takes care of a cat, and (e) creating collages that represent the different things people do to care for their cats.

Step 7. Assign each activity to one of the six curricular domains described in this text. Make sure to have no less than one activity per domain per week. You might have a different number of theme-related activities in each domain. However, you should strive for some balance among them.

Depending on how you structure it, the same activity could be adapted to more than one domain. Thus, a collage designed to help children represent different ways cat owners care for their cats takes on a social focus if children are asked to cooperate as a group to create one large collage. In contrast, giving each child his or her own collage to work on, along with several cutting tools, emphasizes the fine-motor aspects of the activity, which makes it more physical. With this example in mind, you can use the same activity to teach more than one skill on the same day or on different days.

Step 8. Make certain to include the varying types of activities described in chapter 3 (i.e., exploratory play, guided discovery, problem solving, discussions, demonstrations, and direct instruction). If you become aware that watching or listening dominates the activities, redesign them to include more hands-on involvement.

Making a Plan

Once the TFPs and activities are fully developed, assemble them into a thematic plan. Such a plan typically covers no less than 2 weeks' instruction and may be extended for several weeks after that, often in the pursuit of child-initiated projects. The following steps outline the planning process.

Step 9. Commit your ideas to paper, incorporating several theme-related activities into your lesson plans. Some teachers plan each day on a separate sheet of paper; others put an entire week's activities on a single sheet. Consider what time of the day certain activities will take place and whether each will be presented once or on several days. You will also want to consider if certain activities should be presented early to provide a foundation for other activities. Design additional non-theme-related activities to round out the rest of the instructional time and to give children some respite from the theme. Remember, having fewer well-developed theme-related activities is better than contriving to make activities fit.

Step 10. Check your plan to ensure that at least three theme-related activities are included every day and that by week's end all the domains have been included.

Step 11. Consider classroom management issues such as availability of materials, numbers of adults available to help, and special events. Adjust your plan as necessary. For instance, if you have scheduled easel painting and tie-dyeing for the same day and time but have only three smocks in your room, move one of these activities to another time in the day or to another day so that you will have enough smocks for children at both areas.

Step 12. Plan for a portion of group time to focus on the theme each day. Such whole-group activities allow children to become aware of certain concept-related information simultaneously, which provides a common foundation for exploration. Carried out at the beginning of class time, circle activities serve as an introduction to the day's experiences. Conducted at the end, they give children a chance to review and summarize their current understanding of the theme.

Step 13. Make a final check of your written plan, focusing on how well you have addressed the TFPs. Tally how often you have used each. Refer to your original brainstorming list if you need a reminder of which activities relate to which TFPs. Verify that each TFP receives attention at least three or four times during the week. Also make sure that individual TFPs have been addressed within different domains across the plan. If you notice that some domains are seldom theme related or that certain TFPs are always addressed within the same domain, revise your plan to achieve better integration. In addition, if some TFPs have been left out or are underrepresented, either add a few related activities or extend the theme another week, focusing on these TFPs as well as some additional TFPs, to give the children more time to explore the concept. In this way you will create 2-, 3-, and 4-week units.

Step 14. After your plan is complete, gather or create any materials you will need. To minimize preparation time, use some props for more than one activity.

Step 15. Enrich the classroom atmosphere by including theme-related materials throughout the classroom. Post theme-associated pictures at children's eye level. Choose CDs, videotapes, DVDs, audiotapes, books, finger plays, or songs related to the topic.

Implementing the Theme

Once you have a sound plan, implement the theme. Let the following steps guide your actions.

Step 16. Carry out your plan. Also, take advantage of spontaneous events to further children's understanding of the concept they are exploring.

Step 17. Assess and document children's understanding of and interest in the theme through observations, interviews, group discussions, work samples, and constructions. Make note (mentally and through written anecdotes) of times when children talk about the theme, when they exhibit theme-related behaviors and knowledge, and when family members mention incidents illustrating children's awareness of and reactions to the topic. During the free-choice or learning center portion of your day, keep track of the activities children choose and the amount of time they spend there. A participation chart can help maintain this type of record (described in chapter 7). Record evidence of covering any required content and examples of children's learning which may be mandated by local or state standards.

Step 18. Help children reflect on their understanding of thematic content and processes. Invite them to make drawings, graphs, murals, maps, constructions, journal entries, paintings, charts, dramatizations, and reports to represent their learning. Take photographs of the children's work. Keep work samples and include them in portfolios or display them for children's reference. See Figure 16.2 for an example of how one preschool class documented their investigation of a transportation unit.

Step 19. Extend the thematic unit if children's interest remains high. As children demonstrate understanding of and

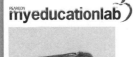

PEARSON
myeducationlab

Go to the Video Examples section of Topic 10: Planning in the MyEducationLab for your course and watch the video entitled *Birds: Part 2*. See how teachers integrated the topic of birds throughout the curriculum.

FIGURE 16.2   Preschoolers Document Their Investigation Using Photos, Drawings, and Words

curiosity about the subject, introduce additional TFPs in subsequent weeks or move into the project phase of investigation. An example of a project carried out by teacher Jennifer Heaton and her kindergarten class at Beech Hill Elementary School, Summerville, South Carolina, is presented in Figure 16.3. It grew out of a unit on transportation and took 2 months to complete.
Step 20. Establish two-way communication with families about the theme. Provide theme- and project-related information to them through newsletters. Invite family members to contribute

FIGURE 16.3 The Truck Project

Introduction

The kindergarten children had been involved in a thematic unit on transportation. They collected ideas in a topic web, generated questions, and shared experiences. Their teacher was able to bring in a tire from a Mack truck. The size of the truck tire captured the children's attention and provided the starting point for the "truck" project.

Phase 1

The teacher scheduled a field experience at the trucking company where her mother worked in the payroll office. The children planned questions to ask at the trucking company field site, ranging from "How do you hook the truck and the trailer?" to "How do you pay for the trucks?" The children's interests were in the truck and the company. The teacher prepared personnel at the field site for the types of questions the children would have and the experiences they were hoping for.

Phase 2

The children had previously learned about questioning, sketching, and investigating. Before leaving school, the children chose specific areas of the truck and the company that they wanted to investigate. They toured the grounds of the company, including the fueling lane, the tire shop, the maintenance shop, the tank-washing area, and the office. The president of the company, a safety specialist, and the comptroller accompanied the class on the tour and answered the children's questions.

One truck was cleaned and parked in an area where the children could examine it thoroughly. The children recorded their observations in field sketches. Some sketched inside the truck, some the tires, and some the tank they saw being washed. A few children tallied how many trucks they saw in the yard. A small group of children went into the office area and investigated the dispatch process.

On returning to their classroom, the children discussed the idea of building their own truck. To begin, they made a basic frame for the truck from cardboard and drew lines for the doors and windows. After several discussions, they designed the hood so that it opened. The engine had to be accessible. They referred to pictures and finally decided where the teacher should cut so that the hood would open correctly. They painted the truck.

A few children worked on making the tires for the truck. They determined how to trace a circle on

cardboard, then painted the circles. Once they made the tires, they wanted to attach them to the truck so that the tires would actually turn. With the teacher's help, they tried four ways and then decided on the one that they could do by themselves.

As their work continued, the children thought about how they could set up a trucking company in the learning centers in the classroom. The children used various materials to make the things they needed, including a toolbox, fan belts, fenders, windshield wipers, tools, forms, money, a fuel tank, and a fuel pump.

Three children worked on the fuel tank and pump. They wanted to make numbers that really turned. It took them several attempts, but they finally achieved what they had envisioned.

The children paid great attention to the details of the truck. They were careful to include the grill, an engine, a steering wheel that turned, a driver's seat that bounced, a bed behind the seats, a fifth wheel, mud flaps, taillights, side mirrors, and a horn that worked (a bicycle horn!).

As the truck was being constructed and the trucking company developed, the children wrote a poem and made books about trucks. One large area of the classroom wall was devoted to a display of the children's work. The wall area displayed the children's field sketches as well as photographs of the areas the children had sketched. This area became the working area for construction of the model truck. The truck eventually became so large—6 feet long and 4 feet tall—that the teacher and the children moved it into the hall to complete work on it.

Phase 3

As a culminating event, the class made a presentation of their truck and gave a tour of their trucking company. The model truck was exhibited in front of the work on the wall display. The truck tire was displayed with the diagram showing its dimensions.

At first, the children wanted to invite everyone at school to see their work. Instead, they agreed with the teacher to give their presentation to four classes ranging from kindergarten to fourth grade, a special education class, and several administrators and office personnel. The teachers also made a video of the presentation for the children's parents to view at home. Each child had a part in sharing his or her knowledge of trucks. It was clear that they enjoyed their involvement and had learned a great deal about the important work done by truck drivers and trucking companies.

Source: Chard, S. C. (2001). *The Project Approach: Taking a Closer Look.* [CD-ROM]

FIGURE 16.3 The Truck Project *(continued)*

The children examine a truck on their field trip.

The number on the tank is 1145.

One kindergartner's field sketch will help the children remember what they saw at the truck company.

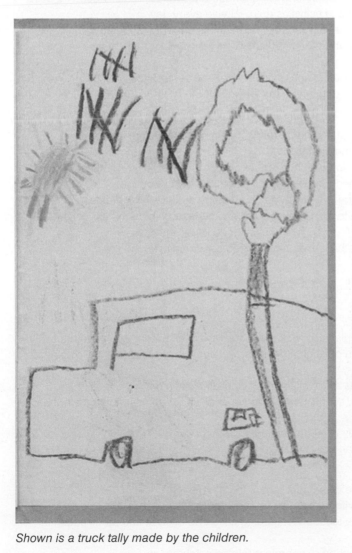

Shown is a truck tally made by the children.

The children point out many things on the truck they made.

materials or their talents to the classroom. Suggest ways for family members to support the theme or project at home. Create opportunities for family members to share the children's discoveries.

Step 21. Evaluate the theme by using the theme-teaching checklist presented in Figure 16.4. Write down the changes you made and how you might alter your plan if you decide to repeat it later.

FIGURE 16.4 Theme-Teaching Checklist

Purpose: To help teachers assess the effectiveness of theme teaching in their classrooms

Directions: Put a *1* by each item that accurately depicts the classroom. Total the items to achieve a final score.

Score	Level of Effectiveness
22–24	Excellent use of themes
19–21	Good use of themes; minor additions could make it better
16–18	Reasonable start; gradually address missing items to improve
15 and less	Poor use of themes; major revisions necessary

Theme-Related Activities

❑ 1. The theme planner can describe the relevance of the theme to the children.
❑ 2. Theme-related information is accurate.
❑ 3. Two or more theme-related *firsthand experiences* are available each week.
❑ 4. At least three theme-related activities are available every day.
❑ 5. Theme-related activities take place at different times throughout the day.
❑ 6. Every week at least one theme-related activity is included for each of the six domains.
❑ 7. Children have opportunities to apply, synthesize, and summarize what they have learned about the theme throughout the week.

Child Involvement

❑ 8. Children are talking about the theme (offering information, asking questions, conversing with peers and adults).
❑ 9. Children are pretending in relation to the theme.
❑ 10. Children are creating theme-related products of their own invention.
❑ 11. Children express a desire to learn more about some aspect of the theme.
❑ 12. Children link the theme to their past or current experiences through their actions and words.
❑ 13. Family members report that children have discussed or played out the theme at home.
❑ 14. Children continue to refer to the concept represented by the theme after the unit ends.

Classroom Environment

❑ 15. Terms, facts, and principles are posted or otherwise available for adult reference.
❑ 16. Children's theme-related creations (projects, writings, sculptures, etc.) are displayed in the room.
❑ 17. Theme-related materials are available to the children each day.
❑ 18. Theme-related pictures, songs, poems, books, and so on are used to create a thematic atmosphere.
❑ 19. One circle time each day is theme related.
❑ 20. Theme-related circle-time activities include active child participation.

Family Involvement

❑ 21. Family members receive information about the theme.
❑ 22. Family members are invited to contribute to the theme.
❑ 23. Family members receive feedback regarding children's interest and participation in the theme.
❑ 24. Families are included in theme- or project-related celebrations.

Adapting "Apples in the Schoolyard": An Apple Theme

All the steps involved in theme planning are illustrated in the following example of an "apple" theme. As you read through this approach, consider how to adapt the theme for the children in your class.

Step 1. The 4- and 5-year-olds in Hannah Solomon's preschool class noticed that two apple trees in the play yard were heavy with fruit. Eager to pick the apples, the children watched each day as the fruit grew riper. Based on her observation of the children's interest, Ms. Solomon decided that a theme about apples would be appropriate and would promote the children's observation skills and problem-solving abilities. Because the children lived in a community known for its apple orchards, she also thought that such a theme would provide a good chance for the children to become more aware of resources in their environment.

Steps 2 and 3. She prepared for the apple theme by looking up information about apples and making a list of TFPs related to the concept. By not simply relying on her own knowledge, she discovered some facts about apples she had not known previously. As the list grew to around 25 items, she divided it into the following subsections: varieties of apples, physical characteristics, apples as food, apples' development from blossom to fruit, and apples' journey from orchard to home.

Steps 4 and 5. Next, she narrowed the list to include 12 TFPs that would provide a general overview for the children to explore for at least 2 weeks. Following are 5 of the 12 she chose:

1. There are many kinds of apples.
2. Apples vary in size, shape, color, texture, smell, and taste.
3. People eat apples in many forms.
4. Apples grow on trees.
5. Apples are the fruit of the apple tree.

Step 6. Ms. Solomon brainstormed activities to go with each TFP. Would you add others to this list?

❏ *There are many kinds of apples.* ACTIVITIES: Select different varieties of apples at an orchard or a store, examine the apples firsthand, match the different apple types to their names, look at paintings that include apples, create apple paintings, and look through seed and fruit catalogs that show various kinds of apples.

❏ *Apples vary in size, shape, color, texture, smell, and taste.* ACTIVITIES: Examine different kinds of apples, make a chart graphing apple differences, generate a list of words that describe apple characteristics, create apple books with one page for each variety—list the characteristics, sort apples, taste apples (seriate the apples from sweetest to most sour; seriate the apples from juiciest to least juicy), and select favorite apples.

❏ *People eat apples in many forms.* ACTIVITIES: Examine different apple products (raw apple, applesauce, apple juice), make an apple product such as applesauce, create a lotto game using apple product pictures or labels, and create a grocery store in which children pretend to buy and sell apple products.

❏ *Apples grow on trees.* ACTIVITIES: Examine an apple tree, examine apple leaves, do a bark rubbing, trace or paint with apple leaves, read fiction and nonfiction books about how apples grow, create a make-believe orchard in which children pretend to pick apples, go on a field trip to pick apples, read a book about how apple trees appear during the different seasons, construct apple trees out of art materials, and make apple-tree puzzles.

❏ *Apples are the fruit of the apple tree.* ACTIVITIES: Examine seeds inside apples, examine dried apple blossoms, read a story about how the blossom becomes fruit, and predict how many seeds will be in the different varieties of apples.

Steps 7 and 8. Ms. Solomon could see that she had a wide array of firsthand activities to support children's learning. Next, she assigned the activities to different domains, referring to the goals for each. For TFP 1 she developed the following list.

❏ Select different varieties of apples at an orchard or a store—affective (focus on the choosing process).

❏ Examine the apples firsthand—record the children's observations—cognitive (focus on observation).

❏ Match the different apple types to their names—language (focus on language labels).

❏ Look at paintings that include different kinds of apples—aesthetic (focus on the color and design elements of the art).

❏ Create paintings that include different kinds of apples—aesthetic (focus on color and design elements while painting).

❏ Look through seed and fruit catalogs that show various kinds of apples—cognition (focus on the social-conventional knowledge related to the different varieties).

Ms. Solomon repeated this process for each TFP. She looked over the complete list to make sure she had included many exploratory-play, guided-discovery, and problem-solving activities as well as some demonstrations, discussions, and direct-instruction activities. Convinced that she had a good selection of activities, she began to commit her ideas to paper.

Steps 9 Through 13.   Ms. Solomon created the weekly plan, presented in Figure 16.5. She made adjustments to ensure that she did not have too many "star" activities (those involving a lot of adult supervision) on any one day and that both theme-related and non-theme-related activities were provided daily. She also paid attention to the sequence of thematic activities throughout the week, so that certain activities could lead up to or build on others. For instance, in the art area on Tuesday, Ms. Solomon hung three still-life paintings of apples by different artists in different styles for the children to enjoy. During the next few days, she drew the children's attention to the paintings, especially their color and design. The following week, Ms. Solomon provided a bowl of apples of different varieties along with watercolors and poster paints for the children to make their own still-life arrangements and paintings. In this way, she used the Week 1 art activity to lead to another activity planned for Week 2.

Steps 14 and 15.   Ms. Solomon gathered relevant materials and prepared the classroom. She asked families to contribute any materials they might have (such as favorite stories or songs) and invited a parent who was a fruit grower to visit the class.

Steps 16 Through 18.   Ms. Solomon implemented the theme according to her written plan. However, on Tuesday a child brought in two pieces of fruit that resembled apples but were actually Korean pears. Intrigued by their similarity, some children spent much of the free-choice time comparing the fruits and discussing their similarities and differences. During the second week, they created pictures, paintings, and stories about their experiences.

Step 19.   After 2 weeks, Ms. Solomon conducted a circle time in which she and the children talked about what they had learned, what they still wanted to learn, and how they might go about doing so. Several children were interested in finding out more about how apples from Oregon went to stores across the United States. Others were interested in finding out people's favorite apple recipes. Some children wanted to know if people had apples everywhere in the world. Ms. Solomon and the children carried out investigative projects to answer these questions. These projects took several weeks and included a field trip to a produce distribution center and visits to the class by family members with recipes to share. The group created a time line that went along one whole wall of the classroom showing the various steps in the distribution process. The children also made a cookbook of classroom recipes with apples as an ingredient. Trying some of the recipes in class and documenting the process was also part of the project phase of this theme.

Step 20.   While the children were involved in learning about apples, Ms. Solomon communicated with families through individual notes home and a classroom newsletter. Family members were invited to provide favorite apple recipes for the class and to join the field trips to the orchard and the distribution center. As the thematic unit neared its conclusion, children, teachers, and family members gathered to see and hear what the children had learned. They examined the time line, marveled over the child-authored apple books, and sampled apple butter made by the class.

Step 21.   Ms. Solomon formally evaluated the theme by using the theme-teaching checklist and anecdotal records in some activity areas each day. She also kept a journal to remind herself of points she wanted to remember and reflect on:

> *September 20: The children enjoyed making apples to put on the trees in the pretend orchard. It was exciting to see them consult the catalogs to determine which variety to make. Having several different catalogs on hand was a good idea. Albert and Johan argued about whether two kinds of apples could grow on the same tree. We added this question to our chart on what we want to know more about. This point will be important to follow up on at the orchard.*

> *October 6: We're putting a lot of time into Phase 1 of the project portion of this theme. The children had several opportunities at circle time and throughout the week to share their knowledge and stories as well as what they continue to wonder about. It became clear today that learning*

FIGURE 16.5 Sample Weekly Plan: Apple Theme, Week 1, Introduction

Time/Routine	Area	Monday	Tuesday	Wednesday	Thursday	Friday
8:30–8:45 A.M. Greeting Time	Group-time rug	Children arrive		Children arrive	Introduction to	Day's activities
8:45–10:00 Free choice	Art area	Easel painting on apple shapes Apple still life pictures to enjoy		Making play dough; tools available include apple cookie cutters and apple shapes to trace	Sponge painting with apple shapes and red, yellow, and green paint (1, 2, 3)	Cooperative color mixing
	Blocks	Vehicles		Unit blocks with	human figures	cardboard trees
	Library	Apple posters Flannel board: "The Apple and the Worm"		Apple catalogs	*How Do Apples Grow?* by B. Maestro *The Seasons of Arnold's Apple Tree*, by G. Gibbons	Big Book: *Down the Road*, by Alice Schertle
	Writing area	Apple adjectives		Class surveys	Apple books	
	Fine motor	Cutting activity		Making apple tree puzzles with a friend Lacing apple shapes	Peeling apples for snack	Cutting activity
	Math and science	Magnets Apple seed estimates	Field trip to the orchard	Numeral bingo Pulleys and levers Apple sorting	Ramps with rollers Seriating apples by taste, touch, smell, size, and look	Counting apple seeds Making applesauce
	Open snack	Dried apples, toast, and low-fat cheese cubes	Snack at orchard	Apple juice, crackers, and peanut butter	Tasting three kinds of apples	Charting apple favorites (juice, sauce, raw)
	Pretend play	Add pie-making materials to house Include cinnamon-scented play dough		Pretend orchard—trees, apples, bushel baskets, cash register, materials for sign making plus housekeeping	Add props to orchard as suggested by children	
9:55—Warning for cleanup				Pairs of children clean up	Children self-select cleanup area and decide what needs to be done	
10:00—10:10 Cleanup						

(continued)

479

FIGURE 16.5 **Sample Weekly Plan: Apple Theme, Week 1, Introduction** *(continued)*

Time/Routine	Area	Monday	Tuesday	Wednesday	Thursday	Friday
10:10–10:30 Large group	Group-time rug	Preparation for orchard field trip Discuss questions we want to answer at orchard		Flannel board: "The Apple and the Worm" Two little apples hanging on a tree	Thank-you note to orchard—group writing experience and reflection on trip	Book: *Down the Road,* by Alice Schertle
10:30–10:35 Transition outdoors						
10:40–11:20 Outdoor time	Apple tree investigations—materials for bark rubbings, magnifying glasses, small plastic bags for collecting apple tree items, chart paper for recording observations	Musical hoops	Return from orchard during this time — transition to playground		Apple tree investigations—materials for bark rubbings, magnifying glasses, small plastic bags for collecting apple tree items, chart paper for recording observations	Wheeled carts
11:20–11:30 Transition indoors	Bathroom hand washing	_____				
11:30 A.M.–12:00 P.M. Lunch	Classroom	Set a place for a friend	Set a place for a friend	Set a place for a friend		
12:00–12:15 Transition home	Saying farewell to friends	_____				_____

Note: Items listed here are provided in addition to the standard materials always available to children indoors and outside. Tally of theme-related activities: Aesthetic activities = 3, affective activities = 2, cognitive activities = 6, language activities = 6, physical activities = 6, social activities = 3, social activities = 4.

480

how apples get from our orchard to stores throughout the country is of keen interest to several children. We'll begin a topic web at circle time tomorrow to see how this plays out.

Later, as the apple unit drew to a close, Ms. Solomon made a note to herself to periodically take the children out to observe the apple trees in the play yard throughout the late fall, winter, and spring. She believed that ongoing observation would promote their interest in the seasonal cycle of the apple trees and in how the trees provide shelter and food for various animals and insects.

The next theme undertaken in this class could be a spin-off from the apple theme, such as "trees," "insects," or "stores." In this way, one theme could lead to another, which would provide conceptual links among several topics and a sense of intellectual coherence for children and teachers. Alternatively, the class's interests may move in an entirely different direction. "Birds," "pottery," or "physical fitness" may be topics that intrigue them next. What prompts the development of each new theme will be unique for each group.

Now that a sample thematic unit has been described from start to finish, let us consider the most common questions teachers have about theme and project planning, implementation, and evaluation.

COMMON QUESTIONS ABOUT THEMES AND PROJECTS

Must Every Activity Relate to the Theme or Project?

As noted, effective daily and weekly plans include both theme-related and non-theme-related activities. However, this question is so commonly asked that the answer bears repeating. Although having several theme-related activities each day is important, creating a mix of theme- and non-theme-oriented activities each week is preferable. Remember, not all children will be intrigued by the topic to the same extent. Some non-theme-related activities interspersed throughout your teaching plan will provide a respite from the topic and enable you to address necessary skills unrelated to the theme. Reprising children's favorites, reviewing past experiences, and including subject-based activities whose content is mandated by the program curriculum are appropriate alternatives. In half-day programs, the minimum number of theme-related activities is three or four, one of which should occur during a group time. For full-day programs, an average of two or three activities in each half day works reasonably well. At least some portion of a group time should also be devoted to an aspect of the theme.

How Long Does a Typical Thematic Unit or Project Last?

The answer to this question is best based upon the needs and interests of the individual children in your group. Generally, the less experience children have with a concept, the more time they need to explore it. Some thematic units and projects may last only a week or two; others will last much longer. For instance, spending several days exploring "pumpkins" might cover the topic well. In contrast, 3 or 4 weeks devoted to "seeds" may barely scratch the surface of possible information or children's curiosity about the topic. Moreover, one class could find 2 weeks devoted to the "kitchen" to be sufficient, whereas another group of children might be so intrigued by the kitchen and what goes on there that they will choose to carry out a variety of projects regarding this important place in their center or school.

Exercise judgment in determining the most fitting approach for your class. Many teachers report that 2- to 3-week themes (with an optional follow-up week or two) work well. If you anticipate that children will become involved in projects as a result of the theme, even more time will be necessary. Some in-depth projects may last several months.

Beware of teaching an entire year of themes that last only 1 week each. One-week thematic units are too brief to do more than survey a few bits of information. The short time frame denies children opportunities to become absorbed in a topic, conduct personal investigations into the concept it represents, and come away with new understanding.

Is There a Difference Between Planning Themes for 3- and 4-Year-Olds and Planning Themes for 6- to 8-Year-Olds?

The process of planning and implementing themes is the same regardless of children's ages. Selecting a topic, creating the TFPs, generating activity ideas, planning the unit, and carrying it out are steps required for every theme. However, themes vary—in terms of the TFPs selected and the concepts chosen for study—according to the children's ages and their prior experience with the theme. To make age-appropriate and individually appropriate differentiations, divide the TFPs into two categories: simple and advanced.

Simple TFPs consist of terms or facts that can be observed or experienced by the children directly through their own activity (although they might not be able to put these terms or facts into words). Existing in the here and now rather than the future or past, simple TFPs do not require teacher explanations. Adult talk may reinforce children's self-discoveries, but it is never a substitute for direct experience. Principles, because they often involve abstractions, are not identified as simple. For example, the theme "clothing" could be supported by the following simple terms and facts:

> *Terms: Specialized names for certain articles of clothing are poncho, helmet, yarmulke, kimono, vest, kilt, turban, kaftan, and so on.*
> *Facts: Certain articles of clothing go on certain parts of the body.*
> *Clothes have different fasteners: buckles, buttons, snaps, zippers, ties, and Velcro.*
> *Clothing comes in a variety of sizes, shapes, colors, patterns, and textures.*
> *People wear clothing for different reasons.*

Children engaged in activities and routines in the classroom could incorporate all these terms and facts into their concept of clothing on the basis of actual experience.

Advanced TFPs are those that children often learn about through secondary sources such as pictures, models, or discussions. Advanced TFPs may refer to past or future events or events that occur outside the classroom and may require children to envision something mentally in order to comprehend them. That cows have four legs is a simple fact because it is readily observable both in real cows and in toy cows in the classroom. The fact that cows have multiple stomachs is advanced because it must be represented by a picture, diagram, or discussion and requires children to envision the internal workings of a cow without experiencing them directly. Advanced TFPs consist of more elaborate or enigmatic vocabulary and more complicated facts and principles. Because of the complexity or abstractness of these TFPs, children generally need more opportunities and time to grasp them than is usually required for simple TFPs. Advanced TFPs related to the theme "clothing" are given in the following examples:

> *Terms: When two pieces of fabric are sewn together, the joining point is called a seam.*
> *Natural fibers are made from animals or plants. Synthetic fibers are made from chemicals.*
> *Facts: People make leather from the skins of various animals. People created synthetic fibers for many reasons: strength, durability, ease of care, and so on.*
> *Principle: When choosing clothing they like, people may be influenced by advertising or others' opinions.*

This designation of simple and advanced TFPs will help you to identify which category of TFPs to emphasize when you are working with a particular group of children. Simple TFPs should be used with 3-, 4-, and 5-year-olds and older children who have little experience with the theme. Advanced TFPs are more appropriate for kindergartners who know the theme well and for children in the early primary grades. This differentiation allows you to choose a subset of TFPs that best corresponds to the needs of your class. Depending on the concept to be addressed, the subset may be composed of TFPs representing either or both levels of difficulty.

The criteria that differentiate simple TFPs from advanced TFPs may also be applied to concepts overall. Concepts that deal with the here and now and that youngsters can explore through numerous hands-on experiences are most suitable for young children. Examples are clothing, water, plants, textures, books, and people at school. Children can explore all these topics in the immediate environment of their classroom, play yard, or neighborhood. These topics do not rely on a one time field trip or visitor as the children's only real experience with the concept. Concepts dependent on these latter forms of experience are more abstract and would be considered advanced. Examples are the circus (this theme depends on children remembering or envisioning a circus experience), communication (this theme depends on children manipulating actions rather than tangible objects), and the eye (this theme depends on representations such as models and diagrams to illustrate how the eye functions). Advanced concepts are better used with children toward the latter phases of the early childhood period and beyond.

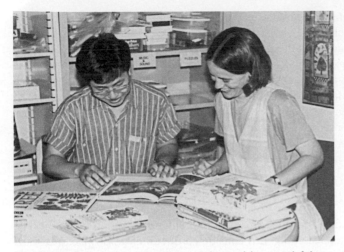

Educators find working together on theme ideas satisfying and stimulating.

How Do I Use Themes and Projects with So Much Required Content to Cover?

Theme teaching and project work are not add-ons. They are not additional strands to be incorporated into the day's instruction, nor are they an extra layer to be added to an already-bursting curriculum. Themes and projects are strategies for breaking away from rigid compartmentalization of subject matter and the traditional use of designated time blocks.

Rather than focusing on teaching children a little about many topics, thematic teaching allows children to investigate topics thoroughly in an integrated manner. One way to ensure you cover required content is to map the purpose of the project onto the curricular standards of your program. Project work has been shown to be a successful method of meeting standards (Benson & Miller, 2008; Helm, 2008). One effective approach is to create some thematic units each year focusing on concepts generally associated with underrepresented portions of the curriculum. Also, by using required content as one source for themes and related projects, you can combine previously isolated subjects or skills (e.g., science and writing; social studies and math; health and reading; speaking, reading, and writing; or art and critical thinking). Doing so makes the day less fragmented, and allows children and teachers more time to explore topics in depth. Covering required content and standards is well suited to the integrated approach of thematic teaching.

Thematic teaching can provide a range of opportunities for children to acquire content and demonstrate learning. Teachers can provide evidence of integrating required content and specified educational standards into theme activities and projects. Helm and Katz (2001) suggest incorporating required content and standards into the planning process by identifying what content and standards will be addressed by specific activities. Required content is presented in a meaningful way to children when various content is integrated into a cohesive theme. Because an integrated curriculum such as theme teaching can address multiple standards at one time, teachers may find it much more feasible and enjoyable than trying to address separate standards individually.

What About Repeating Themes?

Sometimes teachers and family members worry about children's revisiting certain themes as they move from the 3-year-old room to the 4-year-old class or from kindergarten to first grade. Thinking children may get bored or will not learn anything new, they need to remember that children learn through repetition. Each time children participate in a given theme, they glean new insights and skills from the experience. In addition, the projects and activities that evolve out of a theme will vary from one year to the next as children build on what they know to investigate new aspects of the topic. Consequently, repeating some themes from one year to the next is an effective instructional strategy.

By basing the theme around questions a particular group of children are trying to answer and adapting activities to meet the individual needs of children, the theme will necessarily vary somewhat each time it is explored. The same topic can also be investigated by drawing children's attention to different facets of the topic and introducing content in new ways. In contrast, simply rehashing the exact same material year after year without thought to the particular children in the group may not provide enough stimulation to hold children's interest or enhance their concept development. Multiyear themes can be used to help children move from focusing on simple TFPs to more advanced TFPs. For instance, "dinosaurs" is a topic often requested by children throughout the early childhood years. It may be covered 2 or 3 years in a row, which makes it an ideal vehicle for collaborative planning among teachers at different program levels. Such a plan could be formulated, keeping in mind that 6-year-olds are fascinated by the terms associated with dinosaurs, especially their names. Simple facts regarding dinosaurs' physical characteristics are also appealing to these children. Second graders, already familiar with dinosaur names, continue to be intrigued with the physical attributes of dinosaurs as well as where they lived and how they protected themselves. By third grade, children who have experienced the theme twice before tend to be no less enthusiastic about dinosaurs, but they may have moved on to exploring more advanced facts (e.g., why dinosaurs became extinct) as well as considering principles (e.g., attributes of the jaw and teeth are what distinguish meat eaters from plant eaters). Creating a programwide plan that incorporates this developmental progression from simple to complex and from concrete to more abstract supports children's interest in the theme. It also gives each teacher a chance to offer children opportunities for new insights. The more often teachers within the same program talk to and collaborate with one another regarding theme planning, the more likely it is that they will complement rather than duplicate one another's efforts.

How Can I Document Children's Participation in Themes and Projects?

When teachers collect, analyze, and interpret evidence of children's participation in a project or unit and display evidence of children's learning, it is considered **documentation** (Helm & Katz, 2001). Before choosing how to document, review the goals and objectives for the activities planned within the theme or project. Once these goals and objectives have been identified, choose the best method to document children's achievement. Choose a variety of artifacts to support the documentation, including samples of children's work, photographs, and transcriptions of conversations. Consider including plans for documentation within your lesson plans right from the start (Helm, Beneke, & Steinhamer, 2007). To help you determine the artifacts needed for an effective documentation display, plan specific times to observe children and choose methods that are best able to capture evidence of children's knowledge and skills, For example, recording direct quotes of children's questions, comments, and theories about a topic at the beginning and the end of a project can provide convincing evidence of children's learning over time. Including photographs and children's work samples that illustrate the story of a project can enhance the documentation and help to make the children's learning visible to others. Make sure that evidence of children's growth and learning in each developmental domain is documented. Set aside time each day to summarize and reflect on the artifacts you have gathered. This will help you better understand children's thinking and facilitate the next steps for the theme or project. Documentation will also seem more manageable if done regularly versus waiting until the end of the unit or project.

Consider who will be viewing the documentation and tailor the display to the audience (Helm et al. 2007). Is the documentation for school administrators, parents, children, or persons outside the program? Adapt the documentation to the unique needs of each of these audiences. Documentation should include evidence of children's discussing, deciding, predicting, experimenting, and explaining their work and ideas (Katz & Chard, 2000). Effective displays encourage the viewer to study the documentation instead of glancing at it (Helm et al., 2007). Although artifacts may be selected to demonstrate an individual child's learning, when the various pieces are viewed as a whole, it should tell the story of the project. Use a variety of spaces to document children's learning through themes and projects. These spaces may include bulletin boards, shelves, classroom and hallway walls, and tabletops. Collecting and organizing documentation takes commitment and practice on your part. Although time consuming, documentation provides a rich context through which child learning and development can be showcased.

What About Having All My Themes and Projects Revolve Around Holidays?

One practice still common in many early childhood programs is to use holidays as a primary framework for developing curriculum. Weeks at a time revolve around Halloween, Christmas, St. Patrick's Day, Washington's Birthday, Groundhog Day, and so forth. A number of potential problems are inherent in this approach.

First, such themes run the risk of being little more than a convenient backdrop for children's participation in numerous craft projects, with minimal attention paid to either content learning or process learning. Children usually come away from these units without having increased their skills or expanded their conceptualizations.

Second, when children spend an entire month focusing on Halloween or St. Patrick's Day, these times come to dominate children's lives. They take on a disproportionate importance in

FIGURE 16.6   Terms, Facts, and Principles (TFPs): "Family Traditions"

1. A family tradition is an activity families repeat in much the same way time after time.
2. Traditions are an important part of family life.
3. All families have traditions, such as special songs, celebrations, foods, activities, stories, recollections, routines, rules, beliefs, and values.
4. Family celebrations are often influenced by tradition:
   ❏ Particular foods may be prepared.
   ❏ A certain sequence of events may be followed.*
   ❏ Special clothing may be worn.
   ❏ Special songs may be sung.
   ❏ Special stories may be told.
   ❏ People may have special roles within the celebration.*
   ❏ Special activities may be carried out.
5. Families vary in the traditions they observe.
6. A family's religious and/or cultural heritage influences the traditions they adopt.*
7. Traditions help family members feel close to one another.
8. Some family traditions have been carried out for many years, and some are relatively new.*
9. Some traditions are very elaborate; others are quite simple.
10. Sometimes outsiders are invited to participate in a family tradition, and sometimes only the family participates.
11. Every family has stories or anecdotes about how certain traditions developed or how certain family members were involved in family traditions.
12. Photographs, home videos, or cassette recordings are often used to record traditional family events.

Source: These TFPs were developed by Laura C. Stein, M.S., Early Childhood Consultant, Stein Associates, East Lansing, Michigan. Those marked with an asterisk are advanced.

comparison to the more common and relevant phenomena that constitute children's real life experiences. In addition, by devoting much time to particular holidays it erroneously presupposes that every family celebrates that holiday.

Finally, focusing the curriculum on holidays can inadvertently teach cultural or religious stereotypes. For instance, in many schools across the United States, November marks the time when children hear about pilgrims and Native Americans. Thanksgiving is presented as a time of universal celebration and feasting. Although true for many people, to some the "first Thanksgiving" presents a distorted view of history. In fact, many Native Americans fast at this time and view the day as one of mourning in remembrance of the many tragedies suffered by native people following the arrival of the first White settlers (Little-Soldier, 1990; Ramsey, 1979). Equitable treatment of the subject demands a balanced point of view that would be too abstract for most young children. Yet, promoting the traditional stereotypes, assuming they will be altered or undone when children are older, is risky because such corrections may never happen.

Eliminating holidays as the sole basis for theme planning does not mean ignoring them altogether. Just as other topics may stem from the interests of the children, it may be appropriate to study certain aspects of a holiday if children are intrigued. Teachers may incorporate these special times into the context of a larger concept such as "celebrations" or "family traditions." Both of these themes could support a wide array of TFPs, as illustrated in Figure 16.6. In addition, holiday customs need not be confined only to holiday times. Instead, a variety of observances could be highlighted within such generic themes as "clothing," "seasons," "storytelling," or "healthy foods" and could be carried out at any time of the year, with rituals, games, props, and foods associated with various holidays incorporated as appropriate. Exploring holidays in this manner tends to be inclusive rather than exclusive and supports children's growing awareness and appreciation of similarities and differences among people.

How Do I Know That Children Are Developing More Sophisticated, Complex Concepts?

Children show us what they understand in many ways. They reveal their conceptual understandings through play, conversations with peers and adults, questions, errors, methods of investigating objects and events, products, and representations. To find out what children know, observe and talk with them about the concept. Use the KWHLH brainstorming technique described in chapter 4 to give children a chance to describe what they have learned and what they still wonder about. Give children opportunities to talk and interact with their peers, and provide open-ended activities through which they can explore the concept in their own way. Encourage them to represent what they have learned through drawings, charts, writings, dictation, and so forth. Create displays of these items so that children can refer to them as the unit progresses. Make these documentation displays available to family members in an end-of-unit celebration or get-together. Make notes about what you see and hear, using the assessment techniques described in chapter 7.

SUMMARY

Coordinating activities around a central theme has long been a tradition in early childhood education. The benefits to youngsters, practitioners, and programs are many. Nonetheless, the greatest value of thematic teaching lies in its use as a concept organizer. As young children engage in activities permeated by the same basic idea, they connect individual bits of knowledge and perceptions and form more comprehensive, accurate concepts. However, such positive outcomes result only when practitioners keep in mind principles of developmentally appropriate practice as well as those of effective teaching. The latter include relying on children's interests and capacities to influence theme selection and direction; focusing on the conceptual nature of thematic teaching; using an accurate, thorough body of factual information to support the theme; emphasizing firsthand learning as well as real objects in carrying out the theme; integrating thematic activities across domains, subject areas, and parts of the day; and using the theme as a foundation for child-initiated and child-directed projects.

Creating effective thematic units involves several steps. The first is to select a topic. Ideas for topics most often originate from the children. Themes may also reflect special events or unexpected happenings, school-mandated content, or teacher or family interests. The best themes are relevant to children and include many hands-on experiences. They contribute to diversity and balance across the curriculum, include a variety of topic-oriented resources, and prompt children to engage in projects of their choosing in order to extend their learning.

Once an idea has been selected, the second step is to create a topic web as well as an accurate information base to support the concept under study. To do this, teachers must research relevant terms, facts, and principles (TFPs). These serve as the basis for developing activities. To increase their educational value further, activities should also address a variety of domains and modes of learning.

Creating a plan is the third phase of theme teaching. It involves distributing theme-related activities throughout your weekly lessons and across all parts of the day. Although having several theme-related activities in the plan is important, not every activity in a day or week must focus on the theme.

The last phase of theme teaching involves implementing, evaluating, and revisiting the theme as children become engaged in the topic. Themes may evolve into child-initiated projects. Projects have three phases: (1) beginning the project, (2) developing the project, and (3) concluding the project. Within this chapter, a theme-teaching checklist is provided as a tool for assessing theme implementation in classrooms as well as children's theme-related learning. Educators' potential questions regarding theme teaching and project work are also posed and answered.

In sum, theme teaching and project work are valuable instructional tools when used properly. Practitioners who have never engaged in this kind of teaching may find it time consuming at first. In fact, it may feel more complicated and demanding than a more traditional teacher-directed approach. Nevertheless, as familiarity with the process increases, so will the teacher's speed and efficiency in carrying it out. Helping to make sense of what could otherwise be fragmented educational events is an advantage both children and teachers will enjoy.

Key Words

concepts	principles	theme
documentation	project	web
facts	secondary sources	
primary sources	terms	

Applying What You've Read in This Chapter

1. **Discuss**
   a. The children in your classroom are excited about the new apartment building under construction across the street from the early childhood program building. What thematic ideas does this suggest? On the basis of what you learned in this chapter, how would you plan a thematic unit?
   b. Your colleague is planning to develop a thematic unit about the circus. Is this a developmentally appropriate theme for 3-year-olds in your community? Is it a developmentally appropriate theme for 7-year-olds in your community? How do you know?
   c. Using the apple activities generated by Hannah Solomon for the children in her preschool class, create a 1-week overview of activities for a class of children you know. Add or subtract activities as necessary. How does your plan compare with Hannah's? What is the rationale behind your plan?

2. **Observe**
   a. Observe a group of children in a classroom that uses theme planning. What do you notice about the children's involvement in the theme? What implications do your observations have for your approach to theme planning?
   b. Observe a group of children carrying out a project. What do you notice about their involvement with the project? What implications do your observations have for your approach to facilitating projects?

3. **Carry out an activity**
   a. Interview two early childhood educators who work with children of different ages. Ask these teachers to describe some of the topics their students are most interested in learning more about. Ask them to talk about how they incorporate children's interests into their teaching.
   b. Participate in a classroom in which thematic teaching or projects are offered to children. Describe how you supported children's involvement with these topics.
   c. Using the guidelines in this chapter, choose a thematic topic for a specific group of children. Explain why you selected the topic, and discuss how it is age appropriate, individually appropriate, and socioculturally appropriate for these children.
   d. Using the guidelines in this chapter, create a thematic unit for a specific group of children in which you identify a topic, TFPs, a week's activities, and methods for evaluating the plan's effectiveness.

4. **Create something for your portfolio**
   a. Take pictures of and record children's reactions to a theme or project you supervised.

5. **Add to your journal**
   a. What is your initial reaction to the idea of theme planning or project implementation with young children?
   b. List the most pressing concerns you have about planning and implementing appropriate themes or projects for children. Describe how you will address your concerns.

6. 🖐 **Consult the standards**
   a. Obtain your local or state educational standards for the age group you addressed in Activity 3d. Identify which standards you will address for each activity you have planned.

PRACTICE FOR YOUR CERTIFICATION OR LICENSURE EXAM

The following items will help you practice applying what you have learned in this chapter. They can help to prepare you for your course exam, the PRAXIS II exam, your state licensure or certification exam, and for working in developmentally appropriate ways with young children.

Teaching with Themes and Projects

You have noticed several children in your class spending time on the playground catching various insects, observing ant hills, and chasing butterflies. You have overheard children asking questions and sharing their theories about insects. The time seems ripe to introduce an insect theme or project.

1. **Constructed-response question**
   a. Describe *one* developmentally appropriate, insect-related activity that integrates the following disciplines:
   Science
   Math
   Language arts

   b. Discuss the conceptual understanding that the activity will address in each content area.

2. **Multiple-choice question**

   Which of the following is the best rationale for theme teaching?

   a. It is more efficient for teachers to plan activities around one topic than several different topics.
   b. Theme teaching provides a way to integrate content learning and process learning around a topic that interests children.
   c. Most teachers have sufficient personal knowledge to develop activities quickly and easily, making theme teaching enjoyable and simple.
   d. Children enjoy theme activities and actively participate in what teachers have planned.

Appendix

A

Sample Lesson Plans

SAMPLE GUIDED-DISCOVERY PLAN

Domain: Cognitive   **Activity Name:** Sea Life Observations

Goal: Examine natural objects by using their multisensory abilities.

Objectives

The child will
1. Examine an object by using multiple senses.
2. Talk about what he or she discovered.
3. Record his or her observations for future reference.
4. Describe how he or she examined the object.

Content

1. People learn about objects in nature by examining them closely.
2. Some ways to examine an object include looking at it, touching it, smelling it, and listening to it.
3. The more senses people use in their investigations of natural objects, the more they learn.
4. People improve their investigative skills through practice and by thinking about how they will remember what they observed.
5. People record their observations so that they can refer to them later.

Materials: One large, dead starfish; a Dungeness crab or another hard-shelled crab, preserved on ice; strands of wet seaweed on a tray; a horseshoe crab shell free of insects; paper towels that cover the objects prior to use and that the children can use to wipe their hands on as necessary; pads of paper for the children to use; pencils or markers.

Procedures

Examine and Talk

1. Gather the children in a large circle. Begin the activity with a discussion about all the ways that the children have been examining objects during the week. Remind the children of some of the strategies they have used.
2. Divide the children into four small groups, each assigned to a different table.
3. Give each group a towel-covered tray that holds a natural object. Explain that everyone will have a chance to examine the natural object very closely. Make sure that the children know that the objects are safe to touch. Invite the children to examine the object *before* taking off the paper towels. Ask this question: "What did you find out?" Paraphrase the children's comments.
4. Ask the children, "How did you discover?" Paraphrase the children's comments.
5. Tell the children to remove the towels and continue their investigation. Ask open-ended questions to prompt the children's use of various senses. Paraphrase the children's discoveries. Add factual information if the children desire it.

Record

6. After several minutes, give each child a piece of paper and ask him or her to make a mark on the paper as a reminder of what he or she discovered. Such marks could take the form of pictures, words, or symbols. They need have no meaning to anyone other than the child.

Describe

7. Invite the children to return to the large-group area with their marked papers. Conduct a discussion of what the children discovered. Create on chart paper a master list of the children's discoveries. Post this list where the children can refer to it and add to it throughout the day. During this discussion, continually refer to the investigative methods the children used and how they used them.
8. Tell the children that all the trays will be in the science/math center so that they can explore items they did not have a chance to investigate.

Simplification: Divide the large group of children into small groups; give each group a specimen of a similar object (e.g., give all the groups a starfish).

Extension

1. Have the children examine a different object each day, keeping a journal of the properties of the object.
2. Ask the children what they would still like to know but have not yet discovered about the objects. Brainstorm with them about how they could find out.
3. Adapt the activity to involve natural objects the children find outdoors or those in which they spontaneously express interest.

Evaluation

1. What properties were the most common among the children's observations?
2. What different strategies did the children use to investigate the objects?
3. What different ways did the children use to record their observations?
4. How might you revise the activity in the future and why?

SAMPLE PROBLEM-SOLVING PLAN

Domain: Affective   **Activity Name:** Making Plans

Goal: Make a plan and carry it out.

Objectives

The child will
1. Establish a goal.
2. Create a plan for meeting the goal.
3. Carry out the plan.
4. Evaluate the plan.

Content

1. A *plan* is a guide for decision making and action.
2. A *goal* is something a person wants and tries to reach.
3. A goal can be better accomplished when we have thought about a plan of action to reach the goal.

Materials: A wide array of art materials; scraps of wood or cloth; glue, paste, and other fasteners; scissors, markers; crayons; paint.

Procedure

1. Invite the children to look at the materials available.
2. Tell the children they will have a chance to make something of their choosing.
3. Ask each child to think of something he or she would like to make from the materials. This can be an object, such as a car, or something abstract, such as a collage.
4. Ask the children what they would have to do first, second, and third to make their projects. Write down their ideas, making a simple plan.
5. Have the children implement their plan.
6. After the children have made something, review their plan with them and ask them if they kept to their plan or changed it.

Simplification: Work with the child to scaffold a two- or three-step plan.

Extension: Invite the children to make plans of four or more steps.

Evaluation: Complete the following evaluation sheet by putting a check mark beside the objectives that each child demonstrated. Note how many steps each child included in his or her plan.

Children's Names	Established a Goal	Created a Plan	Carried Out the Plan	Evaluated the Plan	Number of Steps in the Plan
Alonzo					
Cathy					
David					
Dwayne					
Hallie					
Jorge					
Mark					
Maureen					
Olivia					
Rita					
Talia					
Veronica					

SAMPLE DISCUSSION PLAN

Domain: Social   **Activity Name:** Rules for the Block Area

Goal: Create rules for the classroom and identify reasons for their rules.

Objectives

The child will

1. Participate in a group discussion about classroom rules.
2. Identify reasons for classroom rules.
3. Suggest an idea for a rule.
4. Provide a reason for his or her rule.

Content

1. A rule is a guide for behavior.
2. People make rules to protect property, to protect people's rights, and to ensure safety.
3. People in groups agree to follow certain rules to help them get along with one another.
4. People discuss things to better understand them and to reach agreement about them.
5. In a discussion, sometimes people talk, and sometimes they listen.

Materials: Easel and easel pad; dark, thick-tipped marker.

Procedure

1. Open the discussion by talking about some of the current problems in the block area (people running, blocks all over the floor). Introduce the idea of rules as guides for behavior.
2. Invite the children to suggest ideas for rules that might involve play in the block area.
   a. Paraphrase the children's ideas.
   b. Use questions to stimulate the children's thinking.
3. Guide verbal turn taking.
   a. Remind the children to listen carefully when another child is speaking.
4. Record the children's ideas on a large sheet of easel paper.
   a. Restate each idea after it has been written.
5. Draw the discussion to a close by summarizing the children's rules.
6. Post the children's rules in the block area.

Simplification: If the children cannot think of ideas, offer suggestions to get the discussion started.

Extension: After a week, ask the children to evaluate their rules and revise them as necessary.

Evaluation

1. Who contributed to the group discussion?
2. Which children met which objectives?
3. What surprised you about the discussion?

SAMPLE DEMONSTRATION PLAN

Domain: Cognitive   **Activity Name:** Body Patterns

Goal: Reproduce patterns.

Objectives

The child will
1. Explore a variety of body movements.
2. Imitate simple body movement patterns consisting of two elements.
3. Imitate complex body movement patterns consisting of more than two elements.
4. Suggest, create, or demonstrate a pattern of their own to the rest of the group.

Content

1. A *pattern* refers to the ways in which colors, shapes, lines, sounds, or actions are arranged or repeated in some order.
2. The way that the elements of a pattern are organized determines the pattern's design or how it sounds. A pattern can be a set of repeated actions.
3. The same elements may be organized in a variety of ways to create different patterns.

Materials: None

Procedures

Explore

1. Invite the children to participate in the activity. Gain their attention by asking them to explore different ways to move their bodies.
2. Encourage the children to imitate a single motion that you or another child makes.

Imitate Simple Patterns

3. Invite the children to watch as you show them a body movement pattern. Create a simple pattern of movements and words involving two body parts and single motion. For instance, tap your body and say the word for the body part in a rhythmic fashion: "Head, head, shoulders, shoulders, head, head, shoulders, shoulders."
4. Using a do-it signal, have the children respond by imitating your actions.
5. Repeat steps 3 and 4 using two different body parts and different number combinations. Keep the numbers the same for each body part, such as two taps and two claps.

Imitate Complex Patterns

6. Gradually increase the complexity of the patterns by increasing the number of body parts and motions (tapping your head, clapping your hands, and stomping your feet). Another way to increase complexity is to vary the number of motions (two taps, three claps, one stomp). Have the children imitate the pattern you create.

Simplification: Use simple patterns slowly. Use major body parts such as head, hands, and feet.

Extension

1. Increase the complexity of the pattern and the speed of your movements, using body parts such as wrist, neck, and ankles.
2. Demonstrate a repetitive movement. Ask the children to predict what comes next, and then do it.

Evaluation

1. Which children participated in this activity?
2. What objectives did each child achieve?
3. Was the procedure carried out as described? If so, what was the result? If not, what did you change and why?

SAMPLE DIRECT INSTRUCTION PLAN

Domain: Cognitive   **Activity Name:** Earthworm Facts

Goal: Acquire scientific knowledge related to life sciences, specifically animal life.

Content

1. Earthworms are cylindrically shaped, segmented animals.
2. Earthworms have a mouth (no teeth), a headed end, and a tailed end (the head is more pointed than the tail).
3. Earthworms have no ears, eyes, legs, or skeleton.
4. Earthworms live and burrow in the soil.
5. Earthworms move by waves of muscular contractions traveling along the body.

Materials: A shovel full of soil in a bucket or in the water table; worms; a large picture of an earthworm depicting its segments, specifically, head end and tail end; a children's reference book about earthworms that includes pictures and simple facts about earthworm movement and habits; a clean piece of white paper on which to place an earthworm to watch its movements more easily; paper on which to write and markers or pens; cheesecloth.

Procedures

Preparation: To prepare for this activity, dig up some large earthworms or buy some at a bait store. Keep the soil moist and covered with cheesecloth prior to asking the children to participate.

Learning Phase	Immediate Objectives	Adult Does	Adult Says
Explore	Given a shovelful of soil containing some earthworms, the child will	Invite the children to participate.	Hi. Look at what's in this water table. It's not water! Today we have some soil dug out of our yard.
	1. Gently pick through the soil, searching for earthworms.	Remind children to be gentle.	Look carefully through it and tell me what animals you find.
Acquire	2. Talk about the earthworms as he or she observes them.	Ask children what they are noticing about the earthworms. Paraphrase the children's comments.	Tell me what you see. You noticed that some of these worms are red and some are black. You see skinny worms. The worm in your hand is very thick all the way around.
	Given an opportunity to observe and handle an earthworm while hearing an adult describe some of its features, the child will.	Provide information to the children as they examine the earthworms. Talk about the shape, size, and movements of the earthworms.	Earthworms have a mouth at the head end of their bodies. Look for the mouth on your earthworm.
	3. Differentiate the head end from the tail end of the worm.	Ask the children to look for the earthworm's mouth.	Earthworms move head first. Look at that worm. Show me the head end.
		Refer to the picture of the earthworm to help children know at which end to look.	Look at this picture. See if your earthworm has segments on it like this.
		On a piece of paper, record the parts of the worm the children are able to identify.	So far, we have found heads and tails on these earthworms. Let's write that on our earthworm facts chart.
	4. Identify body parts earthworms do not possess.	Ask the children to tell you what body parts people or other animals have that they do not see on the earthworms they are examining.	Look to see if your earthworm has legs. Look at this picture; this earthworm has no ears. Look to see if that is true for your earthworm.

Learning Phase	Immediate Objectives	Adult Does	Adult Says
		Ask simple questions to help children focus on the body parts earthworms do not possess.	
		Provide correct information to children who have erroneous ideas.	You think your earthworm has eyes. Those dark colors on the tail are not eyes.
	5. Describe ways the earthworms move.	Show the children how the earthworms move by contracting their bodies. This may be done in the soil and on a clean piece of paper where the worm's undulating motion is easily seen. In addition, the worm will leave a faint imprint on the paper that will show the wavy way in which it propels itself.	Let's look closely at how these earthworms get from place to place. Tell me what you see. Notice how the earthworm pulls in and then stretches out to move.
Practice	6. Observe and talk about earthworms outside on the playground throughout the week.	Guide the children's attention to earthworms outside. Review what the children discovered earlier in the week. Add new information to the chart the children had dictated.	Let's see if any earthworms are out here today. You remembered that earthworms come in different colors. You discovered that earthworms have tiny bristles on the underside of their bodies. Let's add that to our list of earthworm facts.

Simplification: Focus primarily on color and shape and the variety among earthworms.

Extension: Have the children compare earthworms with garter snakes, identifying similarities and differences.

Evaluation

1. What strategy was most successful in engaging the less assertive children in the activity? the more assertive children?
2. Which children achieved which objectives?
3. What did the children seem to know about earthworms in the exploration stage? What erroneous information did the children possess? About what were they most curious? What new facts did the children acquire during the week?

Appendix

B

Field Trips

Excursions into the community broaden children's understanding of the world in which they live and offer ways to diversify the curriculum through firsthand experience. Such trips may be as simple as visiting the mailbox on the corner or as elaborate as a day at the museum. Use the following questions to guide your field trip decision making.

FIELD TRIP PLANNING

1. What is the purpose of the trip? How will the trip promote children's learning?
   - ❏ Determine a curricular focus for the trip. Choose one domain and one goal to highlight. For example, a field trip to a garden could focus on plant identification (cognitive domain) or emphasize children's sensory exploration (aesthetic domain). The activities you carry out at the garden will differ depending on the goal you choose. For instance, to foster the cognitive objective of plant identification, you might organize a plant scavenger hunt to stimulate children's interest in recognizing certain plants. To highlight the aesthetic objective of sensory exploration, you might have children sit in a circle, close their eyes, listen quietly, and then describe the sounds they hear. Later, the children could explore textures, scents, and visual characteristics of the plants.
2. What is your destination? Is the site suitable for your group of children?
   - ❏ Make a preliminary visit to the site to determine site suitability.
   - ❏ Consider to what extent the site allows children to act like children—move about freely, make noise, and participate in hands-on activities.
   - ❏ Determine how well the site supports your educational goals. Preview what children will actually see, hear, and do. If on-site personnel are to be involved, talk with them in advance, discussing the developmental needs of the children involved, the amount of time available, and the group size.
   - ❏ Determine how long the trip will take. Inexperienced and younger children as well as children enrolled in half-day programs should spend no more than 20 minutes walking or riding (one way) to the site. Older, more experienced youngsters enrolled in full-day programs can occasionally tolerate as much as 1 hour of riding time in one direction without ill effect (Eliason & Jenkins, 2003; Michigan Family Independence Agency, 1996).
   - ❏ Consider how to meet children's biological needs such as using the toilet, having access to food and water, and resting periodically. If meeting these needs is not possible, choose another place to visit.
   - ❏ Check the site for accessibility to persons with special needs. Will everyone have easy access to all areas of the site where the group will be visiting? Excluding any member of your party because of inaccessibility is not acceptable. In addition, think through how children, family members, or staff members with special needs will benefit from traveling to this site. If the benefits are few, choose another site.
   - ❏ Check for potential safety hazards, both at the site and getting there and back. Make every effort to ensure all participants' safety. Any site with questionable safety is inappropriate.
   - ❏ Determine a potential meeting place outside or inside the facility, suggest a sequence through the facility, identify where to take shelter in case it rains or is too hot, and describe what to be sure to see or avoid.
3. When will the trip occur?
   - ❏ Consider site availability, access to transportation (if necessary), availability of adult support, and the time of day when children are most alert and comfortable. Determine whether the trip will serve as an introductory learning experience or a summary experience to help children synthesize what they have learned.

4. How will children get to the site?
   - ❏ Think through the route you will take (whether walking or riding) and anticipate any problems that might arise on the way.
   - ❏ If you require transportation, obtain permission from appropriate program supervisors to arrange for drivers and vans/buses. If you are soliciting drivers from children's families, provide advance notice so you can be sure enough vehicles and seat belts are available. Make sure every driver has a legal driver's license and appropriate insurance. Obtain backup drivers in case someone cannot go at the last minute. If you are going by car, each vehicle should have these items:
     a. A map showing the route between the program and the field trip site
     b. A written record of the telephone numbers of the early childhood program and the site you will be visiting
     c. A list of all persons riding in the vehicle
     d. A seat belt for each person
     e. A field trip first-aid kit (bandages, soap, moist towelettes, paper cups, a fresh container of potable water)
     f. An emergency card for each child riding in the vehicle, listing a place to reach the parent and emergency medical information (these are required by law for all children enrolled in most state-licensed preschool programs and are a good idea for elementary children, too)
     g. A list of songs to sing or information for adults to share with children on the way to the site or while returning to the program
     h. A schedule for the day, including specified times for gathering, such as snack and lunch times; a designated time for leaving; and a list of procedures in case someone gets lost or becomes ill
5. What kind of supervision will be necessary? How will you keep children safe? How will you draw children's attention to relevant features of the trip, extend concepts, and answer questions?
   - ❏ For children ages 3 to 5, plan to have one adult for every 3 to 4 children; for children 6 to 8 years of age, plan to have one adult for every 5 to 6 children. Increase adult numbers if you have to cross busy streets or take children to large, crowded environments.
   - ❏ If possible, do not be responsible for a particular group of children yourself. This will enable you to keep a global view of the group as a whole, to more easily address unexpected problems that may arise, and to interact with resource people at the site as necessary.
   - ❏ If you are going to a site by car, van, or bus, plan to have two adults in each vehicle: one to drive and one to supervise the children.
6. How will you obtain permission for children to participate in the trip?
   - ❏ Assume no child may go on a field trip without written permission from his or her parent or guardian. In some programs, families are asked to sign a blanket form once a year to allow children to take part in program-sponsored field trips; in other programs, separate permission slips are required for each trip. Even when parents provide blanket permission, they must be notified before each field trip and told when and where the children will be going. Make follow-up telephone calls or write reminders to acquire all appropriate permissions.
7. In what ways might parents or other family members become involved in the field trip?
   - ❏ Determine what adults need to do to support safety and educational aims.
8. What is your backup plan?
   - ❏ Anticipate what might go wrong and have an alternative strategy in mind for these dilemmas. Plan in advance what you will do if a driver calls in sick; how you will handle someone's getting lost en route; what you will do if at the last minute a parent says his or her child cannot participate.
9. How will you prepare adults and children for what to expect on field trip day?
   - ❏ Plan to clarify the educational purpose of the trip and provide a few ideas of things adults might do or say in keeping with the focus. Provide such guidelines in writing as well as orally.
   - ❏ Ask volunteers to arrive a few minutes early so that there is enough time to orient them to the trip, and allow them to ask questions as necessary.
   - ❏ Plan to inform adults of any rules and special considerations, such as how to interact with a child who moves only with the aid of a walker or strategies to help an easily frustrated child feel more relaxed during the trip.
10. What will you do on field trip day?
    - ❏ *Count.* Know exactly how many youngsters are in the group. Count the children frequently throughout the time you are away.
    - ❏ *Teach.* Draw children's attention to relevant cues in the environment, and respond to children's remarks with this focus in mind.
    - ❏ *Remain flexible.* Take advantage of spontaneous events from which children might learn something new.
    - ❏ *Enjoy.*
11. How will you evaluate the field trip?
    - ❏ Ask these questions of adults/children: What did the children gain from the trip? How well was the educational purpose of the trip fulfilled? To what extent did the trip proceed as expected? What were some things you did not anticipate? What were the strengths of the trip? How could the trip have been improved? Would you

recommend returning to the same place another time? Why or why not? What follow-up activities would best support the children's learning? What might family members like to know about the children's experience?

❑ Incorporate the answers to these questions in your future planning.

12. How will the lesson continue after the field trip?

❑ Look at pictures or make an album of pictures taken on the trip.

❑ Draw pictures or make a collage related to the trip.

❑ Dictate stories about what they experienced.

❑ Write in their journals or create a group newsletter to send home to family members, outlining the key concepts they learned.

❑ Reconstruct the field trip experience during pretend play or with blocks.

❑ Role-play in relation to the trip.

❑ Use items collected during the trip to create something back at the center or school (e.g., children make soup from vegetables purchased at the grocery, or they make a classroom reference book from the leaves they gathered on a nature walk).

❑ Visit the site again, with a new goal in mind (e.g., children make repeated visits to a pond during the year, attending to different details each time).

❑ Invite the children to draw pictures or write letters thanking volunteers who provided supervision on the trip or people who guided their visit at the field trip site. These tokens of appreciation can be created individually or generated by the group.

Appendix C

The Big, Big Turnip

Once upon a time, a farmer planted a turnip seed in the ground. After many days of sun and rain, warm days and cool nights, the turnip grew until it was very big. Finally, the farmer said, "It's time to pull that big, big turnip out of the ground."

He ran out to the garden and grabbed the turnip's long green leaves. He pulled and pulled, but the big, big turnip would not come out.

The farmer called to his wife, "Help me pull this big, big turnip out of the ground." The wife ran over and wrapped her arms around the farmer's waist. Together the farmer and his wife pulled, but still the big, big turnip would not come out.

The farmer's wife called to his daughter, "Help us pull this big, big turnip out of the ground." The daughter ran over and wrapped her arms around the wife's waist. Together the farmer, the wife, and the daughter pulled and pulled, but still the big, big turnip would not come out.

The daughter called to the dog, "Help us pull this big, big turnip out of the ground." The dog ran over and wrapped his paws around the daughter's waist. Together the farmer, the wife, the daughter, and the dog pulled and pulled, but still the big, big turnip would not come out.

The dog called to the cat, "Help us pull this big, big turnip out of the ground." The cat ran over and wrapped her paws around the dog. Together the farmer, the wife, the daughter, the dog, and the cat pulled and pulled, but *still* the big, big turnip would not come out.

The farmer scratched his head, the wife and daughter and cat and dog puffed and panted. Then the daughter had an idea. She ran into the house and put a little piece of cheese by a mouse hole. Soon a hungry little mouse popped its head out of the hole. The daughter said, "Help us pull this big, big turnip out of the ground."

The mouse ran over and held onto the cat. Together the farmer, the wife, the daughter, the dog, the cat, and the mouse pulled and pulled. Then POP!!! that big, big turnip came flying out of the ground.

That night, the farmer and his wife made a huge pot of turnip stew. Everyone ate as much as they wanted. And do you know what? The hungry little mouse ate the most of all!

Glossary

Introduction

Division for Early Childhood of the Council for Exceptional Children (DEC): One of 17 divisions of the Council for Exceptional Children (CEC), the largest international professional organization dedicated to improving educational outcomes for individuals with exceptionalities, students with disabilities, and/or the gifted. DEC is especially for individuals who work with or on behalf of children with special needs, birth through age 8, and their families.

Early childhood education: Any group program, serving children from birth to age 8 designed to promote children's intellectual, social, emotional, language, and physical development and learning.

Individuals with Disabilities Education Act (IDEA): Initially passed in 1997, this federal legislation provided protections to people with disabilities, including freedom from discrimination and equal access to public programs. IDEA was updated in 2004, governing how states and public agencies provide early intervention, special education, and related services to more than 6.5 million infants and toddlers (from birth to age 2) and children and youth (ages 3 to 21) with disabilities.

Least restrictive environment: This refers to the Individuals with Disabilities Education Act (IDEA) mandate that children with disabilities be educated to the maximum extent appropriate with nondisabled peers.

National Association for the Education of Young Children (NAEYC): With nearly 100,000 members, this is the world's largest professional membership organization dedicated to improving the well-being of young children, with particular focus on the quality of educational and developmental services for all children from birth through age 8.

Chapter 1

Behavioral perspective: An educational philosophy that focuses on children's achieving specific behavioral outcomes (e.g., reciting the alphabet, tying a bow, counting to 10) rather than internal affective processes.

Constructionist perspective: An educational philosophy that focuses on children as holistic beings whose development and learning are influenced both by biology and by children's interactions with the physical world and other people.

Developmentally appropriate practices (DAP): Refers to judgments early childhood professionals make based on what they know about how children develop and learn; what they know about the strengths, needs, and interests of individual children; and what they know about the social and cultural contexts in which children live.

Individualized education plan (IEP): Describes what services children with special needs will receive, how services will be provided, and the outcomes a child might reasonably be expected to accomplish in a year. Every IEP includes these elements: a description of the child's strengths, needs, goals; short-term objectives; special education services and program modifications; and the frequency, duration, and location of the services to be provided.

Maturationist perspective: An educational philosophy that focuses on the natural unfolding of children's developmental capacities.

Mental health perspective: An educational philosophy that emphasizes using play to prevent mental illness.

Pushdown curriculum: Teaching practices traditionally not encountered by children until first grade or later such as long periods of whole-class instruction, written instruction out of workbooks, and letter grades.

Chapter 2

Academic standards: Describe what children should know and be able to do.

Behavior reflections: Verbal descriptions of what children are doing, also called information talk or descriptive feedback.

Chaining: The process of introducing a series or "chain" of behaviors one step at a time. As children master the first step, a new step is added and so forth until they successfully demonstrate total completion of a task.

Close-ended questions: These questions can be answered yes or no or with one word.

Cortisol: A hormone secreted by the adrenal glands that occurs naturally in the body, sometimes called the stress hormone. High, prolonged levels of cortisol in the bloodstream and the brain (like those associated with chronic stress) have been shown to have negative effects on memory and cognitive functioning.

Cycle of learning: The process whereby children move from initial awareness, to exploration, to acquiring new knowledge and skills, to practicing, to generalizing knowledge and skills, to a variety of situations on their own.

Effective praise: Specific individualized acknowledgements of children's actions and progress.

Frames of mind: A concept developed by Howard Gardner, also called multiple intelligences. The eight intelligences are linguistic, logical-mathematical, musical, spatial, bodily-kinesthetic, intrapersonal, interpersonal, and naturalistic.

Guided practice: The process of giving children many opportunities to master a skill through rehearsals, repetition, and gradually elaborating on what children already know and can do.

Open-ended questions: These questions have more than one possible answer, and encourage children to offer opinions and think in new and different ways.

Paraphrase reflections: Nonjudgmental restatements of what children are saying, also called verbal expansions or active listening.

Scaffolding: The process of providing and then gradually removing external support for children's learning. During the scaffolding process, the original task is not changed, but how the child participates in the task is made easier with assistance. As children take more responsibility for pursuing an objective, assistance is gradually withdrawn.

Successive approximation: The process of shaping behavior by rewarding children for gradually approximating desired goals (getting more and more accurate).

Task analysis: The process of identifying a sequence of steps a child might follow to achieve some multistep behavior such as setting the table, getting dressed, or completing a long-division problem.

Chapter 3

Developmental direction: Principles that describe the typical advancement of the learning process beginning with basic demonstrations to more advanced levels.

Domain: One of the six curricular areas associated with whole-child learning. The six domains are aesthetic, affective, cognitive, language, physical, and social.

Goals: Identify desirable behaviors relevant to children's development and learning.

Objectives: The specific learning behaviors children might logically display in relation to a goal.

Chapter 4

Body: The main purpose of the whole-group instruction time.

Closing: When the teacher summarizes the activity and guides children to the next portion of the day.

Opening: Strategies used to signal the beginning of group time and capture children's attention.

Transition: A strategy that links an activity with the next activity or step.

Whole-group instruction: Those portions of the day when all or most of the children in a class gather in one place to share the same learning experience simultaneously.

Chapter 5

Boundaries: Physical or psychological barriers that indicate the edges of a center or learning space.

Large-group space: An area where all of the children may gather at one time.

Learning center: A planned and organized space where specific activities that implement curriculum goals occur.

Loose parts: Anything that is small and can be manipulated by children; often what adults call junk (e.g., stones, seeds, sticks or other natural materials).

Natural playscape: A space that may be landscaped to include a variety of surfaces (hills and gullies), and be planted to promote learning. Natural materials are used predominantly.

Pathways: Areas between centers or workspaces where children can move easily.

Private space: A planned location for one child to work alone.

Small-group space: A planned location, or learning center, for up to six children to work together.

Vertical space: Space at a right angle to the floor. Up and down space. Usually walls, windows, or dividers.

Chapter 6

Adherence: The most basic form of behavioral regulation; the individual responds to external controls such as physical guidance, rewards, and negative consequences.

Authoritarian discipline style: Adults who are high in control and maturity demands and low in communication and nurturance.

Authoritative discipline style: Adults who are high in control, communication, maturity demands, and nurturance.

Communication: How much information adults provide children throughout the guidance process.

Control: The way and extent to which parents and teachers enforce children's compliance with their expectations.

Identification: Intermediary level of behavioral regulation; the individual adopts code of conduct of someone he or she admires.

Internalization: Highest level of behavioral regulation; the individual constructs a personal sense of right and wrong based on what he or she thinks is right, not to gain a reward or the approval of others.

Logical consequences: Teach children logical alternatives to mistaken behavior; supports development of self-regulation.

Maturity demands: The level at which adults set their expectations for children's behavior and compliance.

Nurturance: How much caring and concern is expressed toward children.

Permissive discipline style: Adults who are high in nurturance, but low in control, make few maturity demands, and use minimal communication with children.

Punishment: Consequences that are harsh and shameful, causing children to feel demeaned or fearful; does not lead to internalization.

Rehearsal: When children approximate or practice a desirable behavior in response to some inappropriate action.

Restitution: Children make amends for a mistaken behavior.

Uninvolved discipline style: Adults who are low on control, maturity demands, communication, and nurturance.

Chapter 7

Anecdotal records: Narrative, descriptive, continuous, or specimen records; jottings.

Assessment: A systematic procedure for obtaining information from observation, interviews, portfolios, projects, tests, and other sources that can be used to make judgments about characteristics of children or programs.

Authentic assessment: The innumerable and complex ways in which early childhood teachers measure children's learning without the use of standardized tests, developmental inventories, and/or achievement tests.

Ecomap: A visual overview of a child's experience in the family and community.

Evaluation: The measurement, comparison, and judgment of the value, quality, or worth of children's work and/or of their schools, teachers, or a specific education program based upon valid evidence gathered through assessment.

Frequency counts: Tallies of specified behaviors.

Halo effect: Rating individual performance of a child more positively than may be warranted.

Leniency factor: Rating all subjects more highly than may be warranted.

Oral reading tests: Running records to note quality of a child's reading (comprehension, fluency, expressiveness), mistakes, and ability to self-correct.

Readiness: Characteristics that equip children with the knowledge of how to learn.

Reliability: The extent to which a test consistently yields the same results when readministered within a reasonable time frame or by another person.

Rubrics: Scoring tools that list clearly defined and observable criteria.

Screening: Identifying children who may need diagnostic assessment and intervention.

Sensitivity: Accuracy of a test in identifying delayed development.

Specificity: Accuracy of a test in identifying children who do not have delays.

Validity: The extent to which a test measures what it is intended to measure.

Chapter 8

Collaboration: The act of working jointly together; to willingly cooperate.

Family members: Parents, grandparents, stepparents, domestic partners; adults who are raising the particular child.

Jargon: Technical terminology.

Chapter 9

Aesthetics: A person's ability to perceive, be sensitive to, and appreciate beauty in nature and creations in the arts.

Arts: Both the creative work and the process of producing the creative work.

Creative movement: Physical movement that represents the inward state.

Literary arts: Creative writing such as writing stories, poems, plays, jokes, or skits.

Performing arts: Art carried out through the artist's body face or presence such as dancing, singing, or puppetry.

Usable arts: Creation of art that is functional or practical in some way (e.g., weaving, ceramics, or knitting).

Visual arts: The creation of art that is primarily visual in nature such as painting, drawing, or sculpture.

Chapter 10

Attention deficit hyperactivity disorder (ADHD): Neurological condition characterized by hyperactivity, inability to concentrate, and impulsive behavior.

Autism: Condition disturbing perceptions and the formation of relationships.

Autonomy: Freedom from dependence or control by another; ability to be self-regulated.

Down syndrome: Genetic disorder resulting from an extra chromosome and characterized by unique physical features and learning difficulties.

Emotion: A strong feeling triggered by internal or external events.

Emotional intelligence: Concrete skills required to identify and manage emotions, make reasonable decisions, and develop social relationships.

Empathy: The ability to understand another person's emotions by feeling the same emotion.

English language learner (ELL): A person acquiring English who has a different primary language; also NEP (non-English proficient), LEP (limited-English proficient).

Global self-concept: All the beliefs a person has about himself or herself.

Resilience: Ability to rise above difficult circumstances and to move forward with reasonable optimism and confidence.

Self-awareness: Capacity to view oneself honestly and to interact effectively with others.

Self-esteem: One's perceptions of how competent one is intellectually, physically, emotionally, and so forth.

Sensory processing disorder: Condition where there may be over- or underresponsiveness in any or all sensory areas involving touch, sound, sight, taste, or smell.

Chapter 11

Abstraction principle: Counting part of a mixed set of items, for example, counting the red blocks in a building made of multicolored blocks.

Axon: Extension of a neuron that transmits impulses outward from the cell body.

Cardinal principle: Using the last number name spoken to describe the number of objects in the set (e.g., "one … two … three … three snakes").

Cognition: Complex mental processes of the human mind for acquiring knowledge via reasoning, intuition, or perception.

Cognitive processing: The way in which human beings actually think, reason, and develop language.

CREB: Gene that stimulates neural connections.

Dendrite: Branched extension of a nerve cell that receives electrical signals and conducts those signals to other neurons.

Inquiry: Effective and systematic observation of objects and materials in one's world.

Logical-mathematical knowledge: Understanding of relations between objects and phenomena deriving from observation; organization of incoming information.

Metacognition: Proficient strategies for monitoring one's thinking processes.

Mirror neurons: Type of brain cell that fires equally when we perform a certain action or when we observe others performing the same action; neurons that allow us to "feel" what others may be feeling in a certain situation.

Myelin: Fatty substance that surrounds and insulates nerve fibers, ensuring smooth transmission of nerve impulses.

Neuroimaging technologies: Includes functional magnetic resonance imaging (fMRI), positron emission tomography (PET), electroencephalography, and magnetoencephalography methodology to study areas and dynamic functions of the brain.

Neuron: A cell, usually consisting of a cell body, axon, and dendrite that transmits neural impulses.

Neuroscience: Study of the human brain.

One-to-one principle: Using one and only one number name for each number counted.

Order-irrelevance principle: Recognizing that the order in which objects are counted is irrelevant (e.g., six balls are always six balls, no matter which one you count first).

Physical knowledge: Understanding of observable attributes of objects and physical phenomenon.

Pruning: Elimination of infrequently used or weak neural pathways.

Representational knowledge: Understanding of ways to express symbolic or abstract thought.

Social conventional knowledge: Understanding of cultural and societal conventions, rules, viewpoints transmitted from generation to generation.

Stable-order principle: Using the number names in a stable order, such as "one … two … three" even though the order may be unconventional, such as "six … eleven … fifteen …".

Synapse: Junction between two nerve cells that transmit signals.

Synaptogenesis: Growth of connections between neurons and brain circuitry; also known as arborization.

Chapter 12

Alliteration: A string of words that begin with the same sound.

Alphabetic awareness: Knowledge of letters of the alphabet and understanding that they correspond to spoken sounds in the language.

Balanced literacy: A language arts program that contains components of oral language, reading strategies, and writing experiences.

Basal readers: Published anthologies of stories chosen to illustrate and develop certain reading skills.

Differentiating: Using strategies to move toward the same learning goal with different age groups of children or children of varying learning capacities and/or experiences.

Emergent literacy: Development and association of print with meaning.

Graphemes: The letter symbols in an alphabet.

Guided reading: Grouping students on the basis of strengths and limitations; using leveled books.

Literacy rotations: Block of time that includes both large- and small-group activities where children are rotated from one to another in definitive time sequences.

Onset and Rime: Onsets are the beginning sounds of words. Rimes consist of phonograms beginning with a vowel and sharing the same spelling endings (e.g., -at, -ack, -ing).

Phonemes: Discrete sounds in a language.

Phonemic awareness: Awareness that the speech stream consists of a sequence of sounds or phonemes.

Phonics: Tool to help make concrete connections between individual graphemes and their associated sounds.

Phonological awareness: Ability to consciously reflect on and manipulate the sounds of language; awareness of sounds or groups of sounds within words.

Prosody: The rhythmic sounds or "music" that constitute a particular language.

Scripted reading instruction: Reading lesson where teachers are expected to follow step-by-step teaching scripts.

Chapter 13

Body awareness: Names and functions of various body parts.

Body relationship awareness: Where one's body is in relation to another person such as a leading/following relationship.

Coordination: The use of more than one set of muscle groups and sensory systems.

Directional awareness: Understanding the pathway of movement (e.g., up/down; around or zig-zag).

Dynamic balance: Maintaining a posture while moving.

Fine-motor skills: Controlled and efficient use of the hands or feet, usually detailed or challenging controlled movement of the hands such as writing and sewing.

Fundamental motor skills: The basic movement from which more complex movements are made in sports, dance, and games.

Locomotor movement: Moving from one place to another (e.g., rolling, jumping, galloping).

Manipulative movement: Involves the controlled moving an object with hands or feet (e.g., throwing a bean bag or kicking a ball).

Physical fitness: A condition which the body is in a state of well-being and readily able to meet the physical challenges of everyday life.

Sedentary: Refers to a condition of physical inactivity.

Self space: The space near one's body or within reach of arms and legs when stretched out.

Sensory integration: Using all sensory data simultaneously.

Shared space: The space where two or more persons are moving at the same time.

Static balance: Maintaining a posture while remaining still.

Chapter 14

Attitude goals: These social studies goals emphasize respecting individuals both similar to and different from ourselves, understanding and appreciating one's own and others' culture and traditions, and caring for the world around us.

Inclusive environments: Environments in which all forms of diversity are fairly and consistently represented.

Knowledge goals: The goals relate to the content of social studies, such as the uniqueness of all people, the interdependence of people, the influence of the environment on people's choices of habitats and work, and the function and operation of social groups. Other knowledge goals deal with the structure of the social science disciplines, such as what and how we learn about human history and how people make decisions. Additional knowledge goals reflect similarities and differences among individuals and groups and how people learn to live together.

Prosocial behavior: Acts of kindness such as helping, sharing, sympathizing, rescuing, defending, cooperating, and comforting.

Skill goals: These goals focus on children's mastery of social studies techniques related to gathering information, improving their interpersonal interactions within their group, and problem solving, both in terms of content and social relations.

Social competence: How well children perceive, interpret, and respond to the variety of social situations they encounter.

Social responsibility: Developing respect for individual differences and functioning as contributing members of the communities in which they live.

Social skills: Learning to interact with others.

Social studies: Exploring people's interactions in and with their social and physical environments, now and in the past. The social studies are derived from a variety of disciplines, such as anthropology, history, geography, sociology, economics, and political science.

Socialization: Learning the values, beliefs, customs, and rules of society.

Chapter 15

Construction play: Something that is made or built to represent something else. Representational thinking is required.

Make-believe: Pretend, altering reality via words and imagination.

Metacommunication: A message about the nature of the communication. It is used to describe what is play, to construct a play frame, define roles, begin a pretend narrative, and transform objects and settings.

Object invention: Using actions or gestures as if one were using the object invented.

Object substitution: Using one object as if it were another.

Play frame: The space, materials, and people engaged in a play scenario.

Rough-and-tumble play: Consists of laughing, running, smiling, jumping, open-hand beating, wrestling, play fighting, chasing, and fleeing. It looks aggressive to many adults.

Sociodramatic play: Pretend play with two or more children with shared goals and a theme that lasts more than 10 minutes.

Transformation: The act of changing one thing to another. In play, the setting, time, and place are transformed from the here and now to an alternate reality.

Chapter 16

Concept: Fundamental ideas children form about concepts and events in the world.

Documentation: The process of collecting, analyzing, and presenting evidence.

Facts: Something known to exist or have happened.

Primary source: Firsthand sources of information such as real life objects, field sites, or topic experts.

Principles: A basic generalization that is accepted as true and that can be used as a basis for reasoning or conduct. Principles involve deduction and are more abstract than terms or facts.

Project: An in-depth study of a real world topic.

Secondary source: Indirect sources of information such as books, models, or photographs.

Terms: Vocabulary that describes theme- or projected-related objects and events.

Theme: A unifying idea.

Web: A graphic representation of related learning activities.

References

Abrams, H. (1985). *The Museum of Modern Art, New York*. New York: Author.

Adams, P., & Nesmith, J. (1996). Blockbusters: Ideas for the block center. *Early Childhood Education Journal, 24*(2), 87–92.

The Adventures of Sherlock Holmes [Motion picture]. (1939). United States: 20th Century Fox Studios.

Allen, W. R., Brookins, G. K., & Spencer, M. B. (Eds.), *Beginnings: The social and affective development of black children* (pp. 185–200). Hillsdale, NJ: Erlbaum.

Allen, E. K., & Edwards Cowdery, G. (2008). *The exceptional child: Inclusion in early childhood education*. Boston: Cengage Learning.

Allen, K. E., & Marotz, L. R. (2007). *Developmental profiles: Pre-birth through twelve* (6th ed.). Clifton Park, NY: Delmar Learning.

Allen, S. K., & Johnson, R. R. (1995, June). A study of hazards associated with playgrounds. *Journal of Environmental Health, 57*, 23–26.

Allington, R. L. (2004). Setting the record straight. *Educational Leadership, 61*(6), 22–25.

Alvino, F. J. (2000, May). *Art improves the quality of life: A look at art in early childhood settings*. East Lansing, MI: National Center for Research on Teacher Learning. (ERIC Document Reproduction Service No. ED447936)

American Psychiatric Association. (2000). *Diagnostic and statistical manual of mental disorders* (4th ed., Text Revision). Washington, DC: Author.

American Public Health Association & American Academy of Pediatrics. (2002). Caring for our children: National Health and Safety Performance Standards: Guidelines for out-of-home care. Washington, DC: American Public Health Association.

Americans with Disabilities Act (ADA). (2008). Retrieved November 11, 2008, from http://www.ada.gov/childq%26a.htm.

Amsterlaw, J. (2006). Children's beliefs about everyday reasoning. *Child Development, 77*, 443–464.

Anderson, S., Corr, M., Egertson, H., & Fichter, C. (2008, July 23). A call to action. Paper presented at the Working Forum on Nature Education: New Tools for Connecting the World's Children with Nature, Nebraska City, Nebraska.

Anghileri, J. (2006). *Teaching number sense*. New York: Continuum.

Archbald, D. A., & Newmann, F. M. (1988). *Beyond standardized testing*. Reston, VA: National Association of Secondary School Principals.

Armstrong, T. (2006). *The best schools: How human development research should inform educational practice*. Alexandria, VA: ASCD.

Arts Education Partnership. (2004). *Strategic plan 2004–2006*. Retrieved February 21, 2009, from aep-arts.org

Association for Supervision and Curriculum Development. (2008). Teaching to the brain. *ASCD Update, 33*(8), 1–8.

Aunola, K., & Nurmi, J. E. (2005). The role of parenting styles in children's problem behavior. *Child Development, 76*(6), 1144–1159.

Baghban, M. (2007). Scribbles, labels, and stories. *Young Children, 62*(1), 20–26.

Bagnato, S. J. (2007). *Authentic assessment for early childhood intervention–best practices*. New York: Guilford Press.

Baker, R. J., & McMurray, A. M. (1998). Contact fathers' loss of school involvement. *Journal of Family Studies, 4*(2), 201–214.

Bandura, A. (1989). Social cognitive theory. In R. Vasta (Ed.), *Annals of child development* (Vol. 6, pp. 1–60). Greenwich, CT: JAI.

Bandura, A. (1997). *Self-efficacy: The exercise of control*. New York: W.H. Freeman.

Banks, J. (2007). Approaches to multicultural curriculum reform. In J. Banks & C. Banks (Eds.), *Multicultural education: Issues and perspectives*. Boston: Allyn & Bacon.

Banks, J. A. (1988, Spring). Approaches to multicultural curriculum reform. *Multicultural Leader, 1*(2), 1–4.

Barab, S. A., & Landa, A. (1997, March). Designing effective interdisciplinary anchors. *Educational Leadership, 54*(6).

Barbarin, O., Bryant, D., McCandies, T., Burchinal, M., Early, D., Clifford, R., & Pianta, R. (2006). Children enrolled in public Pre-K: The relation of family life, neighborhood quality, and socioeconomic resources to early competence. *American Journal of Orthopsychiatry 76*, 265–276.

Barbour, C., Barbour, N. H., & Scully, P. A. (2008). *Families, schools, and communities*. Upper Saddle River, NJ: Merrill/Prentice Hall.

Barbour, N. H. (1990). Flexible grouping: It works! *Childhood Education, 67*(2), 66–67.

Barclay, K., Benelli, C., Campbell, P., & Kleine, L. (1995). Dream or nightmare? Planning for a year without textbooks. *Childhood Education, 71*(4), 205–211.

Barnett, W. S. (2008). *Preschool education and its lasting effects: Research and policy implications*. Boulder and Tempe: Education and the Public Interest Center & Education Policy Research Unit. Retrieved March 30, 2008 from http://epicpolicy.org/publication/preschool-education.

Barnett, W. S., & Yarosz, D. J. (2007). *Who goes to preschool and why does it matter?* New Brunswick, NJ: National Institute for Early Education Research.

Baroody, A. J. (1987). *Children's mathematical thinking*. New York: Teachers College Press.

Baroody, A. J., & Dowker, A. (Eds.). (2003). *The development of arithmetic concepts and skills*. Mahwah, NJ: Erlbaum.

Barrera, I., Corso, R. M., & Macpherson, D. (2003). *Skilled dialog*. Baltimore: Brookes Publishing Co.

Bateson, G. (1971). The message "This is play." In R. Herren & B. Sutton-Smith (Eds.), *Child's play* (pp. 261–266). New York: Wiley.

Batshaw, M. L., Pellegrino, L., & Roizen, N. J. (2007). *Children with disabilities* (6th ed.). Baltimore: Brookes.

Batzle, J. (1992). *Portfolio assessment and evaluation: Developing and using portfolios in the classroom*. Cypress, CA: Creative Teaching Press.

Baum, S., Viens, J., & Slatin, B. (2005). *Multiple intelligences in the elementary classroom: A teacher's toolkit*. New York: Teachers College Press.

Baumrind, D. (1967). Child care practices anteceding three patterns of preschool behavior. *Genetic Psychology Monographs, 75*, 43–88.

Baumrind, D. (1973). Current patterns of parental authority. *Developmental Psychology Monographs, 4*, 1.

Baumrind, D. (1978). A dialectical materialist's perspective on knowing social reality. In W. Damon (Ed.), *Moral development* (pp. 349–373). San Francisco: Jossey-Bass.

Baumrind, D. (1983). Rejoinder to Lewis's reinterpretation of parental firm control effects: Are authoritative families really harmonious? *Psychological Bulletin, 94*, 132–142.

Baumrind, D. (1991). The influence of parenting style on adolescent competence and substance use. *Journal of Early Adolescence, 2*, 56–95.

Baumrind, D. (1995). *Child maltreatment and optimal care-giving in social contexts*. New York: Garland.

Begley, S. (1997, Spring/Summer). The brain. *Newsweek*, (Special ed.), 28–31.

Bell, S. H., Carr, V., Denno, D., Johnson, L. J., & Phillips, L. R. (2004). *Challenging behaviors in early childhood settings: Creating a place for all children*. Baltimore: Brookes.

Bellows, L., & Anderson J. (2006). Encouraging preschoolers to try new foods. *Young Children, 61*(3), 37–39.

Beneke, S. J., Ostrosky, M. M., & Katz, L. G (2008). Calendar time for young children: Good intentions gone awry. *Young Children 63*(3), 12–16.

Bennett, B. (2008, September). Personal communication.

Bennett, J. (2008). Early childhood services in the OECD countries: Review of the literature and current policy in the early childhood field. Innocenti Working Paper No. 2008-01. Florence: UNICEF Innocenti Research Centre.

Bennett-Armistead, S., Duke, N., & Moses, A. (2007). *Beyond bedtime stories: A parent's guide to promoting reading, writing and other literacy skills from birth to 5*. New York: Scholastic.

Benson, J., & Miller, J. L. (2008). Experiences in nature: A pathway to standards. *Young Children, 63*(4), 22–28.

Bergen, D. (1988a). *Play as a medium for learning and development*. Portsmouth, NH: Heinemann.

Bergen, D. (1988b). Using a schema for play and learning. In D. Bergen (Ed.), *Play as a medium for learning and development* (pp. 169–180). Portsmouth, NH: Heinemann.

Bergen, D. (1993). Teaching strategies: Facilitating friendship development in inclusion classrooms. *Childhood Education, 69*(4), 234–236.

Bergen, D. (1994). Should teachers permit or discourage violent play themes? *Childhood Education, 70*(5), 302–303.

Berger, E. H. (2008). *Parents as partners in education: Families and schools working together* (7th ed.). Upper Saddle River, NJ: Merrill/Prentice Hall.

Berk, L. (2007). *Infants and children: Prenatal through middle childhood* (6th ed.). Boston: Allyn & Bacon.

Berk, L. (2008). *Infants, children, and adolescents* (6th ed.). Needham Heights, MA: Allyn & Bacon.

Berk, L. (2009). *Child development* (8th ed.). Boston: Allyn & Bacon.

Berndt, T. J., & Keefe, K. (1995). Friends' influence on adolescents' adjustment to school. *Child Development, 66*(5), 1312–1329.

Berkowitz, M. W. (2002). The science of character education. In W. Damon (Ed.), *Bringing in a new era of character education* (pp. 43–63). Stanford, CA: Hoover Institution Press.

Berndt, T. J., & Murphy, L. M. (2002). Influences of friends and friendships: Myths, truths, and research recommendations. *Advances in Child Development and Behavior, 30,* 275–310.

Bernero, T. (2003). *Intermediate results of a school-wide discipline policy.* Report on the Community School, East Lansing, MI.

Berns, R. M. (2009). *Child, family, school, community: Socialization and support* (5th ed.). Fort Worth, TX: Harcourt College.

Bickart, T. S., Dodge., T. D., & Jablon, J. R. (1997). *What every parent needs to know about 1st, 2nd, and 3rd grades.* Naperville, IL: Sourcebooks.

Biddle, B. J., & Berliner, D. C. (2002, February). Small class size and its effects. *Educational Leadership, 59*(5), 12–23.

Bjorklund, D. F. (2005). *Children's thinking: Cognitive development and individual differences.* Belmont, CA: Wadsworth/Thomson Learning.

Bjorklund, D. F, & Brown, R. D. (1998). Physical play and cognitive development: Integrating activity, cognition, and education. *Child Development, 69*(3), 604–606.

Bobbitt, N., & Paolucci, B. (1986). Strengths of the home and family as learning environments. In R. J. Griffore & R. P. Boger (Eds.), *Child rearing in the home and school* (pp. 47–60). New York: Plenum.

Bodrova, E., & Leong, D. (2007). *Tools of the mind: The Vygotskian approach to early childhood education* (2nd ed.). Upper Saddle River, NJ: Merrill/Prentice Hall.

Bogart, J. (1994). *Gifts.* Richmond Hill, Ontario, Canada: Scholastic Canada.

Bollin, G. G. (1989, Summer). Ethnic differences in attitude towards discipline among day care providers: Implications for training. *Child & Youth Care Quarterly, 18*(2), 111–117.

Bornstein, M. C. (2007). On the significance of social relationships in the development of children's earliest symbolic play: An ecological perspective. In A. Göncü & S. Gaskins (Eds.), *Play and development: Evolutionary, sociocultural, and functional perspectives* (pp. 101–129). Mahwah, NJ: Erlbaum.

Bornstein, M. H., Haynes, O. M., O'Reilly, A. W., & Painter, K. M. (1996). Solitary and collaborative pretense play in early childhood: Sources of individual variation in the development of representational competence. *Child Development, 67*(6), 2910–2929.

Bowman, B. (1994). The challenge of diversity. *Phi Delta Kappan, 76*(3), 218–225.

Bowman, B. T., Donovan, M. S., & Burns, M. S. (2001). *Eager to learn: Educating our preschoolers.* Washington, DC: National Academy Press.

Boyatzis, C. (1997). Of Power Rangers and v-chips. *Young Children, 52*(7), 74–79.

Boyd, B. J. (1997). Teacher response to superhero play: To ban or not to ban? *Young Children, 74*(1), 23–27.

Bracey, G. W. (2001). School involvement and the working poor: Summary of research by S. J. Heymann and A. Earle. *Phi Delta Kappan, 82*(10), 795.

Brainard, A., & Wrubel, D. H. (1993). *Literature-based science activities.* New York: Scholastic.

Brandt, R., & Epstein J. (1989, October). On parents and schools: A conversation with Joyce Epstein. *Educational Leadership, 47*(2), 24–27.

Bredekamp, S. (1987). *Developmentally appropriate practice in early childhood programs serving children from birth through age 8.* Washington, DC: National Association for the Education of Young Children.

Bredekamp, S., & Rosegrant, T. (Eds.). (1992). *Reaching potentials: Appropriate curriculum and assessment for young children* (Vol. 1). Washington, DC: National Association for the Education of Young Children.

Bredekamp, S., & Rosegrant, T. (Eds.). (1995). *Reaching potentials: Transforming early childhood curriculum and assessment* (Vol. 2). Washington, DC: National Association for the Education of Young Children.

Brendtro, L. K., Brokenleg, M., & Van Bockern, S. (1997). *Reclaiming youth at risk: Our hope for the future* (Rev. ed.). Bloomington, IN: National Educational Service.

Brewer, J. A. (2007). *Introduction to early childhood education: Preschool through primary grades* (6th ed.). Upper Saddle River, NJ: Pearson Education, Inc.

Briggs, N. R., Jalongo, M. R., & Brown, L. (2006). Working with families of young children: Our history and our future goals. In J. P Isenberg & M. R. Jalongo (Eds.), *Major trends and issues in early childhood education* (pp. 56–69). New York: Teachers College Press.

Bronfenbrenner, U. (1989). Ecological systems theory. In R. Vasta (Ed.), *Annals of child development* (Vol. 6, pp. 187–249). Greenwich, CT: JAI.

Bronson, M. B. (2006). Developing social and emotional competence. In D. F. Gullo (Ed.), *K Today: Teaching and learning in the kindergarten year* (pp. 47–56). Washington, DC: NAEYC.

Brouette, C. (2004). Aesthetics in the classroom setting. *Child Care Information Exchange,* January/February (155), 42–45.

Brown, G., Scott-Little, C., Amvade, L., & Wynn, L. (2007). A review of methods and instruments to build in state and local school readiness evaluations. IES National Center for Educational Evaluation and Regional Assessment. Washington, DC: U.S. Department of Education Institute of Educational Science.

Bruer, J. T. (2003). *The myth of the first three years.* New York: Free Press.

Bugental, D. B., & Goodnow, J. J. (1998). Socialization processes. In N. Eisenberg (Ed.), *Handbook of child psychology* (Vol. 3, pp. 389–462). New York: Wiley.

Bukatko, D. (2008). *Child and adolescent development: A chronological approach.* Boston: Houghton Mifflin Harcourt Publishing Company.

Bukowski, W. M., Sippola, L. K., & Bolvin, M. (1995, March). *Friendship protects "at risk" children from victimization by peers.* Paper presented at the meeting of the Society for Research in Child Development, Indianapolis, IN.

Bullard, J. (2010). *Creating environments for learning.* Upper Saddle River, NJ: Merrill.

Burningham, L. M., & Dever, M. (2005). An interactive model for fostering familiy literacy. *Young Children, 60*(5), 87–93.

Burns, M. (2007). *About teaching mathematics: A K–8 resource* (3rd ed.). Sausalito, CA: Math Solutions Publications.

Burts, D. C., Hart, C. H., Charlesworth, R., & Kirk, L. (1990). A comparison of frequencies of stress behaviors observed in kindergarten children in classrooms with developmentally appropriate versus developmentally inappropriate instructional practices. *Early Childhood Research Quarterly, 5,* 407–423.

Burts, D. C., Hart, C. H., Charlesworth, R., & Kirk, L. (1992). Observed activities and stress behaviors of children in developmentally appropriate and inappropriate kindergarten classrooms. *Early Childhood Research Quarterly, 7*(2), 297–318.

Butler, Y. Fox News.com. Retrieved January 29, 2009.

California Department of Education. (2002). *State study proves physically fit kids perform better academically.* Report of the 2001 California Standardized Testing and Reporting Program. Report #02-37. Sacramento, CA: Author.

Cardellichio, T., & Field, W. (1997, March). Seven strategies that encourage neural branching. *Educational Leadership, 54*(6), 33–36.

Carin, A. A., Bass, J. E., & Contant, T. L. (2005). *Activities for teaching science as inquiry.* Upper Saddle River, NJ: Merrill/Prentice Hall.

Carlisle, A. (2001). Using the multiple intelligence theory to assess early childhood curricula. *Young Children, 56*(6), 77–83.

Carlson, K., & Cunningham, J. L. (1990). Effect of pencil diameter on the graphomotor skill of preschoolers. *Early Childhood Research Quarterly, 5*(2), 279–293.

Carlson, S. A., Fulton, J. E., Lee S. M. & Maynard, L. M. (2008). Physical education and academic achievement in elementary school: Data from the early childhood longitudinal study, American Journal of Public Health, Vol 98 Issue 4 721–728.

Carnegie Foundation for the Advancement of Teaching. (1988). *The conditions of teaching: A state by state analysis.* Princeton, NJ: Author.

Carta, J., Schwartz, L., Atwater, J., & McConnell, S. (1993). Developmentally appropriate practices and early childhood special education: A reaction to Johnson and McChesney Johnson. *Topics in Early Childhood Special Education, 13*(3), 243–254.

Casey, E. A. & Nurius, P. S. (2006) Trends in prevalence and characteristics of sexual violence: a cohort analysis, *Violence and Victims* Vol 21 #5, 629–645.

Casey, M., & Lippman, M. (1991, May). Learning to plan through play. *Young Children, 46*(4), 52–58.

Cassidy, D. (1989). Questioning the young child: Process and function. *Childhood Education, 65*(3), 146–149.

Castle, K. (1991). Children's invented games. *Childhood Education, 67*(2), 82–85.

Caughy, M. O., Huang, K., Miller, T., & Genevro, J. L. (2004). The effects of Healthy Steps for Young Children Program: Results from observations of parenting and child development. *Early Childhood Research Quarterly, 19*(4), 611–630.

Center for Civic Education. (1994). *National standards for civics and government.* Washington, DC: Author.

Chafel, J. (1986). Call the police, okay? Social comparison by young children during play in preschool. In S. Burrows & R. Evans (Eds.), *Play, language and socialization* (pp. 115–130). New York: Gordon & Breach.

Chaille, C. (2008). *Constructivism across the curriculum in early childhood classrooms: Big ideas of inspiration.* Boston: Pearson Education, Inc.

Chalufour, I., & Worth, K. (2003). *Discovering nature with young children.* St. Paul, MN: Redleaf Press.

Chamberlain, S. (2008). Effective practices for students with disabilities in inclusive classrooms. In Y. S. Freeman, D. E. Freeman, & R. Ramirez (Eds.), *Diverse learners in the mainstream classroom* (pp. 77–100). Portsmouth, NH: Heinemann.

Chang, H., Salazar, D., & DeLeong, C. (1994). *Drawing strength from diversity: Effective services for children, youth and families.* Sacramento: California Tomorrow.

Chapin, J. R. (2009). *Elementary social studies* (7th ed.). Boston: Pearson.

Chard, D. J. and Dickson, S. (May, 1999). Phonological awareness: Instructional and assessment guidelines. *Intervention in School and Clinic, 34*(5), 261–270.

Chard, S. C. (1998a). *The project approach: Making curriculum come alive.* New York: Scholastic.

Chard, S. C. (1998b). *The project approach: Managing successful projects.* New York: Scholastic.

Chard, S. C. (1999, Spring). From themes to projects. *Early Childhood Research and Practice, 1*(1). Retrieved June 10 from http://ecrp.uiuc.edu/vlnl/chard.html

Chard, S. C. (2001). *The project approach: Taking a closer look* [CD-ROM].

Chard, S. C. (2002). The challenges and the rewards: Teachers' accounts of their first experiences with the project approach. In D. Rothenberg (Ed.), *Issues in early childhood education: Curriculum, teacher education, and dissemination of information.* Proceedings of the Lilian Katz Symposium, Champaign, IL.

Charles, C. M., Seuter, G. W., & Barr, K. B. (2008). *Building classroom discipline* (9th ed.). Upper Saddle River, NJ: Merrill/Prentice Hall.

Charlesworth, R. & Lind, K. (2010). *Math & Science for Young Children* (6th ed.). Belmont, CA: Wadsworth/Cengage Learning.

Charlesworth, R. & Lind, K. K (2009). *Math and science for young children.* New York: Delmar Learning.

Charney, R. S. (2002). *Teaching children to care: Management in the responsive classroom.* Greenfield, MA: Northeast Foundation for Children.

Chen, L., & Mara-Flores, E. (2006). *Balanced literacy for English language learners, K–2.* Portsmouth, NH: Heinemann.

Children's Defense Fund. (2006). *State of America's children: 2005.* Washington, DC: Author.

Clarizio, H. (1980). *Toward positive classroom discipline.* New York: Wiley.

Clark, C., & Gross, K. H. (2004). Adolescent health-risk behaviors: The effect of perceived parenting style and race. *Undergraduate Research Journal for the Human Sciences, 3,* 1–11.

Clay, M. (1979). *Reading: The patterning of complex behaviour* (2nd ed.). Auckland, New Zealand: Heinemann.

Clay, M. M. (1995). *Reading recovery: A guidebook for teachers in training* (Rev. ed.). Portsmouth, NH: Heinemann.

Clayton, M. K. (1989). *Places to start: Implementing the developmental classroom.* Greenfield, MA: Northeast Foundation for Children.

Clayton, M. K., & Forton, M. B. (2001). *Classroom spaces that work.* Greenfield, MA: Northeast Foundation for Children.

Clements, R. D., & Wachowiak, F. (2010). *Emphasis art: A qualitative art program for elementary and middle schools.* Boston: Allyn & Bacon.

Coates, E. (2002). I forgot the sky: Children's stories contained within their drawings. *International Journal of Early Years Education, 10*(1), 21–35.

Cochran, M., & Henderson, C. R., Jr. (1986). *Family matters: Evaluation of the parental empowerment program.* Ithaca, NY: The Comparative Ecology of Human Development Project.

Codell, E. R. (2001). *Educating Esme: Diary of a teacher's first year.* Chapel Hill, NC: Algonquin Books.

Cohen, M., & Gross, P. (1979). *The developmental resource: Behavioral sequences for assessment and program planning* (Vol. 2). New York: Grune & Stratton.

Cohen, S. (1977). Fostering positive attitudes toward the handicapped: New curriculum. *Children Today, 6*(6), 7–12.

Cohen, S. (1994). Children and the environment: Aesthetic learning. *Childhood Education, 70*(5), 302–303.

Coie, J. D., & Dodge, K. A. (1998). Aggression and antisocial behavior. In N. Eisenberg (Ed.), *Handbook of child psychology* (Vol. 3, pp. 779–862). New York: Wiley.

Coladarci, T. (2002, June). Is it a house . . . or a pile of bricks? Important features of a local assessment system. *Phi Delta Kappan, 83*(10), 772–774.

Colbert, C. (1997). Visual arts in the developmentally appropriate integrated curriculum. In C. H. Hart, D. C. Burts, & R. Charlesworth (Eds.), *Integrated curriculum and developmentally appropriate practice: Birth to age eight* (pp. 201–223). Albany: State University of New York Press.

Cole, E. (1990). An experience in Froebel's garden. *Childhood Education, 67*(1), 18–21.

Commeyras, M. (2007). Scripted reading instruction? What's a teacher to do? *Phi Delta Kappan, 33*(5), 404–407.

Consortium of National Arts Education Associations. (1994). *Dance, music, theatre, visual arts: What every young American should know and be able to do in the arts: National standards for arts education.* Reston, VA: Author.

Cooper, J. L., & Dever, M. T. (2001). Sociodramatic play as a vehicle for curriculum integration in first grade. *Young Children, 56*(3), 58–63.

Copple, C. (Ed.). (2003). *A world of difference: Readings on teaching young children in a diverse society.* Washington, DC: NAEYC.

Copple, C. & Bredekamp, S. (2006). *Basics of developmentally appropriate practice: An introduction for teachers of children 3 to 6.* Washington, DC: NAEYC.

Copple, C. & Bredekamp, S. (2009). *Developmentally appropriate practice in early childhood programs serving children from birth through age 8* (3rd ed.). Washington, DC: National Association for the Education of Young Children.

Cost, Quality, and Child Outcomes Study Team. (2000). *Cost, quality, and child outcomes in child care centers* (Public Rep.). Denver: Economics Department, University of Colorado at Denver.

Costa, A. L., & Kallick, B. (2004). Launching self-directed learners. *Educational Leadership, 62*(1), 51–55.

Council of Chief State School Officers. (2009, January). *Assessment terminology.* Washington, DC: Author.

Crary, E. (1996). *Help! The kids are at it again: Using kids' quarrels to teach "people" skills.* Seattle, WA: Parenting Press.

Creech, N., & Bhavnagri, N. (2002). Teaching elements of story through drama to 1st-graders. *Childhood Education, 78*(4), 219–223.

Crews, D. (1991). *Bigmama's.* New York: Trumpet.

Cross, T. (1995). The early childhood curriculum debate. In M. Fleer (Ed.), *DAP centrism: Challenging developmentally appropriate practice* (pp. 87–108). Watson, Australia: Australian Early Childhood Association.

Cross, W. E. (1985). Black identity: Rediscovering the distinctions between personal identity and reference group orientations. In M. B. Spencer, G. K. Brookins, & W. R. Allen (Eds.), *Beginnings: The social and affective development of black children* (pp. 155–172). Hillsdale, NJ: Erlbaum.

Crosser, S. (1992). Managing the early childhood classroom. *Young Children, 47*(2), 23–29.

Crosser, S. (1994). Making the most of water play. *Young Children, 49*(5), 28–32.

CTB/McGraw–Hill. (2003). *Pre-K standards: Guidelines for teaching and learning.* New York: Author.

Cunha, F., & Heckman, J (2007, September 9–10). Investing in disadvantaged young children is good economics and good public policy. Telluride, CO: Telluride Economic Summit on Early Childhood Investment.

Cunningham, P. (2008). *Phonics they use: Words for reading and writing* (5th ed.). New York: Longman.

Currie, J. R. (1988, Winter). Affect in the schools: A return to the most basic of basics. *Childhood Education, 65*(2), 83–87.

Curry, N. E., & Johnson, C. N. (1998). *Beyond self-esteem: Developing a genuine sense of human value* (2nd ed.). Washington, DC: National Association for the Education of Young Children.

Curtis, D., & Carter, M. (2003). *Designs for living and learning. Transforming early childhood environments.* St. Paul, MN: Redleaf Press.

Curwin, R. L., & Mendler, A. N. (2000). *Discipline with dignity.* Upper Saddle River, NJ: Pearson.

Curwin, R. L., Mendler, A. N., & Mendler, B. D. (2008). *Discipline with dignitiy: New challenges, new solutions.* Alexandria, VA: ASCD.

D'Addesio, J., Grob, B., Furman, L., Hayes, K., & David, J. (2005). Learning about the world around us. *Young Children, 60*(5), 50–57.

Daniel, J. (2009) Intentionally thoughtful family engagement in early chidlhood education, *Young Children,* vol 64 #5, 10–14.

Darling-Hammond, L., & Hammerness, K. (2005). The design of teacher education programs. In L. Darling-Hammond & J. Bransford (Eds.), *Preparing teachers for a changing world* (pp. 390–441). San Francisco: Jossey-Bass.

Deasy, R. J. (2002). *Critical links: Learning in the arts and student academic and social development.* Washington, DC: Arts Education Partnership.

Deegan, J. G. (1993). Children's friendships in culturally diverse classrooms. *Journal of Research in Childhood Education, 7*(2), 91–101.

DeFrain, J., Jones, J. E., Skogrand, L., & DeFrain, N. (2003). Surviving and transcending a traumatic childhood: An exploratory study [Electronic version]. *Marriage & Family Review, 35.*

DeHart, G. B., Sroufe, L. A., & Cooper, R. G. (2000). *Child development: Its nature and course* (4th ed.). New York: McGraw-Hill.

Delisio, E. R. (2008). Home visits forge school, family links. *Education World.* Retrieved January 31, 2009, from http://www.educationworld.com/a_admin/admin/admin342.shtml

Delpit, L. (1995). *Other people's children: Cultural conflict in the classroom.* New York: The New Press.

Dempsey, J., & Frost, J. (1993). Play environments in early childhood education. In B. Spodek (Ed.), *Handbook of research on the education of young children* (pp. 306–321). New York: Macmillan.

Denham, S. A. (1995, September). Scaffolding young children's prosocial responsiveness: Preschoolers' responses to adult sadness, anger and pain. *International Journal of Behavioral Development, 18*(3), 485–504.

Derman-Sparks, L., & Edwards, J. O. (2010). *Anti-bias education for young children and ourselves.* Washington, DC: NAEYC.

Derscheid, L. E. (1997, Spring/Summer). Mixed-age grouped preschoolers' moral behavior and understanding. *Journal of Research in Childhood Education, 11,* 147–151.

Developmentally Appropriate Practice in Early Childhood Programs Serving Children from Birth through Age 8. In C. Copple & S. Bredekamp (Eds.) *Developmentally Appropriate Practice in Early Childhood Programs.* E3. Washington DC: NAEYC, 1–31.

DeVogue, K. (1996, March). *Conflict resolution with children in grade school.* Presentation, Forest View Elementary School Teachers, Lansing, MI.

DeVries, R., & Kohlberg, L. (1990). *Constructivist early education: Overview and comparison with other programs.* Washington, DC: National Association for the Education of Young Children.

DeVries, R., Zan, B., Hildebrandt, C., Edmiaston, R., & Sales, C. (2002). *Developing constructivist early childhood curriculum.* New York: Teachers College Press.

Deyell-Gingold, P. (2006). Successful transition to kindergarten. *Early Childhood NEWS,* May/June, 14–19.

Dickinson, D. K. (2002). Shifting images of developmentally appropriate practice as seen through different lenses. *Educational Researcher,* January/February, 26–32.

Dickinson, D. K., & Tabors, P O. (2001). *Beginning literacy with language: Young children learning at home and school.* Baltimore: Paul H. Brookes.

Dinkmeyer, D., Sr., McKay, G. D., Dinkmeyer, J. S., Dinkmeyer, D., Jr., & McKay, J. L. (1997). *Parenting young children: Systematic training for effective parenting (STEP) of children under six.* Circle Pines, MN: American Guidance Service.

Dodge, D. T. (2003). *The creative curriculum for early childhood.* Washington, DC: Teaching Strategies.

Dodge, D. T., Colker, L. J., Heroman, C., & Bickart, T. S. (2008). *The creative curriculum for preschool* (3rd ed.). Washington, DC: Teaching Strategies.

Doherty-Derkowski, G. (1998). *Quality matters: Excellence in early childhood programs* (2nd ed.). Reading, MA: Addison-Wesley.

Donegan, M., Hong, S. B., Trepanier-Street, M., & Finkelstein, C. (2005). Exploring how project work enhances student teachers' understanding of children with special needs. *Journal of Early Childhood Teacher Education, 26*(1), 37–46.

Douglas-Hall, A., & Chau, M. (2007). *Basic facts and low-income children birth to age 6* (pp. 1–4). New York: National Center for Children in Poverty, Columbia University.

Doyle, R. P. (1989, November). The resistance of conventional wisdom to research evidence: The case of retention in grade. *Phi Delta Kappan, 71*(3), 215–220.

Dreikurs, R., & Soltz, V. (1991). *Children: The challenge* (Reprint ed.). New York: Plume/Penguin Books. (Originally published in 1964, New York: Hawthorn Books)

Dresden, J., & Lee, K. (2007). The effects of project work in a first-grade classroom: A little goes a long way. *Early Childhood Research and Practice, 9*(1).

Drew, W. F., & Rankin, B. (2004). Promoting creativity for life using open-ended materials. *Young Children, 59*(4), 38–45.

Driscoll, A., & Nagel, N. G. (2008). *Early childhood education birth–8: The world of children, families and educators* (4th ed.). Boston: Allyn & Bacon.

Duckworth, E. (1987). *The having of wonderful ideas and other essays on teaching and learning.* New York: Teachers College Press.

Duffelmeyer, F. A. (2002, April). Alphabet activities on the Internet. *The Reading Teacher, 55*(7), 631–634.

Dunn, L., Beach, S. A., & Kontos, S. (1994). Quality of the literacy environment in day care and children's development. *Journal of Research in Childhood Education, 9,* 24–34.

Dyson, A. (1990, January). Symbol makers, symbol weavers: How children link play, pictures, and print. *Young Children, 45*(2), 50–57.

Eastman, W. (2002, May/June). Working with families around nutritional issues. *Child Care Information Exchange, 145,* 42–45.

Eaton, M. (1997). Positive discipline: Fostering self-esteem in young children. *Young Children, 52*(6), 43–46.

Educational Materials Center. (2005). *Michigan model for comprehensive health education.* Retrieved May 6, 2006, from www.emc.cmich.edu/mm/default.htm

Educational Productions. (1998). *Supergroups.* Portland, OR: Author.

Edwards, C. H. (2007). *Classroom discipline and management.* New York: John Wiley and Sons.

Edwards, C. P. (2005, November 19). *Showing that early childhood education works: Lessons from around the world.* College of Education and Human Sciences Student Research Conference, Lincoln, NE.

Edwards, C. P., Gandini, L., & Forman, G. (Eds.). (1998). *The hundred languages of children: The Reggio Emilia approach—advanced reflections* (2nd ed.). Greenwich, CT: Ablex.

Edwards, L. (2003). Writing instruction in kindergarten: Examining an emerging area of research for children with writing and reading difficulties. *Journal of Learning Disabilities, 36*(4), 136–148.

Egertson, H. (2008). *Assessment in early childhood: A primer for policy and program leaders.* Arlington, VA: National Association of State School Boards of Education. Available at http://www.nasbe.org.

Ehlert, L. (1989). Eating the alphabet: Fruits & vegetables from A to Z. San Diego: Harcourt Brace Jovanovich.

Eisenberg, N., Fabes, R. A., & Spinrad, T. L. (2006). Prosocial development. In N. Eisenberg, W. Damon, & R. M. Lerner (Eds.), *Handbook of child psychology* (pp. 646–718). Hoboken, NJ: Wiley.

Eisenhauer, M. J., & Feikes, D. (2009). Dolls, blocks and puzzles: Playing with mathematical understandings. *Young Children, 64*(3), 18–24.

Eldridge, D. (2001). Parent involvement: It's worth the effort. *Young Children, 56*(4), 65–69.

Elgas, P., Prendeville, J., Moomaw, S., & Kretschmer, R. (2002, January). Early childhood classroom setup. *Child Care Information Exchange, 143,* 17–20.

Elias, C. L., & Berk, L. E. (2002). Self-regulation in young children: Is there a role for socio-dramatic play? *Early Childhood Research Quarterly, 17*(2), 216–238.

Elias, M. J. (2006). The connection between academic and social-emotional learning. In M. J. Elias and H. Arnold. The Educator's Guide to Emotional Intelligence and Academic Achievement. Thousand Oaks, CA: Corwin Press. [table 10.2]

Eliason, C., & Jenkins, L. T. (2007). *A practical guide to early childhood curriculum* (8th ed.). Upper Saddle River, NJ: Merrill/Prentice Hall.

Elkind, D. (1989, October). Developmentally appropriate practice: Philosophical and practical implications. *Phi Delta Kappan, 7*(2), 113–117.

Elkind, D. (2005). Early childhood amnesia: Reaffirming children's need for developmentally appropriate programs. *Young Children, 60*(4), 38–40.

Elkind, D. (2007). *The power of play: How spontaneous imaginative activities lead to happier, healthier children.* Cambridge, MA: Da Capo Press.

Elkind, D. (2007). *The power of play: Doing what comes naturally.* Cambridge, MA: De Capo Press.

Epstein, A. S. (2007). *The intentional teacher: Choosing the best strategies for young children's learning.* Washington, DC: National Association for the Education of Young Children.

Epstein, A. S. (2008). An early start on thinking. *Educational Leadership, 65*(5), 38–43.

Epstein, A. S. (2009). *Me, you, us: Social-emotional learning in preschool.* Ypsilanti, MI: HighScope Educational Research Foundation.

Epstein, J. L. (1978). Growth spurts during brain development: Implications for educational policy and practice. In J. Child and A. Mersey (Eds.), *Education and the brain* (pp. 135–161). Chicago: University of Chicago Press.

Epstein, J. L. (1984, April). *Effects of parent involvement on student achievement in reading and math.* Paper presented at the annual meeting of the American Research Association, Washington, D.C.

Epstein, J. L. (1986). Parents' reactions to teacher practices of parent involvement. *Elementary School Journal, 86,* 277–293.

Epstein, J. L. (2002). *School, family, and community partnerships: Your handbook for action. Preparing educators and improving schools.* Boulder, CO: Thousand Oaks, CA: Corwin Press.

Espinosa, L. M. (2008). *Challenging common myths about young English language learners: FDC policy brief advancing PK–3, No. 8.* New York: Foundation for Child Development.

Essa, E. (2007). *Introduction to early childhood education* (4th ed.). Clifton Park, NY: Delmar Learning.

Evans, B. (2002). *You can't come to my birthday party: Conflict resolution with young children.* Ypsilanti, MI: High/Scope Press.

Evans, E. D. (1975). *Contemporary influences in early childhood education* (2nd ed.) New York: Holt, Rinehart & Winston.

Evans, G. W., & Rosenbaum, J. (2008). Self-regulation and the income-achievement gap. *Early Childhood Research Quarterly, 23*(4), 504–514.

Faber, A., & Mazlish, E. (1995). *How to talk so kids can learn at home and school.* New York: Simon & Schuster.

Fabes, R. A., Martin, M. C., & Havish, L. D. (2003). Children at play: The role of peers in understanding the effects of child care. *Child Development, 74*(4), 1039–1043.

Fagen, J. (2000). African American and Puerto Rican American parenting styles, paternal involvement, and Head Start children's social competence. *Merrill-Palmer Quarterly, 46*(4), 592–612.

Farver, J. A. M., & Shinn, Y. L. (1997). Social pretend play in Korean- and Anglo-American preschoolers. *Child Development, 68*(3), 544–556.

Feuerstein, A. (2000). School characteristics and parent involvement: Influences on participation in children's schools. *Journal of Educational Research, 94*(1), 29–39.

Fields, M. V., & Spangler, K. L. (2000). *Let's begin reading right: A developmental approach to emergent literacy* (4th ed.). Upper Saddle River, NJ: Merrill/Prentice Hall.

File, N. (2001). Family–professional partnerships: Practice that matches philosophy. *Young Children, 56*(4), 70–74.

Filler, J., & Xu, Y. (2006). Including children with disabilities in early childhood education programs: Individualizing developmentally appropriate practices. *Childhood Education, 83*(2), 92–99.

Finkelhor, D. (1984). *Child sexual abuse: New theory and research.* New York: Free Press.

Finkelhor, D., & Baron, L. (1986). High-risk children. In D. Finkelhor & Associates (Eds.), *A sourcebook on child sexual abuse* (pp. 60–88). Beverly Hills, CA: Sage.

FitzGerald, D. P., & White, K. J. (2003). Linking children's social worlds: Perspective-taking in parent-child and peer contexts. *Social Behavior and Personality, 31*, 509–522.

Fleer, M. (1995). *DAP centrism: Challenging developmentally appropriate practice.* Watson, Australia: Australian Early Childhood Association.

Fleer, M., & Careen, L. (1995). *What do I look like on the inside? Developing children's understanding about their bodies.* (Australian Early Childhood Association Resource Book Series, Vol. 2, No. 1). Watson, Australia: Australian Early Childhood Association.

Ford, S. (1993). The facilitator's role in children's play. *Young Children, 48*(6), 66–69.

Forman, G. (1996). A child constructs an understanding of a water wheel in five media. *Childhood Education, 72*(5), 269–273.

Forman, G., & Kuschner, D. S. (1983). *The child's construction of knowledge: Project for teaching young children.* Washington, DC: National Association for the Education of Young Children.

Fountas, I. C., & Pinnell, G. S. (1996). *Guided reading: Good first teaching for all children.* Portsmouth, NH: Heinemann.

Fox, L., & Lentini, H. (2006). You got it!: Teaching social and emotional skills. *Young Children, 61*(6), 36–42.

Franklin, M. (1994). Art, play, and symbolization in childhood and beyond: Reconsidering connections. *Teacher's College Record, 95*(4), 526–541.

Franz, C. E., McClelland, D. C., & Weinberger, R. L. (1991). Childhood antecedents of conventional social accomplishment in mid-life adults. A 36-year prospective study. *Journal of Personality and Social Psychology, 60*, 586–595.

Freeman, N. K., & Feeney, S. (2006). The new faces of early care and education: Who are we? Where are we going? *Young Children, 61*(5), 10–16.

Freyd, J. Putnam, F.W., Lyon, T.D., Becker-Blease, K.A., Cheit, R.E., Siegal, N. B., Pezdek, K. (2005) Science of child sexual abuse, *Science.* Vol 308 Issue 5721, p. 501.

Freiberg, H. J., & Driscoll, A. (2005). *Universal teaching strategies* (3rd ed.). Boston: Allyn & Bacon.

Friedman, S. (2005). Environments that inspire. Retrieved December 5, 2008, from www.journal.naeyc.org-btj-200307

Friedrich, L. K., & Stein, A. H. (1973). Aggressive and pro-social television programs and the natural behaviors of preschool children. *Monographs of the Society for Research in Child Development, 38*(4), serial no. 151.

Fromberg, D. P. (2002). *Play and meaning in early childhood education.* Boston: Allyn & Bacon.

Frost, J. (1991). *Play and playscapes.* Albany, NY: Delmar.

Frost, J. L., & Sweeney, T. (1995). *Causes and prevention of playground injuries and litigation case studies* (pp. 60–88). Washington, DC: ERIC Clearinghouse. (ERIC Document Reproduction Service No. ED394648)

Frost, J. L., Brown, P., Sutterby, J. A., & Thornton, C. P. (2004). *The developmental benefits of playgrounds.* Washington, DC: ACEI.

Frost, J. L., Wortham, S., & Reifel, S. (2008). *Play and child development* (3rd ed.). Upper Saddle River, NJ: Merrill/Prentice Hall.

Frost, L., Talbot, J., & Monroe, M. (1990). Playgrounds. In L. Ard & M. Pitts (Eds.), *Room to grow: How to create quality early childhood environments* (pp. 149–160). Austin: Texas Association for the Education of Young Children.

Gabbard, C., Le Blanc, E., & Lowy, S. (1994). *Physical education for children: Building the foundation* (2nd ed.). Upper Saddle River, NJ: Prentice Hall.

Gable, S., & Cole, K. (2000, October). Parents' child care arrangements and their ecological correlates. *Early Education and Development, 11*(5), 549–572.

Gage, N. L., & Berliner, D. C. (1998). *Educational psychology* (6th ed.). Boston: Houghton Mifflin.

Gallagher, K. C. (2005). Brain research and early childhood development: A primer for developmentally appropriate practice. *Young Children, 60*(4), 12–20.

Gallagher, K. C., & Mayer, K. (2006). Teacher-child relations at the forefront of effective practice. *Young Children, 61*(6), 44–49.

Gallahue, D. (1993). Motor development and movement skill acquisition in early childhood education. In B. Spodek (Ed.), *Handbook of research on the education of young children* (pp. 24–41). New York: Macmillan.

Gallahue, D. (1995). Transforming physical education curriculum. In S. Bredekamp & T. Rosegrant (Eds.), *Reaching potentials: Transforming early childhood curriculum and assessment* (Vol. 2). Washington, DC: National Association for the Education of Young Children.

Gallenstein, N. L. (2003). *Creative construction of mathematics and science concepts in early childhood.* Olney, MD: Association for Childhood Education International.

Gandini, L., & Edwards, C. P. (1988). Early childhood integration of the visual arts. *Gifted International, 5*(2), 14–18.

Garbarino, J. (2008). *Children and the dark side of human experience.* New York: Springer.

Garcia, C., Garcia, L., Floyd, J., & Lawson, J. (2002). Improving public health through early childhood movement programs. *Journal of Physical Education, Recreation and Dance, 73*(1), 27–31 [+].

Gardner, H. (1993a). *Frames of mind* (Rev. ed.). New York: Basic Books.

Gardner, H. (1994). *The arts and human development.* New York: Basic Books.

Gardner, H. (1997). *Extraordinary minds: Portraits of exceptional individuals and an examination of our extraordinariness.* New York: Basic Books.

Gardner, H. (1998). Are there additional intelligences? The case for naturalist, spiritual, and existential intelligences. In J. Kane (Ed.), *Education, information, and transformation: Essays on learning and thinking* (pp. 111–131). Upper Saddle River, NJ: Merrill/Prentice Hall.

Gardner, H. (2001, January 15). Constant testing isn't the way to measure education. *Lansing State Journal,* 5A.

Gardner, H., Kornhaber, M. L., & Wake, W. K. (2006). *Intelligence.* Fort Worth, TX: Harcourt Brace.

Gartrell, D. (2004). *The power of guidance: Teaching social-emotional skills in early childhood classrooms.* Albany, NY: Thomson, Delmar Learning.

Gartrell, D. (2006). Guidance matters. *Young Children, 61*(2), 88–89.

Gartrell, D. (2007). *A guidance approach for the encouraging classroom* (3rd ed.). Clifton Park, NY: Delmar.

Gazda, G. M. (1999). *Human relations development: A manual for educators* (6th ed.). Boston: Allyn & Bacon.

Gazda, G. M., Balzer, F., Childers, W., Nealy, A., Phelps, R., & Walters, W. (2006). *Human relations development—a manual for educators* (7th ed.). Boston: Allyn & Bacon.

Geist, K., & Geist, E. (2008). Do re mi, 1-2-3 that's how easy math can be: Using music to support emergent mathematics. *Young Children, 63*(2), 20–25.

Gelnaw, A. (2005) Belonging: Including children of gay and lesbian parents—and all children in your program. *Exchange, 163,* 42–45.

Genisio, M., & Drecktrah, M. (2000–2001). Emergent literacy in an early childhood classroom: Center learning to support the child with special needs. In K. M. Paciorek (Ed.), *Annual editions: Early childhood education* (22nd ed.). Guilford, CT: McGraw-Hill/Dushkin.

George, M. A., & Sellers, W. (Eds.) (1984). *Michigan model for comprehensive health education.* Mt. Pleasant: Central Michigan University Educational Materials Center.

Gestwicki, C. (1997). *The essentials of early education.* Albany, NY: Delmar.

Gestwicki, C. (2005). *Developmentally appropriate practice: Curriculum and development in early education.* Albany, NY: Delmar.

Gillon, G. (2002). Phonological awareness intervention for children. *The ASHA Leader Online Archive.*

Ginsburg, K. R. (2006). *A parent's guide to building resilience in children and teens.* Elk Grove Village, IL: American Academy of Pediatrics.

Ginsburg, K. R. (2007). The importance of play in promoting healthy child development and maintaining strong parent-child bonds. *Pediatrics, 119*(1), 182–191.

Glasgow, N. A., & Hicks, C. D. (2003). *What successful teachers do: Research-based classroom strategies for new and veteran teachers.* Thousand Oaks, CA: Corwin Press.

Glasser, W. (1985). *Control theory in the classroom.* New York: Perennial Library.

Glickman, C. (1991). Pretending not to know what we know. *Educational Leadership, 48*(8), 4–8.

Golbeck, S. L. (2006). Developing key cognitive skills. In D. F. Gullo (Ed.), *K Today: Teaching and learning in the kindergarten year* (pp. 37–46). Washington, DC: NAEYC.

Goldberg, S. (1997). *Parent involvement begins at birth.* Boston: Allyn & Bacon.

Goldhaber, J., Lipson, M., Sortino, S., & Daniels, P. (1996–1997). Books in the sand box? Markers in the blocks? Expanding the child's world of literacy. *Childhood Education, 73*(2), 88–91.

Goleman, D. (1997). *Emotional intelligence: Why it can matter more than IQ* (Reprint ed.). New York: Bantam Books.

Goleman, D. (2006). *Social intelligence: The new science of social relationships.* New York: Bantam Books.

Gonzalez-Mena, J., & Widmeyer Eyer, E. D. (2009). *Infants, toddlers, and caregivers* (8th ed.). Mountain View, CA: Mayfield.

Gordon, A., & Browne, K. W. (1996). *Guiding young children in a diverse society.* Boston: Allyn & Bacon.

Gould, J. C., Thorpe, P., & Weeks, V. (2001, November). An early childhood accelerated program. *Educational Leadership, 59*(3), 47–50.

Grace, C., & Shores, E. F. (1991). *The portfolio and its use: Developmentally appropriate assessment of young children.* Little Rock, AR: Southern Association on Children under Six.

Graves, S., Gargiulo, R., & Sluder, L. (1996). *Young children: An introduction to early childhood education.* St. Paul, MN: West.

Gray, A., & McCutchen, D. (2006). Young readers' use of phonological information. *Journal of Learning Disabilities, 39*(4), 325–333.

Green, C. R. (1998). This is my name. *Childhood Education, 74*(4), 226–231.

Greenman, J. (1988). *Caring spaces, learning places: Children's environments that work.* Redman, WA: Exchange Press.

Greenman, J. (1995). Of culture and a sense of place. *Child Care Information Exchange, 101,* 36–38.

Greenman, J. (2004). The experience of space, the pleasure of place. *Child Care Information Exchange,* January/February (155), 34–35.

Greenman, J. (2005). *Caring spaces, learning places: Children's environments that work.* Redmond, WA: Exchange Press.

Gregory, K., Kim, A. S., & Whiren, A. (2003). The effect of verbal scaffolding on the complexity of preschool children's block structures. In D. Lytle (Ed.), *Play theory, children's playfulness, and educational theory and practice.* Westport, CT: Praeger.

Griffore, R. J., & Bubolz, M. (1986). Family and school as educators. In R. J. Giffore & R. P. Boger (Eds.), *Child rearing in the home and school* (pp. 61–104). New York: Plenum.

Grollman, S. (1994, September). Fantasy and exploration: Two approaches to playing. *Child Care Information Exchange,* 48–50.

Gronlund, G. (2006). *Make early learning standards come alive.* Washington, DC: NAEYC.

Gross, T., & Clemens, S. G. (2002). Painting a tragedy: Young children process the events of September 11. *Young Children, 57*(3), 44–55.

Grusec, J. E., Davidov, M., & Lundell, L. (2002). Prosocial and helping behavior. In P. K. Smith, & C. H. Hart (Eds.), *Blackwell handbook of childhood social development* (pp. 457–474). Malden, MA: Blackwell Publishing Ltd.

Guild, P. (2001). *Diversity, learning style and culture.* Seattle, WA: New Horizons for Learning.

Gullo, D. F. (Ed.). (2006). *K Today: Teaching and learning in the kindergarten year.* Washington, DC: NAEYC.

Guralnik, M., Neville, B., Hammond, M., & Conner, R. T. (2007). The friendships of young children with developmental delays: A longitudinal analysis. *Journal of Applied Developmental Psychology, 28*(1), 64–79.

Haberman, M. (1994, Spring). Gentle teaching in a violent society. *Educational Horizons, 72,* 131–135.

Halle, T., Forry, N., Hair, E., Perper, K., Wadner, L., Wessel, J. & Vick, J. (2009). *Disparities in Early Learning and Development:Lessons fro the Early Childhood Longitudinl Study—Birth Cohort (ECLS-B).* Washington, DC: Child Trends.

Harms, T., Clifford, R. M., & Cryer, D. (1998). *Early childhood environment rating scale-revised.* New York: Teachers College Press.

Hart, C. H., Burts, D. C., & Charlesworth, R. (1997). Integrated developmentally appropriate curriculum: From theory to research to practice. In C. H. Hart, D. C. Burts, & R. Charlesworth (Eds.), *Integrated curriculum and developmentally appropriate practice: Birth to age eight* (pp. 1–27). Albany: State University of New York Press.

Hart, C. H., Burts, D. C., Durland, M. A., Charlesworth, R., DeWolf, M., & Fleege, P. O. (1998). Stress behaviors and activity type participation of preschoolers in more or less developmentally appropriate classrooms: SES and sex differences. *Journal of Research in Childhood Education, 12*(2), 176–196.

Hart, C. H., Newell, L. D., & Olsen, S. F. (2003). Parenting skills and social/communicative competence in childhood. In J. O. Greene, & B. R. Burleson (Eds.), *Handbook of communication and social interaction skills* (pp. 753–797). Mahwah, NJ: Erlbaum.

Harter, S. (1999). *The construction of the self: A developmental perspective.* New York: Guilford Press.

Hartup, W. W. (1998). Cooperation, close relationships, and cognitive development. In W. M. Bukowski, A. F. Newcomb, & W. W. Hartup (Eds.), *The company they keep: Friendships in childhood and adolescence* (pp. 213–237). Cambridge, UK: Cambridge University Press.

Hatch, T. (1997, March). Getting specific about multiple intelligences. *Educational Leadership, 54*(6), 26–29.

Hatch, T., & Gardner, H. (1988, November/December). New research on intelligence. *Learning, 17*(4), 36–39.

Haubenstricker, J. (1990). *Summary of fundamental motor skill characteristics: Motor performance study.* Unpublished document, Michigan State University, East Lansing, MI.

Haubenstricker, J. (1991, May). *Gross motor development in preschoolers.* Paper presented to Michigan Council of Cooperative Nurseries, East Lansing, MI.

Haywood, K. M., & Getchell, N. (2001). *Life span motor development* (3rd ed.). Champaign, IL: Human Kinetics.

Hearron, P., & Hildebrand, V. (2004). *Guiding children's social behavior.* Upper Saddle River, NJ: Prentice Hall.

Hearron, P., & Hildebrand, V. (2009). *Guiding young children* (8th ed.). Upper Saddle River, NJ: Merrill/Prentice Hall.

Hein, G. E., & Price, S. C. (1994). *Active assessment for active science.* Portsmouth, NH: Heinemann.

Helm, J. H. (2008). Got standards? Don't give up on engaged learning! *Young Children, 63*(4), 14–20.

Helm, J., Beneke, S., & Steinhamer, K. (2007). *Windows on learning: Documenting young children's work* (2nd ed.). New York: Teachers College Press.

Helm, J., & Katz, L. (2001). *Young investigators: The project approach in the early years.* New York: Teachers College Press.

Helm, J. H. (2008). Got standards? Don't give up on engaged learning! *Young Children, 63*(4), 14–20.

Helwig, C. C., & Turiel, E. (2002). Children's social and moral reasoning. In C. Hart, & P. Smith (Eds.), *Handbook of childhood social development* (pp. 475–490). Oxford: Blackwell Publishers.

Hemmeter, M. L., Ostrosky, M. M., Artman, K. M., & Kinder, K. A. (2008). Moving right along ... Planning transitions to prevent challenging behavior. *Young Children, 63*(3), 18–25.

Henderson, T. L., & Stevenson, M. L. (2003). Grandparents rearing grandchildren: Rights and responsibilities. Blacksburg, VA: Virginia Cooperative Extension Publication. Retrieved May 5, 2006, from www.ext.vt .edu/pubs/gerontology/350-255/350-255 .html

Hendrick, J., & Weissman, P. (2007). *Total learning: Developmental curriculum for the young child* (7th ed.). Upper Saddle River, NJ: Merrill/Prentice Hall.

Hendrick, J., & Weissman, P. (2010). *The whole child: Developmental education for the early years* (9th ed.). Upper Saddle River, NJ: Merrill/Prentice Hall.

Henninger, M. L. (2009). *Teaching young children: An introduction* (4th ed.). Upper Saddle River, NJ: Pearson.

Herner, T. (1998). President's message. *Counterpoint, 4*(4), 2.

Herr, J., & Libby, Y. (2000). Creative resources for the early childhood classroom. New York: Delmar.

Heroman, C., & Copple, C. (2006). Teaching in the kindergarten year. In D. F. Gullo (Ed.), *Teaching and learning in the kindergarten year* (pp. 59–72). Washington, DC: NAEYC.

Hetherington, E. M., Parke, R., Gauvin, M., & Otis Locke, V. (2006). *Child Psychology: A contemporary viewpoint.* Boston: McGraw-Hill.

High/Scope Curriculum. (1998). *Supporting children in resolving conflicts.* Ypsilanti, MI: High/Scope Press.

High/Scope Educational Foundation. (2005). Plan-Do-Review in the High/Scope Demonstration Preschool. Ypsilanti, MI: Author.

Hildebrand, V. (1997). *Guiding young children: A center approach.* Palo Alto, CA: Mayfield.

Hirsch, E. S. (1996). *The block book* (3rd ed.). Washington, DC: National Association for the Education of Young Children.

Hirsh, R. A. (2004). *Early childhood curriculum: Incorporating multiple intelligences, developmentally appropriate practices and play.* Boston: Pearson.

Hirsh-Pasek, K., & Golinkoff, R. (2004). *USA Today.* Available at www.usatoday.com/news/opinion/editorials/2004-12-15-toy-edit_x.htm

Hoffman, M. L. (1990). Empathy and justice motivation. *Motivation and Emotion, 14*(2), 151–172.

Hoffman, M. L. (2000). *Empathy and moral development.* New York: Cambridge University Press.

Hohmann, M., & Weikart, D. P. (2002). *Educating young children.* Ypsilanti, MI: High/Scope Press.

Holleman, A., Wood, C., & Sheehy, K. (2008). Sensitivity to speech rhythm explains individual differences in reading ability independently of phonological awareness. *British Journal of Developmental Psychology, 26*(3), 357–367.

Holt, B. G. (1989). *Science with young children.* Washington, DC: National Association for the Education of Young Children.

Honig, A. S., & Wittmer, D. S. (1996). Helping children become more prosocial: Ideas for classrooms, families, schools, and communities. *Young Children, 51*(2), 62–70.

Horowitz, F. D., Darling-Hammond, L., & Bransford, J. (2005). Educating teachers for developmentally appropriate practice. In L. Darling-Hammond & J. Bransford (Eds.), *Preparing teachers for a changing world* (pp. 88–125). San Francisco: Jossey-Bass.

Hsue, Y., & Aldridge, J. (1995). Developmentally appropriate practice and traditional Taiwanese culture. *Journal of Instructional Psychology, 22,* 320–323.

Huber, L. K. (1999). Woodworking with young children: You can do it! *Young Children, 54*(6), 32–34.

Hudson, S., Thompson, D., & Mack, M. (1997). Are we safe yet? A twenty-five year look at playground safety. *Journal of Physical Education, Recreation and Dance, 68*(8), 32–34.

Huettig, C. I., Sanborn, C. F., DiMarco, N., Popejoy, A., & Rich, S. (2004). The O generation: Our youngest children are at risk for obesity. *Young Children, 59*(2), 50–55.

Huffman, L. R., & Speer, P. W. (2000). Academic performance among at-risk children: The role of developmentally appropriate practices. *Early Childhood Research Quarterly, 15*(2), 167–184.

Huntsinger, C. S., Schoeneman, J., & Ching, W. (1994, May). *A cross-cultural study of young children's performance on drawing and handwriting tasks.* Paper presented at the Midwestern Psychological Association, Chicago, IL.

Hurley, R. S., & Blake, S. (1997). Animals and occupations: Why theme-based curricula work. *Early Childhood News, 9*(1), 20–25.

Hymes, J. (Narrator). (1980). *Hairy scary* [Film]. Silver Spring: University of Maryland.

Hymes, J. L. (1998, May). A child development point of view: Excerpts from the writings of James L. Hymes, Jr. *Young Children, 53*(3), 49–51.

Hyson, M. C. (Ed.). (2003). *Preparing early childhood professionals: NAEYC's Standards for Programs.* Washington, DC: NAEYC.

Hyson, M. (2003). Putting early academics in their place. *Educational Leadership, 60*(7), 20–23.

Hyson, M. (2004). *The emotional development of young children: Building an emotion-centered curriculum.* New York: Teachers College Press.

Hyson, M. (2008). *Enthusiastic and engaged learners: Approaches to learning in the early childhood classroom.* New York: Teachers College Press.

Hyson, M. C., Hirsh-Pasek, K., & Rescorla, L. (1990). The classroom practices inventory: An observation instrument based on NAEYC's guidelines for developmentally appropriate practices for 4- and 5-year-old children. *Early Childhood Research Quarterly, 5,* 475–494.

IDEA. (2004). Statutes and regulations. Available at http://www.wrightslaw.com/idea/law/htm.

Ignico, A. (1994). Early childhood education: Providing the foundation. *Journal of Physical Education, 65*(6), 25–56.

Ignico, A. (1998, May). Children's sedentary lifestyle: A forerunner of unhealthy adulthood. *USA Today, 126*(2636), 58–59.

Inhelder, B., & Piaget, J. (1964). *The early growth and logic in the child.* London: Routledge & Kegan Paul.

International Reading Association & National Association for the Education of Young Children. (2005). Overview of learning to read and write: Developmentally appropriate practices for young children. A joint position paper of the IRA and the NAEYC. Washington, DC: NAEYC.

International Reading Association & National Council of Teachers of English (1996). Standards for the English Language Arts. Newark, Delaware: International Reading Association and Urbana, Illinois: National Council of Teachers of English.

Isaacson, W. (2009). How to raise the standard in America's schools. *Time, 173*(16), 32–37.

Isbell, R., & Raines, S. (1991). Young children's oral language production in three types of play centers. *Journal of Research in Childhood Education, 5*(2), 140–146.

Jackman, H. (2001). *Early education curriculum: A child's connection to the world.* Albany, NY: Delmar Learning.

Jackson, P. W. (1997). Child-centered education for Pacific-rim cultures? *International Journal of Early Childhood Education, 2,* 5–18.

Jalongo, M. R. (2007). Beyond benchmarks and scores: Reasserting the role of motivation and interest in children's academic achievement. An ACEI Position Paper. *Childhood Education, International Issue,* 395–407.

Jalongo, M. R. (2008). *Learning to listen, listening to learn.* Washington, DC: NAEYC.

Jalongo, M. R., & Stamp, L. N. (1997). *The arts in children's lives: Aesthetic education in early childhood.* Needham Heights, MA: Allyn & Bacon.

Janz, K. E, Dawson, J. D., & Mahoney, L. T. (2000). Tracking physical fitness and physical activity from childhood to adolescence: The Muscatine study. *Medicine and Science in Sports and Exercise, 32*(7), 1250–1257.

Jenkins, J. M. (2000). Theory of mind and social behavior: Causal models tested in a longitudinal study. *Merrill-Palmer Quarterly, 46*(2), 203–220.

Jensen, E. (1998). *Teaching with the brain in mind.* Alexandria, VA: Association for Supervision and Curriculum Development.

Jensen, E. (2008, February). A fresh look at brain-based education. *Phi Delta Kappan, 89*(6), 408–417.

Jesse, P O., Wilson, H., & Morgan, D. (2000). Medical play for young children. *Childhood Education, 76*(4), 215–218.

Johnsen, E. P., & Christie, J. F. (1984). Play and social cognition. In B. Sutton-Smith & D. Kelly-Bryne (Eds.), *The masks of play* (pp. 109–118). New York: Leisure Press.

Johnson, J. E., Christie, J. F., & Yawkey, T. D. (2005). *Play and early childhood development* (2nd ed.). Boston: Allyn & Bacon.

Justice, L. M., & Vukelich, C. (2008). *Achieving excellence in preschool literacy instruction.* New York: Guilford Press.

Kagan, J. (1997/1998). The realistic view of biology and behavior. In K. L. Freiberg (Ed.), *Human development annual editions* (pp. 54–56). Sluice Dock, Guilford, CT: Dushkin.

Kagan, S. (2000). The changing face of parenting education. In M. Jensen & M. A. Hannibal (Eds.), *Issues, advocacy and leadership in early education* (pp. 156–157). Boston: Allyn & Bacon.

Kalb, C., & Namuth, T. (1997, Spring/Summer). When a child's silence isn't golden. *Newsweek: Your Child* (Special ed.), 23.

Kamii, C. (1985, September). Leading primary education toward excellence: Beyond worksheets and drills. *Young Children, 40*(6), 3–9.

Karoly, L. A., Kilburn, M. R., & Cannon, J. S. (2005). *Early childhood interventions: Proven results, future promise.* Santa Monica, CA: Rand.

Katz, L. G. (1987). *What should young children be learning?* Urbana, IL: ERIC Clearinghouse on Elementary and Early Childhood Education.

Katz, L. G. (1995). The benefits of mixed-age grouping. *ERIC Digest,* No. ED382411. Retrieved from http://www.ericfa-cility.net/ericdigests/ed382411.html

Katz, L. G., & Chard, S. C. (1989). *Engaging children's minds: The project approach.* Norwood, NJ: Ablex.

Katz, L. G., & Chard, S. C. (2000). *Engaging children's minds: The project approach* (2nd ed.). Norwood, NJ: Ablex.

Katz, L. G., Evangelou, D., & Hartman, J. A. (1990). *The case for mixed-age grouping in early education.* Washington, DC: National Association for the Education of Young Children.

Katz, L. G., & McClellan, D. E. (1997). *Fostering children's social competence: The teacher's role.* Washington, DC: National Association for the Education of Young Children.

Katz, P. (1982). Development of children's racial awareness and intergroup attitudes. In L. G. Katz (Ed.), *Current topics in early childhood education* (Vol. 4, pp. 17–54). Norwood, NJ: Ablex.

Kauffman, J. M., & Burbach, H. J. (1997, December). On creating a climate of classroom civility. *Phi Delta Kappan, 79*(4), 320–325.

Keeler, R. (2008). *Natural playscapes.* Redmond, WA: Exchange Press.

Kellogg, R. (1969). *Analyzing children's art.* Palo Alto, CA: National Press Books.

Kellogg, R. (1979). *Children's drawings/children's minds.* New York: Avon Books.

Kemple, K. M., & Johnson, C. A. (2002, Summer). From the inside out: Nurturing aesthetic response to nature in the primary grades. *Childhood Education, 78*(4), 210–218.

Kendall, J. S., & Marzano, R. J. (2004). *Content knowledge: A compendium of standards and benchmarks for K–12 education.* Aurora, CO: Mid-continent Research for Education and Learning. Online database: www.mcrel.org/standardsbenchmarks/

Kendrick, A., Kaufmann, R., & Messenger, K. (1988). *Healthy young children: A manual for programs.* Washington, DC: National Association for the Education of Young Children.

Kennedy, L. M., Tipps, S., & Johnson, A. (2009). *Guiding children's learning of mathematics* (11th ed.). Belmont, CA: Wadsworth.

Kessler, S. (1991). Alternative perspectives on early childhood education. *Early Childhood Research Quarterly, 7*(2), 183–197.

Kibbey, M. (1988). *My grammy.* Minneapolis, MN: Carolrhoda.

Kieff, J. E., & Casbergue, R. M. (2000). *Playful learning and teaching: Integrating play into preschool and primary programs.* Needham Heights, MA: Allyn & Bacon.

Kilmer, S. J., & Hofman, H. (1995). Transforming science curriculum. In S. Bredekamp & T. Rosegrant (Eds.), *Reaching potentials: Transforming early childhood curriculum and assessment* (Vol. 2, pp. 43–63). Washington, DC: National Association for the Education of Young Children.

Kim, S. (1999). The effects of storytelling and pretend play on cognitive processes, short-term and long-term narrative recall. *Child Study Journal, 29*(3), 175–191.

Kindergarten Curriculum Guide and Resource Book. (1985). Victoria, British Columbia: Curriculum Development Branch, Ministry of Education.

King, M., & Gartrell, D. (2004). Guidance with boys in early childhood classrooms. In D. Gartrell, *The power of guidance: Teaching social-emotional skills in early childhood classrooms* (pp. 106–124). Albany, NY: Thomson Delmar Learning.

King, M. L., & King, C. S. (1984). *The words of Martin Luther King, Jr.* New York: Newmarket Press, 92.

Kizlik, R. (2009, January). Measurement, assessment and evaluation in education. Available from http://www.adprima.com.

Klein, E. L., Murphy, K. L., & Witz, N. W. (1996). Changes in preservice teachers' beliefs about developmentally appropriate practice in early childhood education.

International Journal of Early Childhood Education, 1, 143–156.

Klein, J. (1990). Young children and learning. In W. J. Stinson (Ed.), *Moving and learning for the young child* (pp. 23–30). Reston, VA: American Alliance for Health, Physical Education, Recreation and Dance.

Kline, S. (1985). *Don't touch.* New York: The Trumpet Club.

Kluth, P., & Schwarz, P. (2008). *Just give him the whale!* Baltimore: Paul H. Brookes Publishing Co.

Knapczyk, D. R. (2004). *Self discipline for self-reliance and academic success.* Verona, WI: Attainment.

Knapczyk, D. R., & Rodes, P. G. (1996). *Teaching social competence: A practical approach for improving social skills in students at-risk.* Pacific Grove, CA: Brooks/Cole.

Knapczyk, D. R., & Rodes, P. G. (2001). *Teaching social competence: Social skills and academic success.* Madison, WI: Attainment.

Kniepkamp, J. (2005). Calling all parents . . . successful methods of involving parents in the educational process. *Connections, 34*(1), 16–18.

Kochanska, G., Aksan, N., Prisco, T. R., & Adams, E. E. (2008). Mother-child and father-child mutually responsive orientation in the first two years and children's outcomes at preschool age: Mechanisms of influence. *Child Development, 79,* 30–44.

Kochanska, G., Gross, J. N., Lin, M., & Nichols, K. E. (2002). Guilt in young children: Development, determinants and relations with a broader system of standards. *Child Development, 73I,* 461–482.

Koff, S. R. (2000). Toward a definition of dance education. *Childhood Education, 77*(1), 27–31.

Kohlberg, L. (1964). Development of moral character and moral ideology. In M. L. Hoffman & L. W. Hoffman (Eds.), *Review of child development research* (Vol. 1, pp. 381–431). New York: Russell Sage Foundation.

Kohn, A. (1996). *Beyond discipline: From compliance to community.* Alexandria, VA: Association for Supervision and Curriculum Development.

Kolbe, U., & Smyth, J. (2000). *Drawing and painting with under-threes.* Watson ACT, Australia: Australian Early Childhood Association.

Kolodziej, S. (1999). Block building: Architecture in early childhood art education. In J. K. Guilfoil & A. R. Sandler (Eds.), *Built environment education in art education* (pp. 151–152). Reston, VA: National Art Education Association.

Kontos, S., & Wilcox-Herzog, A. (1997). Teacher's interactions with children: Why are they so important? *Young Children, 52*(2), 4–12.

Kornhaber, M., Fierros, E., & Veenema, S. (2005). *Multiple intelligences: Best ideas from research and practice.* Boston: Allyn & Bacon.

Kostelnik, M. J. (1990, February). *Standards of quality for early childhood education: Implications for policy makers.* Keynote address, Michigan Department of Education Early Childhood Conference, Detroit, MI.

Kostelnik, M. J. (Ed.). (1991). *Teaching young children using themes.* Glenview, IL: Good Year Books.

Kostelnik, M. J. (Ed.) (1996). *Themes teachers use.* Glenview, IL: Good Year Books.

Kostelnik, M. J. (1997, October). *Spaces to learn and grow: Indoor environments in early education.* Paper presented at the Samsung

International Early Childhood Conference, Seoul, Korea.

Kostelnik, M. J. (2005). Modeling ethical behavior in the classroom. *Child Care Information Exchange,* Nov/Dec., 17–21.

Kostelnik, M. J., & Grady, M. (2009). *Getting it right from the start: The principal's guide to early childhood education.* Thousand Oaks, CA: Corwin Press.

Kostelnik, M. J., Onaga, E., Rohde, B., & Whiren, A. (2002). *Children with special needs: Lessons for early childhood professionals.* New York: Teachers College Press.

Kostelnik, M. J., & Stein, L. C. (1986, November). *Effects of three conflict mediation strategies on children's aggressive and prosocial behavior in the classroom.* Paper presented at the annual meeting of the National Association for the Education of Young Children, Washington, DC.

Kostelnik, M. J., & Stein, L. C. (1990). Social development: An essential component of kindergarten education. In J. S. McKee (Ed.), *The developing kindergarten: Programs, children, and teachers* (pp. 145–179). Saginaw: Mid-Michigan Association for the Education of Young Children.

Kostelnik, M. J., Whiren, A. P., Soderman, A. K., & Gregory, K. (2009). *Guiding children's social development: Theory to practice* (6th ed.). Albany, NY: Delmar.

Koster, J. B. (2009). *Growing artists: Teaching art to young children* (4th ed). Albany, NY: Thomson Delmar Learning.

Kovalik, S., & Olsen, K. (2001). *Integrated thematic instruction.* Kent, WA: Susan Kovalik & Associates.

Kranowitz, C. S. (2005). *The out-of-sync child.* New York: The Berkley Publishing Group.

Kreidler, W. J. (2005). *Creative conflict resolution* (2nd ed.). Tucson, AZ: Good Year Books.

Kuschner, D. (2007). Children's play in the journal. Young children: An analysis of how it is portrayed and why it is valued. In D. J. Sluss, & O. S. Jarrett (Eds.), *Investigating play in the 21st century; Play and Culture Studies* (vol. 7, pp. 55–67).

Kwon, J. Y., & Yawkey, T. D. (2000). Principles of emotional development and children's pretend play. *International Journal of Early Childhood, 32*(1), 9–13.

Ladd, G. W. (2005). *Children's peer relations and social competence.* New Haven, CT: Yale University Press.

Ladd, G. W., & Coleman, C. C. (1993). Young children's peer relationships: Forms, features, and functions. In B. Spodek (Ed.), *Handbook of research on the education of young children* (pp. 54–76). New York: Macmillan.

Landy, S. (2002). *Pathways to competence: Encouraging healthy social and emotional development in young children.* Baltimore: Brookes.

Lantieri, L. (2008). *Building emotional intelligence.* Boulder, CO: Sounds True.

Larsen, J. M., & Haupt, J. H. (1997). Integrating home and school. In C. H. Hart, D. C. Burts, & R. Charlesworth (Eds.), *Integrated curriculum and developmentally appropriate practice: Birth to age eight* (pp. 389–415). Albany: State University of New York Press.

Lawton, J. T. (1987). The Ausubelian preschool classroom. In J. L. Roopnarine & J. E. Johnson (Eds.), *Approaches to early childhood education* (pp. 85–108). Upper Saddle River, NJ: Merrill/Prentice Hall.

Lay-Dopyera, M., & Dopyera, J. (1993). *Becoming a teacher of young children.* New York: McGraw-Hill.

Lee, L. (1997). Working with non-English speaking families. *Child Care Information Exchange, 116,* 57–58.

Lee, V. E. & Burkham, D. T. (2002). *Inequality at the starting gate: Social background differences in achievement as children begin school.* Washington DC: Economic Policy Institute.

LeFrançois, G. R. (2001). *Of children: An introduction to child and adolescent development* (9th ed.). Belmont, CA: Wadsworth.

LePage, P., Darling-Hammond, L., & Akar, H. (2005). Classroom management. In L. Darling-Hammond & J. Bransford (Eds.), *Preparing teachers for a changing world: What teachers should learn and be able to do* (pp. 327–357). San Francisco: Jossey-Bass.

Lcong, D. J., & Bodrova, E. (1995, Fall). Vygotsky's zone of proximal development. *Of Primary Interest, 2*(4), 1–4.

Leppo, M. L., Davis, D., & Crim, B. (2000). The basics of exercising the mind and body. *Childhood Education, 76*(3), 142–147.

Levin, D. (2003). *Teaching young children in violent times: Building a peaceable classroom* (2nd ed.). Cambridge, MA: Educators for Social Responsibility; Washington, DC: National Association for the Education of Young Children.

Levine, J. (2004). Creating a father-friendly environment. *Exchange, 155,* 58–61.

Levy, A. K. (1984). The language of play: The role of play in language development. *Early Child Development and Care, 17,* 49–62.

Lewin, K., Lippitt, R., & White, R. (1939). Patterns of aggressive behaviors and experimentally created "social climates." *Journal of Social Psychology, 10,* 271–299.

Lightfoot, C., Cole, M., & Cole, S. R. (2008). *The development of children* (6th ed.). New York: Worth Publishers.

Lind, K. K. (2004). *Exploring science in early childhood education.* Albany, NY: Delmar/Cengage Learning.

Lind, K. K. (2007). Science in the developmentally appropriate integrated curriculum. In C. H. Hart, D. C. Burts, & R. Charlesworth (Eds.), *Integrated curriculum and developmentally appropriate practice: Birth to age eight* (pp. 75–101). Albany: State University of New York Press.

Lipkin, P. H. (2006, June). Developmental surveillance and screening. American Academy of Pediatricians. Available at http://www.medicalhomeinfor.org/screening.

Little-Soldier, L. (1990, January). *Anthropology in education.* Keynote address, Michigan Association for the Education of Young Children, Grand Rapids, MI.

Loeffler, M. H. (2002, Winter). The essence of Montessori. *Montessori Life, 14*(1), 34–36.

Louv, R. (2005). *Last child in the woods: Saving our children from nature deficit disorder.* Chapel Hill: Algonquin Books.

Love, J. M., Ryer, P., & Faddis, B. (1992). *Caring environments: Program quality in California's publicly funded child development programs.* Portsmouth, NH: RMC Research Corp.

Lowenfeld, V., & Brittain, W. L. (1965). *Creative and mental growth* (4th ed.). New York: Macmillan.

Lubeck, S. (1994). The politics of developmentally appropriate practice: Exploring issues of culture, class and curriculum. In B. L. Mallory & R. S. New (Eds.), *Diversity and developmentally appropriate practices: Challenges for early childhood education* (pp. 17–43). New York: Teachers College Press.

Lubeck, S. (1998). Is developmentally appropriate practice for everyone? *Childhood Education, 74*(5), 283–292.

Lumeng, J. (2005, January). What can we do to prevent childhood obesity? *Zero to Three,* 13–19. Also in K. Paciorek (Ed.). (2009). *Annual editions: Early childhood education* (pp. 85–91). New York: McGraw-Hill.

Maag, J. W. (2004). *Behavior management: From theoretical implications to practical applications* (2nd ed.). Belmont, CA: Wadsworth/Thomson.

Maccoby, E. E. (1984). Socialization and developmental change. *Child Development, 55,* 317–328.

Machado, J. M. (2009). *Early childhood experiences in the language arts* (9th ed.). Albany, NY: Delmar Cengage Learning.

Machado, J. M. & Meyer Botnarescue, H. (2008). *Student teaching: Early childhood practicum guide.* (6th ed.) Albany, NY: Cengage Learning.

Macrina, D. (1995). Educating young children about health. In C. Hendricks (Ed.), *Young children on the grow: Health, activity and education in the preschool setting* (pp. 33–42). Washington, DC: ERIC Clearinghouse on Teacher Education.

Magid, K., & McKelvey, C. A. (1990). *High risk: Children without a conscience.* New York: Bantam Doubleday Dell.

Malott, R. W., & Trojan, E. A. (2008). *Principles of behavior.* Upper Saddle River, NJ: Pearson-Prentice Hall.

Mantzicopoulos, P. Y., Neuharth-Pritchett, S., & Morelock, J. B. (1994, April). *Academic competence, social skills, and behavior among disadvantaged children in developmentally appropriate and inappropriate classrooms.* Paper presented at the annual meeting of the American Educational Research Association, New Orleans, LA.

Marcon, R. A. (1992). Differential effects of three preschool models on inner-city 4-year-olds. *Early Childhood Research Quarterly, 7,* 517–530.

Marcon, R. A. (1995). Fourth-grade slump: The cause and the cure. *Principal, 74*(5), 17–20.

Marcon, R. A. (1999). Differential impact of preschool models on development and early learning of inner-city children: A three-cohort study. *Developmental Psychology, 35,* 358–375.

Marion, M. (2007). *Guidance of young children* (7th ed.). Upper Saddle River, NJ: Merrill/Prentice Hall.

Marion, M. (2010). *Introduction to early childhood education.* Upper Saddle River, NJ: Merrill.

Martin, R. L., Bucholz, M. B., & Nemphie, S. (2001). Brain breaks: A physical activity idea book for elementary classroom teachers. [unpublished document]

Martin, S. (2007). *Take a look: Observation and portfolio assessment in early childhood.* Toronto: Pearson.

Marzano, R. J. (2003). *What works in schools: Translating research into action.* Alexandria, VA: Association for Supervision and Curriculum Development.

Maslow, A. H. (1954). *Motivation and personality.* New York: Harper & Row.

Matthews, K. (2002). Building a community experience. *Young Children, 57,* 86–89.

Mason, J. M., & Sinha, S. (1993). Emerging literacy in the early childhood years: Applying a Vygotskian model of learning and development. In B. Spodek (Ed.), *Handbook of research on the education of young children* (pp. 137–150). New York: Macmillan.

Mawhinney, T. S., & Sagan, L. L. (2007). The power of personal relationships. *Phi Delta Kappan, 88*(6), 460–464.

Maxim, G. W. (2006). *Dynamic social studies for elementary classrooms* (8th ed.). Upper Saddle River, NJ: Merrill/Prentice Hall.

Maxwell, L. E. (2000). A safe and welcoming school: What students, teachers, and parents think. *Journal of Architectural and Planning Research, 17*(4), 271–282.

Mayesky, M. (2009). *Creative activities for young children* (9th ed.). Albany, NY: Thomson Delmar Learning.

McAfee, O., & Leong, D. J. (2007). *Assessing and guiding young children's development and learning* (4th ed.). Boston: Allyn & Bacon.

McBride, B. A., Rane, T. R., & Bae, J. H. (2001). Intervening with teachers to encourage father/male involvement in early childhood programs. *Early Childhood Research Quarterly, 16*(1), 77–93.

McClellan, D., & Katz, L. (2001). Assessing young children's social competence. ERIC Clearinghouse on Elementary and Early Childhood Education, Champaign, IL (Eric document Reproduction Service No. ED450953).

McDevitt, S. C., & Carey, W. B. (1978, July). The measurement of temperaments in 3–7 year old children. *Journal of Child Psychology and Psychiatry, 19*(3), 245–253.

McGann, J. F., & Clark, P. (2007). Fostering positive transitions for school success. *Young Children, 62*(6), 77–99.

McGee, L. M., & Richgels, D. J. (2008). *Literacy's beginnings: Supporting young readers and writers* (5th ed.). Boston: Allyn & Bacon.

McGuinness, D., Olson, A., & Chaplin, J. (1990). Sex differences in incidental recall for words and pictures. *Journal of Learning and Individual Differences, 2,* 263–286.

McIntyre, E., & Pressley, M. (1996). *Balanced instruction: Strategies and skills in whole language.* Norwood, MA: Christopher-Gordon.

Medina, J. (2008). *Brain rules.* Seattle, WA: Pear Press.

Meisels, S. J., & Atkins-Burnett, S. (2005). *Developmental screening in early childhood: A guide* (5th ed.). Washington, DC: National Association for the Education of Young Children.

Meisels, S. J., & Provence, S. (1989). *Screening and assessment: Guidelines for identifying young disabled and developmentally vulnerable children and their families.* Washington, DC: National Center for Clinical Infant Programs.

Mellor, S. (2007). *Australian education review no. 50.* Camberwell, Victoria: Australian Council for Educational Research.

Mellou, E. (1994). Factors which affect the frequency of dramatic play. *Early Child Development and Care, 101,* 59–70.

Michigan Department of Human Services. (2006). *Michigan child care licensing standards.* Lansing, MI: Author. Retrieved May 5, 2006, from www.michigan.gov/dhs/0, 1607, 7-124-5455_27716_27718—,00.html

Michigan Family Independence Agency. (1996). *Child care licensing regulations.* Lansing: Author.

Michigan State University Child Development Laboratories. (1997). *LPS parent handbook.* East Lansing: Author.

Mid-continent Research in Education and Learning. (2005). *PreK–12 Standards: Keys to Learning* [Web site]. Aurora, CO: Author. (www.mcrel.org)

Milevsky, A., Schlechter, M., Netter, S., & Keehn, D. (2007). Maternal and paternal parenting styles in adolescence: Associations with self-esteem, depression, and life satisfaction. *Journal of Child and Family Studies, 16,* 39–47.

Miller, D. F. (2009). *Positive child guidance* (6th ed.). Clifton Park, NY: Delmar Learning.

Miller, E. & Almon, J. (2009). *Crisis in the kindergarten: Why children need to play in school.* College Park, MD: Alliance for Childhood.

Miller, S., Fernie, D., & Kantor, R. (1992). Distinctive literacies in different preschool play contexts. *Play and Culture, 5,* 107–119.

Mills, R. S. L. (2005). Taking stock of the developmental literature on shame. *Developmental Review, 25,* 26–63.

Milne, A. A. (1995). *Pooh's little instruction book.* New York: Dutton Books, 24.

Mindes, G. (2006). Social studies in kindergarten. In D. F. Gullo (Ed.), *K Today: Teaching and learning in the kindergarten year* (pp. 107–115). Washington, DC: NAEYC.

Mischel, W., & Ayduk, O. (2004). Willpower in a cognitive-affective processing system: The dynamics of delay of gratification. In R. F. Baumeister, & K. D. Vohs (Eds.), *Handbook of self-regulation: Research, theory, and applications* (pp. 99–129). New York: Guilford.

Mitchell, L. C. (2005). *Making the MOST of creativity in activities for young children with disabilities. Spotlight on young children and the creative arts.* Washington, DC: National Association for the Education of Young Children.

Mitchell, S. Foulger, T. & Wetzel, K. (2009). Ten tips for involving families through internet-based communication. *Young Children* (64)5 pp. 46–49.

Moll, L. (1996). *Vygotsky and education.* Cambridge, MA: Cambridge University Press.

Monighan-Nourot, P. M. (1998). Sociodramatic play: Pretending together. In D. Fromberg & D. Bergen (Eds.), *Play from birth to twelve and beyond: Contexts, perspectives, and meanings* (pp. 378–391). New York: Garland.

Monke, L. (2007, September/October). Unplugged schools. *Orion Magazine, 26*(5), 18–25.

Montie, J. E., Claxton, J., & Lockhart, S. D. (2007). A multinational study supports child-initiated learning. *Young Children, 62*(6), 22–26.

Moore, S. G. (1986). Socialization in the kindergarten classroom. In B. Spodek (Ed.), *Today's kindergarten* (pp. 110–136). New York: Teachers College Press.

Moriarty, R. F. (2002, September). Helping teachers develop as facilitators of three- to five-year-olds' science inquiry. *Young Children, 57*(5), 20–25.

Morrison, G. S. (2009). *Early childhood education today* (11th ed.). Upper Saddle River, NJ: Merrill/Prentice Hall.

Morrow, L. (1990). Preparing the classroom environment to promote literacy during play. *Children's Quarterly, 5,* 537–554.

Moskal, B. M. (2003). Recommendations for developing classroom performance assessments and scoring rubrics. *Practical Assessment, Research, and Evaluation, 8*(14). Retrieved May 6, 2006, from http://pareonline.net/getvn.asp?v=8 &n=14

Moyer, J. (1990). Whose creation is it, anyway? *Childhood Education, 66*(3), 130–131.

Mulcahey, C. (2002). Take-home art appreciation kits for kindergartners and their families. *Young Children, 57*(1), 80–88.

Music Educators National Conference. (1994). *Opportunity to learn standards for music instruction, preK–12.* Task force chair P. Lehman. Reston, VA: Author.

Myers, S. S., & Pianta, R. C. (2008). Developmental commentary: Individual and contextual influences on student teacher relationships and children's early problem behaviors. *Journal of Clinical Child & Adolescent Psychology, 37*(3), 600–608.

National Academy of Science. (1996). *National science education standards.* Washington, DC: Author.

National Arbor Day Foundation. (2007). *Learning with nature idea book.* Lincoln, NE: Author.

National Association for Sport and Physical Education. (2002). Available at www.aahperd.org/NASPE.

National Association for the Education of Young Children. (1986). *Early childhood teacher education guidelines for four- and five-year programs.* Washington, DC: Author.

National Association for the Education of Young Children. (1995). *Responding to linguistic and cultural diversity: Recommendations for effective early childhood education.* Washington, DC: Author.

National Association for the Education of Young Children. (1996). *Guidelines for preparation of early childhood professionals.* Washington, DC: Author.

National Association for the Education of Young Children. (2005a). *Guidelines for appropriate curriculum content and assessment in programs serving children ages 3 through 8.* Position statement of the National Association for the Education of Young Children and the National Association of Early Childhood Specialists in State Departments of Education. Washington, DC: Author.

National Association for the Education of Young Children. (2005b). *Standards for assessment of child progress.* Washington, DC: Author.

National Association for the Education of Young Children. (2005; revised 2007). *NAEYC early childhood program standards and accreditation criteria: The mark of quality in early childhood education.* Washington, DC: Author.

National Association for the Education of Young Children. (2006a, September). *Early childhood program standards and accreditation criteria.* Washington, DC: Author.

National Association for the Education of Young Children. (2006b, September). *Program portfolio (plans, documents, and records that provide evidence of program implementation of the NAEYC accreditation criteria.* Washington, DC: Author.

National Association of Elementary School Principals. (1998). *Early childhood education & the elementary principal: Standards for quality programs for young children.* Alexandria, VA: Author.

National Association of Elementary School Principals. (2005). *Leading early childhood learning communities: What principles should know and be able to do.* Alexandria, VA: Author.

National Association for Music Education. (2004). *National standards for music education.* Reston, VA: Author.

National Association of State Boards of Education. (1988). *Right from the start.* Alexandria, VA: Author.

National Center for History in the Schools. (1994). *National Standards: History for grades k–4.* Los Angeles: Author.

National Council on Economic Education. (2002). *Economics America.* Bloomington, IN: Author.

National Council for the Social Studies. (1998). *Expectations of excellence.* Washington, DC: Author.

National Council for the Social Studies. (2009). Expectations of Excellence: Curriculum Standards for Social Studies–Executive Summary. Retrieved April 30, 2009, from http://www.socialstudies.org/standards/execsummary

National Council of Teachers of Mathematics. (2000). Standards for grades pre-K–2. In *Principles and standards for school mathematics* (pp. 73–78). Reston, VA: Author.

National Dissemination Center for Children with Disabilities. (2004, January). Deafness and hearing loss, Fact Sheet 3, 1–5.

National Health Education Standards. Retrieved March 18, 2009, from http://www.aahperd.org/aahe/pdf_files/standards.pdf.

National Institute of Child Health and Human Development & Duncan, G. J. (2003). Early Childcare Research Network and Modeling the impacts of childcare quality on children's preschool cognitive development. *Child Development, 74*(5), pp. 1454–1475.

National Institute of Child Health and Human Development, Early Childcare Research Network (Ed.). (2005). *Childcare and child development: Results from the NICHD study of early childcare and youth development.* New York: Guildford Press.

National Parent Teacher Association. (1988). *School is what we make it!* [planning kit]. Chicago, IL: Author.

National Research Council. (2000). *How people learn: Brain, mind, experience, and school* (Expanded ed.). Washington, DC: National Academy Press.

National Research Council. (2001). *Eager to learn: Educating our preschoolers.* Washington, DC: National Academy Press.

National Research Council and Institute of Medicine. (2000). *From neurons to neighborhoods: The science of early childhood development.* Washington, DC: National Academy Press.

National Research Council and National Academy of Science. (1996). *National science education standards: Observe, interact, change, learn.* Washington, DC: National Academy Press.

National Scientific Council on the Developing Child. (2004, December). *Young children* develop in an environment of relationships. Working paper no. 1. Cambridge, MA: Center on the Developing Child, Harvard University.

National Scientific Council on the Developing Child. (2007). *The science of early childhood development: Closing the gap between what we know and what we do.* Cambridge, MA: Center on the Developing Child, Harvard University.

Nebraska Department of Education. (2005). *Nebraska's Early Learning Guidelines 3 to 5 Year Olds.* Lincoln, NE: Author.

Neill, D. M., & Medina, N. J. (1989). Standardized testing: Harmful to educational health. *Phi Delta Kappan, 46*(8), 688–697.

Nelson, C. A., Thomas, K. M., deHaan, M. (2006). Neural bases of cognitive development. In W. Damon, R. Lerner, D. Kuhn, & R. Siegler (Eds.), *Handbook of child psychology* (6th ed., Vol. 2). New York: Wiley.

Nelson, R. R., Cooper, P., & Gonzales, J. (2007). *Stepping stones to literacy: What works clearinghouse.* Washington, DC: Institute of Education Sciences, U.S. Department of Education.

Neuharth-Pritchett, S. M., Hamilton, C. E. & Schwanenflugel, P. J. (2005, Spring). Revisiting early literacy practices for pre-kindergarten children: Systematic strategies that promote preliteracy skills. *ACEI Focus on Pre-K & K,* pp. 1–8.

Neuman, S. (2007). Changing the odds. *Educational Leadership, 65*(2), 16–21.

Neuman, S., & Roskos, K. (1990). Peers as literacy informants: A description of young children's literacy conversations in play. *Early Childhood Research Quarterly, 6,* 233–248.

Neuman, S. B., & Roskos, K. (2007). *Nurturing knowledge.* New York: Scholastic.

New, R. (1990, September). Excellent early education: A city in Italy has it. *Young Children, 7,* 4–8.

New, R. S. (1994). Culture, child development, and develop-mentally appropriate practices: Teachers as collaborative researchers. In B. L. Mallory & R. S. New (Eds.), *Diversity and developmentally appropriate practices: Challenges for early childhood education* (pp. 65–83). New York: Teachers College Press.

New Jersey State Department of Education. (2004). *Preschool Teaching & Learning Expectations: Standards of Quality.* PTM# 1503.18. Trenton, NJ: Author.

Newberger, J. J. (2008). *Brain development: What we know about how children learn.*

Newcomb, & W. W. Hartup (Eds.), *The company they keep: Friendships in childhood and adolescence* (pp. 289–321). Cambridge, UK: Cambridge University Press.

Newman, J. (1996). Teachers' attitudes and policies regarding play in elementary schools. *Psychology in the Schools, 33*(1), 61–69.

Newman, J. M., & Church, S. M. (1990). Myths of whole language. *The Reading Teacher, 44*(1), 20–26.

Newman, P. R., & Newman, B. M. (2003). *Childhood and adolescence.* Pacific Grove, CA: Brooks/Cole.

Nickelsburg, J. (1976). *Nature activities for early childhood.* Menlo Park, CA: Addison-Wesley.

Nieto, S. (2007). *Affirming diversity: The sociopolitical context of multicultural education* (3rd ed.). New York: Longman.

Obenchain, K. M., & Morris, R. V. (2007). *50 social studies strategies for K–8 classrooms*

(5th ed.). Upper Saddle River, NJ: Merrill/Prentice Hall.

Oliver, S. J., & Klugman, E. (2002). Playing the day away. *Child Care Information Exchange, 145,* 66–70.

Ong, W., Allison, J., & Haladyna, T. M. (2000). Student achievement of thirdgraders in comparable single-age and multiage classrooms. *Journal of Research in Childhood Education, 14*(3), 205–215.

Orb, A., & Davey, M. (2005). Research: Grandparents parenting their grandchildren. *Australasian Journal on Aging, 24*(3), 162–168.

Ordonez-Jasis, R., & Ortiz, R. W. (January 2006). Reading their worlds: Working with diverse families to enhance children's early literacy development. *Young Children, 61*(1), 42–47.

Otto, B. (2009). *Language development in early childhood* (3rd ed.). Upper Saddle River, NJ: Merrill/Prentice Hall.

Oyserman, D., Bybee, D., Mobray, C., & Hart-Johnson, T. (2005). When mothers have serious mental health problems: Parenting as a proximal mediator. *Journal of Adolescence, 28,* 443–463.

Paasche, C. L., Gorrill, L., & Strom, B. (2004). *Children with special needs in early childhood settings: Identification, intervention, inclusion.* Albany, NY: Delmar/Thomson Learning.

Paciorek, K., & Munro, J. H. (1995). *Notable selections in early childhood education.* Guilford, CT: Dushkin.

Paley, V. (1981). *Wally's stories: Conversations in the kindergarten.* Cambridge, MA: Harvard University Press.

Paley, V. (1988). *Mollie is three.* Chicago: University of Chicago Press.

Paley, V. (1993). *You can't say, "You can't play."* Cambridge, MA: Harvard University Press.

Paley, V. (1995). *Kwanzaa and me.* Cambridge, MA: Harvard University Press.

Palincsar, A. S., & Brown, A. L. (1989). Classroom dialogues to promote self-regulated comprehension. In J. Brophy (Ed.), *Advances in research on teaching* (Vol. 1, pp. 35–71). Greenwich, CT: JAI.

Parten, M. B. (1932). Social participation among preschool children. *Journal of Abnormal and Social Psychology, 27,* 243–269.

Partnership for 21st Century Skills. (2009). *Framework for 21st century learning.* Retrieved January 5, 2009, from http://www.21stcenturyskills.org/documents/frameworkflyer_072307.pdf.

Payne, V. G., & Isaacs, L. D. (2007). *Human motor development: A lifespan approach* (7th ed.). New York: McGraw-Hill.

Payne, V. G., & Rink, J. (1997). Physical education in the developmentally appropriate integrated curriculum. In C. H. Hart, D. C. Burts, & R. Charlesworth (Eds.), *Integrated curriculum and developmentally appropriate practice: Birth to age eight* (pp. 145–170). Albany: State University of New York Press.

Payton, J., Weissberg, R. P., Durlak, J. A., Dymnicki, A. B., Taylor, R. D., Schellinger, K. B., & Pachan, M. (2008). *The positive impact of social and emotional learning for kindergarten to eighth-grade students: Findings from three scientific reviews.* Chicago: Collaborative for Academic, Social and Emotional Learning.

Peaslee, A., Snyder, I., & Casey, P. B. (2007). Making our thinking visible: Using

documentation for professional development. *Young Children, 62*(4), 28–29.

Pellegrini, A. D., & Bjorklund, D. F. (2002). Should recess be included in a school day? In Paciorek, K. (Ed.), *Taking sides: Clashing views on controversial issues in early childhood education* (pp. 174–175). Guilford, CT: McGraw-Hill.

Pellegrini, A. D., & Glickman, C. D. (1990). Measuring kindergartners' social competence. *Young Children, 45*(4), 40–44.

Pellegrini, A. D., & Perlmutter, J. C. (1988). Rough and tumble play. *Young Children, 43*(2), 14–17.

Pena, D. C. (2000). Parent involvement: Influencing factors and implications. *Journal of Educational Research, 94*(1), 42–54.

Perry, B. D. (2005). Self-regulation: The second core strength. Available at http://teacher.scholastic.com/professional/bruceperry/self_regulation.htm

Peterson, R., & Felton-Collins, V. (1991). *The Piaget handbook for teachers and parents.* New York: Teachers College Press.

Petrakos, H., & Howe, N. (1996). The influence of the physical design of the dramatic play center on children's play. *Early Childhood Research Quarterly, 11*(1), 63–77.

Phaidon. (1994). *The art book.* New York: Phaidon Press.

Phelps, P., & Hanline, M. F. (1999). Let's play blocks! Creating effective learning experiences for young children. *Teaching Exceptional Children, 32*(5), 62–67.

Phillips, C. B. (1991). *Culture as process.* Unpublished paper.

Phillips, P. (1997, May). The conflict wall. *Educational Leadership, 54*(8), 43–44.

Piaget, J. (1962). *Play, dreams and imitation in childhood.* New York: Norton.

Pica, R. (2000). *Experiences in movement with music, activities, and theory* (2nd ed.). Albany, NY: Delmar.

Pica, R. (2006). Physical fitness and the early childhood curriculum. *Young Children, 61*(3), 12–19.

Pica, R. (2009). What makes a game developmentally appropriate? *Young Children, 64*(2), 66–67.

Pickett, L. (1998). Literacy learning during block play. *Journal of Research in Childhood Education, 12*(2), 225–230.

Podlozny, A. (2000). Strengthening verbal skills through the use of classroom drama: A clear link. *Journal of Aesthetic Education, 34*(3–4), 239–275.

Powell, D. (1994). Parents, pluralism and the NAEYC Statement on Developmentally Appropriate Practice. In B. L. Mallory & R. S. New (Eds.), *Diversity and developmentally appropriate practices: Challenges for early childhood education* (pp. 166–182). New York: Teachers College Press.

Powell, R. (1989). *Families and early childhood programs* (Research Monographs of the National Association for the Education of Young Children, Vol. 3). Washington, DC: National Association for the Education of Young Children.

Powell, W., & Napoliello, S. (2005). Using observation to improve instruction. *Educational Leadership, 62*(5), 52–55.

Puckett, M. B., & Black, J. K. (2009). *The young child: Development from prebirth through age eight* (4th ed.). Upper Saddle River, NJ: Pearson.

Pulkkinen, L. (1982). Self-control and continuity from childhood to adolescence. In P. B. Baltes & O. G. Brim, Jr. (Eds.), *Lifespan development and behavior* (Vol. 4, pp. 63–105). Orlando, FL: Academic Press.

Quintero, E. P. (2005). A source of meaningful content for kindergartners. *Young Children, 60*(6), 28–32.

Raikes, H., Torquati, J., Hegland, S., Raikes, A., Scott, J., Messner, L., et al. (2004). Studying the culture of quality: A cumulative approach to measuring characteristics of the workforce and child care quality in four Midwestern states. In I. Martinez-Beck & M. Zaslow (Eds.), *Early childhood professional development and training and children's successful transition to elementary school* (pp. 111–139). Baltimore, MD: Brookes.

Raikes, H. H. & Edwards, C. (2009). *Extending the dance in infant & toddler caregiving: Enhancing attachment & relationships.* Baltimore: Paul H. Brookes Publishing.

Railsback, J. (2002). *Project-based instruction: Creating excitement for learning.* Portland, OR: Northwest Regional Educational Laboratory.

Raines, S. C. (1990). Representational competence: (Re)presenting experiences through words, actions, and images. *Childhood Education, 66*(3), 139–144.

Ramachandran, V. S. (January, 2006). Mirror neurons and the brain in the vat. Edge.

Ramsey, P. G. (1979). Beyond "Ten Little Indians" and turkey: Alternate approaches to Thanksgiving. *Young Children, 34*(6), 28–52.

Ramsey, P. G. (2006). Early childhood multicultural education. In B. Spodek, & O. N. Saracho (Eds.), *Handbook of research on the education of young children* (2nd ed.). Mahwah, NJ: Erlbaum.

Ranweiler, L. W. (2004). *Preschool readers and writers: Early literacy strategies for teachers.* Ypsilanti, MI: High/Scope Press.

Ratcliff, N. (2001). Use the environment to prevent discipline problems and support learning. *Young Children, 56*(5), 84–88.

Read, K., Gardner, P., & Mahler, B. (1993). *Early childhood programs: Human relationships and learning.* New York: Harcourt Brace Jovanovich.

Readdick, C. A., & Park, J. (1998). Achieving great heights: The climbing child. *Young Children, 53*(6), 14–19.

Reifel, S., & Greenfield, P (1983, Spring). Part-whole relations: Some structural features of children's representational block play. *Child Care Quarterly, 12*(1), 144–151.

Reineke, J., Sonsteng, K., & Gartrell, D. (2008). Should rewards have a place in early childhood programs? Viewpoint. *Young Children, 63*(6), 89–97.

Reisman, B. (1996). What do parents want? Can we create consumer demand for accredited child care programs? In S. Bredekamp & B. Wilier (Eds.), *NAEYC accreditation: A decade of learning and the years ahead* (pp. 139–148). Washington, DC: National Association for the Education of Young Children.

Resnick, L. (1996). Schooling and the workplace: What relationship? In *Preparing youth for the 21st century* (21–27). Washington, DC: Aspen Institute.

Revicki, D. (1982). The relationship among socioeconomic status, home environment, parent involvement, child selfconcept and child achievement. *Resources in Education, 1,* 459–463.

Reynolds, E. (2001). *Guiding young children: A problem-solving approach* (3rd ed.). New York: McGraw-Hill.

Rief, S. F., & Heimberge, J. A. (2007). *How to reach and teach all children through balanced literacy.* San Francisco, CA: Jossey Bass.

Rightmeyer, E. C. (2003, July). Democratic discipline: Children creating solutions. *Young Children, 58*(4), 38–45.

Rivkin, M. (1995). *The great outdoors: Restoring children's right to play outside.* Washington, DC: National Association for the Education of Young Children.

Roberts, R. (2006). *Self-esteem and early learning.* Thousand Oaks, CA: Sage.

Robertson, B. (2007). Getting past "inquiry versus content." *Educational Leadership, 64*(4), 67–70.

Rogers, L., & Steffan, D. (2009). Clay play. *Young Children, 64*(3), 78–81.

Roskos, K. (1990). A taxonomic view of pretend play activity among four and five year old children. *Early Childhood Research Quarterly, 5,* 495–512.

Rothlein, L., & Brett, A. (1987). Children's, teachers', and parents' perceptions of play. *Early Childhood Quarterly, 2,* 45–53.

Routman, R. (1996). *Literacy at the crossroads.* Portsmouth, NH: Heinemann.

Routman, R., & Butler, A. (1991). *Transitions.* Portsmouth, NH: Heinemann.

Rubin, K. H., Bukowski, W. M., & Parker, J. G. (2006). Peer interactions, relationships and groups. In N. Eisenberg, W. Damon, & R. M. Lerner (Eds.), *Handbook of child psychology* (pp. 571–645). Hoboken, NJ: Wiley.

Rushton, S. (2001). Applying brain research to create developmentally appropriate learning environments. *Young Children, 56*(5), 76–82.

Russell, A., Mize, J., & Bissaker, K. (2004). Parent-child relationships. In P. K. Smith, & C. H. Hart (Eds.), *Blackwell handbook of childhood social development* (pp. 204–222). Madden, MA: Blackwell.

Rylant, C. (1985). *The relatives came.* New York: Bradbury.

Sanders, S. W. (2002). *Active for life: Developmentally appropriate movement programs for young children.* Washington, DC: National Association for the Education of Young Children.

Sanders, S. W. (2006). Physical education in kindergarten. In D. F. Gullo (Ed.), *Teaching and learning in the kindergarten year.* Washington, DC: National Association for the Education of Young Children.

Santos, R. M. (2004). Ensuring culturally and linguistically appropriate assessment of young children. *Young Children, 59*(1), 48–51.

Santrock, J. (2008). *Child development.* Boston: McGraw-Hill.

Santrock, J. W. (2007). *A topical approach to life span development* (3rd ed.). Boston: McGraw-Hill.

Santrock, J. W (2010). *Children* (10th ed.). Boston: McGraw-Hill.

Saracho, O. N. (1993). Preparing teachers for early childhood programs in the United States. In B. Spodek (Ed.), *Handbook of research on the education of young children* (pp. 412–426). New York: Macmillan.

Sarama, J., & Clements, D. H. (2006). Mathematics in kindergarten. In D. F. Gullo (Ed.), *Teaching and learning in the kindergarten year* (pp. 85–94). Washington, DC: NAEYC.

Sattler, J. (2001). *Assessment of children: Cognitive applications* (4th ed.). La Mesa, CA: Sattler.

Schickedanz, J. A. (2008). *Increasing the power of instruction: Integration of language, literacy, and math across the preschool day.* Washington, DC: National Association for the Education of Young Children.

Schirrmacher, R. (1986). Talking with young children about their art. *Young Children, 41*(5), 3–7.

Schirrmacher, R., & Fox, J. E. (2009). *Art and creative development for young children* (6th ed.). Albany, NY: Thomson Delmar Learning.

Schmidt, H. M., Burts, D. C., Durham, R. S., Charlesworth, R., & Hart, C. H. (2007, April 1). Impact of developmental appropriateness of teacher guidance strategies on kindergarten children's interpersonal relations. *Journal of Research in Childhood Education.* Retrieved March 30, 2009, from http://www.encyclopedia.com/doc/1P3-1282389631.html

Schmoker, M. (1996). *Results: The key to continuous school improvement.* Alexandria, VA: Association for Supervision and Curriculum Development.

Scholastic, Inc. (2002). *September 12th we knew everything would be alright.* Written and illustrated by first-grade students of H. Byron Masterson Elementary in Kennett, Mo.

Schulman, K., & Blank, H. (2009). State child care assistance policies 2008: Most states hold the line, but some lose ground in hard times. Washington DC: National Women's Law Center.

Schweinhart, L. J., Montie, J., Xiang, Z., Barnett, W. S., Belfield, C. R., & Nores, M. (2005). *Lifetime effects: The HighScope Perry Preschool study through age 40.* (Monographs of the HighScope Educational Research Foundation, 14). Ypsilanti, MI: HighScope Press.

Sciarra, D. J., & Dorsey, A. G. (2007). *Developing and administering a child care center.* Albany, NY: Delmar.

Scott-Little, C., Brown, E. G., Hooks, L., & Marshall, B. J. (2008). Classroom quality rating systems; How do teachers prepare and what do they think about the process? *Young Children, 63*(6), 40–45.

Scott-Little, C., Kagan, S. L., & Frelow, V. S. (2005). *Inside the content: The breadth and depth of early learning standards.* Greensboro, NC: SERVE.

Seefeldt, C. (Ed.). (1987). *The early childhood curriculum: A review of current research.* New York: Teachers College Press, 144–197.

Seefeldt, C. (2005). *How to work with standards in the early childhood classroom.* New York: Teachers College Press.

Seefeldt, C., Castle, S. D., & Falconer, R. (2010). *Social studies for the preschool/primary child* (8th ed.). Upper Saddle River, NJ: Merrill/Pearson Hall.

Seefeldt, C., & Galper, A. (2007). *Active experiences for active children: Science.* Upper Saddle River, NJ: Merrill/Prentice Hall.

Seefeldt, C., & Wasik, B. A. (2006). *Early education: Three, four and five-year-olds go to school* (2nd ed.). Upper Saddle River, NJ: Pearson.

Seefeldt, V., & Vogel, P. G. (1986). *The value of physical activity.* Reston, VA: American Alliance for Health, Physical Education, Recreation & Dance.

Seligman, M. E. (1995). *The optimistic child.* New York: Houghton Mifflin.

Selman, R. L., Levitt, M. Z., & Schultz, L. H. (1997). The friendship framework: Tools for the assessment of psychosocial development. In R. Selman, C. L. Watts, & L. H. Schultz (Eds.), *Fostering friendships* (pp. 32–52). New York: Aldine DeGruyer.

Sendak, M. (1963). *Where the wild things are.* New York: Harper & Row.

Seven styles of learning: Clip-and-save chart. (1990, September). *Instructor Magazine,* 52.

Shaffer, D. R. (2008). *Social & personality development* (6th ed.). Belmont, CA: Wadsworth.

Shaffer, D. R., and Kipp, K. (2009). *Developmental psychology: Childhood and adolescence* (9th ed.). Belmont, CA: Wadsworth.

Shapiro, L. (1997). *How to raise a child with a high EQ.* New York: Harper Collins.

Sherman, C. W., & Mueller, D. P. (1996, June). *Developmentally appropriate practice and student achievement in innercity elementary schools.* Paper presented at Head Start's Third National Research Conference, Washington, DC.

Shiller, V. M., & O'Flynn, J. C. (2008). Should rewards have a place in early childhood programs? Viewpoint. *Young Children, 63*(6), 88–93.

Shoemaker, C. J. (1995). *Administration and management of programs for young children.* Upper Saddle River, NJ: Merrill/Prentice Hall.

Shonkoff, J. P. (2009, April 1). Early childhood science and policy: Closing the gap and creating the future. Paper presented as part of the Creating Connections Series, Lincoln, NE: University of Nebraska.

Shonkoff, J. P., Boyce, W. T. & McEwen, B. S. (2009). Neuroscience, molecular biology, and the childhood roots of health disparities, JAMA, 301 (21), 2252–2259.

Shonkoff, J. P., & Phillips, D. A. (Eds.). (2000). *From neurons to neighborhoods: The science of early childhood development.* Washington, DC: National Academy Press.

Shore, R. (2003). *Rethinking the brain: New insights into early development.* New York: Families at Work Institute.

Shore, R., Bodrova, E., & Leong, D. (2004). *Preschool policy matters: Child outcome standards in pre-K programs.* New Brunswick, NJ: National Institute for Early Education Research.

Shotwell, J., Wolf, D., & Gardner, H. Y. (1979). Exploring early symbolization: Styles of achievement. In B. Sutton-Smith (Ed.), *Play and learning* (pp. 127–156). New York: Gardner Press.

Sigsgaard, E. (2005). *Scolding: Why it hurts more than it helps.* New York: Teachers College Press.

Singer, D. G., & Singer, J. L. (2005). *Imagination and play in the electronic age.* Cambridge, MA: Harvard University Press.

Slentz, K. L., & Krogh, S. L. (2001a). *Early childhood development and its variations.* Mahwah, NJ: Erlbaum.

Slentz, K. L., & Krogh, S. L. (2001b). *Teaching young children: Contexts for learning.* Mahwah, NJ: Erlbaum.

Smart, M. S., & Smart, R. C. (1982). *Children: Development and relationships* (Rev. ed.). New York: Macmillan.

Smilansky, S. (1968). *The effects of sociodramatic play on disadvantaged preschool children.* New York: Wiley.

Smith, J. (1990). *To think.* New York: Teachers College Press.

Smith, K. A., & Gouze, K. R. (2004). *The sensory-sensitive child.* New York: HarperCollins.

Smith, S. S. (2009). *Early childhood mathematics* (4th ed.). Needham Heights, MA: Allyn & Bacon.

Snow, C., & Kang, J. Y. (2006). Becoming bilingual, biliterate, and bicultural. In W. Damon, R. M. Lerner, K. A. Renninger, & I. E. Sigel (Eds.), *Handbook of child psychology* (6th ed., pp. 75–103). New York: John Wiley & Sons.

Snow, C. E., Tabors, P. O., & Dickinson, D. K. (2001). Language development in the preschool years. In D. K. Dickinson & P. O. Tabors (Eds.), *Beginning literacy with language: Young children learning at home and school* (pp. 1–25). Baltimore: Paul H. Brookes.

Snow, C. E., & Van Hemel, S. B. (Eds.) *Early childhood assessment: Why, what, and how.* Washington, DC: The National Academies Press.

Snow, V. R., Burns, M. S., & Griffin, P. (Eds.). (1998). *Preventing reading difficulties in young children.* Washington, DC: National Academy Press.

Soderman, A. (1997, August). *Multi-age classrooms: Accommodating gender differences among children.* Paper presented at the Michigan Multi-Age Conference, Kalamazoo, MI.

Soderman, A. K. (2001, Fall). Statewide testing: Problem or solution for failing schools? *Michigan Family Review, 6*(1), 55–66.

Soderman, A. K., & Farrell, P. (2008). *Creating literacy-rich preschools and kindergartens.* Boston: Allyn & Bacon.

Soderman, A. K., Gregory, K. S., & McCarty, L. (2005). *Scaffolding emergent literacy.* Boston: Allyn & Bacon.

Soderman, A. K., Gregory, K. S., & O'Neill, L. T. (2005). *Scaffolding emergent literacy: A child-centered approach for preschool through grade 5* (2nd ed.). Boston: Allyn & Bacon.

Soderman, A. K., & Oshio, T. (2008, September). Social and cultural contexts of second language acquisition. *European Early Childhood Research Journal (EECER),* 297–311.

Soderman, A. K., Wescott, B. L., & Shen, J. (2007, November). Bridging two languages: Engaging activities for bilingual immersion programs. *Beyond the Journal—NAEYC Young Children on the Web.*

Sorte, J. M., & Daeschel, I. (2006). Health in action, A program approach to fighting obesity in young children. *Young Children, 62*(3), 40–46.

Spangler, C. B. (1997). The sharing circle: A child-centered curriculum. *Young Children, 52*(5), 74–78.

Spiegel, A. (2008, February 28). Creative play makes for kids in control. National Public Radio. Available at www.npr.org/templets/story.php?storyld=76838288

Spodek, B. (1973). *Early childhood education.* Upper Saddle River, NJ: Prentice Hall.

Spodek, B. (1985). *Teaching in the early years* (3rd ed.). Upper Saddle River, NJ: Prentice Hall.

Spodek, B., & Brown, P. C. (1993). Curriculum alternatives in early childhood education: A historical perspective. In B. Spodek (Ed.), *Handbook of research on the education of young children* (pp. 91–104). New York: Macmillan.

Spodek, B., Saracho, O. N., & Davis, M. D. (1991). *Foundations of early childhood education.* Upper Saddle River, NJ: Prentice Hall.

Starbuck, S., & Olthof, M. (2008). Involving families and community through gardening. *Young Children, 63*(5), 74–79.

State of America's Children: Yearbook 1997 (1997). Washington, DC: Children's Defense Fund.

Stein, L. C., & Kostelnik, M. J. (1984, Spring). A practical problem solving model for conflict resolution in the classroom. *Child Care Quarterly, 13*(1), 5–20.

Steinberg, L., Blatt-Eisengart, I., & Cauffman, E. (2006). Patterns of competence and adjustment among adolescents from authoritative, authoritarian, indulgent, and neglectful homes: A replication in a sample of serious juvenile offenders. *Journal of Research on Adolescence, 16,* 47–58.

Steiner, J., & Whelan, M. S. (1995, December 29). *For the love of children: For people who care for children.* St. Paul, MN: Redleaf Press.

Stephens, K. (1996, May). You can make circle time developmentally appropriate. *Child Care Information Exchange,* 40–43.

Stephens, K. (2009). Imaginative play during childhood: Required for reaching full potential. *Exchange,* March/April (186), 53–56.

Stephens, T. J. (2006). *Discipline strategies for children with disabilities.* Sioux Falls, SD: School of Medicine & Health Sciences, Center for Disabilities, University of South Dakota.

Sternberg, R. J. (2006). *Cognitive psychology* (4th ed.). Belmont, CA: Wadsworth.

Stiggins, R. J. (2002, June). Assessment crisis: The absence of assessment for learning. *Phi Delta Kappan, 83*(10), 758–765.

Stiggins, R. (2007). *An Introduction to Student-Involved Assessment FOR Learning* (5th ed.). Upper Saddle River, NJ: Pearson.

Stipek, D., Feiler, R., Daniels, D., & Milburn, S. (1995). Effects of different instructional approaches on young children's achievement and motivation. *Child Development, 66,* 209–223.

Stocking, S. H., Arezzo, D., & Leavitt, S. (1980). *Helping kids make friends.* Allen, TX: Argus Communications.

Stone, C. A., Silliman, E. R., Ehren, B. J., & Apel, K. (Eds.) (2004). *Handbook of Language and Literacy Development and Disorders.* New York: Guilford Press.

Stone, S. J., & Christie, J. F. (1996). Collaborative literacy learning during sociodramatic play in a multiage (K-2) primary classroom. *Journal of Research in Childhood Education, 10*(2), 123–133.

Stritzel, K. (1995). Block play is for all children. *Child Care Information Exchange,* 42–47.

Stronge, J. H. (2002). *Qualities of effective teachers.* Alexandria, VA: Association for Supervision and Curriculum Development.

Stroud, J. (1995). Block play: Building a foundation for literacy. *Early Childhood Education Journal, 23*(1), 9–13.

Stuber, G. M. (2007). Centering your classroom: Setting the stage for engaged learners. *Young Children, 62*(4), 58–60.

Sullivan, M. (1982). *Feeling strong, feeling free: Movement exploration for young children.* Washington, DC: National Association for the Education of Young Children.

Sunal, C. S. (1993). Social studies in early childhood education. In B. Spodek (Ed.), *Handbook of research on the education of young children* (9th ed.). Upper Saddle River, NJ: Merrill/Prentice Hall.

Sutterby, J. A., & Thornton, C. P. (2005). It doesn't just happen! Essential contributions from playgrounds. *Young Children, 60*(3), 26–30, 32–33.

Sutton-Smith, B. (1992). *Toys as culture.* New York: Gardner Press.

Swartz, M. I. (2005). Playdough: What's standard about it? *Young Children, 60*(2), 100–109.

Swiniarski, L., Breitborde, M. L., & Murphy, J. A. (1999). *Educating the global village: Including the young child in the world.* Upper Saddle River, NJ: Merrill/Prentice Hall.

Sylva, K. et al. (2003). *The effective provision of pre-school education (EPPE) project: Findings from the pre-school period.* London: Institute of Education, University of London.

Sylwester, R. (2006, December). Cognitive neuroscience discoveries and educational practices: Seven areas of brain research that will shift the current behavioral orientation of teaching and learning. *School Administrator, 63*(11), 32.

Tabors, P. O., & Snow, C. E. (2001). Young bilingual children and early literacy development. In S. B. Neuman & D. K. Dickinson (Eds.), *Handbook of early literacy research* (pp. 159–178). New York: Guilford Press.

Taras, H. (1992). Physical activity of young children in relation to physical and mental health. In C. Hendricks (Ed.), *Young children on the grow: Health, activity and education in the preschool setting* (pp. 33–42). Washington, DC: ERIC Clearinghouse on Teacher Education.

Tarr, P. (2001). Aesthetic codes in early childhood classrooms: What art educators can learn from Reggio Emilia. *Art Education, 54*(3), 33–39.

Taylor, B. J. (2004). *A child goes forth: A curriculum guide for preschool children.* Upper Saddle River, NJ: Prentice Hall.

Taylor, B. J. (2003). *Science everywhere: Opportunities for very young children.* New York: Harcourt Brace Jovanovich.

Taylor, J. A., & Baker, R. A., Jr. (2002, January). Discipline and the special education student. *Educational Leadership, 59*(4), 28–30.

Teaching Tolerance Project. (1997). *Starting small: Teaching tolerance in preschool and the early grades.* Montgomery, AL: Southern Poverty Law Center.

Tegano, D. (1996). Designing classroom spaces: Making the most of time. *Early Childhood Education Journal, 23*(3), 135–144.

Tegano, D., Sawyers, J., & Moran, J. (1991, Winter). Problem finding and solving in play: The teacher's role. *Childhood Education, 68*(2), 92–97.

Theimer, C. E., Killen, M., & Stangor, C. (2001). Young children's evaluations of exclusion in gender-stereotypic peer contexts. *Developmental Psychology, 37*(1), 18–27.

Thelen, P., & Soderman, A. K. (2002). *Running a successful kindergarten round-up: A guide for elementary principals and teachers.* Lansing, MI: Lansing School District Safe Schools/Healthy Students Initiative.

Thomas, A., & Chess, S. (1977). *Temperament and development.* New York: Brunner/Mazel.

Thomas, A., & Chess, S. (1980). *The dynamics of psychological development.* New York: Brunner/Mazel.

Thomas, A., & Chess, S. (1984). *Origins and evolution of behavior disorders.* New York: Brunner/Mazel.

Thomas, A., Chess, S., Birch, H. G., Hartzig, M. E., & Korn, S. (1963). *Behavioral individuality in early childhood.* New York: New York University Press.

Thompson, R. A. (2006). The development of the person: Social understanding, relationships, conscience, self. In N. Eisenberg (Ed.), *Handbook of child psychology* (6th ed., vol. 3, pp. 24–98). Hoboken, NJ: Wiley.

Tierney, R., & Simon, M. (2004). What's still wrong with rubrics: Focusing on the consistency of performance criteria across scale levels. *Practical Assessment, Research & Evaluation, 9*(2). Retrieved May 6, 2006, from http://pareonline.net/getvn.asp.?v=9&n=2

Tisak, M. S., & Block, J. H. (1990). Preschool children's evolving conceptions of badness: A longitudinal study. *Early Education and Development, 4,* 300–307.

Trawick-Smith, J. (1988, July). Play leadership and following behavior of young children. *Young Children, 43*(5), 51–59.

Trawick-Smith, J. (2009). *Early childhood development: A multicultural perspective* (5th ed.). Upper Saddle River, NJ: Merrill/Prentice Hall.

Trepanier-Street, M. (1991). The developing kindergartner: Thinking and problem solving. In J. McKee (Ed.), *Developing kindergartens: Programs, children and teachers* (pp. 181–199). East Lansing: Michigan Association for the Education of Young Children.

Turbiville, V. P., Umbarger, G. T., & Guthrie, A. C. (2000, July). Fathers' involvement in programs for young children. *Young Children, 55*(4), 74–79.

Turiel, E. (1998). The development of morality. In N. Eisenberg (Ed.), *Handbook of child psychology* (Vol. 3. pp. 863–932). New York: Wiley.

Turner, J. S. (1992). Montessori's writings versus Montessori practices. In M. H. Loeffler (Ed.), *Montessori in contemporary American culture* (pp. 17–47). Portsmouth, NH: Heinemann.

UNESCO—Education for All Global Monitoring Report Team. (2007). *Strong foundations: Early childhood care and education.* Paris, France: Author.

UNICEF. (2008). The childcare transition: A league table of early childhood education and care in economically advanced countries. Innocenti Report Card 8, UNICEF.

U.S. Census Bureau. (2007). *America's children: Key national indicators of well-being.* Washington, DC: Author.

U.S. Census Bureau. (2007). *Current population survey, annual social and economic supplement.* Retrieved January 5, 2008, from http://www.childstats.gove/americaschildren07/famsoc1.asp.

U.S. Department of Education. (1986). *What works: Research about teaching and learning.* Washington, DC: U.S. Government Printing Office.

U.S. Department of Education. (2009). Building the legacy of IDEA 2004. hhtp://idea.ed.gov.

Valentini, N. C., Rudisill, M. E., & Goodway, J. D. (1999). Incorporating a mastery climate into physical education: It's developmentally appropriate! *Journal of Physical Education, Recreation and Dance 70*(7), 28–32.

Van Hoorn, J., Monighan-Nourot, P. M., Scales, B., & Alward, K. R. (2007). *Play at the Center of the Curriculum* (4th ed.). Upper Saddle River, NJ: Prentice Hall (Pearson Education Ltd.).

van Kleeck, A., Gillam, R. B., & Hoffman, L. M. (2006). Training in phonological awareness generalizes to phonological working memory: A preliminary investigation. *Journal of Speech-Language Pathology—Applied Behavior Analysis, 1*(3), 228–243.

Vance, B. (1973). *Teaching the prekindergarten child: Instructional design and curriculum.* Pacific Grove, CA: Brooks/Cole.

Vasta, R., Haith, M. M., & Miller, S. A. (2004). *Child psychology: The modern science* (3rd ed.). New York: Wiley.

Viadero, D. (1997). Fathers play unique role in schooling, study finds. *Education Week, 17*(13), 3–5.

Vos, K. D., & Baumeister, R. F. (2004). Understanding self-regulation: An introduction. In R. F. Baumeister, & K. D. Vohs (Eds.), *Handbook of self-regulation: Research, theory, and applications* (pp. 1–12). New York: Guilford.

Vygotsky, L. (1929). The problem of the cultural development of the child. *Journal of Genetic Psychology, 36,* 415–434.

Vygotsky, L. S. (1962). *Thought and language* (E. Hanfmann & G. Vakar, Eds. & Trans.). Cambridge, MA: MIT Press, (original work published 1934).

Vygotsky, L. (1967). Play and its role in the mental development of the child. *Social Psychology, 12,* 62–76.

Vygotsky, L. (1979). The genesis of higher mental functioning. In J. V. Wertsch (Ed.), *The concept of activity in Soviet psychology.* Armonk, NY: Sharpe.

Wagner, T. (1996, October). Bringing school reform back down to earth. *Phi Delta Kappan, 78*(2), 145–149.

Waite-Stupiansky, S. (1997). *Building understanding together: A constructionist approach to early childhood education.* Albany, NY: Delmar.

Ward, S. (1986). *Charlie and grandma.* New York: Scholastic.

Warner, L., & Sower, J. (2005). *Educating young children from preschool through primary grades.* Boston: Allyn & Bacon.

Warren, S. L., Emde, R. N., & Sroufe, L. A. (2000). Internal representations: Predicting anxiety from children's play narratives. *Journal of the American Academy of Child and Adolescent Psychiatry, 39*(1), 100–107.

Washington, V., & Andrews, J. D. (Eds.). (1998). *Children of 2010.* Washington, DC: National Association for the Education of Young Children.

Watson, R. (2001). Literacy and oral language: Implications for early literacy acquisition. In S. B. Neuman & D. K. Dickinson (Eds.), *Handbook of early literacy research* (pp. 43–53). New York: Guilford Press.

Wellhousen, K., & Crowther, I. (2004). *Creative effective learning environments.* Clifton Park, NY: Delmar.

Weikart, P. S. (1998, May/June). Facing the challenge of motor development. *Child Care Information Exchange, 121,* 60–62.

Wein, C. A. (2004). *Negotiating standards in the primary classroom: The teacher's dilemma.* New York: Teachers College Press.

Weinraub, M. , Horvath, D. L., & Gringlas, M.B. (2002). Single parenthood, In M. H. Bornstein (Ed.), *Handbook of Parenting* (2nd ed., Vol. 3, pp. 109–140). Mahwah, NJ: Erlbaum.

Weinstein, C. S., Tomlinson-Clarke, S., & Curran, M. (2004). Toward a conception of culturally responsive classroom management. *Journal of Teacher Education, 55*(1), 25–38.

Weinstein, C. S., & Mignano, A., Jr. (2007). *Elementary classroom management: Lessons from research and practice* (4th ed.). New York: McGraw-Hill.

Weissberg, R. P., Shriver, T. P., Bose, S., & DeFalco, K. (1997). Creating a districtwide social development project. *Educational Leadership, 84*(8), 37–40.

Weissbourd, R. (1997). *The vulnerable child: What really hurts America's children and what we can do about it.* Reading, MA: Addison-Wesley.

Wellhousen, K., & Kieff, J. (2001). *A constructivist approach to block play in early childhood.* Albany, NY: Delmar.

Wenner, M. (2009, January 28). The serious need for play. *Scientific American.* Retrieved February 25, 2009, from http://www.sciam.com/article.cfm?id=the-serious-need-for-play.

Wheeler, E. J. (2004). *Conflict resolution in early childhood.* Upper Saddle River, NJ: Merrill/Prentice Hall.

Which Hand. (2007, Spring). *Texas child care.* Texas Workforce Commission; also in *Annual editions, Early childhood education,* 2009, 77–80.

Whitin, D. J., & Piwko, M. (2008). Mathematics and poetry: The right connection. *Young Children, 63*(2), 34–39.

Wieder, S., & Greenspan, S. I. (1993). The emotional basis of learning. In B. Spodek (Ed.), *Handbook of research on the education of young children* (pp. 77–104). New York: Macmillan.

Wilcox, E. (1994). Unlock the joy of music. *Teaching Music, 2,* 34–35.

Williams, K. C., & Cooney, M. H. (2006). Young children and social justice. *Young Children, 61*(2), 75–82.

Willis, C. (2009). *Creating inclusive learning environments for young children.* Thousand Oaks, CA: Corwin Press.

Wilson, H. K., Pianta, R. C., & Stuhlman, M. W. (2007). Typical classroom experiences in first-grade: The role of classroom climate and functional risk in the development of social competencies. *Elementary School Journal, 108*(2), 29–48.

Wilson, R. (1995). Environmental education: Environmentally appropriate practices. *Early Childhood Education Journal, 23*(2), 107–110.

Wiltz, N. W., & Klein, E. L. (2001). "What do you do in child care?" Children's perceptions of high and low quality classrooms. *Early Childhood Research Quarterly, 16*(2), 209–236.

Winfrey, O. (1996). *About us: The dignity of children.* Fred Berner Films and the Children's Dignity Project: CDP Films.

Winsler, A., De Leon, J. R., Walace, B. A., Carlton, M. P., & Wilson-Quayle, A. (2003). Private speech in preschool children: Developmental stability and change, across-task consistency, and relations with classroom behavior. *Journal of Child Language, 30*(3), 583–608.

Winsler, A., Naglieri, J., & Manfra, I. (2006). Children's search strategies and accompanying verbal and motor strategic behavior: Developmental trends and relations with task performance among children age 5 to 17. *Cognitive Development, 21,* 232–248.

Wittmer, D. S., & Honig, A. S. (1994, July). Encouraging positive social development in young children. *Young Children, 4,* 4–12.

Wolery, M., Strain, P., & Bailey, D. (1992). Reaching potentials of children with special needs. In S. Bredekamp & T. Rosegrant (Eds.), *Reaching potentials: Appropriate curriculum and assessment for young children* (Vol. 1, pp. 92–111). Washington, DC: National Association for the Education of Young Children.

Wolfgang, C. H. (1996). *The three faces of discipline for the elementary school teacher.* Boston: Allyn & Bacon.

Wolfgang, C. H. (2008). *Solving discipline and classroom management problems: Methods and models for today's teachers* (7th ed.). New York: Wiley.

Wolfgang, C. H., & Sanders, L. (1986). Teacher's role: A construct for supporting the play of young children. In S. Burroughs & R. Evans (Eds.), *Play, language and socialization* (pp. 49–62). New York: Gordon & Breach.

Wolfgang, C. H., Stannard, L. L., & Jones, I. (2001). Block play performance among preschoolers as a predictor of later school achievement in mathematics. *Journal of Research in Childhood Education, 15*(2), 173–180.

Woodard, R. J., & Yun, J. (2001). The performance of fundamental gross motor skills by children enrolled in Head Start. *Early Child Development and Care, 169,* 57–67.

Worth, K., & Grollman, S. (2003). *Worms, shadows, and whirlpools: Science in the early childhood classroom.* Portsmouth, NH: Heinemann.

Wortham, S. C. (2008). *Assessment in early childhood education* (5th ed.). Upper Saddle River, NJ: Pearson.

Worthington, M., & Carruthers, E. (2004). *Children's mathematics.* Thousand Oaks, CA: Sage.

Woyke, P. (2004). Hopping frogs and trail walks: Connecting young children to nature. *Young Children, 59*(1), 82–85.

Wurtele, S. K., Gissispie, G., Currier, L., & Franklin, C. (1992). A comparison of teachers vs. parents as instructors of a personal safety program for preschoolers. *Child Abuse & Neglect, 16,* 127–137.

York, S. (2009). *Roots and wings: Affirming culture in early childhood settings.* St. Paul, MN: Toys'n Things Press.

Zaichkowsky, L., & Larson, G. (1995). Physical, motor, and fitness development in children and adolescents. *Journal of Education, 177*(2), 55–79.

Zavitkovsky, D. (1986). *Listen to the children.* Washington, DC: National Association for the Education of Young Children.

Name Index

Subject Index